BISMARCK

AND THE DEVELOPMENT OF GERMANY

VOLUME III

The Period of Fortification, 1880–1898

BISMARCK, MARCH 1885. (INTER-NATIONES, BONN.)

BISMARCK

AND THE DEVELOPMENT OF GERMANY

VOLUME III

The Period of Fortification, 1880–1898

Otto Pflanze

PRINCETON UNIVERSITY PRESS

PRINCETON, NEW JERSEY

✱

Bismarck and the Development of Germany

VOL. 1: THE PERIOD OF UNIFICATION, 1815–1871

VOL. 2: THE PERIOD OF CONSOLIDATION, 1871–1880

VOL. 3: THE PERIOD OF FORTIFICATION, 1880–1898

✠ ✠ ✠

Copyright © 1990 by Princeton University Press
Published by Princeton University Press, 41 William Street,
Princeton, New Jersey 08540
In the United Kingdom: Princeton University Press, Oxford

Library of Congress Cataloging-in-Publication Data
(Revised for volume 3)

Pflanze, Otto.
Bismarck and the development of Germany.
Previously published in 1963 in one volume.
Contents: v. 1. The period of unification, 1815–1871
—v. 3. The period of fortification, 1880–1898.
1. Bismarck, Otto, Fürst von, 1815–1866. 2. Germany
—History—1815–1866. 3. Germany—History—1866–1871.
DD218.P44   1990   943'.07   89-11004
ISBN 0-691-05587-4 (v. 1 : alk. paper)

This volume was furthered by a research year at
the *Historisches Kolleg* (Munich), which is supported by
the *Stiftungsfond Deutsche Bank zur Förderung der Wissenschaft
in Forschung und Lehre im Stiftverband für
die deutsche Wissenschaft.*

This book has been composed in Linotron Goudy

Princeton University Press books are printed
on acid-free paper, and meet the guidelines for
permanence and durability of the Committee on
Production Guidelines for Book Longevity
of the Council on Library Resources

Printed in the United States of America by
Princeton University Press, Princeton, New Jersey

1   3   5   7   9   10   8   6   4   2

For

STEPHEN, CHARLES, AND KATRINE

✠

✢ CONTENTS ✢

✤ ABBREVIATIONS ✤
Used in the Footnotes

AWB   Heinrich von Poschinger, ed., *Aktenstücke zur Wirtschaftspolitik des Fürsten Bismarcks* (2 vols., Berlin, 1890).

BA   Bundesarchiv der Bundesrepublik Deutschlands (Koblenz).

BFA   Bismarck Family Archive (Friedrichsruh).

BGB   *Bundes-Gesetzblatt des Norddeutschen Bundes* (1867–1871).

BP   Heinrich von Poschinger, ed., *Fürst Bismarck und die Parlamentarier* (2d ed., 3 vols., Breslau, 1894–1896).

BR   Horst Kohl, ed., *Die politischen Reden des Fürsten Bismarck* (14 vols., Stuttgart, 1892–1905).

DDF   Ministère des Affaires Étrangères, *Documents diplomatiques français, 1871–1914*, 1re Série (1871–1900, 16 vols., Paris, 1929–1959).

DZA   Das Zentralarchiv der Deutschen Demokratischen Republik (Potsdam and Merseburg).

GP   Johannes Lepsius, Albrecht Mendelssohn Bartholdy, Friedrich Thimme, eds., *Die grosse Politik der europäischen Kabinette 1871–1914* (39 vols., Berlin, 1922–1927).

GSA   Geheimes Staatsarchiv der Stiftung Preussischer Kulturbesitz (Berlin-Dahlem).

GSP   *Gesetzsammlung für die königlich preussischen Staaten* (Berlin, 1851ff.).

GW   Herman von Petersdorff and others, eds., *Bismarck: Die gesammelten Werke* (15 vols., Berlin, 1923–1933).

HW   Julius Heyderhoff and Paul Wentzcke, eds., *Deutscher Liberalismus im Zeitalter Bismarcks: Eine politische Briefsammlung* (2 vols., Bonn, 1925–1927).

RGB   *Reichsgesetzblatt* (1871ff.).

SBHA   *Stenographische Berichte über die Verhandlungen des Landtages: Haus der Abgeordneten*

SBHH   *Stenographische Berichte über die Verhandlugen des Landtages: Herrenhaus*

SBR   *Stenographische Berichte über die Verhandlungen des Reichstages.*

SEG   Heinrich Schulthess, ed., *Europäischer Geschichtskalender* (81 vols., Nördlingen and München, 1860–1940).

This volume is the last of three. The preceding volumes are Bismarck and the Development of Germany: The Period of Unification, 1815–1871 (Princeton, 1st ed., 1963, 2nd ed., 1990) and Bismarck and the Development of Germany: The Period of Consolidation, 1871–1880 (Princeton, 1990). The author's acknowledgments and an account of the genesis of the entire work are in the preface to the new edition of the first volume. In the introduction to the same volume is a statement of the "Bismarck problem" as it developed after 1945 and a "discourse on method" relevant to all three volumes. Since the events of 1870–1871 constituted a greater caesura in German history than those of 1879–1880, volumes two and three have a common introduction, to be found at the beginning of volume two. Chapter 15 of this volume contains the conclusion to the entire work.

✠

BOOK ONE

A Time for Conservatism,

1880–1884

I have often been reproached for doing nothing to fortify the Reich, for failing to solidify my position so that it can stand alone, quite independently of the personality of my successor, if I must have one. The reproach is very unjust. I work day and night toward this end, and it is the only concern in this world that I still have. . . . I seek the fortification of the Reich in a strong army, good finances, and the contentment of all the Reich's citizens in their various organic formations. . . . To achieve their common contentment is in my opinion one of the preconditions for the solidity of the Reich, if difficult crises should occur.

—*Bismarck to the Reichstag,*
March 1886

✠

CHAPTER ONE

The Empire of Rye, Iron, and Ink

N THE LATE 1870s Bismarck scored some of his greatest triumphs. He confounded the liberal opposition, created new options for forming a majority in the Reichstag, reconstructed the Reich executive, established his power over the Prussian cabinet, oriented German politics away from ideology toward materialism, welded a firmer union of German elites in support of the Prussian-German establishment, launched a more determined effort to interdict subversion, found national issues with which to bring together a divided country, created a tariff wall behind which he hoped German industry and agriculture would prosper, and negotiated the Dual Alliance with Austria. These successes were more than adequate to obscure the failure of his attempt to destroy the Center party in the Kulturkampf. He could look forward to the 1880s with renewed confidence in his mastery of the dominant forces in both domestic and foreign affairs. Yet the experience of that decade did not measure up to his expectations.

The first half of the 1880s was marked, to be sure, by further triumphs in foreign affairs. Bismarck succeeded in reconstructing the combination of eastern powers that he preferred. It enabled him to stabilize once more the European balance of power and buttress the aristocratic-monarchical order in central and eastern Europe. His personal hegemony in European diplomacy made possible a new venture—the acquisition of a colonial empire that he hoped would be another contribution to German economic prosperity.

But the record of those same years in domestic affairs was dismal. Although the deep depression of the 1870s was overcome, the German and world economies did not return to the standard of prosperity and progress set in 1850–1873. A mood of pessimism continued to plague businessmen and statesmen. The relief expected of protectionism did not materialize, and whatever benefits colonialism might bring lay in the future. But the greatest disappointment lay in the failure of the Reichstag (though not the Landtag) to become the subservient instrument he had expected. From 1881 to 1886 the difficulties Bismarck encountered in parliament approximated those of 1862–1866. He succeeded neither in smashing the Social Democratic party through antisocialist legislation nor in seducing its labor support through social insurance legislation. Interest-group politics worked where the business class was concerned, but failed with the proletarians. The cleavages in the German social structure and in its political life remained, although those of particularism declined.

In the year 1887 the lines of development in foreign and domestic affairs crossed once more. The final collapse of the Three Emperors League caused by renewed crises in the Balkans put the Bismarckian system of foreign policy to its greatest test, one which its architect was able to surmount only at considerable cost. Yet that same crisis, coupled with the Boulanger episode in France, enabled the chancellor to accomplish his last great coup in domestic politics. In 1887 he exploited the danger of war and the sentiment of national patriotism to achieve, as in 1866–1867, 1871, and 1878, a stunning victory in a national election that gave him for a time the subservient majority he required for his objectives in domestic affairs. But not even this triumph was lasting. Both in foreign and domestic affairs he faced in 1890 at the age of seventy-five formidable problems whose solution would have taxed the strength of a younger and healthier man.

Industrial Expansion

The crash of 1873 introduced an era in German and world capitalism that has been called "the great depression." The decline over two decades in average prices for the products of heavy industry led Nikolai Kondratieff, Josef Schumpeter, and others to conclude that this was a downward "long wave," lying between two upward "long waves"—evidence of the cyclical pattern of capitalist economic development. Recently other economic historians have pointed to factors that, beginning in the late 1870s, contradict this conclusion: expansion in the production of heavy industry; significant growth in the work force, wages, and labor productivity; and a climbing net social product.[1]

And yet the period 1873–1894 was undeniably marked by business cycles of short duration, whose psychological, social, and political consequences demarcate it from earlier and later phases of industrialization. After six years deep in the trough, the German economy began to ascend during the winter of 1879–1880. The recovery was propelled by a resumption of railway construction in the United States. Twenty-five thousand miles of lines were constructed in two years, creating a voracious demand for rails and block iron that could be met only by imports from England and Germany. Compared with previous German recoveries, that of 1880–1882 was short and weak. It

[1] On the problem of the "great depression," see Karl Erich Born, *Wirtschafts- und Sozialgeschichte des deutschen Kaiserreiches (1867/71–1914)* (Stuttgart, 1985), pp. 107–119; Knut Borchardt, "Wirtschaftliches Wachstum und Wechsellagen, 1800–1914," in Hermann Aubin and Wolfgang Zorn, eds., *Handbuch der deutschen Wirtschafts- und Sozialgeschichte* (Stuttgart, 1976), II; Hans Rosenberg, *Grosse Depression und Bismarckzeit* (Berlin, 1967); Hans Ulrich Wehler, *Bismarck und der Imperialismus* (Cologne, 1969); U. Weinstock, *Das Problem der Kondratieff-Zyklen* (Berlin, 1964); J. G. Adelman, "Long Cycles—Fact or Artifact?" *American Economic Review*, 60 (1965); S. B. Saul, *The Myth of the Great Depression, 1873–1896* (London, 1969); T. Spree, *Wachstumstrends und Konjunkturzyklen in der deutschen Wirtschaft von 1820 bis 1913* (Göttingen, 1978).

ended abruptly with the collapse of the American boom and a crisis on the Paris bourse marked by scandal. Five years passed before a general recovery began in 1887 that reached boom proportions in 1889, only to collapse once more in 1890. In summary, there were two upward (1879–1882 and 1888–1890) and three downward movements (1873–1879, 1883–1887, 1890–1894).[2] The brevity of the upswings and longevity of the downswings, along with intensified competition and uncertain profit margins, produced a mood of insecurity and pessimism throughout the business world. The German experience was shared by other countries. Industrial capitalism had produced a worldwide economy so interlocked by the exchange of goods and capital that no segment could long escape the common fate.[3]

The lower level of prices for goods produced by heavy industry reflected these short cycles. From 145.5 marks per ton in the peak year of 1873, the price of pig iron fell to 56.2 marks in 1879, rising to 60.4 marks in the recovery period that ended in 1882. Then came a steady retreat to 45.7 marks in 1887, followed by a brief ascent to 64 marks in 1890, a price that was not reached again until 1899. Pig iron production followed these fluctuations only in the beginning, falling from 2,240,575 tons in 1873 to 1,846,345 tons in 1876; thereafter, output rose in steady crescendo to 8,521,000 tons in 1900. Only twice (1886, 1891) during this long period did production fail to exceed that of the year before, and even then only by a small margin.

In order to dispose of this constantly rising tide of iron, steel, coal, and other goods German manufacturers had to conquer an increasing proportion of the home market and improve their position in the export market as well.[4] Advocates of protectionism naturally took credit for their success, but the behavior of prices indicates that other factors were at work. Prices fell because of cutthroat competition and lowered costs made possible by improved technology and mass production. Improvements occurred in blast furnaces, rolling

[2] Arthur Spiethoff, *Die wirtschaftlichen Wechsellagen: Aufschwung, Krise, Stockung* (Tübingen, 1955), I, 146–147 and II, tab. 1.

[3] Spiethoff, *Die wirtschaftlichen Wechsellagen*, I, 124–127; Max Wirth, *Geschichte der Handelskrisen* (4th ed., Frankfurt a. M., 1890), pp. 653–654; Rosenberg, *Grosse Depression*, pp. 51–52. For the attitudes of businessmen see Wolfram Fischer, *Herz des Reviers* (Essen, 1965), pp. 193–230, and "Konjunkturen und Krisen im Ruhrgebiet seit 1840 und die wirtschaftspolitische Willensbildung der Unternehmer," *Westfälische Forschungen*, 21 (1968), pp. 44–51.

[4] Spiethoff, *Die wirtschaftlichen Wechsellagen*, II, tabs. 20 and 25. The prices given by Spiethoff are those at Hamburg. Naturally they differ, owing to transportation costs, from those at other centers. See, for example, the Breslau statistics of Max Sering, *Internationale Preisbewegung und Lage der Landwirtschaft in den aussertropischen Ländern* (Berlin, 1929), p. 173, the indices of Walther G. Hoffmann, *Das Wachstum der deutschen Wirtschaft seit der Mitte des 19. Jahrhunderts* (Berlin, 1965), p. 546, and the statistics of Das Kaiserliche Statistische Amt, *Statistisches Handbuch für das deutsche Reich* (Berlin, 1907), I, 259. For the trade balance between Germany and other countries see *Statistisches Handbuch*, II, 8ff., also the export-import indices of Hoffmann, *Wachstum der deutschen Wirtschaft*, pp. 533–538, and Spiethoff, *Die wirtschaftlichen Wechsellagen*, II, tab. 14.

mills, foundries, and the like. But the most dramatic technological innovation of the period was the swift introduction after 1879 of the Gilchrist Thomas process for extracting phosphorus from iron ore. This permitted the exploitation of enormous beds of phosphorus-rich ore in Lorraine and Luxemburg, a benefit unforeseen at the time Lorraine was annexed.

"Big industry," wrote the economist Franz Huber in 1883, "shows a double character previously unknown—on the one hand, brisk activity, lively business, copious orders, higher production, and increased numbers of workers; on the other hand, a serious decline in prices, a mass production that often becomes overproduction, and a heightened competition that frequently disintegrates into selling below cost and the attempt to attract new orders through ever greater concessions on price. 'More sales, but less profit'—that is the signature of big industry since 1880. In many branches sales are more lively only because the gain is smaller. More and more industries are falling under the dominion of the law of mass turnover." To the heavy industrialist of the 1880s expansion in production was not evidence of a sound economy. On the contrary, he appeared to be caught in a vicious circle. Fierce competition forced him to cut prices and profit margins in order to find internally the capital for technological improvements that would lower costs and increase production, which again depressed prices as inventories piled up and goods had to be dumped.[5]

> Ixion on his restlesse wheele to which his limmes were bound
> Did flie und follow both at once in turning ever rouund.[6]

To Max Wirth, another contemporary economist and student of business crises, the five years from 1883 to 1887 were for both America and Europe a period of decline worse than that following the crash of 1873. "The prices of many wares continued to decline to a low point unknown to the living generation. Interest rates sank to a level unheard of in the entire history of finance, and remained so long in the trough that many believed Proudhon's prediction was coming true—a no-interest condition that would lead simultaneously to the fall of capitalism and, as a necessary consequence, the fall of culture. Capital piled up in conformity with this development to such an extent that the large banks, unlike any earlier period, often had more bullion

[5] F. C. Huber, _Fünfzig Jahre des deutschen Wirtschaftslebens_ (Stuttgart, 1906), pp. 43–44. See the yearly statistics on net profits by the major German iron and steel producers after 1878 in Wilfried Feldenkirchen, _Die Eisen- und Stahlindustrie des Ruhrgebiets, 1879–1914_, in Hans Pohl and Wilhelm Treue, eds., _Zeitschrift für Unternehmensgeschichte_, Beiheft 20 (Wiesbaden, 1982), pp. 277ff. and appendix tab. 113. Carl-Ludwig Holtfrerich pointed out in his review of this book that the statistics do not support the author's rejection of the "great depression" thesis. _Historische Zeitschrift_, 238 (1984), pp. 191–193. What the statistics explain is the depressed state of entrepreneurial minds; businessmen perceived the period to be one of economic depression because their profit margins were much lower and improvements were short-lived.

[6] Ovid, _Metamorphoses_, bk. 4, ll. 571–572, trans. Arthur Golding (1567).

in their safes than notes in circulation. Only the workers knew how, by hold-ing firmly together, to maintain during the decline most of the increased pay achieved during the period of prosperity. . . . The puzzling phenomenon—that the entrepreneurial spirit seemed to have disappeared at a time when the interest rate in London, the center of the money market, fluctuated for years between 2 and 3 percent and when prices for raw and supplementary materials reached their deepest point of the century—concerned for a long time the theoreticians as much as it did the practitioners, statesmen, and leaders of the economic parties."[7]

The consequences of such conditions were a decline in the number of firms through merger, liquidation, or bankruptcy; the founding of vertical cartels controlling the successive phases of production; and the creation of syndicates (lateral cartels) to control prices and allot markets. The depression of the 1870s had already taken a heavy toll of smaller enterprises in banking and heavy industry. Thirty out of 40 new banks established at Berlin during 1870–1873 were liquidated between 1873 and 1881; at Dresden, the figures were 13 out of 14; at Hamburg, 9 out of 15; at Frankfurt, 8 out of 13; at Breslau, 7 out of 10. As the small banks became less numerous, the larger grew. The *Deutsche Bank* was the first to grasp that bank liquidation could be profitable, and the *Dresdner Bank* and others quickly followed. The result was another surge of expansion and concentration in the structure of German banking.

In heavy industry the same process was evident. Of 244 iron smelting works existing in 1873, only 127 were left in 1879. During the recovery of 1879–1881 the number increased to 139, of which 110 remained in 1887 and 108 in 1890. The number of operating furnaces in these works increased but slightly from 210 in 1879 to 222 in 1890, but their output rose by 156 percent in the same period. Steel production also underwent a consolidation. The number of open hearth steelworks fell from 351 in 1879 to 255 in 1890, while total production increased by 6 percent. Works equipped with Bessemer con-verters numbered 57 in 1879, 75 in 1882, 94 in 1887, and 115 in 1890, rep-resenting an increase of 107 percent in the number of plants and 433 percent in production. Many of these works were owned or controlled by giant enter-prises (vertical cartels) that combined the successive phases of production—coal and iron mines, pig iron and steel plants, rolling mills, and fabricating plants—under one management. To name a few: Krupp, Phönix, Haniel, Thyssen, Stumm, Klöckner, Aachener.[8]

The necessity for secrecy among partners makes the history of syndicates difficult to trace. Although the earliest attempts to establish a united front on

[7] Wirth, *Geschichte der Handelskrisen*, pp. 654–655.

[8] Manfred Pohl, *Konzentration im deutschen Bankwesen, 1848–1980* (Frankfurt a. M., 1982), pp. 119ff.; Rolf Sonnemann, *Die Auswirkungen des Schutzzolls auf die Monopolisierung der deutschen Eisen- und Stahlindustrie, 1879–1892* (Berlin, 1960), pp. 96–99; *Statistisches Handbuch*, I, 258–267.

prices came as early as the 1840s, the greatest activity arrived during the 1880s. Before 1886 the syndicates were regional and tended to be short-lived. In that year the *Rheinisch-westfälischer Roheisenverband* was founded at Düsseldorf. This syndicate included seventeen of twenty-one iron and steel firms in the Rhineland-Westphalian region, and it became the model for other syndicates in associated industries such as coal mining, rolling mills, and the fabrication of rails, wire, and pipes. These syndicates soon expanded into national organizations for the purpose of dominating the domestic market and gaining competitive advantage abroad. Unlike the United States, which adopted antitrust statutes, and unlike Britain, France, Austria-Hungary, and smaller European states, which passed statutes limiting agreements in restraint of trade, the German government encouraged monopolistic development as a contribution to the rationalization of production and order in the marketplace. Nevertheless, the founding of syndicates was not always easy. The road was cluttered with broken agreements, dissolutions, price cutting by outsiders like Krupp, and the demoralizing collapse of the recovery of 1888–1890.

"Children of necessity" in the 1880s, cartels and syndicates were reborn as "children of convenience" in the more prosperous period that followed. Monopolies offered escape from the risks and anxieties of two decades. Originally based on informal agreements, many took on firmer outlines as time passed, until they assumed corporate form on the pattern of early American trusts. The protective tariff did not produce the cartels; both were products of depressed conditions, whose principal victim was economic liberalism—free enterprise as well as free trade.[9]

These developments speeded the nationalization of the German economy during the last decade of Bismarck's chancellorship. The uniquely German concentration of banking and industrial capital in large, interlocking enterprises counteracted the centrifugal tendencies of German particularism and imperial federalism to a far greater degree than Bismarck himself appreciated. Another aspect of nationalization was the reduction of Germany's dependence upon foreign capital and assistance. By the 1880s it had ceased to rely upon technical help from British mechanics, engineers, and managers (like William Mulvany) and upon funding by French, British, Belgian, and Dutch capitalists. Instead, Germany itself had become an important exporter of capital and technology as well as of industrial products.[10]

During the period of rapid expansion in 1850–1873, the trend of German economic development had been away from the autarchic practices of mercantilism toward laissez-faire and internationalism (Zollverein, low tariffs,

---

[9] Sonnemann, *Die Auswirkungen des Schutzzolls*, pp. 48–49, 55ff.

[10] Walther G. Hoffmann, "The Take-Off in Germany," in W. W. Rostow, ed., *The Economics of Take-Off into Sustained Growth* (London, 1964), pp. 106–112.

free enterprise). In April 1866 Georg Siemens, soon to be the founder and president of the *Deutsche Bank*, explained the significance of this development in a letter to his father: "From the moment when we changed our entire trade policy by concluding the commercial treaty with France, making the transition from protectionism to free trade, we joined the west European system to form just one country with France, England, and Belgium."[11] To liberals like Siemens, Germany's economic union with the west was at least a surrogate for its failure to achieve political institutions like those of its Atlantic neighbors. But now even the surrogate was lost. The shift to protectionism in 1879 signaled a return to autarchy, but with an important difference. This time it was not the state acting as entrepreneur and paternalistic authority that cooled the fires of free enterprise. Germany's businessmen themselves put together the corporate monopolies, the giant banks and industries, the cartels and syndicates that came to dominate the German economy. The quest for order and security became the nemesis of economic freedom, as earlier it had been the nemesis of political freedom.

Agrarian Stagnation

Events were to prove that German landowners had even more cause for alarm during the 1880s than did German businessmen. German manufacturers were affected by a cyclical decline, agrarians by a structural change in agricultural markets. Bad harvests in the late 1870s supported the price of grain but reduced the output and income of German farmers, while encouraging Russian and American imports.[12] After 1881 it became apparent that the invasion of foreign wheat from the steppes and prairies was not a temporary phenomenon. Without massive imports Germany could not feed her growing millions. Despite better domestic harvests, German wheat imports mounted from 362,000 to 572,400 tons from 1881 to 1885, more than half coming from Russia and about a quarter from North America. During the same period German grain exports sank from 53,000 to 14,000 tons.[13]

The inundation of grain markets by cheap wheat forced down prices throughout Europe. In free-trading Britain, for example, the price of wheat in 1894 was one-third of what it had been in 1867–1868.[14] In Germany the comparatively modest tariff of 1879 acted as a brake that slowed, but could

[11] Karl Helfferich, *Georg von Siemens: Ein Lebensbild aus Deutschlands grosser Zeit* (2d ed., Berlin, 1923), pp. 46–47. Siemens's point was that, if Prussia were to be competitive with Britain, France, and Belgium, it must possess Schleswig-Holstein and Hamburg; otherwise its industry would be "ruined." "Freedom is only possible in industrial, not commercial states."

[12] See vol. 2, pp. 7–9, 283–285.

[13] Max Sering, *Die landwirtschaftliche Konkurrenz Nordamerikas in Gegenwart und Zukunft* (Leipzig, 1887), p. 545.

[14] Wilhelm Abel, *Agrarkrisen und Agrarkonjunktur* (2d ed., Hamburg, 1966), p. 259.

not halt the descent. Rye was by far Germany's largest grain crop, and much less of it was imported than wheat, as was also true of oats and barley. Yet the price of all cereals fell in sympathy with wheat. Between 1881 and 1886 wheat dropped from 213.7 to 148.5 marks per ton, rye from 196.4 to 107.1 marks. Naturally, the consequence was renewed agitation for protection. Tariff rates on wheat and rye were raised from 10 to 30 marks per ton in 1885 and to 50 marks per ton in 1887. Prices rose in the late 1880s, wheat reaching 184 marks in 1891, rye 173.1 marks. But the relief was temporary. Wheat fell to 100.7 and rye to 88.2 marks per ton in 1894. Thereafter, prices moved generally upward, although the level of 1891 was not reached again before the First World War.[15]

Unlike heavy industrialists, German landowners of the 1880s could not immediately increase production to compensate for the narrowing gap between price and cost. Most arable land had already been put under cultivation by 1865. Not until after 1890 were higher grain yields achieved through the use of fertilizers, better cultivation, and improved machinery.[16] Meanwhile, the owners of the grain fields east of the Elbe were confronted with stagnating production and falling prices. After a thorough study of North American conditions, economist Max Sering warned that German agriculture was engaged in a "battle of intelligence" as well as of climate and soil conditions. German farmers and estate owners had virtues—"a chivalric attitude, readiness to sacrifice for the common good, a love for the native sod"—that were more valuable than "money-making as an end in itself and as the main aim of existence." Yet anyone who had observed American conditions, Sering concluded, had to recognize that the "undoubtedly existing superiority" of American farmers over central European agrarian producers was owed to the farmers' "respected social position." To compete successfully against them, German landowners would have to recognize the necessity for hard work and industriousness that could not be harmonized "with an all-too smug or extravagant life of pleasure." He urged German agrarians to concentrate on crops and products less vulnerable to foreign competition than wheat and to learn

---

[15] Theodor Freiherr von der Goltz, Agrarwesen und Agrarpolitik (Jena, 1904), p. 269; Spiethoff, Die wirtschaftlichen Wechsellagen, II, tab. 27. See also Hoffmann, Wachstum der deutschen Wirtschaft, pp. 522–554. Again the prices cited are derived from Spiethoff and are the average for imported grain at Hamburg. Hoffmann's figures are somewhat higher, being an estimate of the average price received by German producers. Because of Bismarck's interests, the price of timber is significant. After reaching a peak of 13.18 marks per cubic meter in 1875, the price of lumber (Nutzholz) sank to 10.08 marks in 1877–1878, recovering slightly to 10.24 marks in 1879, only to fall again despite the protective tariff. It hovered between 7.91 marks (1882) and 8.44 marks (1883–1884) until 1886, when an ascent began that reached its peak at 11.79 marks in 1889. In conformity with the business cycle, it declined thereafter to 9.15 marks in 1894, after which it followed the upward trend to the First World War. Ibid., pp. 563–564.

[16] Hans Wolfram Graf Finck von Finckenstein, Die Entwicklung der Landwirtschaft in Preussen und Deutschland, 1800–1930 (Würzburg, 1960), pp. 98–108.

from the American cooperative movement the virtues of mutual help, bringing together big and small landowners in a common effort to raise the productivity of German agriculture.[17]

Many big landowners were ill prepared to cope with the problems that now arose. They were former army officers or state officials who knew little about agriculture and often left the management of their estates to overseers. Being accustomed to command, they sometimes intervened with unfortunate results that earned them the ill will and even indifference of subordinates. Many were distracted from their own affairs by involvement in local government and in parliament. Their social status, furthermore, demanded an expensive life-style. Of the large allodial estates 42.9 percent were estimated in 1896 to have been mortgaged at more than 60 percent of their value.[18] Max Weber warned that the average noble estate of 400 to 500 acres could "no longer support a lordly aristocratic existence." The Junker, observed Friedrich Engels, had the same problem as Mr. Micawber: how "to have an annual income of say 20,000 marks, an annual expenditure of 30,000 marks and not make any debts."[19] Yet most landowners managed to survive. In Prussia 5,650 properties totaling about 548,000 acres went into bankruptcy between 1883 and 1900. But this constituted only 0.2 percent of all such properties and 0.7 percent of all cultivated land in Prussia.[20]

The threat of failure was greater than the reality in agriculture as well as in industry, but the anxieties engendered by the struggle to survive sufficed to perpetuate the coalition of "rye and iron" first established by the tariff act of 1879 and extended by that of 1885. This so-called solidarity bloc was not, as Alexander Gerschenkron observed, an alliance between agriculture and industry as such, but rather between the most powerful pressure groups within both, between the big landowners of trans-Elbia (League of German Farmers, founded in 1893) and the big industrialists of Rhineland-Westphalia, Saar-Lorraine, and Upper Silesia (Central Federation of German Industrialists, founded in 1876). More properly speaking, the solidarity bloc was an uneasy compromise within which each member yielded something in order to gain something. After propping up grain prices, the industrialist had to raise wages to assure the subsistence of his workers and the continuing in-migration of rural labor. After propping up industrial prices and wages, the big landowner was compelled to pay more for farm implements and machinery and to raise rural wages in order to keep peasants on the land. Both, furthermore, had to buy off allied segments of the economy; for example, the big industrialist had

[17] Sering, Konkurrenz Nordamerikas, pp. 715–716.
[18] Theodor Freiherr von der Goltz, Geschichte der deutschen Landwirtschaft (Stuttgart, 1903), II, 402–404, and Agrarwesen und Agrarpolitik, pp. 124–140.
[19] Quoted in Alexander Gerschenkron, Bread and Democracy in Germany (Berkeley, 1943), pp. 45–46.
[20] Abel, Agrarkrisen und Agrarkonjunktur, p. 260.

to strike bargains with the machine manufacturer who needed cheap steel, the big landowner with the small farmer who had an interest in cheap fodder. Internationally, furthermore, protectionism could only be a losing game in the end, for, as trade agreements expired, other countries prepared to hike their tariffs in retaliation, threatening German industrialists with the loss of dumping grounds for surplus merchandise.[21]

Within the solidarity bloc the economic weight of big industry grew inexorably at the cost of big agriculture. According to the best available estimates, the net domestic product of Germany during 1850–1854 was derived 45.2 percent from agriculture, forestry, and fisheries as against 20.4 percent from industry and handicraft production. In 1870–1874 the contrast was 37.9 to 29.7 percent and in 1900–1904, 29 to 36.6 percent. During the same half century the percentage of workers employed in agriculture, forestry, and fishing sank from 54.6 to 38.0 percent, while those employed in industry and handicraft pursuits rose from 24.3 to 34.4 percent; during the same period the percentage of capital invested in agriculture is believed to have declined from 51.2 to 30.1 percent, while that invested in industry and railways rose from 29.3 to 45.3 percent.[22] The aristocratic landowners, whom Bismarck considered to be the backbone of the Prussian-German state, were by the end of his life no longer the backbone of its economy. How long could social mores and political institutions, conceived when rye was king, endure in an economy dominated by iron and steel?

Social Consolidation

The union between big business and big agriculture that Bismarck consummated with the protective tariff of 1879 was not the result of a sudden courtship eased by an advantageous marriage contract. A rapprochement had long been under way. Bourgeoisie and aristocracy had found common ground early in the nineteenth century in the state service, whose officials had been molded into a common bureaucratic estate (*Beamtenstand*). The breach that occurred during the middle decades in the solidarity and isolation of the bureaucratic estate followed generational more than caste lines and paralleled economic and social conflicts in society at large.[23] Bismarck's achievements in the 1860s, his ascendancy over the bureaucratic apparatus, the relentless pressure upon bureaucratic opponents by Bismarck, Eulenburg, Puttkamer, and other ministers effectively closed the political gap within the service and insulated the bureaucratic estate once more from ideological currents. Thereafter, officials sat in parliament as supporters of the regime, not as members of

---

[21] Gerschenkron, *Bread and Democracy*, pp. 44ff. After 1887 the favorable balance of trade that Germany gained in 1880 turned unfavorable. *Statistisches Handbuch*, II, 8–9.

[22] Hoffmann, *Wachstum der deutschen Wirtschaft*, pp. 33, 35, 44.

[23] See vol. 1, pp. 103–126.

either a liberal or conservative opposition. Agrarian difficulties led more sons of the gentry to seek bureaucratic careers during the last part of the century. Those of aristocratic lineage continued to receive preference for higher posts, although the proportion of those they held (somewhat more than 50 percent in 1914) tended to decline as the service expanded. Their presence certainly strengthened the influence of agrarian interests on government policy, but it also reflected a continued ascription to the nobility of values that qualified them better for high office than their bourgeois colleagues.[24]

Bureaucratic families with more than one generation of service to the state continued to supply recruits for its ranks. Their sons and daughters (like Wilhelmine Mencken) often married into the nobility, but an increasing number also sought careers in business, academia, and the officer corps. By favoring candidates with inherited wealth for the service, the bureaucracy made progress in overcoming the internal class conflict of the middle decades. Naturally this aided those sons of the new industrial elite who sought status by becoming officials, regular army officers, or reserve corps officers. Wealth became a criterion of personal capacity and social acceptability to a degree unknown in the academically oriented bureaucracy of earlier years. "A new ruling class was emerging, which combined the formerly separate elements of industrial and agrarian wealth with the professional elites and cut across all provincial boundaries."[25]

Despite their disparate origins, Prussian officials of the late nineteenth century possessed a high degree of homogeneity based on wealth, social elitism, and general acceptance of authoritarian government. In other European countries (England is the best example) imposition of high academic standards and professionalization of the state service tended to detach the bureaucracy from the old ruling caste, democratize it, open it up to new social and political concerns, and guarantee its neutrality in the political struggle. But in Prussia the state service reflected the fusion of the old agrarian and new industrial elites. The old establishment expanded to accommodate and to include within its ranks the new elite of culture and property (*Bildung und Besitz*) and thereby perpetuated itself.[26] Although by no means a radical, Rudolf Gneist described in bitter words the pressures for conformity that characterized the system. "To learn how one can serve a system against one's conscience and convictions for an entire lifetime, one must be a Prussian official; to know how one covers the disgrace of abandoned conviction with a title or a decoration, one must know the secrets of the higher bureaucracy."[27]

[24] John R. Gillis, *The Prussian Bureaucracy in Crisis, 1840–1860* (Stanford, 1971), pp. 200ff.; Nikolaus von Preradovich, *Die Führungsschichten in Österreich und Preussen, 1804–1918* (Wiesbaden, 1955), pp. 107–108, 160ff.

[25] Gillis, *Prussian Bureaucracy*, p. 207.

[26] Gillis, *Prussian Bureaucracy*, pp. 221–214.

[27] Quoted in Gillis, *Prussian Bureaucracy*, p. ii.

The latifundia east of the Elbe provided another common ground for aristocracy and bourgeoisie. The abolition of legal restrictions on the purchase of
noble estates in 1807, followed by a period of agrarian crisis, released a flow
of mercantile capital into agriculture. The sons and grandsons of successful
merchants and bankers from western cities made the leap from urban patrici-
ate to gentry by buying east-Elbian estates. As Bismarck observed, these parvenus adopted the social and political stance of the Junkers, whose status they
hoped to achieve. The agrarian revolution, on the other hand, changed the
character of the aristocracy. The transformation of land into a commodity,
the step-by-step dissolution of manorial powers and ties, the transition from
subsistence to capitalistic agriculture, and the ownership of rural industries
transformed a governing aristocracy into a landowning interest group that no
longer had the attributes of the feudal nobility they still conceived themselves
to be. Earlier Prussian noblemen had given leadership to the liberal as well as
conservative political parties. But the gradual amalgamation of bourgeois and
noble estate owners produced a homogeneous class of rural gentry animated
by a common *Korpsgeist*. The old political elite was replaced by "men who
thought according to stereotype, rigidly followed the standardized conventions of their caste, draped their robust materialism in idealistic and 'national'
terms, and stubbornly clung to their privileged position."[28]

The "pseudo-democratization" of the aristocracy proceeded simultaneously
with the "pseudo-feudalization" of the upper *Mittelstand*. Despite consistent
support from Bismarck and the government, the gentry were outstripped in
wealth by other interest groups in industry, finance, and commerce. Yet they
continued to possess the primary status in German society, a prestige born of
their feudal origin. By virtue of birth they took precedence over the captains
of industry and finance at court and over bourgeois officers and officials in the
competition for high positions in the service of the state. Although their actual function in German society was rapidly changing, Prussian noblemen
continued to act the role of feudal lords and to be accepted in that role by a
rank-conscious society.

The achievements of the Hohenzollern monarchy under Bismarck's leadership in 1866 and 1871 and the fears of social unrest produced by the depression of 1873–1879 and by the rise of proletarian socialism changed the attitudes of the German businessmen toward the nobility. Although they still
grumbled on occasion at the social and political dominance of the aristocracy,
the chief aspiration of the wealthy *arrivistes* of German capitalism was not to
destroy the old elite, but to enter it through the student corps, reserve officer
corps, marriage, and ennoblement. In 1866 Hermann Baumgarten described

---

[28] Hans Rosenberg, "Die Pseudodemokratisierung der Rittergutsbesitzerklasse," in Hans Ulrich
Wehler, ed., *Moderne deutsche Sozialgeschichte. Neue wissenschaftliche Bibliothek: Geschichte*, vol.
10 (Cologne, 1966), p. 298.

the scene: "Merchants who became rich in a hurry had the satisfaction of surpassing officials and nobles financially and soon, in individual cases, socially as well. They displayed their wealth by riding in the most elegant equipages with liveries like those of a baron; they gave dinners to which diplomats and ministers were glad to come; they received decorations and titles. Yes, if it went very well, they became barons."[29]

The rapprochement of nobility and upper *Mittelstand* after 1871 was speeded by "*commercium and connubium*, i.e., by their common participation in the boom period following the Franco-Prussian war, and further by intermarriages that relieved the financial necessities of the aristocracy and satisfied the social ambition of the enriched bourgeoisie."[30] Unlike the English aristocracy, which regularly sent its younger sons into the business world, the Junkers had in the past remained largely aloof from business enterprise. Although increasingly capitalistic in their attitude toward land and its uses, they continued to regard entrepreneurial activity as incompatible with a noble's status and honor. From heavily mortgaged estates they watched with contempt laced with envy as the businessmen of Berlin and the Ruhr amassed fortunes. Although their duties remained, their privileges diminished and likewise their relative wealth. But they also noted that birth and lineage did not immunize the great nobles of Silesia from the temptation to make money as industrial entrepreneurs. As the German "take-off" reached its climax in the early 1870s, disdain for money-grubbing capitalists gave way to greed. During the *Gründerjahre* the great lords, rural gentry, and public officials joined bankers, industrialists, journalists, shopkeepers, porters, and cab drivers in seeking fortunes on the bourse, bidding up the price of corporate shares without regard to present earnings or future prospects. Company promoters, aiming at higher stock prices rather than operating profits, sought public confidence by enlisting titled nobles as board members.

Aristocrats shared the boom, but also the bust. As early as 1869–1870 the collapse of the Rumanian railway scheme of Bethel Henry Strousberg jeopardized the fortunes of some of Prussia's highest-ranking nobles, including the Prince of Putbus, Duke of Ujest, and Duke of Ratibor. In his ironic mode Bismarck described their predicament and their salvation to the French ambassador: "Our greatest lords and our bootblacks believed that Strousberg would present them with a gold mine, and a great many risked the best part of what they possessed, believing the promises of this adventurer. All that is buried now in the Rumanian mud, and, one fine day, two dukes, one general who is an aide-de-camp, a half-dozen ladies-in-waiting, twice that many chamberlains, a hundred coffeehouse owners and all the cabmen of Berlin

[29] Ernst K. Bramsted, *Aristocracy and the Middle Classes in Germany* (rev. ed., Chicago, 1964), pp. 228ff.

[30] Bramsted, *Aristocracy*, p. 230.

found themselves totally ruined. The Emperor took pity on the dukes, the aide-de-camp, the ladies-in-waiting, and the chamberlains, and charged me with pulling them out of the trouble. I appealed to Bleichröder who, on condition of getting a title of nobility, which as a Jew he valued, agreed to rescue the Duke of Ratibor, the Duke of Ujest, and General Count Lehndorf; two dukes and an aide-de-camp saved—frankly, that is worth the 'von' bestowed on the good Bleichröder. But the ladies-in-waiting, the cabmen, and the others were left drowning."[31] Strousberg himself languished in a Russian jail, despite Bismarck's efforts to gain his freedom. Yet his collapse did not serve as a sufficient warning to the Prussian aristocracy. Three years later Bleichröder was again called to the rescue, this time to bail out two of Bismarck's subordinates, Hermann Wagener and Count Paul von Hatzfeldt. In 1873 Gerson von Bleichröder—"the first Prussian Jew who had been so honored without having previously converted to Christianity"—fittingly capped his ascent into the aristocracy by purchasing Field Marshal Roon's estate in the neighborhood of Potsdam.[32]

What Bleichröder achieved a host of others aspired to—a social status for themselves and their descendants commensurate with their accumulated wealth. The various routes to this goal were well charted during the reign of Wilhelm I. In addition to that taken by Bleichröder, Prussian businessmen eased their way into the nobility by nourishing personal connections with the royal family, making munificent gifts to favored royal charities, purchasing either entailed estates or *Herrschaften* east of the Elbe, and marrying the daughters of aristocrats—often those seeking rescue from indigent or modest financial circumstances.[33] Two examples reported by Werner Sombart show how quickly the process of amalgamation between the young capitalistic nobility (*Geldadel*) and the old landowning nobility (*Grundadel*) proceeded. "The Cologne banker Simon Oppenheim, who held the [honorary] title of Prussian privy counselor of commerce [*Geheimer Kommerzienrat*], was made a baron by Austria in 1867, an elevation that Prussia recognized a year later. The granddaughters of the first Baron von Oppenheim—children of his two oldest sons—all married into families of the old nobility; their names are Baroness Plancy, Countess Bredow, Frau von Frankenberg, Baroness von Hammerstein, Countess Arco, Countess Matuschka, Countess Pocci. One of their brothers is married to a Russian countess, the other to a baroness from an old

[31] Fritz Stern, "Money, Morals, and the Pillars of Bismarck's Society," *Central European History*, 3 (1970), pp. 55–58.

[32] Fritz Stern, *Gold and Iron: Bismarck, Bleichröder, and the Building of the German Empire* (New York, 1977), pp. 167ff., 351ff.; and Gordon R. Mork, "The Prussian Railway Scandal of 1873: Economics and Politics in the German Empire," *European Studies Review*, 1 (1971), pp. 35–48.

[33] Lamar Cecil, "The Creation of Nobles in Prussia, 1871–1918," *American Historical Review*, 75 (1970), pp. 757–795; Werner Sombart, *Die deutsche Volkswirtschaft im neunzehnten Jahrhundert* (2d ed., Berlin, 1909), p. 508.

Bavarian noble family. In Bavaria King Max Joseph I awarded his court banker Aaron Elias Seligmann the baronial name 'von Eichtal.' His descendants, except for one branch that settled in Paris, have all been absorbed by the old native nobility of Bavaria. They are chamberlains, estate owners, officers, and are closely related by marriage to the Barons von Rummel, Podewils, Seckendorff, Godin, Moreau, Imhof, and Gumpenberg."[34]

Not every industrialist succumbed to the lure of ennoblement. Bismarck was both "impressed and amused" when Friedrich Krupp refused a patent in 1888 because it would "damage his business reputation."[35] A recent study shows, moreover, that Wilhelm I, Friedrich III, and even Wilhelm II, who cultivated relationships with wealthy capitalists like the shipping magnate Albert Ballin, conferred predicates and titles less as a means of bringing new blood into the nobility from the business world than of legitimating bourgeois officers of high rank (particularly under Wilhelm I) and of providing "aristocratic shelter to marginal members of the older noble class." Most of the patents conferred went to the husbands or fiancés of noblewomen, their sons or grandsons, close relatives of noble families, holders of foreign patents or of unauthenticated claims to ancient titles, and illegitimate sons of noblemen and the sons of life peers. "Thus the nobles created by Wilhelm I and his successors were a tightly constituted group with strong material, marriage, or occupational ties to the older aristocracy."[36] *Connubium* rather than *Commerzium* was the surest way up the social ladder.

Ennoblement was not, however, the only or even principal way in which bourgeois were "feudalized." Only big capitalists, generals, and high officials had a realistic possibility of such recognition. The sons of *Mittelstand* families with sufficient means to "study" at the universities gained their indoctrination in the Junker "sense of honor" and "capacity for giving satisfaction" from dueling fraternities and the reserve officer corps. Suspicion of the loyalty of bourgeois officers had led Wilhelm and Roon to reduce the role of the *Landwehr* in the Prussian army; hence the execution of the military reform of the early 1860s was undoubtedly a defeat for the Prussian *Mittelstand* and its values. In the late 1880s the expansion of the German army created a need for more officers than Junker families could supply. Yet the proportion of bourgeois to noble officers could not be increased in the reserve regiments without reintroducing the threat that Wilhelm and Roon had seen in the old *Landwehr*. The victories of 1864, 1866, and 1870–1871 had given the Prussian army and its leadership a glamor that impressed philistines; the proletarianization of labor and the spread of socialism made the army appear to be a necessary bulwark of internal law and order. A commission in the reserves

[34] Quoted in Sombart, *Deutsche Volkswirtschaft*, p. 509.

[35] Freiherr Lucius von Ballhausen, *Bismarck-Erinnerungen* (Stuttgart, 1920), pp. 448, 450.

[36] Cecil, "Creation of Nobles," pp. 791–793.

became a valued status symbol. Instead of civilianizing the army, the typical bourgeois reserve officer tended to militarize society. He aped the social pretensions and opinions, arrogance and swagger, of the aristocratic line officer. The bourgeois of modest means found in an officer's rank a surrogate for the aristocratic title that was beyond his reach.[37]

In the judgment of Max Weber there was little by 1914 to distinguish the Prussian aristocracy from the upper bourgeoisie. "Those who know the much vilified (often unjustly so) and much apotheosized (with equal injustice) 'Junker' of the east will find much to like about him in purely personal terms. On the hunt, having a good drink, at card playing, in the hospitality of his estate—there everything is genuine. Everything first becomes artificial when this purely economic, entrepreneurial, hence essentially bourgeois business stratum is categorized as an 'aristocracy.' Although oriented toward agrarian entrepreneurial activity, this stratum of society is as heavily and unreservedly engaged in the social and economic conflict of interests as any manufacturer. Ten minutes in the company of these people suffices to show that they are plebeians, particularly so in their virtues, which have a thoroughly plebeian character. . . . *They* are not the only stratum of which this is true, for the lack of the forms of cosmopolitan upbringing is evident among us not only in the character of the Junkers, but also in the penetrating bourgeois character of *all* those which have been the special bearers of the Prussian state in the periods of its poor but glorious ascent. The old officer families, which cultivated the tradition of the old Prussian army with a high sense of honor and often in very needy circumstances, the old families that similarly supplied the state with officials are [today] economically and socially, as well as in outlook, a *bourgeois middle class* [*Mittelstand*], whether or not they belong to the nobility." It was futile, Weber concluded, to attempt to manufacture an aristocracy out of an ennobled bourgeoisie. For the sons of parvenus to copy the old aristocracy by aping its traditions as dueling students and reserve officers, and its politics as voters and public servants, could only produce a caricature of the original model, which the processes of economic and social change had already liquidated.[38]

The German bourgeoisie never achieved a fully developed class consciousness. Its capitalists failed to act the role Marx assigned them in the dialectic of the class struggle. Instead of overthrowing the aristocracy, they tended to join it and accept its standards. From the indemnity bill of 1866 to the tariff act of 1879 the blending of nobility and upper bourgeoisie was a principal aim

[37] Eckart Kehr, "Zur Genesis des königlich preussischen Reserveoffiziers," in Hans-Ulrich Wehler, ed., *Der Primat der Innenpolitik* (3rd ed., Berlin, 1976), pp. 57–63.

[38] Max Weber, "Wahlrecht und Demokratie in Deutschland," in *Gesammelte politische Schriften* (2d ed., Tübingen, 1958), pp. 265–267. The issue that gave rise to this political tract was a proposal to increase the number of noblemen by creating new entailed estates. See *ibid.*, pp. 178ff.

of Bismarck's domestic policy. In contrast to many people of his social standing, he understood that in this dynamic century the aristocracy alone could no longer provide an adequate social foundation for the Hohenzollern monarchy and Prussian bureaucratic state. Yet his success in widening their base of support created another fissure that was to be their principal weakness. By the 1880s the alienation of many German workers presented a far greater threat to the stability of the Prussian-German establishment than the bourgeoisie had ever been, even in the revolution of 1848.

The Quest for Consensus

In promoting the fusion of the empire's financial and social elites, Bismarck did not intend that the process of social consolidation should end there. His actions suggest that he aimed at a broader consensus of social forces in which all "productive" classes and interest groups would be won to the state and the existing order through the cultivation of their material interests. There appears to be no good reason to doubt that he truly believed that the tariffs of 1879 and 1885 would benefit everyone and harm no one. That prices for industrial and agrarian products continued to fall proved to his satisfaction the correctness of his assumption that the burden of customs duties was borne by foreign producers, not German consumers. Yet he also clung to the conviction, however inconsistent, that tariffs constituted a genuine protective shield that sheltered the domestic market, providing greater profits for employers and higher wages for employees. Those who were engaged in the processes of production, whether as owner-managers or laborers, were the worker bees of German society, whom the state must nurture and protect, in contrast to the few drones who contributed nothing. Among the drones were absentee landlords and rentiers ("coupon clippers") living off invested capital, but also academically trained editors, journalists, officials, and politicians who by their impracticality and divisiveness obstructed the nation's progress.[39] His aim, he declared, was "the protection of national labor, protection of the entire wealth of the nation, that of the poor as well as the rich."[40]

To these same ends Bismarck, who had long turned a deaf ear to the entreaties of colonial enthusiasts, reversed himself in 1883–1885 by acquiring colonies in Africa and the South Pacific. As in the case of the protective tariff, he aimed to preserve for Germany a secure market for its products in the era of "new imperialism." He thought to protect the interests of merchants engaged in overseas trade and of manufacturers and laborers who produced the goods they sold. Yet he was by no means uncritical of German

---

[39] Reichstag speech of May 9, 1884. BR, X, 129ff. This conception of society is evident in many other sources; see, for example, his Reichstag speech of Feb. 6, 1885. BR, XI, 25.

[40] Reichstag speech of Feb. 10, 1885. BR, X, 473.

capitalism or unwilling, where he thought it necessary, to contravene the interests of German businessmen. On the contrary, he sought the nationalization of German railways, fought for government monopolies over the tobacco and liquor industries, and advocated public ownership of fire and hail insurance companies and of the coal-mining industry. For the benefit of German labor, urban and rural, he established a revolutionary system of social insurance that differed substantially from the wishes of much of the business community. Still his concessions to labor in the way of protective legislation were limited by what he believed to be the vital interests of employers. He did not succeed in integrating labor into the national consensus.

There is no reason to doubt the genuineness of Bismarck's conviction that the monarchy must achieve the "reconciliation of different interests whose conflicts limit our economic and political development." "I hope that ever wider circles of our population will come to recognize that the social reform undertaken by the governments, which seeks to secure the worker against the vicissitudes of fate, is motivated by the spirit of reconciliation and equalization of class interests. As long as my strength lasts, I will not cease to work for the completion of this reform."[41] That he did not achieve this was partially the consequence of his own limited experience. Although he prided himself on being a man of practical affairs in close touch with the real world, he was largely unfamiliar with the new industrial regions of the Ruhr and Silesia and the industries that were in his lifetime transforming Berlin from a governmental into a major industrial city. The industries he knew by personal experience were the small distilleries and paper mills at Varzin and the sawmill, distillery, and gunpowder factory at Friedrichsruh. Only twice apparently did he visit a major industrial complex—"the largest machine factory in the world" at Manchester in 1842 and the Krupp works at Essen in 1864. If the scores of workers who tended the blast furnaces and giant hammers made any impression on him, we have no record of it. (In 1864 he was probably more interested in Krupp's products than his work force.) As far as we know, he never descended a mine shaft to see miners at work, their faces grimy with coal dust and streaked with sweat, or entered a textile mill, where harried women and children served the whirling spindles and flying shuttles.[42]

And yet Bismarck firmly believed that he was in closer contact with working men and women and better acquainted with their wants and needs than were most of his contemporaries. In the Reichstag he pontificated, "Gentlemen, I believe that I usually see in every year more workers and exchange more words with workers than I do with other people, if I may perhaps exclude the Reichstag. When I am in the country, where I spend much of my time,

[41] Bismarck to Evangelischer Arbeiterverein in Herne, Nov. 4, 1884. GW, XIV, 955–956.

[42] Otto to Ferdinand von Bismarck, July 28, 1842. GW, XIV, 18–19. Telegrams, Krupp to Bismarck, Bismarck to king, Oct. 26, 1864. BFA, Bestand B, Mappe 65/1.

no worker's dwelling is unknown to me. I know most of the workers personally, and I speak with them personally; I am not at all shy of having contact
with them. There is no worker who, when I come, does not meet me at the
threshold, extend his hand trustingly, invite me inside, wipe off a chair and
invite me to sit down. Hence I know the opinion of the workers rather
well."[43] By his own unwitting confession Bismarck's personal knowledge of
workers was that of a grand seigneur who talked about crops, timber, weather,
and buttermilk with the peasants on his estates.

Agriculture remained Bismarck's favorite child. Undoubtedly this was true
for subjective reasons: personal background, investment in fields and forests,
and involvement in their management. But he also believed that rural landlords were the bulwark of the existing social and political order, the class
whose destruction would be an irreparable loss to the monarchy, bureaucracy,
and army. Despite the feudal terminology he often used, especially when addressing the Kaiser, his was not a romantic vision. His compromises with industrial capitalism, plans for the Prussian House of Lords, and intentions in
the Kreisordnung of 1872 show that he was no ordinary agrarian reactionary.
He was aware of the changing character of the agrarian landowning class and
believed that class distinctions were easing in rural Prussia.

In the 1880s Bismarck maintained that the term "big landlord" (Gross-
grundbesitzer) was losing its original social connotation. Many farmers with
large holdings, larger than some knights' estates, considered themselves to be
"estate owners" and sat in county diets. Increasingly the gentry and farmers
thought of themselves as members of the same status group (Stand). To the
disappointment of those who promoted class conflict, "this amalgamation is
proceeding gradually and inexorably. This is the wholesome consequence of
legislation, which many privileged persons initially found painful—namely,
the abolition of all prerogatives (whether based on law or principle) belonging
to the larger landed estates or, to be exact, to the old nobility. We owners of
the larger estates are today nothing more in our industry than the largest farmers, and the farmer is nothing but the owner of a smaller estate." In principle
he favored dividing the land in order to increase the number of landowners.
Yet he was not opposed to the accumulation of large holdings, if the owners
resided on and managed their estates. Big landowners, with sweaty faces
brown from the sun, who themselves oversaw the cultivation of their fields,
who purchased land out of "passion for their trade," were "the good fortune
of our country." If this "race" were ever destroyed, the result would be the
"crippling of our entire economic and political life."[44]

For all his reliance on material factors Bismarck did not lose sight of the
psychological dimension of consolidation through national consensus. This

[43] BR, XII, 244.
[44] Reichstag speeches of Feb. 14–16, 1885. BR, XI, 16–25.

can be seen in his continual effort to "Germanize" ethnic minorities and his use of German patriotism to overcome regional particularism and party cleavages. By attacking ultramontanism, but not Catholicism,[45] international socialism but not proletarians, he aimed to remove what were by his diagnosis cancerous growths on the otherwise healthy body of the nation. His mistake was to assume that both could be excised as effectively as were Denmark in 1864 and Austria in 1866. In the protective tariff and colonial acquisitions he expected to find new currents with which to galvanize national sentiment. Yet his greatest successes in pulling the nation together were achieved by exploiting frictions and dangers in foreign affairs. During the last decade of his chancellorship, the opportunities for such actions came briefly from Britain (1884–1885) and then from France and Russia (1886–1888).

Although the goal of consensus is apparent, his tactics for arriving at it were often self-defeating. In attacking ultramontanes and socialists he overestimated the appeal of dynastic loyalty and German patriotism and underestimated the degree of alienation felt by his targets, the moral power of their religious and social ideals, and the effect of persecution (the limited kind available to constitutional governments) in stiffening the will of the persecuted. The moral and material consensus he sought was also endangered by the ferocity of his verbal assaults upon those who would not do his bidding. Resistance to his will and the questioning of his indispensability induced in him a narcissistic rage that spilled out in his parliamentary speeches and the articles he inspired in the press. Those who opposed him for whatever reason, whether in parliament or palace, were labeled as *Reichsfeinde* (enemies of the Reich). Support was equated with patriotism, opposition with disloyalty.

Bismarck could not accept that the composition of parliament was a true reflection of the views and feelings of most Germans. Instead, he believed that it reflected the capacity of journalists and agitators to mislead the nation. Hence he constantly appealed to the nation over the heads of the deputies assembled before him. His aim was to educate the voters, inducing them to sweep away ultraconservatives, left-liberals, centrists, social democrats, and the like at election time, in order that the true opinions of the nation could be heard. The worker bees were urged to expel the drones from the hive. During the 1880s the thought was never far from his mind that the replacement of universal male suffrage by corporative representation was perhaps the only way to achieve that end.

During the last decade of his chancellorship Bismarck spoke often of the long-term benefits of universal public education and compulsory military service as perhaps the only effective means of building the national consensus he sought. "I share completely your majesty's faith in the future of our military

---

[45] That the Kulturkampf tended to become an attack upon Catholicism as such he blamed on the policies of Falk.

BISMARCK, JULY 3, 1871. (BILDARCHIV PREUSSISCHER KULTURBESITZ.)

WILHELM I, ABOUT 1880. (BILDARCHIV PREUSSISCHER KULTURBESITZ.)

training and see in it a counterweight to many of the evil consequences of our
civilian education," he wrote to Wilhelm in 1881.[46] By increasing the dispar-
ity between benefits received by educators in state schools over those received
by teachers employed in local community schools (*Communalanstalten*), he
proposed to force the local schools into the hands of the state. "I presume to
have the support of all my colleagues," he told the cabinet, "if I continue the
struggle of the monarchy against the communal republics. He who has the
schools controls the future!"[47]

After two decades of struggle against political opposition stemming from
varied sources, Bismarck came to rely in the long run less on moral, political,
and even physical coercion than on the ultimate influence of patriotic teachers and professors and the habits of discipline and obedience to authority in-
culcated by the army to achieve the national consensus that, reinforced by
material bonds, would consolidate the existing order and preserve it from the
ravages of time and change. "One could achieve concordats acceptable to
Prussia," he remarked, through diplomacy and by "working on Roman prelates," but these "small means" could not "heal the old injury" caused by the
fact that so many Germans trusted the political leadership of their priests
more than that of the king—"priests dependent on a foreign, absolute monarch, who is in turn dependent on the Jesuits and their money. This is a
sickness which only time and above all the *school* can cure, although perhaps
never completely."[48]

Too much education was equally dangerous. Although illiteracy must be
reduced to a minimum, he told Gossler in 1885, the state must in the interest
of social stability limit its appropriations for education. School administra-
tions must not be allowed to increase further the measure of "knowledge and
capacity already established as the norm for compulsory education of the people. I hold that the present norm has been set too high and believe that the
resulting cost of administering our schools puts an excessive burden on local
governments, a burden unjustified by the needs of the state and existing statutes. . . . Your excellency knows what great importance I attach to elementary schools for political reasons. . . . Furthermore, I am convinced that your
excellency shares the concern that I have repeatedly expressed with regard to
the excesses of elementary education. Russian nihilism is in this connection
an instructive phenomenon, because it illustrates the pathological consequences of schooling that exceeds [social] needs. . . . I see in present conditions a danger for our political future."[49] "The nihilists," he told the Reichs-

---

[46] Bismarck to Kaiser, Apr. 2, 1881. *GW*, XIV, 925.

[47] To the Prussian cabinet, Feb. 7, 1882. Lucius, *Bismarck-Erinnerungen*, p. 224.

[48] Bismarck to Crown Prince Friedrich Wilhelm, Dec. 19, 1882. *GW*, VIc, 267. Emphasis is
in the original. See also *BR*, XII, 300.

[49] Bismarck to Gossler, May 31, 1885. *GW*, VIc, 314–315. Bismarck to Puttkamer, June 9,
1885, *ibid.*, pp. 315–316.

tag, "stem from a college [Abiturienten] proletariat of half-educated people" produced by Germany's upper schools, which provided a "learned education" to a far greater number of young people than society could digest.[50]

Although he perceived dangers, Bismarck continued in later years to place his hopes for the future upon Germany's students and their professors. "I have confidence in the German nation," he told the Reichstag, "and especially in our young people, who are studying in the universities. They have studied under the impressions of the great epoch that our Kaiser inaugurated at the head of his army. One day they will look back critically (like contemporary historians writing about the particularism of the 1850s) at the particularism of the ten to twelve factions that now fight each other [in parliament]. That is the hope in which I will peacefully die. I will not live to see it happen myself, but I have that hope when haunted in troubled moments by the thought that we may one day return to the old German confederation."[51] On being congratulated by the social Darwinist Professor Ernst Haeckel for his decision to acquire colonies, Bismarck replied in typical fashion. "I thank you, sir, for your benevolent letter of last month, which proves once again that the national idea is being constantly and faithfully nurtured by teachers in Germany's institutions of higher education. It is chiefly they whom we must thank for the preservation, during difficult times, of national traditions from which we benefit today. The love of Kaiser and Reich shown by our academic youth is worthy testimony for the effectiveness of their teachers."[52] The master of Realpolitik finally placed his reliance for the realization of his vision less upon ministers, bureaucrats, and army officers than upon patriotic professors and their students. In this he was not unjustified.

Conquest of the Intelligentsia

In his search for consensus Bismarck's most notable achievement was conquest of the German academic and academically trained community—that group in German society of which he was generally most contemptuous and made the least effort to placate. Although he accepted their honorary doctorates and eulogies with brief, gracious letters, he had no great interest in their scientific projects and humanistic endeavors, except for the few historians in whose works he rummaged about. His intellectual contacts were limited to a few interviews (notably Rudolf Ihering and Erich Marcks) and a few consultations (Adolph Wagner and Albert Schäffle on social insurance) in which

---

[50] Reichstag speech of May 9, 1884. BR, X, 103–105; also GW, VIc, 406–408.

[51] Reichstag speech of Mar. 14, 1885. BR, XI, 113–114. The parenthetical passage refers to a publication by Heinrich von Poschinger, ed., Preussen im Bundesrat, 1851–1859 (4 vols., Leipzig, 1882–1884), containing diplomatic documents from the Prussian state archives dealing with the problems of the German Confederation during Bismarck's period in Frankfurt.

[52] GW, XIV, 957.

he sought facts and ideas useful to his legislative efforts. Generally he regarded scholars as impractical people remote from the circumstances of real life, that is, the kind of circumstances that he personally experienced daily as a landowner, capitalist, and statesman. Yet the professors and their students became his most enthusiastic and consistent supporters. By contrast, the tsarist regime during these same decades alienated the Russian intelligentsia—with catastrophic results. Subversion in Russia was born not among proletarians and oppressed peasants, but within the educated, professional class, whose alienation from the existing government and society prepared the way for the revolutions of 1905 and 1917.

What Bismarck expected of German schools and universities they largely fulfilled, cementing the academic community—professors, students, and graduates—into the consensus Bismarck sought and providing it with a moral and intellectual legitimation that lasted more than half a century. It was not always so. Signs of alienation in the German intellectual community had been evident after 1815 in the politics of the radical student movement (*Burschenschaft*), the philosophical radicalism of Young Germans and Neo-Hegelians, and after 1840 in the revival of natural law and the growth of constitutionalism. But the failure of the revolution of 1848 largely liquidated radical liberalism, leaving a political void that socialism was later to fill. During the 1850s the German intelligentsia, of moderate liberal and German nationalistic persuasion, provided the backbone of the parliamentary opposition to the Bismarck regime. Its conversion after 1866 was almost total. Through the adoption of constitutionalism, achievement of national unity, and promotion of laissez-faire and private enterprise, Bismarck, without giving the matter special attention, won the German academic community. Foremost among the converts were the historians, who by the mid-nineteenth century had displaced philosophers as Germany's most highly regarded intellectuals. During the Bismarck era students crowded into the historians' classrooms, and the educated public avidly bought their works. History replaced philosophy as the "queen of the disciplines."[53]

So total was the conquest that the captured troops followed Bismarck even when he abandoned laissez-faire and shifted to the interventionist state. Kaiser, chancellor, and Reich became the new trinity of the German academic faith. Political and ideological heretics—Catholics, socialists, and democrats—had little chance to launch academic careers. They were acceptable neither to the ministries that officially made the appointments nor to the professors who under the principle of "academic freedom" retained the right

---

[53] See Wilhelm Lütgert, *Die Religion des deutschen Idealismus und ihr Ende* (3 vols., Gütersloh, 1923–1926); Frederic Lilge, *The Abuse of Learning: The Failure of the German University* (New York, 1948); William J. Brazill, *The Young Hegelians* (New Haven, 1970); Walter Struve, *Elites against Democracy: Leadership Ideals in Bourgeois Political Thought in Germany, 1890–1933* (Princeton, 1973).

RUDOLF VIRCHOW, 1887. (ARCHIV FÜR KUNST   THEODOR MOMMSEN, ABOUT 1902. (BILDARCHIV
UND GESCHICHTE, BERLIN.)   PREUSSISCHER KULTURBESITZ.)

to reject the nominees. The established academic elite guarded its ranks against newcomers whose scholarship was presumed to be tainted by religious or political affiliation. Among the few mavericks were Rudolf Virchow, a famous pathologist and leading figure in the German Progressive party, and Theodor Mommsen, after Ranke Germany's most distinguished historian in the nineteenth century. Like most of his peers, Mommsen was a German nationalist who became an enthusiastic supporter of Bismarck's foreign policy through 1871. Like Virchow, he supported the Kulturkampf. Classical scholar and committed humanist, he never surrendered his fundamental belief in republicanism and popular participation in government. The protectionist issue violated his conviction that politics must be based on ethical conviction rather than material interests. A Reichstag deputy (national liberal and then secessionist), he spoke out against the Bismarck regime, but also attacked a "spineless," "servile" citizenry that failed to perform its Kantian role in public life. But Mommsen was an exception and the cost of his apostasy was political isolation and ironic, deprecatory attacks by the mighty chancellor.[54]

The conquest of the German intellectual class was not exclusively Bismarck's achievement. On the contrary, the way had been long prepared by the tradition of German idealistic philosophy. Although Hegelian metaphysics was formally rejected soon after the philosopher's death by those in the

[54] GW, XII, 286, 326, 612; Alfred Heuss, *Theodor Mommsen und das 19. Jahrhundert* (Kiel, 1956), pp. 129–137, 194–220; and Albert Wucher, *Theodor Mommsen: Geschichtsschreibung und Politik* (Göttingen, 1956), pp. 151–175, 218–219.

mainstream of German intellectual life, the basic presuppositions of German idealism, to which Hegel had given the most powerful expression, continued to dominate German thought about the state, politics, and history. An example can be seen in Ranke's confidence in the existence of "spiritual forces" or "leading ideas" in history and his reverence for states as "spiritual substances" or "thoughts of God." Ranke had a universal mind (his final project was a world history), but he left behind few students, mostly venerators.[55] The "Prussian school" of historiography came to dominate German historical writing. Johann Gustav Droysen, Heinrich von Treitschke, and Heinrich von Sybel—to give the most notable examples—all regarded Bismarck's achievement as the fulfillment of Prussia's destiny to assume leadership in Germany. A persistent opponent of the government during the constitutional conflict, Sybel became the official historian of the period of unification, the author of the most detailed account of Bismarck's triumphs. Characteristic of German historical scholarship was its concentration upon the "power state" (*Machtstaat*) both internally and externally. In the "historical school of law" launched by Friedrich Karl von Savigny early in the century and the "historical school of economics" initiated by Gustav Schmoller and the *Kathedersozialisten* in the 1870s, the state was seen as the protagonist of history. Whether law, politics, economics, society, philosophy, or intellectual life in general was the object of study, the state and its works dominated the stage.[56]

Bismarck was not the initiator of this development, but his achievements confirmed the general conviction that German thought and scholarship were on the right path. Abstract ideas of right and wrong, already discredited by German idealism, appeared all the more inapplicable to historical judgments. Truth and right were the products of history, which was the record of the state's achievements. Whatever they professed to think of Hegel and his system, the German educated class in the bureaucracy, universities, and professions tended toward the conviction that values are historically produced, true because they triumph. Losers were consigned to the scrap heap of history. Through Bismarck, who doubted that man can make history, the German national idea had reached its great goal—the creation of a German nation-state. *Weltbürgertum* had been replaced by *Nationalstaat*.[57]

Bismarck's achievements, furthermore, appeared to confirm the view, now

[55] Theodore von Laue, *Leopold Ranke: The Formative Years* (Princeton, 1950); Ernst Simon, *Ranke und Hegel* (Berlin, 1928); Leonard Krieger, *Ranke: The Meaning of History* (Chicago, 1977).

[56] Günther Birtsch, *Die Nation als sittliche Idee: Der Nationalstaatsbegriff in Geschichtsschreibung und politischer Gedankenwelt Johann Gustav Droysens. Kölner historische Abhandlungen*, vol. 10 (Cologne, 1964), pp. 197ff.; Hermann Heller, *Hegel und der nationale Machtstaatsgedanke in Deutschland* (Leipzig, 1921); Georg Iggers, *The German Conception of History* (Middletown, Conn., 1968). For the enduring influence of this academic tradition, see Bernd Faulenbach, *Ideologie des deutschen Weges: Die deutsche Geschichte in der Historiographie zwischen Kaiserreich und Nationalsozialismus* (Munich, 1980).

[57] Friedrich Meinecke, *Weltbürgertum und Nationalstaat* (Munich, 1908).

called the *Primat der Aussenpolitik*, that foreign policy must take precedence over domestic affairs. As expressed by Ranke, "The position of a state in the world depends on the degree of independence it has attained. It is obliged therefore, to organize all its internal resources for the purpose of self-preservation. This is the supreme law of the state."[58] Bismarck's achievements in diplomacy and those of the Prussian army on the battlefield appeared to verify in the real world the presumption that Germany, given its geopolitical situation in central Europe, could survive only under a mixed constitution. The vital powers of the executive—diplomatic, military, administrative, and financial—must be concentrated in the hands of the monarch and his ministers. Because the monarch had failed to yield to parliament in the constitutional conflict, but had pursued his own independent course by reorganizing and strengthening the Prussian army and by choosing and keeping in office an unpopular minister of great capacity, Prussia had succeeded in unifying Germany and establishing it as the continent's leading power. As a consequence of these achievements, the mixed constitutional system, elsewhere in Europe but a passing stage in the development of parliamentary government, appeared to be the only possible form of government for Germany. In 1911 Otto Hintze proclaimed it to be "the uniquely Prussian-German system" of constitutionalism.[59]

[58] Ranke, "A Dialogue on Politics," in Von Laue, *Ranke*, p. 167.

[59] Otto Hintze, "Das monarchische Prinzip und die konstitutionelle Verfassung.," reprinted in Fritz Hartung, ed., *Otto Hintze: Staat und Verfassung, Gesammelte Abhandlungen zur allgemeinen Verfassungsgeschichte*, vol. 1 (Leipzig, 1941), pp. 349–379. See also E. R. Huber, *Deutsche Verfassungsgeschichte seit 1879*, vol. 3 (1963), 4–26, and Ernst-Wolfgang Böckenförde, "Der Verfassungstyp der deutschen konstitutionellen Monarchie im 19. Jahrhundert," in Wolfgang Böckenförde, ed., *Moderne deutsche Verfassungsgeschichte (1815–1914). Neue wissenschaftliche Bibliothek*, vol. 51 (2d ed., Königstein, 1981), pp. 146–170.

CHAPTER TWO

Apogee and Perigee of the Bismarck "Dictatorship"

T THE END of the 1870s Bismarck's personal authority reached a new peak within Germany. His prestige in foreign affairs was never higher. At the Congress of Berlin he appeared to be the arbiter of Europe. The Dual Alliance that followed was highly popular among Germans everywhere, for it restored the historic connection between the German Reich and the Habsburg Empire severed by the war of 1866. In domestic affairs the chancellor had attained conclusive control over the executive branches of both the imperial and Prussian governments. His supremacy over the Bundesrat and the state governments was reaffirmed by the "Fischer affair" and the inclusion of Bremen and Hamburg in the imperial customs union. A two-year upswing in the business cycle that began in 1879 seemed to justify his abandonment of liberal economics. Through the anti-socialist act he expected to quell radical agitation and through social reform to seduce urban labor. By jettisoning some Kulturkampf statutes, he hoped to reconcile Catholics and end his dependence upon the liberals. He had finally succeeded in ridding the National Liberal party of its left wing. In Landtag and Reichstag he had the option of combining conservatives and free conservatives with either the national liberals or centrists, depending on the issue.

And yet Bismarck remained dissatisfied with the parliamentary situation. The system of alternative majorities had been responsible for significant legislative successes since 1879, but the failures were equally notable. What the chancellor wanted most was a reliable parliamentary majority, unfailing in its loyalty to his policies. The Center party, he concluded, would never become a government party, any more than would the progressives. There was danger, in fact, that centrists and progressives might actually ally, drawn together by common hostility toward the government. But it was also true that right-wing conservatives preferred cooperating with the centrists rather than with the national liberals. Bismarck's own preference was for a majority composed of moderate conservatives, free conservatives, and national liberals. Yet Rudolf von Bennigsen and his associates resisted both his blandishments (a promise not to seek legislation upon which the coalition was in disagreement) and his threats (a warning that without such a coalition Germany was "headed directly toward absolutism").[1] They desired the role of a "middle party" capable

---

[1] Hermann Oncken, *Rudolf von Bennigsen* (Stuttgart, 1910), II, 447–448.

of supporting the government on some issues, but opposing it on others, particularly where the power of parliament was concerned.[2] One of the consequences was that the "tax reform" for which Bismarck had striven since 1875 remained incomplete. What was accomplished in the tariff bill of 1879 had been achieved under the duress of protectionism. The general shift from direct taxes levied by the states to indirect taxes levied by the Reich had not been attained. Bismarck had "fortified" the Reich neither by giving it a solid financial base nor by weakening its parliamentary institutions.

The failure of his tax program in the Reichstag session of February–May 1880 markedly increased Bismarck's doubts about the efficacy of the parliamentary process itself.[3] He was weary of the constant frictions normal to the business of politics, particularly in a multiparty system of the kind his own actions had helped to create. To him party politics appeared to be but a new form of particularism, another manifestation of the divisiveness that had marked German history for centuries. Again and again, he depicted himself as elevated above the arena of political strife, concerned only with the public welfare, particularly the consolidation of the Reich.[4] He gave credit neither to the wisdom nor honesty of those who disagreed with him. At court and in parliament he perceived only circles of conspiracy—old enemies still intriguing for his downfall, younger men eager to have him yield to the ravages of age and ill health. For more than a decade some had waited impatiently for evidence that even Wilhelm was mortal. But the old Hohenzoller not only survived Nobiling's buckshot; he also seemed better for it. Wilhelm celebrated his eighty-third birthday on March 22, 1880; Bismarck, his sixty-fifth on April 1. Their relationship seemed as solid as ever. In February 1881 Bismarck warned the Chamber of Deputies not to reckon on his own departure. "A good horse never dies in harness. . . . J'y suis, j' reste."[5]

Hegemony over the Prussian Cabinet

Indeed Bismarck's health improved during the last half of 1880. In May he had complained to the Kaiser that opposition from the state governments, in addition to his struggles with political parties and the press abetted by "dynastic and court influences," had sapped his strength. His physicians prescribed a long period of "rest and isolation" free of all state business.[6] That

[2] Ibid., pp. 451ff.

[3] BP, I, 197–198; BR, VIII, 249, 325–329; GW, VIII, 394. See also his reputed remarks to an anonymous diplomat reported in the Kölnische Zeitung, June 6, 1880. SEG (1880), pp. 180–182.

[4] See particularly his Reichstag speeches of Feb. 24 and Mar. 3, 1881. BR, VIII, 329, 345–346.

[5] Freiherr Lucius von Ballhausen, Bismarck-Erinnerungen (Stuttgart, 1920), p. 209; BR, VIII, 249.

[6] GW, VIc, 1882–1883. Bismarck to King Ludwig of Bavaria, June 1, 1880. DZA Potsdam, Reichskanzlei, 656, p. 3.

summer he spent a month at Friedrichsruh (June 29–July 24) and another at Bad Kissingen (July 26–August 27), after which he returned via Berlin to Friedrichsruh for four months (August 31–January 8). In June Baroness Spitzemberg thought him in relatively good condition, not particularly disturbed by the fate of the enabling act. At Friedrichsruh in mid-July Lucius found him "in an excellent mood, free of irritation, fresh, hearty, penetrating in his conversation and able to bear contradiction."[7] The cure at Kissingen (twenty-five baths) was declared a success, despite complaints about facial pains and neuralgia. He still spoke of insomnia, of nights when he debated acrimoniously in half-sleep. He had, however, learned to cope with it better. He arose to order the sheets and comforters, fluffing up the pillows, until other thoughts came and he slept again. Smoking had lost some of its appeal, but his appetite remained voracious. Visiting Friedrichsruh in October, Tiedemann reported that dinner consisted of six heavy courses plus dessert. "Now as before, they eat here until the walls burst."[8]

From September 1880 until his death in 1884 a local physician, Dr. Eduard Cohen of Hamburg, was in frequent attendance at Friedrichsruh, while the prince's regular doctor, Heinrich Struck, remained in Berlin. Apparently Cohen was able for a time to change the prince's daily routine: bedtime at about 11:00 P.M., rising at 9:00 A.M., and a diet that ended heartburn, but caused the patient to sing, "*Mich fliehen alle Freude.*" Bismarck could again take long walks in the woods and even mount a horse; riding, he joked, made him feel upper class once more. In early December his horse stepped in a hole on a dark forest path, threw the rider, and fell on him. Bismarck complained of "pains in all his limbs," but kept the cause secret from Johanna. To Baroness Spitzemberg, who arrived on December 4, he "looked downright rosy, not at all bloated." Cohen recorded in his diary on December 13: "Bismarck is most pleased, almost jovial, because today he endured with complete ease extraordinary physical exertions. He feels again as elastic and strong as he did years ago and can get ready for the trapeze."[9]

The one episode that disturbed him during this period was a dispatch from Berlin on July 17 that aroused him to a fit of anger at Karl von Hofmann. Eight days later, so he claimed, his mouth was still bitter from the gall he had "spewed." Although reduced in status in 1879, when the chancellor's office was abolished, the Hessian remained, after Bismarck, the most important official of the Reich, being state secretary of the new Imperial Office of the interior, Prussian minister of commerce, and Bismarck's chief deputy as pre-

---

[7] Rudolf Vierhaus, ed., *Das Tagebuch der Baronin Spitzemberg* (Göttingen, 1960), pp. 184–185; Lucius, *Bismarck-Erinnerungen*, pp. 184, 189.

[8] Moritz Busch, *Tagebuchblätter* (Leipzig, 1899), II, 592–593; GW, XIV, 920; GW, VIII, 370; Lucius, *Bismarck-Erinnerungen*, p. 190; Christoph von Tiedemann, *Sechs Jahre Chef der Reichskanzlei unter dem Fürsten Bismarck* (2d ed., 1910), pp. 411–412, 415–418.

[9] GW, VIII, 375, 381, 384, 386, 389. Spitzemberg, *Tagebuch*, pp. 185–186.

siding officer in the Bundesrat. His sin was to secure passage in the Bundesrat of a bill requiring employers to report industrial accidents as a step toward the extension of their liability. When Bismarck heard of this action, he fired off a dispatch that forced Hofmann to recall the bill. The prince insisted that, as Prussian minister of foreign affairs, he alone had the right to introduce Prussian bills in the Bundesrat through his power to instruct the Prussian delegation; as Prussian minister-president and as imperial chancellor, he could not defend and countersign statutes with which he disagreed.[10] Passing through Berlin on July 25, 1880, he told Lucius, "Hofmann must go. I cannot use a deputy who misuses his position and makes difficulties for me either because he lacks judgment or is malevolent. Hofmann is my creation. He is simple and knows nothing at all about practical matters. He is a horse that anyone can saddle, mount, and ride wherever he wants." In August Hofmann was demoted to the post of state secretary in the administration of the Reichsland and shipped off to Strassburg.[11]

What ruined Hofmann was not merely a matter of procedure; it was also a fundamental disagreement about social policy between Bismarck and those officials in the Ministry of Commerce from whom Hofmann, a man of few ideas, got his advice. Bismarck had made the decision to launch a revolutionary new system of state social insurance, beginning with an accident insurance statute, which he believed more compatible with the needs of both capital and labor than the "impractical" course Hofmann and his subordinates had chosen. In preparation for this task, he wanted a firmer grip on the latchkey to legislation. He replaced Hofmann as imperial state secretary with Karl von Boetticher, a provincial administrator (governor-general of Schleswig) whom he expected, and rightfully so, to be a better tool for the purpose. Like Hofmann, Boetticher was also appointed to the Prussian cabinet, but as minister without portfolio rather than as minister of commerce. Bismarck himself assumed the latter position in addition to his other duties! It was, he declared a "lasting arrangement" that would enable him to "conquer the ministry for the Reich," establishing his personal authority over those officials who had given Hofmann such bad advice.[12] From the Ministry of Commerce and other min-

---

[10] Hans Goldschmidt, *Das Reich und Preussen im Kampf um die Führung* (Berlin, 1931), pp. 71, 277–279; GW, VIc, 190–191. In March Hofmann had already received a warning on this problem. Goldschmidt, *Reich und Preussen*, pp. 271–273. In the Reichstag on Feb. 24, 1881, Richter maintained, with some justification, that in failing to represent to the Reichstag a bill approved by the Bundesrat the chancellor had exercised a personal veto not provided by the constitution. SBR (1881), I, 19–29.

[11] Lucius, *Bismarck-Erinnerungen*, pp. 189–190. See also Bismarck to Hofmann, July 31, 1880. GW, VIc, 192–194. Wilhelm to Bismarck, Aug. 23, 1880. Horst Kohl, ed., *Anhang zu den Gedanken und Erinnerung von Otto Fürst von Bismarck* (Stuttgart, 1901), I, 301.

[12] Rudolf Morsey, *Die oberste Reichsverwaltung unter Bismarck, 1867–1890* (Münster, 1956), pp. 210–212; AWB, II, 1–6; Goldschmidt, *Reich und Preussen*, pp. 279–281; GW, VIc, 196; Kohl, ed., *Anhang*, I, 301–302.

istries he selected a number of officials equipped with the required technical skills for a new department within the Imperial Office of the Interior, where they were to draft social insurance laws under Boetticher's leadership. Since they remained on the Prussian payroll and no authorization was sought from the Reichstag, this was probably a violation of the imperial constitution. In October 1880, furthermore, Bismarck deputized Boetticher to administer for him what was left of the Ministry of Commerce.[13]

Here was another of those improvisations in executive policy that had marked the chancellor's course since 1867. By occupying a third ministerial post and by securing the appointment of Boetticher, an imperial official, as minister without portfolio and as his personal deputy in the Ministry of Commerce, he completed his conquest of the Prussian cabinet and its constituent ministries. The Ministry of Commerce, he claimed, caused him no additional work; on the contrary, it lightened his burden. "I had to keep that bureaucratic pack from my throat. Now I have taken possession of the terrain and can execute my plans." He would see to it that the imperial side of Janus-faced Prussian officials grew more distinct, while the Prussian side faded. There was no such thing as "Prussian," only "imperial" commerce.[14] Officials of the ministry were not the only ones to feel the heavy hand of the new minister. Among the conquered were the urban chambers of commerce (Handelskammer), which enjoyed a semiofficial status under the law. In annual reports to the ministry, they were accustomed to editorialize about the mistakes of the government's new economic policy: for free trade against protectionism, for free enterprise against the guild system, for "self-help" against state socialism. In November 1881 Bismarck ordered these reports sent to the ministry for "corrections" well in advance of publication. This decree produced a wave of protest from the chambers, which subsided after the minister threatened their abolition. During the ensuing years Bismarck sought to reconstruct these bodies by widening their base of representation to include agriculture, industry, and artisanry, as well as commerce. As business chambers (Gewerbekammer) they were to become the foundation for a new corporative organization embracing all "productive forces."[15]

Bismarck's increasing stranglehold over the Prussian cabinet soon forced the departure of other ministers. In February 1881 Minister of Interior Botho

---

[13] See particularly Bismarck's explanation of his decisions to the Prussian cabinet on Aug. 28, 1880. DZA Merseburg, Rep. 90a, B, III, 2b, Nr. 6, Vol. 92. See also Goldschmidt, Reich und Preussen, pp. 280–288; Morsey, Reichsverwaltung, pp. 212–213; Walter Vogel, Bismarcks Arbeiterversicherung: Ihre Entstehung im Kräftespiel der Zeit (Braunschweig, 1951), pp. 111–113.

[14] GW, VIII, 377.

[15] Minister of Commerce Bismarck to Minister-President Bismarck, Nov. 30, 1881. Heinrich von Poschinger, ed., Fürst Bismarck als Volkswirth (Berlin, 1889–1890), II, 92–94, also pp. 83–88, 97–99, 145–146; AWB II, 69–70, 102–103; and particularly SEG (1881), pp. 206–207, 254–256, 304–306, 315–318; SEG (1882), pp. 20, 84, 145–146; and SEG (1883), p. 77.

BISMARCK, AS A CIRCUS PERFORMER, KEEPING ALL THE CABINET PORTFOLIOS IN THE AIR (THE FOREIGN
OFFICE ON HIS NOSE), WITH A LITTLE HELP FROM ROBERT VON PUTTKAMER AND KARL BITTER, THE NEW
MINISTERS OF INTERIOR AND FINANCE. THESE THREE ARE "THE POWERFUL ONES." "ACTUALLY NO ONE
ELSE IS NEEDED." WILHELM SCHOLZ IN *KLADDERADATSCH*, 1881.

Eulenburg was seemingly the victim of a "comedy of errors" resulting from the multiple roles that Bismarck played. As minister of commerce, the prince approved amendments to a bill for administrative reform that Eulenburg strongly supported in the Landtag, amendments that Bismarck disapproved a few days later in his capacity as minister-president. Although Bismarck discovered the contradiction in time, his attempt to rectify it was frustrated. Too ill to appear in the House of Lords, where the bill was being discussed, he chose to send an underling, Privy Counselor Rommel of the Ministry of Commerce, who could not be found immediately. When Rommel appeared, blissfully unaware of the crisis, the chancellor yelled at him "until the windows rattled" and sent him flying "red-faced and utterly consternated" to the chamber, where, uncertain of his chief's intentions, he reinforced rather than dispelled the impression of a basic disagreement between the two ministers. The House of Lords adjourned amid confusion; Eulenburg resigned and stuck to his resolve even after Bismarck appeared in the chamber to disavow any material difference in their views on the impending legislation. His post was filled by Robert von Puttkamer, who was replaced as *Kultusminister* by Gustav von Gossler, an under secretary of state, to the dismay of other cabinet members, who had no high regard for Gossler's abilities. Obviously Eulenburg had seized upon the episode as an opportunity to depart. From good sources Lucius had heard of sharp disagreements between him and Bismarck. Recently the chancellor had accused the minister of "wanting to govern."[16]

In March 1881 Count Otto zu Stolberg-Wernigerode, for three years deputy of the imperial chancellor and vice-president of the Prussian cabinet, also resigned. Stolberg had served Bismarck successfully as governor-general of Hanover during the period of its integration into Prussia and thereafter as German ambassador in Vienna. In 1878 he had given up the ambassadorship reluctantly. His fear that as "vice-Bismarck" he would have little authority and little chance to exercise his talents proved all too true. No one replaced him in his dual role, although Puttkamer was appointed cabinet vice-president in addition to his post as minister of interior. Bismarck treated Stolberg's departure lightly, but Lucius believed it would injure the prestige of the cabinet and nurture the view that Bismarck could not tolerate an independent personality as colleague.[17] That others thought the same is shown by Bismarck's difficulty in replacing the highly capable Bernhard Ernst von Bülow, state secretary of the Imperial Foreign Office since 1873 and Prussian minister without portfolio since 1876, who died suddenly in 1879. His first choice was Prince Chlodwig zu-Hohenlohe Schillingsfürst, then German ambassador in

---

[16] Tiedemann, *Sechs Jahre*, pp. 442–453, 459; Lucius, *Bismarck-Erinnerungen*, pp. 196–203, 558–560; GW, VIc, 206–208, 229–230; BR, VIII, 286ff. After Eulenburg's departure Bismarck fed Busch material for a critical attack on him in *Grenzboten*. Busch, *Tagebuchblätter*, III, 31–34.

[17] Lucius, *Bismarck-Erinnerungen*, pp. 135–136, 146, 207–208; GW, VIc, 215–216, 229–230; VIII, 338–339; XIV, 920–921; Horst Kohl, ed., *Bismarck-Jahrbuch*, IV (1897), 231–236.

Paris, who accepted it only on a temporary basis, as did his successor Count Paul von Hatzfeldt. Hatzfeldt agreed to take the position permanently only after considerable hesitation, much to Bismarck's disgust, and he did not serve to the chancellor's satisfaction. In 1885 he was replaced by Bismarck's son Herbert, who held the post until 1890.[18]

Even ministers more pliable than Botho Eulenburg found it hard to cope with the narcissistic personality in Wilhelmstrasse 76. Consider, for example, the dilemma of Karl Bitter who, as minister of finance, had to execute the chancellor's idiosyncratic tax program. "Bitter's situation is becoming steadily more difficult," Lucius observed in February 1881. "He is confused and senile, changes his opinions on important financial questions overnight and yields to every pressure from the prince in order to stay in office."[19] But Bitter did attempt to stand up to Bismarck on what mattered most to him. Imbued with the Prussian tradition of conservative public finance, he abhorred unbalanced budgets. For Bismarck, however, Prussian deficits were a political weapon with which to force the passage of new imperial taxes. In January 1882 Bitter found himself hopelessly isolated on this issue within the Prussian cabinet.[20] In June 1882 he resigned in protest over the issuance of imperial rescripts on tax matters that had been drafted without his knowledge. Bismarck found him "inadequate" and was glad to see him go.[21]

In Bitter's successor, Adolf Scholz, chief of the Imperial Treasury, Bismarck finally acquired a finance minister to his liking—one capable, as a contemporary remarked, "of accepting the role of a reliable aide of the great statesman, even at the cost of renouncing his own convictions and endangering his own reputation as a financier and lawmaker."[22] What others criticized Bismarck praised. Scholz was, he wrote in August 1884, "the first finance minister in twenty-two years with whom I have been privileged to work together in mutual understanding."[23]

With the departure of Botho Eulenburg, Stolberg, and Bitter only two thorns remained in Bismarck's flesh: Georg von Kameke and Albrecht von Stosch. As Prussian minister of war and delegate to the Bundesrat, Kameke had the duty of defending military legislation before the Reichstag. Bismarck

---

[18] Morsey, *Reichsverwaltung*, pp. 118–121. Hohenlohe claimed that he did not have an income adequate for the position, which he estimated would cost him more than the Paris embassy. Friedrich Curtius, ed., *Memoirs of Prince Chlodwig of Hohenlohe-Schillingsfuerst* (New York, 1906), II, 256ff.

[19] Lucius, *Bismarck-Erinnerungen*, p. 194; Tiedemann, *Sechs Jahre*, p. 459.

[20] Cabinet Meeting of Jan. 4, 1882. DZA Potsdam, Reichskanzlei, 223, pp. 27–31. See also *ibid.*, 222, pp. 128–132, 160–163; 223, pp. 68–110; 2082, pp. 98–100; and 2083, pp. 14ff., 81ff.

[21] Lucius, *Bismarck-Erinnerungen*, pp. 233–234; GW, VIc, 257–258.

[22] Baron Octavio von Zedlitz und Neukirch, free conservative deputy and *Vortragender Rat* in the Ministry of Public Works, quoted in Wilhelm Gerloff, *Die Finanz- und Zollpolitik des deutschen Reiches* (Jena, 1913), p. 182.

[23] Bismarck to Scholz, Aug. 31, 1884. GW, XIV, 954.

thought him too eager to maintain good relations with parliament by allowing the parties some influence in military matters—"a parliamentary general on active service is always a disagreeable phenomenon, but as war minister he is dangerous."[24] But Kameke had other, equally formidable enemies in Emil von Albedyll, chief of the military cabinet since 1871, and Count Alfred von Waldersee, newly appointed quartermaster-general and deputy to Moltke on the general staff. Both generals aimed to establish the independence of the agencies they served from the Prussian Ministry of War, which was their only bond to the constitution and to parliament. In February 1883 Kameke, under heavy fire from centrist and liberal critics of the military in the Reichstag, advised the Kaiser to accept some of their demands, including elimination of the tax exemption on private income enjoyed by officers. Bismarck was outraged not only by Kameke's willingness to make concessions, but also by his failure to proceed through the proper channels. He maintained that, as chancellor, he was the Reich's only minister and as such responsible for military as well as other affairs.[25]

Albedyll and Waldersee did their part by persuading Wilhelm that Kameke's actions encouraged parliamentary government. Thinking he had lost the confidence of the Kaiser, Kameke resigned and was replaced by Paul Bronsart von Schellendorf, who promised greater resistance to parliament and soon permitted the severing of the military cabinet and general staff from the Ministry of War. The reduction of the war ministry heightened Bismarck's influence, but it also destroyed the administrative unity of the army. "The war ministry, the military cabinet, and the general staff had become mutually independent agencies, but it was virtually impossible to define the limits of their spheres of competence and, between 1883 and 1914, disputes were frequent, acrimonious, and damaging to the efficiency of the army."[26]

Kameke's resignation confirmed the chancellor's status as "imperial war minister," but it also removed from the scene an old foe, Albrecht von Stosch, who had supported Kameke's recommendations. Since his failure to oust Stosch as chief of the Imperial Admiralty in 1876–1877, Bismarck had been compelled to tolerate him.[27] Stosch even survived the scandal that followed the sinking in 1878 of the battle cruiser *Der Grosse Kurfürst* which collided with a sister ship in the English Channel in broad daylight. As the responsible official, Stosch came under heavy attack in parliament and press, including rather vicious articles inspired by Bismarck. Yet he retained the confidence of the Kaiser, who refused his repeated offers of resignation. Even

[24] Quoted in Gordon A. Craig, *The Politics of the Prussian Army, 1640–1945* (Oxford, 1955), p. 226.

[25] GW, VIc, 273–274.

[26] Craig, *Prussian Army*, pp. 228–230.

[27] See vol. 2, pp. 138–139, 359–363. For an example of Bismarck's sensitivity concerning Stosch, see GW, VIc, 261–262.

the Reichstag, furthermore, rejected the chancellor's attempt, through friendly deputies, to limit Stosch's authority by creating the post of inspector general of the navy. In March 1883 Stosch, worn out in defending himself against these many slings and arrows, chose to depart with Kameke, and the Kaiser agreed.[28]

"I must say," Bismarck told Mittnacht in April 1883, "that the Kaiser has always stuck by me. Since everyone in the Prussian cabinet came to understand the probability that any minister will be dismissed on my request, a discipline has predominated within the government that never before existed."[29] By 1883 the collegial character of the Prussian cabinet had been destroyed by the ascendancy of the chancellor and minister-president. "The hard grind stones, about which Prince Bismarck used to complain so vigorously, have given way to soft ones," wrote a contemporary observer. "Prussia is different from the Reich only in appearance. The state secretaries of the Reich function, even when acting under their own responsibility, only as deputies of the imperial chancellor; formally Prussian ministers are equal colleagues of the minister-president, but actually they exercise their functions under the presumption that they are in agreement with the minister-president."[30]

Through the ministers Bismarck strove to discipline the state service as a whole and, with its help, the voters. We shall see that in the Reichstag elections of 1881 the Prussian bureaucracy intervened in behalf of progovernment candidates as shamelessly as in the reactionary 1850s and 1860s. Nor did the grip of Bismarck and Puttkamer relax once the election was over. On January 4, 1882, the king issued a royal rescript drafted by Bismarck that made clear what was expected. "The task of my ministers is to protect my constitutional rights against doubt and obfuscation. I expect the same from all officials who have sworn an oath to me. To infringe the freedom of the ballot is far from my intention, but those officials charged with the execution of my acts of government and subject to discharge from the service under the official discipline statute have the sworn duty under their oaths of office to support the policy of my government also at the polls. Those who loyally fulfill that duty will receive my gratitude."[31]

[28] Frederick B. M. Hollyday, *Bismarck's Rival: A Political Biography of General and Admiral Albrecht von Stosch* (Durham, 1960), pp. 176–215. In July 1884 Friedrich von Schauss, a Bavarian lawyer and national liberal who had lost his Reichstag seat in 1881 and was running for reelection, charged that in 1879 Rickert and other future secessionists had planned, once Bismarck had been ousted, to secure the appointment of Stosch as chancellor. The "intrigue" was supported by free traders from Baltic ports who feared the consequence of protective grain tariffs for the export of mixed Russian and German grain. Rickert denied the charge, which received wide publicity. SEG (1884), pp. 80–81.

[29] GW, VIII, 493.

[30] SEG (1884), p. 63.

[31] GW, VIc, 240 (fn. 1); XII, 324. To Bismarck's mind even the conservative and autocratic

Political reliability became the principal criterion for appointment and promotion in the Prussian bureaucracy and imperial service. On Bismarck's orders personnel records were scrutinized to detect "harmful and unworthy elements." Political conformity was not in itself sufficient. Those known to be free traders by conviction, not to speak of those active in opposing the new economic policy of the government, were singled out for purge or punishment. A talented official whom Lucius wished to promote was passed over because he had the temerity to vote for the secessionist Heinrich Rickert. Even the Bundesrat was "purified," when Karl Oldenburg, delegate from Mecklenburg, was bumped, because of his free trade views, from the committee on trade and customs by an adverse vote of the Prussian delegation. The days when Prussian officials dared, whether as deputies in the Landtag or Reichstag or in any other capacity, to oppose the government came to an end. The bureaucracy lost its status as a separate *Stand* in German society. "Everyone who is not with us," Bismarck declared, "is against us."[32]

The Prussian (German) Economic Council

Still, the latchkey to legislation was only partly secured by domination of the two executive branches; there was the additional problem of Landtag and Reichstag. Simultaneously with his final conquest of the Prussian cabinet, Bismarck proposed creation of a corporative body called the Prussian Economic Council (*Preussischer Volkswirtschaftsrath*). The need for such a body, he asserted, had been raised by the German Commercial Association, the Central Federation of German Industrialists, and the German Agricultural Council. The economic council would represent "the productive classes of the population" by giving them a consultative voice in the legislative process. In contrast to the ministries, whose officials lacked practical experience, and the Reichstag, where political considerations were paramount, the council would provide expert advice in drafting tax, social insurance, and other economic bills.[33]

The Prussian Economic Council was created on November 17, 1880, by an evasion of the legislative process that it was intended to assist. Bismarck pro-

---

Puttkamer was not sufficiently vigorous in following up on this warning. See Lucius, *Bismarck-Erinnerungen*, pp. 255ff.; *GW*, VIII, 500–501.

[32] Morsey, *Reichsverwaltung*, pp. 262ff. See especially Eckart Kehr, "Das soziale System der Reaktion in Preussen unter dem Ministerium Puttkamer," in Hans-Ulrich Wehler, ed., *Der Primat der Innenpolitik* (Berlin, 1965), pp. 64–86.

[33] Oct. 15, 1880. *AWB*, II, 10–18. On Sept. 17, 1880, the chancellor had made public his intention to establish such a council in replying to a petition from the chamber of commerce in Plauen. See Poschinger, ed., *Volkswirth*, II, 4–5; *BR*, VIII, 195ff. The date given this document in *GW*, XIV, 915, is inaccurate. See also Julius Curtius, *Bismarcks Plan eines deutschen Volkswirtschaftsrats* (Heidelberg, 1919), pp. 11ff.; and Heinrich Herrfahrdt, *Das Problem der berufständischen Vertretung von der französischen Revolution bis zur Gegenwart* (Stuttgart, 1921), pp. 58–83.

posed, the Prussian cabinet disposed, and the king decreed.[34] It was composed of seventy-five representatives, of whom forty-five (fifteen each for industry, trade, and agriculture) were chosen by the ministers for trade, public works, and agriculture from a list of ninety candidates nominated by local chambers of commerce, merchant corporations, and agricultural associations. The remaining thirty (including at least fifteen artisans and workers) were named by the ministers directly. A standing committee, composed of ten members chosen by the government and five members selected by each of the council's subsections (trade, industry, and agriculture), could be summoned for longer sessions than the full council.

In the documents leading to its creation and in his public remarks to the delegates, Bismarck made clear that the Prussian Economic Council was but the first step and "quickest way" toward the creation of a German economic council by the addition of fifty representatives for the rest of the nation.[35] Although Bismarck denied it, suspicion was widespread that he expected the German economic council to become a counterweight to, or even replacement for the Reichstag. That its members were to be paid per diem costs, a right that the Reichstag had been repeatedly denied, was alienating. But centrist and liberal deputies also detected in the council another effort by the chancellor to divert parliamentary life toward material and away from political, idealistic, and legal concerns. In June and December 1881 the Reichstag twice rejected a German economic council by refusing to fund it. Bismarck declared that the Bundesrat could create the body by its ordinance power independently of the Reichstag.[36] But he never took this step, for the Prussian Economic Council soon disappointed him.

In January–February 1881 the council deliberated upon and approved two bills, providing accident insurance for workers and strengthening artisan guilds. While the second bill became law, the accident insurance bill failed because of amendments introduced by the Reichstag. In March 1882 the council was summoned to consider bills for both accident and health insurance and for nationalization of the tobacco industry. It passed the insurance bills but, to Bismarck's surprise and dismay, rejected the tobacco monopoly, a project that had long been the heart of his fiscal reform program. Rejection by the council contributed later to the monopoly's overwhelming defeat in the Reichstag.[37]

Opposition deputies were correct in surmising that the proposed German economic council was intended to become a surrogate Reichstag. As in the case of the customs parliament of 1867–1870, Bismarck obviously anticipated

[34] Cabinet meeting of Nov. 13, 1880. DZA Merseburg, Rep. 90A, B, III, 2b, Nr. 6, Vol. 92.

[35] GW, VIc, 199–203; AWB, II, 22–25, 39–40; BR, VIII, 211–16, and IX, 176–181; BP, I, 196–198.

[36] SBR (1881), II, 1268–1290, 1589–1611, and (1881–1882), I, 130–146; Curtius, Bismarcks Plan, pp. 24–50; Herrfahrdt, Berufständische Vertretung, pp. 72–81.

[37] Curtius, Bismarcks Plan, pp. 21–22; Herrfahrdt, Berufständische Vertretung, pp. 65ff.

that the council would develop organically. While becoming familiar to the public and the special interests, it would stand by for the day when a deadlock between crown and Reichstag might require the latter's abolition.[38] But after the Prussian council betrayed him on the issue of the tobacco monopoly, the prince lost interest.[39] In 1883 the Chamber of Deputies deleted from the Prussian budget the per diem and travel allowances for the council. Rather than finance it from the Guelph fund, Bismarck let the Prussian Economic Council expire after its last meeting in January 1884.[40] He did not mourn its demise because he had meanwhile found another, far subtler approach to his goal—corporative associations formed originally as administrative organs for social insurance funds, but intended ultimately to form the basis for a national diet. To the end of his life Bismarck never surrendered the thought that a corporative legislature might provide relief from the frustrations of party politics by making possible the revocation of the gift of universal male suffrage.[41]

The Politics of Bread and Taxes

The good harvest of 1878 had depressed the price of grain and converted German farmers to protectionism, but it was a boon for urban dwellers who enjoyed the lowest prices for rye and wheat since 1865. During the next two years, however, the wheel of fortune turned 180 degrees. Bad harvests in 1879 and 1880 drove up food prices throughout Europe. At Berlin the wholesale price of rye, the chief staple in the German diet, rose yearly: 132.8 marks per ton in 1879, 187.9 in 1880, 195.2 in 1881. Not even at the height of the *Gründerjahre* had the wholesale price of food reached the level of 1880–1881.[42] The dire predictions by free traders about the probable adverse effects of the grain tariffs for urban dwellers appeared to have come true. To compound the distress, the relief of direct taxes in Prussia that Bismarck had promised as part of the total "tax reform" package remained unfulfilled. The revenues Prussia gained from the new tariffs imposed in 1879 had to be used to balance its budget.[43]

The political consequences of this double bind for low-income voters be-

[38] Lucius, *Bismarck-Erinnerungen*, p. 196.

[39] *BP*, I, 199.

[40] Bismarck to Boetticher, Jan. 13, 1884. Goldschmidt, *Reich und Preussen*, pp. 298–300, also pp. 80–82; *SEG* (1884), p. 13.

[41] In his memoirs Bismarck wrote, "My ideal has always been a monarchical power so controlled by an independent representative body organized along corporative or occupational lines that neither monarch nor parliament can change existing laws unilaterally. Changes should be made only by common consent in the open, with public criticism by press and Landtag of all state proceedings." *GW*, XV, 15. See the other references given for the 1890s by Herrfahrdt, *Berufständische Vertretung*, pp. 64–67.

[42] Alfred Jacobs and Hans Richter, *Die Grosshandelspreise in Deutschland von 1792 bis 1934. Sonderhefte des Instituts für Konjunkturforschung*, vol. 37 (Berlin, 1935), pp. 53, 107.

[43] Gerloff, *Finanz- und Zollpolitik*, p. 168.

came evident in Reichstag by-elections during 1880 to fill seats left vacant by death or resignation. The progressives easily retained two seats in Berlin and another in Potsdam-Havelland; at Hamburg the national liberals lost a seat to socialists, the progressives scoring a close second; in Kassel and Lübeck the progressives took away two seats hitherto regarded as safe by the national liberals; and in Sachsen-Altenburg they took a seat from the free conservatives. Buoyed by these returns, the progressive leader Eugen Richter decided to launch at an early date his party's campaign for the Reichstag election due in 1881. It began in June 1880 with a confident manifesto. "The signs are growing that wide circles of the population are changing their opinions. The government is accelerating that change by heaping mistake upon mistake, arousing one group of people after another against itself. The tactical skills that once helped the chancellor achieve his greatest successes have been missing in recent events. Judging from his most recent pronouncements in behalf of his domestic policies, he has already begun to doubt the understanding of the masses of the population—the same masses to whom he was still attempting to appeal last year in every possible way." During the following months Richter and his progressive colleagues unleashed a massive effort through speakers, meetings, correspondence, new local organizations, and the public press to exploit what they correctly sensed was the best opportunity for left-liberals to influence the electorate since 1861.[44]

Indeed, Bismarck's reaction to the food crisis of 1880–1881 demonstrated how partisan he was to the financial interests of the landowning class and how faulty was his understanding of economics and taxation, the policy for which he had now assumed chief responsibility. In August 1880 he wrote Lucius that the interests of farmers and foresters, already injured by bad weather, would only be damaged further by tariff reductions to encourage imports and reduce prices. "We must not yield to the screaming of the progressives, if we do not want to ruin our election chances with the rural population. The latter expect *their* minister, more than any other, to protect agrarian interests, and doubtless they have a right to expect that." Bismarck discounted reports of a harvest disaster and opposed emergency relief, except for measures to expedite railway grain shipments to the affected towns. The government must be concerned about the welfare of "producers, not consumers." He hoped, however, that the agitation against grain tariffs could "be converted into an agitation against the unequal taxation of domestic agriculture."[45]

By tax inequity Bismarck meant "the double taxation imposed on income from farming through the combination of real estate and income taxes and the further double taxation that results when the mortgage appraisal of an

---

[44] Eugen Richter, *Im alten Reichstag: Erinnerungen* (Berlin, 1914), II, 168–172.

[45] Bismarck to Lucius, Aug. 20 and Sept. 26, 1880. Lucius, *Bismarck-Erinnerungen*, pp. 191, 555; GW, XIV, 919. Bismarck to Prussian cabinet, Aug. 28, 1880. DZA Merseburg, Rep. 90a, B, III, 2b, Nr. 6, Vol. 92. Later he told Busch that "the opinion that low grain prices mean happiness, well-being, and contentment is a superstition." Busch, *Tagebuchblätter*, III, 90.

estate is affected by the income tax to be paid by the mortgagee as well as by the land and building tax [paid by the mortgagor]." He regretted that the efforts of the government to achieve a more equitable system of taxation through Reichstag and Landtag had escaped the understanding of the voters; "among the latter the only residue that will remain is dissatisfaction with the government and an inclination to vote for the opposition." The voters, he predicted, would migrate to the extremes, to either the ultraconservatives or the progressives. From the progressives one could expect an attempt to form a parliamentary majority in alliance with the Center party and "a corresponding government." Skillful speakers would know how to "stupefy" the public.[46]

Bismarck continued, nevertheless, to push forward on his charted course in the hope of distracting voters from the price of bread. His strategy was to take advantage of the fact that the Landtag session (opening October 28, 1880) preceded that of the Reichstag (opening February 15, 1881). As in the previous year, he would show the "bright side" of his tax reform to the Prussian Landtag (reduction of direct taxes) in order to make its "dark side" (imposition of new indirect taxes) more acceptable to the German Reichstag. If the Reichstag's opposition parties persisted in rejecting the taxes needed to execute tax relief in Prussia, their neglect would, he hoped, draw the wrath of the voters in the upcoming national election.[47]

The bright side was presented to the Landtag in the form of two bills. The first proposed to employ a Prussian treasury surplus of 14 million marks (expected under the Franckenstein clause) to remit for one year three monthly payments of the class tax (paid by low-income groups) and of the five lowest brackets of the classified income tax (paid by middle-income groups).[48] More drastic was the second bill, a new utilization statute (*Verwendungsgesetz*) establishing in advance how Prussia would spend its share (about 65 million marks) of 110 million marks expected from new imperial taxes, yet to be legislated. Nicknamed "*Verschwendungsgesetz*" by its critics, the second bill would have suspended the four lowest brackets of the class tax (incomes to 1,200 marks) and allocated to local governments (urban and rural) revenues from the remaining eight brackets and up to one-half of the revenues from land and building taxes. The four lowest brackets of the class tax included 4,378,000 persons, 86 percent of those who paid the tax. Their occupations were listed as industrial workers, artisans, shopkeepers, schoolteachers, lesser government officials, and small landowners. Other beneficiaries were to be

[46] Bismarck to Director Burchard of the Imperial Treasury, Aug. 11, 1880. AWB, I, 342–344. Bismarck to Scholz, Jan. 17, 1881. AWB, II, 37.

[47] Bismarck to Bitter, Aug. 29, 1880. DZA Potsdam, Reichskanzlei, 2082, pp. 206–214. Bismarck to Bitter, Sept. 29, 1880. Ibid., 2083, pp. 37–42. Bismarck to Scholz, Oct. 10, 1880. GW, VIc, 197–198.

[48] SBHA (1880–1881), Anlagen, I, No. 29. See also the report of Finance Minister Bitter to the Prussian cabinet on the state of Prussia's finances, Sept. 18, 1880. DZA Merseburg, Rep. 90a, B, III, 2b, Nr. 6, Vol. 92. On the Franckenstein clause see vol. 2, pp. 487–489, 517–518.

local governments and property owners (abolition of surtaxes), particularly rural landlords.[49]

During deliberation on the first bill it became evident that the increased cost of the imperial army under the new *Septennat* would require additional assessments on the states (*Matrikularbeiträge*), of which Prussia's share was to be more than 15 million marks, wiping out the Prussian surplus intended to pay for the tax cut. Nevertheless, Eugen Richter, ordinarily a fiscal conservative, perceived the chance to outtrump the government and moved that the reduction be made permanent.[50] Bismarck was not dismayed at the prospect of a 14 million mark deficit in the Prussian budget. "We must not permit ourselves to be outbid in this connection by the opposition," he explained to a reluctant cabinet, "and we must document our will to accomplish tax relief by deeds. I am basically against a tax remission for only one year. . . . Abhorrence of a vacuum will fill the gap created by a permanent tax cut."[51] The first bill, as amended by Richter, was passed by a strange majority composed of conservatives, centrists, and progressives over national liberal opposition. Yet progressives, national liberals, and centrists combined ultimately to bury the second bill in committee. To have passed the second utilization bill would have obligated the liberals morally to accept in the Reichstag fiscal legislation that they had rejected in early 1880—including, they correctly surmised, a government tobacco monopoly.[52]

Bismarck's defense of his tax program in 1881, while covering much familiar ground, offers new insights into his views on taxation. His tax reform, he

[49] *SBHA* (1880–1881), Anlagen, II, No. 98. The estimates of those affected are in the *Motive*, pp. 8–9. For the benefits to rural landlords, see Bitter to Bismarck, Oct. 28, 1880, with Bismarck's numerous marginalia. DZA Potsdam, Reichskanzlei, 2083, pp. 101–104. From Count Helldorff and other leading conservatives Bismarck had warnings that, if the promised tax cuts were not achieved, rural voters would desert the conservatives and the government in the coming imperial election. Helldorff to Bismarck, Aug. 11, 1880. DZA Potsdam, Reichskanzlei, 2082, pp. 186–187. Bismarck to Bitter, Aug. 29, 1880. *Ibid.*, pp. 210–211. Bismarck to the Prussian cabinet, Aug. 28, 1880. DZA Merseburg, B, III, 2b, Nr. 6, Vol. 92. For the first utilization act see vol. 2, pp. 522–523.

[50] *SBHA* (1880–1881), I, 16–22, 126–202, 203ff., 1347ff., 1409ff.; Anlagen, II, Nos. 154, 185; Richter, *Im alten Reichstag*, II, 184–187. Also Scholz to Bismarck, Dec. 4, 1880. DZA Potsdam, Reichskanzlei, 2084, pp. 28–34. Lucius, *Bismarck-Erinnerungen*, pp. 191–192.

[51] Bismarck to Foreign Office and Tiedemann, Nov. 11, 1880. DZA Potsdam, Reichskanzlei, 2083, pp. 138, 141–145. Cabinet meeting of Jan. 24, 1881. DZA Merseburg, Rep. 90a, B, III, 2b, Nr. 6, Vol. 93; Lucius, *Bismarck-Erinnerungen*, pp. 193–194. Bitter to Bismarck, Feb. 20, 1881. DZA Potsdam, Reichskanzlei, 2084, pp. 219–221. Actually Prussia ended fiscal 1881–1882 with a surplus of 2,850,000 marks, despite the tax reduction and increased assessment paid to the Reich. A surplus of 14,357,000 marks from the state railways was the biggest factor in this outcome. Bitter to Bismarck, June 16, 1882. DZA Potsdam, Reichskanzlei, 223, pp. 133–134.

[52] *SBHA* (1880–1881), II, 1385–1388, 1511–1564. Statute of Mar. 10, 1881. GSP (1881), pp. 126–127. Scholz believed that the tobacco monopoly was the only means of producing the revenue needed to defray the full cost of the Prussian tax reform. Scholz to Bismarck, Aug. 28, 1880. DZA Potsdam, Reichskanzlei, 2082, pp. 219–220. Also Bismarck to Tiedemann, Nov. 11, 1880. *Ibid.*, 2083, p. 145.

told the Chamber of Deputies on February 4, 1881, was an act of justice to both urban and rural property owners, but particularly to the latter, who, he claimed, bore a disproportionate share of the tax burden. Being subject only to the personal income tax, "coupon clippers" paid only 3 percent of net income in direct taxes, and even this amount could easily be reduced by concealing assets. But he, as an estate owner, paid an additional 6 to 7.5 percent in real estate taxes on assets that could not be concealed, although "neighborly" tax assessors might underestimate their value. While disclaiming any ambition to abolish the land and building taxes imposed by the new era government, Bismarck again denounced the tax act of 1861 as a "great injustice," which had been compounded by the practice of permitting local governments to assess surtaxes that added 10 to 20 percent to the total bill. Because his own estates were largely unmortgaged, Bismarck estimated his total burden from all direct taxes to be about 10 percent of net income. For the owner of heavily mortgaged estates, he claimed, the burden was "easily" 20 percent. Bismarck denied any self-interest in his tax reform—"I have become so rich through the grace of the king that I have no need of petty tax advantages."[53]

The failure of the second utilization bill in the Prussian Chamber of Deputies presaged a Reichstag session (February 15–June 15, 1881) that was nearly catastrophic for the Bismarck program. Again the government presented constitutional amendments providing for biennial budgets and Reichstag sessions and extending the period between imperial elections from three to four years. Only the latter amendment carried.[54] Three tax bills from the preceding year (increases in the brewing tax, new stamp taxes, and a graduated income tax on citizens excused from military service) were reintroduced, all equipped with revenue-sharing provisions in the style of the Franckenstein clause. Again Bismarck advanced the view that direct taxes on income and real estate were excessively high and that indirect taxes on high consumption items were more equitable and less burdensome to taxpayers generally, including low-income groups. He was undaunted by Lasker's charge that what the government actually intended was tax relief for noble landlords. Why not solve the government's fiscal needs, Lasker asked, by imposing an inheritance tax, following the example of England and France? Why not relieve the poor by reforming the class and income taxes, shifting the burden from the lowest to the highest income brackets? To the charge that consumption taxes were regressive, more burdensome to the poor than to the rich, Bismarck re-

[53] BR, VIII, 227–285. See also the "Zur Geschichte der Steuerreform im Reiche und in Preussen," in BR, VIII, 297–310. Prussian landlords had long maintained that the land and building tax imposed in 1861 was unjust, for mortgaged real estate was not actually the property of the title holder. Real estate taxes should apply only to that portion of the assessed property's value that remained unmortgaged. To tax mortgaged property was to impose a double burden on the owner—interest on the mortgage and tax on the property. The author thanks Thomas Kohut for this information.

[54] SBR (1881), pp. 180–232, 953–999, 1028–1045.

sponded that this was a purely theoretical view of impractical professors, journalists, and professional politicians out of touch with economic reality. But
the deputies refused to accept Bismarck's economics. Except for small concessions of modest yield (stamp taxes on notes, securities, and private lotteries
and increased tariffs on meal and grapes) the government's tax program was
decisively rejected.[55]

The Reichstag deputies also handed the chancellor stinging defeats on two
other matters. They rejected his attempt to fund a German economic council
and amended Boetticher's accident insurance statute so drastically as to make
it unacceptable to the chancellor.[56] The most notable statute passed was
dubbed the *Lex Tiedemann*, a product of Bismarck's ongoing feud with the
Berlin city government dominated by the Progressive party. The chancellor
of the German Reich—who claimed to be "so rich through the grace of the
king" that he was above quibbling over taxes—sought to lower by imperial
law the city's graduated rent tax upon dwellings occupied rent-free by imperial
officials. By insisting that the rental value of the dwellings be established at
10 percent of the occupant's salary, rather than upon rents paid for comparable dwellings, he expected to lower the tax paid by only 1,200 marks. The
chief beneficiaries were the chancellor himself (rent tax reduction from 746
to 120 marks) and his aide Christoph von Tiedemann (252 to 30 marks). For
days this petty bill, first introduced but ignored in 1880, occupied the attention of the parliament of the German Reich. The deputies, who received no
remuneration for parliamentary service, listened to the rich and mighty chancellor complain even about the 3.50 marks assessed by the city for the number
of horse stalls in his stable. In his rage at the "progressive ring" that allegedly
discriminated against him, he threatened to remove the Prussian and imperial
governments from Berlin. With the help of the Center party, angling for favors in church legislation, the conservatives upped the percentage of salary
from ten to fifteen and passed the bill over the opposition of the liberal parties, including two of Bismarck's former colleagues, Falk and Delbrück.[57]

Rebellion of the Little Man

The legislative debates of 1880–1881 were conducted with an eye on the upcoming Reichstag election. Bismarck's campaign was aimed primarily at urban and rural property owners, but also at the urban lower classes. By remit-

[55] *SBR* (1881), pp. 551ff., 1057, 1340ff., 1677ff., 1696ff., 1710ff. *BR*, VIII, 316ff., 332ff.,
398ff. Bismarck's ideal taxes were the notorious milling and slaughter taxes imposed by Prussian
cities in lieu of the class tax until abolished in 1873.

[56] *SBR* (1881), pp. 1589–1611, 1746–1783.

[57] *SBR* (1881), pp. 159–176, 889–931, 999–1005; *RGB* (1881), p. 99; *BR*, VIII, 353ff., IX,
44–60; Richter, *Im alten Reichstag*, II, 198–207; Busch, *Tagebuchblätter*, III, 32–37. Bismarck
branded "the social and political republicans of Berlin the most dangerous enemy of the monarchy." To the Kaiser, June 22, 1881. GSA, Hausarchiv, Rep. 51, Nr. 10.

ting taxes, seeking accident insurance, announcing his intention to expand social security into other areas, he posed as the "advocate of the little man," an image that was reinforced by the official press.[58] In parliament he also inveighed against party politics and professional politicians, preached the virtues of "interest politics," and thumped the drums of national patriotism. He denied that his tax bills, proposed constitutional amendments, and the economic councils were intended to reduce parliamentary power. Yet the threats they posed sufficed to keep the National Liberal party from being a docile member of the progovernment coalition that Bismarck wished to construct. Eager though they were to remain in harmony with the government, Bennigsen and his associates still could not participate in the emasculation of popular institutions. Hence they voted with progressives, centrists, and socialists in frustrating the chancellor's legislative program.[59]

The election campaign was complicated by an upsurge of anti-Semitic agitation, one of whose protagonists was Adolf Stöcker, court chaplain and founder of the Christian Social Labor party.[60] Unable to woo Berlin workers away from the social democrats in 1878, Stöcker dropped the word "labor" from the party title and focused instead upon the constituency of the progressives (petty officials, shopkeepers, small businessmen) by concentrating on anti-Semitism. In this way he also hoped to counterattack liberal publishers, journalists, and politicians—many of them Jewish—who had dealt harshly with his movement from its inception. The shift in strategy made Stöcker more sympathetic to conservatives, who had earlier disliked his populism and attacks on property.[61]

Furthermore, anti-Semitism had now become popular among Germans who felt threatened by both Polish and Jewish migration from the east. In the pages of the *Preussische Jahrbücher*, Heinrich von Treitschke—professor at Berlin, celebrated historian, dynamic orator, and Reichstag deputy—denounced the presumption, avarice, and unassimilability of Jews. Despite protests by Theodor Mommsen and a few other colleagues, Treitschke's assault made anti-Semitism academically and socially respectable.[62] In the fall of 1880 anti-Semites launched a petition demanding that Bismarck sponsor legislation to suspend Jewish immigration, bar Jews from governmental and teaching positions, and reestablish a Jewish census. By the time it reached Bismarck in April 1881 the petition bore 250,000 signatures, far short of the one million anticipated, but still impressive.[63]

Anti-Semitic agitation on this scale was new in German public life. How

[58] *AWB*, II, 57–58; Lucius, *Bismarck-Erinnerungen*, p. 191; SEG (1881), pp. 166–167.

[59] Oncken, *Bennigsen*, II, 451ff.

[60] For the earlier history of the Stöcker movement, see vol. 2, pp. 292–293.

[61] Peter G. Pulzer, *The Rise of Political Anti-Semitism in Germany and Austria* (New York, 1964), pp. 90–97.

[62] See pp. 199–203.

[63] SEG (1881), p. 148.

would the Bismarck government react? In June 1880 Stöcker attacked Gerson Bleichröder and his wealth in a public meeting. When the banker petitioned the Kaiser for "patriarchal protection," the preacher escalated his rhetoric, accusing the banker of having amassed his fortune by cheating Christians.[64] In 1875–1877 the anti-Semitic attack on Bleichröder was also directed at Bismarck and the laissez-faire, procapitalist policy of his government. But the chancellor's reversal in policy during 1878–1879 had removed him from the line of fire.[65] In a message to Puttkamer, to whom the matter of Stöcker's conduct was referred, Bismarck did object to the chaplain's attack on rich Jews who supported the state, but not to his anti-Semitism as such. He wished that Stöcker would turn his attention instead to the unpropertied Jews who opposed the government in the press and parliament. What most alarmed him was Stöcker's advocacy of a "normal work week," which would "ruin our industry," and full compensation for unemployed workers, which was "unattainable."[66] He wanted to prosecute Christian socialists for instigating class conflict, but not for slandering Jews.

In November 1880 the Reichstag progressives tried to compel the government to take a stand on the anti-Semitic petition. Their interpellation produced a two-day debate that starkly revealed how much progress anti-Semitic agitation had made in the upper circles of German society. Conservatives, free conservatives, centrists, and even some national liberals joined the assault in varying degrees; even the progressives tended to be apologetic in their defense of Jewish civil rights.[67] For Bismarck the interpellation posed a dilemma, for he could neither support nor oppose it. From Friedrichsruh he angrily instructed his colleagues to ignore the interpellation and, when that proved to be impossible, to avoid at least any support for Stöcker. He was forced, nevertheless, to give up any thought of prosecuting the chaplain under the antisocialist act of 1878, for such an action would have identified the government with the progressives. Hence he joined Puttkamer in advising Wilhelm merely to rebuke Stöcker for committing "excesses" by attacking rich men, criticizing government policy, and arousing insatiable expectations for social reform. Bismarck had no objection to anti-Semitism as long as it was used against his foes.[68]

<hr/>

[64] Fritz Stern, Gold and Iron: Bismarck, Bleichröder, and the Building of the German Empire (New York, 1977), pp. 513–517.

[65] See vol. 2, pp. 285, 316–321.

[66] Bismarck to Puttkamer, Oct. 16, 1880. GW, VIc, 198–199.

[67] SBHA (1880–1881), I, 226–299.

[68] See particularly Stern, Gold and Iron, pp. 517–524. "I make distinctions among Jews," Bismarck told Busch (Jan. 21, 1881). "The rich ones are not dangerous. They do not put up barricades, and they pay their taxes punctually. The ambitious ones who have nothing are something else, especially those active in the press. Still the Christians are the worst, not the Jews." Busch, Tagebuchblätter, III, 13. After the election turned out badly, Bismarck deplored the "untimeliness" of the anti-Semitic movement; it had diverted the aims of the election campaign. "I am

During the election year Bismarck responded politely to addresses sent him by anti-Semitic groups and assemblies. When pressed to explain his position, he told the Reichstag that he had no time to check out the character of the groups of citizens that sent telegrams and petitions on public issues streaming into the Wilhelmstrasse; he deplored agitators who stirred up "class hatred" (no mention of ideological or religious hatred) and spoke vaguely of his desire as chancellor to keep his distance from all "undesirable" movements.[69] In the absence of any censure from the chancellor and Prussian ministers, the public could assume that the government did not disapprove of the anti-Semitic clamor. In the pages of *Grenzboten* they could read unrestrained attacks on Jews by Moritz Busch, Bismarck's journalistic pistol. No disciplinary action was taken by the government against schoolteachers and pastors involved in the anti-Semitic movement. The Guelph fund was believed to be financing anti-Semitic newspapers that suddenly sprouted across the land.[70] The general atmosphere encouraged rowdyism, including some noisy demonstrations and attempts to break up meetings of socialists and progressives. Anti-Semitic leaflets were distributed on Berlin streets—"*Juden 'raus!*" In the northeastern cities of Thorn, Neustettin, and Stolp riots broke out. Jewish homes and a synagogue were burned. At Stolp the army intervened to restore order, leaving sixteen wounded and thirty under arrest. Only then did the government forbid anti-Semitic agitation in the provinces of Pomerania and West Prussia.[71] But in May 1881 the Prussian cabinet inaugurated on Bismarck's instigation those sharpened passport controls that presaged the expulsion of alien Jews from Berlin and the eastern provinces.[72] One year after he contemplated legal action against Stöcker, Bismarck advised his son Wilhelm to support the preacher's candidacy for the Reichstag, but without involving the government. "Stöcker's election is urgently desirable, both to defeat his opponent and because he is an extraordinary, militant, and useful ally."[73]

With Puttkamer's appointment as minister of interior in June 1881 a hard-fisted official assumed control of Prussia's administrative structure, including provincial governors, district presidents, county counselors (*Landräte*), and police. The "Puttkamer system" of rigid discipline and undeviating loyalty was soon evident in the Reichstag election campaign of that year. On his orders state officials, especially the county counselors, actively campaigned in

---

against progressive, not conservative Jews and their newspapers." To the cabinet, Nov. 14, 1881. Lucius, *Bismarck-Erinnerungen*, p. 216.

[69] *BR*, IX, 14–15.

[70] Richter, *Im alten Reichstag*, II, 176–183.

[71] *SEG* (1881), pp. 155, 230, 240. Jews were prosecuted for burning down their own synagogue to collect insurance. Their conviction was overturned by an appeals court. *SEG* (1883), p. 143; (1884), p. 31.

[72] See pp. 201–202.

[73] Bismarck to Wilhelm Bismarck, Oct. 14, 1881. *GW*, XIV, 932. Also Busch, *Tagebuchblätter*, III, 55.

behalf of favored candidates, whether conservative or national liberal. Through Maybach and Bitter Bismarck extended the system to include tax and railway officials. From the Guelph fund came a steady stream of cash for conservative journals and journalists; from press officials of the foreign office and Prussian cabinet came a flood of articles and leaflets either dictated by or written on guidelines laid down by the chancellor.[74] After the election protests from the Reichstag were met by an assertion of the government's right and duty to assure that the correct side won. With Bismarck's approbation Puttkamer bluntly told the angry deputies, "The government wants its officials to support it in elections within the limits of the law, and I can add that those officials who did that loyally during the last election can count on the government's thanks and recognition and—what is more valuable—the certain gratitude of his imperial majesty. . . . In my opinion the essence of a monarchical state system is that its officials form a single organic whole also in political affairs." Never before, remarked Lasker, had the government's system been so nakedly described.[75]

Both the progressives and the government viewed the election of 1881 as a plebiscite "for or against Bismarck." Bismarck ordered his press agents to make clear to the voters that he would never accept progressive "swine" as colleagues in the government. If the progressives brought about his fall, Germany would lose the secure position in European politics that the chancellor alone had created. "To vote for the government and for Bismarck is to vote for peace."[76] As election day approached, Rickert and Lasker, true to the original aim of the Secession, sought to unite all three liberal battalions under a single banner. But the extremes were too far apart. Bennigsen was unwilling to commit himself never to cooperate with Bismarck, and Richter was resolute in his conviction that "Bismarck must go!" Some national liberal leaders sensed that to hang on to Bismarck's coattails was potentially disastrous. In August 1880 Miquel, now mayor of Frankfurt am Main, wrote to Bennigsen, "Thousands of individual dissatisfactions continually produced by Bismarck have combined into a single current, even sweeping many national groups along with it." Stephani feared that, if the chancellor continued the "stormy,

---

[74] Walter Bussmann, ed., *Staatssektretär Graf Herbert von Bismarck: Aus seiner politischen Privatkorrespondenz* (Göttingen, 1964), pp. 98–109; *BP*, I, 193–194; *SEG* (1881), pp. 238–239. On Bismarck's request the railway station newsstands were pressed into service to distribute an anonymous pamphlet (written by Lothar Bucher) attacking Cobdenism. *GW*, XIV, 926–927; Busch, *Tagebuchblätter*, III, 47. Bismarck himself orchestrated the campaign against two secessionist candidates in Lauenburg, threatening to sell the Sachsenwald and move away if his Lauenburg neighbors were so "conceited, stupid, and mean" as to elect sessionist deputies. *BP*, I, 101. When Lauenburg voters disobeyed, he chose a milder form of punishment—skipping his fall visit to Friedrichsruh. Spitzemberg, *Tagebuch*, pp. 193–194.

[75] *SBR* (1881–1882), I, 359–377, 383–411; Anlagen, II, No. 38. See also Bismarck to Bennigsen, Dec. 17, 1881. *GW*, VIII, 440–441.

[76] Herbert Bismarck to Rantzau, Sept. 12 and 15, 1881. Bussmann, *Herbert von Bismarck*, pp. 102–103.

restless, whimsical agitation" that had characterized his course during the last year and a half, he would drive three-quarters of Germany into extreme opposition and destroy the middle parties. Yet Bennigsen, remembering the blows suffered by liberals in the campaigns of 1878–1879, still believed in Bismarck's capacity for detecting the "quiet undercurrents present in Germany for years. The phenomenal and historical importance of Bismarck is to be found in his great sensitivity for, and quick observation of, the shifting movements within the minds and hearts of the people."[77]

Since 1866 Prussian and German voters had seemingly tried to please Bismarck. In successive elections over a decade and a half most had cast their ballots in accordance with what the architect of German unity seemed to want, although his purposes were not always clear. They had given him majorities with which to complete the work of unification, expedite the growth of industrial capitalism, fight the Kulturkampf, avenge Wilhelm's wounds, save Germany from socialism, and protect "national labor" against invasions of alien iron, rye, and timber. But on October 27, 1881, the electorate deserted him. The middle parties, upon which he had staked his hopes, were decimated, the free conservatives sinking from 57 to 28 seats, national liberals from 99 to 47. What the national liberals lost the secessionists won (46 seats), while the progressives more than doubled their strength from 26 to 60 seats. (Bismarck's instruction that conservatives vote for socialists against progressives in the runoff elections did not affect the outcome.)[78] The centrists also benefited, growing from 94 to 100 seats, while their Polish allies expanded from 14 to 18. The Guelphs kept their 10 seats and the Alsatians their 15. On the extremes the conservatives dropped from 59 to 50 and the social democrats regained the 3 seats lost in 1878 for a total of 12.[79] In Berlin the anti-Semitic movement won no seats, although it replaced the social democrats as the second strongest party in the capital.[80]

While this success was beyond their wildest expectations, secessionists, progressives, and the People's party (9 seats) controlled only 125 seats in a chamber of 397. Even if they managed to establish with the national liberals a "great liberal" coalition (172 seats), which was unlikely, they still could not create a majority. For Bismarck, on the other hand, the old system of alter-

[77] Oncken, Bennigsen, II, 438–474; Felix Rachfahl, "Eugen Richter und der Linksliberalismus im neuen Reiche," Zeitschrift für Politik, 5 (1912), p. 317. On the "Secession" see vol. 2, pp. 534–537.

[78] Herbert Bismarck to Count Rantzau, Oct. 29, 1881. Bussmann, Herbert von Bismarck, pp. 108–109; Lucius, Bismarck-Erinnerungen, p. 216.

[79] Bernhard Vogel, Dieter Nohlen, and Rainer-Olaf Schultze, Wahlen in Deutschland: Theorie-Geschichte-Dokumente, 1848–1970 (Berlin, 1971), p. 291.

[80] During the election campaign the anti-Semites joined with the conservatives in a coalition (the Conservative Central Committee) that garnered 46,000 votes compared to the progressives' 89,000; the social democrats, hampered by the antisocialist act, attracted 30,000 voters. Stöcker was elected at Siegen in Westphalia, running as a conservative. Pulzer, Rise of Political Anti-Semitism, p. 99.

native majorities was no longer possible. The two conservative parties could not form a majority with the national liberals (125 seats). But neither could they form one with the centrists (178 seats)—unless the coalition included Poles, Alsatians, Guelphs, and some national liberals. The mere possibility of such a combination meant that the Center party was the chief beneficiary of the election of 1881. Either by giving or withholding its support, the Center and its political allies could make or break the chancellor's program. Bismarck now faced an imperial parliament dominated by oppositional elements, which, though united in nothing else, had a common hostility toward his regime. Those whom the prince had branded as *Reichsfeinde*—left-liberals, social democrats, centrists, Poles, Alsatians, Danes, and Guelphs—occupied no fewer than 272 seats!

Why this result? Unfortunately, no historian has made an in-depth study of this significant election. A contemporary analysis concluded that the victories of secessionists and progressives were owed largely to the votes of urban "little people"—workers of the lowest stratum and "the petty bourgeois" of the lower-middle stratum.[81] But what moved them? Uncontrolled increases in the price of bread and other foodstuffs? The government's failure to deliver the promised class tax relief? The threat of price increases on tobacco, owing to the government's plan for monopoly? Bismarck's patent favoritism toward rural interests, especially the gentry? The protectionist alliance of big industry, big banking, and big agriculture that Forckenbeck and Richter denounced? Economic issues affecting everyone's pocketbook probably played the primary role in turning out the left-liberal vote. Prominent protectionists were decisively defeated, and prominent free traders were returned by big majorities. But politically minded voters may also have been unsettled by the progressives' charge that Bismarck had lost his grip on domestic affairs, by recurrent cabinet crises and the chancellor's growing "dictatorship" over the administrative apparatus of two governments, by his attempts to weaken the power of the Reichstag and Chamber of Deputies and his threat to overthrow universal and equal male suffrage. Whatever their reasons, the voters produced in 1881 the greatest reversal in German politics since 1866. Although the total liberal vote was no greater than in the previous election, Richter and his associates were euphoric over the possibility that the election might signal the beginning of a new trend in German politics.[82]

Family Crisis and Political Misfortune

When Bismarck returned to Berlin in January 1881, his health was much improved over previous years. But that condition did not last. During the

---

[81] See the analysis of the election in the *Augsburger Allgemeine Zeitung*, No. 306, Nov. 2, 1881; *SEG* (1881), pp. 271–272.

[82] *SBR* (1881), II, 1706; James Sheehan, *German Liberalism in the Nineteenth Century* (Chicago, 1978), pp. 208–210.

following months a family crisis jeopardized the one secure bastion in his continuing war with the political world. The wish of his oldest son to follow his heart's desire in choosing a wife produced a serious disruption in their relationship. Herbert had for years been passionately in love with the Princess Elisabeth Carolath. The beautiful daughter of the Prince of Hatzfeldt-Trachenberg, a wealthy Silesian magnate, and a prominent figure in Berlin society, Elisabeth divorced her husband, Prince Carolath-Beuthen, in April 1881 and took up residence in Venice to await her lover.

But Herbert never came, for his father took violent exception to their marriage. Bismarck objected not only to her status as a divorced woman, but also to her family connections. She was related by marriage to the von Loë family, one of whose members was a partisan of Harry von Arnim and had followed the renegade diplomat into exile under threat of a prison sentence. But she was also stepsister to Mimi von Schleinitz, wife of Royal House Minister Alexander von Schleinitz, long an object of Bismarck's hatred. Schleinitz was one of those "unresponsible" people at court, whom the chancellor suspected of intrigues against his person and policies. The possibility that a woman with these family associations could become a member of his family and frequent resident in his household was more than the prince could bear.

In impassioned confrontations between father and son Bismarck, by Herbert's testimony, was reduced to tears and threats of suicide. He had, he said, placed all of his hopes and plans upon Herbert's future. If Herbert should take

HERBERT BISMARCK, 1885. (BILDARCHIV PREUSSISCHER KULTURBESITZ.)

the train to Venice, Bismarck would go with him; to prevent the marriage was "more important than the entire German Reich." Johanna joined the laments of her husband by predicting that the marriage would be the death of her. But Bismarck also placed his son in an impossible financial situation by conniving with the Kaiser to change the primogeniture statutes to prevent sons who married divorced women from inheriting entailed estates. A disinherited Herbert and his wife would have been forced to live from her alimony, which their marriage would have reduced by half. Herbert chose to abandon his sweetheart, although she also threatened suicide, and to accept the social stigma of having compromised her. Whether this shattering experience was responsible for his alcoholism and misanthropy in following years is naturally unverifiable. [83]

But it seems certain that the Carolath affair had a most adverse effect on Bismarck's own mental and physical health. His violent opposition to Elisabeth Carolath was grounded in the threat that such a union posed to the hearth that he wished "to protect and to shelter against all that is evil and foreign."[84] In March 1881 he suffered from grippe, and in May his old leg injury returned to haunt him, forcing him for weeks to walk with a cane and to lie on a sofa during conferences. In February and again in June he was attacked by "nervous facial pains," the prelude to a serious new malady (trigeminal neuralgia). To Lucius he appeared "old and trembling." In a broken voice the chancellor complained, "I can't do it any more and must give up. Once I take hold of something, I can't turn it loose again." During June he was afflicted by severe stomach cramps, followed by bleeding. "He attributed all of this to his many vexations, although everything points to the presence of stomach ulcers." Again he was agitated by "thoughts about future ministerial combinations" and suspicions of plots by Stosch, secessionists, and progressives to oust him from power. Lucius wrote, "To determine how much of this is reality and how much is fantasy is scarcely possible." Even minor matters aroused his ire, such as the "theory" held by veterinarians that rabies epidemics were spread by canine biting; cooler weather, he insisted, would moderate the disease. [85]

An attack of hemorrhoids that began in June and lasted four months added to his misery, "burning like hellfire." To Busch he complained of "weakness and oppression, and pains all over, in the body, chest, and face," of teeth that

[83] Erich Eyck, Bismarck: Leben und Werk (3 vols., Zurich, 1941–1944), III, 389–392; Philipp zu Eulenburg-Hertefeld, Aus 50 Jahren (Berlin, 1923), pp. 81–107; Louis L. Snyder, "Political Implications of Herbert von Bismarck's Marital Affairs, 1881, 1892," Journal of Modern History, 36 (1964), pp. 155–169.

[84] Bismarck to Johanna von Bismarck, May 14, 1851. GW, XIV, 211–212. See vol. 2, pp. 61–62.

[85] Bismarck to Kaiser, Mar. 13, 1881. GSA, Hausarchiv, Rep. 51, Nr. 10; Busch, Tagebuchblätter, III, 13–14; Lucius, Bismarck-Erinnerungen, pp. 208–210, 214; Tiedemann, Sechs Jahre, p. 458.

pained him, "tugging and tearing above and below and all round."[86] In late June he wrote to the Kaiser that "every involvement in state business, regardless how minor, brings painful and debilitating relapses."[87] Another concern was his Johanna's heart trouble, for which Struck advised the baths at Kreuth. This meant a separation of weeks, which she resisted as did her spouse. The prince gave Struck such "an excessively rude reception" that the doctor resigned, declaring that his own health was too poor "to endure the convulsions that come with practicing medicine in the Bismarck household."[88]

On June 15, 1881, the prince felt compelled to ask the Kaiser for another extended leave. But he was too weak to leave Berlin until July 1, when he departed for Bad Kissingen without Johanna, who went to Bad Kreuth.[89] Daily baths supplemented by bottles of Rakoczy water diminished but did not end his pains. On August 14 he was back in Berlin, leaving, after a day in Schönhausen, for Varzin on August 18. There his rest was interrupted by the necessity of attending (September 8–10, 1881) a meeting of Emperors Wilhelm and Alexander at Danzig. The effort was costly. Increased pain forced him to stay in bed and incapacitated him for business. A week later vexation over a "harsh" letter from the Kaiser, the result of a misunderstanding (or was it another palace intrigue?), produced a relapse that caused his household grave concern.[90] Bismarck's health, Herbert reported, "has *never* been so bad." Another doctor had to be summoned from Berlin, and in October the patient was temporarily better.[91]

Despite his considerable effort to influence the voters, Bismarck expressed indifference over the outcome of the October election, predicting gains by conservatives and progressives at the cost of the "moderate parties."[92] Imme-

---

[86] Busch, *Tagebuchblätter*, III, 40, 54, 55, 91; Spitzemberg, *Tagebuch*, p. 192. Tiedemann described the symptoms as "sleeplessness, no appetite, general exhaustion." To Bleichröder, June 15, 1881. *Bleichröder Archive*, Kress Library of Business and Economics, Harvard, Box 1, Folder 14.

[87] Bismarck to Kaiser, June 22, 1881. GSA, Rep. 51, Nr. 10.

[88] Norman Rich and M. H. Fisher, eds., *The Holstein Papers: The Memoirs, Diaries and Correspondence of Friedrich von Holstein, 1837–1909* (4 vols., Cambridge, Eng., 1955–1963), II, 110–111. Bismarck was outraged that this man, "whom I found and made," could give him an ultimatum. Lucius concluded, "Dr. Struck has learned something from Bismarck's style!" Lucius, *Bismarck-Erinnerungen*, p. 213.

[89] GW, VIc, 215. Tiedemann to Bleichröder, June 15, 26, and July 1, 1881. *Bleichröder Archive*, Kress Library of Business and Economics, Harvard, Box 1, Folder 14.

[90] GW, XIV, 926, 931; Lucius, *Bismarck-Erinnerungen*, pp. 213–214; Bussmann, *Herbert von Bismarck*, pp. 104–105. Wilhelm was justifiably outraged to learn that Bismarck had been negotiating with the Vatican without his knowledge through a "vacationing" Prussian envoy, Kurd von Schlözer. But he also assumed, on the basis of a newspaper clipping sent him anonymously, that the chancellor had agreed to the appointment of a papal nuncio at Berlin. GW, VIc, 224–229.

[91] Rich and Fisher, eds., *Holstein Papers*, III, 51–52.

[92] Busch, *Tagebuchblätter*, III, 44; GW, VIII, 422–423. See also his memorial to Gossler, July 22, 1881. GW, IVc, 218–219.

diately after the election he announced that he was "neither surprised nor discouraged; chronic illnesses demand time and patience for their cure."[93] But on November 8 the free conservative *Post*, often an outlet for his views, claimed that the chancellor—"tired of being the butt of all the malice, villainy, slander, and envious suspicion that a population of millions can discharge"—would hand over to someone else the responsibility of forming a majority with the Center party, made necessary by the desertion of the liberals. Other reports were that he would restrict himself in the future to foreign policy, deputizing parliamentary leaders like Franckenstein, Bennigsen, or Forckenbeck to carry the burdens of internal affairs. He preferred to cling to constitutionalism; although not an evil in itself, absolutism could bring the wrong person to power.[94]

Lothar Bucher complained to Busch about the "nonsense" emanating from "backwoods" Varzin, which he attributed to Herbert rather than to the father. Yet Bismarck spoke in the same petulant, half-joking vein to the cabinet and members of the Bundesrat after his return to Berlin on November 12, 1881. His mood was expressed most bluntly to Busch. "They hate and slander me because I am a Junker and not a professor, and because I have been a minister for twenty years. They take advantage of my attachment to the emperor and pretend that I am clinging to office, that I am devoured by love of power. It may turn out differently, however, and I may say to them, 'Here you take it! Now let's see you govern!' "[95] If these fantasies served no other purpose, they did make Wilhelm anxious. In an audience at the palace Bismarck again relieved the octogenarian's fear of being deserted. Afterward Lucius found the chancellor confident that he, as far as the Kaiser was concerned, was "fully master of the situation" and could take "the parliamentary situation lightly." On November 17 the chancellor appeared in full uniform, flanked by the crown prince and other royal princes, to read the Kaiser's speech from the throne opening the first session of the new Reichstag. "Bismarck is now shoving the person of his majesty into the foreground," Lucius observed, "and is making him personally the bearer of the prince's own social and fiscal plans."[96]

Bismarck's mood in the fall of 1881 was not unlike that of 1862. He sum-

---

[93] Horst Kohl, ed., *Fürst Bismarck: Regesten zu einer wissenschaflichen Biographie des ersten Reichskanzlers* (Leipzig, 1891), II, 246; SEG (1881), p. 273.

[94] *BP*, I, 231–238; SEG (1881), pp. 275–276, 278. On Bismarck's threat to restrict his activities to foreign affairs, see also the report by a "highly placed diplomat" of his interview with Bismarck, published in the *Kölnische Zeitung*, June 6, 1880. SEG (1880), pp. 180–182. Also Hohenlohe, *Memoirs*, II, 292.

[95] Moritz Busch, *Bismarck: Some Secret Pages of His History* (New York, 1898), II, 292–295. The entire entry for Nov. 9, 1881, which contains the quoted passage, was expurgated from the German version of Busch's diary. Busch, *Tagebuchblätter*, III, 55. Lucius, *Bismarck-Erinnerungen*, pp. 215–217; Spitzemberg, *Tagebuch*, p. 193.

[96] Lucius, *Bismarck-Erinnerungen*, pp. 216–217.

moned the Reichstag to meet in November, fully determined to insist upon his legislative program despite the certainty of rejection. Since August he had pressed upon Scholz, head of the Imperial Treasury, and upon the Prussian cabinet his view that only an imperial monopoly of the manufacture and sale of tobacco could provide funds adequate to finance a system of social insurance and the revenue-sharing needed to relieve the burden of direct taxation in Prussia.[97] During the election campaign the *Kathedersozialist* Adolph Wagner described the scheme at Bismarck's request. The "patrimony of the disinherited," the professor declared, was to be provided by the tobacco monopoly without increasing the price of the product. "The entire profit, which is now lost en route from the manufacturers through wholesalers to the consumers, shall devolve upon the state." Even after tobacco merchants and manufacturers had been indemnified, the monopoly was expected to yield 130,000,000 to 150,000,000 marks, a sum sufficient to launch an imperial program of old-age and disability insurance for workers.[98]

As finally drafted, however, the tobacco monopoly was unhooked from the social insurance bill. The entire yield (now estimated at 163,600,000 marks) was to be distributed to the state governments, leaving the social insurance program to be financed by state assessments and new imperial taxes.[99] For the third time Bismarck sought to prejudice the Reichstag's consideration of his tax program by securing passage, in advance of its debates on the tobacco monopoly, of a utilization bill in the Prussian Landtag. Prussia's share of the funds to be derived from the monopoly and from still other new imperial revenues (totaling 188,000,000 marks) was to be allocated to the same purposes listed in the previous bill, with certain seductive additions: up to 25,000,000 marks for pay increases to state officials, a reduction in the tax burden for education (that is, the surtax on real estate), and abolition of "school money" paid locally by families with children in public schools.[100]

But again the Chamber of Deputies refused to do Bismarck's bidding, despite the fact that its composition was considerably more favorable to the government than that of the Reichstag. They would not appropriate funds to

[97] GW, VIc, 220, 222; AWB II, 61–63; DZA Potsdam, Reichskanzlei, 2085, pp. 66–77. Nationalization of the tobacco industry was not a new idea with the Bismarck government. As early as 1872 the government had sought to prepare the way "very quietly" by imposing a tobacco tax as the initial step toward a tobacco monoply. In 1877 Bismarck had revived the idea, but without success. Cabinet meeting of Mar. 9, 1877. DZA Merseburg, Rep. 90a, III, B, 2b, Nr. 6, Vol. 89.

[98] SEG (1881), pp. 228–229, 258. At a cabinet meeting on December 22, Bismarck disclaimed responsibility for Wagner's initiative, but the ministers were unconvinced. Lucius, *Bismarck-Erinnerungen*, pp. 219–220. They were right. See Herbert Bismarck to Adolph Wagner, end of July 1881. Poschinger, ed., *Volkswirth*, II, 78–80, and Heinrich Rubner, ed., *Adolph Wagner: Briefe, Dokumente, Augenzeugenberichte, 1851–1917* (Berlin, 1978), p. 203.

[99] SBR (1882–1883), Drucksachen, No. 7; GW, VIc, 247; AWB, II, 90–94, 104–105; Poschinger, ed., *Volkswirth*, II, 101–102.

[100] SBHA (1882), Anlagen, II, No. 135.

be derived mainly from a fiscal source that appeared to be highly unpopular, judging by the cries of affected merchants and manufacturers and the protests of governments and legislatures in states where the tobacco industry was concentrated. They doubted that a nationalized tobacco industry would yield the enormous sum promised, without price increases that would alienate millions of smoker-voters. Progressives and national liberals alike charged that the government's tax program would benefit the wealthy at the cost of the poor; whatever tax relief the lower classes received would be outweighed by the new burdens imposed.[101] When they lost the first test of strength on the utilization bill (May 6, 1882), the cabinet withdrew it—much to the distress of Bismarck, who tried desperately to rally the ministers from his sickbed at Friedrichsruh.[102]

That the tobacco monopoly was in jeopardy was already evident from the actions of the Prussian Economic Council. This body of "practical experts," which contained but one representative of the tobacco industry, rejected the monopoly proposal, 33 to 31, on March 21, 1882.[103] During April, while Bismarck lay ill at Friedrichsruh, there were also signs of revolt in the Bundesrat. Except for Württemberg, all of the medium states and many of the small states—where the tobacco industry was important—voted against the measure; still it passed, 36 to 22.[104] Although the statute was obviously doomed, Bismarck obstinately insisted that the Reichstag be summoned to deliberate on it in May and June, if only to clarify the issue.[105] The tobacco monopoly had to come, Bismarck told his physician Cohen. Even his opponents would some day have to adopt it in order to ease the intolerable burden of direct taxation.[106]

If there was any hope for passage of the tobacco monopoly in 1882, it lay with the Center party, which had some reason to be satisfied with the government's new direction in religious matters. Prussian officials had made use of the enabling act of June 1880 to relax restrictions placed on the Catholic church at the height of the Kulturkampf. Only 133 of approximately 1,000 parishes vacated during the struggle were still without priests; of twelve bishoprics only three were still unoccupied. During 1881 alone Kultusminister Gossler permitted seventeen hundred priests to resume religious instruction

[101] SBHA (1882), II, 1705–1737, 1749–1769. See particularly the speeches by Robert von Benda and Eugen Richter. Ibid., pp. 1708, 1730.

[102] Bismarck to Puttkamer, Apr. 25, 26, and May 6, 1882. GW, XIV, 935–936; VIc, 253–255. Also Lucius, Bismarck-Erinnerungen, pp. 229–230, and GW, VIII, 447.

[103] SEG (1882), p. 58.

[104] Heinrich von Poschinger, ed., Fürst Bismarck und der Bundesrat, 1867–1890 (Stuttgart, 1901), V, 94–102.

[105] Lucius, Bismarck-Erinnerungen, p. 226; AWB, II, 107.

[106] GW, VIII, 445–446.

BISMARCK DISCOVERING THAT THE WALLS OF THE CHURCH (THE NEWLY COMPLETED COLOGNE CATHE-
DRAL) ARE OF STONE AND HIS FOREHEAD NOT OF IRON. "WHY SHOULD I RUN MY HEAD THROUGH THE
WALL?" THE CHICKEN IS A REFERENCE TO LUDWIG HAHN, AUTHOR OF AN EARLY WORK ON THE KUL-
TURKAMPF. WILHELM SCHOLZ IN *KLADDERADATSCH*, 1881.

in the schools (except in Posen).[107] In June 1881 Bismarck assigned to the Vatican his old colleague of Petersburg days, Kurd von Schlözer, who negotiated the resumption of formal diplomatic relations on April 24, 1882. But Leo continued to insist that the May laws be repealed before the church made concessions on the *Anzeigepflicht* (the church's obligation to notify the state of nominations for ecclesiastical offices and the state's right to veto the same).[108]

In the spring of 1882 Gossler presented to the Prussian Chamber of Deputies a second enabling act, to replace that of 1880, which had expired. At Bismarck's direction the minister permitted a coalition of conservatives and centrists to amend the bill, rejecting the state's request for more authority to veto ecclesiastical appointments and permitting prospective priests to evade the hitherto obligatory state "cultural examinations" by proving that they had graduated from a "German *Gymnasium*" and had studied "with industry" philosophy, history, and German literature "on the university level." Although the chancellor nurtured relations with the right wing of the Center party, he believed that no concessions could buy the support of Windthorst and the party as a whole. "The government," he wrote, "can rely upon no one but itself."[109] Indeed the Center joined the liberal parties in overwhelming (277 to 43) the tobacco monopoly on June 15, 1882. By its intervention in the recent election, Windthorst remarked, the government had shown what political use it could make of 30,000 state-owned tobacco shops and their employees.[110]

Two Parliaments Out of Control

In the Prussian election of October 1882 the government eschewed the massive intervention that had marred the Reichstag election of 1881. Bismarck anticipated that the Conservative party, his most dependable parliamentary ally, would benefit politically from his perennial efforts at direct tax relief. Publicists for both conservative parties thought it wise, nevertheless, to stress their independence from the government. Free conservatives even criticized the "fantasies" of the Bismarck tax program.[111] The progressive campaign was marred by open feuding between Albert Hänel, who desired to cooperate with the Secession and National Liberal party, and Eugen Richter, who obdurately

---

[107] Erich Schmidt-Volkmar, *Der Kulturkampf in Deutschland, 1871–1890* (Göttingen, 1962), pp. 168, 187.

[108] Schmidt-Volkmar, *Kulturkampf*, pp. 267ff., 285ff.

[109] *SBHA* (1882), Anlagen, Nos. 7, 149, 188, 258; I, 138ff.; II, 1307ff., 1739ff.; GW, VIc, 244–251; Rich and Fisher, eds., *Holstein Papers*, II, 7–8. For the first enabling act, see vol. 2, pp. 531–537.

[110] *SBR* (1882–1883), I, 104–197, 353–470.

[111] *SEG* (1882), pp. 165–166, 173, 176.

opposed cooperation and campaigned actively to unseat national liberal incumbents.[112] In October balloting conservatives increased their strength from 110 to 122, free conservatives from 51 to 57, and centrists from 97 to 99 seats. Progressives retained 39 seats but lost, primarily to conservatives, 10 more of their traditional constituencies in East Prussia. In their first Prussian election the Secession won 19 seats, evidently at the cost of national liberals, who declined from 85 to 66 seats. In a chamber of 433 deputies the Center had retained its swing position; it could combine with either the conservative or liberal parties to gain a majority. With the help of part of the National Liberal party, the two conservative parties could form a majority. But the three liberal parties alone could not dominate the chamber.[113]

In the past the three-class voting system, oral voting, and indirect election had not sufficed to make the conservatives consistently the major party in the Prussian Chamber of Deputies. The increasing divergence in the political compositions of the Reichstag and Prussian lower chamber produced by the elections of 1879, 1881, and 1882 may have stemmed from other causes: increasing disparities in the wealth and size of the voting population in Prussian electoral districts (established in 1849) that favored rural districts; increased government intervention at election time; and the partnership between landowners and farmers established by protectionism and by the shift from ideological to interest politics. At first sight a major difference in political composition between the two legislatures should have given Bismarck a choice: the possibility of using one chamber as leverage against the other or of achieving in one parliament what was denied by the other. But what had worked in the case of the May laws and public ownership of railways failed where Bismarck's tax program was concerned. Despite persistent nagging from the official press, not even the conservatives could be relied upon to give Bismarck what he wanted.

In 1881 the Prussian lower chamber, elected in 1879, had failed to deliver a utilization act that might have helped to secure either new indirect taxes or a tobacco monopoly in the Reich. In amending the government's third utilization bill, the chamber elected in 1882 ignored the advice of the *Provinzial-Korrespondenz* that it should accept "the wisdom of the king and the insights of his advisers."[114] As submitted by Minister of Finance Scholz, the bill would have suspended the four lowest brackets of the class tax (incomes below 1,200 marks), covering the loss of revenue by imposing provisional licensing taxes on the sale of alcoholic beverages and tobacco products in Prussia until such time as revenues shared by the Reich attained "the necessary level."[115] Con-

---

[112] SEG (1882), pp. 176–179.

[113] Vogel et al., *Wahlen in Deutschland*, p. 287; SEG (1882), pp. 186–190.

[114] SEG (1882), p. 197.

[115] SBHA (1882–1883), Anlagen, I, No. 25. For Bismarck's role in the drafting of this bill see DZA Potsdam, Reichskanzlei, 2086, pp. 55ff.

servatives riled Bismarck by voting with centrists and liberals against the two license taxes and by helping Bennigsen rewrite the bill. Bismarck railed at those "blockheads" who thought themselves wiser than the government. "What is the use of their conservatism if they will not support us?"[116]

As finally passed on March 3, 1883, the statute suspended the two lowest brackets of the class tax (to 900 marks). Although less than the government wanted, the law gave tax relief to 75 percent of all persons subject to the class tax, including most mine and factory workers, and to 85 percent of the more than one million persons annually charged with tax deliquency. Excluded from the suspension were small farmers, tradesmen (Gewerbetreibende), government officials, and schoolteachers who fell in the third and fourth brackets and whose circumstances, the government claimed, were often worse than those of workers. The 25 percent general reduction in the class tax in the statute of March 10, 1881, remained in effect for the other ten brackets. To compensate for lost revenue, the bill reduced the tax cut provided by that statute for the first two brackets (3,000 to 4,200 marks) of the classified income tax and abolished the tax cut for brackets three through five (4,200 to 6,000 marks). Baron Wilhelm von Hammerstein, conservative deputy and editor of the Kreuzzeitung, charged that the bill, while favorable to labor and unfavorable to the middle-income groups, "carefully spared the really well-to-do and rich classes of the population." Again those who possessed political power had used it to shift the fiscal burden to the backs of those who lacked it.[117]

After five years of effort Bismarck had achieved only partial success in his attempt to liquidate direct taxation, now his major objective in internal policy. This was not the only frustration that the "Bismarck dictatorship" experienced in 1882–1883 at the hands of the Reichstag and Chamber of Deputies. During the spring of 1882 he summoned the Reichstag to meet on April 27, although the Landtag remained in session until May 11 while debating the utilization bill. Because so many deputies sat in both chambers it was difficult to preserve quorums during the period of overlap. In the following winter the problem was much worse, for the Reichstag convened from November 30, 1882, until June 12, 1883, the Landtag from November 14, 1882, to July 2, 1883. By deliberately creating chaos, Bismarck intended to demonstrate the necessity of biennial Reich budgets.[118] Having failed to attain this end by constitutional amendment in 1881, he now tried a different route. In December 1882 the government presented to the Reichstag a single budget

116 To Busch, Dec. 20, 1882. Busch, Tagebuchblätter, III, 135.

117 GSP (1883), pp. 37–38; SBHA (1882–1883), I, 327ff.; II, 771ff., 1123ff.; Anlagen, I, Nos. 91, 103, 108.

118 Lucius, Bismarck-Erinnerungen, pp. 227–228; GW, VIc, 253 (fn.), 254–255.

bill for two fiscal years (1883–1884 and 1884–1885). But all parties, except for the conservatives, refused to consider the two budgets in tandem.[119]

In April 1883 the issue was revived in a message from the throne (*Kaiserliche Botschaft*) introducing a separate budget bill for 1884–1885. By a narrow margin (105 to 97) the Reichstag at first dodged the issue by referring the bill to committee.[120] In a bitter interview with Bennigsen on June 5, Bismarck spilled out all his resentments over the repeated failure of the rump National Liberal party to become a government satellite. As a consequence the Hanoverian leader, who had always tried even under the most stressful circumstances to maintain contact with the chancellor, retired from politics, resigning his seats in both Reichstag and Landtag.[121] Still Bismarck, on the surface, got his way. Under threat of dissolution the Reichstag finally did accept the budget bill for 1884–1885 immediately before adjournment in June 1883. But the deputies pared appropriations so drastically that the government would be compelled to seek supplementary funding during the budget year.[122] For Bismarck it was a Pyrrhic victory.

This was not, furthermore, his only humiliation during the legislative year 1882–1883. By a new tariff on imported grapes and increased rates on meal and woolen goods in 1881, the government had breached the assumption that the tariff act of 1879 was final. As other countries shifted to protectionism, moreover, pressures by German producers increased. Petitions flooded the Reichstag; no session was without proposals for new or increased tariffs. Government bills alternated with Reichstag resolutions. "Rarely was a bill rejected; many were amended, to be sure, but the government and the protectionist majority were united concerning the line of march: away from free trade and toward the general protection of national labor." The list of protected items grew steadily longer: wax, honey, bees, paving blocks, roof shingles, granite slabs, marble, iron and asbestos wares, cordage, mineral oil, lard, lamps, etc.[123]

Yet when the owner of the Saxon and Varzin forests initiated a bill increasing threefold the rates on lumber—in order, he said, to protect German consumers from "inferior" lumber imported from Russia, Scandinavia, and Austria-Hungary—the Reichstag balked.[124] The majority was not moved by statistics showing that sales of timber from Prussian state forests were declining. Even the government had to admit that the needs of the German market could not be met entirely by German timber production, and the deputies

[119] SBR (1882–1883), pp. 659ff., 1391–1392; Drucksachen, No. 92.

[120] SBR (1882–1883), pp. 2323–2385; Drucksachen, Nos. 249, 291.

[121] Oncken, *Bennigsen*, II, 495ff.

[122] SBR (1882–1883), pp. 2834–3022; RGB (1883), pp. 127–146.

[123] Gerloff, *Finanz- und Zollpolitik*, pp. 198ff.

[124] Bismarck to Lucius, Dec. 29, 1881. AWB, II, 88–90. Lucius diary, Apr. 6, 1882 and Apr. 13, 1883. *Bismarck-Erinnerungen*, pp. 226, 262, 264. See also AWB, II, 115–116 and 123–125.

were not convinced by Bismarck's old argument that a higher tariff on the required imports would be absorbed by foreign producers through reduced profits rather than by domestic consumers through increased prices. To liberals the bill looked like special-interest legislation, designed to benefit big landowners at the cost of thousands of building contractors and hundreds of thousands of construction workers. Although supported by the two conservatives parties and some centrists, the bill was defeated by a comfortable margin (178 to 150).[125]

Scholz's Tax Reform

Deputies in all parties recognized that the class tax relief granted in 1883, five years after passage of the antisocialist statute, was inadequate to remove stark inequities in the income tax structure. During debates on the third utilization bill the Chamber of Deputies passed by a great majority a resolution calling upon the government to draft an organic reform of the class and income tax system, providing tax relief for all incomes below 6,000 marks and for the taxation of income derived from invested capital.[126]

During the following months Scholz and his subordinates at the Ministry of Finance drafted a bill in response to this demand that was dramatically different from any other proposed by the Prussian government in Bismarck's time. The statute would have freed all incomes under 1,200 marks from the class tax. Incomes above 1,200 marks were to be taxed progressively, beginning with 0.5 percent and rising to the old rate of 3 percent above 10,000 marks. Tax reductions owing to "adverse economic circumstances" were to be allowed on incomes below 9,000 marks, in contrast to the old level of 6,000 marks, and the deductions allowed were to be more generous. The cost of these benefits was to be defrayed by taxing corporate income for the first time and by imposing a "moderate" tax on unearned income from capital investments above 600 marks (excluding gross incomes under 1,200 marks, and widows, orphans, and handicapped persons earning less than 3,000 marks). Further fiscal benefits were expected from improvements in the tax assessment system, including self-assessment in the case of the tax on unearned capital income.[127]

Scholz's tax plan of late 1883 represented a major departure in Prussian tax policy—tax relief to the working and lower middle classes, adoption of the principle of progressive taxation, taxation of corporate income, additional tax on unearned income, and adoption of the principle of self-assessment. During the months in which this bill was drafted, Bismarck was at Friedrichsruh.

[125] SBR (1882–1883), pp. 1603–1647, 2388–2419, Anlagen, No. 194.

[126] SBHA (1882–1883), pp. 771–787, Anlagen, Nos. 25 and 91.

[127] Scholz to Puttkamer and Bismarck, Nov. 23, 1883. DZA Potsdam, Reichskanzlei, 2087, pp. 26–27.

Although the bill contained features (for example, progressive income tax) that he resisted six years later, there is no indication that he disapproved of them in 1883. When he first saw the bill in late November 1883, Bismarck's main concern was merely to make sure that the proposed tax on unearned income did not apply to interest received from mortgages on land (which would have driven up mortgage interest rates). He also advised Scholz for tactical reasons to make that tax a separate bill, in order better to defend it as parallel to the land and building tax. Capitalists were to understand that the special tax was being levied on securities income in order, as a matter of equity, to make their burden equivalent to that long borne by landowners.[128]

At the end of November news of Scholz's tax plan seeped through to the press. Scholz was certain that Gerson Bleichröder was the source of attacks that began in the *Nationalzeitung* (whose journalists were known to be close to the banker) and quickly spread to other journals.[129] By the time the bills came up for discussion in the Prussian parliament, an open struggle between big capital and big agriculture was well under way. For three days (January 15, 16, and 17, 1884) the opposing interests hammered away at each other during the first reading of the bill in the Prussian Chamber of Deputies. The Junker landlord and *Landrat* Wilhelm von Rauchhaupt defined the issue: "In the last thirty years our entire system of production has shifted so importantly to the capitalistic side that the earlier basis of our tax system [that is, landownership] has also shifted significantly. Today the power of capital has become so important and has surpassed landownership to such a degree that the latter has essentially fallen into a position of dependence on the former. As a consequence it is a complete misunderstanding of the financial capacities of individual classes in the population of this country to want to preserve any longer a system of taxation that, in the end result, is based on landownership." Rauchhaupt rejoiced that the government had finally found the "courage to take the offensive against the power of capital," while former Minister of Finance Hobrecht and the secessionist leader Heinrich Rickert deplored the bill's "unfair prejudice against capital." Adolph Wagner argued that the bill, by unburdening the "little people (workers, petty merchants, artisans, small farmers, the middle classes)" at the cost of the "well-to-do classes" was an essential part of the government's new social policy, as important as social insurance. The bill was referred to committee, where after forty meetings, it was buried.[130]

[128] Scholz to Bismarck, Nov. 26, 1883. *DZA* Potsdam, Reichskanzlei, 2087, pp. 24–25. Bismarck to Scholz, Nov. 28, 1883. *Ibid.*, pp. 82–85. Cabinet meeting of Nov. 29, 1883. *Ibid.*, pp. 86–91. Scholz to Bismarck, Dec. 8, 1883. *Ibid.*, pp. 93–96. Bismarck had rejected the idea of a progressive income tax as "unjust" in December 1882. Busch, *Tagebuchblätter*, III, 135.

[129] Scholz to Bismarck, Nov. 26, 1883. *DZA* Potsdam, Reichskanzlei, 2087, p. 25. Stern, *Gold and Iron*, p. 216.

[130] *SBHA* (1883–1884), pp. 675–781, Anlagen, Nos. 42 and 290.

Henry Axel Bueck, probably the most important single spokesman for industry and finance, explained what happened with brutal frankness. "Despite long and strenuous labor, two bills fell by the wayside that had been drafted in response to resolutions passed overwhelmingly by the Chamber of Deputies. The reason for this is to be found in the circumstance that the conflicts between interests were not sufficiently resolved. One side fought against the effort to clear the way for reform by imposing a special tax on capital. The other side sought to realize at any cost its aim to establish for exalted and affluent circles a privileged position with regard to the taxation of their property and income. Another difficulty was the attempt to exploit the reform of tax legislation to expand the power of parliament. But chiefly one can say the difficulties show that the conflicting interests of eastern and western regions of the monarchy have not yet been resolved."[131]

Agrarians had the satisfaction, nevertheless, of realizing one of their tax objectives—imposition of a new imperial levy on stock market transactions. Drafted by Scholz's ministry, the bill was introduced in the Bundesrat in May 1884 as a revision of the stamp tax imposed in 1881 on stock and bond issues. "The proposal immediately aroused heavy and almost universal opposition from the business community."[132] While the affected interests attempted to influence the government by storming the Reichstag and Bundesrat with petitions, Bleichröder tried to exploit his private channel to the center of power. In a long letter to Bismarck he reported that the bill had immediately depressed stock prices by 2 to 10 percent. The tax rate proposed and the requirement that businessmen open their books to tax collectors, he predicted, would drive "frightened capital" abroad. Scholz could not have presented the bill to the Bundesrat without Bismarck's prior approval, and yet observers got the impression initially that the chancellor was not eager to accept public responsibility for it.[133]

The stock market bill was evidently too hot an issue for the Bundesrat, which referred it to committee and took no further action during 1884. In the 1884–1885 legislative session Reichstag conservatives rescued the bill by introducing it independently in the Reichstag. National liberal deputies countered with a rival bill more favorable to the interests of financiers.[134] But the conservative version won out on critical points. The final draft taxed bourse transactions involving mobile wealth in accordance with their worth (one-tenth per thousand marks on securities and two-tenths per thousand on goods) rather than at a standard rate per transaction as in the stamp act of

[131] Henry Axel Bueck, "Die bevorstehende Änderung der Gesetzgebung bezüglich der Einkommensbesteuerung," in publication no. 20, Verein zur Wahrung der wirtschaftlichen Interessen von Handel und Gewerbe (Berlin, 1889), p. 47.

[132] SEG (1884), pp. 60, 63.

[133] Stern, Gold and Iron, pp. 220–222.

[134] SBR (1884–1885), Anlagen, Nos. 25, 122, 286, 376.

1881. Bismarck intervened only to insist on features protecting producers and arbitrage brokers from the effects of the tax. Most national liberals joined conservatives and free conservatives in voting for the bill, which passed by a great majority, 214 to 41. Members of the Social Democratic and German Freedom (*Freisinnige*) parties formed the minority. (While they favored taxes on capital, social democrats were opposed in principle to the grant of new taxes to the Bismarck government.)[135]

The *Börsensteuer* of 1885 represented a limited victory for agrarian interests in their battle with industrial capitalism for equalization of the tax burden. Nevertheless, the conflict between those interests had frustrated the greater reform attempted by Scholz in 1884–1885, the necessity of which was admitted by both interest groups. The additional tax relief needed to halt tax delinquency executions among low-income groups was not achieved, and landowners were still compelled to pay the surtaxes on income and property taxes of which they and Bismarck had so often complained.

[135] *SBR* (1884–1885), pp. 763–791, 2517–2586, 2631–2655; *RGB* (1885), pp. 171–194.

CHAPTER THREE

Internal Failure and External Success

URING 1880–1883 the domestic political life of Germany seemed almost at a standstill. While the chancellor's personal authority over the executive branches of Prussia and the Reich reached a new height, his parliamentary influence virtually collapsed. Despite their differing composition, both the Reichstag and Chamber of Deputies resisted the tax program that had been the major goal of Bismarck's domestic policy since 1876—a tax program that was intended to consolidate the Reich by making it financially self-sufficient, weaken the power of the Reichstag over the purse, and grant relief from direct taxation to workers, the lower middle class, and property owners. Bismarck's frequent assaults upon factionalism in political life and the particularism of party politics, coupled with appeals to national unity and patriotism, had been rebuffed by both deputies and voters. His attempt to introduce biennial imperial budgets had been repeatedly rejected, and his experiment with an economic council as a potential corporative substitute for the Reichstag had been a disappointment. Despite the antisocialist law, the social democrats had elected the same number of deputies in 1881 (twelve) as in 1877. The social insurance statutes, with which Bismarck intended to woo the proletarians, were slow in coming. Despite two enabling acts (1880, 1882), progress toward peace with the Catholic church and the Center party had been minimal. In the Bundesrat the medium-sized states dared on occasion to oppose the chancellor when their interests were jeopardized. In the opinion of Lucius these parliamentary checks, for which Bismarck's own tactics were partly responsible, damaged the prestige of the government and increased that of parliament.[1]

In the midst of these many woes the brief economic recovery that began in 1880 came to an end. During February–March 1882 the European money market was disturbed by the collapse of the financial empire of Eugen Bontoux. His *Union Generale* was a relatively new banking enterprise deeply engaged in the promotion of railway, banking, and industrial enterprises in France, the Habsburg Empire, and the Balkans. Bontoux's manipulations had driven up the price of its shares far beyond their actual worth, producing a speculative bonfire that finally ran out of fuel and leaving behind many bank-

---

[1] Freiherr Lucius von Ballhausen, *Bismarck-Erinnerungen* (Stuttgart, 1920), pp. 227–228.

ruptcies and thousands of ruined investors.[2] More fundamental to the capitalistic economy in general was the decline of the railway construction boom in the United States. German exports of rails across the Atlantic, which had reached 45,531,000 tons (value: 5,500,000 marks) in 1881, fell precipitously to a mere 6,335,000 tons (value: 700,000 marks) by 1883, while pig iron exports declined by 50 percent in the same period. Nowhere on the domestic front, neither in political nor in economic life, were there signs of progress.[3]

Withdrawal Symptoms

Following the Reichstag election of October 27, 1881, Bismarck spilled out his narcissistic rage to Busch. "The elections have shown that the German Philistine still lives and allows himself to be frightened and led astray by fine speeches and lies. He will not hear of the protection of labor against the foreigner, nor of insurance against accident and old age, nor of any reduction of school and poor rates, but wants to retain surcharges on direct taxes. Well, he can have that, but not from me as chancellor. . . . Folly and ingratitude on all sides! I am made the target for every party and group, and they do everything they can to harass me, and would like me to serve as a whipping boy for them. But when I disappear they will not know which way to turn, as none of them has a majority or any positive views and aims. They can only criticize and find fault—always say, 'No.' "[4]

As he defended his policies to the Reichstag on November 28–29, 1881, January 11 and 24, and June 12 and 14, 1882, private thoughts and injured feelings seeped into his public statements. Again he depicted himself as a great German patriot, who had striven during his whole life for national unity and welfare, only to be misunderstood, reviled, and slandered. Glaring contemptuously at the parties arrayed in front of him, he denounced their factionalism, their lack of practical experience in the real world of farms and factories, their unjustified conceit that they, not he, represented the masses. "I am a supporter of the majority, but the majority in the German empire consists of big farmers, small farmers." Yet he also lashed the deputies for their "Byzantine" servility to public opinion, their unwillingness to accept unpopularity in behalf of what he deemed to be good for the country. Throughout

[2] G. W. F. Hallgarten, *Imperialismus vor 1914* (Munich, 1951), I, 211–213.

[3] Das Kaiserliche Statistische Amt, *Statistisches Handbuch für das deutsche Reich* (Berlin, 1907), I, 87, 93.

[4] Nov. 15, 1881. Moritz Busch, *Bismarck: Some Secret Pages of His History* (London, 1898), II, 295–296. Corrections have been made in the translation. See Moritz Busch, *Tagebuchblätter* (Leipzig, 1899), III, 55–56. Baroness Spitzemberg heard Bismarck compare himself to a big dog who conducts himself with dignity while being nipped and barked at by smaller dogs, but finally breaks down and replies in kind. He was disappointed in his own conduct. Spitzemberg diary, Nov. 20, 1881. Rudolf Vierhaus, ed., *Das Tagebuch der Baronin Spitzemberg* (Göttingen, 1960), p. 194.

these speeches his tone was one of personal reproach—at their disloyalty to him and their longing for power. "My person irritates you, my manner of speaking irritates you; for you I am staying on this spot too long."[5] To Interior Minister Puttkamer he wrote in May 1882 that there was "not much time to lose." "The opposition reckons from season to season on a change in rulers and on the removal of the present government, in order to gain for itself the merit for accomplishing reforms and *thereby fortifying its position.*"[6]

Inability to bend the parliaments to his will on the most important issues of domestic policy (at a time when his influence in foreign affairs was never higher) produced in Bismarck heightened symptoms of withdrawal. "For three weeks," Lucius reported on March 5, 1882, "Bismarck [has been] unwell, sees no one, lets matters go, and gives no directives, neither on church nor on tax policy."[7] On March 25, four days after the Prussian Economic Council voted against the tobacco monopoly, he left Berlin for Friedrichsruh, where he remained for more than two months, complaining of sciatica and lameness, so incapacitated that he could not return to participate in the debates of the second utilization bill. The cabinet's decision to withdraw the bill after the first adverse vote left him unhappy and morose.[8] "Bismarck now has a downright distaste for people," observed his physician Eduard Cohen. "He only feels well in the solitude of the forest, where even his driver is too much."[9]

On June 5, 1882, he returned to Berlin, still ailing, but determined to take part in the debates on the tobacco monopoly. Again he thought of retiring from domestic affairs and limiting himself to diplomacy; he was getting old, and "the machine does not want to function anymore."[10] Yet he pulled himself together for the Reichstag debate, delivering on June 12 and 14 speeches lasting several hours, in which he again reviewed his basic policies and achievements and responded to attacks by Richter and Bamberger. To Lucius he looked "astonishingly fresh," but the effort exhausted him. Five days later he wrote to the Kaiser, "I can't talk and must write drafts of messages myself, because I can't dictate them."[11] He resolved to skip the cure at Bad Kissingen, which had done him little good in the previous year. On June 20 he departed for Varzin, where he remained for more than five months—often "in tormentis . . . plagued by pains of several kinds" to the point of incapacitation.[12]

---

[5] BR, IX, 105–437, especially 425. On Dec. 17, 1881, Bennigsen found him "in a pessimistic and almost pensive mood. He spoke of reports from envoys about the attention paid by foreigners to our domestic events and complained that everything was going to pieces." Hermann Oncken, *Rudolf von Bennigsen* (Stuttgart, 1910), II, 483.

[6] GW, VIc, 254–255.

[7] Lucius, *Bismarck-Erinnerungen*, p. 225. See also GW, VIII, 442–444, and Horst Kohl, ed., *Anhang zu den Gedanken und Erinnerung von Otto Fürst von Bismarck* (Stuttgart, 1901), I, 309.

[8] Lucius, *Bismarck-Erinnerungen*, p. 229; Kohl, ed., *Anhang*, I, 311–313.

[9] GW, VIII, 446–447, also 449.

[10] GW, VIII, 448.

[11] Lucius, *Bismarck-Erinnerungen*, p. 232; GW, VIc, 258.

[12] Bismarck to Scholz, Sept. 30, 1882. DZA Potsdam, Reichskanzlei, 2086, p. 102.

The difficulty in speaking that Bismarck reported to the Kaiser was the consequence of a new ailment, which, first mentioned in August 1880 and again in February and June 1881, became a major problem following the election disaster of October 1881. For two years thereafter, and occasionally in later years, the prince suffered attacks of a facial ache "like a sword being shoved through my cheek, now from the right, now from the left." The morning hours before the noonday meal were the worst. He sought relief by pressing his hands against both cheeks. In a cold sweat he paced the floor until the pain diminished. He feared to speak in parliament lest an attack compel him to break off.[13] At the end of 1882 Johanna wrote that her husband had "suffered so terribly from facial neuralgia in recent months that I am in despair. Nothing helps him, and his nerves are in worse condition than ever." Abscessed teeth were suspected, but a dentist hammered on each tooth and found them sound—for Bismarck a depressing result, for it meant that he might never be free of the pain. Shaving became a trial, and by the time Bismarck returned to Berlin on December 3, 1882 ("like a convict to his cell") he had grown a full white beard.[14] What afflicted him was trigeminal neuralgia (tic douloureux), an ailment known to produce severe depression and thoughts of suicide in its victims. No sooner was he back in Berlin than he longed "to escape" once more "from this constant confusion." "I would be very glad not to see anyone for one full year other than my wife, my children, and my grandchildren. . . . The yearning for peace wells up in me like a real sickness, of which I cannot rid myself because of my other illnesses."[15]

In this condition he made errors of the kind that drove him to fury when committed by others. In September 1880 he forgot to record and report to Russian Ambassador Peter Saburov a highly important concession made by Baron Heinrich von Haymerlé, Andrássy's replacement as Austro-Hungarian foreign minister, during the discussions that led to the reconstitution of the Three Emperors League. Three weeks later he had to apologize to Saburov with obvious chagrin for this serious lapse. "I was," he lamented, "very ill at

[13] Christoph von Tiedemann, *Sechs Jahre Chef der Reichskanzlei unter dem Fürsten Bismarck* (2d ed., Leipzig, 1910), pp. 412, 484; GW, VIII, 442; BP, I, 253.

[14] To Philipp zu Eulenburg, Dec. 2, 1882. Philipp zu Eulenburg, *Aus 50 Jahren* (Berlin, 1923), pp. 76–77; Norman Rich and M. H. Fisher, eds. *The Holstein Papers: The Memoirs, Diaries and Correspondence of Friedrich von Holstein, 1837–1909* (4 vols., Cambridge, Eng., 1955–1963), II, 19–20. Although Bismarck accepted the dentist's judgment, the Bismarck family and physicians Cohen, Frerichs, and Schweninger remained unconvinced. Marie suspected that her father merely feared the extractions and let Schweninger pull four of her own at one sitting to prove that the procedure was not so bad. But Bismarck refused to sacrifice a tooth "for the sake of peace in the family." GW, XIV, 937–939; Busch, *Tagebuchblätter*, III, 93–94, 137; GW, VIII, 499; Spitzemberg, *Tagebuch*, p. 200. Struck spoke of "incipient arteriosclerosis" and Frerichs of "either a tooth or senile decay." The pain "provoked states identical with hysteria in women." Rich and Fisher, eds., *Holstein Papers*, II, 22. For once Bismarck's medical instinct was correct. The unnecessary extraction of teeth is a common mistake in cases of trigeminal neuralgia. See Henry B. Clark, Jr., *Practical Oral Surgery* (Philadelphia, 1955), pp. 46–48.

[15] BP, I, 255; Busch, *Tagebuchblätter*, III, 89, 164–165.

BISMARCK, JANUARY 30, 1883. (BILDARCHIV PREUSSISCHER KULTURBESITZ.)

that time."[16] During the winter a series of errors (failure to read or remember a document recently signed, inattention at a cabinet meeting, failure to instruct a subordinate properly) produced the Botho Eulenburg crisis of February 1881. Another mistake in August 1882 compelled him to write the only genuine letter of apology in his collected works. "It is," he explained, "a symptom of the decline in my capacity for business."[17] To Moritz Busch Bismarck complained in the summer of 1882 that he could "scarcely work for a couple of hours without losing hold of my ideas." In December 1882 Friedrich von Holstein found him not only aged, but also "in a state of nervous depression." He recalled that for years the chancellor had feared a "softening of the brain" like that which had incapacitated Friedrich Wilhelm IV.[18]

Bismarck traced his health problems to the usual causes—the "intrigues" of Kaiserin Augusta and of the conservatives. What depressed him, he told Lucius, were "the enemies in my own camp, the envy, the ill will, the lack of understanding among friends. Since they can do nothing, no one else shall do anything either. The struggle against political friends is the exhausting thing—as in the case of the school inspection act [in 1872]." But he also grumbled about obstructionism from other parties in both parliaments. "At present social and economic questions are dominant, and on such issues political partisanship is unjustified. The best fortification of the Reich would come from common finances, common sources of income and revenues, which the individual states can share. That there is so little understanding for this [program] is the greatest evil. It is shameful and causes me to lose courage."[19]

"I have no intention of going to the Reichstag," Bismarck told a deputy in January 1883. "They can get along without me." He made but one, brief speech during the long Reichstag session that began on November 30, 1882, and ended on June 12, 1883. Not once did he appear in the Landtag during the sessions of November 14, 1882, to July 2, 1883, and November 20, 1883, to May 19, 1884. "I no longer read their speeches and brawling," he admitted to Busch. "The imperial machine works fine," he claimed, "and I rejoice that the atmosphere is conflict free. If I still had to lose my temper, I would no longer be able to hold out."[20] Illness, anger, and misanthropy also reduced his contacts with ministers and subordinates. "He continues to live completely withdrawn," Lucius reported in February 1883. "He receives almost no one and usually transmits his decisions and directives through Rottenburg." Hol-

---

[16] Wolfgang Windelband, *Bismarck und die europäischen Grossmächte, 1879–1885* (Essen, 1942), p. 174.

[17] To Adolf Scholz, Aug. 18, 1882. GW, XIV, 937–938. See also his letter to Scholz, Sept. 30, 1882. *Ibid.*, p. 939.

[18] Busch, *Tagebuchblätter*, II, 89; Rich and Fisher, eds., *Holstein Papers*, II, 19.

[19] Lucius, *Bismarck-Erinnerungen*, pp. 239–240.

[20] BP, I, 255; May 15, 1883. Busch, *Tagebuchblätter*, III, 147.

stein concluded that long periods of seclusion and self-imposed isolation were costing Bismarck his "mental elasticity." "His mind is a spring that flows incessantly. If there is no outlet, the natural result is stagnation." On May 31, 1883, he presided over a cabinet meeting for the first time in almost a year. "He has really aged," Lucius wrote, "face white and fallen, body bloated."[21] On July 2, 1883, Bismarck left Berlin on another "extended leave" from which he did not return until March 12, 1884.

Thoughts of a Staatsstreich

As political frustrations multiplied and his mental and physical health deteriorated, Bismarck contemplated not the surrender of his objectives, but other ways to attain them. Some way had to be found to convert important interest groups to his cause and put pressure upon their representatives to support the government. One tactic was to exploit the popularity of the Kaiser, who since 1866 had become a "father figure" to millions of Germans. To this end Bismarck rewrote history for the benefit of the Reichstag and the public. On January 24, 1882, he described to parliament how during the constitutional conflict Wilhelm had held firm to "*his own* policy," to the "traditions of the Prussian dynasty," and to the ideals dictated by "his German heart, his German sentiment"; how, when his minister-president did not move fast enough "in the German, national sense" during the Schleswig-Holstein affair, Wilhelm had asked in vexation, "Aren't you then also a German?" Germany owed her unity, Bismarck asserted, "only to the political insight of his majesty" and to the success of the army under his command. The cabinet had merely executed the king's will.[22]

During 1881–1883 the chancellor secured Wilhelm's signature on no less than three imperial and royal rescripts (*Botschaften* and *Erlasse*), a category ordinarily reserved for documents of greatest importance. The first imperial rescript was read to the newly elected Reichstag on November 17, 1881. It began with the traditional formula reminiscent of the age of absolutism, "We, Wilhelm, by the Grace of God German Kaiser, King of Prussia, etc., do proclaim that all men shall know by these presents . . ." What followed in each case was a vigorous statement of the government's policies, couched as the will of the monarch himself. When the procedure was challenged as incompatible with constitutionalism, the official press responded with a lesson on the "monarchical principle" in Prussia and Germany and on the "blessings" that flowed from "the power and vitality of the crown." In Prussia and Ger-

---

[21] Lucius, *Bismarck-Erinnerungen*, pp. 249, 265. See Spitzemberg, *Tagebuch*, p. 195; Walter Bussmann, ed., *Staatssekretär Graf Herbert von Bismarck: Aus seiner politischen Privatkorrespondenz* (Göttingen, 1964), pp. 152–153; and Rich and Fisher, eds., *Holstein Papers*, II, 22, 35.
[22] *BR*, IX, 236.

many the monarch both "reigned and governed." The idea that he "reigned, but did not govern" was an alien concept born on "foreign soil."[23]

Simultaneously Bismarck began to consider the most drastic action of all: a coup against the constitution (Staatsstreich). Shortly before the Reichstag election of October 1881 he told Hohenlohe "that the Germans did not know how to handle the Nuremberg toy he had given them; they are ruining it. If this continues, the allied governments would return again to the old Frankfurt Diet, giving up the Reichstag and retaining only the military and customs alliances."[24] This was not a solitary thought, as is shown by his remarks to Busch shortly after the election, "The defectiveness of our institutions is shown by the credulity of the electors. It may come to this: that we shall some day have to say of the German constitution—after all attempts to govern under it and to reform it have failed—what Schwarzenberg said at Olmütz, 'This arrangement has not stood the test.' But that must not be printed now. It is only for yourself."[25] Yet he shared the same idea a few days later with the Württemberg envoy, Baron Mittnacht: "It is possible that a moment may come when the German princes must consider whether the present parliament is still compatible with the welfare of the Reich."[26]

What Bismarck said privately he soon declared in public. In concluding a long speech in defense of the tobacco monopoly in the Reichstag on June 12, 1882, he declared that only a sense of duty and obligation, his oath to the Kaiser, and his concern for the future kept him in office. "On sleepless nights I cannot ward off the thought that our sons may again sit around the familiar round table of the Frankfurt Bundestag. The way in which our affairs are going does not exclude that possibility from being realized, if the respect and prestige that we today enjoy abroad should ever suffer a blow. We have won a great authority, but it would be easy to shatter." Once he had regarded the dynasties as the greatest danger to the "national idea" and the Reichstag as the "anchor of rescue and the cement for our unity." For that reason he had tried to make the Reichstag "as strong as possible." But now he had reversed himself. "Today the German dynasties are national in outlook. To stand together, back to back, against all foreign dangers is for them a necessity. But they are also determined not to permit their monarchical rights, as they exist under the constitution, to be undermined."[27]

Bismarck's threat of a Staatsstreich against the Reichstag came only two

---

[23] BR, IX, 84–88 (Nov. 17, 1881), 219–222 (Jan. 24, 1882), 442–444 (Apr. 14, 1883).

[24] Friedrich Curtius, ed., Memoirs of Prince Chlodwig of Hohenlohe-Schillingsfuerst (New York, 1906), II, 292.

[25] Busch, Tagebuchblätter, III, 57–58 (see also 73, 151); the translation is from Busch, Secret Pages, II, 297.

[26] GW, VIII, 433–434. See also his remarks to Cohen, June 4, 1882. Ibid., p. 449.

[27] BR, IX, 366–368.

years after he had threatened the federated states with the same fate![28] Now
he maintained that, since the federated states had created the North German
Confederation and German Reich, they could also destroy or, at least, revise
the union. By withdrawing their approval of the constitution, they could liquidate the Reichstag, replacing it with some other kind of assembly, probably
corporative in character, that would produce the majorities needed for the
Bismarck legislative program. Such an interpretation would hardly satisfy any
hardheaded legal authority and probably not the courts. But the softheaded
kind (Rudolf Ihering?) would vouch for its legitimacy. More important, a
loyal army, sworn to the Kaiser, would legitimize it—if necessary, by force.
During the early 1880s, furthermore, Germany's foreign relations appeared to
be ideal for the reconstruction of her constitutional order. "We have a firm
bond with the great monarchies that lie outside the borders of the German
Reich," he told the Reichstag on June 12, 1882, "monarchies that have the
same interest as we in preserving peace and stability. I also believe that these
bonds will be lasting . . . and that there will be a great, firm, conserving
power in the middle of Europe."[29]

The New Three Emperors League

In overcoming the Kaiser's objections to the Dual Alliance with Austria in
August–September 1879, Bismarck had asserted repeatedly that his aim was
not to alienate Russia but to prepare the way for a reestablishment of the old
relationship on a more secure basis. One of the purposes of the Dual Alliance
was to convince the Russians of the necessity of again coming to terms with
the central European powers.[30] From the experience of the Balkan war and
the Congress of Berlin Gorchakov had drawn the conclusion that Russia
could now depend on no one but itself.[31] But Bismarck calculated that cooler
heads would prevail in Petersburg, once it became evident that Germany had
the option of enlarging the dual into a triple alliance by coming to terms with
England and even of bringing a newly republican France into the German
orbit. To escape isolation the Russians would have no choice but to come to
treat once more with Austria and Germany.

Following the eclipse of Peter Shuvalov in the summer of 1879, Bismarck
found in Peter Saburov a person willing to pursue such a policy within the
counsels of the Russian government. A career diplomat, Saburov had served

[28] See vol. 2, p. 525.

[29] BR, IX, 368.

[30] See vol. 2, pp. 501–510. What Bismarck said privately he also trumpeted to the world in
the pages of the Kölnische Zeitung on October 7, 1879. The article had an obviously official
character and had in fact been written by the foreign office press bureau on Bismarck's orders and
edited by him. Windelband, Grossmächte, pp. 93–95, also 111ff.

[31] See vol. 2, pp. 499–500.

as counselor at London and minister at Athens; he had just been appointed ambassador at Constantinople. In July 1879 Saburov and Bismarck vacationed at Bad Kissingen at the same time. Naturally Bismarck used the opportunity to reiterate his grievances of recent months against the Russian government and newspaper press and to express his regret that three years earlier the Russians had ignored his offer of an alliance. In 1876, he declared, he had been "prepared to put the German army at your service" and "follow you whatever happens [durch dick und dünn]," provided Russia guaranteed Germany's possession of Alsace-Lorraine. But Gorchakov had turned a "deaf ear" to the proposal, and now Russia seemed bent upon sacrificing the relationship with Berlin and Vienna, which in past decades had been so fruitful for all three.[32] Saburov's record of these conversations and his memorial arguing for continuation of the Three Emperors League reached Tsar Alexander at Alexandrovo in September 1879, at a time when the monarch was shocked by the consequences of his unguarded utterance to Schweinitz and his personal letter to Wilhelm in August. Aware of the fact but not the content of Bismarck's negotiations with Andrássy at Gastein and Vienna, Alexander dispatched Saburov to Berlin to reconnoiter the terrain.

To Saburov's surprise he was immediately granted a three-hour interview with the German chancellor (September 27). Although bound to secrecy (on Andrássy's insistence) as to the terms of the Dual Alliance, Bismarck left Saburov in no doubt as to the content of the paragraph that dealt with Russia. He spoke of the necessity of "reassuring Austria" and of a "guarantee that we might perhaps be under obligation to give Austria with regard to her territorial status quo." At another point he declared, "I thus succeeded in carrying out what I call the first act of my political system—that of placing a barrier between Austria and the western powers. In spite of this summer's clouds (passing ones in my opinion), I do not despair of realizing the second act— the reconstitution of the League of Three Emperors, the only system offering . . . maximum stability for the peace of Europe." The two men then worked out the general outlines of an agreement under which each country guaranteed its neutrality under certain conditions, Germany in the event of war between Russia and England, Russia in the event of war between Germany

---

[32] J. Y. Simpson, *The Saburov Memoirs or Bismarck and Russia* (New York, 1929), pp. 50–64, also 81–82 (with the wrong date of 1877); and *GP*, III, 139–140. This extraordinary claim, which could not be verified in the files of the Russian foreign office, astonished Giers and Alexander, who later interrogated Schweinitz about it. Wilhelm von Schweinitz, ed., *Denkwürdigkeiten des Botschafters General von Schweinitz* (Berlin, 1927), II, 87–90, 224. The Russians were not alone in their confusion about the "alliance offer" of 1876. Wilhelm von Bismarck, who was with his father at Kissingen in Aug. 1879, thought he remembered documents recording negotiations at that time between State Secretary Bernhard von Bülow and Russian Ambassador Paul d'Oubril. This recollection caused Bismarck to order a search of memories and files. Bussmann, ed., *Herbert von Bismarck*, pp. 91–94. For an explanation of the "alliance offer of 1876," see vol. 2, pp. 423–426.

and France; the neutral power in either case would restrain "by force if need be" any fourth power from entering the conflict; Russia would respect Austria's territorial integrity, but Austria must fulfill its obligations under the Treaty of Berlin.[33]

Considering the hurry with which Bismarck pushed through the Dual Alliance in August–September, his treatment of the Russian overture can only be classified as dilatory. Wilhelm had demanded that Alexander be told the terms of the Dual Alliance, but Bismarck pointed out that Andrássy was adamantly opposed to such a disclosure, which in any case was ill advised because Russia was named in the agreement as the potential foe. Hence Wilhelm had to be content with a letter (October 20, 1879) to Alexander in which he described the Austrian-German entente in general terms as the restoration of a centuries-old relationship that had been interrupted by liquidation of the German Confederation in 1866. If nihilists, in concert with Panslavists, should move the Russian government to take aggressive action abroad, the result would be a "solidarity of resistance" on the part of Austria and Germany. He enclosed a harmless memorandum signed by Andrássy and Bismarck, which denied that either power had hostile intentions toward Russia.[34] Speculation on the real contents of the treaty was rife in the European press and diplomatic corps. To Bismarck's irritation, Salisbury had heightened the assumption that Russia was its target by referring publicly to "good tidings of great joy" from Berlin and Vienna. Despite these provocations Alexander's response to Wilhelm (November 14) was mild. The tsar declared that he would like "to see the return of that perfect entente of the three emperors" that had rendered such a great service to Europe.[35] To facilitate agreement he appointed Saburov Russian ambassador to Berlin, replacing Oubril, whom Bismarck distrusted and detested.

Bismarck was in no haste to come to terms with Russia because he valued the possibility of choice that the Dual Alliance had given Germany in the European balance of power. Once again Germany was in the position of the fulcrum, able to control the balance by shifting from one side to the other. The Dual Alliance had not limited but restored the mobility of German policy between east and west. The weapon that Bismarck sometimes carried on his person or placed on his desk became a metaphor with which he explained the alliance's purpose to both the Russian and British ambassadors. "I regarded you," he told Saburov, "as a dear friend with whom I was taking a solitary walk and who suddenly had gone mad. I rushed off to provide myself with a

33 Saburov, Memoirs, pp. 65–88; Hajo Holborn, ed., Aufzeichnungen und Erinnerungen aus dem Leben des Botschafters Joseph Maria von Radowitz (Stuttgart, 1925), II, 97–102; Bruce Waller, Bismarck at the Crossroads: The Reorientation of German Foreign Policy after the Congress of Berlin, 1878–1880 (London, 1974), pp. 219–221.

34 GP, III, 99–100, 124–127.

35 GP, III, 132–134; IV, 14.

pocket pistol, and now I am come back to continue my walk with you in the same amicable manner, but in a more comfortable state of mind as to my own safety."[36]

By steadily reinforcing Russian isolation in 1879–1880, Bismarck strove to heighten the Russian desire to escape it by coming to terms with Berlin and Vienna. To this end he cultivated better relations with France and encouraged cooperation between England and France in the Mediterranean. An entente between those powers, he often said, was the best guarantee of European peace. When Haymerlé expressed the fear that the entente might become "too intimate," Bismarck tried to calm him by explaining that their rapprochement would keep both from dangerous enterprises. Britain would hardly support a French attempt to regain Alsace-Lorraine, and France would certainly not go to war against Russia in behalf of British interests in the Balkans. Collaboration with Britain, furthermore, ought to deter France from coquetry with Russia. Although Bismarck always liked to keep available the option of a link between Germany, Austria, and Britain—for the eventuality of a warlike crisis with Russia—he tried to make sure that such a combination would not be exploited for exclusively British interests. "Naturally our sympathy for English policy," he instructed the foreign office staff, "will grow to the degree that it proves to be peace-loving and Russian policy proves to be dangerous for the peace of Europe." When Haymerlé proposed that the dual powers dispel British "mistrust" by supporting London's Balkan policy against Russia, Bismarck demurred: "For what? Our relationship with Austria is defensive, and we must not permit ourselves to be harnessed for aggressive English purposes."[37]

Bismarck's vision of the desirable situation in the Balkans was still a division into spheres of influence that would regulate and defuse, but not eliminate conflicts among the great powers. To that end he believed that the dual powers should not contest Russia's ambition to unite the two Bulgarias and create a client state. But beyond that he was inclined to hold to the "correct and useful principle" that Germany should "be a secure and helpful friend to our friends, but also an active opponent of our adversaries." Not knowing whether Russia was to be friend or foe, he measured carefully the amount of support Germany gave to Russia's effort to force the Porte to observe the dictates of the Treaty of Berlin. But he resisted any suggestion that the dual powers should interfere with Russia's plans for the unification of Bulgaria and

---

[36] Alfred Lyall, *The Life of the Marquis of Dufferin and Ava* (London, 1905), I, 305. For other versions of the same metaphor, see Hohenlohe, *Memoirs*, II, 257; Schweinitz, *Denkwürdigkeiten*, II, 80; and GW, VIII, 339.

[37] Windelband, *Grossmächte*, pp. 60–61, 108–110; GP, III, 127–136; DDF, II, 45off. Germany could defeat France, he told Hohenlohe, even if the English sided with her. Hohenlohe, *Memoirs*, II, 291.

its conversion into a client state.[38] Simultaneously, however, the prince was active in securing the predominant influence of the dual powers in Rumania and Serbia.

For more than a decade the Rumanian connection had been a source of vexation to Bismarck. Elevation of the Hohenzollern Prince Karl to the throne in Bucharest had led to heavy involvement by unwary German investors (particularly aristocrats of high title) in the railway construction schemes of Bethel Henry Strousberg. To rescue them Bismarck called upon the services of Gerson Bleichröder and Adolf Hansemann, who were ennobled for their pains. By 1879 the two bankers were eager to escape from this costly enterprise by selling the railways to the Rumanian government, whose venality and inefficiency had contributed to their problems and aroused Bismarck's anger and contempt. To prevent the Bleichröder–Hansemann consortium from having to sell at a great loss, Bismarck exploited Rumanian vulnerability on another issue, namely, the failure of the Bucharest government to grant the guarantees of civil equality to Jews stipulated in the Treaty of Berlin. By denying German recognition of Rumanian independence until those guarantees had been legislated, Bismarck both appeased Bleichröder, who had become the spokesman of European Jewry in protesting anti-Semitism in Rumania, and garnered support on moral grounds from the French and British governments.

Behind the scenes, however, Bismarck intimated to the Rumanian government a willingness to paper over the issue of civil rights in return for an advantageous settlement of the railway issue, in other words, to sell out Rumania's Jews in order to bail out Prussia's bankers and Junker investors. And these were the grounds for the ultimate settlement in February 1880, a settlement that was warmly welcomed in Vienna, which regarded Rumania as within its Balkan sphere of influence.[39] The Rumanian railway episode is a striking example of Bismarck's willingness to engage German foreign policy in behalf of influential private financial interests—not ethical or moral interests—when that could be accomplished without injury to his country's fundamental political concerns.

Meanwhile, he kept open at least the possibility of renewing the arrangement with Russia that he regarded as basic to German foreign relations. On leaving Berlin, October 8, 1879, Saburov promised to return in December to resume their exploratory talks at Varzin. His appointment as Russian ambassador to Berlin delayed his return until January but placed him in a much better position to finish the negotiation.[40] Yet he found Bismarck now in no apparent hurry to conclude an agreement. Several developments had led the

[38] Windelband, Grossmächte, pp. 127–130, 133–136.

[39] See particularly Fritz Stern, Gold and Iron: Bismarck, Bleichröder, and the Building of the German Empire (New York, 1977), pp. 351–393.

[40] Saburov, Memoirs, pp. 85, 88–92.

German chancellor to cool the discussion. The continuing redeployment on the Austrian and German borders, of Russian troops, particularly cavalry regiments, was disturbing to both Moltke and Bismarck. As in the case of France in 1875, Bismarck attempted, again in vain, to persuade and even frighten the Russian government into giving up its troop concentrations by presenting (one year early) a bill for the renewal of the military (iron) budget and stimulating a newspaper polemic against the Russian threat. Through diplomatic channels, furthermore, he strove to get Alexander to disavow Minister of War Dmitry A. Milyutin, whom he held responsible for the military threat.[41]

Another irritant was a report about General Nikolay Obruchev, the chief of staff of the Russian army, who had, while on a trip to Paris the preceding August, sounded out Premier Waddington and French generals about the possibility of a French-Russian alliance. Apparently Obruchev had not been commissioned to engage in any such discussions, but his reputed démarche revealed again the disarray and factionalism at the center of the Russian government.[42] Nor was the return of Gorchakov to his post in the Russian foreign ministry reassuring. At the time of Bismarck's first frank discussion with Saburov in September 1879, Gorchakov had been on another extended leave at spas in western Europe. For months the Russian chancellor had played little part in the conduct of foreign relations, and many had assumed that his retirement was imminent. But in December he was again in Petersburg and potentially in a position to wreck any serious negotiation with Berlin—if conducted through normal channels.[43]

When Bismarck and Saburov conferred again (January 31–February 5, 1880), the ambassador was struck by Bismarck's initial unwillingness to continue the discussion on the same plane as in September. This was the occasion on which the prince lectured Saburov on the geometry of the European balance of power. "All politics reduces itself to this formula: to try to be one of three, so long as the world is governed by the unstable equilibrium of five great powers." The Dual Alliance, he maintained, had been negotiated "in order to return afterwards to the triple entente with you, if you are sincerely disposed towards it." But he described Haymerlé, as a "skittish horse." "Every time you make a proposal to him he asks himself, 'Where is the trap?' " Saburov saw the point: At Vienna there was "a skittish minister," at Petersburg

---

[41] Saburov, Memoirs, pp. 97–106; Windelband, Grossmächte, pp. 116–122; Waller, Crossroads, pp. 224ff.; Schweinitz, Denkwürdigkeiten, II, 107–110. Milyutin was not the sinister man of Bismarck's press propaganda. He was realistic about Russia's internal weaknesses (its economy and public finance) and against adventurism in foreign policy (particularly in the west). The troop movements into Poland "were the make-shift defensive posture of a ponderous army and not a reflection of Russia's readiness for war." Dietrich Geyer, Russian Imperialism: The Interaction of Domestic and Foreign Policy, 1860–1914 (New Haven, 1987), p. 104.

[42] Schweinitz, Denkwürdigkeiten, II, 68, 75–77, 92–93, 97–98; Saburov, Memoirs, pp. 106–109; GP, III, 141–142; Waller, Crossroads, pp. 239–242.

[43] Waller, Crossroads, pp. 223–224.

a "senile chancellor." The two men agreed not to engage in official negotiations but to explore informally the possible basis for a triple entente in pourparlers, whose critical content Saburov would communicate only to the tsar and Bismarck would keep from Wilhelm ("Formerly he kept secrets well, but at eighty-three this is not the case").[44]

Once he made this commitment, Saburov found Bismarck again ready to negotiate. The ambassador's purpose, shared by Alexander and Assistant Foreign Minister Nikolay Giers, was to escape the isolation created by the Dual Alliance and the French-English entente. To that end they wished an agreement with Germany that would weaken both the alliance, by ending Austria's monopoly of Germany's support, and the entente, by putting pressure on France not to cooperate with Britain in the Mediterranean. In view of the continued friction with Britain and Turkey over the execution of the Treaty of Berlin, furthermore, the Russians wanted help in compelling the Porte to keep the Straits closed to alien, particularly British warships.[45] With Germany as an ally, Bismarck told Saburov, Russia could be "morally certain" that France would not enter a hostile alliance against her. "But the mathematical certainty will only be secured by attracting Austria into this system. Forming a permanent coalition ourselves, we shall have no fear of one against us." Austria, furthermore, was the only power capable of supporting Russia's need to keep the British out of the Black Sea by forcing Turkey to keep the Straits closed. Again Bismarck refused to mediate between Russia and Austria on Balkan problems, directing the Russians to negotiate directly with Vienna.[46]

On returning to Petersburg in early February 1880, Saburov found men of like conviction in Giers and Milyutin, who advocated a defensive posture on all fronts that would give Russia a period of peace in which to gain financial and military strength. Only Germany and Austria could provide the needed stability and security.[47] Behind Gorchakov's back the three conferred at length with the tsar, who sent the ambassador back to Berlin authorized to negotiate along the lines Bismarck had outlined.[48] But again Bismarck was dilatory, chiefly because Austria was far from ready to come to terms with Russia. On the contrary, Haymerlé sent an emissary in early February 1880 to tell Bismarck that his chief aim was to block Russia "permanently" in the Balkans, a policy requiring British and Italian support. For this reason the Austrian foreign minister was unsympathetic to Bismarck's suggestion that he

---

[44] The accounts of these negotiations by Bismarck and Saburov differ in detail. Saburov, *Memoirs*, pp. 110–126; *GP*, III, 141–147.

[45] Saburov, *Memoirs*, pp. 123–126.

[46] *GP*, III, 141–142.

[47] Charles Jelavich, *Tsarist Russia and Balkan Nationalism: Russian Influence in the Internal Affairs of Bulgaria and Serbia, 1879–1886* (Berkeley, 1958), pp. 16–27.

[48] Saburov, *Memoirs*, pp. 123, 127.

deal harshly with the rising irredentist agitation in Italy, a movement that demanded that Italy be compensated at Trieste and in the Trentino for Austria's occupation of Bosnia and Herzegovina.[49]

Bismarck's unbridled disdain for Italy stemmed from its rather clumsy attempt in 1877 to gain Germany's alliance for this objective and its coquetry with Russia in the critical month of August 1879, apparently to the same end. The Italians were like jackals, he once said, drawn by the "odor of corruption and calamity—always ready to attack anybody from the rear and make off with a bit of plunder." As in the case of France, he sought to divert Rome toward North Africa (or possibly Albania). To keep Italy in check required the assistance of the British navy, another reason for Berlin to continue looking westward as well as eastward.[50] In February 1880 Bismarck had even suggested to Count Waldersee that he would prefer Britain to Russia as the third partner in a triple entente.[51]

In mid-April 1880 the western end of Bismarck's diplomatic seesaw was unbalanced and his quest for a revived German-Russian-Austrian entente was disrupted by the victory of the liberals over the conservatives in a British general election. The fall of Disraeli and the return of Gladstone to Downing Street introduced a new factor into the equation of European politics. In speeches to his Midlothian constituents in November 1879 and in campaign speeches during March and April 1880, Gladstone had charted a new course in European politics. He called for a revival of the concert of Europe, for a return to mutual cooperation among the great powers that would "neutralize and fetter and bind up the selfish aims of each." He expected not only to reduce tensions and promote peace but also to further the cause of liberty in Europe by supporting self-determination among the peoples of Europe's great multinational empires. In practical terms this meant hostility toward the Habsburg and Ottoman Empires and an entente with Russia in support of the emerging Balkan states—a complete reversal of the foreign policy of Disraeli and Salisbury in the eastern question. Austria, he denounced, as the "unflinching foe of freedom in every country of Europe." "There is not an instance—there is not a spot upon the whole map where you can lay your finger and say, 'There Austria did good.' "[52]

[49] Helmut Krausnick, *Neue Bismarck-Gespräche* (Hamburg, 1940), pp. 24–25; William L. Langer, "The European Powers and the French Occupation of Tunis," *American Historical Review*, 31 (1925–1926), pp. 68–71, and *European Alliances and Alignments, 1871–1890* (New York, 1956), pp. 200–201.

[50] GW, VIII, 215–220; A. F. Pribram, *The Secret Treaties of Austria-Hungary, 1879–1914* (Cambridge, Mass., 1920), II, 5–6; Langer, *Alliances and Alignments*, p. 201; Waller, *Crossroads*, pp. 228–229.

[51] GW, VIII, 344–345.

[52] W. N. Medlicott, *Bismarck, Gladstone, and the Concert of Europe* (London, 1956), pp. 29–33; Harold Temperley and Lillian M. Penson, *Foundations of British Foreign Policy from Pitt (1792) to Salisbury (1902)* (London, 1966), pp. 391–394.

Gladstone's "idealistic" vision of a federative Europe bound to keep the peace by a web of common interests, a Europe in which the interests of the whole would outweigh particular interests, was diametrically opposed to Bismarck's "realistic" appraisal of the European balance of power system as composed of competing states, whose natural inclination was the pursuit of self-interest, producing frictions the exploitation of which was the key to German security and, coincidentally, to the preservation of peace. Under Disraeli the conflict of interests between Russia and Britain had appeared unresolvable, even structural in character; under Gladstone they now found a common interest in supporting national self-determination at the cost of the Ottoman and, conceivably, Habsburg Empires. To Bismarck, Gladstone was that "crazy professor" and "dilettante," the "most incompetent" British leader since the American revolution. Gorchakov, Garibaldi, Gambetta, and Gladstone were "the revolutionary quartet on the G string."[53]

Bismarck's rage at Gladstone arose not only from his differing conception of the very nature of international politics, but also from the threat to his own political strategy posed by Britain's change of course. It also had a tactical purpose. In messages to Petersburg and Vienna he sought to stir up anxiety with a "red scare." Gladstone, he warned, had resurrected the antimonarchical policy of Palmerston but with a far greater prospect of success, owing to the growth of revolutionary movements in Russia and eastern Europe. But the Russians were teased by the possibilities for Russia's self-interest laid open by Britain's offer of an entente and disinclined, as a consequence, to rush into a new Three Emperors League. On entering Whitehall, furthermore, Lord Granville hastened to repair the damage done by Gladstone's campaign rhetoric by assuring Vienna that Britain had no hostile objectives toward Austria.[54] In Berlin Lord Odo Russell reported to Bismarck that the Gladstone government approved of the Dual Alliance and desired to cooperate with Germany and Austria. Bismarck responded by talking out of both sides of his mouth. If the peace party triumphed in Petersburg, he would seek to re-create the Three Emperors League, but even so Germany would prefer Britain as an ally![55]

[53] Windelband, *Grossmächte*, p. 181; GW, VIII, 379, 381–382, 387. For Bismarck's criticism of Gladstone and his policies, see GP, IV, 25ff., and Bussmann, ed., *Herbert von Bismarck*, pp. 110ff. Historians differ, no less sharply than the statesmen themselves, in their judgments on the conceptions of foreign affairs held by Bismarck and Gladstone. The German historian Windelband, writing in the shadow of the Nazi regime, praised Bismarck's position; the English historian Medlicott, writing in the era of the European Common Market and the movement for European unity, favored Gladstone's. Windelband, *Grossmächte*, p. 186; Medlicott, *Bismarck, Gladstone*, pp. 10–34, 339–337.

[54] Saburov, *Memoirs*, pp. 129, 132; Waller, *Crossroads*, pp. 243–245; John Morley, *The Life of William Ewart Gladstone* (New York, 1903), III, 8; Medlicott, *Bismarck, Gladstone*, pp. 53–54.

[55] Lord Edmond Fitzmaurice, *The Life of Lord Granville* (London, 1905), II, 208–212; GP, IV, 14–15.

Bismarck had no choice but to suspend negotiations with Austria and Russia and look on while Gladstone seized the initiative in European politics. In May 1880 the prime minister called upon the European concert to preserve the sanctity of treaties and force Turkey to fulfill its remaining obligations under the Treaty of Berlin by ceding territory promised to Montenegro and Greece. Meeting at Berlin on June 16, the great powers decided to appease Montenegro by substituting for the promised territory (held by Albanian tribesmen backed by the Turks) a segment of the Dalmatian coast, including the town of Dulcigno. When the Turks refused this settlement, the powers staged a naval demonstration opposite Dulcigno, with no effect. Russia and Britain favored military action to end Turkish intransigence, and in London there was talk of occupying Smyrna and ordering the fleet to the Dardanelles. But Austria, Germany, and France would neither join such an enterprise nor extend to the two powers a mandate to act in the name of the European concert.

Although potentially serious, the crisis was unnecessary, Bismarck told his subordinates in the foreign office. "I do not accept the proposition that Europe cannot back down, since I do not recognize the concept of 'Europe's' solidarity." Obviously he found malicious pleasure in the collapse of the "crazy professor's" illusion that common interest could replace self-interest in the conduct of foreign policy. He disdained Gladstone's request for advice on what to do ("I'm happy when I can advise myself"). With French support, however, he secretly advised the Turks to yield, and they did. In November 1880 Turkish troops subdued Albanian resistance, and Montenegro received Dulcigno and the adjacent coast.[56] The question of Greece's frontiers remained, however, a serious threat to European peace.

Britain's change of course under Gladstone appears to have convinced Bismarck of the necessity of expediting restoration of the Three Emperors League at the first opportunity. Earlier the instability at the center of the autocratic Russian empire, as rival interests struggled for control over foreign policy, had led him to insist on the Dual Alliance; now the uncertainties of foreign policy in Britain's constitutional monarchy, as two political parties with differing conceptions of foreign policy alternated in power, convinced him that Germany's security required a close bond with Russia and Austria. Although the conflicting interests and fluctuating combinations of European politics still offered opportunities for anyone capable of exploiting them, he concluded in 1879–1880 that the risks had begun to outweigh the rewards. War with Russia would be "dangerous" and without "acceptable war aims"; in the event of war between Russia and Austria, Germany could permit neither to crush the other. Hence the time had come to lower the level of conflict and fluctuation

[56] Windelband, *Grossmächte*, pp. 150–158, 176–191; Langer, *Alliances and Alignments*, pp. 203–204; *GP*, IV, 15ff.; Temperley and Penson, *Foundations*, pp. 394–412.

by establishing firm commitments with Austria and Russia that would keep either from entering an alliance hostile to Germany and reduce, although it could not eliminate, the rivalry between them.[57] Germany's task in the eastern question, he suggested, was "to maintain peace wherever possible among all [the powers]—especially to prevent conflict between Austria and Russia and likewise to prevent, if possible, the chance of warlike action by England and Russia alone against Turkey."[58]

While at Kissingen in August 1880 Bismarck responded to renewed feelers from the tsar by directing the Imperial Foreign Office to resume negotiations, dormant now since February, for a tripartite pact with Russia and Austria. Almost simultaneously Haymerlé grew alarmed over Gladstone's disruptive policy toward the Balkans and sought out Bismarck at Friedrichsruh in early September to propose an agreement with Russia. During the next nine months Bismarck and his diplomats mediated between Vienna and Petersburg in difficult negotiations (the details of which need not be recounted here) repeatedly threatened by failure.[59] Once fully satisfied that an agreement was essential, Bismarck was relentless in his effort to obtain it. The primary negotiation was between Germany and Russia, since it was apparent that Austria would be the main obstacle to an agreement. Naturally Haymerlé was reluctant to dilute Austria's new relationship to Germany by including Russia. The purpose of that agreement had been, after all, to obtain German backing for Austrian interests in the Balkans threatened by Russia. But Haymerlé also lacked the decisiveness of Andrássy. He was so timid, Bismarck jibed, that he always said "no" three times on waking in the morning "for fear of having undertaken some commitment in his sleep."[60]

At Friedrichsruh in late November 1880 Bismarck and Saburov worked out a draft proposal, to which Alexander agreed with minor changes and Wilhelm, still unhappy over the anti-Russian stance forced upon him in August–September 1879, consented with relief. In January 1881 Bismarck assumed the delicate task of gaining Austria's consent. The best course, it appeared, was to approach Franz Joseph directly, lest Haymerlé prejudice the Kaiser against the agreement while explaining it to him. The Grand Duke of Saxe-Weimar, who was asked to act as intermediary, thought it beneath the dignity of a "reigning prince" to act as a diplomat. Finally a dual approach was arrived at—a letter from Wilhelm to Franz Joseph timed to arrive simultaneously with

[57] GP, III, 151–153, 159; Saburov, Memoirs, p. 74.

[58] GP, IV, 19.

[59] Windelband, Grossmächte, pp. 165ff.; GP, III, 147ff., Saburov, Memoirs, pp. 142ff.; W. R. Bridge, From Sadowa to Sarajevo: The Foreign Policy of Austria-Hungary, 1866–1914 (London, 1972), pp. 114–119.

[60] Windelband, Grossmächte, pp. 173–176, 192–196; Bridge, Sadowa to Sarajevo, p. 108; and Saburov, Memoirs, pp. 172–173.

an official dispatch to Haymerlé.[61] The Austrian Kaiser reacted favorably, but Haymerlé was again "skittish." Indeed the terms that Bismarck presented exceeded those he had discussed with Haymerlé at Friedrichsruh in September 1880. To the Austrian chancellor it appeared as though Austria would always be at a disadvantage in any tripartite agreement with Germany and Russia. Bismarck seemed to be asking him to give away the advantages Andrássy had built into the Dual Alliance.[62] While Haymerlé temporized, the quarrel between Greece and Turkey over their mutual frontier approached the flash point, and Bismarck saw in it the opportunity to demonstrate once again that Berlin was the center of European diplomacy.

Gladstone found that it was easier to condemn than to improve upon the foreign policy of the Disraeli government. His attempt to organize collective action by European powers to force Turkey to execute the Treaty of Berlin, as modified by the Berlin conference of June 1880, had merely provided new proof of the demise of the European concert. To British, French, and Russian suggestions that he take the lead in seeking a solution of the problem, Bismarck warily responded, as so often in the past, that Germany would initiate no action in a matter that did not directly involve German interests but would cooperate in any common step decided upon by the interested powers.[63] Still he sensed danger—the possibility that foreign chancelleries, if constantly rebuffed in Berlin, might accuse him of deliberately fomenting strife. To avoid this impression, he finally responded to a British appeal in February 1881 by proposing that the ambassadors of the six great powers at Constantinople be empowered to negotiate a new frontier, which, once accepted by Greece, would be forced upon Turkey. But the other powers did not follow the Bismarck scenario at Constantinople, with the consequence that the outcome he feared—isolation and censure by the disappointed powers if the action was unsuccessful—appeared imminent. Hence he jettisoned the common front with Britain and instructed Germany's ambassador to the Porte, Count Paul von Hatzfeldt, to join any four powers that included Austria and Russia, or the latter two alone if necessary, in any collective step they proposed. Otherwise Hatzfeldt should keep a low profile.[64]

The Greek affair, which finally ended in May 1881 when the Turks and Greeks accepted the border imposed by the powers, was now for Bismarck just one means among many with which to cement relations between the three empires. The continuing negotiations for reconstitution of the Three Emperors League had become mired, meanwhile, in Vienna, and beginning in March 1881 Bismarck subjected Haymerlé to a brutal pressure, forcing the

---

[61] Saburov, Memoirs, pp. 171–197; GP, III, 156–165.

[62] Saburov, Memoirs, pp. 198–215; GP, III, 148.

[63] GP, IV, 17–22.

[64] GP, IV, 22–24; Gerhard Ebel, ed., Botschafter Paul Graf von Hatzfeldt: Nachgelassene Papiere, 1838–1901 (Boppard am Rhein, 1976), I, 364–388; Windelband, Grossmächte, pp. 207–219.

Austrian to retreat, step by step.[65] In June, when the negotiation again bogged down, Bismarck, whose health and nervous condition were fast deteriorating, announced his intention to withdraw and leave the other two powers without his mediation. Austria and Russia quickly resolved their remaining differences.[66]

The "Second Three Emperors League," signed on June 18, 1881, reached much further than its predecessor, being a formal alliance between governments rather than an agreement by monarchs to consult in time of crisis. The alliance, whose exact terms remained secret until 1919, provided that, if one of the three powers should find itself at war with a fourth, its allies would maintain benevolent neutrality and seek to localize the conflict. This stipulation should apply in the case of war with Turkey only if the three powers had agreed in advance concerning the results of the war. Russia agreed to respect the "new position" gained by Austria-Hungary in the Treaty of Berlin, while all three governments guaranteed the closure of the Straits to warships. They agreed to take into account their respective interests on the Balkan Peninsula and to reach accord on all new modifications in the territorial status of European Turkey. To facilitate that accord the three powers approved a list of specific agreements: Austria could annex Bosnia and Herzegovina whenever she found it "opportune"; Austria could garrison, but not administer or annex the Sanjak of Novi-Bazar in accord with prior agreements; the three powers would discourage the Porte from invading Eastern Rumelia; they were not opposed to the union of Bulgaria and Eastern Rumelia, if the "force of circumstances" made that necessary; but they would deter Bulgaria from aggression against Macedonia and other Turkish possessions.[67]

Finally Bismarck had repaired the damage suffered by his system of foreign relations in 1877–1878. Once again Germany was one of three in an unstable system of five great powers. At last he had a formal guarantee that Germany would not have to face a two-front war in the event of conflict with France. Although Austria insisted that the treaty last only three years, he did not doubt that Haymerlé would come to appreciate its advantages and renew it in 1884.[68] For Russia the agreement provided an opportunity to escape from isolation, consolidate what gains remained from the recent war with Turkey, close the Straits to British warships, and buy time to put its finances in order. For Austria the agreement offered a chance to consolidate gains made at the Congress of Berlin, assurance of a voice in any future decisions with regard to

---

[65] Saburov, Memoirs, pp. 219–222; GP, III, 167–172; Windelband, Grossmächte, p. 221; Radowitz, Aufzeichnungen und Erinnerungen, II, 159–183.

[66] Saburov, Memoirs, pp. 233–255; GP, III, 173–176.

[67] Saburov, Memoirs, pp. 296–299; GP, III, 176–179. On the internal weaknesses (economy and public finance) that induced the Russian autocracy to come to terms again with Germany and Austria, see especially Geyer, Russian Imperialism, pp. 101–105.

[68] Saburov, Memoirs, pp. 220, 232.

the Balkans, and freedom to continue its economic penetration of the western Balkans through Macedonia to Saloniki. As long as they did not challenge Russian political supremacy in Bulgaria, the Austrians might even strengthen their economic and financial position in Bulgaria itself. Hence the treaty reduced the areas of friction and the possibility of a violent confrontation that might ultimately force Germany to fight for the interests of other powers. And yet Bismarck was under no illusion that the new harmony among the three empires would end the struggle for power and influence in the Balkan region. On the contrary, such a result was neither within his power nor in Germany's interest, for the continuing involvement of the great powers in that region tended to distract them from issues closer to Germany's borders.[69]

The Triple Alliance

During the final stages of the negotiation for the Three Emperors League, Alexander II, a frequent target for assassins, fell victim to a terrorist bomb in a Petersburg street. Since Saburov's initiatives with Bismarck were owed entirely to the tsar's desire to reestablish the relationship with Berlin and Vienna, everything now depended upon the attitude of his successor. Alexander III loyally completed what his father had begun, and in September 1881, attended by Giers, he met Kaiser Wilhelm and Bismarck at Danzig, where the new alliance was toasted and reinforced by expressions of goodwill.[70] And yet the new tsar's choice of close advisers gave cause for nervousness about the steadiness of his course. "Because of his limited knowledge of men and affairs," wrote Schweinitz, "the tsar could some day be moved in a critical moment to actions whose consequence he does not foresee, then perhaps regret, but can no longer avoid."[71] Although he soon dismissed Milyutin as minister of war, Alexander III chose as minister of interior none other than Nikolay Ignatyev and as director general of the Holy Synod Konstantin Pobedonostsev—both committed Slavophils and Panslavs imbued with a strong hatred for Austria. Giers, Gorchakov's deputy at the foreign office, did not share this fanaticism and was a supporter of Saburov's efforts to revive the Three Emperors League, but he lacked charisma and influence. Officially Gorchakov was still Russian foreign minister, furthermore, and it was by no means certain that Giers would succeed him. Ignatyev longed for the post and, while waiting for the appointment, exploited his control over the newspaper press to promote Panslav agitation against Austria and Germany.[72]

[69] See especially GP, III, 153; Kohl, ed., Anhang, I, 260.

[70] Windelband, Grossmächte, pp. 220ff., 256–264.

[71] Schweinitz, Denkwürdigkeiten, II, 168–169. For Bismarck's adverse judgment of Alexander III, his ministers, and advisers, see Helmut Rogge, Holstein und Hohenlohe (Stuttgart, 1957), pp. 174–175.

[72] On the struggle for power and policy at the Russian court, see especially George Kennan,

During these same months of 1881 a change of government at Paris raised again the possibility that a revanchist policy might triumph in France. Since the victory of moderate republicans in 1877, French foreign policy had been oriented more toward North Africa than Alsace-Lorraine. In April 1881 the cabinet of Jules Ferry, with Bismarck's encouragement, sent troops into Tunis and established a protectorate in execution of the secret agreement reached by the great powers at the Congress of Berlin.[73] When Léon Gambetta succeeded Ferry in November, however, the question arose whether France would again look north rather than south for the satisfaction of its national interests. To many Frenchmen Gambetta was the symbol and spirit of revanche. For this reversal of policy the natural course would have been rapprochement with Russia.

The signs of such a turnabout were not long in appearing. Despite wide ideological differences, the radical republicans under Gambetta and autocratic conservatives under Alexander III began to measure the advantages of cooperation. One straw in the wind was the appearance at Paris in January–February 1882 of General Mikhail Skobelev. Much celebrated in Russia for his victories over the Turks in 1877–1878 and the tribesmen of central Asia in January 1881, Skobelev was an impassioned Panslav, given to oratorical outbursts about the inevitability of a sanguinary struggle between Teuton and Slav—this at a time when Austria was fighting insurrections in Bosnia and Herzegovina. Although Skobelev had no official mission in France, he talked privately with Gambetta and made contact with pro-Russian sympathizers in military and press circles.[74]

Once again Bismarck had to worry that anti-German and anti-Austrian circles might gain the upper hand in both Russia and France and that all of his efforts to prevent such a turn of affairs might end in frustration. On a visit to Varzin in late October 1881, Schweinitz discussed with Bismarck the likelihood that Ignatyev would become foreign minister and the possibility of war with France and Russia. Moltke, Bismarck reported, wanted to go on the offensive in the east, depending on the fortresses at Strassburg, Metz, Mainz, and Koblenz to ward off a French attack. Bismarck favored the opposite strategy, for in Russia there were no objectives whose seizure would end the war.[75] And yet Bismarck did not overreact to the signs of new trouble from east and

The Decline of Bismarck's European Order: Franco-Russian Relations, 1875–1890 (Princeton, 1979), pp. 60–68. Schweinitz wrote of Gorchakov in June 1881: "The prince retains his 40,000 rubles and 100 rooms, travels abroad and reads novels, and Giers continues to work without rank, increase in pay, and suitable quarters." Schweinitz, Denkwürdigkeiten, II, 166, also 103, 115–116, 175, 194.

[73] Langer, "European Powers and Tunis," pp. 55–78, 251–265.

[74] Windelband, Grossmächte, pp. 277–285, 303–315; Hans Rogger, "The Skobelev Phenomenon: The Hero and His Worship," Oxford Slavonic Papers, New Series, 9 (1976), pp. 46–78.

[75] Schweinitz, Denkwürdigkeiten, II, 173–174.

west. He judged accurately that Gambetta, whom he found interesting and had invited—secretly and vainly—to visit him at Varzin in the autumn of 1881, would distinguish between words and deeds.[76] On January 26, 1882, the Gambetta cabinet fell and was replaced by a moderate republican government. Bismarck also handled the Skobelev provocation with restraint, persuading an outraged Wilhelm that it would be a mistake to demand that the Russian government disavow and reprimand the "White General."[77] In April Schweinitz could report that Giers had replaced Gorchakov as foreign minister instead of Ignatyev, who in June, furthermore, was dismissed as minister of the interior. Except for a lingering press war, the flurry of hostility and fear subsided.[78]

There was, however, a major consequence—the signing of an alliance between Germany, Austria, and Italy. The Italian government headed by Benedetto Cairoli was torn between two irreconcilable objectives: the hope of gaining compensation in the Trentino and Trieste for Austria's expansion in the Balkans and the desire for commercial and strategic reasons to acquire Tunis. The former objective required close relations with France and conceivably Russia, the latter with Germany and Austria. Each of these mutually exclusive courses had its partisans within the Italian government, press, and public. Cairoli, a fiery patriot of minimal political judgment, was reluctant to abandon either, and the result was frustration and isolation. France's occupation of Tunis in April–May 1881 and the signing of the Three Emperors League in June 1881 were undeniable proof of the bankruptcy of Italian policy and led to the fall of the Cairoli government. Under the influence of irredentist agitation, the new prime minister, Agostino Depretis, settled on a pro-French, anti-Austrian direction in foreign affairs, only to be overwhelmed by the national outcry over Tunis.[79] In the last half of 1881 the Italian scene was complicated still more by rioting and general tumult in Rome against the Catholic church by radical anticlericals. Bismarck exploited the opportunity to curry favor with German Catholics by painting in the Reichstag an unsympathetic picture of the drift of the Italian government toward republicanism and raising in the press the possibility that the pope might have to seek refuge abroad and the European powers might have to intervene to assure the independence of the Holy See by restoring the Papal States. Faced by these several

[76] Hohenlohe, Memoirs, II, 291; Rogge, Holstein und Hohenlohe, pp. 90–91, 164–166.

[77] The Skobelev episode ended when Alexander III, concerned over German and Austrian protests and suspicious of the general's popularity and political ambitions, recalled him from France. Although he did not discipline Skobelev, Alexander put him "on the shelf." In June 1882 at the age of 39 Russia's Boulanger died of a heart attack in a brothel. Rogger, "Skobelev Phenomenon," pp. 64–66. See also Hans Herzfeld, "Bismarck und die Skobelev-Episode," *Historische Zeitschrift*, 142 (1930), pp. 279–302.

[78] Schweinitz, Denkwürdigkeiten, II, 185–186, 194, 198–199.

[79] Windelband, Grossmächte, pp. 272–276; Langer, Alliances and Alignments, pp. 220–230; C. J. Lowe, Italian Foreign Policy, 1870–1940 (London, 1975), pp. 18–27.

crises, the Depretis government ran for cover. In late October 1881 King Humbert I paid a state visit to Vienna, a symbolic act that was the prelude to negotiations.[80]

Bismarck had by no means lost his scorn for the Italians. His reaction to their overtures in the fall of 1880 was decidedly negative. Rapprochement with the Italian government was purposeless, he wrote to Vienna. It would merely strengthen the tendency evident in the "Italian character" to exaggerate Italy's international importance. Italy could not be trusted to keep its commitments, which were "absolutely worthless" for the preservation of peace. To further Italian ambitions to recover "the islands and coasts where the flags of Venice, Genoa, and Savoy once waved" would antagonize France. Russia, not France, should be the target of an Italian-Austrian agreement.[81] One year later, however, Bismarck was inclined to yield to Italian entreaties for support. With Gambetta premier in Paris and Ignatyev angling for the foreign ministry in Petersburg, it seemed wise not to discourage Count Gustav von Kálnoky, Austro-Hungarian foreign minister following the death of Haymerlé, from negotiating with Rome. Kálnoky wanted to secure Austria's Alpine frontier in the event of trouble with France, but he also feared the domino effect of Gambetta's regime in Paris upon the monarchical order in Europe—"the gradual collapse of one throne after another and the appearance of a group of republics of Latin race, followed perhaps by a group of Slavic republics." The Italian monarchy was next in line, and the papacy would suffer from its fall and the triumph of Italy's republicans.[82]

Bismarck did not share Kálnoky's domino theory. He believed, furthermore, that the interests of the papacy could be harmonized with the republican form of government. A confederation of republics headed by the pope had been, after all, one of the solutions proposed for Italian unity. "Any form of a republic, however, would bring republican Italy into a close and lasting relationship to its sister republic France." Hence he proposed that the request of the Italian monarchy for a "treaty of guarantee" be used as a means of persuading the monarchists to reach a modus vivendi with the church that would have granted the papacy a "worthy and independent existence in Rome." Kálnoky was taken with this suggestion, which, if realized, would have provided Bismarck with yet another tool in his effort to resolve the German Kulturkampf![83] But the inhabitants of the Quirinal were eager for a guarantee precisely because it would have confirmed their possession of Rome against the claims of the papacy. Stalemated on the issue of a territorial guarantee, the negotiators turned to a second proposal advanced by the Italians, that of a treaty of neutrality. Bismarck directed Rome to seek the "key to the

[80] Langer, *Alliances and Alignments*, pp. 231–234; BR, IX, 153ff.
[81] GP, III, 183–189.
[82] GP, III, 194.
[83] GP, III, 195–199.

door" in Vienna rather than Berlin, for the critical issues concerned Italy's relations with Austria, not Germany. But he followed with keen interest in February–April 1882 the negotiations in Vienna and approved most of the results in the belief that what mattered most was not the exact wording of the treaty but that the alliance itself be accomplished.[84]

In a secret treaty signed on May 20, 1882, the three powers pledged not to enter into hostile alliances against each other. Germany and Austria would assist Italy militarily if she were attacked by France without provocation, while Italy would reciprocate in the event of an unprovoked attack by France on Germany. If attacked without provocation by two or more great powers not signatory to the treaty (read "Russia and France"), any member of the alliance could count on the support of the others. If "menaced" by one such power (read "France") and forced to war against it, a member of the alliance (read "Germany") could count on the benevolent neutrality of its partners.[85] Although the Italians were refused an outright guarantee of their territorial possessions (including Rome), they could now at least be sure that neither of the central powers would intervene in behalf of the papacy. If attacked by Russia, Austria could concentrate all of its forces on the Galician frontier. If attacked by France, Germany could expect Italy to hold down some enemy forces in southern France. Bismarck believed that Italy's military assistance to the dual powers would be minimal in wartime. What mattered was not her troops but her neutrality. As when urging restoration of the alliance with Russia, Bismarck argued negatively. It was better to have a treaty with Italy than not to have one.[86]

[84] GP, III, 205–210, 238–243, 247; Pribram, *Secret Treaties*, II, 3–43; Bridge, *Sadowa to Sarajevo*, pp. 128–133.

[85] GP, III, 245–247.

[86] GP, III, 222–225, 237; Langer, *Alliances and Alignments*, pp. 244–245.

CHAPTER FOUR

❧❧❧

Connections and Disconnections

A Missed Opportunity?

THE DUAL ALLIANCE, Three Emperors League, and Triple Alliance (supplemented by Austria's alliance with Serbia signed in 1881 and the Austro-German alliance with Rumania signed in 1883) represented a significant departure in European international politics. Heretofore alliances had been formed usually for specific ad hoc purposes; even the word "alliance," like "entente," had signified a loose combination of temporary duration. That Bismarck departed from that tradition was owed to his desire to stabilize somewhat the ever-fluctuating configurations of European politics in the interest of German security. His secondary aim was to buttress the existing social and political establishments in Germany, Austria, Russia, and perhaps Italy (certainly this was an aim of Kálnoky) against social disorder, political radicalism, and revolutionary terrorism. In this aspect the alliance system was an extension of the reversal in domestic policy that produced his plan for general tax reform, the protective tariff, his assault on the unity of the National Liberal party, the liquidation of the Kulturkampf, and the antisocialist statute. "The three emperors combination," said Wilhelm, "presents a firm barrier against revolution and is so strong that no one can attack it."[1]

That a connection existed between German foreign and domestic policies during the years 1878–1883 is hardly surprising, for the formulation of both occurred in a single intellect working simultaneously, or nearly so, on the entire range of problems confronting the German state and society. It is a mistake, nevertheless, to assume that in Bismarck's mind there was but one arena rather than two and that, as a consequence, his domestic policy can be explained by the imperatives of foreign affairs (once a common view) or his foreign policy by the dictates of domestic interests (a more recent view). Actually each arena contained a largely autonomous system of competing forces, whose dynamic relationships and interactions were affected but not necessarily determined by those occurring in the other. Each system had requirements that did not necessarily coincide with and at times even contradicted those of the other. The most notable fact about the German experience during 1878–1883 was the absence of a connection between foreign and domestic affairs that might well have occurred but did not. During those years Bismarck

---

[1] Walter Bussmann, ed., *Staatssekretär Graf Herbert von Bismarck: Aus seiner politischen Privatkorrespondenz* (Göttingen, 1964), p. 190.

passed up the opportunity provided by his successes in foreign affairs to "refound" the German Reich through an internal *Staatsstreich*.

One of the striking attributes of Bismarck's intellect was his capacity to see manifold interconnections between politicial phenomena, not only their actual but also their potential links, that is, their mutual vulnerability to common manipulation. His virtuoso command of such relationships in international affairs is what made Bismarck a grand master of foreign policy. In December 1880 he exulted to Eduard Cohen, "Our position has never been so brilliant as it is today." Earlier Germany had been confronted, he said, with the danger of a hostile triple alliance (Russia, France, Austria). Now the threat was gone. Even Russia was seeking to be on a good footing with Germany, and foreign statesmen (including the Queen of England) were turning to Berlin for advice.[2]

In domestic politics, however, Bismarck's position was hardly brilliant. Here his tactical skills had proven to be quite inadequate for the tasks he set himself. His manipulations had altered the face of German politics, but they had not produced the constellation of economic, social, and political forces that was his aim. And the frustration that came with that failure had upset still further the quivering balance of his nervous system and left him in constant fear of a stroke and final collapse. Having established for Germany an unparalleled, almost controlling position in European politics, why did he not exploit the security and stability it provided to launch the great coup in domestic politics that he often threatened and that seemed to offer a way out of his dilemma in this arena? Why did he not use this highly favorable moment in foreign affairs—a time when he no longer needed the backing of German public or parliamentary opinion for any moves abroad—to rid himself of the barriers in his way at home? Since he blamed his bad health on the opposition, obstructionism, and malevolence of his adversaries, why did he not sweep away the political system that fostered those ills and thereby effect his own cure?

The moment was undeniably propitious. The outcome of the Reichstag election of 1881 provided an adequate provocation. The Kaiser was not an obstacle, and his advancing age was another reason not to delay; Crown Prince Friedrich Wilhelm could not be expected to start his reign with a reactionary coup. In earlier years poor health had not prevented Bismarck from engaging in major actions in either domestic or foreign affairs. The drafting of the constitution in late 1866, the Hohenzollern candidacy for the Spanish throne in early 1870, and the Kulturkampf legislation of 1872–1873 had all occurred at times of severe illness. In 1875 he had doubted his physical capacity to deal with the problems that lay ahead, and yet he had launched in late 1875, after the king denied his request for retirement, a fundamental change of course in German internal affairs. In 1877–1878 he undertook,

[2] GW, VIII, 390.

despite bad health, the fiscal reform, Congress of Berlin, antisocialist act, and Reichstag election. On some occasions (for example, the war of 1870 and the tariff debate of 1879) the prospect of decisive action seemed even to revive and refresh him.

We have seen that during 1881–1883 Bismarck began to prepare the base— accident insurance act, business chambers, and economic council—for a national diet with which to replace the Reichstag. In public and private discussions he had charted the legal course for such an action by reinterpreting the constitution as a sovereign union not of the German people but of federal states. But something kept him from taking the final step of a Staatsstreich. Was he dissatisfied with his progress in building the organic base for a surrogate parliament? Did he fear to reopen the question of Prussia's hegemony in the federal union and of Prussia's relationship to the lesser states that such an action would entail? Did he shrink from a "preventive war" of this magnitude in internal affairs even as he did in foreign affairs? Whatever the reasons, Bismarck did not choose the route of the Staatsstreich in 1882–1883. He sought his cure not in another revolution from above, but in a new medical and psychological treatment; not in the overthrow of the imperial constitution, but in its administrative revision.

Schweninger to the Rescue

In March 1882 the Baroness Spitzemberg watched Bismarck "slink through his garden," amid blooming crocuses, "very tired and old and unable to get rid of his maladies despite arsenic."[3] Since Struck's rebellion, he had begun to consult other doctors and try other cures. For about a year (1882–1883) he was treated by Friedrich Frerichs, professor of medicine at Berlin and head of the famous Charité hospital. Summoned on Bleichröder's recommendation, Frerichs prescribed various English medicines (pills to be swallowed and a "strong-smelling yellow liquid" to be rubbed on the cheek) that afforded temporary relief from facial neuralgia.[4] In late January 1883 the leg injury of Petersburg days produced another attack of phlebitis. The infection spread from the calf to the knee and completely immobilized the chancellor, who lay for weeks in pajamas and dressing gown on a chaise longue in the garden room of the chancellery, scarcely able to climb the stairs to his bedroom at nighttime. To Johanna's fury that "dumbbell" Frerichs declared the leg ailment "unim-

---

[3] Rudolf Vierhaus, ed., Das Tagebuch der Baronin Spitzemberg (Göttingen, 1960), p. 195. In a letter to Herbert, undated but apparently written in January 1883, Johanna wrote of Bismarck taking arsenic again to deaden his neuralgia, a treatment that appeared to have had some effectiveness earlier at Friedrichsruh. BFA, Bestand C, Box 8.

[4] Freiherr Lucius von Ballhausen, Bismarck-Erinnerungen (Stuttgart, 1920), p. 244; BP, I, 253; Moritz Busch, Tagebuchblätter (Leipzig, 1899), III, 141, 144; Wilhelm Treue, Doctor at Court (London, 1958), pp. 181–182.

portant and secondary." The prince's "chief problem was nerves," for which "no work and much sleep, food, and fresh air" were the best prescription.[5]

In March the phlebitis disappeared, but the facial neuralgia returned and with it a severe cold followed by a racking cough. Irritated by his reception in the Bismarck household, Frerichs ceased to call. Holstein was sent to mediate, but Frerichs was unmoved by the diplomat's warning that his professional reputation would suffer if the German chancellor had to seek help from a rival physician. Bismarck, said Frerichs angrily, was "actually in good health," except for catarrh. His neuralgia was an "odd business," for the pains, which never appeared when the doctor was present, were much less severe than supposed. Yet Frerichs did not believe that the prince was shamming. "No, no. . . . It depends on his mood. . . . His family has no idea how to handle him. . . . I tell you there's nothing wrong with the chancellor; it's just that he's showing signs of wear."[6]

At the end of April tic douloureux was joined by a persistent stomachache, a combination that hindered both sleeping and eating. These symptoms brought Frerichs back to the Wilhelmstrasse. To reduce the pain and induce sleep the doctor prescribed five teaspoons of morphine nightly, a dosage that Johanna declared to be ineffective. In addition, the doctor prescribed pills that Johanna denounced as "full of filth" (the containers read "bismuth, pepper, aloe, nex vonica, belladonna, enzian, calmus, often calen[dula] powder" and once "calen[dula] oil"). Neither Frerich's pills nor the drops (content undisclosed) administered by yet another physician, Dr. Zwiegenberg, improved the patient's condition. And so a despairing Johanna, to whom all doctors were "dumb sheep," began to dose her husband with her own homeopathic remedy (spigelia).[7] Not to be outdone, Bismarck prescribed for himself—champagne. Only "slight intoxication," he declared, was effective against the neuralgia that now extended, he said, "over the entire body," limiting his capacity "to think and work to two hours at the most."[8] About this time Bismarck began to put his financial affairs in order for the benefit of his heirs.[9]

[5] Johanna to Herbert von Bismarck, Feb. 1, 5, 13, 19, and 24, 1883. BFA, Bestand C, Box 8.

[6] Johanna to Herbert von Bismarck, Mar. 13, 24, and 28, 1883. BFA, Bestand C, Box 8; Norman Rich and M. H. Fisher, eds., *The Holstein Papers: The Memoirs, Diaries and Correspondence of Friedrich von Holstein, 1837–1909* (4 vols., Cambridge, Eng., 1955–1963), II, 38, 41.

[7] Johanna to Herbert von Bismarck, Apr. 26, May 7, 13, 18, and 26, 1883. BFA, Bestand C, Box 8. Contributing to the *Götterdämmerung* atmosphere in the Bismarck household in May–June 1883 was the sickness and death of another family dog, Flörchen. Her body was shipped to Varzin to be buried beside Sultan. Johanna to Herbert, May 26 and June 3, 1883. *Ibid.* In a rare appearance at a cabinet meeting on May 31, 1883, Bismarck told his colleagues that for six months he had taken opium, as prescribed by Frerichs. Lucius, *Bismarck-Erinnerungen*, p. 265.

[8] Lucius, *Bismarck-Erinnerungen*, p. 264.

[9] To facilitate the division of his estate among his heirs, Bismarck increased his liquid assets by borrowing money on his estates (*Pfandbriefe und Amortisationshypotheken*), investing the

In the first half of 1883 both Bismarck and his doctors believed that he did not have long to live. (Frerichs, it is said, suspected cancer.) The person who changed this prognosis was Dr. Ernst Schweninger. This physician, then resident in Munich, first appeared in the Bismarck household to treat the younger son Wilhelm. By age twenty-eight "Bill" had eaten his way to 260 pounds. Gout and heart trouble followed. Schweninger prescribed a ten-month diet, to which Bill held, despite contrary advice from family and friends. When Schweninger saw Bill again, nearly a year later, he did not recognize the patient, who had lost 60 pounds and considerable girth. In early October 1882 Bill brought the doctor to Varzin, where he had the chance to observe the chancellor for three days.[10] Under Cohen's care at Friedrichsruh the prince had adopted a more sensible daily routine after his "stroke" in 1880: rising at 8:30–9:00 A.M., retiring at 11:00 P.M., and eating a low-fat diet that reduced his weight from 272 (1879) to 255 (1881) pounds.[11] Yet the effort was spasmodic.[12] Schweninger observed that "he ate and drank whenever and whatever he wanted. Little exercise but a lot of exhausting work." A few days after the doctor's departure, Johanna wrote to Herbert, "We liked him very much, and now he has sent all kinds of little bottles for Papa."[13]

In late May 1883 Schweninger came to Berlin for a medical exhibit and Johanna immediately invited him to dinner. On the following morning he examined Bismarck and was shocked by how far the prince had deteriorated in six months. The doctor reduced Johanna to despair by the decisiveness with which he opposed all further medication and ordered drastic changes in the chancellor's life-style. *Papachen*, she thought, would find it "quite impossible" to conform. Schweninger ordained a spartan diet for the entire family:

money raised in interest-bearing securities. Bismarck to Scholz, Nov. 28, 1883. DZA Potsdam, Reichskanzlei, 2087, p. 84.

[10] Ernst Schweninger, *Dem Andenken Bismarcks* (Leipzig, 1899), pp. 34–35.

[11] Lucius, *Bismarck-Erinnerungen*, pp. 239–240; Spitzemberg, *Tagebuch*, pp. 194, 196. On Bismarck's weight, see Otto Pflanze, "Toward a Psychoanalytic Interpretation of Bismarck," *American Historical Review*, 77 (April 1972), p. 435, fn. 49, and Augustin Cabanès, "La Medecine Anecdotique: Bismarckiana," *La Chronique Medicale*, 5 (1898), p. 354. Unfortunately Cabanès does not give his source for these figures. Schweninger claimed that he first weighed Bismarck at 272 lb. (247 *Pfund*), but appears to want to attribute to himself what Cohen had already partially achieved. Schweninger, *Dem Andenken*, p. 35.

[12] See Alfred von Kiderlen-Wächter's humorous account of a meal at the chancellery in early December 1881. GW, VIII, 439–440.

[13] Johanna to Herbert von Bismarck, Oct. 10, 1882. BFA, Bestand C, Box 8. This letter, written only a few days after Schweninger's visit, does not verify Schweninger's own account, written years later, that he uttered on this occasion a dire warning that the chancellor's health was fast deteriorating. Given the nature of their correspondence, Johanna would certainly have confided it to her son, as indeed she did when Schweninger actually delivered the prognosis eight months later. Schweninger, *Dem Andenken*, pp. 36–37. Georg Schwarz, *Ernst Schweninger: Bismarcks Leibarzt* (Leipzig, 1941), gives no sources and generally follows uncritically Schweninger's own published statements.

tea or milk with eggs for breakfast, "a little" fish and roast meat (no vegetables) at noon, a "small jug" of milk about 4:00 P.M., and yet another in the evening. To eat "less and more frequently" and avoid everything bilious was the rule. As recounted earlier, Bismarck surprised his wife by yielding to the "ordinances" of the Bavarian physician, who established his psychological dominance over the patient.[14] Within days the stomach pains diminished. But still Bismarck could not sleep regularly without morphine. Fearing addiction, Schweninger substituted a weak injection for the five full teaspoons of the drug that Frerichs had nightly "poured" into the patient's stomach to no avail. By June 8 Johanna had already developed a "mighty trust" in Schweninger's judgment and prayed that this "pleasant, modest, cheerful, and unspeakably demanding" personality would remain by her husband's side for the rest of the summer.[15]

Schweninger's victory over Frerichs was not, however, as immediate or total as the Bavarian later claimed. Johanna reported that her husband was still receiving visits from Frerichs but no longer took his pills. In medicine as in

ERNST SCHWENINGER, IN THE 1880S. ARTHUR REHBEIN, *BISMARCK IM SACHSENWALD* (BUCHVERLAG DER GESELLSCHAFT ZUR VERBREITUNG KLASSISCHER KUNST G.M.B.H., BERLIN, 1925), P. 69.

[14] See vol. 2, pp. 53–55.

[15] Johanna to Herbert von Bismarck, June 8 and 28, 1883. *BFA*, Bestand C, Box 8. Again Johanna's account varies somewhat from Schweninger's recollection in *Dem Andenken*, pp. 36–37.

politics the master of *Realpolitik* kept his options open. At the end of June
Baroness Spitzemberg heard from the family that the chancellor was taking
from the prescriptions of both doctors "whatever suits him." Dietary trans-
gressions followed. One morning he consumed two tall glasses of buttermilk,
circled the chancellery garden three times without tiring, and toasted this feat
with two more large glasses of buttermilk, which he chased with cognac. The
punishment was severe: "unbearable" stomach pains and heavy vomiting,
signs of peritoneal irritation, and a bad attack of jaundice. "The poor princess," Spitzemberg reported, "is even more distressed and her despair has increased [Bismarck's] moroseness to the point that the physician and children
don't know what to do next." There was, however, a welcome by-product—
a thumb-sized gallstone, whose passage relieved the abdominal pains.[16]

Schweninger vanquished Frerichs not only by superior psychological insight and more accurate diagnosis but also by neglecting for a time his own
medical practice. When Bismarck left for Friedrichsruh on July 2, 1883,
Schweninger went along, likewise to Bad Kissingen on July 28, Bad Gastein
on September 1, and back to Friedrichsruh on September 28. "I determined
as far as possible," the physician wrote later, "the working time and tasks to
be undertaken during it; regulated the time and amount of recreation, exercise, and rest; supervised eating and drinking according to time, quantity, and
quality; regulated getting up and going to bed; intervened whenever necessary
either to moderate or to stimulate; and finally had the satisfaction of noting
real progress in body and spirit."[17]

During the autumn at Friedrichsruh, while Schweninger was absent, Bismarck suffered a fresh, but milder attack of jaundice and stomach pains, intensified by anger over "court intrigues by people who have not the slightest
understanding of politics." When his Hamburg physician Cohen refused him
morphine, the prince telegraphed for Schweninger, who came and injected
it. Cohen felt insulted and threatened not to return, but let himself be pla-
cated by the prince and princess. (Bismarck continued his two-platoon system
of doctors until Cohen's death in 1884.)[18] As the winter progressed, the jaundice, facial neuralgia, and migraines vanished for the time being, the patient's
sleep became regular and sufficient, the digestive and hemorrhoidal problems
disappeared, and the varicose veins and injured leg became less bothersome.
His weight dropped to 222 pounds, and his clothing drooped from his body.

[16] Johanna to Herbert von Bismarck, June 8 and 22, 1883; *BFA*, Bestand C, Box 8. Spitzemberg, *Tagebuch*, pp. 199–200; Lucius, *Bismarck-Erinnerungen*, pp. 267–268.

[17] Schweninger, *Dem Andenken*, pp. 37–38. Philipp Eulenburg, who dined with the Bismarcks
at Bad Kissingen, August 20, recorded the diet: no soup and no drink during the meal, a trout,
cold roasted rabbit and partridge. *GW*, VIII, 478–479.

[18] *GW*, VIII, 484, 496, 499, 512; Lucius, *Bismarck-Erinnerungen*, p. 273; Moritz Busch, *Bismarck: Some Secret Pages of His History* (London, 1898), II, 362.

The patient could walk and, to his great joy, ride again.[19] In December 1883 he wrote to Wilhelm that physically he felt better than he had for years.[20] On returning to Berlin on March 12, 1884, he told the Prussian ministers that he felt "much better than two years ago, when he had not expected to survive the winter."[21]

Reduction of the Bismarck "Dictatorship"?

At dinner on June 12, 1884, Bismarck suddenly turned to the Baroness Spitzemberg and said, "Do you understand anything about dreams? Last night I dreamt that I was on a road; on the right was a city (it looked like Naugard), to the left a lake. Suddenly the water began to roar; waves dashed upward, as though big fish agitated the water, which threatened to come over the road. I told myself that I would either drown or at least get very wet and should avoid that. So I turned around! To which of my measures should I assume that this dream pertains?" "Retreat does not seem like you," exclaimed the baroness, "but you are a fatalist!" "Not quite," Bismarck replied, "but I pay attention to the signs that voiceless nature gives us; she is often smarter than we."[22] What the chancellor took to be a sign from nature was a sleeping expression of a waking anxiety. Under Schweninger's regime he could look forward to a few more years in office, despite his sixty-nine years. But the Kaiser had reached eighty-seven, and what would happen after his death was now a matter of daily speculation, especially among those whose careers were likely to be affected. Naturally Bismarck began to consider how, by retreating to safer ground, he might prevent the conversion of the regime he had created into a parliamentary government under the next Kaiser. Germany had to be protected against the flood.

During the preceding December he had discussed with Lucius and others the necessity of "reducing" the position of imperial chancellor (except for foreign affairs) to the dimensions given it in his original draft of the constitution (1866–1867): that of presiding officer over the Bundesrat, without the obligation of appearing in the Reichstag to defend government policy. "The Bundesrat with its unresponsible majority decisions" should move into the foreground; the Prussian government should occupy "a position no different from that of other governments."[23] Lucius did not take the suggestion seriously, but within a few days Bismarck began to implement it. He ordered

[19] Cabanès, "Bismarckiana," p. 354. Thereafter his weight rose to 227 lb. in 1886 and remained at that level until 1890.

[20] Horst Kohl, ed., *Anhang zu den Gedanken und Erinnerung von Otto Fürst von Bismarck* (Stuttgart, 1901), I, 320.

[21] Lucius, *Bismarck-Erinnerungen*, p. 284.

[22] Spitzemberg, *Tagebuch*, pp. 207–208.

[23] GW, VIII, 494–495.

imperial agencies to discontinue the practice of presenting "presidential bills" to the Bundesrat. Under the constitution, he maintained, neither the Kaiser nor the chancellor, only the allied governments, had the right of legislative initiative. Presidential bills were reducing the weight of the Bundesrat, increasing that of the chancellor, and they raised the possibility that the German government would one day be composed of a unicameral legislature based on universal and secret male suffrage and a single responsible minister serving a monarch with "incomplete rights."[24]

After returning to Berlin in mid-March 1884, Bismarck revealed more about his intentions to Oswald von Nostitz-Wallwitz, Saxon envoy at Berlin. The program of the new German Freedom party, he pointed out, called for a "responsible imperial ministry." Under the crown prince, whom he did not intend to serve, there was danger that this aim might be realized. To prevent such a development the governments must repeatedly stress their opposition to it; otherwise the "liberalizing advisers and ministers" surrounding Friedrich Wilhelm would have their way. "The unity of Germany," he reaffirmed, "rests much less on the feeling of national cohesiveness, which usually flares up only in times of great crises like those produced by military threats, than on the bond established by the governments." To reduce the importance of the chancellorship, he intended to withdraw entirely from the Prussian cabinet and remove the imperial state secretaries from the Bundesrat, thereby keeping them out of contact with the Reichstag. This would end the anomaly that the heads of Reich agencies and even their subordinates sat in the Bundesrat and chaired its committees as Prussian delegates. Their places were to be taken by Prussian ministers, whose presence would heighten the importance of the Bundesrat and encourage ministers of the lesser states to participate in it.[25]

By the time Bismarck met the cabinet on March 16, rumors of his newest intent to give up his Prussian offices were already abroad. In the past Bismarck's resignations had usually been the prelude to the departure of other ministers. But the prince hastened to say that he had "never been in such close agreement with his colleagues as in the last three years." Reasons of health, he declared, required him to restrict his activities to foreign policy,

---

[24] Bismarck to Hermann von Schelling, state secretary of the Imperial Office of Justice, Dec. 21, 1883. Hans Goldschmidt, *Das Reich und Preussen im Kampf um die Führung* (Berlin, 1931), pp. 295–297. "The danger of falling into direct government by alternating parliamentary majorities lies in the intervention of legislative bodies in the affairs of the executive and its administration," he wrote to Boetticher on January 13, 1884. "Experience shows that the weight of such intervention is growing and arises from the direct participation by administrative officials in the public deliberations of law-making bodies." *Ibid.*, pp. 298–300.

[25] Nostitz-Wallwitz to Saxon Foreign Minister General von Fabrice, Mar. 14, 1884. Goldschmidt, *Reich und Preussen*, pp. 300–303. As the chancellor requested, the Saxon, Württemberg, and Bavarian governments led the Bundesrat in a public declaration of their intention to hold to the federal treaties by resisting the creation of responsible ministries. Heinrich von Poschinger, ed., *Fürst Bismarck und der Bundesrat, 1867–1890* (Stuttgart, 1896–1909), V, 149–152.

but it was also politically desirable at this juncture to separate the chancellorship from the Prussian cabinet. The interests of the Reich, he asserted, would
be nurtured in the cabinet by the minister of war and by imperial state secretaries who would be appointed as Prussian ministers (he spoke of Boetticher
as minister of commerce and of Count Hatzfeldt as Prussian minister of foreign
affairs).[26]

On the surface it would appear that Bismarck intended to demolish the
position of authority he had labored so hard to construct for himself. Holstein, who always looked for the hidden motive and sometimes found it,
thought the prince's purpose was to make it impossible for Friedrich Wilhelm,
once Kaiser, to oust him as chancellor. All factions, even the democratic
liberals, believed that Bismarck was indispensable in foreign affairs. By surrendering offices and functions, Bismarck would sacrifice some power but
would remain a force to be reckoned with throughout the government. The
next Kaiser would have to be "very wary" in choosing ministers who were to
work with him. That Bismarck considered making Scholz, his most obedient
colleague in the cabinet, minister-president would seem to support this
view.[27] As state secretary of the Imperial Foreign Office, Hatzfeldt would have

CONCERNING THE DIMINUTION OF BISMARCK, "THE PRINCE WILL ALWAYS REMAIN BIG ENOUGH TO
CAST A SHADOW INTO THE PRUSSIAN CABINET WHEN HE STANDS IN THE CHANCELLOR'S OFFICE." WIL-
HELM SCHOLZ IN *KLADDERADATSCH*, 1884.

[26] Cabinet meeting of Mar. 16, 1884. DZA Merseburg, Rep. 90a, B, III, 2b, Nr. 6, Vol. 96.
Goldschmidt, *Reich und Preussen*, pp. 303–306; also Lucius, *Bismarck-Erinnerungen*, pp. 284–286.
[27] Rich and Fisher, eds., *Holstein Papers*, II, 74, 100–102. The plan had to be abandoned
because the indispensable Maybach would have resigned in protest at being passed over for the
higher office.

been under Bismarck's thumb and hardly free in his role as Prussian minister of foreign affairs to follow his own or the cabinet's judgment in instructing Prussia's delegates on how to vote in the Bundesrat.[28] During the cabinet meeting of March 16 Bismarck assured the ministers that he would keep "in touch with"—surely to be read as "keep an eye" on—them. But could even this "disciplined" cabinet be expected to continue indefinitely in the designated orbit, particularly given the difficulty of knowing and interpreting the intentions of an absentee chancellor?

In the plan he formed at Friedrichsruh during the winter of 1883–1884 Bismarck thought to solve this dilemma by creating yet another governmental organ. Writing to Boetticher on January 13, he announced his intention to establish an "imperial council" (Reichsrat) to advise the Kaiser on national affairs. "The members of this consultative agency, over which the imperial chancellor will preside [!], would in my view be, first of all, the Prussian ministers and heads of the Reich's offices and, secondarily, those personalities whom his majesty may summon as in the case of the [Prussian] State Council [Staatsrat]. Furthermore, those persons who now meet in the economic council can be added. Representation by other allied governments is not to be excluded."[29] By the time he reached Berlin in March Bismarck had modified this proposal to "a reactivation of the Prussian State Council, to which the heads of the Reich's offices are to be appointed; later this body will be enlarged and become an imperial council."[30] To Lucius this "fantastic project" meant a diminution of the Prussian cabinet, and it was so interpreted in the public press.[31]

Established in 1817 as a consultative body in legislative matters, the Prussian State Council had lapsed with the revolution of 1848. Revived in 1852, it did not meet until 1854 and thereafter existed only on paper. Now Bismarck proposed that this moribund institution, historically associated with bureaucratic absolutism, should replace the defunct Prussian Economic Council. He expected the state council, composed of high officials of the Reich and Prussia, "other distinguished persons," and representatives from various interest and occupational groups, to be in closer touch with practical affairs than ministers and privy counselors and free from the factionalism and political considerations that marred the work of the Prussian and German parliaments. Neither the Kaiser, the crown prince, nor the Prussian ministers were taken with this idea. But as usual Bismarck overcame Wilhelm's doubts. Friedrich Wil-

[28] That Bismarck still considered this post vital is shown by his instruction to the Prussian cabinet of June 28, 1884, in which he again instructed his colleagues on the proper procedure for forwarding Prussian bills to the Bundesrat. He insisted that the Prussian minister of foreign affairs alone should sign such bills, not the entire cabinet. GW, VIc, 302–303.

[29] Goldschmidt, Reich und Preussen, p. 299.

[30] Ibid., p. 305.

[31] Lucius, Bismarck-Erinnerungen, pp. 280, 288; SEG (1884), p. 49.

helm he won over by proposing that the crown prince assume the presidency of the council, with himself as vice-president.[32]

On this occasion, according to Holstein, the two men discussed what would happen on Wilhelm's death. Friedrich Wilhelm declared his intention to retain Bismarck as chancellor. "He would then appoint Bennigsen and Miquel to direct Prussian affairs." Bismarck voiced no objection, but warned against a further step to the left "to Forckenbeck and his friends," which would "lead to republicanism."[33] A week later Holstein curried favor with the chancellor by remarking "that his enemies, Stosch and Co., are completely thunderstruck; now they realize that the present chancellor is not so near fading out as they thought." Bismarck replied "with no trace of melancholy, 'They've not even begun to realize the implications of my retirement from Prussian affairs. This is the price for my remaining under the crown prince, who is extraordinarily keen to keep me on as *chancellor*.' "[34]

His own health somewhat restored, Bismarck was preparing for the continuation of his regime in altered form under the next reign. But his plan to revise the constitution "backward" to December 1866 was not realized. Wilhelm obdurately refused to release him from his Prussian posts.[35] Wilhelm's resistance had never been an insuperable obstacle to what Bismarck firmly wanted. That the prince did not force the issue in March 1884, as he did in resuscitating the Prussian State Council, causes one to wonder how firm he was about his own plans. In May Boetticher made the mistake of acting independently, and Holstein reported that Bismarck "said he is again wavering in his decision to free himself from Prussian affairs, because to do so he would need to leave behind at least one person in the cabinet on whose judgment and tact he could rely absolutely. Hitherto he had supposed Boetticher was that person, but now he had doubts."[36]

To Lucius the revived Prussian State Council was "a waste of time and a neutralization of the Prussian cabinet! A new friction machine."[37] The Kaiser's reaction was similar, for he had participated in the sessions of the council

---

[32] BR, X, 225–226; Rich and Fisher, eds., *Holstein Papers*, II, 117–123.

[33] Holstein diary, Apr. 14, 1884. Rich and Fisher, eds., *Holstein Papers*, II, 112–113.

[34] Holstein diary, Apr. 21, 1884. *Ibid.*, II, 123. Another possible motive for the rapprochement was to undercut Crown Princess Victoria, who wished to marry one of her daughters off to Prince Alexander of Battenberg, the reigning prince of Bulgaria. Bismarck opposed the match because of Prince Alexander's feud with Russia.

[35] To Mittnacht, Mar. 28, 1884. GW, VIII, 506. Bismarck to Kaiser Wilhelm I, June 24, 1884. GW, VIc, 301–302. Rich and Fisher, eds., *Holstein Papers*, II, 119–121. Bismarck's plan for reorganization of the two governments and their relationship was not a passing fancy, but one that continued to concern him. In Feb. 1889, when newspapers again rumored his resignation, he outlined a similar plan "theoretically" to the Prussian cabinet, to be acted upon "if the blow hits me." Lucius, *Bismarck-Erinnerungen*, p. 490.

[36] Holstein diary, May 2, 1884. Rich and Fisher, eds., *Holstein Papers*, II, 135.

[37] Mar. 20, 1884. Lucius, *Bismarck-Erinnerungen*, p. 288.

before 1848 and thought the Landtag had made it superfluous.[38] By the time it met (October 25–November 13, 1884) Bismarck too sensed that he had merely complicated the machinery of government. Hence he revived the practice of "presidential bills" in order to bypass it and get fast action on a matter he considered vital.[39] At the opening session the crown prince spoke poorly, stressing the wrong words and phrases, as though he did not understand the address written for him. "Bismarck looked bad and out of sorts."[40] Not until 1890 did the council meet again. Its only benefit in 1884, so far as Lucius could see, was to bring the heir to the throne temporarily into closer contact with the current business of state and into a "more intimate relationship with the chancellor."[41] But Friedrich Wilhelm felt differently about the matter. He too recognized that the council was "a completely superfluous institution." Nor could he see any value in being president, for Bismarck left him no chance to influence decisions; "nothing happened in the council of state against [the chancellor's] wishes."[42]

Indeed it was unlike Bismarck to retreat. The position of power that he had secured was a means with which to satisfy his personal need to dominate and control, but also to expedite the consolidation of the German Reich and the stabilization of its social and political order. Yet he had begun to sense that his success in dominating the executive branches of the Prussian and German governments was a danger for the future. At a time when a crown prince with liberal contacts and sympathies stood at the foot of the throne and an oppositional majority, in which left-liberals were the largest element, dominated the Reichstag, it behooved Bismarck to reconsider the institutional structure he had erected. Although he wrestled with the problem during the winter of 1883–1884, he was unable to solve it. The plan he conceived was of doubtful practicality, but it also involved a sacrifice of his direct authority that the Kaiser opposed and upon which Bismarck himself did not insist.

Requiem for Lasker

Bismarck was hardly alone in calculating on the approaching reign of the crown prince. In parting from the National Liberal party in 1880 the secessionists hoped to become the nucleus of a "great liberal party," uniting na-

[38] Wilhelm I to Bismarck, Apr. 13 and 17, 1884. Goldschmidt, *Reich und Preussen*, pp. 306–308.
[39] Bismarck to Boetticher, Oct. 9, 1884. GW, VIc, 307. At a cabinet meeting on Oct. 23, 1884, Bismarck spoke of the state council "as though he were already uncomfortable with it." Lucius, *Bismarck-Erinnerungen*, p. 302.
[40] Lucius, *Bismarck-Erinnerungen*, p. 303. Rich and Fisher, eds., *Holstein Papers*, II, 166.
[41] Lucius, *Bismarck-Erinnerungen*, pp. 298, 302. On the preparations for the meeting of the council, see GW, VIc, 304–306; XIV, 952–953.
[42] Holstein diary, Nov. 17, 1884. Rich and Fisher, eds., *Holstein Papers*, II, 167.

tional liberals and progressives in one powerful phalanx in preparation for a change of regime. Within the Progressive party Albert Hänel and Rudolf Virchow worked steadily for fusion with the Secession, but their colleague Eugen Richter resisted. A brilliant debater and presumed expert on public finance, Richter was an autocrat eager to preserve the dominance he had attained over the party. He symbolized the uncompromising spirit that had led the party to stand against the Bismarck government on every basic issue except the Kulturkampf: the constitution, the iron budget and *Septennat*, the antisocialist statute, the protective tariff, and finally the liquidation of the Kulturkampf. What Richter demanded of the secessionists was tantamount to capitulation: full acceptance of the progressive program and abandonment of any thought of reunion with the national liberals. The three liberal caucuses still found common ground in opposing government intervention at the polls, biennial Reich budgets and Reichstag sessions, and Bismarck's tax program. But the attempt to establish a common front for the Landtag elections of October 1882 was only a limited success owing to Richter's resolute opposition.[43]

As Richter prepared for the Reichstag election of 1884, however, he too realized the necessity of coming to terms with the secessionists. Intoxication over the victory of 1881 had given way within the Progressive party to sobriety and even exhaustion. Money was short; candidates were difficult to find; some local committees were inclined to back secessionists. Richter had to face the prospect that, having been given credit for the victory of 1881, he would bear the blame for defeat in 1884. His prodigious labors as a deputy in two parliaments, journalist, and party dictator had worn him down to where he felt the need of support from men of the stature of Forckenbeck, Stauffenberg, Bamberger, and Rickert. Hence he yielded to Hänel's desire to negotiate. Some secessionists were reluctant to turn their backs on the national liberals and ally with Richter. But Rickert and Bamberger argued for it. Some decisive step was needed to galvanize the liberal movement for the coming election. They wished to be ready, moreover, to take advantage of the liberal current that was expected on the ascension of Friedrich Wilhelm. United and one hundred strong, the left-liberals would become the "government party" in the post-Bismarckian era. From these common pressures and expectations was molded the German Freedom party (*Deutsche Freisinnige Partei*), formally established on March 16, 1884.[44]

In drafting the new program Hänel and Bamberger still hoped that the fusion would attract members of the National Liberal party, badly demoralized by the Secession and Bennigsen's retirement from politics. But the actual effect was to revive it. Under the leadership of Johannes Miquel the party ac-

[43] Felix Rachfahl, "Eugen Richter und der Linksliberalismus in neuen Reiche," *Zeitschrift für Politik*, 5 (1912), pp. 311–312; SEG (1882), pp. 178–179, 212.

[44] Rachfahl, "Eugen Richter," pp. 321–324.

centuated the contrast between itself and the left-liberals. The *Freisinnige* program called for a responsible imperial cabinet, maintenance of the rights of
parliament (especially budget rights), preservation of the basic human free-
doms, rejection of state socialism and all restrictions on free enterprise, lower
tariffs on the necessities of life and no favors for special interests, reduction of
the term of military service, and annual review by parliament of the size of
the armed forces. The response of the national liberals, as drafted by south
Germans at Heidelberg on March 23, 1884, and ratified at a party congress in
Berlin, May 18, 1884, included preservation of a strong army, praise for Bismarck's foreign policy, support of his social security program, defense of the
protective tariff system as established, renewal of the antisocialist statute, and
higher taxes on brandy, sugar, and bourse transactions in order to reduce the
burden of direct taxes.[45] As Felix Rachfahl observed, the National Liberal
party gambled on the present, the Freedom party on the future. The former
announced its attachment to the existing government, the latter its expectation of a close relationship with the regime that would replace it.[46]

Bismarck may have expedited the secret negotiations that led to fusion of

EDUARD LASKER, 1884. (BILDARCHIV PREUSSISCHER KULTURBESITZ.)

[45] Felix Salomon, *Die deutschen Parteiprogramme* (Leipzig, 1907), pp. 33–37. On the drafting
of the new party program, see James Sheehan, *German Liberalism in the Nineteenth Century* (Chicago, 1978), pp. 199–202, 210–213.

[46] Rachfahl, "Eugen Richter," p. 332.

the left-liberals by insulting the memory of Eduard Lasker. On January 4, 1884, Lasker died of a heart attack in New York at the end of a six-month visit to the United States, during which he visited a brother in Galveston, was widely acclaimed by German immigrants, and was a guest at the formal opening of the Northern Pacific Railway's transcontinental line. Four days after his death the U.S. House of Representatives passed a resolution of condolence to the German Reichstag. "Resolved that this House has heard with deep regret of the death of the eminent German statesman Edward Lasker. That his loss is not alone to be mourned by the people of his native land, where his firm and constant exposition of and devotion to free and liberal ideas have materially advanced the social, political, and economic conditions of those peoples, but also by the lovers of liberty throughout the world." Transmitted by the American minister in Berlin to the German foreign office, the message was returned by the chancellor on the grounds that its description of Lasker's contribution to his country was erroneous.

When the Reichstag opened on March 7, this action was protested by Rickert, Hänel, and Richter and defended by Boetticher, creating a scene so turbulent that the speaker adjourned the chamber. On March 13, the day after his return from Friedrichsruh, Bismarck reopened the issue in the Reichstag. His tongue lubricated by one and a half bottles of Mosel wine,[47] he attacked the dead man for having opposed his policies and those of the Kaiser "from the outset." To the anger of the liberals he reminisced about those years when "no government bill could be passed without the stamp of Lasker on it." Lasker, he charged, had spoiled the negotiations with Bennigsen in 1878, split the party, and led its left wing into the progressive current. Hänel protested that Lasker had always recognized the chancellor's achievements. "In principle, he was my friend, in actuality my opponent—the one did not exclude the other," Bismarck replied. "He praised me but fought me. When someone stabs me relentlessly on the political dueling floor, while heaping me with praise, I naturally can't be very thankful to him."[48] Five members of the Prussian cabinet desired to attend Lasker's funeral, but Bismarck responded, "Most certainly not."[49]

---

[47] Rich and Fisher, eds., *Holstein Papers*, II, 103. The information came from Schweninger, Mar. 14, 1884.

[48] *SBR* (1884), I, 7–11, 28–34. See also Richard W. Dill, *Der Parlamentarier Eduard Lasker und die parlamentarische Stilentwicklung der Jahre 1867–1884* (Erlangen, 1956), pp. 200–204, and especially Louis L. Snyder, "Bismarck and the Lasker Resolution, 1884," *The Review of Politics*, 29 (1976), pp. 41–64.

[49] Rich and Fisher, eds., *Holstein Papers*, II, 67–68. According to Holstein, another purpose was to "teach a lesson" to the government of the United States, whose communications, "always uncivil," had become "positively boorish in recent years." In an article for the *Norddeutsche Allgemeine Zeitung*, which the editors refused to publish, the German chancellor declared *inter alia* that Lasker's mourners were mostly "American swine and trichinae." *Ibid.*, pp. 72, 86–87. Relations with the United States had become unsettled by the German prohibition in 1880 and 1882

No act of Bismarck's career illustrates better his need for universal support than this furious and inaccurate attack on a dead man for having had the temerity to follow his convictions even when they ran counter to those of the unifier of Germany. And yet even this assault had a tactical purpose. It was directed not merely at Lasker's memory but also at Lasker's associates in the leadership of the left-liberals. The chief purpose of his speech had been to give the group of moderates around Bennigsen more courage. "Now that Forckenbeck, Stauffenberg, and company have become *open* enemies," he told Holstein, "I want to attempt again the formation of a large middle party."[50]

---

of imported American pork, believed unsafe for consumption in Germany where pork was served with minimal cooking. The American minister in Berlin, Aaron Sargent, aggravated the dispute by threatening retaliation and insisting that the ban stemmed from Bismarck's desire to protect German pig farmers, not German consumers. Suellen Hoy and Walter Nugent, "Public Health or Protectionism? The German-American Pork War, 1880–1891," *Bulletin of the History of Medicine*, 63, pp. 198–224.

[50] Bussmann, ed., *Herbert von Bismarck*, p. 225.

CHAPTER FIVE

+|+|+|+|+|+|+|+|+|+|+|+|+|+|+|+|+|+|+|+|+|+|+|+|+|+|+|+|+|+|+|+|+|+|+|+|+|+

Expansion Overseas

S HIS HEALTH improved during the winter of 1883–1884, Bismarck found the energy to attack two new problems: the protection of German overseas trade in the era of "new imperialism" and the completion of the first stage of a new system of social insurance. Even as he sought ways to reduce the power of parliament and create obstacles that would diminish its chances of controlling the executive, he launched new initiatives that, contrary to his original intent, not only heightened executive authority in the Reich, but also gave to the Reichstag new angles of attack upon that authority in the critical areas of state finance and foreign policy. These initiatives were acts of state intervention designed to meet Germany's economic-social-political crisis of the late 1870s and early 1880s. They must be seen as but two aspects of an effort to build up a general combination of interest groups, hopefully even a popular consensus, that would undercut oppositional movements, severing the roots of the discontent that fed them and leaving them to wither on the vine. Earlier that effort was expended upon protective tariffs for the benefit of agriculture and industry and tax relief for property owners; now its aim was to secure foreign markets for Germany's excess industrial production and to attain social security for factory and mine workers in the form of health, injury, and old-age insurance.

Early Attitudes toward Colonies

Since the early nineteenth century German explorers, missionaries, geographers, historians, and publicists had occasionally argued for colonies on both commercial and patriotic grounds. In his *Das nationale System der politischen Ökonomie* (1841) Friedrich List wrote, "The fullest bloom of [a nation's] manufacturing strength, of the domestic and foreign commerce that grows from that strength, of a significant coastal and seagoing merchant fleet and large fishing industry, and finally of an imposing sea power is colonies."[1] During the following decades Germany's industrialization, the search for markets and materials, the expansion in overseas trade, and the exodus of German emigrants to foreign lands gave weight to List's theoretical argument. By the 1860s Hanseatic firms and joint-stock companies had prosperous investments in Africa

[1] Friedrich List, *Das nationale System der politischen Ökonomie*, in Artur Sommer, ed., *Friedrich List: Schriften, Reden, Briefe* (Berlin, 1930), VI, 289.

and the South Seas and commercial connections with Japan and China for which they sought government support and protection. In February 1867 the semiofficial *Norddeutsche Allgemeine Zeitung* published a series of articles advocating a colonial empire that some believe were written or fostered by Lothar Bucher, Bismarck's secretary and aide.[2]

If Bucher was involved, his views did not reflect those of the Bismarck government. In a letter to Roon of January 1868, Delbrück assessed the claimed advantages of colonies for German industry as "illusions for the most part." The experience of Britain and France showed that the cost often exceeded the value. It would be difficult to justify taxing "the entire nation in behalf of individual branches of trade and industry." The fledgling German navy was not equal to conflicts with other colonial powers and a conscript army could hardly be expected to serve in the tropics. It was best to leave the field to private enterprise; state intervention was out of place.[3] In 1871 Bismarck dismissed the proposal to take either Pondicherry or Vietnam from France with sarcasm: "I don't care for colonies at all. They are only good as supply posts." For Germany they would be "like sable coats worn by Polish noblemen who don't have shirts."[4] In 1873 Odo Russell reported him as saying that "colonies would only be a cause of weakness, because colonies could only be defended by powerful fleets, and Germany's geographical position did not necessitate her development into a first-class maritime power. . . . Many colonies had been offered him—he had rejected them, and wished only for coaling stations acquired by treaty from other nations."[5] For nearly two decades the foreign office received a steady flow of proposals for colonial ventures in various parts of the world. But the prince remained unmoved. "He will not hear of colonies, now as at other times," wrote Hohenlohe in 1880. "He says

---

[2] *Norddeutsche Allgemeine Zeitung*, Feb. 16–22, 1867. For descriptions of the colonial movement to 1882, see Mary E. Townsend, *The Rise and Fall of Germany's Colonial Empire, 1884–1918* (2d ed., New York, 1966), pp. 1–53; Alfred Zimmermann, *Geschichte der deutschen Kolonialpolitik* (Berlin, 1914), pp. 1–44; Maximilian von Hagen, *Bismarcks Kolonialpolitik* (Berlin, 1923), pp. 1–41; Woodruff Smith, *The German Colonial Empire* (Chapel Hill, 1978), pp. 3–27. On Hanseatic investments and trading activities overseas, see Helmut Washausen, *Hamburg und die Kolonialpolitik des deutschen Reiches 1880 bis 1890* (Hamburg, 1968), pp. 12ff.

[3] Delbrück to Roon, Jan. 9, 1868. DZA Potsdam, Reichskolonialamt, 7155, pp. 11–12. Historians have become unnecessarily confused about the date and authorship of this document. Contrary to Hans-Ulrich Wehler, *Bismarck und der Imperialismus* (Cologne, 1969), p. 191, the date is January 9, not 6. Wehler and others have attributed the letter to Bismarck, although the author is clearly Delbrück. At Bismarck's request Delbrück sent him a copy, referring to it as "my letter of the 9th of this month addressed to the naval minister." Delbrück to Bismarck, Jan. 11, 1868. DZA Potsdam, Reichskolonialamt, 7155, p. 10. Although the margins of the document contain question marks in Bismarck's hand, there is no reason to assume that the chancellor was in disagreement with the thrust of Delbrück's argument.

[4] Diary entry, Feb. 9, 1871. Moritz Busch, *Tagebuchblätter* (Leipzig, 1899), II, 157.

[5] Odo Russell to Lord Granville, Feb. 11, 1873. Lord Edmond Fitzmaurice, *The Life of Granville* (2d ed., London, 1905), II, 337.

we do not have an adequate fleet to protect them and our bureaucracy is not skillful enough to direct their management."[6]

Difficulties with the Reichstag during the next two years only deepened Bismarck's distrust. In November 1881–February 1882 Louis Baare, one of Germany's biggest industrialists, and Adolf André, Baare's brother-in-law and an old China hand, proposed that Germany purchase Formosa. Bismarck's marginalia show what he thought of that proposition. "Colonies require a mother country in which national feeling is stronger than the spirit of partisanship. With *this* Reichstag it is difficult enough just to maintain the Reich as it is, even to maintain the army within the country. As long as the Reich has not been consolidated financially, we cannot think of launching such difficult undertakings. Samoa is an example. A colonial administration would only provide parliament with a larger drill field. We cannot administer colonies directly, only support companies. But even for that we need a national Reichstag, one that has other purposes than to make speeches and difficulties for the government."[7]

Bismarck's disinterest was not shared by an increasing segment of the German public. The most vocal and successful propagandists for colonies were Ernst von Weber, Wilhelm Hübbe-Schleiden, and Friedrich Fabri. In numerous books, pamphlets, articles, and lectures they and others pounded home the thesis that the desperate conditions of German industry and the radicalization of the urban lower classes required colonies to drain off excess goods and people. Weber was a wealthy Saxon estate owner who had spent four years in South Africa; Hübbe-Schleiden was a former consular official who had managed a trading post in Equatorial Africa for three years; Fabri was the

---

[6] Diary, Feb. 22, 1880. Friedrich Curtius, ed., *Memoirs of Prince Chlodwig of Hohenlohe-Schillingsfuerst* (New York, 1906), II, 267. The assumption by some historians that Bismarck's conversion to colonialism can be traced back to 1876 rests on an "interview" that is presumed to have occurred in June of that year between Bismarck and two colonial zealots, one of whom was Ernst von Weber. This document first surfaced in *Kolonialpolitische Korrespondenz*, Jan. 7, 1885, a publication of the German Colonial Association, and quotes Bismarck as saying, "Such a great nation as Germany cannot dispense with colonies indefinitely." Heinrich von Poschinger, ed., *Fürst Bismarck als Volkswirth* (Berlin, 1889), I, 117–118. Every other source for this period quotes Bismarck as unqualifiedly against acquiring colonies. In *Vier Jahre in Afrika, 1871–1875* (Leipzig, 1878), II, 329, 339ff., 543–545, Weber wrote of submitting memoranda to the Kaiser and chancellor proposing acquisition of Delagoa Bay for the purpose of Germanizing the Transvaal, Orange Free State, and "the greater part of south Africa." He published Bismarck's letter of June 13, 1876, rejecting the proposal. There is no mention here of an interview. Maximilian von Hagen, *Bismarcks Kolonialpolitik* p. 52, fn. 2, speculated that the other participant in the interview was Adolf Lüderitz, and many historians have followed him in this. But Wilhelm Schüssler, Lüderitz's best biographer, knew of no such relationship between Weber and Lüderitz and dated the merchant's first interview with Bismarck on April 19, 1884. *Adolf Lüderitz* (Bremen, 1936), pp. 36–37, 91, 144–146.

[7] Baare to Bismarck, Nov. 29, 1882, and Eck to Bismarck, Feb. 10, 1883 (transmitting the foregoing document). DZA Potsdam, Reichskolonialamt, 7159, pp. 150–155.

chief executive of the *Rheinische Mission*, Germany's largest Protestant missionary organization, which had a post in Southwest Africa. "We live on a
volcano in the truest sense of the word," wrote Weber, "and it could easily
happen that on the hundredth anniversary of the French Revolution our
beautiful fatherland will be flooded by a sea of blood." Colonies would absorb
the surplus goods that flowed from German factories, provide investment for
surplus capital, and act as a "safety valve" (a common metaphor in the literature) to relieve social unrest. They would provide homes under the German
flag for millions of emigrants who would otherwise strengthen the United
States, already a formidable economic rival. They were as necessary as tariff
walls to secure the fruits of "national labor" from other foreign competitors.
In the Darwinian "struggle for existence" Germany could survive only by establishing German states overseas and a colonial empire like those of Britain,
France, Spain, Belgium, and the Netherlands.[8]

The appeal for economic growth was paired with the call for cultural expansion and the need to reawaken the German national spirit. "The final
goal, gentlemen, the end goal toward which all of our efforts have been
aimed," Hübbe-Schleiden declared, "is nothing less than to elevate our German people from a continental military power to a world cultural power—to
make a divided, embrangled European folk into an active nation that ener-
getically spans the globe and creatively promotes the civilization of mankind."[9] Economic and social, patriotic and national, humanistic and universal motivations were poured into the common crucible along with fear, hope,
pride, and avarice. But the emphasis throughout the literature is decidedly on
the patriotic and national motive. "The expansion of the German nationality
abroad on other continents," wrote Weber in a typical passage, "is to me from
the patriotic standpoint still more important" than the "expansion of our economic realm." The German people must secure for themselves "for all time"
a position in the world equal to that held by the Anglo-Saxon and Slavic-
Russian peoples.[10]

[8] Ernst von Weber, *Die Erweiterung des deutschen Wirtschaftsgebiets und die Grundlegung zu über-
seeischen deutschen Staaten* (Leipzig, 1879), pp. 7, 60, and *Vier Jahre*, II, 535ff.

[9] Wilhelm Hübbe-Schleiden, "Weltwirtschaft und die sie treibende Kraft, Vortrag gehalten in
der General-Versammlung des Westdeutschen Vereins für Colonisation und Export zu Köln, 4.
März 1882" (an undated leaflet), p. 3. See also his *Ethiopien: Studien über Westafrika* (Hamburg,
1879) and *Deutsche Kolonisation* (Hamburg, 1881).

[10] Weber, *Erweiterung*, p. iii, and *Vier Jahre*, II, 574. For a general description of the developing
agitation during the late 1870s and early 1880s, see Hans-Ulrich Wehler, *Imperialismus* (Cologne,
1969), pp. 142–157. Because his model emphasizes the disposal of excess industrial production
as the motivation for imperialism, Wehler largely ignores other motives. For a critique of Wehler's social imperialism model, see Otto Pflanze, "Bismarck's Herrschaftstechnik als Problem der
gegenwärtigen Historiographie," *Historische Zeitschrift*, 234 (1982), pp. 561–599. Fabri based the
case for colonies more on the glut of people than goods. Overpopulation, he wrote, was the
"heart of our economic crisis." Friedrich Fabri, *Bedarf Deutschland der Colonien? Eine politisch-*

As the number of interested persons grew, organizations were established and pressure groups formed. The first of significance was founded in 1868 by a group of economists, geographers, and explorers who chose the unwieldy title, Central Association for Commercial Geography and for Promotion of German Interests Abroad. Two organizations of geographers, the German African Society and the Society for Research on Equatorial Africa, fused in 1878 to become the African Society in Germany. Through their publications and conventions the Central Association and African Society sought to awaken entrepreneurs, politicians, and officials to the potentiality of overseas trade and colonies for the solution of Germany's economic and social problems. Branches of the Central Association sprang up in Barmen, Chemnitz, Freiburg, Jena, Kassel, Stuttgart, and other cities; allied organizations were located in Leipzig and Munich. Among its members by 1880 were a few prominent names from industry, banking, and government, for example, Adolf von Hansemann, Werner Siemens, Albrecht von Stosch, and Heinrich von Kusserow. Still the Central Association represented primarily north German shipping interests and the small and medium-sized manufacturers of finished goods in the Rhineland, southern Germany, Saxony, and Thuringia.

Organizations of greater potency came into being with the founding at Düsseldorf in January 1881 of the West German Association for Colonization and Export by "sixty of the most prominent representatives of the Rhenish-Westphalian large industry and wholesale trade" and at Frankfurt in late 1882 of the German Colonial Society, whose leadership included magnates from the aristocracy (Baron Hermann von Maltzan, Prince Hermann zu Hohenlohe-Langenburg, Count Adolf von Arnim-Boitzenburg), prominent officials (Prussian Minister of Agriculture Karl Friedenthal, Württemberg Minister-President Baron Friedrich von Varnbüler, Lord Mayor Johannes Miquel of Frankfurt), and the ubiquitous publicists Fabri and Hübbe-Schleiden.

ökonomische Betrachtung (3d ed., 1884), p. 22. In an Exkurs of three pages Wehler recognized the persistence of this argument in the literature, but concluded weakly that as a "direct motive for German colonial policy, emigration has often been overvalued." Wehler, Imperialismus, pp. 155–157. Wehler's summary does not show that Fabri in his concluding pages based his case for colonialism on the requirements of the German Kulturstaat and Machtstaat. In the final sentence, Fabri wrote: "If the new German Reich wishes to build and preserve a long-lasting foundation for its rewon power position, it must comprehend that position as a cultural mission and delay no longer in reactivating its colonizing task." Fabri, Bedarf Deutschland Kolonien?, p. 112. The works of Wilhelm Hübbe-Schleiden, furthermore, stress the national, cultural, and spiritual (in the Hegelian sense) motivation as much as, if not more than, the economic and social. For a more balanced analysis of motives expressed by the propagandists for colonies than that given by Wehler, see Klaus J. Bade, Friedrich Fabri und der Imperialismus in der Bismarckzeit (Freiburg im Breisgau, 1975), particularly pp. 21–24, and "Imperial Germany and West Africa: Colonial Movement, Business Interests, and Bismarck's 'Colonial Policies,' " in Stig Förster, Wolfgang J. Mommsen, and Ronald Robinson, Bismarck, Europe, and Africa: The Berlin Africa Conference 1884–1885 and the Onset of Partition (Oxford, 1988), pp. 121–147.

The German Colonial Society quickly outdistanced the rival Central Association to become a cover organization for the many associations and societies that had mushroomed in Germany during these years for similar purposes. By 1884 it possessed forty-three branches and nine thousand members. Although owners of small and medium-sized businesses predominated in numbers, the membership included most of Germany's big industrialists and financiers (Krupp, Haniel, Hoesch, Kirdorf, Baare, Hammacher, Röchling, Stumm, Schwartzkopff, Kardorff, Ujest, Ratibor, Pless, Schaffgotsch, Donnersmarck, Oppenheim, Hansemann, Salomonsohn, Schwabach, Bleichröder, Mendelssohn, and others). Corporate memberships were held by the Central Federation of German Industrialists, Association of German Iron and Steel Manufacturers, Union of German Iron Founders, twenty-three chambers of commerce, fifteen trade associations, and sixteen city councils and mayors of large municipalities. On the roster were names of prominent academicians and intelligentsia (Treitschke, Sybel, Ranke, Ratzel, Kirchoff, Schmoller, A. Wagner, Nasse, Wislicenius, and Schliemann) and prominent deputies, officials, and ministers (Kusserow, Lucius, Friedenthal, Hobrecht, Bennigsen, Varnbüler, Stolberg-Wernigerode, Arnim-Boitzenburg, Stöcker, Frankenberg-Tillowitz, Mirbach-Sorquitten). Judged by membership alone, the German Colonial Society quickly became the most formidable pressure group yet assembled in Germany.[11]

The views of the colonialists did not go uncontested. Although adherents of laissez-faire shared the belief that overproduction was the source of the economic problem that plagued Germany and the entire capitalist world, their solution was lower tariffs, free trade, and private initiative. And yet the Manchester school recognized that the tools and methods of what is now known as "laissez-faire expansionism" or "informal empire" were appropriate to the normal expansion of trade. They were consular services, coaling and naval stations, patrol squadrons, diplomatic pressure on native governments, and trade agreements either to secure most favored nation status or to perpetuate monopolies already enjoyed by German traders. What the free traders objected to was establishment of German sovereignty and direct rule over alien lands. Writers like Friedrich Kapp and F. C. Philippson regarded the acquisition of colonies as quixotic and anachronistic, a product of "confused, unclear, foggy, unhistorical, romantic" intellects. Men of this conviction still dominated the Congress of German Economists, which debated the issue at its annual meeting in 1880. Yet they lost the struggle in the German Commercial Association (*Handelstag*), whose annual convention approved the government's new colonial policy in 1885.[12]

[11] Wehler, *Imperialismus*, pp. 158–168; Bade, *Fabri*, pp. 102–105, 136–189; Fritz F. Müller, *Deutschland-Zanzibar-Ostafrika* (Berlin, 1959), pp. 51ff.

[12] Wehler, *Imperialismus*, pp. 147–148, 153; Bade, *Fabri*, pp. 109–120.

Bismarck's Conversion to Colonialism

Bismarck's shift to colonialism in 1883–1884 cannot be explained by public agitation and the pressure of business interests.[13] He was never loathe to oppose public opinion and private pressure when occasion demanded it, particularly in matters of foreign policy.[14] Ultimately the public clamor, like that for German unity in the 1860s, did provide him with a justification for decisions reached on other grounds. Nor does the "conspiracy thesis" suffice to explain his new interest in colonies and foreign trade. To be sure, family relationships existed between the Godeffroys and Bernhard von Bülow, state secretary of the Imperial Foreign Office until his death in October 1879, and between Adolf von Hansemann, chief of the *Disconto-Gesellschaft*, and Heinrich von Kusserow, senior official of the foreign office in charge of commercial affairs. And there were business links between Gustav Godeffroy, Adolf Hansemann, Gerson Bleichröder, and others.[15] That these businessmen sought to

[13] A wide variety of opinion exists concerning the motivation of Bismarck's decision to acquire colonies in 1883–1884. Mary E. Townsend concluded in *Origins of Modern German Colonialism, 1871–1885* (New York, 1921) and *The Rise and Fall of Germany's Colonial Empire, 1884–1918* (New York, 1930) that the chancellor had intended to acquire colonies since 1876, but guilefully concealed his intent until the opportunity came. The weakness of this view, also held by earlier German historians, is shown in William O. Aydelotte, "Wollte Bismarck Kolonien?" in Werner Conze, ed., *Deutschland und Europa: Festschrift für Hans Rothfels* (Düsseldorf, 1951). Those who believe he changed his mind in 1883–1884 are divided into two schools as to whether the decision arose from the dynamics of domestic or foreign affairs. Defenders of the first school differ as to which domestic concern was primary. For Marxist-Leninist historians "imperialism" (a word so propagandistically abused as to have become virtually meaningless) is a natural function of the late, monopoly stage of finance capitalism. A good example is Müller, *Deutschland-Zanzibar-Ostafrika*. Pointing in the same direction is G. W. F. Hallgarten, *Imperialismus vor 1914: Die soziologischen Grundlagen der Aussenpolitik europäischer Grossmächte vor dem ersten Weltkrieg* (2 vols., 2d ed., Munich, 1963). Wehler, *Imperialismus*, and Hans Rosenberg, *Grosse Depression und Bismarckzeit* (Berlin, 1967), are exponents of the view that the depression (with its attendant problems of overproduction, social distress, and fear of revolution) led to the decision both in the country and the chancellery. Aydelotte, on the other hand, believes that Bismarck inaugurated a colonial policy "in the hope of pleasing German public opinion, stimulating national sentiment and securing by this means a working majority in the insubordinate Reichstag." William O. Aydelotte, *Bismarck and British Colonial Policy* (Philadelphia, 1937), p. 18. The most extreme statement of the second school (dynamics of foreign policy) came from A. J. P. Taylor, who maintained that Bismarck needed a quarrel with England in order to cultivate closer relations with France and that to accomplish this end he raised a "provocative claim to ownerless lands, in which the German government had hitherto shown no interest." See his *Germany's First Bid for Colonies, 1884–1885* (London, 1938), pp. 1–15. An effective critique of this view is Henry Ashby Turner, Jr., "Bismarck's Imperialist Venture: Anti-British in Origin?" in Prosser Gifford and William Louis, eds., *Britain and Germany in Africa* (New Haven, 1967), pp. 47–82.

[14] During 1879–1882 Bismarck ignored mounting agitation for colonies in the press and decisively rejected petitions for military and naval intervention in Africa and other parts of the world. Bade, *Fabri*, pp. 121–133.

[15] Historians of Marxist orientation have stressed these personal connections. Although he aspired to present a broad "sociological" approach, Hallgarten focused on Kusserow as the man

use their contacts to influence government policy was only natural. Whether they influenced Bismarck is another matter.

As in drafting the constitution and the social insurance bills, Bismarck took from those whose advice he sought only what he wanted for his own purposes. In no area of public policy was he more sensitive toward and suspicious of influence peddlers than in foreign affairs. None of the three entrepreneurs whose interests he initially supported—Godeffroy, Woermann, and Lüderitz—possessed great wealth. Nor were they known to him personally before he took up their causes. His conferences with interested businessmen stemmed from his conviction that economic policies were more likely to be effective if shaped in consultation with "men of practical affairs" than with professional civil servants and legislators. When a subordinate in the foreign office warned that a Hamburg merchant was inclined to exploit "the interest of the fatherland" to advance his personal interests, Bismarck rebuked the official with the remark that business activity is "by its nature egoistic." The business interest of the merchant concerned was "also an interest of the fatherland and a fragment of the national interest."[16]

It has been persuasively argued that the "new imperialism" of the 1880s was but a natural extension of "laissez-faire expansionism."[17] Since 1862 the Bismarck government, like its predecessors, had promoted the growth of external as well as internal trade. Laissez-faire did not require the total rejection of government assistance either at home or abroad. The flood of economic legislation after 1867 was designed to create more favorable conditions for private enterprise. Equivalent actions abroad were the negotiation of trade treaties, establishment of consular services, creation of naval depots (Yokohama in 1867, Samoa in 1879), and the regular dispatch of war vessels to patrol the South Atlantic and the Pacific from China to the South Seas. Bismarck's desire to save the commercial empire of Godeffroy in Samoa during 1880 was a logical extension of the same policy—a practical attempt to preserve an enterprise upon whose survival rested the preponderance of German trade in the Polynesian Islands.[18]

---

who "created the entire German colonial policy." Kusserow's mother was an Oppenheim; one sister was the wife of banker Adolf Hansemann, another was married to iron merchant Louis Ravené. *Imperialismus*, I, 169, 211. See also Hans-Peter Jaeck, "Die deutsche Annexion," in Helmuth Stoecker, ed., *Kamerun unter deutscher Kolonialherrschaft* (Berlin, 1960), I, 52–61, and Müller, *Deutschland-Zanzibar-Ostafrika*, pp. 135ff. Turner has effectively rebutted this thesis in "Bismarck's Imperialist Venture," pp. 67–68. See also Wehler, *Imperialismus*, pp. 418–419, whose critique of Hallgarten inspired the latter to reply in "Wehler, der Imperialismus, und Ich: Eine geharnischte Antwort," *Geschichte in Wissenschaft und Unterricht*, 197 (1972), pp. 295–303.

[16] Krauel to Herbert von Bismarck, Mar. 20, 1885. Quoted in Wehler, *Imperialismus*, pp. 438, 444–445.

[17] Ronald Robinson and John Gallagher, "The Imperialism of Free Trade," *The Economic History Review*, 6 (1953), pp. 1–15, and *Africa and the Victorians, The Official Mind of Imperialism* (London, 1961).

[18] Wehler, *Imperialismus*, pp. 194ff.

The collapse throughout the capitalist world in late 1882 of the short-lived recovery in industry and finance, coupled with a sharp decline in grain prices, raised doubts about the continued adequacy of laissez-faire expansionism. It accelerated the scramble for secure markets and heightened the concern of governments everywhere for the preservation of foreign trade. The result was a new wave of protectionism at home and colonialism abroad. The "open doors" in Africa and the Pacific began to close, as the older colonial powers staked out new territories and expanded old frontiers. The prospect emerged that German exporters might be excluded not only from markets in which they had until now successfully competed, but also from vast new markets that were commonly presumed to lie waiting in the interiors of the African and Asian continents. If Germany was to have its India, the time had come to acquire it. What has been aptly described as *Torschlusspanik* developed— the anxiety that once sent villagers scurrying for the town gates at sunset. As the depression deepened in 1883–1884, the fear of being too late penetrated the foreign office and chancellery. Bismarck was not immune.[19]

Anxiety about the state of Germany's economy, concern about social stability, the search for secure and growing markets, and the dynamics of European and world politics were the principal conditions that led to Bismarck's change of policy on colonies in 1883–1884. But they were not the only ones. Colonialism offered yet another opportunity to extend the base of interest groups upon which the Prussian-German establishment rested. The shift to protectionism had embittered merchants to whom the maximum exchange of goods was both a matter of economic doctrine and financial survival. By dragooning Hamburg and Bremen into the Zollverein during 1883–1884, furthermore, the prince had dealt important mercantile interests another heavy

[19] In explaining to the public the "genesis" of his new policy, Bismarck stressed the need to "acquire new markets for our industry, even for the smallest industries . . . which feed very many Germans and provide them with work." Reichstag speech of Jan. 10, 1885. BR, X, 395. He expected that coastal protectorates would become routes of access into the African interior, where lived "hundreds of millions" of natives who would gradually become accustomed to purchasing European goods. Reichstag speech of Mar. 13, 1885. BR, XI, 72ff. (particularly p. 78). But other motives are also evident in his discourses. "The government . . . ascertained that the moment had come to hold open a door for German labor, German civilization, and German capital. If nothing proves to be behind the door, it will always be possible to surrender [protectorates]. . . . When the German nation senses within itself an excess of strength, entrepreneurial spirit, and spirit of discovery, we should at least open for it a door, through which it can realize [those feelings]." Reichstag speech of Mar. 16, 1885. BR, XI, 141–142. Bismarck's expressed motives followed those of the propagandists—with one important exception. He did not hold that, by directing German emigration either to imperial colonies or to regions like South Africa, Paraguay, or southern Brazil, the government and private enterprise could contribute to the "Germanization" of regions on other continents and hence enlarge the area of "German civilization." He held emigrating Germans in contempt for the speed with which they adapted themselves to other cultures. See particularly Bade, *Fabri*, pp. 191–200, 234, 354–360. Documentary evidence of this attitude is in DZA Potsdam, Auswärtiges Amt, 29768, pp. 42–45, 57–59, 140–144, 150–160, 165.

blow. Colonialism offered a way to attract the support of several interest groups in a critical election year: industrialists seeking to dump their products, merchants eager to expedite the exchange of goods, Hanseatic cities whose lifeblood was maritime commerce, and patriots who swelled with pride at the thought that Germany had the prospect of becoming a world power. It offered to the chancellor, beleaguered by oppositional majorities in two parliaments, the chance to demonstrate that the state under his leadership was still capable of positive action in behalf of capital as well as labor.

Yet Bismarck would never have joined the scramble for colonies if the international situation during 1883–1885 had not permitted their acquisition without serious harm to Germany's foreign relations in Europe. At no other time during his years of power did the constellation of European politics appear so favorable to colonial ventures. Every European great power during these years had some need of German friendship. Austria was bound to Germany by the Dual Alliance, Russia by the Three Emperors League. Conflicts of interest on two continents divided England and Russia, increasing the desire of both for German support. Under the government of Jules Ferry France turned its attention away from the Rhine in the quest for colonies, a quest that soon embroiled her with Britain at Suez and in northern Africa. Since 1881 Britain had been grateful for Germany's passive support for its policy in Egypt, which left London in a poor position to block German ambitions elsewhere in Africa.[20] For the time being it was possible to conduct a diplomatic struggle for territories and spheres of influence overseas without jeopardizing Germany's position in Europe. The door to colonial empire stood open and the vista beyond was tempting.

Into the Colonial Morass

Bismarck's decision to participate in the "new imperialism" ripened between August 1883 and April 1884, the period of his rejuvenation at the hands of Schweninger. By August 1883 he no longer had cause to fear imminent death from cancer. After eight months recuperating at Kissingen, Gastein, and Friedrichsruh he returned to Berlin in March 1884 refreshed and reinvigorated. A rapprochement with Crown Prince Friedrich Wilhelm, furthermore, gave him the prospect of remaining at the helm long enough to inaugurate a major departure in foreign policy. Undoubtedly he was teased by the possible advantages of colonialism: expectations of material prosperity and social stability, the gratitude of important mercantile and industrial interests, a new boost to national pride, and the chance to shore up the government's sagging political fortunes at the polls. Yet the master of *Realpolitik* had long ago perceived most of the reasons why colonies were not worth the effort: the ex-

[20] GP, IV, 25–50.

pense of their administration, inadequate benefits for the economy as a whole, diversion of naval and military power, and danger of a new dependence on the Reichstag. What led him to suppress these doubts was not only the fear of being too late but also the conclusion that a way could be found to enjoy the benefits of colonies without the disadvantages of possessing them. This was the mirage—for so it proved to be—that drew him step by step into the morass of colonialism, where he became mired in a policy whose adverse effects he had foreseen, but could not avoid. On one of the few occasions when Bismarck clearly permitted domestic concerns to dictate foreign policy (*Primat der Innenpolitik*) he came to regret the consequences.

From March to July 1883 officials of the German foreign office waxed increasingly apprehensive about the activities of other powers in regions where German traders had established themselves. From Adolf Woermann, head of a prominent firm engaged in the West African trade, and from the Hamburg chamber of commerce, usually a bastion of free trade, came warnings that the British were showing interest in the Cameroons; even the Spanish and Portuguese appeared ready to join the scramble for territories as yet unclaimed. Hamburg merchants called for the acquisition of strategically located islands and harbors, stationing of consuls, and dispatch of warships to patrol the coast.[21] In March was published the text of an Anglo-French convention, negotiated in June 1882, that defined the respective rights of the two powers on the West African coast. As interpreted by Kusserow to Bismarck, this somewhat ambiguous document appeared more menacing than the content justified.[22] In April 1883 the Australian colony of Queensland attempted to annex eastern New Guinea, where German traders were engaged, but its action was disavowed by the Gladstone government. The consequences of foreign annexation were brought home to the German government in April by London's repeated refusal, after extended negotiation, to honor the claims of German merchants for property expropriated after British annexation of the Fiji Islands in 1874.[23]

The impact of these developments on Bismarck can be seen in his shifting response to appeals from yet another Hanseatic businessman. In November 1882 Adolf Lüderitz, a Bremen tobacco importer, announced to the foreign office his intention to set up a trading post on the southwestern African coast

---

[21] Washausen, *Hamburg und die Kolonialpolitik*, pp. 141–154. Despite this appeal, which was influenced largely by Woermann, Hanseatic businessmen were, as Washausen showed, by no means sanguine about the immediate economic benefits of colonization.

[22] The scholar who discovered the discrepancy in Kusserow's analysis of the treaty text believed it intentional. Hans-Peter Jaeck, "Die deutsche Annexion," in Stoecker, *Kamerun*, I, 53ff. More likely, it was an error induced by Kusserow's zeal for the colonial cause. See Turner, "Bismarck's Imperialist Venture," pp. 53–54. The text is in G. Martens, ed., *Nouveau Recueil General de Traités*, 2d ser., vol. 18 (1893), pp. 613–617.

[23] Turner, "Bismarck's Imperialist Venture," pp. 56–57; GP, IV, 48ff.

and requested consular protection and an occasional visit by a German warship.[24] But Bismarck turned to the British, suggesting in February 1883 that London might wish to extend its protection to German settlers in the region; he added that, if this were not the case, Germany would provide "the same measure of protection that it gives to its subjects in other remote parts of the world—but without having the least desire to establish any footing in southern Africa."[25]

At the time Bismarck would genuinely have preferred to let Britain bear the expense of providing law and order in the region. By August, however, his attitude was different. During that month Lüderitz reappeared in the Wilhelmstrasse with the information that he had purchased the bay of Angra Pequena from a Hottentot chieftain, but his rights were being disputed by a British trader operating in the same area. Since no reply had been received to his démarche of February, Bismarck ordered a "cautious inquiry" in London to discover whether Britain claimed sovereignty over the southwest coast and, if so, on what grounds. No longer was there any suggestion that Germany would welcome British protection for German traders. In fact, the chancellor ordered the German consul at Cape Town to extend support and protection to the Lüderitz settlement and instructed the official press to emphasize that "the Bremen firm could count on the protection of the German government as long as its enterprise did not collide with the rights of foreigners."[26]

Bismarck's policy had changed. Instead of seeking the extension of British sovereignty over Angra Pequena and its environs, he now wished to extract from London an admission that Britain had no claims over that territory. Neither the foreign nor colonial offices in London had any plans for that desolate stretch of land. But the Cape Colony persuaded the government to reply, after a long delay, that, although the "Queen's sovereignty" had been proclaimed only over Walfish Bay and islands off Angra Pequena, the British government considered that "any claim to sovereignty or jurisdiction by a foreign power" over the rest of the coast between Angola and Cape Colony "would infringe their legitimate rights." This preposterous reply irritated Bismarck, who on December 27 instructed Münster to point out that it contradicted earlier British statements and to inquire upon what title the claim was based and what steps Britain had taken to make its rule effective.[27]

[24] Adolf Lüderitz to Foreign Office, Nov. 23, 1882. C. A. Lüderitz, ed., *Die Erschliessung von Deutsch-Südwest-Afrika durch Adolf Lüderitz* (Oldenburg, 1945), pp. 14–15. In 1878 Lüderitz, his tobacco business threatened by Bismarck's plan for a state monopoly, had decided to diversify, establishing a trading station in Lagos. *Ibid.*, pp. 12–13.

[25] Quoted in Taylor, *First Bid*, p. 24. For the dispatch of Feb. 4, 1883, from Berlin that was the basis for Herbert Bismarck's discussion with Pauncefote, see Aydelotte, *Bismarck and British Colonial Policy*, p. 38.

[26] Aydelotte, *Bismarck and British Colonial Policy*, pp. 32–34, 38–39. Lüderitz's first business at Angra Pequena was not tobacco but arms—two boatloads of rifles and revolvers for the use of Nama tribesmen in their war with the Herero. Bade, *Fabri*, p. 203.

[27] Aydelotte, *Bismarck and British Colonial Policy*, pp. 35–37. Turner has taken issue with Ay-

For more than a year this inquiry remained unanswered. Granville delegated the matter to Colonial Secretary Lord Derby, whose office was embarrassed to find that indeed Britain had no basis for the claim advanced. From the Cape Colony came pressure for annexation, but no willingness to assume the cost. Derby let the matter drift. As the months passed, Bismarck grew suspicious that the delay masked British preparations for annexation.[28] In late February 1884 Britain and Portugal shocked Europe by signing a treaty that gave Portugal sovereignty over the mouth of the Congo River. Since Portugal was considered a British client state, the treaty appeared to be the prelude to an expansion of British influence into central Africa. On March 12 Bismarck returned to Berlin convinced that Britain intended to extend its empire, jeopardizing the interests of about fifteen German firms with sixty factories on Africa's west coast.[29]

These suspicions made Bismarck vulnerable to renewed appeals from Lüderitz reinforced by Kusserow. In late February 1884 Lüderitz returned from Africa armed with documents substantiating his claims to acquisitions in the Angra Pequena region; on March 21 he turned them over to the foreign office and again asked for the protection of the German Reich. Kusserow, an indefatigable drafter of memoranda and a German patriot whose imagination was fired by the thought of overseas empire, produced at this critical moment the formula that offered his chief the chance—so it appeared—to pursue a colonial policy without acquiring colonies. In a memorandum dated April 8, 1884, he proposed that the Reich negotiate treaties with native chieftains guaranteeing their independence against other powers and issue to Lüderitz an imperial charter, one that followed the model of the royal charter recently granted by the British government to a company holding North Borneo. The charter would commission Lüderitz's company to govern (excluding foreign policy) as well as exploit the Angra Pequena region. Expense to the Reich would be minor, consisting merely of the appointment of a professional consul and the stationing of warships.[30] Kusserow's carefully calculated memorandum succeeded in dissolving Bismarck's lingering skepticism. Years later, after these measures had proved to be insufficient, he charged that Kusserow was the one who "dragged me into the colonial whirl."[31]

---

delotte's conclusion that Bismarck's aim as of September 1883 was to take possession of Angra Pequena. Rather he hoped, by securing a British disclaimer of ownership, to leave open to Lüderitz or a native chieftain the exercise of sovereignty under German protection. This would seem to be consistent with his later policy. Turner, "Bismarck's Imperialist Venture," pp. 60–61.

[28] Aydelotte, *Bismarck and British Colonial Policy*, pp. 24, 40ff.

[29] Alfred Zimmerman, *Geschichte der deutschen Kolonialpolitik* (Berlin, 1914), pp. 60–61.

[30] DZA Potsdam, Reichskolonialamt, 1995, pp. 155–169; also *Deutsches Kolonialblatt*, vol. 9 (Sept. 1, 1898), Beilage, pp. 1–4.

[31] Bismarck to Wilhelm Probst and others, Jan. 18, 1890. E. W. Pavenstedt, "A Conversation with Bismarck," *Journal of Modern History*, 6 (1934), p. 38. Kusserow's post was that of *Vortragender Rat* in division II (legal-commercial affairs) of the foreign office. In 1882–1883 Bismarck tried him out in the more prestigious division I (political affairs). Holstein, who disliked him,

Spurred by further warnings that British annexation was imminent, Bismarck resolved to act. On April 19, 1884, he summoned Lüderitz, assured him of the Reich's protection, and requested his plans for the territory.[32] Two days later the chancellor gained the approval of the Kaiser for whatever action was deemed necessary. On April 22 Lüderitz, obviously well coached by Kusserow, submitted a memorandum requesting "imperial protection" (*Reichsschutz*), the first use of this concept; no imperial colony (*Reichskolonie*) was intended and the Lüderitz company would both finance and administer the territory. The extension of *Reichsschutz* was to be officially announced at Cape Town by the German consul, made evident through frequent visits by German warships, and buttressed by treaties with native rulers.[33] On April 24, later regarded as the birthday of Germany's colonial empire, Bismarck telegraphed the German consul in Cape Town and Count Münster in London, announcing that Lüderitz had "a claim on the protection of the German Reich for his holdings."[34] The message was cryptic, concealing the importance of what was transpiring, while giving the chancellor a basis for claiming later that interested parties had been informed.

What Bismarck did for Lüderitz he intended to do for Woermann and other German traders in similar situations. Encouraged by the foreign office, Woermann and his associates acquired rights to extensive territories in the Cameroons in late 1883. On May 19, 1884, an "imperial commissioner" (the African explorer and German consul general at Tunis, Gustav Nachtigal, then standing by in Lisbon) was dispatched aboard a German gunboat to Togoland,

---

used the chance to unload upon Kusserow his most troublesome responsibility—Balkan affairs. Bismarck soon decided that the counselor was "not suited for political work" and shunted him back to division II, "the safest place for a tactless person." To Holstein's dismay, this put Kusserow unexpectedly in a key position, where in 1883–1884 he worked closely with the chancellor on the fast-breaking problems of overseas affairs. During the summer of 1884 Kusserow fell out with Caprivi, whose complaint led Bismarck to order Hatzfeldt to exercise strict control over him and to cut off his direct contacts with Lüderitz. "He works hard and knows a thing or two," was Bismarck's assessment, according to Holstein, "but I shouldn't sleep quietly a single night if he were a minister, even in Lisbon." In 1885 Kusserow was demoted to the post of Prussian envoy to Hamburg. Norman Rich and M. H. Fisher, eds., *The Holstein Papers: The Memoirs, Diaries and Correspondence of Friedrich von Holstein, 1837–1909* (4 vols., Cambridge, Eng., 1955–1963), II, 14, 27–29, 32, 159. Bismarck used Kusserow, knowing his limitations. To reverse the relationship is to distort it. Letters published as long ago as 1908 also show clearly that Bismarck generally held Kusserow at arms's length, much to the latter's distress. Heinrich von Poschinger, "Aus den Denkwürdigkeiten von Heinrich von Kusserow," *Deutsche Revue*, 33 (1908), pp. 63–72, 186–197, 267–274.

[32] Lüderitz to Foreign Office, Mar. 15, 21, and Apr. 8, 1884. DZA Potsdam, Reichskolonialamt, 1995, pp. 90–92, 98–126.

[33] Lüderitz to Foreign Office, Apr. 22 and May 1, 1884, with Bismarck marginalia. Lüderitz, *Die Erschliessung*, pp. 65–72. See also Turner, "Bismarck's Imperialist Venture," p. 70; Schüssler, *Lüderitz*, pp. 91–97.

[34] DZA Potsdam, Reichskolonialamt, 1995, pp. 153–154. Lüderitz, *Erschliessung*, pp. 72–73; Friedrich Prüser, "Carl Alexander von Weimar und Adolf Lüderitz," *Tradition*, 4 (1959), p. 181.

the Cameroons, and Angra Pequena. His orders were to conclude treaties of friendship, commerce, and protection with native rulers and, where appropriate, endorse agreements reached by the Hanseatic merchants. Again Bismarck eschewed imperial colonies, but his instructions contained words that went significantly beyond the term *Reichsschutz*, including "suzerainty" (*Oberhoheit*), "take possession" (*Besitzergreifung*), and "protectorate" (*Protektorat, Schutzherrschaft*).[35] On July 5 Nachtigal raised the German flag in Togoland and on July 14 in the Cameroons, five days before the arrival of British Consul Hewett bent on the same mission. While Nachtigal and Hewett competed for the allegiance of neighboring chieftains, the German corvettes *Leipzig* and *Elisabeth* steamed to Angra Pequena, where the German flag was raised on August 7. By the time Nachtigal arrived on October 7, Lüderitz and his agents had already extracted several "requests for protection" from native rulers.[36] At home the telegram announcing that Germany had established a huge "protective region" [*Schutzgebiet*] in western Africa came "like an electric shock."[37] The agitators who had propagated "colonial fever" so assiduously for five years were astounded to learn that the Bismarck government was not immune. Patriots rejoiced at this new exercise of German power. A decade and a half after Germany's unification, the nation appeared to have found a new mission far beyond the shores of Europe.

The German-French Entente

Needless to say, the British were bewildered by this sudden eruption of German activity. From their ambassador in Berlin, Lord Ampthill (Odo Russell), Granville had received repeated assurances that Bismarck was quite opposed to colonial ventures. His counterpart in London, Count Münster, was of the same belief, for Bismarck did not trust him with the truth. The British thought of the German chancellor as clever, but not devious; they failed to detect several clues that came their way. Until the summer of 1884 they were still under the illusion that Berlin was encouraging them to take Angra Pequena. Not until Herbert Bismarck arrived in London during the third week of June temporarily to supersede the perplexed Münster did Granville learn what the German chancellor actually wanted. Nor did the British suspect that further surprises awaited them in July. Ampthill had been led to believe that Nachtigal's journey was only a fact-finding mission, and London had ordered

[35] Hans Delbrück, ed., *Das Staatsarchiv: Sammlungen der officiellen Actenstücke zur Geschichte der Gegenwart*, vol. 43 (1885) (Leipzig, 1885), pp. 246–353.

[36] Lüderitz, *Erschliessung*, pp. 81ff.; Harry R. Rudin, *Germans in the Cameroons, 1884–1914* (New Haven, 1938), pp. 17ff. Bismarck was not pleased by Nachtigal's reports. In the margin of one he wrote, "A lot of words, little business content! No proposition, no proposal, just the diary of a traveler!" DZA Potsdam, Reichskolonialamt, 2035, p. 27.

[37] Heinrich von Treitschke quoted in Bade, *Fabri*, p. 233.

colonial authorities to render it assistance. "Too late Hewett" had been sent to forestall French, not German, acquisitions in West Africa. Nachtigal's flag-raising flabbergasted both the consul and his superiors in London.[38]

The lands that became German protectorates in June–July 1884 were not vital to Britain, and the wisest course would have been to relinquish them gracefully, welcoming Germany as a colonial neighbor and potential ally against France in the game of imperialism. Indeed Granville and his colleagues readily agreed to recognize the German protectorate at Angra Pequena. But the foreign and colonial offices were poorly coordinated under Lords Granville and Derby, and they were soon beset by complaints from the Cape Colony, traders, missionaries, and pro-British chieftains on the west coast who feared for their rights under German rule. The term "protective region" (Schutzgebiet) was new and left open many legitimate questions as to German intentions. Boundaries remained to be established and in this vast area that problem alone offered plenty of opportunity for misunderstandings and conflicts. The result was that the Gladstone cabinet bungled the matter, irritating Bismarck and the German public with obstacles and petty requirements (such as the stipulation that no penal colony be established at Angra Pequena) as the price for accepting German presence in Africa.[39]

Relations between London and Berlin deteriorated as Britain discovered that the protective regions established in July–August were not the end of German aspirations. Emboldened by his success on the southwest coast, Lüderitz dispatched an agent to acquire parts of Zululand and to claim Santa Lucia Bay on the east coast; he had visions of a German sphere stretching from the Atlantic though Bechuanaland and the Transvaal to the Indian Ocean.[40] The examples of Lüderitz and Woermann inspired other Hanseatic firms to launch projects during the winter of 1884–1885 on the Guinea coast west of the Niger River, north of Sierra Leone at the mouth of the Dubréka River, at Sangareah Bay in the region of French Senegambia, and on the opposite side of the continent at Witu in Kenya. To Bismarck these scattered claims were useful pawns to be exchanged in future negotiations with Britain and France for more important pieces on the African chessboard.[41]

One of those pieces was the protectorate established in East Africa opposite the Sultanate of Zanzibar. The race for colonies made Hanseatic firms long established on the island of Zanzibar anxious about continued access to the neighboring coast and the inland regions beyond. In September 1884 Bismarck responded to their appeals by dispatching an African traveler, Gerhard

---

[38] GP, IV, 64–93; Walter Bussmann, ed., Staatssekretär Graf Herbert von Bismarck: Aus seiner politischen Privatkorrespondenz (Göttingen, 1964), pp. 239–247; Aydelotte, Bismarck and British Colonial Policy, pp. 59ff.

[39] For a description of the way in which foreign policy was formulated in Britain under the Gladstone cabinet, see Aydelotte, Bismarck and British Colonial Policy, pp. 2ff.

[40] Schüssler, Lüderitz, pp. 141ff.

[41] Wehler, Imperialismus, pp. 292–298, 328–333, 367–372.

Rohlfs, newly appointed German consul general, to negotiate a new trade treaty with the Sultan of Zanzibar guaranteeing free transit for German goods. But Rohlfs's mission was quickly overshadowed by the exploits of Karl Peters. Son of a Protestant minister and not yet 30 years old, Peters had in March 1884 led in the founding of the Company for German Colonization to finance an expedition to Africa. His career shows better than anything else that the forces behind the new imperialism were not entirely economic. A man of towering ego with a pathological thirst for power, Peters expounded an imperial ideology based on a mixture of German nationalism and social Darwinism. His closest associates were Count Felix Behr, a wealthy landowner, and Friedrich Lange, a newspaper editor. Peters's company was more successful in raising capital than in deciding what to do with it. His quixotic schemes for establishing German colonies in areas of West Africa already claimed by the British were denied foreign office support.

Bent on engraving his name in German and world history, Peters finally set out with two companions for Zanzibar in September 1884 without the blessing of the German foreign office. Informed at Zanzibar that he could not expect imperial protection, he crossed undeterred to the mainland with three associates and in less than a month (November 23 to December 17, 1884) concluded about twelve treaties with African headmen, mostly village chiefs whom he promoted to "sultans." For small presents and vague promises they committed an area of 140,000 square kilometers to the Company for German Colonization. Back in Berlin on February 5, 1885, Peters requested and this time got imperial protection for the "last African paradise," which he proposed to enlarge to the dimensions of a German India. "The acquisition of land is very easy in East Africa," Bismarck sneered. "For a couple of guns one gets a piece of paper with several Negro crosses." Certainly Bismarck was not impelled here by pressure from German commercial interests but by the desire to gain for Germany secure routes of access to the interior of Africa, where he and his foreign office associates assumed lay a potentially huge market for German goods.[42]

Africa was not the only area over which the German eagle spread its wings during 1884. The news from Africa caused the Gladstone cabinet finally to respond favorably to numerous demands from Australia for the annexation of eastern New Guinea. German firms active in the region appealed to the Wilhelmstrasse for preemptive action. Among them was the Godeffroy firm (German South Seas Trading and Plantation Company) that had been rescued from insolvency in 1880 by a group of Berlin bankers, headed by David von Hansemann and Gerson von Bleichröder, despite the unwillingness of the Reichstag to guarantee its dividends "in the national interest." Well informed

[42] H. P. Merritt, "Bismarck and the German Interest in East Africa, 1884–1885," *The Historical Journal*, 21 (1978), pp. 97–116; Wehler, *Imperialismus*, pp. 333–342; Müller, *Deutschland-Zanzibar-Ostafrika*, pp. 97ff.

by Kusserow concerning the government's change of policy in Africa, the two bankers formed a "New Guinea Consortium," which in June 1884 despatched a secret expedition to duplicate Nachtigal's feat on the opposite side of the globe in New Guinea, adjacent New Britain, and the Solomon Islands. After being officially informed by London that Britain had decided to annex eastern New Guinea, Bismarck secretly gave the Bleichröder-Hansemann venture official approval.[43] When news arrived of the expedition's success, he informed the European powers in a circular note on December 23 of the new German protective region in the Pacific.[44] In London there was again surprise and indignation. As Joseph Chamberlain expressed it, "I don't care about New Guinea, and I am not afraid of German colonization, but I don't like to be cheeked by Bismarck or anyone else."[45]

For many months Bismarck had anticipated and begun to prepare for a confrontation with England. His technique was the familiar one: "to present Lord Granville with the necessity of either securing our political support by adopting a position toward our overseas interests that, if not altogether benevolent, is at least correct or looking on while we seek to further our interests in cooperation with other powers." In May 1884 Münster was ordered to utter this threat to Granville, while Nachtigal was under way down the African coast. But the pro-British ambassador ignored the menacing words, the meaning of which had been kept secret from him, and, to his chief's annoyance, engaged the foreign secretary instead in a gentlemanly discussion on the German desire for Helgoland, a secondary issue mentioned in the same dispatch.[46] That Bismarck's words were not idle can be seen in the messages that had been passing between Berlin and Paris since April. For years Bismarck had encouraged the government of Jules Ferry to indulge itself in colonial ventures; now he actually proposed that the two ancient enemies form an entente against England. "I do not want war with England," he told the French ambassador, "but I desire her to understand that, if the fleets of other nations unite, they will form a counterbalance on the ocean and oblige her to reckon with the interests of others. To that end it is necessary to accustom her to the thought that a Franco-German entente is not impossible."[47] By July the Paris *Figaro* and the *Kölnische Zeitung* (often a Bismarck mouthpiece) were openly discussing the possibility of an "alliance."[48]

Naturally the French government was wary. Yet the course of its relations with Britain during the latter part of 1884 compelled Paris to respond to Bis-

---

[43] Wehler, *Imperialismus*, pp. 223, 391–397.

[44] *Staatsarchiv*, vol. 44 (1885), pp. 205–216, 219–224.

[45] Quoted in Taylor, *First Bid*, p. 71.

[46] Bismarck to Münster, June 1, 1884. *GP*, IV, 59–62. See also the preliminary dispatches of May 5, 8, 24, and 25. *Ibid.*, pp. 50–59.

[47] *DDF*, ser. 1, vol. V, 424; see also pp. 264ff. Translation by Pearl Boring Mitchell, *The Bismarckian Policy of Reconciliation with France, 1875–1885* (Philadelphia, 1935), p. 154.

[48] Mitchell, *Policy of Reconciliation*, p. 152.

marck's enticements. In August an international conference at London over the foreign debts of the Egyptian government, which was close to bankruptcy, broke up because of differences between France and Britain. Bismarck's tactic was to support the French position in this dispute sufficiently to alarm, without alienating, the Gladstone cabinet in the expectation of softening its resistance to the German position in the continuing disputes over rights and frontiers in Africa.[49] To the same end he continued to work for an entente with France directed against the British-Portuguese attempt to control the Congo. During June–September these efforts bore fruit when Paris and Berlin joined in summoning an international congress on the Congo with the purpose of guaranteeing freedom of commercial access to central Africa, including King Leopold's newly established Congo Free State.[50] From November 15, 1884, to February 26, 1885, representatives of the European powers and the United States met at Berlin under Hatzfeldt's chairmanship. The result was an agreement securing free trade in both the Congo and Niger basins, creating an international commission to oversee freedom of navigation on the Congo, and defining the principle of effective occupation as the basis for colonial claims. Bismarck's statesmanship, it appeared at the time, had kept open for German business interests the vast heartland of the African continent and the enormous potential markets presumed to exist there. Where he could not establish "protective regions" for Germany, he could at least preserve an "open door."[51]

In March 1885 another London conference finally resolved the issue of Egypt's finances on terms satisfactory to France, which had the backing not only of Germany, but also of Russia, Austria, and Italy. By facing England in concert with other continental powers, the French avoided becoming dependent on Germany. Bismarck, on the other hand, constantly stressed to the London cabinet that his support of France on the Egyptian issue was entirely due to Britain's hostility to German aims elsewhere in the colonial world. Although eager to profit from their accord, neither Germany nor France was willing to antagonize Britain to the point that they must ally against her. Such was the nature of the "French-German entente" of 1884–1885.

Again the German chancellor operated on two fronts simultaneously, supporting France in the conference on Egypt, while sending Herbert to London to negotiate with Granville a settlement of colonial differences. The course of Herbert's visit in March 1885 was similar to that of June 1884—a series of interviews that began with recrimination and ended with a general agreement in which the British yielded most of what his father wanted. Eastern New Guinea was partitioned by the two powers; Britain recognized German claims in the Cameroons; Germany surrendered the pawn of Santa Lucia Bay; the

[49] GP, IV, 93–99.
[50] GP, III, 420–426; Mitchell, Policy of Reconciliation, pp. 157ff., 180ff.
[51] Staatsarchiv, vol. 45 (1886), pp. 47–242.

BISMARCK, THE PROUD PEACOCK IN (MODIFIED) MILITARY UNIFORM, SHOWING OFF HIS FEATHERS: "EU-
ROPEAN PEACE, CONGO CONFERENCE." THE FAMOUS THREE HAIRS, BELOVED OF CARTOONISTS, ARE LA-
BELED "COLONIAL POLICY," "FOREIGN POLICY," AND "TRADE POLICY"; HIS BOOTS, "INTERIOR AFFAIRS."
WILHELM SCHOLZ IN *KLADDERADATSCH*, 1884.

independence of the Sultanate of Zanzibar was recognized; and Britain recognized German acquisitions in Tanganyika. Herbert was sent home with many assurances of English friendship, and Gladstone made it official in the House of Commons on March 12, when he bestowed his blessing on Germany's colonial ventures and expressed his willingness to redress future grievances as they arose.[52]

Although the Ferry government fell at the end of March 1885, the last fruit of its rapprochement with Germany was harvested by its successor in an agreement signed December 24, 1885, which settled French and German colonial differences. The treaty fixed the boundary line between the Cameroons and the French Congo and recognized France's claim to Senegal, Germany's claim to Togoland, and the rights of both in certain South Sea islands. The mutual benefits of their collaboration led some even to hope for lasting reconciliation. But to Frenchmen with long memories, kept alive by the right-wing press, the entente was a "sellout" to the victor of 1871, whose sole aim was to seduce France into forgetting the loss of Alsace-Lorraine.[53]

End of the Mirage

In outlining his vision of overseas expansion to the Reichstag during 1884–1885, Bismarck stressed that he was opposed to colonization à la Française, that is, the acquisition of land, followed by colonists, officials, garrisons, etc.[54] The flag should follow trade, not precede it. "That is my aim. Whether we can attain that immediately or whether we must first nurture companies that are strong enough [to precede the flag] I don't know, but my goal in those regions is the governing merchant and not the governing bureaucrat—not the governing military and Prussian official. Our privy counselors and junior officers are outstanding at home, but out there in colonial regions I expect more from Hanseatics who have been abroad, and I am taking pains to push the obligation of governing off on these entrepreneurs. My goal is government by merchant companies, over whom hovers the supervision and protection of the Reich and Kaiser."[55] Nevertheless, all the German *Schutzgebiete* ultimately became "hothouse colonies" of the sort he disdained.

The story of the *Schutzgebiet* Southwest Africa is illustrative. Control over an area half again the size of Germany itself required far greater resources than Lüderitz possessed. To keep the British, who already possessed Walfish Bay,

[52] GP, IV, 100–107. Taylor, *First Bid*, pp. 78–79; Mitchell, *Policy of Reconciliation*, pp. 191–192.

[53] *Staatsarchiv*, vol. 46 (1886), pp. 243–245; Mitchell, *Policy of Reconciliation*, pp. 162–167.

[54] Reichstag speeches of June 26, 1884, and Mar. 16, 1885. BR, X, 193ff., and XI, 137ff.

[55] Reichstag speech of Nov. 28, 1885. BR, XI, 282ff. See also BP, I, 231, and his instruction to Nachtigal in Kurt Herrfurth, *Fürst Bismarck und die Kolonialpolitik* (Berlin, 1917), pp. 122–123.

from taking the northern part, Bismarck had to order German warships to "raise the flag" at some points months before company agents arrived with their land contracts. Quick action by Cecil Rhodes, who initiated a British protectorate over Bechuanaland in December 1884, cut off the German *Schutzgebiet* from the Transvaal and restricted it in the west to a largely barren "sandlot" (in Eugen Richter's contemptuous words). Lüderitz had to recognize that the region was unsuitable for trade or colonists. He hoped for minerals, but the best mineral prospects were in the north behind Walfish Bay. In June 1884 the mineral rights in that region were purchased by a consortium formed by Hansemann, Bleichröder, and a Bremen merchant named Dyes. Discouraged by reports from his own geologists about prospects in the south and running short of capital, Lüderitz offered to sell his mineral rights to the Hansemann group for 500,000 marks and 5 percent of the profits of the consortium. When refused, he threatened to sell out to British interests! Less than a year after he had extended the Reich's protection to Lüderitz's company, Bismarck had to intervene to prevent it from being sold to foreign capitalists.[56]

In September 1883 none other than Fabri, whose mission was located in the new *Schutzgebiet*, had warned that the prospects for trade and settlement at Angra Pequena were poor in a series of articles published by the *Kölnische Zeitung*. "It is," he wrote, "one of the least economic coasts on earth—no tree, no bush, no leaf is to be seen, nothing but sand, eternally clear sky and the deep blue sea."[57] "What a terrible desert we have acquired," was Nachtigal's first reaction to Angra Pequena.[58] His reports to the foreign office about economic development were pessimistic, except for the possibility of mining in the Walfish Bay region.[59] Even the Hansemann-Bleichröder-Dyes consortium was soon disillusioned about the chance for profits. It took pressure from the foreign office, patriotic talk from the German Colonial Society, and armtwisting by Hammacher, Miquel, Schwabach, and others to get a group of bankers and industrialists to capitalize (April 1885) the German Colonial Company for Southwest Africa, which bought out both Lüderitz (300,000 marks) and the consortium (213,000 marks). Declaring that the enterprise

[56] Schüssler, *Lüderitz*, pp. 212–221; Lüderitz, *Erschliessung*, pp. 102ff.; L. Sander, *Geschichte der deutschen Kolonial-Gesellschaft für Südwest-Afrika* (Berlin, 1912), I, pp. 12ff.

[57] "Deutsche Untersuchungen in Südwest-Afrika," *Kölnische Zeitung*, Sept. 9, 10, 11, and 12, 1883; Schüssler, *Lüderitz*, pp. 62–64. Fabri was appalled and angered by the success of Lüderitz, the arms smuggler, at the chancellery and foreign office, which had been deaf to his own entreaties. He feared the disillusionment that would result from the attempt to attract German settlers and traders to an arid region, where mining was the only promising activity, and only at Walfish Bay, not at Angra Pequena. Bade, *Fabri*, pp. 204–207.

[58] Max Buchner, *Aurora Colonialis: Bruchstücke eines Tagebuchs aus dem ersten Beginn unserer Kolonialpolitik 1884–1885* (Munich, 1914), p. 206. Since Angra Pequena had none, water had to be shipped in from Cape Town, a journey of three weeks. DZA Potsdam, Reichskolonialamt, 1995, pp. 135–136.

[59] DZA Potsdam, Reichskolonialamt, 2007, pp. 5–8; 2035, pp. 2–27, 48–71.

was "for the public interest" rather than private gain, the company demanded and got exemption from the stamp tax. "We have had to bite into this sour apple because the foreign office urgently wished it," fumed Hammacher.[60] In October 1888 the Herero tribe, disappointed by the German failure to provide real military assistance against their native foes, renounced the German "protectorate." The imperial commissar and company officials fled ignominiously to the safety of English guns at Walfish Bay. Bismarck's efforts to get the Colonial Company to recruit and arm a native militia were in vain. He had no choice but to send German troops to reestablish control over the hinterland. But that was not all. Appalled by these difficulties, the owners of the company had to be kept from selling it to an English bidder in late 1889. Not until the discovery of a major copper deposit near Tsumeb in 1906 and of diamonds in the Namib Desert in 1908 did German capitalists take a renewed interest in "Lüderitzland."[61]

Although the commercial value of West Africa had been long established, some of the same problems appeared in the *Schutzgebiet* Togoland-Cameroons. The "egoism" that Bismarck had recognized as a natural attribute of business life frustrated attempts of the foreign office to merge the Hanseatic firms operating in the region into a single charter company capable of administering its internal affairs. Summoning Woermann and his competitors to Friedrichsruh in September 1884, the chancellor insisted that they at least form a syndicate to govern what his diplomacy had secured for them. "I cannot transfer a single Prussian *Landrat* to the Cameroons!" The Syndicate for West Africa, founded under Woermann's chairmanship, was willing to assume only advisory functions, insisting on the appointment of a governor to exercise sovereignty (*Landeshoheit*) in the name of the Kaiser.[62] Native unrest led to the dispatch of a naval squadron, which in December 1884 restored "the honor of the German flag" by bombarding and burning several native villages, leaving many dead and wounded. Fever and dysentery attacked the victors, to whom jungles thick with mosquitoes seemed like "hell" itself. Shortly before his death in 1885, Nachtigal recommended that the chancellor abandon the idea that German traders could govern; their trading methods, especially the copious dispensing of spirits, did not inspire respect; seldom would they be uninvolved and impartial on issues of law and justice.[63] On January 13, 1885, the Reichstag passed a government bill—avidly supported by Woermann as deputy for Hamburg—providing the salary for an imperial governor and, some months later, an appropriation to construct buildings and hire officials. West

[60] Sander, *Kolonial-Gesellschaft*, pp. 17ff. The prospectus was candid about the prospects. "For the foreseeable future no interest or, for that matter, gain on the invested capital can be expected. The contribution must be made as a patriotic duty, somewhat like a sacrifice." *Ibid.*, p. 20.

[61] Wehler, *Imperialismus*, pp. 282–292; Bade, *Fabri*, pp. 321–333.

[62] Wehler, *Imperialismus*, pp. 320–328.

[63] Buchner to Bismarck, Apr. 17, 1885. Buchner, *Aurora Colonialis*, pp. 190ff.

Africa soon received its *Landrat*, Baron von Soden, first governor of the Cameroons and commissioner for Togoland. In December 1886 the Syndicate for West Africa dissolved; with it disappeared the last pretence that private enterprise participated in the government of the Cameroons.[64]

Karl Peters's Company for German Colonization received its letter of protection (*Schutzbrief*) on February 26, 1885, the concluding day of the Congo conference, at which Bismarck had the chance to sniff out the aims of the colonial powers. Next Peters founded the German East Africa Company, a commandite enterprise, to raise capital for his venture. An infusion of cash from Karl von der Heydt, a banker at Elberfeld, enabled him to send out ten expeditions in quick succession to enlarge his domain inland through new contracts with native chiefs. Said Bargasch, sultan of Zanzibar, was outraged by the German declaration of a protectorate over a region he claimed and was unappeased by Bismarck's declaration that Germany recognized his sovereignty over the island of Zanzibar and adjacent coast. But the sultan was helpless to fend for his rights without British support. In London and the Cape Colony it was recognized that the German presence in East Africa posed a greater threat to Britain's colonial plans than it did in West and Southwest Africa. Yet the British cabinet, involved in a crisis with Russia over Afghanistan and with France over Egypt, was compelled to yield to Bismarck's repeated threats that he would regard British conduct in East Africa as a "test" of English friendship. Bismarck rejected Peters's argument that the interests of the sultan and the German Empire were so opposed that the success of either meant ruin for the other. Germany must attempt, he wrote, to maintain a good relationship with the sultan "by the right alternation of threat and goodwill." Threatened by a German naval blockade and bombardment, Said Bargasch earned German goodwill by concluding a treaty in December 1885 that recognized the German protectorate. Delimitation of the frontier between sultanate and protectorate and of the routes of access from the coast to the interior was left to a combined British, French, and German commission. Its British representative was compelled by the new Salisbury government, under considerable pressure from Berlin ("Continuing frictions in colonial regions can ultimately lead to political opposition everywhere"), to accept a settlement that violated the sultan's sovereignty in some respects, but satisfied Bismarck. By an exchange of notes on October 29, 1886, the British and German governments achieved a common policy toward the sultanate and a division of East Africa into two great spheres of influence between the lands claimed by the German East Africa Company (Tanganyika) and the British East Africa Company (Kenya). Peters's initiative and Bismarck's diplomacy had won an enormous region for German exploitation.[65]

[64] Rudin, *Germany in the Cameroons*, pp. 120ff., 178ff.; Washausen, *Hamburg und die Kolonialpolitik*, pp. 121–127.

[65] GP, IV, 143–173; SEG (1899), pp. 155ff.; Wehler, *Imperialismus*, pp. 343–358.

Herbert Bismarck, who had won his spurs as a diplomat on the colonial issue during two special missions to London, was already appalled at the prize. On June 12, 1884, he wrote to brother Bill, "I'm afraid that, with the whole of East Africa, Kusserow has led us into a manure pile." On that day Sir Edward Malet, the new British ambassador in Berlin, had warned Herbert, "If you take over such a huge protectorate, then you have to provide protection, and that will be expensive and difficult." On its borders, so Herbert had heard, were "wild, man-eating tribesmen," possibly millions of them. Even the Arab inhabitants and their sultan were untrustworthy and might well turn on the Germans when it served their interests to do so.[66] Herbert's fears and Malet's observation proved to be prophetic.

Again the German foreign office encountered difficulty in creating a charter company. The Hamburg firms of O'Swald and Hansing, long established at Zanzibar and capitalized at more than a million marks, found "impertinent" Peters's suggestion that they permit themselves to be absorbed by the German East Africa Company, with 50,000 marks in resources. Like Lüderitz, Peters had to be restrained from selling out his interests to English capitalists. In this case Wilhelm Oechelhäuser, president of the *Deutsche Kontinental Gas-Gesellschaft* and national liberal deputy, took over Hammacher's role, appealing to patriotism as well as profit in an effort to tap the needed capital. Such was the distrust of Peters in the German financial community that little could be accomplished before he was ousted. Even so, it required 500,000 marks from the Kaiser's private funds, disguised as a *Seehandlung* investment, to prime the pump that ultimately produced 3,480,000 marks in new capital for the East Africa Company from an assortment of big bankers, big industrialists, and Hamburg merchants. Reorganized in February 1887 as a corporation under the Prussian law code of 1791, the company scored an early success when the sultan agreed to lease to it all of his coastal lands and customs collections.[67]

By the spring of 1888 Bismarck finally appeared to be on the verge of achieving in East Africa a self-financed, self-governing *Schutzgebiet*. But again the mirage evaporated. When the German East Africa Company attempted in August to establish its governing authority under the treaty with the Sultan of Zanzibar, Moslem traders, who feared loss of trade and influence, and African natives, resentful of heavy-handed treatment by company employees, rose in revolt. Company agents fled for their lives to the safety of gunboats on the coast. The uprising presented Bismarck with a difficult choice. To abandon the protectorate meant a catastrophic loss of prestige at home and abroad. His government had expended four years of hard diplomatic effort to secure the *Schutzgebiet* and had put pressure on German capitalists to invest the capital with which to exploit and govern it. Reconquest, on the other hand,

---

[66] Herbert to Bill Bismarck, June 12, 1885. Bussmann, ed., *Herbert von Bismarck*, p. 283.

[67] On the financial manipulations of Peters, Behr, and associates, including fraudulent land sales to German farmers, see Müller, *Deutschland-Zanzibar-Ostafrika*, pp. 134ff.

would require a military expedition (expected to cost 10,000,000 marks), garrisons to hold the territory, and a colonial administration to govern it. There was, furthermore, the problem of obtaining funds from the Reichstag at a time when colonial fever had diminished.[68]

But here Fabri, whose continuing memorials to the government Bismarck had finally begun to take seriously, provided him with a solution. One of the by-products of the new imperialism during the 1880s was a renewed humanitarian concern about the slave traffic in central Africa. At the Berlin conference of 1885 on the Congo, the European powers pledged to abolish slavery and the slave trade in Africa. Public agitation over the issue, fueled by Catholic demands for a "crusade" against slave merchants, continued to mount in Germany. Bismarck had never taken an interest in the slave problem, ordering his officials not to become involved. But Fabri pointed out to him that the agitation could be manipulated to reinvigorate the fading popular interest in colonialism, consolidate the progovernment majority (cartel) in the Reichstag, convert the Center party to the cause of imperialism, and thereby secure a large majority in parliament for a colonial war.

In late 1888 Bismarck became a sudden convert to the antislavery cause. In secret collaboration with the publicist Fabri, he helped fuel the popular demand for an end to the barbarities of the slave trade, so luridly and inventively described in the daily press. "Can't we scare up some vivid details about inhuman treatment?" he asked subordinates. The strategy worked, for the Center joined the national liberals and two conservative parties of the majority coalition in voting for the funds to launch the expedition, over the bitter opposition of the Freedom party and social democrats. In January 1889 Bismarck could despatch the explorer Hermann von Wissmann to Africa with just one instruction: "Be victorious!" With a mercenary force raised in Egypt and Mozambique, Wissmann reconquered the lost protectorate and rid it not of slavery—already formally abolished in the region, as both Fabri and Bismarck knew—but of its Muslim rebels.[69]

Not even in the South Pacific did the *Schutzgebiet* develop according to plan. Certainly the New Guinea Company, established in 1885, did not lack experienced leadership. Headed by David Hansemann, the company's investors were Bleichröder, Oppenheim, Hammacher, Prince Donnersmarck, Prince Hohenlohe-Öhringen, Prince Hatzfeldt-Trachenberg, Count Stolberg-Wernigerode, the Duke of Ujest, Werner von Siemens, Louis Ravené, and Adolf Woermann. Being devoted primarily to the "common good" and only secondarily to "profit and gain," Hansemann's enterprise followed the example of the German East Africa Company by incorporating under the

[68] Wehler, *Imperialismus*, pp. 350–352, 359–367; Müller, *Deutschland-Zanzibar-Ostafrika*, pp. 357ff. See his defense of the government's East African policy in the Reichstag debate of Jan. 15, 1889. *BR*, XII, 531ff.

[69] Bade, *Fabri*, pp. 326–328.

Prussian law code of 1791, a device less restrictive than the joint-stock principle. By exaggerating its monopolistic privileges under the Kaiser's *Schutz-brief* granted in May 1885, Hansemann succeeded in forcing participation by its only major competitor, the firm of Robertson and Hernscheim, with properties in New Britain. The Anglo-German agreement of April 1886 was a disappointment to the company because it guaranteed free trade, a great advantage to nearby Australia. Protests to Bismarck, however, were of no avail, for the chancellor was no longer in a position to beard the British lion. By November of that year the company had expanded into the Solomon Islands and had invested about 2,000,000 marks in the enterprise. But the return was disappointing. In 1896 the company sold out to the Reich for 4,000,000 marks. The last charter company gave way to an imperial colony. [70]

In Samoa as well, overseas ventures went sour for the chancellor. Fears for the continued preponderance of German commercial interests there led him after 1884 to seek exclusive control over the islands, with governmental authority to be exercised through a native ruler. But first Britain and then the United States persisted in holding on to treaty rights. The German consul, furthermore, tended to act independently of Berlin, taking sides in the endemic civil wars between native rulers and factions. In late 1888 a native ambush cost fifty German casualties. The consul declared war on the rebels and martial law for all westerners. This foolhardy action produced a dangerous diplomatic crisis with the United States. As American warships headed for Samoa, Bismarck disavowed and publicly reproved the consul; for him the *furor consularis* had become an annoyance and an unnecessary disturbance to German foreign relations. [71] From April to June 1889 Berlin was the scene of a tripartite conference in which the three powers established their coprotectorate over the islands. This proved to be just a step toward partition (1899) and ultimate founding of another imperial colony of the type Bismarck had striven from the outset to avoid. [72]

Colonies did not provide the safety valve for excess production either in goods or people that colonial zealots expected. Between 1887 and 1906, 1,085,124 persons left Germany as emigrants, of whom 1,007,574 chose the United States rather than German colonies. In 1903 only 5,125 Germans lived in the colonies, including 1,567 soldiers and officials; by 1913 the number was only 19,696, of whom 3,000 were soldiers and gendarmes. Nor did overseas possessions prove valuable as a habitat for German capital. By 1914 German capitalists had invested a mere 500,000 marks in colonies (chiefly railways, harbors, plantations, and mining)—only about 2 percent of all German capital invested abroad. In 1891 Germany imported from its colonies

[70] Wehler, *Imperialismus*, pp. 396–398.

[71] Paul M. Kennedy, *The Samoan Tangle: A Study in Anglo-German-American Relations, 1878–1900* (New York, 1974), pp. 1–38.

[72] *Ibid.*, pp. 87–239.

goods valued at 59,000,000 marks, constituting only 0.13 percent of all imports (46,560,000,000 marks). In the same year the colonies absorbed German products worth 60,000,000 marks or only 0.17 percent of all exports (35,039,000,000 marks). By 1910 the proportions were only slightly higher—0.54 percent of all imports and 0.73 percent of all exports.[73]

The German goods that Africans most preferred were not those of heavy industry, on the whole, but liquor, weapons, and gunpowder, which constituted from 30 to 60 percent of all goods shipped to the colonies. The proportionate weight of spirits in cargoes departing from Hamburg for Africa was 64 percent in 1884, 58 percent in 1885, 52 percent in 1886, 56 percent in 1887. West Africa was the chief consumer, East Africa having a large Moslem population.[74] In the Reichstag Adolf Woermann argued that to civilize required some kind of stimulus. "Who is closer to us?" he asked, "Thousands of Germans who earn their bread and livelihood by this trade or the small number of Negroes who fall victim to liquor."[75] Although he did not express himself so crudely, Bismarck, the Pomeranian distiller, was not loathe to promote the drinking habits of Africans. When Great Britain, supported by Belgium, proposed at the Congo conference that trade in liquor and weapons be discouraged on humanitarian grounds by imposing import duties, Bismarck instructed the German delegation (which included Woermann) to oppose the measure because it was not among the purposes of the congress.[76]

By the end of his career, nevertheless, Bismarck wished that he had never become involved in the "colonial swindle." He doubted the capacity of German merchants to "make money" out of colonies and of German officials to govern them and considered selling the German interest in Southwest Africa, East Africa, and Samoa.[77] He was vexed not only because of the failure of the colonies to become important assets to the German economy, but also because of the dangers they produced for German foreign relations and the burdens they imposed on the foreign office and imperial budget. In March–June 1889 he was receptive to a proposal from British Prime Minister Lord Salisbury that Germany accept Helgoland in exchange for the whole of Southwest Africa.[78] In September of the same year Bismarck attempted to persuade the

[73] Washausen, Hamburg und die Kolonialpolitik, pp. 181–184.

[74] Ibid., pp. 183–184.

[75] Quoted in Wehler, Imperialismus, p. 327.

[76] Bade, Fabri, pp. 274–275. On Bismarck and the distillery industry see pp. 212–215, 242–243.

[77] Arthur von Brauer, Im Dienste Bismarcks (Berlin, 1936), pp. 289–290; Freiherr Lucius von Ballhausen, Bismarck-Erinnerungen (Stuttgart, 1920), pp. 500–501.

[78] GP, IV, 408–417. Rather than lead Britain by precipitate action to the conclusion that Germany was eager to strike a bargain, Bismarck ordered the Berlin foreign office to await a concrete proposal from London. GP, IV, 408–417. But there can be no doubt that the chancellor was indeed eager for a swap. Herbert, now state secretary in the foreign office, expressed his father's opinion when he wrote, "I lay no great weight on Southwest Africa because of the lack

city of Hamburg and its merchants to assume the burden of administering the colonies, of which they were the chief beneficiaries. "If the merchants have no interest in the colonies, then neither do I." But he stopped short of threatening the immediate liquidation of Germany's new colonial empire, if the Hanseatic city should decline. "We are not yet that far along." The Hamburg Senate did refuse, and in March 1890, shortly after Bismarck's dismissal, a colonial department was established within the Imperial Foreign Office. In 1907 it became a separate agency, the Imperial Colonial Office.[79] Neither Bismarck nor his successors had the nerve to face a Reichstag and public angered by the abandonment of colonial possessions.

What Germany experienced so did other countries. Colonies acquired during the era of "new imperialism" were generally expensive and the rewards inadequate. Yet once the burden had been shouldered, it remained because no government, not even Bismarck's, dared cast it off. In Hamburg a few merchants like Adolf Woermann reaped immediate benefits. But the business elite of Germany's largest port, accustomed to think in terms of *Soll und Haben*, were probably the least sanguine of all concerning the virtues of the "colonial idea." On the Elbe it was "almost a matter of good taste" to scoff at colonialism. "Enthusiasm for colonies grows the further one is from the sea," wrote Karl Braun. "It is strongest in Swabia, of whose population most have never seen the ocean."[80] Once acquired, colonies were retained not for economic gain, but as symbols of national pride and power, proof that Germany was a *Weltmacht* with far-flung possessions and a rival, if not the equal, of Britain, whose achievements had so often and in so many ways incited Germans to envy and emulation.

If untouched by such emotions, Bismarck was well aware of the colonies' appeal to the German public and of the political effect of that appeal. By 1886, long before colonies had lost their attraction for him as investments, he had begun to lose interest in them for another reason. The configuration of European politics was no longer favorable to such diversions. In France the fall of the Ferry cabinet in late March 1885, the strengthening of the right in elections held later that year, and the growth of chauvinistic and revanchist agitation during 1886 made it hazardous politically for any government in Paris to collaborate with Berlin. In late 1885 revolution in Eastern Rumelia

---

of German entrepreneurial spirit for the investment of capital overseas. Our countrymen would rather purchase insecure foreign state bonds than follow the English example." *Ibid.*, p. 416.

[79] Washausen, *Hamburg und die Kolonialpolitik*, pp. 127–134; Brauer, *Im Dienste Bismarcks*, pp. 289–290; H. Nirrnheim, "Hamburg als Träger der deutschen Kolonialverwaltung. Ein Plan des Fürsten Bismarck," *Zeitschrift des Vereins für Hamburgische Geschichte*, 34 (1934), pp. 184–195. By 1891 the *Schutzgebiete* had produced tax revenues of 123,605 marks and required expenditures of 13,518,717 marks. In 1907 the cost of administering and defending the *Schutzgebiete* that Bismarck acquired swallowed up 99,000,000 marks, of which 84,700,000 were supplied by German taxpayers. Herrfurth, *Kolonialpolitik*, pp. 190ff., 299ff.

[80] Washausen, *Hamburg und die Kolonialpolitik*, p. 180.

followed by its union with Bulgaria ushered in a new period of tension in the Balkans and of renewed difficulties between Russia and Austria that during 1886 threatened the solidarity of the Three Emperors League. A new crisis was brewing in Europe that no longer made it advisable for Germany to risk antagonizing Britain for objectives that lay outside the European continent. How drastically the scene had changed can be seen in Bismarck's rebuff of the colonial plans of Hermann von Wissmann. Ordered to command a German military expedition to restore order in East Africa in 1888, Wissmann dreamed of carving out a great new sphere of influence for Germany in central Africa. "That takes us too far," was the chancellor's sharp reply. "The English sphere of interest extends to the source of the Nile. Your map of Africa is certainly very beautiful, but my map of Africa lies in Europe. Here lies Russia and there," he said, motioning to the left, "lies France, and we are in the middle. That is my map of Africa."[81]

[81] Bismarck interview with Eugen Wolf, Dec. 5, 1888. GW, VIII, 646.

BOOK TWO

The Climactic Years,

1884–1887

I will remain chancellor as long as my health can endure this drudgery and his majesty, the Kaiser, commands it. As for why I have not yet provided for a suitable successor, dear Firks, that question has often been asked of me. The answer is very simple—I would then have to be already dead in my own lifetime.

—*Bismarck to Baron August von Firks-Samiten,*
April 1, 1885

✠

State Socialism

URING THE WINTER of 1883–1884 Bismarck recovered his sense of realism about how to handle parliament. For three years he had tilted at windmills with utilization bills in the Landtag, revenue bills in the Reichstag, and attempts to persuade the Reichstag to injure itself by granting biennial budgets. Now he ceased to insist that the government "do its duty" by continually presenting bills that had no chance of passage. In his thoughts a *Staatsstreich* remained a possible option (all that it had ever been), and he continued to seek ways to build up a corporative basis for a national diet with which, if necessary, to replace the Reichstag. He also speculated about ways to modify universal male suffrage to assure the right election results: indirect election, compulsory voting, holding the polls open for several days. An abnormally low voter turnout, he believed, had been responsible for the adverse results of the 1881 election.[1] For the time being, however, he limited the government to bills that had some chance of approval in the Reichstag and to policies capable of reviving the support of interest groups and voters in general. Colonialism was one such policy, but so also were higher tariffs, renewal of the antisocialist statute, and the attempt to seduce labor through social insurance.

Social Repression

By 1884 it was evident to some that the "exceptional law" against socialists, passed in 1878 and renewed for three years in 1881, was not achieving the desired effect. Not that the authorities lacked vigor in its execution.[2] Armed with sweeping powers to suppress publications and dissolve organizations and assemblies deemed dangerous to public order and "harmony among the social classes," the police quickly liquidated the three most important socialist newspapers: *Vorwärts*, *Berliner Freie Presse*, and the *Hamburg-Altona Volksblatt*. By June 30, 1879, 127 newspapers and periodicals and 237 other publications had been closed throughout Germany. The movement was without a press

[1] Diary of Eduard Cohen, Dec. 14, 1883. GW, VIII, 497. Lucius diary, Dec. 15, 1884. Freiherr Lucius von Ballhausen, *Bismarck-Erinnerungen* (Stuttgart, 1920), p. 307.

[2] The imperial government prepared to execute the statute by conducting an extensive inquiry into socialist clubs, press, and agitators throughout Germany. Stolberg (for Bismarck) to state governments, Aug. 6, 1878. DZA Potsdam, Reichskanzleramt, 1293, pp. 6–15. On execution of the statute, see also *ibid.*, 1292/3.

and hundreds of employees were without jobs. Immediately after the law was passed, party leaders met and officially dissolved the party. By demonstrating their compliance with the law, they hoped to save many organizations loosely affiliated with the party: consumers' cooperatives, mutual welfare funds, educational associations, and glee clubs and other recreational groups. But the police were relentless in harassing persons and organizations even slightly tinged with socialist views or working-class sympathies—except, of course, for those of pronounced liberal or conservative orientation, such as the Schulze-Delitzsch cooperatives, Hirsch-Duncker trade unions, and Stöcker's Christian Social party. Other trade unions were often suppressed, whether or not they were affiliated with the Social Democratic party. With them disappeared many of the welfare funds for strike benefits, unemployment relief, and sickness, disability, and burial insurance. Limited martial law was imposed on Berlin in 1878, permitting the police to expel sixty-seven well-known socialists from the city and environs. Later, socialists in Hamburg, Leipzig, Spremberg, Frankfurt am Main, and Stettin suffered the same fate.[3]

The consequence of this assault upon socialist and working-class organizations in general was to reinforce the conviction among victims and their sympathizers that the socialist movement was the only true defender of working-class interests. As in the case of the Center party and the Catholic population in the Kulturkampf, the antisocialist statute and the manner of its execution merely heightened the sense of alienation and solidarity among the oppressed. Still this effect was not immediately apparent. As their organizations and press disintegrated, socialist and trade union leaders became demoralized, while those who felt threatened by them rejoiced that the evil spirit had been so easily exorcised.[4] The demoralization, however, was temporary and before long the spook of subversion began to reemerge through every crack and loophole that the police and the courts could not cover under the law.

The largest loophole was the continued presence of the social democratic caucus in the Reichstag. Following demolition of the party organization, the nine-member caucus assumed leadership of the movement as a whole. Although divided in the beginning on questions of aims and tactics, the group fell increasingly under the dominance of August Bebel and Wilhelm Liebknecht. With the financial backing of Karl Höchberg, son of a Jewish banker in Frankfurt am Main, they founded a new party journal, Der Sozialdemokrat. Published in Zurich, Der Sozialdemokrat was regularly smuggled with great in-

---

[3] On the operation and consequences of the antisocialist law, see Vernon Lidtke, The Outlawed Party: Social Democracy in Germany, 1878–1890 (Princeton, 1966), pp. 70–1c5. See also Ernst Engelberg, Revolutionäre Politik und rote Feldpost, 1878–1890 (Berlin, 1959); Dieter Fricke, Bismarcks Praetorianer: Die Berliner politische Polizei im Kampf gegen die deutsche Arbeiterbewegung (1871–1898) (Berlin, 1962); Alexander Hellfaier, Die deutsche Sozialdemokratie während des Sozialistengesetzes, 1878–1890 (Berlin, 1958).

[4] Lidtke, Outlawed Party, pp. 80–81.

genuity across the border into Germany and later printed by underground presses in Germany itself. Under the editorship of Eduard Bernstein, a close collaborator of Bebel, the journal became the chief medium for rallying and holding together the socialist movement in the decade ahead. It attained a press run of 9,000 copies by 1884 and 11,000 by 1890. Disguised and secret organizations were soon established that, although constantly harried by the police and occasionally infiltrated by informers and agents provocateurs, proved to be remarkably effective. At election time candidates were supported by temporary election committees that dissolved afterward to avoid prosecution. In 1880, 1883, and 1887 party congresses were held abroad; within Germany regional meetings became frequent.[5] In the first election held under the antisocialist act (1881) the social democrats increased their seats in the Reichstag to twelve, despite a decline from 437,000 to 312,000 in voting strength.

Bismarck was well aware of the role played by the social democratic caucus in frustrating his attempt to interdict the socialist movement. He would have preferred in 1878 to deny those "legally proved to be socialists" the rights to vote, become candidates, and sit in parliament.[6] Failing in this, he sought the arrest and incarceration of two socialist deputies, Friedrich Fritzsche and Wilhelm Hasselmann, who had been banned from Berlin under the declaration of limited martial law, but returned to resume their seats in the Reichstag for the session of 1879. The state's attorney at Berlin, Hermann Tessendorff, contended that the decree of limited martial law took precedence over Article 31 in the imperial constitution, which granted deputies immunity from arrest while the Reichstag was in session. But the chamber, antisocialist though it was, rejected this draconian view (March 21, 1879).[7] During the same session Bismarck again failed in his attempt to silence social democrats by a new statute that would have authorized the Reichstag to purge deputies guilty of being "abusive."[8] Nor did he succeed in moving the Reichstag to authorize legal proceedings against newspapers allegedly slandering the chamber.[9]

The limited means at Bismarck's disposal prevented him from liquidating an oppositional minority. If autocratic, the Prussian-German constitutional monarchy was hardly totalitarian. The chancellor himself, moreover, was still capable of musing about the values of "publicity and freedom of the press" as the "most important" means of preventing government "by mistresses and favorites."[10] The freedom that he required for the preservation of his own

---

[5] Lidtke, *Outlawed Party*, pp. 89–105.
[6] See vol. 2, p. 414.
[7] Lidtke, *Outlawed Party*, pp. 85–86; SBR (1879), I, 23–38, 536; IV, Anlagen, Nos. 19, 22.
[8] SBR (1879), I, 248–318; IV, Anlagen, No. 15.
[9] SBR (1879), III, 2361–2362; see also SBR (1884), I, 440–441.
[10] To Eduard Cohen, Dec. 14, 1883. GW, VIII, 497.

power against the political intrigues of women and courtiers could not be denied generally, only selectively, to others.

Bismarck's battle against socialists was simultaneously an assault on left-liberals. At times, in fact, the latter seemed to be the primary target. In January 1884 he outlined to the Prussian cabinet his strategy for the approaching Reichstag session and the imperial election scheduled for the fall. As the first item of business, the deputies were to be confronted with the necessity of renewing the antisocialist bill, scheduled to lapse in 1884. "If need be, we may let the antisocialist law lapse and thereby cure the liberal bourgeoisie of its progressive inclinations through fear of social democracy."[11] During the critical debate on the bill (May 9, 1884), the chancellor directed his fire primarily at the *Freisinnigen*, whom he compared to Russian nihilists and accused of glorifying Ferdinand Cohen-Blind, his would-be assassin in 1866. Progressives, he declared, were more dangerous than socialists; his duty to king and country was to fight this kind of liberalism "to the last breath." He concluded with a dramatic appeal to the voters: "If you want to be rid of the socialist danger, do not vote for progressive deputies!" Under this pressure twenty-five left-liberals and thirty-nine centrists voted with conservatives and national liberals to produce a majority, 189 to 157, for renewal of the exceptional law for two more years.[12] Bismarck had the satisfaction of receiving the Kaiser's congratulations on this "unexpected" victory.[13]

Bismarck celebrated in his own way. More than five hundred individuals (deputies, peers, Bundesrat delegates, etc.) received personal notes from the chancellor requesting their presence in the Wilhelmstrasse at 8:00 P.M. on May 11 "for a confidential consultation." The effect was electric. Most of the invited had never had a private talk with the German chancellor. With boosted self-esteem they hastened to the Wilhelmstrasse at the appointed hour, eager to find out why Europe's mightiest statesman sought their advice, only to find the street crowded with carriages discharging guests clutching identical invitations. The chancellor wanted full attendance at his first parliamentary soirée in many months, including those centrists who had previously stayed away.

That evening he singled out Ludwig Windthorst for special attention. Throughout the salon the common subject of discussion was the chancellor's

[11] Jan. 10, 1884. Lucius, *Bismarck-Erinnerungen*, p. 280.

[12] SBR (1884), I, 143–195, 441–532; RGB (1884), p. 53. The issue was regarded as so dangerous for the Progressive party that its leadership advised opponents of the statute not to attend the crucial vote at the end of the second reading of the bill. SEG (1885), p. 31.

[13] Horst Kohl, ed., *Anhang zu den Gedanken und Erinnerungen von Otto Fürst von Bismarck* (Stuttgart, 1901), I, 327. On September 1, the anniversary of the victory at Sedan, Wilhelm demonstrated his gratitude again by presenting to Bismarck, as "soldier," the highest military order he could bestow, *Pour le Mérite*—with oakleaf in recompense for not having bestowed it earlier. Kohl, ed., *Anhang*, I, 327–329.

assertion of labor's "right to work," a phrase he had launched like an errant
torpedo, apparently for its shock value, in his speech of May 9.[14] In convers-
ing with Windthorst and Adolph Wagner, Bismarck enlarged on the subject.
According to Wagner, he spoke of public works projects for the unemployed.
"If we now carry out appropriate projects at public cost, that would certainly
be justified. For the worker such assistance would be richer and worthier than
public charity. Although I am reproached for proceeding too impetuously, I
prefer to see the task of a leading statesman as that of a locomotive stoker,
whose job it is to provide sufficient heat to move the machine forward at the
right speed. Otherwise we stand still in everything."[15]

Bismarck's endorsement of the "right to work" principle resounded through
the newspaper press. The *Vossische Zeitung* called it "the most revolutionary
principle in its implications ever pronounced by anyone in such an exalted
position."[16] The *Berliner-Börsen-Courier* declared that the attempt to realize
this goal—to be expected in view of the source—would destroy the foundation of German industry.[17] Reverberations continued for many days but finally
abated when no concrete program for full employment was launched by the
government.[18] The reaction of the *Börsen-Courier* shows, nevertheless, how
shocking the chancellor's words were to the industrial and financial half of
the alliance assembled by Bismarck's alleged *Sammlungspolitik*.[19] At the very

[14] GW, VIII, 508–509; BP, I, 256ff.

[15] Heinrich Rubner, ed., *Adolph Wagner: Briefe, Dokumente, Augenzeugenberichte, 1851–1917*
(Berlin, 1978), p. 225. Apparently the source of Bismarck's inspiration was a book by Emil
Witte, *Die soziale Krankheit und ihre naturgemässe Behandlung durch wirtschaftliche Massregeln* (Leipzig, 1883). In a chapter entitled "The Right to Work" Witte wrote that, although a system of
health, disability, and old-age insurance was "under present circumstances" only a matter of
justice, such institutions were, if realizable, of secondary importance, for unemployed laborers
could not contribute to the system. But if work were provided, the demand for labor would exceed
the supply, wages would rise, and workers could pay for social insurance without the help of the
state. Witte proposed subsidies by the imperial government, in some cases by state and communal
governments, for the construction of "production facilities" (*Produktionsanlagen*), like the North
Sea (Kiel) Canal, which would eventually become independent establishments, capable of creating job opportunities and ending vagabondage. For Bismarck's enthusiastic reaction to this
book, see Heinrich von Poschinger, ed., *Stunden bei Bismarck* (Vienna, 1910), pp. 75–79.

[16] The "right to work" concept had been discussed in late April in the pages of Moritz Busch's
Grenzboten, where it caught the attention of the *Vossische Zeitung* because of Busch's well-known
relationship to the chancellor. *Vossische Zeitung*, No. 201, Apr. 30, 1884, and No. 218, May 10,
1884.

[17] *Der Berliner-Börsen-Courier*, No. 243, May 14, 1884; also No. 249, May 17, 1884.

[18] DZA Merseburg, Rep. 120, BB, VII, 1, 1, Bd. 3, pp. 134ff.

[19] For a discussion of the applicability of the model *Sammlungspolitik* to the policies of the
Bismarck government's in these years, see Otto Pflanze, " 'Sammlungspolitik' 1875–1886; Kritische Bemerkungen zu einem Modell," in Otto Pflanze, ed., *Innenpolitische Probleme des Bismarck-Reiches: Schriften des Historischen Kollegs, Kolloquien 2* (Munich, 1983), pp. 155–193, and
"Bismarcks Herrschaftstechnik als Problem der gegenwärtigen Historiographie," *Historische Zeitschrift*, 234 (1982), pp. 561–599.

moment when he appealed to their representatives in parliament for further support against social democracy, he openly propounded his most radical proposal for social reform. That he did nothing to implement it, as far as we know, suggests that it was but a propaganda weapon aimed at labor—another application of his stick-and-carrot approach to proletarian discontent—in view of the imperial election due in October 1884. But the fright he produced in capitalistic circles shows how seriously they now felt compelled to take any idea thrown out by this often unpredictable statesman. By 1884 they were already appalled by the direction his social insurance plans were taking.

Health and Accident Insurance

Since appointment as Prussian minister-president in 1862, Bismarck had repeatedly toyed and tinkered with social reform. From the outset his motivation was dual: to achieve social justice for the lower classes of an increasingly industrial society and to outflank the entrepreneurial elite that backed liberal causes. But in 1866 he chose a different course toward social and political stability, one more in harmony with his ambition to expand the power of Prussia in German and European affairs. He placed the Hohenzollern monarchy at the head of the national movement and promoted the "moral and material interests" (in Wagener's words) of the business and professional classes.[20] By the time he was ready to return to the social question in 1878, the dimensions of the problem had changed. Now his task was that of detaching labor from the leadership of the social democratic movement rather than from that of middle-class liberals. He had simultaneously to destroy a movement that rejected monarchism for republicanism, Christianity for atheism, and capitalism for socialism and to win the loyalties of proletarians by demonstrating that the "Christian state" was capable of looking after their interests as a matter of social justice, not charity. But he complicated his task, perhaps even predestined it to failure, by applying the stick before holding out the carrot.

Bismarck blamed the delay of his social reforms on his own absorption in foreign affairs, the pervasiveness of laissez-faire in the economic thought of imperial and Prussian officials, and his reliance in economic matters upon incompetent and obstructionist colleagues and subordinates. Not until he had eased Delbrück and others out of office and had himself assumed the Prussian Ministry of Commerce, he claimed, was he able to throw the switches on the bureaucratic machine that produced the medical insurance act of 1883, the accident insurance act of 1884, and the old-age and disability insurance act of 1889.[21] This is yet another example of his talent for exploiting partial truths

[20] For Bismarck's views on the social question, see vol. 1, pp. 223–233 and vol. 2, pp. 301–310.
[21] GW, VIII, 377.

and his need to blame others for his own mistakes in judgment. Before late 1875 he was not ready to abandon the liberal course begun in 1867, and during the next five years he was deeply involved in other actions that absorbed his limited energies (state ownership of railways, protective tariffs, a state tobacco monopoly, and tax reform), actions of little or no benefit to labor. Even the antisocialist act of 1878 had the ulterior motive of weakening and dividing the liberals, a motive that did more to dictate its timing than the actual progress of subversive activity.

Still, it must be granted that the delay in social reform also arose from a dearth of information. There were no precedents and little statistical data that could serve as guides. That Bismarck sponsored numerous inquiries into the conditions of labor during the 1870s testifies both to his uncertainty about what course to take and to his distrust of the proposals being fed him by men like Hermann Wagener, the *Kathedersozialisten*, and Prussian officials. Ultimately he turned to interested entrepreneurs for advice under the assumption that their experience would assure the practicality of what he undertook and its compatibility with private enterprise.

Like their foreign counterparts, many German industrialists of the nineteenth century exploited labor shamelessly in the interest of greater profits, higher dividends, capital accumulation, and competitive survival. Among the wealthiest and most successful, nevertheless, were some genuinely concerned about the physical effects of factory work, child and female labor, bad living conditions, and inadequate health care and about the fate of the unemployed, injured, disabled, and elderly. Entrepreneurs such as Friedrich Harkort, Werner Siemens, August Borsig, Friedrich König, Alfred Krupp, and Karl Stumm sought to improve the circumstances of their workers by providing or fostering welfare chests, improved housing, better working conditions, higher-than-average pay, nurseries for working mothers, and the like. In return, they expected greater productivity, loyalty, discipline, no unions, and no strikes.[22] They conceived of themselves as officers commanding battalions of workers in a fierce struggle for economic survival.

Indeed, the army was the only model or precedent they knew for an enterprise such as Krupp's, where in the early 1880s nineteen thousand workers performed tasks in an established routine, at set hours, and at the direction of a staff headed by a single person. In such an enterprise "authority, training, discipline are necessary," wrote Henry Axel Bueck, director of the Central Federation of German Industrialists. Krupp in the Ruhr and Stumm in the Saar, he said, commanded their works and laborers like Prussian generals on the battlefield; survival was a "daily" matter of "bitter seriousness."[23] "Just as

[22] Walter Vogel, *Bismarcks Arbeiterversicherung: Ihre Entstehung im Kräftespiel der Zeit* (Braunschweig, 1951), p. 34ff.

[23] "Bericht des Geschäftsführers über die Verbandsangelegenheiten," in *Verhandlungen, Mitt-*

the worker is obligated to obey his employer," wrote Stumm, "the employer has to care for his workers far beyond the limits of the work contract both as a matter of justice and religion. The employer should feel like the head of a large family, whose individual members have a claim on his solicitude for as long as they prove themselves worthy of it."[24]

With the support of other big industrialists Stumm, often dubbed "king of the Saar," agitated in press and parliament (he was a free conservative deputy in the Reichstag) during 1878–1879 for an imperial system of compulsory old-age and disability insurance.[25] In August 1879 Bismarck began to press his ministerial colleagues for practical suggestions on the implementation of such a system, conceived as a revision of the imperial social insurance acts of April 7–8, 1876, whose inadequacies had now become glaringly apparent.[26] Consideration of Stumm's proposition, however, was handicapped by a lack of vital statistics, without which actuarial tables could not be calculated.[27] In the spring of 1880 Bismarck took up instead the more limited proposal of Louis Baare, president of the *Bochumer Verein*, one of the largest mining and iron manufacturing firms of the Ruhr basin. On Hofmann's invitation Baare drafted a plan for a national system of accident insurance, based not only on his own views but also on those of Rhenish-Westphalian big industrialists generally.[28] This interest group, which had played such an important role in fashioning the tariff of 1879, again found an opportunity to influence national legislation. If altruism played a role, so did enlightened self-interest and fear of social upheaval. They hoped to head off unfavorable legislation. "If industry now demonstrates a willingness to sacrifice," Baare wrote to his fellow entrepreneurs, "it will receive the sympathy of the imperial government in the struggle against an extension of the law on employers' liability for job-related accidents."[29]

Bismarck valued the initiatives of Stumm and Baare because they stemmed from men outside the government who were "involved in practical affairs."

heilungen und Berichte des Centralverbandes deutscher Industrieller, Nr. 17 (Berlin, 1882), pp. 22–23. DZA Merseburg, Rep. 120, BB, VIa, 1, Bd. 1.

[24] Quoted in Vogel, *Bismarcks Arbeiterversicherung*, p. 41.

[25] SBR (1879), IV, Nos. 16, 28; VI, No. 314.

[26] Bismarck to cabinet, Aug. 5, 1879. DZA Merseburg, Rep. 120, BB, VIII, 4, 1, Bd. 1, pp. 140–141. On Bismarck's insistence Hofmann canvassed the federal government for advice. Hofmann to state governments, Sept. 19, 1879. Ibid., pp. 142–159.

[27] On the problem of statistics, see Becker (director of the Imperial Statistical Office) to Boetticher, Nov. 11, 1880. Ibid., pp. 309–310.

[28] Memorial of Louis Baare, Apr. 30, 1880. Ibid., pp. 77–82. Advice was also procured from Baron Varnbüler, Württemberg's chief delegate to the Bundesrat, who had played an important role in drafting the tariff act of 1879. Ibid., pp. 188–224.

[29] Vogel, *Bismarcks Arbeiterversicherung*, pp. 38–44. Hans-Peter Ullmann has described the variety of motives that inspired the attitudes of business interests in general toward social insurance legislation. See his "Industrielle Interessen und die Entstehung der deutschen Sozialversicherung 1880–1889," *Historische Zeitschrift*, 229 (1979), pp. 588–607.

For this same reason he referred the health and accident insurance bills to the Prussian Economic Council for review before they reached the Bundesrat and Reichstag. Yet bills could be drafted only by officials who possessed the requisite technical expertise. Since September 1878 the problem of social security had been under lively discussion within the Prussian ministries. A driving force for reform was Theodor Lohmann, under secretary of state in the Ministry of Commerce, who had played a key role in drafting the social insurance act of 1876 and industrial code act of 1878. Earnest Protestant and social conservative, Lohmann was genuinely concerned about labor's alienation and acutely aware of the need to build a solid social foundation under the new German Reich. Yet he was strongly opposed to a state socialist solution to the problem with its centralization, bureaucratic control, and public financing— features that, he feared, would stifle labor's sense of corporate identity and Christian individualism. Instead, he favored more statutes to regulate working conditions and protect family life and insurance laws to encourage voluntary participation by both employer and employee in self-governing, local, mutual-aid societies.[30]

Lohmann was the author of the bill drastically extending the liability of employers for industrial accidents that aroused Bismarck's ire and led to Hofmann's dismissal in August 1880.[31] Under Hofmann's replacement, Karl von Boetticher, Lohmann and other technical personnel were transferred to the Imperial Office of the Interior, where they formed a new department specifically charged with drafting social insurance laws according to Bismarck's design. Lohmann was the dominant figure in the group, but he soon discovered, as he wryly expressed it, that *Kommerzienräte* (an honorary title bestowed on businessmen) had more influence than *Geheimräte* (privy counselors in government service). Baare's plan for accident insurance appealed to the chancellor, because it held out the prospect of a direct role for the Reich in social

[30] Hans Rothfels, *Theodor Lohmann und die Kampfjahre der staatlichen Sozialpolitik, 1871–1905. Forschungen und Darstellungen aus dem Reichsarchiv*, vol. 6 (Berlin, 1927), pp. 43ff.

[31] See pp. 33–34. The proposed statute was the fruit of years of agitation for reform of the 1871 statute on accident liability, culminating in a Reichstag resolution of 1878. SBR (1878), 2d sess., *Drucksache* No. 28. The statute of 1871 had placed upon the worker the burden of proving the employer's liability. The reform would have obligated the employer to report accidents that resulted in injuries and have compelled him to prove the worker at fault. Such a statute would have forced the employer to establish insurance chests, whose premiums would be paid equally by employer, employee, and regional poor relief associations (*Armenverbände*). Fortunately for Lohmann perhaps, Bismarck thought the proposal stemmed from a "*Kreuzzeitungsmann*," Under Secretary Jacoby, whom he accused of hostility toward all industry as the product of liberalism. As estate and factory owner, the chancellor declared, he knew that "such a principle was simply ruinous for industry and without help in reviving artisanry." Lucius, *Bismarck-Erinnerungen*, pp. 189–190. See also Bismarck to Hofmann, July 12, 1880, in Hans Goldschmidt, *Das Reich und Preussen im Kampf um die Führung* (Berlin, 1931), p. 278 (fn); Bismarck to cabinet, Aug. 28, 1880, AWB, II, 4–5, also 6–8; and cabinet meeting of Aug. 28, 1880. DZA Merseburg, Rep. 90a, B, III, 2b, Nr. 6, Vol. 92.

security, a role clearly visible to workers whose votes and loyalty he coveted. In late 1883 Lohmann, whose knowledge and ability Bismarck had come to value, resigned rather than continue to draft bills not in harmony with his convictions. Ultimately Bismarck found in Carl Gamp and Anton Bödiker officials more sympathetic to his views and capable of converting those views into practical legislation. Three scholars, Adolph Wagner, Leipzig Professor Karl Heym, and the Tübingen economist and former Austrian minister Albert Schäffle, also made contributions.[32] Yet the basic imprint on the social insurance bills was Bismarck's. As in drafting the constitution of 1867, he took only such advice as fitted his purposes. By choosing advisers whose ideas corresponded to his aims and by extracting bills from unwilling collaborators like Lohmann, Jacoby, and at times even Boetticher, he shaped the laws to fit his own vision.[33]

The first reform that Bismarck launched, the accident insurance bill of March 8, 1881, did not enjoy smooth sailing. It called for compulsory insurance for all factory and mine workers against disabilities resulting from industrial accidents. The insurance was to be administered by an imperial insurance agency. Annual premiums for workers earning less than 750 marks were to be paid by employers (two-thirds) and the Reich (one-third); for those earning between 750 and 1,000 marks by the employers (two-thirds) and the insured (one-third); and for those earning more than 1,000 marks by the employer (one-half) and the insured (one-half). The growth of terrorism—punctuated by the assassinations of Tsar Alexander II on March 13, 1881, and President James Garfield on July 2, 1881—had created a climate favorable for reform. In Bundesrat and Reichstag there was little disposition to question its necessity, although most would have preferred merely to extend existing employers' liability for work-related accidents. Among left-liberals and centrists there was widespread opposition to the unitary and state-socialist features of the government's bill and to the anticapitalistic utterances of ministers and agrar-

[32] Vogel, Bismarcks Arbeiterversicherung, pp. 74–79, 92–117. For documentation on Baare's contribution, see AWB, II, 4–5; GW, VIc, 200–202; on Karl Heym's contribution, see DZA Merseburg, Rep. 120, BB, VIII, 4, 1, Bd. 1, pp. 86, 101; on Wagner's limited contribution, see his Briefe, Dokumente, Augenzeugenberichte, pp. 194, 196, 201, 203–205, 425–426, and Heinrich von Poschinger, ed., Bismarck als Volkswirth (Berlin, 1889–1890), II, 78–80; on Schäffle's contribution, see Albert Schäffle, Aus meinem Leben (Berlin, 1905), II, 174ff., and AWB, II, 66–68; GW, VIc, 230–231; GW, VIII, 433. Concerning Bismarck's first contact with Gamp, see AWB, II, 98 (fn).

[33] For Bismarck's personal role in shaping social insurance legislation, see GW, VIc, 200–202, 204–206, 251; Heinrich von Poschinger, ed., Bismarck-Portefeuille (Stuttgart, 1898), I, 27–28; AWB, II, 68–79, 106, 146–147. With Bismarck breathing down their necks, Lohmann and Jacobi produced the first drafts of bills providing for accident insurance, including invalid, widow, and orphan funds, on September 23, 1880. DZA Merseburg, Rep. 120, BB, VIII, 4, 1, Bd. 1, pp. 1–76, 106–138.

ians in its defense. But even conservatives objected to state-paid premiums, which Richter denounced as "communistic."

Bismarck left no doubt that his further goal was old-age and disability insurance, administered and funded by the Reich. This raised the prospect of deficits in the imperial budget requiring primarily a tobacco monopoly, but also higher tariffs and other disagreeable tax measures. Amendments initiated by the Reichstag transferred the administration of the system to the state governments, ended the Reich's financial contribution, and imposed on even the lowest paid workers the necessity of paying one-third of the premium. In this form the bill was unacceptable to Bismarck, who maintained that poor workers could not afford this burden. Laborers who required no benefits, moreover, would regard the premium as just another imposition by an alien state to which no gratitude was owed.[34]

On reconvening after the election of October 1881, the Reichstag received an imperial rescript in which Bismarck put the Kaiser's prestige and authority on the line in behalf of social reform. "Already in February of this year, we have expressed our conviction that the healing of social ills is not to be sought exclusively in the repression of social democratic agitation but also in positive measures to further the welfare of labor." In addition to a new accident insurance bill, the rescript announced the government's intention to submit a health insurance bill and ultimately an old-age and disability insurance bill.[35]

The health insurance bill was a by-product of deliberations on accident insurance. In cases of nonfatal accidents, benefits were to begin only after thirteen (originally four) weeks; during this interval workers not belonging to welfare chests would have been without assistance. This still constituted the majority since laborers had failed to form the voluntary chests provided for by the statute of 1876. As drafted by Lohmann, the new statute provided for additional compulsory medical insurance chests in all industries covered by the accident insurance statute, with two-thirds of the premium (based on a percentage of income) paid by the worker and one-third by the employer. All illnesses were insured for at least thirteen weeks, not merely those produced by accidents. Sick workers were guaranteed support equivalent to three-quarters of the average wage. To Bismarck's surprise the medical insurance statute was the first to become law (on June 15, 1883), passing the Reichstag by an

[34] SBR (1881), I, 673–756; II, 1441–1556, 1619–1665, 1746–1783; III, Anlagen, No. 41. On the origins of the bill, see Rothfels, Lohmann, pp. 52–54; Bismarck to Tiedemann, Nov. 16, 1880, GW, VIc, 200–201; and Bismarck's note of mid-Dec. 1880 on imperial financing of premiums ("ein staatssozialistischer Gedanke!"), GW, VIc, 230.

[35] BR, IX, 84–88. For another account of the origins of the bill of March 8, 1881, and the rescript of Nov. 17, 1881 (including a facsimile of that document in draft and final form), see Florian Tennstedt, "Vorgeschichte und Entstehung der kaiserlichen Botschaft vom 17. November 1881," in 100 Jahre kaiserliche Botschaft. Zeitschrift für Sozialreform, vol. 27 (1981), pp. 663–774.

overwhelming vote (216 to 99). According to Lohmann, the chancellor considered the act a mere "supposititious child" and was astounded at the degree of public interest it aroused.[36]

After three failures in successive years the accident insurance act finally became law on July 6, 1884. In its final form the statute gave Bismarck the essence of what he wanted: all premiums paid by employers, administration by associations of employers based on individual industries, deficits covered by the Reich, supervision by an Imperial Insurance Office financed by the Reich. His greatest sacrifice was direct payment of part of the premiums by the Reich, but he also permitted the Bundesrat to strike out of the bill provision for workers' committees that would have participated in administering the statute. Efforts of social democrats and left-liberals to revive the provision were defeated. Creation of the employer occupational associations removed some of the original objections to the Imperial Insurance Office by reducing its administrative role. Under the skillful leadership of its first president, Bödiker, the office remained, nevertheless, a highly visible symbol of the Reich's role in social insurance. Bödiker's first achievement was to organize the occupational associations, overcoming the objections of industrialists who balked at the new and unfamiliar tasks of administering mutual accident insurance funds.[37]

There was more to the occupational associations, however, than met the eye. Bismarck had a hidden purpose, which he finally admitted to Lohmann in a long interview on October 5, 1883, that led to Lohmann's resignation. Lohmann was strongly opposed not to the principle of corporative administration itself, but to the compulsory and industry-wide character of the associations on which Bismarck insisted. The counselor expected associations established on this basis to be mechanical and lifeless. Instead he wanted the state to encourage local, voluntary associations that he thought would have a more organic character and hence greater vitality. Bismarck shocked him by declaring, "Accident insurance in itself is for me a secondary consideration. My chief consideration is to use this opportunity to attain corporative associations that must be extended gradually to include all productive classes of the population. In this way we will establish the basis for a future representative body that will become an important participant in the legislative process either as a substitute for, or as a parallel body to, the Reichstag, even if it must be raised to this status by means of a coup d'état."[38]

[36] SBR (1882–1883), I, 199–249, 1966–2236, 2466–2696; RGB (1883), pp. 73–104; Rothfels, Lohmann, pp. 53–55. See also Bismarck's remarks to Busch on June 8, 1882. Moritz Busch, Tagebuchblätter (Leipzig, 1899), III, 89.

[37] RGB (1884), pp. 69–112; SBR (1882–1883), I, 199–251; III, 2257–2272; SBR (1884), I, 35–98; II, 750–953, 1103–1129; Vogel, Bismarcks Arbeiterversicherung, pp. 109–111.

[38] Rothfels, Lohmann, pp. 63–64. The corporative aspect of the statute was derived from suggestions by Albert Schäffle. Bismarck to Schäffle, Oct. 16, 1881. GW, VIc, 230–231.

Social insurance associations were not the only corporative bodies upon which Bismarck hoped to base a future national diet. On becoming minister of commerce in 1880, he inherited from predecessors a bill to resuscitate the guilds (without compulsory membership, for which artisans continued to agitate). He did not expect "very much" from this statute, whose purpose was to protect skilled artisans from the competition of both big industry and amateur craftsmen.[39] Since his Frankfurt years he had looked upon the guild as an anachronistic institution in the age of industrial capitalism, a dying organism that could not be kept alive by artificial devices. But he did believe it possible to cultivate new corporative bodies that might flourish in the modern economic climate.[40] To this end he avidly accepted in May 1882 the proposal of a subordinate in the Ministry of Commerce for the creation of "business chambers" (*Gewerbekammern*) in response to artisan agitation and a recent Reichstag resolution. Bismarck's aim was to effect a radical transformation of existing chambers of commerce (*Handelskammern*), quasi-official bodies composed of big merchants and big industrialists, whose annual reports on business conditions often criticized government economic policy from the laissez-faire standpoint.[41] By expanding them to incorporate all interest groups (including artisans) in business and agriculture, he hoped not only to rid the government of a source of irritation, but also to create a new corporative institution that might eventually become the foundation for a national diet.

In view of the failure of his plan for a German economic council, Bismarck recognized that there was no immediate likelihood that either the Reichstag or Prussian Chamber of Deputies would pass a bill creating and appropriating money for business chambers.[42] So he chose an "administrative route," ordering Prussia's district governments to consult with representatives of the affected interests and submit bills to provincial diets for the creation of business chambers following guidelines from the Ministry of Commerce.[43] This ven-

[39] Bismarck to Prussian cabinet, Aug. 28, 1880. *AWB*, II, 3–4. For the extensive background of this legislation, see DZA Merseburg, Rep. 120, BB, VIa, 1, Bde. 1–3; Rep. 120, BB, I, 1, 1, Nr. 12, Bd. 11; DZA Potsdam, Reichskanzleramt, 454.

[40] See vol. 2, pp. 85–89.

[41] Wilhelm Bismarck to Ministerial Counselor von Moeller, May 4, 1882. DZA Merseburg, Rep. 120, BB, VIa, 1, Bd. 1, pp. 94. Moeller's memorandum of April 27, 1882, proposing the *Gewerbekammern*, with amendments by Bismarck, was published at the chancellor's direction in the south German *Augsburger Allgemeine Zeitung*. By Moeller's count Prussia had 72 chambers of commerce with 1,087 members, of whom 498 were merchants and 589 industrialists. Merchants predominated in 27 chambers, industrialists in 39; they were evenly represented in 6. DZA Merseburg, Rep. 120, BB, VIa, 1, Bd. 1, pp. 95–136. Bismarck outlined his plans for an expansion of the chambers to include representatives of all "branches of business activity" (including artisans and farmers) in a letter to the Osnabrück chamber of commerce, Dec. 18, 1882. *Ibid.*, pp. 257–258.

[42] Cabinet meeting of Dec. 27, 1883. DZA Merseburg, Rep. 90a, B, III, 2b, Nr. 6, Vol. 95.

[43] Rantzau to Rottenburg, Oct. 22, 1883. DZA Merseburg, Rep. 120, BB, VIa, 1, Bd. 2, pp.

ture enjoyed little success. The diets in industrial regions of western Prussia failed to cooperate; although the eastern diets appropriated some funds, the business chambers they created had little appeal for the interests that they were supposed to represent. When the funds ceased in 1892, the institution expired.[44]

Leap in the Dark

Like most Bismarck policies, the social insurance program served more than one purpose. Seen as *Realpolitik*, the program was intended to reconcile labor to the state by showing that the state could "act generously towards the poor." The cost of millions, he said, would be a "good investment," if it averted a revolution in ten to fifty years.[45] But the program was also another attempt to reduce property taxes by relieving local governments of much of the burden of poor relief. Large imperial contributions to the system would unbalance further the imperial budget, creating a persuasive argument for a tobacco monopoly. With the failure of the original bill Bismarck shifted to a corporative structure, whose ulterior purpose was less obvious. The ultimate role he planned (in the event of a *Staatsstreich*) for the occupational associations that were to manage the accident insurance funds explains why he regarded with equanimity the eventual demise of the Prussian Economic Council in 1883–1884.

Still, it is undeniable that Bismarck was also driven by a genuine moral impulse, a real desire to accomplish an important reform in behalf of social justice and "practical Christianity." That his health improved temporarily in the fall of 1880 may have stemmed from excitement over the new vision that opened before him. At a parliamentary soirée on February 1, 1881, five hundred guests found him in an unusual mood. Customarily he moved about from group to group, exchanging pleasantries and small talk, until after the buffet had been served and the company had thinned out; then he commenced a discourse on politics surrounded by a "corona" of remaining guests. But on this occasion, fortified by glasses of Rüdesheimer Berg 1822, he permitted himself to be drawn into a discussion on current issues early in the evening. Surrounded by jostling deputies, ministers, and members of the Prussian Eco-

---

2–3; Ministry of Interior to district governments, July 24, 1884. DZA Merseburg, Rep. 120, BB, VIa, 13, 1, Bd. 1, pp. 1–11. The ensuing correspondence from and to the district governments records the difficulties encountered in gaining the cooperation of local businessmen. *Ibid.*, pp. 12ff. The district governor in Düsseldorf requested and gained Bismarck's approval for the inclusion of five workers in occasional "economic conferences," ordinarily composed of officials and businessmen, when the discussions concerned the interests of workers. This appears to have been an exception. Magdeburg to Bismarck, Apr. 14, 1887. *Ibid.*, pp. 207–211, also pp. 214–216.

44 DZA Merseburg, Rep. 120, BB, VIa, 13, 1, Bd. 2, p. 102.

45 To Busch, Jan. 18, 1881. Busch, *Tagebuchblätter*, III, 10–11.

nomic Council, he became so absorbed in presenting his thoughts on social insurance that, despite repeated admonishments from Johanna, he neglected to eat!

The accident insurance bill, he declared, was but the beginning of a task that might take a decade to complete. Should not the phrase "every German" be substituted for "every worker"? Already it was proposed that coverage be extended to artisans and agricultural workers. But, first, the ice had to be tested, to see how much weight it could bear. "Why shouldn't the idea of old-age insurance be realizable?" Next day the *Berliner Tageblatt* editorialized, "It is a memorable phenomenon that the mightiest statesman of our time brings together in the great hall of the most stately house of the imperial capital princes of industry and simple workmen (four or five were present), leading ministers and elected representatives of the people in order, by the most direct exchange of ideas, to make propaganda for his plans. In truth, the imperial chancellor functions in this way as an apostle of that democratic idea of social 'equality' for which we so often envy the French."[46]

The mixture of realism, idealism, and religion that characterized Bismarck's thoughts about social insurance and his defense of it in parliament is evident in the *Motive* that accompanied the first accident insurance bill. "That the state should assist its needy citizens to a greater degree than before is not only a Christian and humanitarian duty, of which the state apparatus should be fully conscious; it is also a task to be undertaken for the preservation of the state itself. The goal of this task is to nurture among the unpropertied classes of the population, which are the most numerous as well as least informed, the view that the state is not only a necessary but also a beneficent institution. To that end they must be led (through advantages, achieved by legislative action, that are immediately recognizable) to the realization that the state is not to be regarded as an institution invented merely for the protection of the better situated classes of society but as an institution that also serves their own needs and interests. The concern that legislation pursuing this goal contains a socialist element must not be permitted to stop us from proceeding in this direction. Insofar as this is the case, furthermore, the socialist element is not something entirely new but is a further development of the modern idea of the state springing from the Christian tradition, according to which the state, in addition to its obligation to protect existing rights, also has the task of furthering in a positive way the welfare of all its citizens (and especially the welfare of the weak and needy) through the creation of suitable agencies and the employment of all the means available to it. In this sense, specifically, the legislative regulation of poor relief, which the modern state in contrast to those of the ancient and medieval times recognizes to be its obligation, contains a socialist element. In truth, the measures that can be

[46] BP, I, 168–177.

taken to improve the condition of the propertyless classes are but a further development of the established concept of poor relief provided by the state."[47]

Although Stumm and Baare had helped initiate social insurance, they and their fellow manufacturers were not happy over the result. Many industrialists looked upon state intervention in behalf of labor as a "leap in the dark," an experiment in state socialism that would overburden the German economy and establish a precedent dangerous to the free enterprise system. Some opponents were Manchesterites in principle, but others were tariff protectionists who had lobbied enthusiastically for state intervention in behalf of industry in 1878–1879. While supporting accident and health insurance legislation as a whole, the Central Federation of German Industrialists disagreed with many details favorable to labor and complained about the "spirit of mistrust toward employers" that it detected in the statutes.[48] From insurance corporations naturally came a chorus of disapproval. For the state to provide accident insurance, they reasoned, was contrary to its "nature," a radical departure from the *Rechtsstaat*, whose proper function was to protect and further private enterprise, not expropriate or compete with it.[49]

The Conservative and Free Conservative parties of the Reichstag found the argument convincing that social insurance was a natural function of the Christian state and a logical extension of earlier attempts to deal with the problem of the poor. Bennigsen, Miquel, and other national liberals were also easily persuaded that the uprooting of socialist subversion required a major effort to include labor in the national consensus. What the Reich had earlier done for business and for agriculture, it should also do for the socially "disinherited." From the Secession and the Progressive party, on the other hand, came general disapproval. To Bamberger, Richter, and others the bills were an unjustified attack on free enterprise. State socialism was not a "modern idea," but one as old as the Roman Empire, which had fallen in the attempt to provide bread and circuses for the masses. The truly modern state was a "night watchman" that preserved public order, but left room for the development of private enterprise in a free market. State socialism would stifle individual initiative, produce subjects rather than citizens, drones rather than

[47] *SBR* (1881), III, Anlagen, No. 228. For Bismarck's role in drafting the *Motive*, see *GW*, VIc, 204–206. See also Bismarck's speeches in defense of the bill. *BR*, IX, 9–43; X, 40–66.

[48] "Bericht über die Delegierten-Versammlung zu Nürnberg am 18. September 1882," *Verhandlungen, Mittheilungen und Berichte des Centralverbandes deutscher Industriellen*, No. 17 (Berlin, 1882), pp. 18, 30; "Stenographischer Bericht über die am 14. Mai 1884 in Berlin abgehaltene Generalversammlung," *ibid.*, No. 19 (Berlin, 1884). Bochum chamber of commerce to Bismarck, Mar. 31, 1884 (signed Baare), DZA Merseburg, Rep. 120, BB, VIII, 4, Nr. 1, Bd. 5, pp. 65–68, also pp. 100–151. For other reactions, see the numerous clippings from the daily press in DZA Merseburg, Rep. 120, A, XII, 1, Nr. 11, Bd. 3. See also Ullmann, "Industrielle Interessen," pp. 601–610.

[49] Vogel, *Bismarcks Arbeiterversicherung*, pp. 45–50. Ten years later Baare was shocked by the extent of the state social security system he had helped to initiate. *Ibid.*, pp. 41–42.

workers, reduce productivity rather than raise it. That reforms were needed was not denied, but left-liberals saw the solution in an extension of employers' liability, more mutual-aid associations, and more and larger private insurance companies. Social democrats, on the other hand, rejoiced over the "conflict of interests" within the "ruling class" that the bill brought to light and ironically claimed for themselves credit for the reform.[50]

The key to the parliamentary door on social insurance was held by the Center party. Since the 1860s Catholic churchmen, particularly Baron Wilhelm Emanuel von Ketteler, bishop of Mainz, had called for more attention to the social problems of the industrial age. That the electoral base of the Center contained a proletarian contingent also heightened the party's consciousness of social issues. During the late 1870s the Center joined in the agitation for new factory laws and assisted in incorporating the principle of compulsory factory inspection in the industrial code act of 1878. In opposing the antisocialist act of 1878, Windthorst argued that radical ideas could not be defeated by coercion, only by positive steps to remove the distresses upon which they fed. Although sympathetic to social insurance, Windthorst and his associates opposed those features of the 1881 bill that required large increases in the imperial budget and bureaucracy. These centralistic features, repugnant to the Center's federalism, were largely replaced in the bills of 1883 and 1884 by corporative institutions that harmonized with ideas advanced by Ketteler and other Catholic writers for two decades. The dynamics of party politics provided other persuasive reasons for the Center to support social insurance. By joining the two conservative parties to form a majority that warded off liberal amendments, they demonstrated their usefulness to the government and prepared the way for further assaults on the Kulturkampf laws.[51]

This combination placed the National Liberal party in a difficult position. As Bismarck foresaw, the fusion of the Secession with the progressives had driven the party to the right. Although capable of cooperating with left-liberals in opposing the government's attacks on parliamentary power (most recently, Puttkamer's suggestion that the secret ballot be dropped in Reichstag elections), the party came increasingly under the leadership of Johannes Miquel, who desired to work in harmony with the government and in competition with the Center. At Heidelberg on March 23, 1884, south German members of the party drafted a program that reflected these motives and was

[50] SBR (1881), I, 673–756; II, 1441–1556, 1619–1665, 1746–1783.

[51] SBR (1st sess., 1878), I, 205–206. Chairman of the parliamentary committee that recommended critical amendments to the accident insurance bill in 1881 was Baron Franckenstein; the reporter was Count Georg von Hertling. SBR (1881), I, 684–691; II, 1441–1443, 1468, 1488; IV, Anlagen, No. 159. See also Karl Bachem, Vorgeschichte, Geschichte und Politik der deutschen Zentrumspartei (9 vols., Cologne, 1927–1933), IV, 81–101; Eduard Hüsgen, Ludwig Windthorst (Cologne, 1928), pp. 315–333.

accepted by the party's general convention at Berlin in May. It praised Bismarck's foreign policy, advocated social reform (including accident insurance), supported extension of the antisocialist act, denounced "attempts at reaction," declared the tariff system essentially complete, expressed concern over the condition of agriculture, and favored new indirect taxes on security transactions, brandy, and sugar. Finally, the program decisively rejected the idea of "fusion with other parties."[52] After a futile attempt to modify the accident insurance bill in collaboration with left-liberals, they parted from the Freedom party by voting for the statute.

For proletarians the Reichstag election of October 8, 1884, constituted a referendum on the antisocialist and social insurance statutes. In 1881 all that Bismarck had been able to offer them was a commitment to reform; to his disappointment this did not suffice to attract their votes.[53] Now labor had two significant down payments on the commitment, and the question was whether the government's new solicitude for their welfare (including Bismarck's advocacy of their "right to work") would influence the labor vote. Although social democrats voted against both insurance statutes, the party gained in 1884 more ballots than ever before. Almost 550,000 persons (9.7 percent of the electorate) voted for the party of subversion, doubling the number of its deputies from twelve to twenty-four.[54]

Attack on Fire and Hail Insurance Companies

Social insurance for the benefit of workers was not Bismarck's only project in the insurance field during the early 1880s. Less well known is his position with regard to imperial regulation of the insurance business in general and his desire to establish a state monopoly of fire and hail insurance in Prussia for the benefit of property owners, particularly estate owners and small farmers. The state monopoly project provides yet another opportunity incidentally to observe the connection between his personal business experience and his formulation of government policy.

In giving to the central government the power to legislate on insurance, Bismarck and those officials who participated in drafting the constitution of 1867 responded to a general recognition among government officials, insurance companies, and policyholders that a regulatory statute was needed to establish common norms and standards for the industry. In the years that followed businessmen represented in the Prussian chambers of commerce and in the German Commercial Association urged the Reich to exercise its legis-

---

[52] Felix Salomon, Die deutschen Parteiprogramme (Leipzig, 1907), II, 33–36.

[53] BR, IX, 13ff.

[54] Bernhard Vogel, Dieter Nohlen, and Rainer-Olaf Schultze, Wahlen in Deutschland: Theorie-Geschichte-Dokumente, 1848–1970 (Berlin, 1971), pp. 290–291.

lative authority in this field, chiefly in the interest of insurers.[55] In 1869 work on an imperial regulatory statute was begun in the Prussian ministries following passage of a Bundesrat resolution in which the matter was described as "urgent." But the work was suspended in the 1870s, pending changes in the imperial statute on corporate law. Agitation for a regulatory statute and reform of the insurance industry in general reached a peak in 1878–1879. In those years petitions from the affected interests led to discussions in the Prussian Landtag and German Reichstag, ending in a Reichstag resolution calling for government action.[56]

The insurance business in Germany was shared by three types of firms, whose interests were not identical: "public mutual societies" (*öffentliche Societäten*) that enjoyed an official or semiofficial status, having been founded or fostered by the state during the eighteenth century for the protection of the public against disaster; numerous private mutual insurance companies of limited scope and capitalization; and a few large, joint-stock companies established during the nineteenth century. In the field of fire insurance, with which we will be chiefly concerned here, the public societies concentrated primarily on immobile property, the private mutual funds on mobile property, the joint-stock companies on both. Between 1863 and 1878 the amount of fire insurance in force in Prussia tripled for all three types of fire insurance firms. The amount for public mutual societies rose from 4,844,981,274 to 13,465,699,870 marks (including 990,161,406 marks on mobile property); private mutual companies from 623,686,827 to 2,303,046,655 marks (including 351,433,237 marks on immobile property); thirty-three joint-stock companies from 7,377,300,000 to 22,054,458,369 marks.[57] Although of late origin, the joint-stock companies overshadowed their older competitors. Their capacity to raise capital, accumulate reserves, and obtain reinsurance throughout Europe gave them a distinct advantage over mutual companies. As a consequence, the public societies agitated for government support in their struggle for competitive survival. The joint-stock companies, furthermore, were subject in the late 1870s to the same barrage of criticism experienced by their counterparts in other enterprises. They were accused of sharp practices, excessive premiums, and unwarranted profits.

Bismarck's long absences from Berlin during 1878–1879 left those Prussian ministries charged with supervising the insurance business (Ministry of Interior, Ministry of Agriculture, and Ministry of Justice) free, so they thought, to react to growing agitation. In June 1879 Friedberg and Hofmann gained Bismarck's approval for a circular dispatch from the Imperial Chancellery to

[55] DZA Merseburg, Rep. 120, A, XII, 1, Nr. 11, Bd. 1, pp. 1ff.

[56] Hofmann and Friedberg to Bismarck, June 26, 1879. DZA Potsdam, Reichskanzlei, 2309, pp. 14–16. Resolution of Jan. 28, 1878: SBHA (1877–1878), II, 1412; Anlagen, II, No. 158. Resolution of May 14, 1879: SBR (1879), II, 1193; V, No. 150.

[57] Puttkamer to Bismarck, Jan. 31, 1883. DZA Potsdam, Reichskanzlei, 17438, pp. 66–67.

the German governments seeking information and opinions preparatory to the drafting of an imperial regulatory statute.[58] When published on August 4, 1879, under Bismarck's signature as Reich chancellor, this document produced an astonishing reaction. Although nothing in it justified such a conclusion, the dispatch was widely regarded and publicly discussed in the press as the beginning of an effort by the government to nationalize the entire insurance industry. This idea was denounced particularly by liberals of laissez-faire disposition, journals specializing in the insurance trade, and officials, agents, and shareholders of the insurance corporations. The source of the agitation, noted Adolph Wagner, was the conviction that a chancellor who had pushed for nationalization of railways, a state tobacco monopoly, and protective tariffs and who had spoken favorably of Rodbertus and Lassalle and their state-socialist ideas would be quite capable of such an encroachment on the free enterprise system. Hence it was better to sound the tocsin now than to be too late.[59]

By the time the dispatch of August 4 appeared in the newspapers, Bismarck had forgotten having discussed the matter with Hofmann and Friedberg in June. Nevertheless, he did not disapprove—far from it. He wrote to his colleagues in Berlin that he had repeatedly observed "swindling activity" by insurers against hail damage. They had been known to collect premiums for twenty years based on a crop assessment that they then disputed when the hail fell in the twenty-first year. Landowners with official connections or good lawyers were treated generously, but the average farmer was defenseless against "insidious" clauses in company policies.[60] One year later, nevertheless, Bismarck was outraged to discover that Prussian ministers were actually drafting an imperial regulatory statute on the basis of the replies from the state governments to the inquiry of August 4, 1879.[61] During that year he had developed a keen interest in the insurance problem and had begun to pursue objectives different from those of his colleagues. A hint as to the direction of his thoughts can be seen in his positive reaction to an article by Ludwig Büchner advocating nationalization of the life insurance business. After reading the piece in December 1880, not long after he assumed command of the Prussian Ministry of Commerce for the purpose of launching his social insurance program, the prince scrawled in the margin, "No dividends from misery."[62]

[58] Hofmann (for Bismarck) to state governments, Aug. 4, 1879. DZA Potsdam, Reichskanzlei, 2309, pp. 16–21.

[59] Adolph Wagner, "Der Staat und das Versicherungswesen," Zeitschrift für die gesamte Staatswissenschaft, 37 (1881), pp. 102–103.

[60] Bismarck to Hofmann, Oct. 11, 1879, and Hofmann to Bismarck, Oct. 13, 1879. Ibid., pp. 8–13.

[61] Jacobi to Bismarck (with Bismarck's marginalia), Sept. 21 and 25, 1880. DZA Merseburg, Rep. 120, A, XII, 1, Nr. 21, Bd. 1.

[62] Poschinger, ed., Bismarck-Portefeuille, I, 25–26.

As minister of commerce, Bismarck ordered his subordinates to cease all work on the bill; as chancellor, he transferred the matter to the Imperial Office of the Interior.[63] In this way he took it out of the hands of Prussian ministers and counselors and placed it under his direct control. There the regulatory statute appears to have rested for many months, while Bödiker, Lohmann, and their associates proceeded with the accident and health insurance statutes. In November 1881 Bismarck launched another inquiry among the German governments in search of additional information concerning the insurance industry as a whole.[64] But this démarche was followed by another year of apparent inaction. Then suddenly, in December 1882, Bismarck launched a major campaign within the Prussian and German governments not only for the completion and passage of an imperial regulatory statute, but

"EVENTUALLY IT WILL COME TO THIS: ONCE EVERYTHING ELSE HAS BEEN MONOPOLIZED AND NATION-ALIZED, *KLADDERADATSCH*'S TURN WILL COME." BISMARCK SKETCHES HIS FAMOUS THREE HAIRS ON THE JOURNAL'S SYMBOLIC FIGURE, AS FINANCE MINISTER BITTER AND CARTOONIST SCHOLZ LOOK OVER HIS SHOULDER AND INTERIOR MINISTER PUTTKAMER DRAFTS HIS CONDOLENCES IN THE BACKGROUND. WILHELM SCHOLZ IN *KLADDERADATSCH*, 1882.

[63] Bismarck to cabinet, Oct. 16, 1880. DZA Potsdam, Reichskanzlei, 2309, p. 69.

[64] Boetticher (for Bismarck) to state governments, Nov. 17, 1881. DZA Merseburg, Rep. 120, A, XII, 1, Nr. 11, Bd. 2. The dispatch stated that the imperial government had resolved, in view of the replies received to its inquiry of August 4, 1879, to draft a bill requiring all joint-stock insurance companies to apply for licenses from the Imperial Insurance Office, which would regulate the industry. For the working papers on the regulatory statute, see DZA Potsdam, Reichsamt des Innern, 17223–17225.

also for eventual public ownership in the field of fire and hail insurance. What impelled him to take this step (to which historians have given little attention) at a time when the accident and health insurance bills were not under lock and key?

As the owner of three great estates, each with many buildings, Bismarck was a heavy consumer of insurance. In the Sachsenwald, his most extensive possession, were no less than forty-three buildings insured under five-year policies for 704,603 marks with premiums totaling 4,369 marks annually.[65] The owner of Friedrichsruh, so conscious of property taxes, was hardly indifferent toward this burden on his income. In late November 1882 *Die vaterländische Feuer- und Hagel-Versicherungs-Aktiengesellschaft in Elberfeld* informed Bismarck's manager at Friedrichsruh that it proposed to increase its fire insurance premiums on the Sachsenwald properties by 25 to 50 percent under the next five-year contract beginning in 1883. Over a ten-year period, the letter explained, the company had suffered losses in Lauenburg of 168,000 marks (including a loss of 25,191 marks on Bismarck's own property) and in neighboring Schleswig-Holstein of 600,000 marks.[66] On December 20 Bismarck read in the *Reichsanzeiger* that the Elberfeld corporation had paid dividends to shareholders of 20 percent in 1880 and 37.5 percent in 1881.[67]

On December 22, 1882, the Prussian minister of commerce (Bismarck) officially informed the German chancellor (Bismarck) that, at a time when corporate profits in general were modest, the gains of insurance corporations (especially fire insurance) had reached a level out of proportion to their performances. Annual dividends of many major companies (the Elberfeld company was named) ranged from 20 to 70 percent. Such profits, extracted from "the misfortunes of individuals," were a matter of "serious concern" because of their effect on the economy in general. The companies, whose shares were booming on the stock market, were trying continually to increase their rates. Their limited number permitted them to agree on rates and avoid competition. But the companies also improved their earnings by exploiting every opportunity to reduce payments to the insured. If a building was not fully insured and part of it remained standing after a fire, they refused all compensation. Insurers canceled policies but refused to refund premiums paid in advance.

---

[65] *Verzeichnis der Feuerversicherungs-Policen der Fürstlich von Bismarck'schen Fideikommissherrschaft Schwarzenbeck.* Bleichröder Archive, Kress Library of Business and Economics, Harvard, Box IV.

[66] Ebel and Schultze (for *Vaterländische Feuer- und Hagel-Versicherungs-Aktiengesellschaft in Elberfeld*) to Forester Lange, Nov. 24, 1882, *Bleichröder Archive*, Box IV. Expansion of the Bismarck dwelling in the winter of 1882–1883 would have in any case increased Bismarck's insurance bill. By Lange's estimate the mansion was destined to increase in value from 100,800 to 132,000 marks and its inventory from 51,555 to 60,000 marks. Lange to Bleichröder, Dec. 25, 1882. *Ibid.*, Box IV.

[67] *Börsen-Beilage zum deutschen Reichs-Anzeiger und preussischen Staats-Anzeiger*, No. 299 (Dec. 20, 1882), DZA Potsdam, Reichskanzlei, 17438, p. 15.

Companies cheated small farmers out of compensation for hail damage by delaying their assessments until the extent of the damage could no longer be proved. Mutual companies were not guilty of these abuses, but their competitive capacity was limited.

Since "the economic interests of the most numerous classes of the population" were affected, the state must enter into competition with corporate insurers, making possible a redistribution of money absorbed by the insurance business, a considerable reduction in rates, and fairer treatment of the insured. "No risk is involved for the state." The preparations for imperial regulation, under way since 1869, had perhaps been slowed by the attempt to draft a single statute covering all branches of the insurance industry. The difficulties could be reduced by dealing "at least in Prussia" with those branches of the trade, such as fire insurance, that affected all classes of the population and the economy generally.[68] On January 4, 1883, Chancellor Bismarck replied to Minister of Commerce Bismarck that many German states already possessed state-owned or state-controlled companies providing, either directly or indirectly, obligatory fire insurance on immobile property, whose surrender to the Reich they would resist. For that reason a publicly owned fire insurance company should be created for Prussia, leaving to the Reich the regulation of private life, accident, fire, cattle, and hail insurance companies for Germany as a whole.[69]

The proposal that Bismarck sent to Bismarck also went to the pertinent Prussian ministers and the federal governments.[70] Minister of Agriculture Lucius, whose ministry bore responsibility for hail insurance, denied that all hail insurers were guilty of Bismarck's charges; in this field mutual companies, he declared, were already equal to and even superior to joint-stock companies in competitiveness; to found a state hail insurance enterprise would be difficult in view of many practical obstacles standing in the way.[71] Interior Minister Puttkamer, whose ministry was responsible for fire insurance, also objected to Bismarck's proposal. The problems of the insurance business, he declared, did not stem from the large joint-stock companies. Their huge profits were derived not from excessive premiums but from interest on invested reserves accumulated during "luckier or less competitive years." Instead, the problems

---

[68] DZA Potsdam, Reichskanzlei, 17438, pp. 9–14.

[69] Ibid., pp. 16–20, 25.

[70] Bismarck to Lucius and Puttkamer, Jan. 8, 1883, and Bismarck to state governments, Feb. 28, 1883. DZA Potsdam, Reichskanzlei, 17438, pp. 22–25, 45–47. How important the rise in insurance rates was for Bismarck can be seen in his amendment to the draft of this dispatch. Ibid., p. 39. For Boetticher's role in drafting the dispatch, see Boetticher to Bismarck, Feb. 13, 1883. Ibid., pp. 26–32.

[71] Lucius to Bismarck, Mar. 12, 1883. DZA Potsdam, Reichskanzlei, 17438, pp. 50–57. Some months later Lucius saw the wisdom of agreeing with the chancellor and proposed a plan for transforming an existing mutual company into a competing state institution for hail insurance. Ibid., 2309, pp. 144–145.

arose from the small private mutual and joint-stock companies, which for lack of reserve capital were vulnerable to major disasters and inclined to cheat their customers. He proposed that Prussia create a state-owned fire insurance company, which would, in cooperation with the existing public insurance societies, monopolize fire insurance on immobile property (to be made obligatory for all owners), leaving to joint-stock companies all insurance on mobile property. Rather than compete against each other, the state and larger corporations would simply divide the insurance market. The state-owned company that Bismarck proposed would, in Puttkamer's opinion, gradually absorb the smaller, less competitive enterprises (beginning with the public societies and mutual companies) but eventually the larger corporations as well. The final result would be a monopoly of the entire insurance business, a consequence that he presumed Bismarck did not desire.[72]

On March 19 Bismarck carried his initiative to the governors of Prussia's provinces, seeking information on how to strengthen and diversify the public mutual societies in order to make them competitive with the joint-stock companies.[73] Through this channel the news of Bismarck's démarche reached the newspapers and the public, including frightened boards of directors and investors in private insurance corporations.[74] For a decade, the *Nationalzeitung* complained, insurers had waited in vain for a regulatory statute; now suddenly the Prussian minister of commerce had "hurled a thunderbolt" at the fire insurance business.[75] "How could it be," asked a pamphleteer, "that the greatest statesman of our time was presented with drafts and reports that absolutely do not accord with the facts?"[76] That the mighty chancellor may have launched an attack on a major branch of German business without working his way through a pile of pertinent papers did not seem plausible. That his action could have been triggered by a steep hike in his fire insurance bill, no one until now seems to have suspected—except perhaps the officers of his Elberfeld insurer, whose thoughts on the matter are unrecorded. On July 12, 1883, the officers had a chance to measure the length of the chancellor's arm when

[72] Puttkamer to Bismarck, Jan. 31 and Mar. 11, 1883 (with *Denkschrift*). DZA Potsdam, Reichskanzlei, 17438, pp. 58–73, and 17439, pp. 9–16.

[73] DZA Potsdam, Reichskanzlei, 17438, pp. 86, 162–163.

[74] For the reaction of insurers, see *Eingabe des Ausschusses des Verbandes deutscher Privat-Feuerversicherungs-Gesellschaften an den Herren Oberpräsidenten des preussischen Staates*, June 4, 1883. DZA Potsdam, Reichskanzlei, 2309, pp. 104–105, and petition of the Assekuranz-Club zu Leipzig, July 1883, *ibid.*, 17438, p. 158ff. Also *Die Sparcasse*, No. 29, May 19, 1883. *Ibid.*, 17438, p. 85.

[75] *Nationalzeitung*, Sept. 8, 1883. DZA Potsdam, Reichskanzlei, 17438, p. 163.

[76] Hugo Schramm-MacDonald, *Das Feuerversicherungswesen mit Bezug auf den Erlass des preussischen Handelsministers Fürsten von Bismarck vom 19. März 1883* (Dresden, 1883), p. 39. The pamphlet is to be found in DZA Potsdam, Reichskanzlei, 17438, pp. 165–186. The minister of justice also received a copy and promptly sent it on to the ministry library. GSA, Rep. 84a, 11183, p. 142.

the provincial government of Schleswig-Holstein (which included Lauenburg) issued an ordinance requiring local police to register all insurance
agents, record any legal judgments against them, and prevent the sale of insurance policies providing multiple and excessive coverage.[77]

By the end of 1883 Bismarck's thoughts about fire and hail insurance reform
had advanced beyond both his original proposal of January 1883 and Puttkamer's counterproposal of March 11, 1883. He now preferred to replace "*all*"
private companies in this field with a single mutual company supervised by
the state. The result would have been a state-controlled insurance monopoly
"similar to that in accident insurance." He appears, nevertheless, to have
remained isolated within the Prussian government in this objective. Even his
secretaries, Rottenburg and Bill Bismarck, were opposed. The prince could
not "shove" the matter forward and decided as a consequence to accept an
alternative plan offered by Minister of Finance Scholz, namely, to assist public mutual societies in their efforts to meet the challenge of the joint-stock
companies. By consolidating the societies within each province, by extending
their business to include mobile property, and by providing for mutual reinsurance these societies expected to become more competitive. To assist them
the state would provide guidance, exercise stricter control over joint-stock
insurance companies, and hinder the appearance of new private enterprises
in the fire insurance business. "In that way" Bismarck concluded sourly, "we
can at least make some progress in the matter."[78]

But even this modest proposal got nowhere. Puttkamer was the only minister to respond to it; he expressed agreement with the goal but found obstacles.[79] As minister of the interior, his was the responsibility of initiating the
reform, but apparently he did little or nothing. In the summers of 1885 and
1886 Bismarck considered the possibility of forcing Puttkamer to act by reviving his initial plan to create a state institution to sell fire and possibly hail
insurance in competition with joint-stock companies. But in 1886–1887 Bismarck's time and attention were absorbed by other matters, and he did not

[77] *Polizeiverordnung, betreffend des Feuerversicherungswesens*, July 12, 1883. GSA, Rep. 84a,
11183, pp. 145–145v. On Aug. 15 the *Verband Deutscher Privatfeuerversicherungsgesellschaften*
took exception to the ordinance on the grounds that the provincial government had exceeded
its powers—the matter was not a proper subject for police regulation. On Jan. 11, 1884, the
Ministry of Interior revoked the ordinance. SBHA (2d. sess., 1883–1884), Anlagen, No. 217
(Zehnter Bericht der Kommission für Petitionen).

[78] Wilhelm von Bismarck to Rottenburg, Dec. 31, 1883. DZA Potsdam, Reichskanzlei, 2309,
p. 169; Minister of Commerce Bismarck (draft by Boetticher) to Prussian cabinet, Feb. 4, 1884,
ibid., pp. 170–174. For Scholz's proposal, see his *Votum* to Prussian cabinet, Apr. 18, 1883. DZA
Potsdam, Reichskanzlei, 17438, pp. 80–82. The responses to Bismarck's initiative of March 19
by sixteen directors of public mutual societies, proposing ways to increase their competitive effectiveness, also influenced the decision to follow Scholz's suggestion. Rommel to Bismarck, Oct.
7, 1883. DZA Potsdam, Reichskanzlei, 2309, pp. 107–113.

[79] Puttkamer to cabinet, March 4, 1884. DZA Potsdam, Reichskanzlei, 2310, pp. 91–94.

carry out his intention.[80] Nor does he appear to have pushed for completion of the imperial regulatory statute, which did not become law until 1900, years after he left office.

Bismarck enjoyed no greater success when he tried to continue his feud with fire insurance companies in the courts. In early December 1884 he received, as Prussian minister of commerce, the grievance of Heinrich Schlepegrell, a small farmer (*Köthner*) at Oedeme near Lüneburg, against the *Aachen-Leipziger Versicherungsactiengesellschaft*. Schlepegrell had insured for 3,950 marks furniture and equipment valued at 5,000 marks. When the dwelling burned down, the insurance adjusters assessed the loss at 1,465 marks, although few of the insured items escaped the flames. The cotter had many complaints about the conduct of the company agent, adjuster, and damage assessor—not only about the amount they offered in settlement, but the method of assessment, the technical jargon used, their overbearing and threatening manners, their expectation that he should sign the settlement without reading it, and finally their attempt to coerce him physically into signing it. Ultimately he accepted the company offer (minus 46 marks for "costs"), but only after the superior court at Cologne refused to hear his suit against the company. The local state's attorney refused, furthermore, to prosecute (too much time had elapsed, he said) the cotter's charge of fraud against the company's agent and adjustor, who then sued him for libel.[81]

Schlepegrell's appeal for help reached Bismarck's desk at a favorable moment—when his own indignation and frustration were at their peak. (The petitioner was, furthermore, a near neighbor on the Lüneburg heath not far from Friedrichsruh.) He lost no time in forwarding it to the Ministry of Justice, which overrode a negative opinion by the attorney general (*Oberstaatsanwalt*) by deciding to try the case. In June 1885 the criminal court in Lüneburg decided for the defendants; the state had not proven that they intended to profit from the settlement with Schlepegrell.[82]

In the spring of 1887 the Hammermühle, one of the paper mills operated by the Behrends at Varzin, burned to the ground. Reconstruction cost 176,934 marks, of which the insurance paid only 119,462 marks. That Bismarck had to come up with the difference (57,472 marks) could not have improved his feelings about fire insurance companies.[83] Surely it was not mere coincidence that during that same summer the lord of Varzin ordered his estate superintendent, the forester Ernst Westphal, to initiate the prosecution of a local insurance agent who had sold excessive insurance to laborers in the area. The case was dismissed when it was determined that the agent's addi-

[80] Gamp to Bismarck, July 31, 1885. DZA Potsdam, Reichskanzlei, 2310, pp. 39–62. Jacobi to Rottenburg, July 9, 1886. *Ibid.*, pp. 63–65.

[81] Schlepegrell to Bismarck, Nov. 25, 1884. GSA, Rep. 84a, 11183, pp. 148–151v.

[82] Friedberg to Bismarck, June 23, 1885. GSA, Rep. 84a, 11183, pp. 180–196.

[83] Moritz Behrend to Bleichröder, July 27, 1887, *Bleichröder Archive*, Box IV.

tional commission on the unnecessary insurance amounted only to pennies. But Bismarck was not appeased. "The advantage of overinsuring," he wrote acidly to Westphal, "does not accrue to the agent directly but to the company."[84] He sought through the Ministry of Justice to pursue the matter into the appeals courts.[85]

Imperial Election of 1884

The social insurance laws of 1883, 1884, and 1889 (to be discussed later) were path-breaking efforts to achieve social justice, unmatched in other countries for decades and in some features still unequaled in the United States. "That radical politics in America with rare exceptions has been a European import is not greatly to be disputed," Daniel Moynihan wrote in 1973. "But this is true equally of reformist politics. The bold reform programs of the thirties and forties and fifties and beyond (we are just, for example, getting to health insurance) have consisted to a dispiriting degree of ideas Lloyd George borrowed from Bismarck."[86] The lives of millions of Americans have been influenced in some way by legislation that Bismarck and his assistants designed for German workers more than a century ago.

Of Bismarck's many achievements, the national system of social insurance alone survived Germany's debacles in the twentieth century. And yet the reform did not accomplish his immediate objective, for it did not ease class conflict in Germany and close the most serious gap in the social consensus he sought. The reason for that failure probably lay in the tactics he chose and the limitations of the reforms he fostered. He cynically overestimated both the seductive power of the material benefits the program conferred and, as earlier in the Kulturkampf, the capacity of the state to repress a political movement led by determined men and inspired by an intense moral idealism. To the end he remained unwilling to push for labor protection (Arbeiterschutz) as opposed to labor insurance (Arbeiterversicherung), or, to put the matter another way, to take care of the worker inside as well as outside the mine and factory. In the government and Reichstag he continued resolutely to oppose attempts to establish a standard working day, impose new restrictions on child and female labor, prohibit Sunday labor, strengthen the powers of factory inspectors, and the like. Too much regulation of working conditions, he argued, would "kill the goose that laid the golden egg" by increasing the costs of owners to a point where they could no longer compete with foreign pro-

[84] Westphal to Bismarck (with Bismarck's marginalia), Dec. 9, 1887. DZA Potsdam, Reichskanzlei, 2310, pp. 112–113.

[85] Friedberg to Bismarck, Dec. 14, 1887. Ibid., p. 114. I found no documents on this case in the files of the Ministry of Justice.

[86] Daniel P. Moynihan, The Politics of a Guaranteed Income: The Nixon Administration and the Family Assistance Plan (New York, 1973), pp. 4–5.

ducers.[87] He resented incursions by factory inspectors in his own paper mills and sawmills, and he presumed that such intervention would alienate the business class as a whole, which would express its resentments at the polls. His obduracy on the issue of labor protection, coupled with his insistence that indirect taxes were not regressive, injured his credibility among those whose allegiance the social insurance laws were designed to win.

For the upper classes Bismarck had other bait in the Reichstag election campaign of 1884. He hoped to capitalize on the swelling popular interest in Africa arising from the well-publicized exploits of Stanley, de Brazza, Wissmann, and others and from the crescendo of popular agitation produced by the organs and publicists of the colonial movement.[88] Neither Reichstag nor Bundesrat had any voice in the commitment of *Schutzbriefe* to Hanseatic companies—in itself a commentary on the German constitutional order. The purpose of this device, in fact, was to keep the matter out of the fiscal claws of the Reichstag. Yet Bismarck found a way to involve the Reichstag and hence to demonstrate to the voting public that those who opposed him on other issues were enemies of the national interest when it came to protecting German merchants abroad, rescuing German industry from the perils of depression, and proving the virility of the German nation by new and highly visible successes in the game of power politics. Not since 1871 had he found a chauvinistic issue of such appeal with which to belabor the German electorate.

Shortly after he made the final decision to support Lüderitz, Bismarck presented to the Bundesrat (April 23, 1884) a bill appropriating up to 4 million marks annually for fifteen years to subsidize private steamship lines to China, Japan, Australia, New Zealand, and Samoa. The purpose given was to promote exports, carry mail, and build up the shipbuilding industry and merchant marine as a support to the navy. When the bill reached the Reichstag in mid-June, Bismarck had a forum where he could explain the Angra Pequena affair, advertise the fact that the government had launched a major new policy, and establish the policy's character and limits.

On June 14 and 26 he participated in the debates, and on June 23, for the first time since 1871, he appeared before the budget committee to which the bill was referred. Just as the subsidization of railway construction had vivified trade within Germany, he argued, government support for steamship lines would promote exports and benefit "national labor" by producing jobs and

[87] See his negative response to the attempts of the centrist deputy Count von Hertling to extract from the government legislation stiffening factory laws and factory inspection. *BR*, IX, 199–218, and X, 430–439. Also Bismarck to Maybach, *AWB*, II, 95–96, and Bismarck to Boetticher, Apr. 12, 1888. Goldschmidt, *Reich und Preussen*, pp. 314–315.

[88] Boetticher and Caprivi heard him say that "all this fuss about colonies was only being made because of the elections." Diary of Friedrich von Holstein, Sept. 19 and 23, 1884. Norman Rich and M. H. Fisher, eds., *The Holstein Papers: The Memoirs, Diaries and Correspondence of Friedrich von Holstein, 1837–1909* (4 vols., Cambridge, Eng., 1955–1963), II, 161, 163.

staving off starvation. An "overseas policy," he informed the committee, was only possible if the government possessed the enthusiastic support of the nation. Germany had no intention of creating "artificial" colonies by seizing open land, attracting settlers, sending out garrisons and administrators. To protect settlements already established and territories already acquired was a different matter. Neither in the case of the subsidized steamship lines nor in the case of the colonies could one calculate the benefits exactly; one could only judge the utility of both by the experience of other countries. "He considers it presumptuous for us to maintain that Germans are incapable of benefiting from activities that bring profits to other nations." No longer need German citizens stand "hat in hand" to beg for protection from other powers. But these arguments had no effect on Bamberger, Richter, and Rickert, who condemned the bill as a burden on the taxpayers and another infringement of laissez-faire. With the help of the Center the left-liberals succeeded in burying the bill in committee.[89]

Bismarck, however, had gained a new, dynamic election issue. During August news appeared in the German press of the achievements of Nachtigal in Togoland and the Cameroons, followed by reports of additional "flag raising" in Southwest Africa. For a public disturbed since March by the apparent attempt of Britain and Portugal to seal off the Congo basin, there was an official announcement that Berlin itself was to be the site of an international congress, whose aim was to keep that vast region open to the traders of all countries. There can be no doubt that the new role that Germany had assumed in world politics was popular among middle- and upper-class Germans. After initial hesitation the Center party jumped on the bandwagon, and even left-liberals were increasingly reluctant to contest the value of colonies.[90]

Bismarck hoped that the national liberals would be the chief beneficiaries of the twin issues of social reform and overseas expansion. The subsidy bill, he declared, had given them a new platform from which "to spring into the circus." For six years, he told the Prussian cabinet, he had governed without the national liberals, but now it was possible to govern with them, "until they again became too strong and uppity." For Puttkamer's benefit he added, "To accomplish anything with the right is impossible; it is just as incompetent as are the progressives."[91] Although governmental pressure was much less in ev-

---

[89] SBR (1884), II, 719–747; BR, X, 149ff., 166ff., 176ff., 180ff. During the committee hearing Bamberger and Richter charged that the purpose of the bill was to provide transport at public expense for the New Guinea Consortium and German South Seas Trading and Plantation Company in Samoa (that is, Bleichröder, Hansemann, and other big investors). BR, X, 177–183.

[90] The author benefited from an unpublished seminar paper analyzing issues and party attitudes during the Reichstag election of 1884 written by Winfried Seelig. For a description of the colonial issue in the campaign, see Klaus J. Bade, *Friedrich Fabri und der Imperialismus in der Bismarckzeit* (Freiburg, 1975), pp. 237–243.

[91] Lucius diary, July 22, 1884. *Bismarck-Erinnerungen*, pp. 297–298. Also to Eduard Cohen,

idence than in 1881, the official press and bureaucracy favored national liberal candidates.[92] On election eve Lucius judged that Bismarck still thought of appointing Bennigsen to the Prussian cabinet. But the chancellor also had other, blacker thoughts. "If the election results are excessively oppositional, the parliamentary system will be ruined that much faster and the way prepared for saber rule."[93]

In the Reichstag election of October 28, 1884, Bismarck's assault upon left-liberal deputies had some effect on the electorate, but not enough to create a right-wing majority. Although the number of eligible voters casting ballots rose from 56.3 to 60.5 percent, the Freedom party was able to capture only 67 seats in its first national election, a big reduction from the 106 seats (60 progressives and 46 secessionists) the left-liberals had held since 1881. Of

AN AUSTRIAN CARTOONIST'S VIEW OF BISMARCK'S CONDITION AFTER SUCCESSIVE REICHSTAG ELECTORAL DEFEATS IN 1881 AND 1884. *HUMORISTISCHE BLÄTTER*, VIENNA, NOVEMBER 9, 1884.

May 3, 1884. GW, VIII, 303. Since late March Bismarck had been making overtures to Bennigsen and Miquel. Rich and Fisher, eds., *Holstein Papers*, II, 116–117.
   [92] SEG (1884), p. 101.
   [93] Lucius diary, Oct. 27, 1884. *Bismarck-Erinnerungen*, p. 304.

the parties that supported the social insurance laws and the government's new colonial policy, only the conservatives made major gains (50 to 78 seats), while the national liberals enjoyed a modest rise from 47 to 51 and the centrists lost 1 (electing 99 deputies), the Poles 2 (electing 16 deputies).[94]

Again the Center party, the pariah of the 1870s, emerged as the swing party in the chamber. By combining with the two conservative parties, it could produce a slim majority of 205 out of 397 votes even without the help of its Polish allies. By joining other opposition parties—left-liberals, social democrats, Poles, Guelphs (11 seats), Alsatians (15 seats), and Danes (1 seat)—it could create a majority of 240 deputies. The combination that Bismarck favored (conservatives, free conservatives, and national liberals) could muster only 157 votes.[95]

After the election of 1884 Bismarck's interest in social insurance legislation visibly slackened.[96] The old-age and disability bill, announced as imminent in 1883,[97] did not reach parliament until 1888–1889. In discussing the problem of dissident workers, Catholics, Poles, Danes, Alsatians, and Guelphs during these years, he generally expressed confidence in the long-term effects of universal military service and public education. The army, schools, and universities would inculcate the virtues of national patriotism, German culture, social order, and political obedience that would produce the social consensus he sought. This is not to say that he had surrendered the prospect of political coups of more immediate effect in manipulating the electorate. As the mid-1880s arrived, he shifted his attention from tax programs, insurance reform, and social reform to foreign affairs in search of the means with which to garner public support for his regime.

Bludgeoning the Reichstag, 1884–1885

"How Schweninger treats me!" Bismarck exclaimed in March 1884, "Bland soup, bland fish, bland veal, and even bland wine. I am not permitted to have anything from the partridges that are to follow."[98] During the spring numerous appearances in the Reichstag, preparations for the Prussian State Council, and accelerated diplomatic activity took their toll, despite three weeks in Friedrichsruh (May 17–June 7). As the Reichstag neared adjournment in

[94] Vogel et al., *Wahlen in Deutschland*, pp. 290–291. In the runoff election centrists, left-liberals, and social democrats cooperated to defeat national liberal candidates. BR, X, 233–236.

[95] See Bismarck's analysis of the parliamentary situation, BR, X, 289ff.

[96] Lucius, *Bismarck-Erinnerungen*, p. 352; Otto Vossler, "Bismarcks Sozialpolitik," *Historische Zeitschrift*, 167 (1943), p. 344.

[97] Imperial rescript of Apr. 14, 1883. SEG (1883), pp. 59–60. Throne speech read by Boetticher, Mar. 6, 1884. SEG (1884), pp. 29–30.

[98] Julius von Eckardt diary, Mar. 31, 1884. GW, VIII, 503.

June, he requested the Kaiser's permission to recuperate in Varzin.[99] By now Schweninger had become so indispensable that at Bismarck's request *Kultus-minister* Gossler made him chief of a new dermatology (!) clinic at the famed Charité hospital in Berlin and created for him an "extraordinary" professorship at the University of Berlin, a sinecure that allowed him to give up his Munich practice. The Berlin medical faculty, boiling with indignation at this violation of its autonomy, shunned the new colleague.[100] When the renowned physiologist Emil Du Bois-Reymond disdainfully returned Schweninger's calling card, Bill Bismarck challenged the doctor to a duel! The professor refused to shoot it out with the chancellor's son. In the Prussian Chamber of Deputies Gossler defended the funding of the position (3,900 marks) on the grounds that keeping the chancellor healthy was in the national interest.[101]

With Schweninger at his elbow, the prince skipped his usual cure at Kissingen and spent the rest of the summer at Varzin. In mid-September he journeyed to Skierniewicz for a meeting of the three emperors and stood the trip well. On returning to Friedrichsruh, however, he suffered a relapse, blaming it on accumulated work dumped on him by vacationing colleagues. Overseas affairs were particularly burdensome, since he had no separate staff for these matters. But the setback was minor. On October 11 Cohen found him "extraordinarily cheerful, talkative, and amiable; he looked well, has become somewhat heavier." He returned to Berlin on October 21 complaining only of facial neuralgia, which at times impeded his speech. He remained in the capital until June 4, 1885, one of the longest periods in many years. For once, there are few recorded complaints about his health. Bucher reported to Busch in February 1885 that the chancellor looked "quite young and rosy" and was "working fearfully hard." But this meant, as Bismarck himself explained to the Reichstag, only three to five hours a day, in contrast to the twelve to sixteen of which he had once been capable.[102]

Improved health did not change the chancellor's attitude toward parliament. His annual joust with the Reichstag began on November 14, 1884, six days before it convened, when the government curtailed the deputies' right of free passage on German railways, which they had enjoyed since 1873. No longer could the deputies travel anywhere within the Reich while the Reichs-

[99] Horst Kohl, ed., *Fürst Bismarck: Regesten zu einer wissenschaflichen Biographie des ersten Reichskanzlers* (Stuttgart, 1891–1892), II, 318–324.

[100] See Gossler's defense of the appointment in the debates of the Chamber of Deputies. *SBHA* (1885), I, 590ff.

[101] Arthur von Brauer, *Im Dienste Bismarcks* (Berlin, 1936), pp. 145–146; Ludwig Hahn and Carl Wippermann, *Fürst Bismarck: Sein Leben und Wirken* (Berlin, 1891), V, 460–462.

[102] Bismarck to Kaiser, Sept. 29, 1884. GW, VIc, 304; VIII, 512; Busch, *Tagebuchblätter*, III, 172, 184. Lucius, *Bismarck-Erinnerungen*, p. 302; BR, X, 419; Rich and Fischer, eds., *Holstein Papers*, II, 173.

tag was in session; they were limited to the stretch between their homes and the capital. Left-liberal deputies reacted by shoving aside the budget bill, ordinarily the first item of business, to revive an old issue—a constitutional amendment granting per diem and travel costs. Almost every year between 1867 and 1876 they had passed such a bill, only to have it rejected by the Bundesrat. This time Bismarck promised to consent, but only if the majority conceded changes in the suffrage law! Otherwise his words were as uncompromising and venomous as ever. "I do not let myself be impressed by the Reichstag's majority. . . . You are not the men for that. . . . I have not let myself be impressed by all Europe; you will not be the first ones. And, furthermore, of what is this majority composed?" Of radical "republicans" who wished to govern, ultramontanes who wanted priests to govern, and "foreigners" eager to destroy the Reich itself. Only three caucuses mustering 157 votes supported the national interest. At bottom the issue, he declared, was a struggle for power over the state. No bill presented by the government would be considered on its own merits. "The fate of all bills to be presented in this session is clearly already predictable.[103]

The legislative session of 1884–1885, however, was not barren. In colonialism the chancellor had found a national issue with which to batter his opponents. Budget estimates for 1885–1886 showed a prospective deficit for the Reich of nearly 45,000,000 marks (10,000,000 marks of which were for increased military expenditures) to be covered by borrowing rather than by increased state assessments. Included in the budget were 150,000 marks for African exploration, 20,000 marks for a new, high-ranking official to head the colonial section of the foreign office and to raise the pay of subaltern officials in the Imperial Chancellery. During the session supplementary appropriations were requested for colonial purposes: 96,000 marks for various officials in Africa (including a governor for the Cameroons), 152,000 marks for new consulate buildings (including a jail), 180,000 marks for a coastal steamer in Africa, 5,400 marks in subsidies for "mail steamers" in Africa, Asia, and Australia, and 305,750 marks for sundry other purposes. All of the supplementary appropriations were to be covered by increased state assessments.[104]

As usual Richter, the Reichstag's budget expert, subjected the entire balance sheet to critical scrutiny, after which the budget committee voted to eliminate or reduce severely the new appropriations. While the deputies deliberated, the press kept reporting, week after week, a steady stream of new accomplishments in overseas policy: acceptance by the Berlin congress of free trade in the Congo basin and of measures to end the slave trade in Africa: the

---

[103] SBR (1884–1885), I, 17–43, 434–435; BR, X, 239ff. The bill was again passed by the Reichstag (180 to 99) and rejected by the Bundesrat.

[104] SBR (1884–1885), Anlagen, I, Nos. 8, 9, 10, 16, 155.

glorious victory of German gunboats and marines over pro-British black rebels in the Cameroons; and new flag raisings and *Schutzgebiete* in Africa and South Pacific. In addition, the foreign office published a series of "white books" containing documents (some deceptively edited) that revealed the degree of friction between Berlin and London over Germany's acquisition of Angra Pequena, Togo, and the Cameroons and over the claims of German merchants in the Fiji Islands. Although London countered with "blue books," the German public was prone to accept Bismarck's view that Britain had jealously tried to bar Germany from acquiring possessions in "free Africa" and elsewhere. In the Reichstag Bismarck charged that by their resistance to appropriations for the coastal steamer, exploration, and consulates, the deputies had encouraged the British and made his task more difficult. He received the full request in all three instances.[105]

The opposition was also on weak ground in resisting increases in the size and salaries of Bismarck's office personnel. In comparison to chancelleries of other countries, his was unquestionably understaffed, underpaid, and overworked. In the chamber Bismarck and Herbert, now state secretary of the foreign office, described how subordinates worked from 8:00 A.M. to 10:00 P.M., often longer, without Sundays off. An increased volume of business in the foreign office compelled the chancellor himself to perform some routine functions. Of three top officials, one or more was usually ill, the consequence of overwork. "From early until rather late in the day hardly a quarter of an hour passes, often no more than five minutes, without someone opening my door and bringing me a new communication that compels me to make up my mind whether or not the matter requires an immediate treatment."[106] The Reichstag was inundated by telegrams and petitions from outraged citizens throughout Germany supporting the chancellor's request, including a committee in industrial Elberfeld, which offered to contribute the 20,000 marks. Stung by the charge of niggardliness, enough left-liberals deserted the opposition on the third reading of the bill on March 4 to restore what they had deleted on December 15.[107]

Naturally, liberal deputies were disturbed that the government used the device of *Schutzbriefe* issued by the Kaiser to evade the constitution, which granted to Reichstag and Bundesrat the power to legislate on "colonization."[108] Yet the new policy was so popular that they hardly dared refuse appropriations connected with it. This was true of the resurrected steamship line subsidy bill. In the debates Bismarck pulled out all the stops on the organ of

---

[105] SBR (1884–1885), pp. 49–116, 197–920, 1039–1511, 1539–1665; BR, X, 377ff., 394ff.; XI, 53ff.

[106] BR, X, 312–342.

[107] SEG (1884), p. 136; (1885), pp. 1, 19, 51; GW, VIc, 311; XIV, 956–957.

[108] See the interpellation by the Reichstag budget committee on the constitutional issue, Feb. 4, 1885, and Kusserow's reply of Feb. 11, 1885. SEG (1884), pp. 464–466.

public opinion. The special targets of his long speeches, studded with irony and ridicule, were Richter, who doubted the economic value of the new acquisitions, and Windthorst, who suggested that an overseas empire might someday become a mortgage on German foreign policy. Bismarck retorted that without the support of German national sentiment he could not conduct a colonial policy; yet his critics talked the language of particularism and partisan politics. "One thing alone, gentlemen, robs me of my sleep and peace of mind and drives me at my advanced age to use the little bit of breath that remains to me in answering speeches. It is something that comes to me every day and every hour in a hundred different connections. It is love for my nation, love for my fatherland."[109]

Such tactics won passage of the subsidy bill, although the chamber deleted a steamship line to Africa that had been added to the bill of the preceding year. By raising objections, then backing down, by voting no and then reversing themselves, by granting most, but not all of what was requested, the majority exposed itself to the charge that it had participated only unwillingly and under duress in a cause that was regarded as both patriotic and of great potential economic benefit. Bismarck had begun to restock his arsenal for the next election.

In May 1885 he also succeeded in extracting from the Reichstag a major new tariff bill. Earlier it was noted that the price of grain, driven up by bad harvests in 1880–1881, sank catastrophically thereafter under the influence of better harvests and a flood of imports from eastern Europe and the United States.[110] During the period of high prices Bismarck turned a deaf ear to the distress of the urban lower classes, but now he heard loud and clear the anguished cries of farmers and estate owners.[111] The assumption that the tariff wall erected in 1879 would go no higher had already been belied by the tariff of 1882 and by Bismarck's unsuccessful attempt in 1883 to secure a protective rate on timber. Higher tariffs in France and Austria-Hungary led to the drafting in 1883–1884 of a retaliatory tariff bill on a variety of manufactured items, chiefly textiles.[112] But the bill reached the Reichstag on June 15, 1884, much too late for action in that session. During the election campaign the government was silent on its intentions, but soon afterward Bismarck began to push for a major new bill that would include items excised by parliament in the statute of 1882, the lapsed bill of June 1884, and, in addition, much higher

---

[109] BR, XI, 92–93; see also X, 273ff., and XI, 65ff., 87ff., 118ff.

[110] See pp. 9–12 and vol. 2, pp. 283–285.

[111] For examples of his encouragement of rural protest through the creation of *Bauernvereine* that petitioned the government, see AWB, II, 115, 119, 123, 127, 138–139, 151, 156; GW, XIV, 948, 951. See also the article in *Provinzial-Korrespondenz* quoted in AWB, II, 69.

[112] Wilhelm Gerloff, *Die Finanz- und Zollpolitik des deutschen Reiches* (Jena, 1913), pp. 200–201; SBR (1884), Anlagen, IV, No. 130. For Bismarck's role in drafting the bill, see AWB, II, 138–139.

rates on both timber and grain. The owner of Varzin, Schönhausen, and Friedrichsruh now proposed that agriculture, accorded only modest rates in 1879, be granted the same degree of protection given industry.[113]

In the Reichstag Bismarck painted the effects of the 1879 tariff in rosy hues: growth of private capital, expansion of exports and imports, "increasing luxury and consumption." Increased emigration was a sign of greater well-being, not of distress; more people could afford the journey and resettlement than before. Most emigrants came not from the thickly populated manufacturing regions, where industry and agriculture mutually supported one another, but from thinly populated agrarian regions in the east. Peasant farmers sold their land and escaped to America to enjoy there "the blessings of a protective tariff" and to rid themselves of the burden of direct taxation. For three decades, he declared, agriculture had been subjected to steadily increasing burdens by the state; now the time had come for the state to help the farmer. That the government's tariff policy was intended "to burden the poor for the advantage of the well-to-do" he denounced as an untruth born of partisan politics. Both had to be protected from calamity. The ruin of agriculture meant the ruin of industry. When the farmer has money, everybody does.[114]

Industry and agriculture were the twin arteries of the German economy, Bismarck continued. Of 45 million Germans, 25 to 27 million were engaged in farming and forestry.[115] Protective tariffs on timber were in the interest not only of forest owners, but also of thousands of laborers employed in forestry and associated industries who, if unemployed, would become a source of social unrest. Indignantly he rejected the charge that the tariff on grain was a "bread tax" or "blood tax." Although desirable, higher grain prices would not necessarily result from higher tariffs; outsiders could absorb the higher cost of selling in Germany. Their gold would pour into the imperial treasury. If grain prices rose, domestic production would increase accordingly, enabling Germany in normal years to be nearly self-sufficient, a valuable asset in wartime. Cheap grain did not make people happier or the economy more prosperous; otherwise Lithuanians, Russians, and Rumanians would be the happiest and most prosperous people in the world. If the welfare of workers depended on it, why not depress the price of clothing and other consumption goods? Why not, in fact, get rid of protective tariffs on iron and all other products? By what right could the majority of the population, the agrarians, be denied what had already been granted to the minority?[116] The message was clear: Those who in 1879 had clamored for and gotten protection for industrial products must now grant full reciprocity for agriculture.

[113] Poschinger, ed., *Bismarck als Volkswirth*, II, 1–2, 165–166, 192; SBR (1884–1885), Anlagen, II, No. 156.
[114] BR, X, 279–280, 342ff., 433, 473, 479.
[115] BR, X, 129–130, 461–562.
[116] BR, X, 440ff., 474ff.; XI, 3ff., 20ff.

Although he posed as a practical authority on grain and timber on the basis of his experience at Varzin and Friedrichsruh, Bismarck indignantly rejected aspersions that his "liquor," "swine," "sugar," and "timber" policy (as it was variously called) was motivated by his personal finances. Likewise, he denounced as a lie the proposition that higher tariffs on grain and timber would benefit only the owners of large estates. On the contrary, they were in a position to help themselves by diversifying: shifting from grain to cattle and even manufacturing. Nothing favored the growth of great latifundia more than low cereal prices and high income and real estate taxes, which made small holdings uneconomic, forcing their owners to sell and emigrate. Millions of workers in the fields and villages, moreover, depended for their livelihood upon the prosperity of landowners, great and small. Most petitions for higher grain tariffs came not from the northeast, but from regions where medium and small farms predominated. No conflict of interests divided great and small landowners; they belonged to the same *Stand*. Even social distinctions were dissolving. "Peasant farmers and [owners of] the old knights' estates constitute only a minority of the population. But God will preserve both of these classes as long as he wants to maintain an orderly government in our country. If they actually disintegrate, I fear that orderly government will also collapse."[117]

Bismarck was preaching to the converted. In early December 1884, soon after the Reichstag session began, protectionists of all parties revived the "Free Economic Association" of 1878. Led by centrist deputy and estate owner Burghard von Schorlemer-Alst, the association attracted at the outset 180 deputies.[118] Backed by steadily mounting agitation and petitions from farmers' clubs, the protectionist deputies not only granted the government's request that duties on wheat be increased from 10 to 30 marks per ton, but also tripled the duties on rye and other grains, rates that the government bill had proposed only to double. Where timber was concerned, the chamber was less generous. Yet the duty on construction lumber was doubled, that on boards quadrupled, although increases were withheld for types of woods not grown in Germany. The protectionists, furthermore, outdid the government by initiating new duties on horses, cattle, and oxen. As before, bitter opposition came from the seaports, merchants, and left-liberals, who repeated the old arguments for laissez-faire. It was all in vain. For the first time agriculture became a full partner with industry in protectionism.[119]

Although the primary aim was protectionist rather than fiscal, the new

[117] BR, X, 342–376, 462ff., 496, 502; XI, 16, 20.
[118] SEG (1884), p. 134; For the predecessor organization of the same title see vol. 2, pp. 467, 477.
[119] SBR (1884–1885), pp. 1167–1255, 1285–2506, 2695–2831; RGB (1885), pp. 93–156. For the arguments for and against agrarian tariffs see SBR (1884–1885), Anlagen, II, No. 162, pp. 3–7. For an analysis of the contradictions in the arguments for the bill, see Gerloff, *Finanz- und Zollpolitik*, pp. 200–204.

duties soon doubled (1887) and eventually more than quadrupled (1890) tax collections from agrarian imports. Under compulsory revenue-sharing provisions of the Franckenstein clause, this meant a sizeable increase in annual payments by the Reich to the state governments. The amount received by Prussia, 63,338,000 marks in 1885, reached 214,594,000 marks in 1890, outweighing the increase in state assessments paid by Prussia to the Reich, which rose from 40,300,000 to 134,260,000 marks in the same period.[120] As the Reichstag moved toward passage of the agrarian tariff in the spring of 1885, the Prussian Landtag was compelled simultaneously to deal with the problem of what to do with this golden stream flowing from the Reich to the Prussian treasury. The result was the Lex Huene passed by a majority composed of conservatives, centrists, and Poles over liberal opposition and named for the centrist deputy who sponsored it, Baron Karl von Huene. Of the funds received by Prussia from customs revenues under the Franckenstein clause, the Prussian treasury was permitted by the Lex Huene to keep only 15,000,000 marks; the rest was passed on to city and county governments.[121] Although initiated by centrists to protect parliament's budgetary rights and to justify the new tariffs to the public by applying its fiscal benefits to the relief of local government, the Lex Huene harmonized with Bismarck's long-established plan to allocate imperial revenues raised by indirect taxation to the reduction of local direct taxes.[122]

Once again, the social implications of Bismarck's "tax reform" can be seen. His attempt to abolish the class tax and at least part of the classified income tax for the benefit of the working and lower middle classes had achieved only limited success in the statutes of 1881 and 1883. Through the protective tariff of 1879 on industrial products he had sought to improve the balance sheets of the manufacturers and increase employment for industrial workers. By agrarian and timber tariffs in 1879 and 1885 he compensated landowners for the protected prices they paid on manufactured products and reduced the competition they faced from abroad. Through the Lex Huene, moreover, they now had the prospect of property tax relief. The landlords could look forward to double benefits from the legislation, but the urban lower classes were the losers. By bolstering the price of food, the largest item in family budgets, the protective tariff on grain took money from their pockets without compensation. They paid the piper, while others danced.

Bismarck's knowledge of taxation and public finance was faulty, owing to his dependence upon personal experience. In all likelihood he actually believed that all would benefit and none be injured by substituting indirect for

---

[120] Gerloff, Finanz- und Zollpolitik, p. 526.

[121] SBHA (1885), pp. 519–539, 1603–1721; Anlagen, Nos. 59, 202; GSP (1885), pp. 127–130.

[122] SEG (1885), pp. 40–41 (Feb. 18), p. 66 (Mar. 23), pp. 70–71 (Apr. 4), pp. 81–82 (Apr. 30–May 4); Gerloff, Finanz- und Zollpolitik, pp. 254–255, 258–261.

direct taxes. There can be no question, furthermore, that the tax system in Germany, Prussia, and most German states was inequitable and in need of reform. Yet the primary consequence of Bismarck's "reform" was to increase the inequity and to produce one of the more complicated and confusing tax systems in the history of public finance. Annually millions of marks flowed from the states to the Reich, while other millions flowed in the reverse direction from the Reich to the states and county governments. In Prussia, moreover, the villages (*Ortsgemeinden*), whose tax burden was five times greater than that of the counties and cities, had the greatest need for tax relief. Some counties passed the funds on to village governments for use in education and poor relief, while others diverted large sums to purposes not intended by the bill. Since the amount received varied from year to year, orderly planning of expenditures was difficult.[123] "The entanglement of the budgets of public bodies proved to be equally damaging for all concerned, chiefly because the relationship was superficial and not organic, having come about by accident. The financial linkage between Reich, state, and local government did not ease the administration of any of the three. In good years it led to unnecessary expenditures and in bad years it accentuated the financial crisis, for the shortfall in one budget was accompanied by a shortfall or decline in payments from the other. The linkage was a factor for instability rather than security and constancy in public finance."[124]

In Bismarck's defense it should be noted that this structure was not of his design. It was the consequence of his successive efforts to shift the burden of taxation from the states to the Reich, from direct to indirect taxes, and of the resistance of the Reichstag (Franckenstein clause) and the Prussian Chamber of Deputies (*Lex Huene*) to the political and constitutional consequences of that shift. To put the matter in a different way, the crazy-quilt pattern of German and Prussian public finance resulted from Bismarck's attempt to achieve political and social objectives simultaneously: to reduce the budgetary power of both parliaments and to obtain tax relief for workers, lower *Mittelstand*, cities, rural local government, and the landlord class. If Bismarck had succeeded in substituting imperial indirect taxes for Prussian direct taxes, the result would have been, contrary to his own conviction, grotesquely inequitable. The consuming masses, particularly the low-income groups, would have borne a disproportionate share of the state's financial support. The landlord class would have been relieved of its major burden by the near liquidation of the land and building taxes, and capitalist entrepreneurs would have been favored by low personal income taxes, absence of corporate income taxes, and absence of inheritance taxes. During these years the only government tax proposal providing for a more equitable system of taxation was the one pro-

[123] Gerloff, *Finanz- und Zollpolitik*, pp. 259–261.
[124] *Ibid.*, pp. 255, 288ff.

duced by Scholz in 1883–1884, a proposal that Bismarck approved but did not initiate. And that proposal came to naught, as we have seen, not because the parties failed to recognize its wisdom, but because the conflicting interests of big agriculture and big capital stood in the way. They could not agree on features of the bill (*Kapitalrentensteuer*) that affected their interests, and as a consequence tax relief for low-income groups went begging.

❖❖

CHAPTER SEVEN

Political Stagnation and Mental Depression

Chancellor and Kaiser

N APRIL 1, 1885, Bismarck reached his seventieth year, and the event was celebrated throughout Germany and in the colonies in a manner generally reserved for monarchs. The Kaiser and his entire family (with what ambivalent emotions Kaiserin Augusta and Crown Princess Victoria?) came to present their felicitations. Wilhelm's gift was Anton von Werner's huge canvas depicting *The Kaiser Proclamation at Versailles*, a painting that has since been reproduced in hundreds of books. From the Kaiser the prince also received a letter of appreciation, published throughout Germany, expressing the nation's thanks for his achievements. Kaiser Franz Joseph sent a life-size portrait of himself; gifts and medals arrived from other German and European rulers as well. Beginning at Berlin, city councils throughout Germany sent their best wishes and elaborate certificates of honorary citizenship. Universities accorded him honorary degrees in flamboyant Latin, and student corps sent their eulogies. Altogether 3,738 letters (many with multiple signatures), 2,644 telegrams, and 175 addresses from various clubs and corporative bodies were delivered. Of the 560 gifts that arrived, the most munificent, certainly the most appreciated, was the "Bismarck Fund" (2,379,144 marks), raised by public subscription. The appeal for contributions was issued by a committee composed of 116 prominent persons and headed by the Duke of Ratibor, president of the Prussian House of Lords. But less than half of the "Otto pence" collected by the committee went to the charity for which it was ostensibly intended; the rest was used to repurchase ancestral lands at Schönhausen sold during the depressed 1830s to pay off family debts.[1]

An early adjournment of the Reichstag and Landtag in May 1885 enabled Bismarck to depart for Bad Kissingen sooner than usual. From June 4 to July 2 he bathed and breathed salt vapors at the Bavarian spa. Hohenlohe reported him looking well, pleased that he could walk a lot, but still plagued by facial pains. Returning to the Wilhelmstrasse in July, the chancellor found that work tired him quickly. "I wake up with the feeling that I can climb the

---

[1] Horst Kohl, ed., *Fürst Bismarck: Regesten zu einer wissenschaftlichen Biographie des ersten Reichskanzlers* (Stuttgart, 1891–1892), II, 361–366; SEG (1885), pp. 18–19, 66–67, 69–70, 119–120. On the Bismarck fund and its disposition, see vol. 2, pp. 72–74 and fn. 16.

highest mountains but after working for a few hours I can surmount them only with great effort."[2] He attended the wedding of son Bill to niece Sybille von Arnim at Kröchlendorf, then departed on July 9 for Varzin, where he remained until September 19. The vacation did him little good. Initially he restricted himself to two hours of work daily, but the burden kept increasing as Germany clashed unexpectedly with Spain over the Caroline Islands and the Balkan cauldron began to bubble. Cold and rainy weather kept him indoors. Back in Berlin he felt unequal to the burdens thrust upon him. Day by day his health deteriorated and the facial pains increased. On September 27 he retired to Friedrichsruh with the Kaiser's permission to prepare for the "parliamentary winter campaign." He remained there until November 25, 1885. Yet his condition did not improve.[3]

While exercising some control over Bismarck's diet, Schweninger could do nothing for the facial neuralgia, which may have been aggravated by smoking. The doctor restricted him to four pipes of tobacco, to be smoked after dinner,

FAMILY CIRCLE IN THE PARK AT VARZIN, AUGUST 1884. *FROM LEFT*: OSKAR VON ARNIM (BROTHER-IN-LAW), MALWINE VON ARNIM (SISTER), SYBILLE VON ARNIM (NIECE AND FIANCÉE OF WILHELM VON BISMARCK), JOHANNA VON BISMARCK, OTTO VON BISMARCK, WILHELM VON BISMARCK (SON), TYRAS (STÄDTISCHE GALERIE IM LENBACHHAUS.)

[2] GW, VIII, 526; Freiherr Lucius von Ballhausen, *Bismarck-Erinnerungen* (Stuttgart, 1920), pp. 317–318.

[3] GW, XIV, 963–965; Horst Kohl, ed., *Anhang zu den Gedanken und Erinnerungen von Otto Fürst von Bismarck* (Stuttgart, 1901), I, 335–336.

but the patient purchased the largest pipe he could find (three feet long, with an outsized porcelain bowl) and, if no one kept count, he filled it a fifth time. In December the renewal of his feud with the Reichstag opposition aggravated his condition. Throughout the winter of 1885–1886 he was troubled not only by facial pains, but also by his old leg injury. Visitors found him stretched out on a chaise longue, the bad leg propped up, his speech affected by the effort to keep his lower lip out of contact with an aching tooth. Schweninger's treatment, he complained, had relieved his gallbladder problem and prevented him from gaining more weight but nothing more.[4] Holstein detected signs of mental depression and a decreasing capacity to control affairs. More and more, the chancellor became dependent upon Herbert to perform many of the functions of his office. But in April–May 1886 the son was seriously ill with pneumonia, and the father had to resume his full duties. Another source of worry was Johanna's asthmatic condition, made worse by anxiety over her husband and her excessive zeal in nursing him. "The poor old Bismarcks made life difficult for each other out of agitation and concern," noted Baroness Spitzemberg. To Mittnacht the prince confessed "fatigue, no desire to work, and, in contrast to the past, lack of interest for his private affairs, farming, and forestry." Holstein concluded that the chancellor was "losing his grip."[5]

At court some who witnessed the outpouring of patriotic enthusiasm for Bismarck on his seventieth birthday muttered about the Bismarck *Hausmacht* and its hazards for the prestige of the monarchy. At age thirty-six Herbert was patently being groomed to succeed his father. Might not the Bismarcks one day overshadow the Hohenzollern, as had Charles Martel and his successors the Merovingian kings of France?[6] But Wilhelm I does not appear to have had any such concern. In contrast to the grandson who was soon to succeed him, the Kaiser possessed a quiet dignity, a sense of self-worth, and a generosity of spirit that kept him from displaying any apparent jealousy over the tributes paid to his first minister.[7] In the famous corner office of the Berlin palace

[4] GW, VIII, 533, 535, 537; BP, I, 280–281; Moritz Busch, *Tagebuchblätter* (Leipzig, 1899), III, 199; Rudolf Vierhaus, ed., *Das Tagebuch der Baronin Spitzemberg* (Göttingen, 1961), p. 220; Lucius, *Bismarck-Erinnerungen*, p. 352.

[5] Norman Rich and M. H. Fisher, eds., *The Holstein Papers: The Memoirs, Diaries and Correspondence of Friedrich von Holstein, 1837–1909* (4 vols., Cambridge, Eng., 1955–1963), II, 257ff., 274ff.; GW, VIII, 546–547; Spitzemberg, *Tagebuch*, pp. 224–225; Walter Bussmann, ed., *Staatssekretär Graf Herbert von Bismarck: Aus seiner politischen Privatkorrespondenz* (Göttingen, 1964), pp. 360, 366–367. Lucius had an impression similar to Holstein's, although not so strongly put: "It often happens now that Bismarck changes his views, but it would be wrong to seek deep-laid, far-reaching plans in every utterance. That is particularly apparent in church policy." Diary entry of Apr. 14, 1886, Lucius, *Bismarck-Erinnerungen*, p. 347.

[6] Heinrich von Poschinger, ed., *Fürst Bismarck und der Bundesrat, 1867–1890* (Stuttgart, 1897–1901), IV, 167; see also Andreas Dorpalen, *Heinrich von Treitschke* (New Haven, 1957), p. 253.

[7] Friedrich Curtius, ed., *Memoirs of Prince Chlodwig of Hohenlohe-Schillingsfuerst* (New York, 1906), II, 520.

Wilhelm continued routinely to perform the tasks that his station demanded. Dressed in the uniform he always wore when on government business, he conscientiously read the dispatches flowing from the chancellery, war ministry, and general staff. The chancellor was a frequent visitor while in Berlin and during his absences they corresponded on essential matters, but not always without misunderstandings and frictions. Periodically they journeyed together to confer with foreign rulers and ministers. Wilhelm presided over the balls, banquets, and receptions expected of the Kaiser as the leader of German society. Each season he continued to participate in the royal hunts, a sport that Bismarck, although fifteen years his junior, had long since given up.[8]

Since 1867 he had become a highly popular figure throughout the empire. On official visits he was received everywhere with a respect and spontaneous enthusiasm that left no doubt that he had become a German more than a mere Prussian monarch. His figure was tall and erect, his head mostly bald, face adorned with luxuriant muttonchop whiskers. His manner was warm and courteous, dignified but not arrogant, military yet chivalric. He played the part heritage had assigned him, but without unnecessary pomp and theatricality.[9] When he visited the Rhineland in 1880 to help celebrate completion of the famed Cologne cathedral, ultramontanes tried to organize a Catholic boycott of the celebration, but without success.[10] In September 1883 he dedicated the great statue of Germania on the escarpment of the Niederwald overlooking the Rhine. Horror swept the nation when it was discovered that on that day he and his son had narrowly escaped death by dynamite (planted by anarchists) when a wet fuse failed to burn.[11]

Beginning in late August 1884, the Kaiser suffered a series of small strokes (transient ischemic attacks). While some were recorded and widely known,

---

[8] Lucius, *Bismarck-Erinnerungen*, pp. 279, 354–355; SEG (1882), p. 193.

[9] Unfortunately we lack an adequate biography of Wilhelm I. Early attempts to portray him as "Wilhelm the Great" and "the heroic Kaiser," which were intended to diminish Bismarck's role in German unification, faded during the Weimar Republic. The most popular biography (eight editions between 1897 and 1918) sought to bring the contributions of both into balance. See Erich Marcks, *Kaiser Wilhelm I* (9th ed., Berlin, 1943). Neither of the two most recent biographies is satisfying: Franz Herre's flowery and "popular" *Kaiser Wilhelm I.* (Cologne, 1980) and Karl Heinz Börner's comparatively brief and Marxist-oriented *Wilhelm I.: Deutscher Kaiser und König von Preussen, 1797 bis 1888; Eine Biographie* (Berlin and Cologne, 1984). Despite all that divides them ideologically, the Wilhelmian-era Marcks, West German Herre, and East German Börner present much the same view of the Kaiser's personality, character, and ultimate, German-wide popularity that is depicted here.

[10] SEG (1880), pp. 223–225. See also Wilhelm's account of his "triumphal progress" through Hanover, Itzehoe, Hamburg, Kiel, and Stuttgart during Sept. 1881. GW, VIc, 228. His reception was all the more remarkable in view of the adverse outcome of the election at the end of October in the same year.

[11] Adalbert Wahl, *Deutsche Geschichte, 1871–1914* (Stuttgart, 1929), II, 167–169; SEG (1883), p. 136; (1884), pp. 53, 70. Earlier, dynamiters had failed in an attempt to blow up the police station in Frankfurt am Main. SEG (1883), p. 146.

KAISER WILHELM I, ABOUT 1885. FROM A POR-
TRAIT BY PAUL BÜLOW.

KAISERIN AUGUSTA, ABOUT 1885. PAINTING BY
PLOCKHORST.

KAISER WILHELM I AND KAISERIN AUGUSTA AT THE REDEDICATION OF COLOGNE CATHEDRAL, OCTO-
BER 18, 1880. (BILDARCHIV PREUSSISCHER KULTURBESITZ.)

most were not. None was serious enough to incapacitate him for long. One occurred during the Sedan Day parade on September 2, 1884, when he lost consciousness while in the saddle before thousands of onlookers. But at the end of the month he participated in military maneuvers in western Germany and was cheered by massive crowds in Düsseldorf, Münster, and Cologne.[12] In January 1885 Holstein reported that the attacks were becoming more frequent but that for the moment the monarch appeared to be "over the mountain." Other known attacks occurred at Bad Ems in June 1885 and, one month later, at Salzburg en route to Bad Gastein. Holstein wrote that "no one appears to believe that this can last much longer."[13] And yet the monarch continued to be active. In August he dedicated at Potsdam a memorial to King Friedrich Wilhelm I, and in September he visited as usual his daughter and her family in Karlsruhe, interrupted by an excursion to the Zollerburg at Hemmingen, where his Swabian subjects received him jubilantly.[14] In late 1885 Bismarck and the crown prince conferred, obviously in preparation for the succession, and in April 1886 Herbert replaced Hatzfeldt as state secretary in the Imperial Foreign Office, "because it was very questionable whether at his age his majesty will live until Pentecost."[15] The prediction nearly came true.

On May 14, 1886, Wilhelm was "seized by a kind of paralysis, became confused in his utterances, and finally lost the power of speech." Next morning his speech was still confused and his manner "unnaturally excited"; he complained of a headache and exhaustion.[16] In the following months other "little attacks" were reported by members of the royal family.[17] Yet on August 18 the durable old man led the Potsdam garrison, with drawn sword, in the "church parade" that commemorated the hundredth anniversary of the death of Frederick the Great; in September, accompanied by the crown prince, he toured Alsace-Lorraine and was well received by the populace; on October 31 he felled twenty deer at a royal hunt (albeit from a specially prepared blind).[18]

---

[12] SEG (1884), pp. 88, 92–93; Helmuth Rogge, *Holstein und Hohenlohe* (Stuttgart, 1957), pp. 221–227; and Jules Laforgue, *Berlin, la cour et la ville* (Paris, 1922), chap. 4.

[13] Albedyll to Bismarck, July 7, 1885. Kohl, ed., *Anhang*, II, 540–542. Bismarck to Albedyll, July 16, 1885. GW, XIV, 963. Bismarck to Kaiser, July 8, 1885. Kohl, ed., *Anhang*, I, 334–335. Holstein to Hohenlohe, Aug. 14, 1885. Rogge, *Holstein und Hohenlohe*, p. 243.

[14] Ernst Berner, ed., *Kaiser Wilhelms des GrossenBriefe, Reden und Schriften* (Berlin, 1906), II, 407–408; diary entry of Sept. 23, 1885, Spitzemberg, *Tagebuch*, p. 220.

[15] Lucius diary, Dec. 6, 1885. *Bismarck-Erinnerungen*, p. 324. Herbert to Bill Bismarck, Apr. 14, 1886. Bussmann, ed., *Herbert von Bismarck*, pp. 359–360. Julius Heyderhoff, ed., *Im Ring der Gegner Bismarcks* (Leipzig, 1943), pp. 228–231.

[16] Plessen to Bismarck, May 15, 1886. Kohl, ed., *Anhang*, II, 544; translation from Horst Kohl, ed., *The Correspondence of William I and Bismarck* (London, 1903), pp. 217–218.

[17] Crown Princess Victoria to Queen Victoria, Aug. 30, 1886. Frederick Ponsonby, ed., *Letters of Empress Frederick* (London, 1929), p. 243, also pp. 249, 253.

[18] Lucius, *Bismarck-Erinnerungen*, pp. 352, 354–355.

On March 22, 1887, Wilhelm celebrated his ninetieth birthday attended by sixteen hundred bejeweled, uniformed, and titled guests at a banquet in the white salon of the Berlin palace. Flanked by fellow German rulers, the "gray Kaiser" received his guests and accepted the applause of thousands of torch-bearing Berliners who crowded the plaza outside. Most had come, Baroness Spitzemberg reflected, to see their ruler for the last time on such an occasion. "Today we had the proud feeling, and rightly so, of belonging to a powerful, united people."[19] Wilhelm, whose reign in Prussia began in discord and who in 1866 initiated a German civil war, had become for millions the living symbol of German national unity and power. "My ancestors had first of all to create a nation," the Kaiser mused, "for we Prussians are not a born but a created nation. But now a nation is creating me!"[20]

Bismarck responded graciously to the encomiums accorded him in 1885 but appears to have been unaffected by the adulation. What he wanted from the German public was not more honors but responsive voters and obedient parliaments. As Wilhelm's life began to ebb and his own health deteriorated once more, Bismarck strove again to realize in the time left to him his conception of the internal consolidation of the Reich. Even a sick and partially disabled Bismarck was still capable, as in 1875, of pulling the levers that let steam into the political engine. But could he force the train to move down the chosen track? And did the track actually lead toward the stable social and political order that he intended?

Liquidation of the Kulturkampf

In November 1885 Prussia's voters elected the Chamber of Deputies for another three-year term. The result widened still further the contrast between its composition and that of the Reichstag. The so-called national parties were strengthened, the German Conservative party rising from 122 to 133 deputies, the Free Conservative party from 57 to 62, the National Liberal party from 66 to 72. This gain of 22 seats came mostly at the cost of the German Freedom party, which was reduced from 53 to 40 seats, and the Poles, who declined from 18 to 15 seats; the loss of the Center party was minimal (99 to 98).[21] Again Bismarck had the option of combining the conservatives either with the Center or with free conservatives and national liberals to produce a majority. With the help of the first combination he relaxed the May laws: with the help of the second he pursued the Germanization of Polish and other ethnic minorities.

Since 1880 the Prussian government, unable to reach a settlement with the

[19] Spitzemberg, *Tagebuch*, pp. 229–230.
[20] Cited in Herre, *Kaiser Wilhelm I.*, p. 489.
[21] Bernhard Vogel, Dieter Nohlen, and Rainer-Olaf Schultze, *Wahlen in Deutschland: Theorie-Geschichte-Dokumente, 1848–1970* (Berlin, 1971), p. 287.

Vatican, had proceeded unilaterally to ease the Kulturkampf by a series of legislative and administrative actions. Among them was a series of bills (enabling acts) presented to the Prussian Chamber of Deputies. Those passed in 1880 and 1882, already discussed, were followed by a third in 1883.[22] Bismarck's tactic was to accept amendments passed by a coalition of centrists and conservatives, leaving die-hard liberals in the futile position of "defending the state," without the support of the government.[23] Under these statutes the Kultusministerium had permitted the restoration of many priests to vacant parishes and bishops to vacant sees. In April 1882 diplomatic relations had been resumed with the Vatican, and in December 1883 Crown Prince Friedrich Wilhelm paid Leo XIII an official visit. To Prussian legislators and the public these steps were represented as acts of benevolence by the Prussian government to its Catholic citizens rather than as a surrender to Rome.[24]

The end of the Kulturkampf, however, could be achieved only through direct negotiations between Berlin and Rome. Both chancellor and pope were eager to find a mutually acceptable solution, Bismarck in his search for a national consensus including Catholics, Leo in order to gain greater freedom to concentrate on the church's difficulties elsewhere in Europe. The chief obstacle to a settlement lay with neither. Rather it lay with the intransigents in both camps: with the Prussian ministry and the liberal parties and with the curia, the German episcopate, and the Center party (especially Windthorst).

In September 1885 Bismarck, by a brilliant stroke, set negotiations with the Holy See in motion once more by calling upon Leo to arbitrate a dispute between Germany and Spain over rival claims in the Caroline Islands of the Pacific.[25] The islands were of no great consequence to Germany; Catholic Spain could hardly refuse the pope as a mediator; and the pope, who fulfilled the task successfully, could again think of himself as the arbiter mundi. On the successful conclusion of the negotiation the German and Spanish chancellors received from the pope the diamond-studded Order of Christ; Bismarck's award bore the words excelso viro, magno Cancellario. For their efforts Schlözer received the Great Cross of the Order of Pius; Cardinal Jacobini (Vatican secretary of state), the Prussian Order of the Black Eagle. Intransigent Catholics, who had witnessed Windthorst's long struggle in parliament to force repeal of the May laws, were astounded by this exchange of courtesies.[26] Their consternation would have been heightened had they known that an encycli-

[22] For the enabling acts of 1880 and 1882, see pp. 33, 60, 70 and vol. 2, pp. 531–537. The third statute became law on July 11, 1883. GSP (1883), pp. 109–110.

[23] SBHA (1882–1883), pp. 2043–2080, 2103–2142, 2150–2181.

[24] Erich Schmidt-Volkmar, Der Kulturkampf in Deutschland, 1871–1890 (Göttingen, 1962), pp. 267ff.; BR, XII, 48–65, 126–129.

[25] GW, VIc, 324, 325, 327.

[26] Karl Bachem, Vorgeschichte, Geschichte und Politik der deutschen Zentrumspartei (9 vols., Cologne, 1927–1933), IV, 136–138; GW, XIV, 966.

cal of January 6, 1886, in which the pope sought to mollify the German bishops, already lay on Bismarck's desk. Leo had sent him a copy.[27]

In January 1886 Bismarck appeared finally to have succeeded in his long-
standing attempt to establish a direct relationship with the pope that would
leave Catholic intransigents voiceless in negotiations to end the Kulturkampf
and undercut the Center's opposition to the government in other (sectarian)
legislation as well. Through Schlözer he sent to Leo a new bill on ecclesiastical affairs in advance of its presentation to the Landtag, a bill that had been
drafted by Gossler in consultation with Georg Kopp, bishop of Fulda and a
moderate in the Catholic camp. Leo excluded from the subsequent discussions Windthorst, who had led the struggle in parliament for more than a
decade, and all churchmen (including Jacobini) likely to be opposed to the
terms Bismarck offered. He specifically admonished Windthorst, moreover,
to advance no measures dealing with church affairs for the time being, lest
they disrupt the settlement.[28]

In submitting the bill to the papacy, Bismarck had no intention of inviting
Rome to amend it. Even while Leo and the cardinals discussed the contents,
the bill was, much to their surprise, laid before the Prussian House of Lords,
to which Kopp had been appointed in January.[29] If Bishop Kopp, spokesman
for the pope and *persona grata* with Bismarck, could secure approval of an
ecclesiastical bill in the upper chamber, how could the centrists in the Cham-

BISMARCK AND WINDTHORST. "EVEN THOUGH THE FORMER HEATS AS VIGOROUSLY AS THE LATTER
BRAKES, THE ENGINE DOESN'T MOVE." WILHELM SCHOLZ IN *KLADDERADATSCH*, 1884.

[27] Christoph Weber, *Kirchliche Politik zwischen Rom, Berlin und Trier 1876–1888: Die Beilegung
des preussischen Kulturkampfes. Veröffentlichungen der Kommission für Zeitgeschichte bei der katho-
lischen Akademie in Bayern*, ser. B, vol. 7 (Mainz, 1970), pp. 123–125.

[28] Cabinet meetings of Jan. 10 and Feb. 14, 1886, Lucius, *Bismarck-Erinnerungen*, pp. 329,
332; DZA Merseburg, Rep. 90a, B, III, 2b, Nr. 6, Vol. 98; GW, VIc, 327, 330–331; Weber,
Kirchliche Politik, pp. 125–126.

[29] Weber, *Kirchliche Politik*, pp. 127–128; SBHH (1886), Anlagen, Nos. 24, 46, 64, 71.

ber of Deputies oppose it? Bismarck's tactics inserted a wedge within the Catholic camp between the moderates, headed by the pope, who wanted to end the Kulturkampf on the best terms possible, and the hard-liners, like Windthorst and Jacobini, who were inclined to believe that no peace was possible short of the surrender by the Prussian government of all authority over the Catholic church in Germany.[30]

On the surface Gossler's bill went a long way toward final liquidation of the Kulturkampf, but a close reading revealed thorns among the roses. The requirement that new priests either pass a state "cultural examination" or acquire a "German" university education was abolished, but this was the only outright concession. Although the royal tribunal for church affairs was abolished, its appellate jurisdiction in matters of church discipline was assumed by the Berlin *Kammergericht* (including the power to remove priests). Seminaries and other institutions for the training of priests were again permitted and state supervision of them was limited to that imposed on all educational institutions, but professorial appointments still required state approval. Most important of all, the bill left intact the state's power to veto ecclesiastical appointments.

The veto power, as established in the statute of May 11, 1873, required higher clergy to give to Prussia's provincial governors the names of candidates for clerical posts in advance of their appointment and reserved to the state the right to deny the appointment if the candidate failed to meet certain vaguely worded "civil and citizenship" qualifications. In 1880 Leo XIII had offered to concede the requirement for obligatory notification of church appointments (*Anzeigepflicht*), but only for the lower clergy and without specifically yielding to the state the right of veto on any level.[31] With papal approval Bishop Kopp now introduced three amendments to Gossler's bill, abolishing the state's right to veto faculty appointments to the seminaries, the *Kammergericht*'s appellate jurisdiction in ecclesiastical cases, and the state's power to punish priests for saying Mass and administering last rites. Bismarck was willing to accept the Kopp amendments ("I can regain at any time what I now give up"). He had come to regard obligatory notification as "useless" but dared not yield on that issue, lest he expose himself to the charge of having gone *all* the way to Canossa.[32]

On March 22, 1886, he was pleased to learn from Schlözer that the pope had accepted obligatory notification without reservations. But the chancellor's gratification was cut short two days later, when the envoy reported that

[30] Cabinet meeting of Mar. 7, 1886. Lucius, *Bismarck-Erinnerungen*, pp. 336–337; Schmidt-Volkmar, *Kulturkampf*, pp. 298ff.; Weber, *Kirchliche Politik*, p. 125; Anton Kaas, "Zur Geschichte des Kulturkampfes in Preussen: Das Zustandekommen des 1. Friedengesetzes vom 2. Mai 1886, dargestellt auf Grund der Briefe Moslers an Reuss," *Saarbrücke Hefte*, 31 (1970), pp. 5–43.

[31] See vol. 2, pp. 480, 531–532.

[32] To Schlözer, Feb. 2, 1886. GW, VIc, 330–331. For the government's bill and Kopp's amendments, see *SBHH* (1886), II, 329–332, 347.

Leo had backed away from the commitment. Catholic intransigents had gained his ear, and the most Leo would now yield was the obligation to inform the state of candidates for parishes already vacant.[33] Bismarck boiled with anger, at the pope and Kopp but also at Schlözer, whom he blamed for being "too sanguine" in his report of the twenty-second and too yielding in his reaction to the revised position of the twenty-fourth. Limited obligatory notification, he declared, was unacceptable to both the government and the majority in the House of Lords.[34] In quick succession Schlözer was demonstratively recalled from the Vatican, a personal letter outlining the situation was sent by Bismarck to the pope, and Prince Hatzfeldt-Trachenberg, a liberal Catholic and member of both Reichstag and House of Lords, was despatched to Rome as a secret intermediary. "Please tell the pope," he instructed Hatzfeldt, "that as long as the old Kaiser still lives and I remain at the rudder peace can be achieved. What may come after us no one can say."[35]

The pope's response, as communicated by Jacobini on April 4, was to promise that, following passage of the pending bill as amended by Kopp, the Vatican would instruct German bishops to notify the Prussian government of all appointments to parishes then vacant. This reply left in limbo the questions of future vacancies and the government's right to veto undesirable appointments. All that the pope committed the diocesan authority to do was to hear the government's objections to any candidate whose appointment was considered dangerous to "public order."[36] But this sufficed to cover Bismarck's road to Canossa. In return, he promised additional modifications of the May laws in the future.

In the decisive debate on Gossler's bill in the House of Lords on April 12–13, Bismarck supported this solution as indicative of a genuine desire on the part of Leo XIII to end the struggle—in contrast to centrists and left-liberals, whom he accused of wishing to continue it. He assumed responsibility for the May laws but disavowed features incorporated in the statutes by colleagues. Although "fighting statutes" had been necessary, "enemy territory" had been occupied that was "actually worthless." From the start his purpose had been political, not confessional; again he referred to the Guelph and Polish origins of the struggle and to the problem of defending the German language in the eastern provinces. A definitive peace between the German monarchy and the Catholic church would never be completely realizable. "A Catholic priest, from the moment he becomes a priest, is a regimented officer of the pope; he would be pressed to the wall and destroyed if he wished to remain a priest yet fight against the pope and his superiors." For the state to attempt to influence the priesthood against the will of the papacy was "the basic mistake of the

[33] Schmidt-Volkmar, *Kulturkampf*, pp. 307–308.

[34] GW, VIc, 332–335; Lucius, *Bismarck-Erinnerungen*, pp. 343–344.

[35] GW, VIc, 333; Siegfried von Kardorff, *Bismarck im Kampf um sein Werk* (Berlin, 1930), p. 53.

[36] Schmidt-Volkmar, *Kulturkampf*, pp. 308–311; BR, XII, 74, 96–97.

entire May legislation." In contrast to priests in other countries—Spain, Italy, France, Ireland—German priests were lacking in national consciousness; they were priests first and Germans second. This could not be changed by law but only by "the gradual strengthening of national consciousness in every German. If we succeed in fighting Polonism by the route we have recently taken, we will have a substitute for many weapons that would otherwise be indispensable in the religious area." In Leo XIII he claimed to have found "more goodwill and greater interest in the fortification of the German Reich and in the welfare of the German state" than had been displayed by the Center party and "at times" by the Reichstag majority.

It was Bishop Kopp, however, who rescued the situation. In an impassioned speech on April 13, 1886, he warned the liberal opposition, led by Miquel, that Germany had reached a "world-historical" moment. The opportunity for peace was at hand and must be seized. "The great statesman who is in charge of our political fate has extended the hand of peace to the supreme head of the Catholic church." In the decisive vote of the House of Lords Kopp's amendment passed handily, 123 to 46 votes.[37] In the Chamber of Deputies there was minimal debate, for the pope had instructed the Center not to attempt additional amendments. The centrists knuckled under, combining with German conservatives to pass the statute, 259 to 109, over an opposition composed of national liberals, some free conservatives, and most left-liberals. Windthorst sobbed convulsively at what he considered to be a humiliating capitulation.[38]

The ecclesiastical law of 1886 left a number of loose ends. Even Bishop Kopp was unclear about what the pope had granted in the message of April 4. His view that Leo had intended to concede the veto power was quickly challenged by the Catholic newspaper Germania, Windthorst, and much of the German episcopate. Leo temporized, taking the view that there was no problem. "Naturally they will name no one who is unacceptable." He wanted "absolutely no friction" and ordered the bishops to use the registration formula designed by the state. Nor did Bismarck want friction; only in the Polish areas did he expect the veto to be important. But the German bishops were not inclined to put their faith in attitudes; the conduct of the Prussian government on the issue of appointments during the past fifteen years was hardly reassuring. At the annual bishops' conference in Fulda during August 1886 the intransigent majority again denounced the government's veto power and demanded its abolition. Their discontent with Leo XIII was patent.[39]

In 1887 Bismarck followed again the route taken in 1886. He communi-

[37] SBHH (1886), I, 174–219; BR, XII, 75–98.
[38] Margaret Lavinia Anderson, Windthorst: A Political Biography (Oxford, 1981), p. 333; SBHA (1886), pp. 1886–2017; BR, XII, 106–116.
[39] GW, VIc, 337–340; Weber, Kirchliche Politik, pp. 139–144; Anderson, Windthorst, pp. 334–335.

cated the terms of a new "peace law" to the Vatican for its reaction before presentation to the House of Lords. But this time he permitted the Vatican to propose revisions. Although Bismarck was willing to concede the requested revisions, Gossler and the cabinet objected. The prince seemed, Lucius complained, to want "peace at any price." As presented, the bill permitted the training of priests at the diocesan seminaries in Osnabrück and Limburg, allowed the return of most religious orders to Prussia, and redefined, without weakening, the grounds on which the state could veto ecclesiastical appointments. But Catholic intransigents were also dissatisfied because the statute did not liquidate all of the May laws. Passage in the Landtag required intervention by the pope, who ordered the Center party to accept it, and by Bismarck, who put heavy pressure on ultraconservatives to the same end.[40] Bismarck had the satisfaction of being able to call upon both chambers to support the pope against rebellious Catholics, to support the authority of pope and Kaiser in the struggle against subversion, revolution, and anarchy!

Bismarck had gone a long way toward Canossa, but not all the way and not nearly far enough for Windthorst and many German prelates. Important laws remained in the statute books, for example, state supervision of public schools, obligatory civil marriage, ban on the Jesuit order, and revocation of the guarantees of religious freedom in Articles 15, 16, and 18 of the Prussian constitution. Bismarck had accomplished some lasting objectives in the separation of church and state.[41] Had he not feared the political consequences, he would also have completely surrendered the veto power. What the Landtag refused, he committed the government to accept, nevertheless, in a personal letter to Leo on May 28, 1887. If those chosen to wield ecclesiastical authority in Prussia were inspired by the same spirit of reconciliation shown by the Holy See, he wrote, the government would not exercise its veto power.[42]

With this private understanding, he effectively undercut Windthorst's continuing demands for further revision of the May laws. By the diplomatic route Bismarck and Leo XIII resolved what the legislative process had denied. His personal relationship to the pope permitted him in effect to annul what the Prussian cabinet and majorities in both houses of the Landtag had established as the law of the land. Bismarck himself was not convinced that he had achieved a definitive settlement of the centuries-old struggle between church and state. None was possible in his opinion. What he had achieved was merely a modus vivendi, satisfactory to both sides because the Prussian gov-

[40] GW, VIc, 353–358; VIII, 562–563; Lucius, Bismarck-Erinnerungen, pp. 362–364, 367, 370, 375, 384; SBHH (1887), pp. 105–164, Anlagen, Nos. 34, 65; SBHA (1887), pp. 785–843, 879–929, Anlagen, Nos. 118, 127; BR, XII, 330–405; Heinrich Heffter, Die Kreuzzeitungspartei und Bismarcks Kartellpolitik (Leipzig, 1927), pp. 93–94; GSP (1887), pp. 127–130.
[41] Schmidt-Volkmar, Kulturkampf, pp. 356–358.
[42] GW, VIc, 361–362, 366; Weber, Kirchliche Politik, pp. 158–173.

ernment thereafter ceased to exercise its veto power over ecclesiastical appointments (except in Posen).

Bismarck's Final Solution

That the relaxation of the Kulturkampf laws did not apply to the Polish
regions was owing to Bismarck's disappointment with the assimilation program begun in the 1870s. For half a century no progress had been made, he
complained. "We must go forward decisively with Germanization."[43] "The
German and Polish parts of the country are to be measured by different standards."[44] Even as Bismarck and Leo XIII reached their compromise, the Prussian government began a new assault on Polonism marked by the expulsion
of thousands of alien Poles and Jews, a program to purchase the estates of
Polish landlords and resettle them with Germans, and a general cultural offensive designed to employ the army, schools, and government in Germanizing Prussia's linguistic minorities. Bismarck's anxiety concerning the Polish
minority is usually credited to his fears of foreign alliances that might exploit
Polish nationalism to subvert and weaken Prussia-Germany. Undoubtedly
this consideration did figure in his calculations in the early 1870s. But the
years 1881 to early 1885, when a new and vigorous effort to assimilate minorities was launched, were the most halcyon in German foreign relations during
Bismarck's entire career.[45] Not until the fall of the Ferry government in
France (March 31, 1885), the revolution in Eastern Rumelia (September 18,
1885), the rise of Boulanger (after January 1886), and the Austro-Russian
crisis over Bulgaria (August–November 1886) was there cause for renewed

[43] Rottenburg was ordered to relay Bismarck's concern to Minister of Interior Puttkamer. Wilhelm von Bismarck to Franz von Rottenburg, Apr. 28, 1882. DZA Potsdam, Reichskanzlei, 659,
p. 148. Earlier documents in the same file record Bismarck's mounting anxiety. *Ibid.*, pp. 3–4,
25–34, 86, 89. Whether and to what degree the Polish population had actually grown at the cost
of the German is difficult to calculate. The last census taken on the basis of language was conducted in 1861 for Posen and in 1867 for West Prussia and Upper Silesia. Subsequent calculations
had to be based on religious affiliations, correcting for the estimated number of Polish Protestants
and German Catholics. The corrected figures seemed to show that between 1861 and 1885 the
Polish population in the affected governmental districts (*Regierungsbezirke*) had grown by 607,560
(26 percent), the German population by 216,142 (14 percent). DZA Merseburg, Rep. 89H, I,
Preussen 20, Vol. III, pp. 24–31.

[44] Bismarck to Gossler, Nov. 25, 1881. GW, VIc, 234–235. See also pp. 223, 236–240; BR,
X, 294ff.

[45] On May 25, 1884, Bismarck wrote to Kurd von Schlözer, German envoy to the Vatican,
"The Polish question is of interest to us only when our relationship to Russia becomes uncertain,
but that relationship is at present assuming a character that permits the conclusion that the old,
good association will be reestablished for a long time." GW, VIc, 299. Most important among
the works that overemphasize the foreign political aspect of Bismarck's internal policy toward the
Poles is Josef Feldman, *Bismarck a Polska* (Czerwiec, 1947), chaps. 7 and 8 (English summary,
pp. 420–430); see also his "Bismarck et la question Polonaise," *Revue Historique*, 173 (1934).

concern about Germany's position in Europe. We shall see that the new effort to sanitize the eastern frontier of its minority problems began well ahead of the emergence of new problems in foreign affairs.

Since 1815 the Prussian government had been intermittently concerned about illegal immigration of Poles and Jews. Some migrants were young men eager to escape military service in Austria and Russia, but, with the development of agrarian and industrial prosperity in Prussia, others came in search of work. Eastern landowners and Silesian industrialists welcomed the border jumpers as a source of cheap labor. As Prussian peasants—German and Polish—moved west to Berlin, Saxony, Westphalia, the Ruhr, and overseas in search of a higher standard of living, their places were taken in eastern grain fields and Silesian mines and foundries by foreigners who crossed the border by stealth for the same reason. By the 1880s many illegal aliens were sons and even grandsons of the actual immigrants. Some had Prussian wives and mothers. The only home they knew was on the western side of the border.[46]

During 1871–1873, as his government fashioned a Germanizing education for the Polish regions, Bismarck pressed Minister of the Interior Eulenburg to order the gendarmerie to expel from the town and province of Posen "politically active persons," Jesuits, priests, and journalists who could not prove citizenship. By February 1872 he had begun to advocate the "expulsion in principle of *all* Poles who have no claim to citizenship, except those to whom the government may wish to grant dispensation."[47] For the time being, however, the government concentrated on expelling political agitators, on closing off avenues by which Polish immigrants had gained citizenship (usually through other German states), and on sharper control of the border.[48]

As anti-Semitism mounted in the mid-1870s, Jewish immigration also came under attack. For decades (particularly in the 1840s) Russian and Austrian Jews had drifted across the border. After the Russian pogroms began in 1881, thousands took to the road in order to escape persecution and possibly

[46] On the economic motivation for and popular and official reaction to transnational migration in the nineteenth century, see the works by Klaus Bade: " 'Kulturkampf' auf dem Arbeitsmarkt: Bismarcks 'Polenpolitik' 1885–1890," in Otto Pflanze, ed., *Innenpolitische Probleme des Bismarck-Reiches. Schriften des Historischen Kollegs: Kolloquien 2* (Munich, 1983), pp. 121–125; "Massenwanderung und Arbeitsmarkt im deutschen Nordosten von 1880 bis zum Ersten Weltkrieg: Überseeische Auswanderung, interne Abwanderung und kontinentale Zuwanderung," *Archiv für Sozialgeschichte,* 20 (1980), pp. 165–323; "Politik und Ökonomie der Ausländerbeschäftigung im preussischen Osten 1885–1914," in Hans-Jürgen Puhle and Hans-Ulrich Wehler, eds., *Preussen im Rückblick* in *Geschichte und Gesellschaft,* Sonderheft 6 (Göttingen, 1980), pp. 273–299; and " 'Preussengänger' und 'Abwehrpolitik': Ausländerbeschäftigung, Ausländerpolitik und Ausländerkontrolle auf dem Arbeitsmarkt in Preussen vor dem Ersten Weltkrieg," *Archiv für Sozialgeschichte,* 24 (1984), 91–283.

[47] Helmut Neubach, *Die Ausweisungen von Polen und Juden aus Preussen, 1885–1886* (Wiesbaden, 1967), pp. 3–4. Bismarck to Eulenburg, Feb. 7 and 12, 1872. GW, XIV, 827, and Adelheid Constabel, ed., *Die Vorgeschichte des Kulturkampfes* (Berlin, 1956), p. 171.

[48] Neubach, *Ausweisungen,* p. 4.

death. The Prussian border was relatively close, and beyond it, so the grape-vine reported, many Jews had found prosperity and even fortune in Germany's rapidly urbanizing and industrializing society. Assisted by relatives, friends, and fellow Jews, those with experience as artisans, shopkeepers, kosher butchers, and bakers integrated quickly. Having few demands and much in-centive, they were willing to work more hours at less pay than their native counterparts (both Poles and Germans). Often they got ahead faster. In a period of generally hard times and social distress, they became targets of the envious. From towns and villages in the east came petitions protesting the presence of these "unwholesome guests," who had no papers and no obliga-tions to the state.[49]

The issue soon became a matter of general public discussion. Heinrich von Treitschke set the tone in the influential *Preussische Jahrbücher* (1879). Ger-many, he declared, was being inundated by a "horde" of ambitious young Jews, "produced by an inexhaustible Polish cradle," who streamed over the eastern border year after year. He asserted that they were different from the more civilized Jews of western Europe and an older Jewish population that had contributed significantly to German culture. He warned that the children and grandchildren of these new immigrants would one day dominate Germany's newspapers and stock exchanges and claimed that their adverse influence on German economic life had been evident in the recent boom and bust. "In thousands of villages sits the Jew who buys out his neighbors at usurious prices." "What we demand from our Israelite fellow citizens is simple: they shall become German." Treitschke concluded, a "dangerous spirit of pre-sumptuousness" had appeared among Germany's Jews. Many lacked the "goodwill" to become German.[50] In the words of Theodor Mommsen, this essay by the historian and publicist who had made the greatest contribution to German unity had "the effect of an exploding bomb."[51] In the months that followed Treitschke responded to his critics by stoking further the fires of resentment and paranoia against Jewish immigrants, with the consequence that the "Polish question" tended to take on the character of a "Jewish ques-tion."[52]

Many other publicists took up the hue and cry, including Bismarck's *Leib-*

[49] *Ibid.*, pp. 4–7.

[50] "Unsere Aussichten," *Preussische Jahrbücher*, 44 (1879), pp. 559–576, republished in *Deutsche Kämpfe*, Neue Folge (Leipzig, 1896), pp. 1–28.

[51] Theodor Mommsen, *Auch ein Wort über unser Judentum* (5th ed., 1881).

[52] "Herr Graetz und sein Judenthum," *Preussische Jahrbücher*, 44 (1879), pp. 660–670. "Noch einige Bemerkungen zur Judenfrage," and "Zur Judenfrage," *ibid.*, 45 (1880), pp. 85–95, 224–225. "Die jüdische Einwanderung in Deutschland," *ibid.*, 47 (1881), pp. 109–110. Treitschke republished these essays in a pamphlet that reached four editions. *Ein Wort über unser Judentum* (4th ed., 1881). The entire debate between Treitschke and his critics has been reproduced in W. Boehlich, ed., *Der Berliner Antisemitismusstreit* (Frankfurt a. M., 1965). See also Neubach, *Ausweisungen*, pp. 8–10.

journalist Moritz Busch, editor of the widely read *Grenzboten*. Busch dealt with Judaism "not as a religious community, but as a race" and rejected the idea that Jews could ever become German.[53] Outside Germany Russification by the tsarist government and "Magyarization" by the Hungarian government, both of which affected German minorities, added fuel. Eduard von Hartmann, one of Germany's foremost philosophers, called for a response: "When the Slavs extirpate Germanism within their borders, we must have reprisals, that is, extirpate Slavism within our borders, if the influence of Germanism is not to sink considerably in the history of nature's peoples."[54] Contrary voices were not lacking, particularly among progressive and socialist journalists and deputies, but there could be no doubt during these years that the general temper of the country, eager for scapegoats, favored government action against aliens. In early 1881 Bismarck received a petition demanding an end to the immigration of "foreign Jews." It bore 250,000 signatures.[55]

On May 22, 1881, the Prussian cabinet, Bismarck presiding, discussed the illegal immigrant question.[56] Six days later the result was already apparent. Eulenburg ordered the governors of eastern provinces, who had been generally lax in following earlier directives, to strengthen border controls against illegal immigrants and restrict radically the naturalization of foreigners. Alien farm laborers needed in the fields were to be tolerated. Russian subjects who "exploited the need or naivete" of natives or worsened their economic circumstances by their competition were to be denied residence permits.[57]

Evidently the provincial authorities still did not regard the problem with the same urgency as did their superiors in Berlin, and they were subject to the counterpressure of local landlords and other employers who needed Polish labor. Berlin Jews were the chief victims of the new policy. In one year (October 1, 1883, to October 1, 1884), 662 persons (mostly Jews) were expelled from Berlin, as against only 512 persons from the four eastern provinces. To

[53] [Moritz Busch], *Israel und die Gojim: Beiträge zur Beurteilung der Judenfrage* (Leipzig, 1880), pp. 2, 304; see also *Tagebuchblätter*, II, 593.

[54] Helmut Neubach, "Eduard von Hartmanns Bedeutung für die Entwicklung des deutschpolnischen Verhältnisses," *Zeitschrift für Ostforschung*, 13 (1964), pp. 106–159, and *Ausweisungen*, pp. 9, 23–25.

[55] Neubach, *Ausweisungen*, p. 10.

[56] Cabinet meeting of May 22, 1881. DZA Merseburg, Rep. 90a, B, III, 2b, Nr. 6, Bd. 93.

[57] DZA Merseburg, Rep. 77, Tit. 1176, Nr. 2a, Bd. 4, p. 90. Neubach, *Ausweisungen*, p. 13. During 1881–1885 Bismarck received personal reports on the progress of the struggle against Polonism from Christoph von Tiedemann, formerly his principal aide as chief of the Imperial Chancellery and now head of the provincial government at Bromberg. GSA, Rep. 30, Nr. 693. "Acta betr[effend] der erneuerten Bestrebungen für die polnische Nationalität," Polizei Sachen, Aug. 1860–Oct., 1885. It can be presumed that Tiedemann was a major influence on Bismarck's mounting concern over ethnic problems on the eastern frontier during this period. In 1894 Tiedemann was one of the three founders of the *Verein zur Förderung des Deutschtums in den Ostmarken* (commonly known as the *Hakatisten*), which kept alive German consciousness of the "Polish problem" in Wilhelmian Germany.

count the alien population was not easy. The status of many was confused and unclear, and some evaded the poll takers. Not until February 1885 was the government able to arrive at a preliminary picture of the alien immigrant population in the east. Illegal residents of Berlin and the four eastern provinces (as of October 1, 1884) were believed to number 32,306, of whom 22,557 had been granted residence permits and 9,749 were either single persons or heads of families. In the last category were 6,132 Catholics, 2,695 Jews, and 931 Protestants: occupationally, it contained 5,733 field hands, 1,765 artisans, and 1,334 tradesmen.[58]

Bismarck pressed for immediate action.[59] That some regions should suffer a labor shortage was to him less important than the protection of "the state and its future." "The border jumpers of impeccable conduct, who appear to be a burden neither to the police nor to society, are often the most dangerous politically; they provide the revolutionary contacts between Russian Poles and [Polish] emigres in western Europe. But even the masses untouched by political agitation disturb our state organism by Polonizing the border provinces, whose Germanization is the state's task."[60] On March 26, 1885, appeared the fateful order directing four provincial governments to expel without delay persons of Russian origin residing without permission on German soil. In July the order was extended to all aliens, including those of Austrian origin, with or without permits.[61] The problem, about which Bismarck had "complained for years," was finally being attacked.[62]

Within the provincial governments, far closer to the realities than the Prussian cabinet, there was surprise and confusion. Local authorities were ex-

---

[58] Botho Eulenburg to Bismarck, Feb. 26, 1885. DZA Merseburg, Rep. 77, Tit. 1176, Nr. 2a, Bd. 5, pp. 25–42; Neubach, *Ausweisungen*, p. 31.

[59] Bismarck to Puttkamer, Mar. 14, 1885. DZA Merseburg, Rep. 77, Tit. 1176, Nr. 2a, Bd. 5, pp. 100–101. He had the enthusiastic support of *Kultusminister* Gossler, who was convinced that the eastern regions were being Polonized, not Germanized. Gossler to Bismarck, Feb. 12, Mar. 11, and May 2, 1885. *Ibid.*, pp. 25–32, 88–89, 168–169.

[60] Neubach, *Ausweisungen*, pp. 21, 31–32.

[61] Puttkamer to provincial governors (*Oberpräsidenten*), Mar. 26, 1885. DZA Merseburg, Rep. 77, Tit. 1176, Nr. 2a, Bd. 5, pp. 90–93v. On July 26, 1885, Puttkamer ordered provincial governors to include Prussian-born wives of border jumpers, but to exclude mine and foundry laborers who commuted across the border each day and agrarian workers needed during the harvest and planting seasons. *Ibid.*, pp. 400–401. When Puttkamer asked whether the expulsion of Galician Jews should include those that were by speech of German rather than Polish nationality, Bismarck is recorded as replying that to distinguish between these two categories would complicate the matter unnecessarily. "For us Galicians are Poles, whether they belong to one category or the other." He deplored anti-Semitic agitation, yet regarded as an evil the large number of "poor and *culturally non-German* Jews who migrated into Prussia from the east in order to enrich themselves." Cabinet meeting of Sept. 24, 1885. DZA Merseburg, Rep. 90a, B, III, 2b, Nr. 6, Bd. 97. The italicized phrase was inserted by Bismarck into the protocol.

[62] Bismarck marginal note on the document, Gossler to Bismarck and Puttkamer, Feb. 12, 1885. DZA Merseburg, Rep. 77, Tit. 1176, Nr. 2a, Bd. 5, p. 27.

pected to force the departure within one to two weeks of thousands of persons of widely varied status. Some were recent arrivals without roots in the land, but others had lived for decades in Prussia or even been born there. Those who had arrived in an earlier wave of immigration in the 1840s thought that Friedrich Wilhelm IV had granted them citizenship. Some had acquired property, launched careers, and held responsible positions. Their claims and petitions had to be adjudicated by state officials and courts. The Austrian government, eager to preserve good relations with Germany as the eastern crisis developed, expedited its returnees to Galicia. But the Russian government was reluctant to receive and care for thousands of Polish and Jewish refugees, many of whom no longer had roots in Russia or proof of Russian citizenship. During late 1885 pathetic scenes are said to have occurred at border crossings—refugees camping in fields and barns, selling their possessions for food, some destitute and starving. In January 1886 the Russian government agreed to accept those whose Russian citizenship could be established; yet its local officials were dilatory and uncooperative.[63] By April 1886, 16,000 aliens had left Germany; six months later the number was 26,492. By January 1888, when the action was completed, 32,000 aliens, including about 10,000 Jews, had been expelled out of a total now estimated at 44,000.[64]

The expulsion orders aroused bitter debates in Germany. Within the government the four provincial governors were divided. The governor of East Prussia executed the policy with enthusiasm, but the governor of West Prussia opposed it as inhumane and damaging. The governors of Posen and Upper Silesia tended toward ambivalence. Catholics regarded the expulsion as yet another attack on their faith, while left-liberals thought it anti-Semitic and brutal. Universal male suffrage and constitutional government gave the Poles and their allies a national forum from which to stage their protest. In November 1885 the Reichstag's Polish faction—supported by centrists, liberals, socialists, Alsatians, Guelphs, and Danes—interpellated "the imperial government" as to the extent and justification for the expulsion. Because of the support it received, particularly from the centrists, Bismarck chose to make a constitutional issue of the matter. He obtained the consent of the Kaiser, Prussian cabinet, and the Bundesrat to an imperial rescript (*Kaiserliche Botschaft*) that denied the constitutional existence of an "imperial government" empowered to interfere in the internal affairs of Prussia or any other federal state. On behalf of the federal states he declined to answer the interpellation.[65] On January 16, 1886, the Reichstag majority after a two-day, tumul-

---

[63] Neubach, *Ausweisungen*, pp. 76–81, 123. *DZA* Merseburg, Rep. 77, Tit. 250, Nr. 1, Bd. 11, pp. 89ff.

[64] Neubach, *Ausweisungen*, pp. 124, 128; Joachim Mai, *Die preussisch-deutsche Polenpolitik, 1885–1887* (Berlin, 1962), pp. 98, 205.

[65] *SBR* (1885–1886), I, 130–145.

tuous debate censured the Bismarck government by declaring the expulsions "unjustified" and contrary to the Reich's interests.[66]

Bismarck was undeterred. At the time, in fact, he was already well along with another project that he had had in mind for at least a decade. In 1875, when the Kulturkampf was at its height, he had proposed that peasant emigrants, who were steadily deserting the Pomeranian, Mecklenburg, and East Prussian countryside, be diverted from emigration overseas to the Polish regions of Posen, West Prussia, and Silesia by the offer of land on easy terms.[67] As his anxiety over the Poles mounted in 1882, he proposed an appropriation "to buy out the Polish nobility, who are the only hindrance to Germanization."[68] From *Kultusminister* Gossler he heard that many Polish landlords, distressed by falling grain prices, were ready to sell. On September 24, 1885, Bismarck proposed a bill to fund a land purchase program for the "express purpose of Germanization."[69]

For ideas he turned to his old associate Christoph von Tiedemann, now a district governor in Posen, who on January 8, 1886, supplied a long memorandum. As amended by Bismarck, this document was distributed to the king and cabinet and became the platform for a renewed effort to solve the Polish question. The memorandum painted a grim picture of the Polish advance and German retreat. The Polish population was growing faster than the German (10.11 percent as against 4.12 percent annually); many Polish landlords had become equal or superior to their German neighbors in rationally managing their estates; a new bourgeois and professional class (doctors, lawyers, actors), supplemented by an active press and network of voluntary associations, had emerged to support the clergy in the effort "to Polonize the province systematically." Concessions would never win the Poles, to whom they were a sign of weakness. Defense must yield to offense.

Tiedemann recommended several measures for "Germanizing the province of Posen," the most important of which was to revive the land purchase and colonization system attempted by Eduard von Flottwell in the 1830s. Polish estate owners, Tiedemann reported, were on the brink of disaster. Creditors

---

[66] SBR (1885–1886), I, 525–597.

[67] Bismarck to Camphausen, Feb. 27, 1875. GW, IVc, 56; AWB, I, 200. Evidently the initiative came from Posen. In November 1873 the provincial government in Posen reported the failure of a Polish company founded in 1862 for the purpose of keeping Polish landlords solvent and their estates out of German hands. Local Germans hoped that the Prussian government, German rulers, and German capitalists would seize the opportunity to buy estates and settle them with German farmers. DZA Merseburg, Rep. 2.2.1., Nr. 16148, p. 101, also pp. 143–144.

[68] Wilhelm von Bismarck to Franz von Rottenburg, Apr. 28, 1882. DZA Potsdam, Reichskanzlei, 659, p. 148.

[69] Cabinet meeting of Sept. 24, 1885. DZA Merseburg, Rep. 90a, B, III, 2b, Nr. 6, Bd. 97. The discussion was stimulated by a report by *Kultusminister* Gossler that numerous Polish-owned estates were on the market and that his ministry had already made purchases from its own funds. See also the cabinet meeting of Dec. 16, 1884. *Ibid.*, Bd. 96.

could force a third into bankruptcy at any time; another third would sell if the price was right. This unprecedented opportunity might never recur. The state should purchase, subdivide, and lease the distressed properties to German settlers. Coupled with a reform of county government (to reduce the power of the remaining estate owners), this settlement project would be the greatest possible contribution to Germanization of the Polish region.[70]

On January 14, 1886, Wilhelm celebrated his twenty-fifth anniversary as king of Prussia by opening the Landtag with a speech in which he forecast new measures for the protection of Germanism in the east. Two weeks later Bismarck delivered his "great Polish speech" to the Chamber of Deputies—a two-hour exposition of his views on the Polish danger, intermixed with ferocious assaults on the patriotism of his opponents. He called for a state fund with which to purchase estates from financially distressed Polish landlords and also to rescue hard-pressed German farmers who might otherwise sell out to Poles.[71] Later the speech was reprinted in 500,000 copies and distributed throughout Germany.[72] Apparently the attack on the Polish population, which came soon after Germany's first venture into colonialism, was popular in Germany. Bismarck's office was inundated with letters, telegrams, and petitions of support, more than his staff could answer.[73]

Under Bismarck's whip the required legislation was produced with extraordinary speed. A bill cleared the cabinet at the end of January and reached the Chamber of Deputies on February 9, where it was debated on February 22–23 and April 1–2. After the third reading on April 7, the bill passed by a big majority (214 to 120).[74] Passage through the House of Lords was quick, and on April 26, 1886, the bill became law. The "settlement act" established a fund of 100,000,000 marks for the express purpose of "strengthening the German element in the provinces of West Prussia and Posen" by buying up farmland for long-term lease to and ultimate ownership by "German farm workers." The fund was administered by a commission placed directly under the authority of the Prussian cabinet, a device by which Bismarck hoped to "circumvent the bureaucratic tradition" in the interest of effective action.[75]

Bismarck considered even more drastic steps. In the cabinet he talked of

---

[70] Cabinet meeting of Jan. 10, 1886. DZA Merseburg, Rep. 90a, B, III, 2b, Nr. 6, Bd. 98. For the Tiedemann memorandum, including Bismarck's corrections, see DZA Potsdam, Reichskanzlei 661, pp. 68–104.

[71] BR, XI, 407ff.

[72] Neubach, Ausweisungen, p. 112.

[73] Norddeutsche Allgemeine Zeitung, vol. 25, no. 56 (Feb. 3, 1886).

[74] SBHA (1886), II, 683–746; III, 1583–1640, 1707–1742. Bismarck's impatience shows in a marginal note scrawled on a critical document: "We need completed drafts and quickly; otherwise the situation will change before we can act." DZA Potsdam, Reichskanzlei, 661, p. 200.

[75] GSP (1886), pp. 131–134, 159–162. Cabinet meeting of Jan. 24, 1886. DZA Potsdam, Reichskanzlei, 661, pp. 212–219.

"punishing" oppositional Polish landlords by "confiscating" their property.[76] Why should the state not use its power of eminent domain, he asked the Prussian Chamber of Deputies, to "expropriate" Polish property, just as it did farm property for the construction of railways and urban property for public works.[77]

During 1886–1887 "further repressive measures,"[78] voted unanimously by the cabinet on the basis of Tiedemann's recommendations, were implemented in the Polish regions. Polish officials and military recruits were required to serve in the west, where they might "learn the blessings of German civilization."[79] Transferred officials were replaced by Germans from the west, who were given inducements to learn Polish. Polish teachers were transferred to the west and efforts were made (not very successful) to lure Germans eastward by the prospect of better salaries and pension rights. Appropriations totaling 2,400,000 marks paid for new and enlarged schools, more teachers, and higher salaries in the threatened German enclaves. The number of state school inspectors in Polish districts was increased from 66 to 115. Urban academies for the education of German women were improved and increased in number.[80]

New statutes strengthened the state's authority to veto the appointment of teachers by school boards, discipline disloyal teachers, and fine the parents of children absent from school without cause. Trade schools were established in 115 towns and villages to provide Polish apprentices and journeymen with a compulsory "German education" beyond the elementary school (to the age of eighteen).[81] State scholarships were made available to needy German students and to German medical students willing to learn Polish and accept positions in public health in the east. To make sure that only Germans were appointed to public health positions, the authority to fill such positions was taken away from the county diets and given to the district governments.[82] The number of counties in Posen and West Prussia was increased and their

[76] Cabinet meetings of Jan. 10 and Feb. 7, 1886. DZA Merseburg, Rep. 90a, B, III, 2b, Nr. 6, Bd. 98; Lucius, Bismarck-Erinnerungen, p. 331.

[77] BR, XI, 443.

[78] Cabinet to king, Jan. 27, 1886. DZA Merseburg, Rep. 2.2.1., Nr. 15007, Bd. 3, pp. 1–7v.

[79] Bismarck to Chamber of Deputies, Jan. 28, 1886. BR, XI, 444–445. See also the general program for strengthening "German culture" in the region and "fortifying the German spirit" among teachers, officials, and judges. Jan. 27, 1886. GW, VIc, 328.

[80] Kultusminister von Gossler, "Übersicht der Massregeln, welche auf dem Gebiete der Unterrichtsverwaltung im Jahre 1886 getroffen worden sind, um den Bestand und die Entwickelung der deutschen Bevölkerung in den Provinzen Westpreussen und Posen, sowie in dem Regierungsbezirk Oppeln sicherzustellen." This document is a pamphlet dated Feb. 28, 1887, forwarded by Gossler to Bismarck, Mar. 8, 1887. DZA Potsdam, Reichskanzlei, 664, pp. 86ff.

[81] Statutes of May 4, May 6, and July 15, 1886. GSP (1886), pp. 143–145, 185–186. Cabinet to king, Feb. 19, 1886. DZA Merseburg, Rep. 2.2.1, Nr. 15007, Bd. III, pp. 6–8.

[82] DZA Potsdam, Reichskanzlei, 661/1, p. 43. Cabinet meeting of Feb. 7, 1886. DZA Merseburg, Rep. 90a, B, III, 2b, Nr. 6, Bd. 98.

size reduced in order to heighten the effectiveness of the German county counselors who governed them.[83]

The most far-reaching measures, however, were yet to come. The language of government act of 1876 had allowed exceptions to the use of German as the only language for the conduct of public business, to be approved at five-year intervals for no more than twenty years. For ten years minority languages had been permitted in the proceedings of school boards, communal assemblies, and communal councils in several areas: Polish in several counties of the provinces of Posen and West Prussia, Lithuanian in one county of East Prussia, Danish in several counties of northern Schleswig, and French in certain parts of the county of Malmédy in Lorraine. Provincial authorities in Posen and Schleswig-Holstein appealed to the government to continue the exceptions, but in October 1886 the cabinet adamantly refused; the lower classes in Posen, it declared, must be "assimilated into German life and into the Prussian organism of state."[84]

By excluding monolingual Poles (most of the Polish population) in the affected districts from participation in local governmental affairs, this act breached one of the few democratic features of the Prussian constitutional monarchy, the cherished right of "self-administration." But this was not all. On September 7, 1887, the cabinet, acting on the king's authorization, abolished the teaching of the Polish language "without exception" in all elementary schools, the released time to be devoted to additional instruction in German.[85] Prussia's outstanding educational system, Bismarck fretted, had "created" an educated Polish *Mittelstand*, especially doctors and lawyers, that had not previously existed but was now significant in bolstering resistance "to Germanism and the Prussian government."[86]

Certainly Bismarck understood—except at exuberant or ruminative moments[87]—that it was nearly impossible to erase the ethnicity of more than two

---

[83] GSP (1887), pp. 197–207; DZA Potsdam, Reichskanzlei, 661, pp. 114–114v; 661/1, pp. 173–175v; 664, pp. 1–36. A proposal to dismember the province of Posen and join its administrative districts to West Prussia and Silesia was seriously discussed, but never acted upon. Puttkamer to Bismarck, Feb. 20, 1886, DZA Potsdam, Reichskanzlei, 661/2, pp. 93–99v; cabinet meeting of May 8, 1886, DZA Potsdam, Reichskanzlei, 662, p. 64; Tiedemann to Bismarck, Nov. 5, 1886, DZA Potsdam, Reichskanzlei, 661/2, pp. 93–99v.

[84] Cabinet to king, Oct. 8, 1886. DZA Merseburg, Rep. 2.2.1., Nr. 15007, Bd. III, pp. 12–18.

[85] The cabinet orders are in SBHA (1888), Anlagen, II, pp. 1073–1074. The measure was proposed by Gossler, an enthusiastic advocate of Germanization. Gossler to king, July 17, 1887. DZA Potsdam, Rep. 2.2.1., Nr. 15007, Bd. III, pp. 40, 51.

[86] Bismarck to cabinet, June 24, 1887. DZA Potsdam, Reichskanzlei, 664, pp. 127–127v; see also the marginal note on Gossler to Bismarck, June 6, 1887. *Ibid.*, pp. 113–113v. For the first time Bismarck appears here to recognize that the Polish clergy and nobility were not the only sources of Polish resistance.

[87] See vol. 1, pp. 194–195. In late September 1876, Lucius dined with the Bismarck family at Varzin and recorded Bismarck's musings about the uncertainty of Russian aims in the Balkan

million people. Wilhelm was troubled, although more by conscience than by practical difficulties. He feared that his ministers were veering toward a campaign to "root out" (*ausrotten*) the Polish tongue.[88] Yet he kept signing the rescripts his ministers put before him. The king, Bismarck, and cabinet ministers believed it necessary and possible to achieve a substantial shift in the ethnic composition of the eastern region. Bismarck spoke of the policy as "a more vigorous resumption of the defense against Polonization but also of the promotion of Germanization."[89]

Unquestionably Bismarck was the driving force behind the Germanization policy in the 1870s and 1880s. The policy he pursued would, if successful, have eliminated Polish as the language of education, government, politics, the professions, the press, commerce, and military service. Did he really believe that the realm that remained—hearth, home, field, and market—would remain uninvaded? In the great debate on the colonization act of 1886 he declared that the Poles had succeeded in "rooting out" German culture in eastern villages not by fire and sword, as in the case of the Wends, but by "gentle" means such as "the school, religious service, religious instruction, and the superiority of the social position of Polonism."[90] Not all of his means were as "gentle" as those employed by the Poles, but they were of the same order. Obviously he hoped that in time they would effect the same result.

The political assimilation of more than 2,300,000 Poles, separated from 10,000,000 other Poles by frontiers that were less than a century old, was a difficult task in an era of growing ethnic national sentiment. But it was made more difficult by the measures of the Bismarck government. The expulsions of the 1880s not only gave Germany a bad press in Europe but also proved to be economically crippling. After the "German Herod" left office in 1890 the border had to be reopened because of an acute shortage of field hands on east German estates. The efforts of the settlement act commission were countered effectively by Polish agrarian associations that gave financial support to insolvent Polish landlords; in three decades the commission made no headway in

---

crisis. "The Russians themselves don't know what they want, one day war, another day peace. . . . We don't want Warsaw or even Kracow, although we have been offered them on various occasions. But I would not reject a rectification of the frontier that would make Silesia more secure from Russian invasion. The territory gained must not be incorporated [into Germany] but administered independently and ruled absolutely. Germanized *par force*." Lucius, *Bismarck-Erinnerungen*, pp. 90–91.

[88] On approving new repressive measures recommended by the cabinet in early 1886, Wilhelm wrote, "To me it seems important to stress now and then in the discussion concerning these Germanizing plans that we do not aim thereby at the rooting out [*Ausrottung*] of the Polish language." DZA Merseburg, Rep. 2.2.1., Nr. 15007, Bd. III, p. 14.

[89] To the Prussian cabinet, Jan. 10, 1886. DZA Merseburg, Rep. 90a, B, III, 2b, Nr. 6, Bd. 98.

[90] *BR*, XII, 103–104.

changing the ethnic character of the farming population in the east. The attack on their religion and their language only strengthened the loyalty of the Poles to both. To Polish citizens who were denied the use of their mother tongue in so many vital areas of daily life it could have made little difference that the publicly expressed motive was *raison d'état* rather than ethnic or racial intolerance. The result was the same whatever the motive. In his Polish policy, as in other internal affairs, Bismarck seriously miscalculated the efficacy of coercion—at least with the means that he and his age were willing to accept as tolerable.

Final Attempt at Tax Reform

Although the attack on the Polish and Jewish minorities had wide support in Germany, its immediate consequence was a further deterioration in the relationship of the Bismarck government to the Reichstag majority. Soon after the 1885–1886 session began, Bismarck clashed bitterly with Windthorst over a related matter, the government's refusal to allow Jesuit missionary activity in the colonies. "The danger posed by Jesuit activity for Germany, for its unity and its national development lies," the chancellor declared, "not in the Catholicism of the Jesuits but in their whole international organization, in their detachment from and renunciation of all national ties, in their destruction and dissolution of national ties and national sentiments everywhere they encounter them." The "anemic" condition of its national sentiment made Germany vulnerable to the Jesuit bid for world domination.[91]

The chancellor was equally outraged by an attempt of the Polish caucus—supported by centrists, left-liberals, social democrats, Guelphs, Danes, and Alsatians—to interpellate the "imperial government" concerning the expulsions in the east. His use of an imperial rescript to deny both the existence of an imperial government and the Reichstag's constitutional right to interfere in Prussia's internal affairs was, in the opinion of his colleague, "like using cannon to shoot sparrows."[92] The *Vossische Zeitung* called it "one of the greatest surprises in German and Prussian parliamentary history."[93] The rescript failed, furthermore, to keep the Reichstag from discussing and condemning the expulsions.[94]

Bismarck's clash with Windthorst left him feeling "as though he had been fighting with roughnecks in a dirty tavern. I find it hard to do my professional duty by getting into such scraps."[95] As he contemplated the coming struggles

[91] *BR*, XI, 250–251.
[92] *BR*, XI, 298ff.; *GW*, VIII, 535–537; Lucius, *Bismarck-Erinnerungen*, p. 323.
[93] Quoted in Neubach, *Ausweisungen*, p. 89.
[94] See pp. 203–204.
[95] Lucius, *Bismarck-Erinnerungen*, p. 323.

BISMARCK AT HIS DESK IN FRIEDRICHSRUH, DECEMBER 27, 1886.

over the renewal of the antisocialist law and *Septennat*, Bismarck expected the worst: dissolutions, elections, possibly a coup d'état. "The Reichstag," he told Baron Mittnacht, "is showing a rather evil face. If this continues, we will no longer have any legal foundation under our feet. The German rulers may finally discover that it has been an illusion to try to rule Germany with parliament. The Reichstag is more easily dispensable than the army." Mittnacht concluded that, if the chancellor reached the point of having to fear for the monarchy, he would light the fuse under the powder keg "in cold blood."[96]

Despite this angry, tumultuous beginning, the Reichstag session of 1885–1886 was not fruitless for Bismarck's purposes. Without major difficulty the Reichstag renewed the antisocialist statute, although for two rather than the five years requested; appropriated money for construction of the North Sea (Kiel) Canal; and extended health and accident insurance coverage to workers in forestry and agriculture and in the transportation and communication industries (including government-owned enterprises).[97] Yet tax reform, the major goal of Bismarck's domestic policy for a decade, suffered a final, bitter defeat.

Because of the Franckenstein clause the millions in new revenue produced by the protective tariffs were of limited benefit to the Imperial Treasury; because of the *lex Huene*, they were of limited benefit to the Prussian treasury. The steady accumulation of new financial obligations by the Reich—new fortifications, greater outlays for the armed forces, the Kiel Canal, a stately Reichstag building, colonies, new imperial agencies, and an enlarged imperial bureaucracy—produced increasing annual deficits in the national budget, which were covered by borrowing annually up to 410,000,000 marks (in 1885). The borrowing added further burdens in the form of interest and amortization payments.[98] To shift these fiscal obligations to the states by increasing their annual assessments would have thrown their already precarious budgets into further disarray. To compound the problem, the balance of payments between the Reich and the states (that is, the amounts received by the states in excess of annual assessments paid to the Reich) favored the states by 41,000,000 marks in 1885 but only by 17,900,000 marks in 1886 and 5,400,000 marks in 1887.[99]

As was noted earlier, unbalanced budgets were for Bismarck not necessarily evil. On the contrary, financial "vacuums" created coercive situations that might force the Reichstag to accept the solutions he desired.[100] The looming

[96] GW, VIII, 535.

[97] RGB (1885), pp. 159–164, 271–272; (1886), pp. 77, 132–178, 233.

[98] Hans Blömer, "Die Anleihen des deutschen Reiches von 1871 bis zur Stabilisierung der Mark 1924" (unpublished dissertation, Bonn, 1946), pp. 25–26, 90–91.

[99] Wilhelm Gerloff, *Die Finanz- und Zollpolitik des deutschen Reiches* (Jena, 1913), pp. 193, 522.

[100] Lucius, *Bismarck-Erinnerungen*, pp. 309, 314.

financial crisis in 1885–1886 enabled him to launch yet another attempt to tap a major source of revenue that would make possible the "tax reform" that had been his most consistent objective in domestic politics for two decades. What he had failed to accomplish with an imperial tobacco monopoly he now hoped to achieve with an imperial liquor monopoly, a product with which he had considerable experience, both as producer and consumer.

The bill drafted by the Prussian Ministry of Finance under Scholz's direction left the production of raw alcohol in the hands of about three thousand, largely east German estate owners (including Bismarck), who found it useful to convert their potato and grain crops into raw alcohol in their own distilleries. The raw alcohol was to be refined into potable beverages in state distilleries and distributed to state-approved outlets to be sold at controlled prices. The affected interests (beverage distillers) were to be indemnified with 540,000,000 marks. The Reich's gross annual income from this source was expected to be 668,700,000 marks, net income 335,000,000 marks.[101] Once indemnity and start-up costs were amortized, the annual yield was expected to increase six-fold. The flow of funds from the Reich to the states would have been greatly increased, requiring new legislation by state governments as to its disposition. Through Scholz Bismarck outlined how Prussia's share was to be spent: increased salaries for officials, transfer of the real estate tax (Grund- und Gebäudesteuer) to local governments (Kommunalverbände), assumption by the central government of one-half of all school costs, replacement of the remaining steps of the class and classified income taxes by a single income tax not to exceed the old rate of 3 percent.[102]

Raw alcohol distillers did not oppose the monopoly; on the contrary, they gave it enthusiastic support and for good reason. Over the previous decade rural distilleries, such as the four Bismarck owned, had been afflicted by a catastrophic decline in the price for their products. Where once they had received between 60 and 70 marks per hectoliter, they now received 16.[103] The bill would have stabilized the price at 30 to 40 marks and controlled competition by requiring government approval for construction of new raw alcohol distilleries. But neither did beverage distillers oppose the bill, because the price to be paid for their properties was 15,000,000 marks more than market value. It was the publicans who, like the tobacco merchants earlier, were outraged by the monopoly proposal. That higher prices for liquor were expected to induce greater sobriety among workers was for them no recommendation. Within the Reichstag opposition to the proposal was formidable.

[101] BR (1885–1886), Anlagen, Nos. 165 and 208; BR, XI, 314–331.

[102] Gerloff, Finanz- und Zollpolitik, 182–183, pp. 193–195.

[103] SEG (1886), p. 55; Johannes Ziekursch, Politische Geschichte des neuen deutschen Kaiserreiches (Frankfurt a. M., 1927), II, 372. For price fluctuations, see Walther Hoffmann, Das Wachstum der deutschen Wirtschaft seit der Mitte des 19. Jahrhunderts (Berlin, 1965), p. 589.

By opening an uncontrolled source of revenue for the Reich, the monopoly posed another threat to the Reichstag's budgetary power. The national liberals were ambivalent, torn between the desire to appease the government and their dislike of the bill and its constitutional consequences. But even the conservatives were lukewarm in their support. For centrists the bill was too centralistic, for left-liberals too socialistic. Again Richter denounced Bismarck's tax philosophy as relief for the well-to-do at the cost of the poor. Illness prevented Bismarck from defending the bill at its first reading; he promised to appear at committee hearings but did not. At the end of the second reading on March 27, 1886, the vital paragraphs were overwhelmingly rejected, 181 to 3 (the conservatives abstained).[104]

Bismarck's conduct on the issue of the liquor monopoly raises questions about the firmness of his grip on public affairs, despite his successes in the Prussian Landtag during the same period. In November 1885 he was pleased with the bill that Scholz's ministry had drafted, but skeptical about its chances for passage. A month later he spoke to the Prussian cabinet of its rejection as certain, an opinion shared by Lucius and Scholz. Yet by January 1886 Bismarck and Scholz had worked up such enthusiasm for the bill that Lucius concluded with amazement that they had deluded themselves into thinking it would pass.[105] In a cabinet meeting of early March, when the obstacles became apparent, the prince's rage astonished his colleagues. He declared "war to the knife" against the "tyranny" of publicans and denounced the cowardice of the conservatives. He wished to threaten the latter with a distillery tax (Fabrikatsteuer), the former with a Prussian licensing tax (Lizenzsteuer). "I don't want to be fair and equitable. I do not care about the Reich constitution; let it come apart at the joints. I expect your unanimous support, if necessary, to break the constitution." But even Scholz, normally Bismarck's willing collaborator, felt compelled to oppose any such futile attempt at vengeance, and Puttkamer, Lucius, and Boetticher came to his support. All that the chancellor gained from his colleagues was a commitment by Puttkamer and Maybach to make the publicans feel the government's wrath by strict application of building codes. Not since the days of Eulenburg and Bitter had Lucius seen Bismarck so wrathful. "What he actually intended is incomprehensible," Lucius confided to his diary, "since we are not faced with any special financial calamity. We don't at all need the many millions he wishes to conjure up."[106]

Not until the fate of the bill was sealed did Bismarck appear in the Reichs-

[104] SBR (1885–1886), pp. 1295–1374, 1609–1704; Gerloff, Finanz- und Zollpolitik, p. 194.

[105] GW, VIII, 534–535; Lucius, Bismarck-Erinnerungen, pp. 325, 328–329, 331.

[106] Lucius, Bismarck-Erinnerungen, pp. 335–336. The minutes of the cabinet meeting of Mar. 7 confirm the general accuracy of Lucius's account. DZA Merseburg, Rep. 90a, B, III, 2b, Nr. 6, Bd. 98.

tag to defend it. His barbed speech was patently intended more for the public than the deputies. He dismissed the accusation that his *Schnapspolitik* was special-interest legislation for the exclusive benefit of estate owners as just another attack on the nobility and on agriculture in general. In recent decades the tillers of the land had become the stepchildren of tax legislation; they bore far more than their fair share of the state's financial burden. The actual beneficiaries of his monopoly proposal would be the millions of citizens threatened with prosecution and dispossession because of tax delinquencies. But his greatest goal, he said, was to "fortify" the Reich by giving it a firm financial foundation. "I am old and sick and I do not know how much longer I can be active." His opponents would weaken the Reich by introducing parliamentary government. A parliament controlled by the Reich's enemies could not truly represent the nation. He had learned to rely in times of foreign danger not upon the Reichstag but upon the states. The day might yet come when the federated states would demand back the sovereignty that they had surrendered in 1867 and 1871. During the debates he listened to the laughter that followed Richter's ironic attacks on the government with mounting anger. "He who laughs last laughs best," he grimly told the deputies. "You are leading us into a situation that will end your presence here. Then you may laugh differently."[107]

The Reichstag shrugged off this open threat of a coup d'état and rejected yet another Bismarck tax proposal in the spring of 1886. Anticipating the defeat of the liquor monopoly, the chancellor gained his colleagues' approval for a tax bill that was not without an element of revenge against publicans.[108] Producers were to be granted a 10-percent reduction in the existing tax on distilling capacity (*Maischraumsteuer*) at a cost to the state of 6,000,000 marks, while liquor retailers and tavern keepers were to collect a sales tax of 40 pfennig per liter, to be increased in 1888 to 80 pfennig, and in 1889 to 1 mark, 20 pfennig. In addition, the tariffs on imported alcohol were to be increased significantly. The prospective yield was estimated at 210,000,000 marks. In the Reichstag debates left-liberals, centrists, and other oppositional groups disputed the need for such a massive increase in imperial income at the ultimate cost of consumers. They refused to increase the flow of imperial funds to states and local governments without knowing precisely for what purposes the funds were to be used. To distribute such funds on the basis of population alone was to ask the poorer regions in north and east to support the richer regions in the west. Back of these objections loomed the ever-present question of the constitutional consequence of an indirect tax of un-

---

[107] BR, XI, 336–384. For Bismarck's thoughts at this time about the possible necessity of a *Staatsstreich* and changes in the electoral law, see Lucius, *Bismarck-Erinnerungen*, p. 352, and Wilhelm von Schweinitz, *Denkwürdigkeiten des Botschafters General von Schweinitz* (Berlin, 1927), II, 317–318.

[108] Cabinet meeting of Mar. 14, 1886. DZA Merseburg, Rep. 90a, B, III, 2b, Nr. 6, Bd. 98.

limited duration on the Reichstag's parliamentary power. But the distillers were also dissatisfied, grumbling that the tax reduction was insufficient. The "grog parliament," as it was dubbed, ended its session on June 26 by defeating the bill decisively at the end of the second reading.[109]

Bismarck's conduct in the cabinet meeting of March 7 and in the Reichstag on March 26, 1886, made legitimate the question whether he was still able, emotionally and physically, to endure political frustration. He attended none of the debates on the liquor tax bill. In the spring of 1886 he left Berlin much earlier than usual, five weeks before the Reichstag adjourned.

[109] SBR (1885–1886), III, 2121–2173, 2193–2203, VI, Nos. 294, 311. Gerloff, *Finanz- und Zollpolitik*, pp. 195–196.

CHAPTER EIGHT

External Crisis and Internal Conquest

BISMARCK'S itinerary while on leave in 1886 was not that of a sick man. He left Berlin for Friedrichsruh on May 20, 1886, but returned on June 15. After a week in the Wilhelmstrasse he made a three-day trip to Varzin, perhaps to inspect the ruins of one of his paper mills, recently destroyed by fire. If that caused him distress, he undoubtedly enjoyed a one-day excursion to Schönhausen on June 29 to view the ancestral estate, finally restored to its original size by the nation's gift of 1885. On July 3 he was off to Bad Kissingen for the cure, followed by another at Bad Gastein. His stay at Gastein was more political than therapeutic. He conferred there at length with Wilhelm, Emperor Franz Joseph, and Habsburg Foreign Minister Gustav von Kálnoky. On the return journey via Regensburg he stopped at Franzensbad for a talk with Russian Foreign Minister Nikolay Karlovich Giers. Back in Berlin on August 28 he tore a leg muscle, which confined him to quarters and delayed his departure for Varzin until September 14. There he remained during the autumn, proceeding to Friedrichsruh on November 15 by way of Berlin, where he spent only five days. Not until January 8, 1887, did the German chancellor become resident again in the nation's capital. Except for three, fairly brief visits, he had been gone for seven and a half months.[1]

This extended leave is notable because it was not marked by bad health or abnormal physical weakness, except for the torn muscle, a passing ailment. That reports of his condition during this long period are sparse is of itself evidence that he had few complaints. "The prince looks really very good and blooming," Baroness Spitzemberg wrote on July 1, 1886, "and he is uncommonly cheerful."[2] In August and again in November Herbert wrote brother Bill that both parents were getting along well—his father "also insofar as his mood is concerned."[3] Bismarck's mental and physical health may have im-

[1] Horst Kohl, ed., *Fürst Bismarck: Regesten zu einer wissenschaflichen Biographie des ersten Reichskanzlers* (Stuttgart, 1891–1892), II, 406–412.

[2] Rudolf Vierhaus, ed., *Das Tagebuch der Baronin Spitzemberg* (Göttingen, 1961), p. 225; see also entries of Aug. 28 and Sept. 13, 1886. *Ibid.*, p. 226. On July 8, 12, and 27, 1886, Rottenburg reported from Kissingen to Bleichröder that Bismarck's cure was going "extremely well"; on August 14 he reported from Gastein that Bismarck had endured well the considerable strain of the meeting with Wilhelm, Franz Joseph, and Kálnoky. *Bleichröder Archive*, Kress Library of Business and Economics, Harvard, Box III.

[3] Herbert to Bill Bismarck, Aug. 11 and Nov. 24, 1886. Walter Bussmann, ed., *Staatssekretär*

FOREIGN MINISTERS GIERS, BISMARCK, AND KÁLNOKY AT SKIERNIEWICZ, SEPTEMBER 15–17, 1884. (BILD-ARCHIV PREUSSISCHER KULTURBESITZ.)

proved during the last half of 1886 not because of Schweninger's treatment and the cures at Kissingen and Gastein but because of an international crisis and the opportunity it offered him in German politics. Over the years Bismarck had never complained that crises in foreign affairs affected his nerves or ravaged his body, except when coupled with difficulties with Wilhelm (and his generals) as in 1866, 1870, and 1879. Neither the problems nor the personalities of international politics imposed upon him the psychic and resulting physical burdens that he felt in domestic affairs. Indeed, he may have enjoyed the challenge they brought. In 1886–1887 he saw in international affairs the chance to demonstrate that he, not the opposition parties, represented the will of the German nation—a nation awakened to a proper under-

Graf Herbert von Bismarck: Aus seiner politischen Privatkorrespondenz (Göttingen, 1964), pp. 370, 373, 407; see also pp. 414, 416.

standing of its self-interest by the threat of another attack from across the Rhine.

Renewed Turbulence in Continental Affairs

In surveying the European scene for the Reichstag in January 1885, Bismarck noted with satisfaction, "We are surrounded by friends in Europe."[4] During the preceding year the second Three Emperors League had been renewed without difficulty for three more years. A meeting at Skierniewicz in September 1884 (followed by another at Kremsier in August 1885) seemed to demonstrate the solidarity of the alliance, despite continuing uneasiness between Russia and Austria. For nearly two years the greatest threats to peace lay not in eastern Europe but in far-off places: Egypt, Afghanistan, and Caroline Islands. The Gladstone government had found it easier to invade than to withdraw from Egypt. From the "provisional" occupation of Cairo (September 1882) to Gordon's catastrophe at Khartoum in the Sudan (January 1885), Britain's military and administrative commitment grew steadily and planlessly from episode to episode. One consequence was a deterioration in Britain's relationship to France and an increasing dependence of both powers upon German support. Russian expansion toward and into Afghanistan produced rising discord with Britain until in February–April 1885 both countries began to prepare for war. Europe's peace was also threatened in 1885 by conflict between Germany and Spain over the Caroline Islands, intensified, Bismarck believed, by French intrigue. According to Rantzau, he concluded that, if the Carolines dispute could not be settled peacefully, Germany should precipitate the struggle by mobilizing two or three army corps on the Rhine frontier, "and the dance will begin." "For us war with Spain means war with France."[5]

Bismarck's policy in each of these situations, while motivated by his conception of Germany's self-interest, was conducive to the preservation of peace. The Egyptian "apple of discord" was a "gift from heaven," for it provided Berlin with leverage against British resistance to Germany's African policy.[6] While he approved of the French-British entente of the early 1880s (it kept France away from Russia), Bismarck could regard its collapse with composure in view of his success in drawing Russia into the second Three Emperors League. He generally encouraged Russian involvement in Afghanistan, both to prove German fidelity to Russian interests and to relieve Russian pressure on Austria's frontier. When Britain contemplated a defense of India on the shores of the Black Sea, Germany stiffened Turkey's resistance by sending a military commission to advise the Porte on how best to close the

[4] BR, X, 413.

[5] Kuno zu Rantzau to Herbert von Bismarck, Sept. 10 and Oct. 21, 1885. Bussmann, ed., *Herbert von Bismarck*, pp. 315–323.

[6] Herbert to Wilhelm von Bismarck, Sept. 1, 1884. *Ibid.*, p. 259.

Straits to British warships and joined Austria, France, and Italy in insisting that neutrality of the Straits was an international principle.[7] The Afghanistan crisis combined with the Egyptian quagmire threatened Britain with a war that would have to be fought on a distant battlefield with inadequate forces and without allies. Neither the Gladstone cabinet nor its conservative opposition liked this prospect. As the liberal government stumbled toward its end in July conservative politicians were already making overtures to Germany. On Lord Salisbury's succession to Downing Street, he exchanged friendly letters with Bismarck. A new relationship between Britain and Germany appeared to be in prospect.[8] Bismarck also preserved peace with Spain by proposing the pope as arbiter, an offer that the Spanish government could hardly refuse and that simultaneously eased Germany's liquidation of the Kulturkampf.

Never had Germany's position in the European balance of power seemed more unassailable than during the years 1884–1885. As Herbert Bismarck proudly asserted, the quality of his father's diplomacy alone had put her there.[9] By the autumn of 1885, nevertheless, there were already signs of trouble, which multiplied during the following months until by the end of 1886 the powers were again on the verge of a major conflict. In the twilight of their careers Kaiser and chancellor were faced with what was to become their greatest test in international politics.

From the Treaty of Berlin in 1878 to the Triple Alliance of 1882 the European powers had more or less followed, without formally accepting, Bismarck's prescription for the division of the Balkans and eastern Mediterranean into spheres of influence. The critical question now was whether agreements reached at the green table could be converted into political realities. Resentful that the Russians had sacrificed their interests in favor of Bulgaria at the Congress of Berlin, the Serbs turned to Vienna for support. In 1880 they signed a railway convention with Austria and in May 1881 a trade treaty. One month later King Milan accepted the Austrian draft of a secret treaty of alliance in which Serbia agreed to interdict anti-Austrian agitation on its territory. Rumania also slipped into the Austrian orbit. Under a commercial treaty of 1875 Austria had already found in Rumania a good market for its manufactured goods. Like Serbia, Rumania, which had assisted Russia in the war against Turkey, felt betrayed by Russian policy at Berlin in 1878. The Dobruja was not regarded as adequate compensation for the loss of Bessarabia. In the fall of 1883 Bucharest, fearing another Russian military intervention in the Balkans, negotiated a secret treaty with Vienna and Berlin in which the dual powers pledged to defend Rumania against unprovoked for-

[7] Hajo Holborn, ed., *Aufzeichnungen und Erinnerungen aus dem Leben des Botschafters Joseph Maria von Radowitz* (Berlin, 1925), II, 244–247.

[8] *GP*, IV, 131–134; Bussmann, ed., *Herbert von Bismarck*, pp. 245, 261–263.

[9] Bussmann, ed., *Herbert von Bismarck*, pp. 215–216.

eign attack. Russia's plans for a greater Bulgaria had antagonized the Greeks, whose government also sought close relations with Austria and Germany. Even the Turks came calling at the Wilhelmstrasse and Ballhausplatz in the hope of an alliance, but they were refused.[10]

While the Austrians savored their gains in Serbia, Rumania, Greece, and Turkey, the Russians suffered a humiliating disappointment in Bulgaria. On withdrawing their army from Bulgaria after the Turkish war, they left behind a constitution, eighty thousand rifles, and a horde of army officers and officials. They also secured the election as hereditary prince of the tsar's favorite nephew, Alexander of Battenberg, who had served as a volunteer officer in the Russian army during the recent war. But the Bulgarians had not fought for independence against Turkey only to fall under Russian domination, and the twenty-two year old prince was uncomfortable in the role of Russian puppet. By 1884 Russian insensitivity, Alexander's inexperience and ineptitude, rivalry among competing interest groups, personal intrigues, and political factionalism had brought Bulgarian-Russian relations to the crisis stage. In September 1885 a rebellion against Turkey in Eastern Rumelia, whose leaders demanded union with Bulgaria, forced the issue. Battenberg was compelled either to lead an insurrection or suffer one. Tsar Alexander III reacted to his apostasy by recalling the Russian officers serving in Bulgaria and threatening intervention. Bulgaria's stubborn resistance against Russian domination dictated a curious reversal of roles among the great powers. Russia now opposed the greater Bulgaria it had fought to create in 1876–1878, while Britain no longer insisted upon the disunited Bulgaria it had gained at the Congress of Berlin.[11]

British objections frustrated the attempt of the great powers to restore the Treaty of Berlin by forcing Prince Alexander to disgorge Eastern Rumelia. Their failure set off a scramble by Serbia and Greece for compensation. Believing he had Austria's tacit approval, King Milan of Serbia ordered his troops across the Bulgarian border in November 1885, only to be decisively beaten, saved from disaster only by an Austrian ultimatum to Prince Alexander. These turbulent events created a new wave of anxiety in Europe's capitals over the possibility of Austrian and Russian military intervention. Prince Alexander began peace negotiations with the sultan, but the great powers established the terms. In the peace signed on April 5, 1886, the relationship

[10] Willian L. Langer, *European Alliances and Alignments* (2d ed., New York, 1956), pp. 335ff.

[11] Egon C. Corti, *Alexander von Battenberg: Sein Kampf mit den Zaren und Bismarck* (Vienna, 1920), pp. 50ff.; George Kennan, *The Decline of Bismarck's European Order: Franco-Russian Relations, 1875–1890* (Princeton, 1979), pp. 103ff. "Strange reversal of human affairs!" wrote Saburov. "After she had got the Treaty of Berlin signed by us in order to arrest the break-up of the Ottoman Empire, England takes this same Treaty as a starting-point to continue the work of demolition we had begun!" J. Y. Simpson, *The Saburov Memoirs or Bismarck and Russia* (New York, 1929), p. 155.

between Bulgaria and Eastern Rumelia was limited to personal rather than territorial union and the sultan's nominal suzerainty was preserved. The Prince of Bulgaria (on Russian insistence Alexander was not named) was to be appointed governor-general of Eastern Rumelia for five years.[12]

Russia's failure in Bulgaria was not in itself unwelcome to Bismarck, for it presented a new source of friction between England and Russia, who had just resolved their differences over Afghanistan. "Harmony between England and Russia is for us always a danger. If France should become a monarchy again and join that combination, the danger to Germany would immediately become very acute." To have an English protégé and favorite of Queen Victoria on the Bulgarian throne served European peace by keeping Britain and Russia apart. Hence, it was "politically useful" to keep Prince Alexander in Sofia, but only as long as this German motive was hidden from Tsar Alexander (Kaiser Wilhelm: "Is that possible?"). To avoid either offending the tsar or discouraging British support for the prince would require "skillful diplomacy." Bismarck's balancing act, however, was jeopardized by the desire of Prince Alexander to marry the Hohenzollern Princess Viktoria, a match strongly favored by two other Victorias: her mother, the German crown princess, and her grandmother, the British queen. In Bismarck's calculations a dynastic bond between the German Kaiser and Bulgarian king would inevitably create tensions between Germany and Russia that would grow with every successive Balkan crisis. The "Battenberg marriage" threatened to deprive Germany of its freedom of choice between Russia and England and thereby endanger his whole strategy of foreign policy. On Bismarck's advice the Kaiser vetoed the match, which in any case was opposed by Crown Prince Friedrich Wilhelm, who believed the Battenberg family too lowly to marry into the Hohenzollern dynasty. Nevertheless, Crown Princess Victoria and her smitten daughter continued to hope for it.[13]

The collapse of Russian influence in Bulgaria tempted other powers to fill the vacuum—Austria in particular. In October 1886, when the Austrians jumped to the conclusion that Russia was actually backing Prince Alexander's acquisition of Eastern Rumelia, Bismarck urged Kálnoky and his associates not to "pick the Turkish chestnuts out of the fire for England," but to let London take on the task of blocking Russia in the Balkans. In November he was appalled by the report that an Austrian agent, whether with or without instructions from the Vienna government, had encouraged Serbia's attack on Bulgaria. Now he urged Germany's two allies to act in agreement with one

[12] Corti, *Battenberg Kampf mit den Zaren und Bismarck*, pp. 199–257.

[13] Bismarck to Kaiser, Nov. 3 and 10, 1885. Gerhard Ebel, ed., *Botschafter Paul Graf von Hatzfeldt: Nachgelassene Papiere, 1838–1901* (Boppard am Rhein, 1976), I, 458–459. See also GP, III, 342–369; GW, VIII, 509–511; Bussmann, ed., *Herbert von Bismarck*, pp. 237–239, 271–275, 332. On the Battenberg marriage project, see Egon C. Corti, *Alexander von Battenberg* (London, 1954), pp. 116ff.

another, Russia occupying Bulgaria, Austria, Serbia. But Giers and Tsar Alexander declined, and Giers was visibly shocked by this "strange suggestion."[14]

When Bulgaria's counterattack sent the Serbian army fleeing, the Austrians were tempted to march to Serbia's aid. From Bismarck, however, came a warning: Such an action would violate the three emperors agreement, and Germany, furthermore, was not obligated under the alliance of 1879 to back

BISMARCK TO KÁLNOKY: "DON'T SHOOT! SOMETHING LIKE THAT MUST BE CAPTURED ALIVE AND LED AROUND BY THE NOSE." *DER FLOH*, VIENNA, SEPTEMBER 23, 1883.

[14] Bussmann, ed., *Herbert von Bismarck*, pp. 329–336, 339, 343–348.

Austria against Russia in a war "begun in this way."[15] "Loyally and unreservedly as we Germans would back you up if Russia attacked you, we could never contemplate the employment of the Germany army as an auxiliary force in the extension of Austro-Hungarian influence on the lower Danube."[16] Bismarck's bluntness restrained Austria, and Britain assumed its assigned role in Bismarck's scenario by initiating the negotiations that led to the settlement of the Rumelian question in April 1886. Both actions undermined Kálnoky's position in Budapest. The Hungarians could not comprehend why their government, seemingly linked to Germany in an alliance—the limitations of which were secret and not understood—would not exploit the opportunity to root out Russian influence in the Balkans.[17]

In Russia the Bulgarian success was hailed initially as a victory for a Russian- over an Austrian-trained army. Talk of reconciliation with Prince Alexander was general in Petersburg, but "the tsar's rancor was stronger than all political considerations." In Berlin Russia sought assistance in organizing a joint action by the great powers to remove Battenberg from Sofia because of his violation of the Treaty of Berlin. Again Bismarck would not lead, only follow.[18] Unwilling to engage in independent action and unable to obtain a European mandate, the Russians resorted ultimately to bribery and conspiracy, with the consequence that on August 20, 1886, a group of pro-Russian Bulgarian officers forced the prince to abdicate and leave the country—in his bitter words, "dragged like a malefactor through the streets in the dead of night." This coup led within a few days to a countercoup in which the rebels were overthrown and Alexander was recalled. The prince returned, but on September 7, 1886, realizing that Russian hostility made his position untenable, he abdicated a second time and left the country never to return. Again the Russians were frustrated. The leaders who took charge in Sofia after the abdication were even less willing than the departed Battenberg prince to accept Russian tutelage.[19]

In Petersburg this new fiasco produced exasperation, bewilderment, and embarrassment. Were the dogmas preached by Panslavists for a quarter of a century nothing but "humbug?" Who was responsible? The Russians themselves? Austria? England? Germany? And could nothing be done to recoup Russian prestige? Perhaps invade Bulgaria? Strike at Austria? The only concrete action taken by Alexander III was to break off relations with Bulgaria in mid-November by ordering the Russian delegation in Sofia to return to Pe-

[15] GP, V, 24–38; GW, VIII, 529ff.

[16] Corti, *Battenberg Kampf mit den Zaren und Bismarck*, pp. 244–246. The translation is from Joseph V. Fuller, *Bismarck's Diplomacy at Its Zenith* (New York, 1967), p. 51.

[17] GP, V, 123ff.

[18] Bussmann, ed., *Herbert von Bismarck*, pp. 349–356, 359; Hatzfeldt, *Nachgelassene Papiere*, I, 482–484.

[19] Langer, *Alliances and Alignments*, pp. 359–361; Kennan, *Decline of Bismarck's European Order*, pp. 199–202; Hatzfeldt, *Nachgelassene Papiere*, pp. 507–508.

tersburg. Thereafter he appeared to deal with the Bulgarian problem largely by ignoring it.[20]

Bernhard von Bülow, then German counsel of legation at Petersburg, was inclined to attribute Russia's inability to decide which course to take to "the disease of the tsars," a progressive degeneration in the Romanov dynasty of which Alexander III's anger, indecision, apathy, and withdrawal were symptomatic.[21] And yet research has shown that the tsarist regime rejected the actions urged upon it by Russian war hawks and that the grounds for that rejection were realistic. The Balkan position that Russian blood had won in the war of 1876–1878 and retained at the Congress of Berlin, despite the diminution forced by the European powers, could not be buttressed and held during the years that followed. Petersburg could not supply the administrative and diplomatic competence to hold Prince Alexander in check, the capital with which to penetrate Bulgaria and seal it off from the economic incursions of other powers, and the military strength to meet the challenge of the European powers. Driven to the verge of bankruptcy during the Bulgarian crisis, Russia could not risk military intervention and war, a realization shared by the tsar, his ministers of finance and foreign affairs, and the army chief of staff. Failure would have done serious damage to the prestige and power of the Russian autocracy. Outwardly the tsarist regime continued to act like a European great power in these years, but at the critical moments in 1885–1887 its leadership lacked both the means and conviction necessary to convert angry words into punishing deeds.[22]

Naturally the foreign governments were not privy to these discussions and decisions in Petersburg, and, given the precedents of 1853–1856 and 1876–1878, they had reason to doubt that financial exigencies would keep Russia from invading Bulgaria.[23] Austria and Britain discussed the possibility of a common front against Russia, but Lords Salisbury and Randolph Churchill, mindful of their weak position in parliament, insisted that Austria take the lead with Germany's "moral support." The margins of Hatzfeldt's reports of these conversations are studded with Bismarck's cynical comments about the willingness of Britain to let others fight her battles. Austria should not listen to this "old song." Unless London assumed the initiative, Austria should do nothing to block a Russian move on Bulgaria. Only Britain and Austria to-

---

[20] On the vicissitudes and ultimate failure of Russian policy in Bulgaria, see Charles Jelavich, *Tsarist Russia and Balkan Nationalism: Russian Influence in the Internal Affairs of Bulgaria and Serbia, 1879–1886* (Berkeley, 1958).

[21] GP, V, 68–73.

[22] Dietrich Geyer, *Russian Imperialism: The Interaction of Domestic and Foreign Policy, 1860–1914* (New Haven, 1987), pp. 110–118.

[23] Earlier Bismarck judged that lack of money would not make the Russians more peace-loving. They would give out what was necessary for "railways and war whether they have it or not." For a "real" lack of money to become apparent would take a long time in so large a country as Russia, and, meanwhile, the government would operate with paper money, "as it has done in the past." Rantzau to Herbert von Bismarck, Mar. 14, 1884. Bussmann, ed., *Herbert von Bismarck*, p. 220.

gether, with help from Turkey and Italy, could give the Russians pause. Otherwise it was best to let the tsar's army take Bulgaria and the Dardanelles, for the resulting dispersion of its forces could only weaken Russia. By concentrating her army in Transylvania Austria could gain a strategic superiority that Russia would hesitate to challenge.[24]

But Kálnoky, hard pressed by Hungarian critics, declared in the budget committee of the Austro-Hungarian Delegations on November 13 that any attempt by Russia to impose a commissar on Bulgaria or to occupy any part of that country would compel Austria to take "decisive position." Again Bismarck found himself holding the collars of "two savage dogs" eager to spring at each other. Yet he placed the primary blame on the Austrians and Hungarians because of their unwillingness to respect the Russian sphere of influence in the eastern Balkans.[25] Over and over again he reminded Vienna that the Dual Alliance was a defensive, not an offensive alliance and that Austria, if it became involved in war with Russia over Bulgaria, could not count on Germany's support. But he also warned (October 20, 1886) Russia against precipitate action in Bulgaria, which could only lead to an anti-Russian coalition. Germany could not promise to remain neutral in the event of a Russian-Austrian war; to do so would be to run the risk of ultimately having both as enemies. Again he reiterated the formula he had concocted in 1876: Germany could tolerate a war between Russia and Austria in which one combatant lost a battle, but not a war in which either was so badly mauled that its position as a European great power was jeopardized. "We must spin out the Three Emperors League as long as a strand of it remains."[26]

Bismarck's efforts to prevent an eastern war between Germany's allies were all the more pressing because of the emerging threat from France. Public dissatisfaction in France with Ferry's policy toward Germany and with colonialism came out strongly in the election of October 1885, in which royalists and Bonapartists more than doubled the number of popular votes they had received in 1881. Moderate republicans still controlled 220 seats, but they now faced approximately 180 monarchists and as many radicals. The minister of war in the new cabinet of Charles de Freycinet was General Georges Boulanger, appointed on the recommendation of Clemenceau because he was "the only really radical republican general." Within months Boulanger's energy and political instinct made him a popular figure in France; he recalled troops

[24] GP, IV, 265–294, also pp. 138–142; Wilhelm von Schweinitz, *Denkwürdigkeiten des Botschafters General von Schweinitz* (Berlin, 1927), II, 319.

[25] GP, V, 70, 146; Schweinitz, *Denkwürdigkeiten*, II, 327–328; Freiherr Lucius von Ballhausen, *Bismarck-Erinnerungen* (Stuttgart, 1920), p. 359. For some months Bismarck ceased to press for a demarcation of spheres in the Balkans, since neither Austria nor Russia appeared interested in such an arrangement. GP, V, 75.

[26] GP, V, 78 (fn.), 96, 123–153. See also the remarkable exchange of memoranda between Bismarck and son Herbert concerning the importance of Austria to German foreign policy, Oct. 8 and 10, 1886. Bussmann, ed., *Herbert von Bismarck*, pp. 392–394.

stationed overseas, reformed the army and the conditions of service, and reduced the influence of royalist officers.

On July 14, 1886, the general transformed what had hitherto been a modest military review of the Paris garrison on the French national holiday into a
brilliant spectacle. Units were transported to Paris from all the provinces, and
Boulanger himself led the parade. He cut a splendid figure—in full uniform,
hair brushed and pomaded, blond beard and effulgent mustache carefully bar-
bered, astride a handsome black horse whose prancing movements betrayed a
circus background. The republic was dull, and Paris was looking for a hero.
Boulanger caught the imagination of the crowd, and the music halls cashed
in by celebrating him in song. This most republican of all generals seemed to
embody the spirit of *revanche*, and his quest for personal publicity and popularity soon made him vulnerable to the manipulations of antirepublican factions and movements. Among them was Paul Déroulède, poet and publicist
and founder of the League of Patriots, a nationalistic movement hostile to the
republic. The league was the connecting link between hundreds of local rifle,
gymnastic, and patriotic societies. In October 1886 a new journal *La Revanche*
bearing Boulanger's image appeared on the newsstands.[27]

Autocratic Russia and republican France had in common chauvinistic agi-

GENERAL GEORGES BOULANGER. (ARCHIV FÜR KUNST UND GESCHICHTE, BERLIN.)

[27] Langer, *Alliances and Alignments*, pp. 371ff.; Frederic H. Seager, *The Boulanger Affair, Political Crossroad of France, 1886–1889* (Ithaca, 1969), pp. 25–48.

tators angling for influence over foreign policy whom neither government could disregard. In Russia the brilliant and influential journalist Mikhail Katkov, hitherto a supporter of collaboration by the three empires, now denounced their alliance as an unnecessary restraint upon Russian foreign policy. Katkov's widely read editorial, published in his *Moscow Gazette* at the end of July 1886, painted a sinister picture of Bismarck. "The German Chancellor has acquired, together with his deserved fame, a certain mythological quality. His hand is suspected in all the events of our time; he is viewed as the possessor of the talisman before which all obstacles dissolve and all locks open. Without his agreement, one is given to understand, one may neither lie down nor stand up; he runs the whole world." Germany, not Russia, Katkov declared, had been the chief beneficiary of the association between the two powers. The time had come to restore Russia's "free hand" in European politics.[28]

An embarrassed Giers attributed Katkov's turnabout to "personal participation in the undertakings and speculations of ultraconservative industrialists" displeased at the prospect of still higher German coal and iron duties. According to Giers, even the tsar suspected that "material considerations and purposes were often decisive in determining Katkov's political direction." To Peter Shuvalov Katkov explained that he wanted "to make the Germans anxious" (Bismarck: "clumsy and dumb"), and more "pliant" (Bismarck: "on the contrary"). Shuvalov found Katkov's attitude "childish" (Bismarck: "In foreign policy threats create not only irritations but also counterirritations that cannot be erased and that set the course").[29] Whatever the cause, Katkov's editorial evidently struck a responsive chord inside as well as outside the government, and the conviction spread that a French-Russian alliance was not an unnatural combination. Geographically remote, Bulgaria and Alsace-Lorraine began to seem politically adjacent. In October 1886 Alexander III, humiliated by the complete bankruptcy of his Bulgarian policy, took the first steps to restore normal relations with Paris, interrupted since January by the clumsiness and indifference of the Freycinet government.[30]

From Count Münster, now German ambassador in Paris, and Jules Herbette, the new French ambassador in Berlin, Bismarck received assurances of France's peaceful intent. But he did not believe Herbette and dismissed Münster as an "optimist," unable to grasp the dynamics of French politics. The French, he said, did not know what to do with their republic and might at any time find in war the best way out of their embarrassment; Boulanger might easily become the "fuse" for the explosion, perhaps without wanting to be.

[28] Quoted in Kennan, *Decline of Bismarck's European Order*, p. 177.

[29] GP, V, 45–50.

[30] Kennan, *Decline of Bismarck's European Order*, pp. 158–182, 203–219. In Kennan's judgment, Alexander III's restoration of contact with Paris was a critical turning in Russian-French relations that led ultimately to the alliance of 1894. *Ibid.*, pp. 203–204.

Political movements in France had always been the work of energetic minorities. All nations preferred peace, but that was not always true of their leaders. The Paris government's requests for military credits far exceeded normal needs; reports had accumulated of French purchases of picric acid and lumber in Germany and the construction of barracks and enlarged railway stations in France at points near the German border.[31] German generals conceded that French military preparations might well be of defensive rather than aggressive intent, but they discussed, nevertheless, the advisability of a preventive strike. As one officer expressed it, "Two strong armies standing face to face attract each other like magnets." Again Bismarck condemned preventive war as hubristic; no one could anticipate "divine providence." In the course of time many events might intervene to prevent the outbreak of a French-German war.[32]

No evidence suggests that Boulanger deliberately sought a military confrontation with Germany during his first year as minister of war. And yet his efforts to improve France's military preparedness and his growing popularity in France, when coupled with anti-German agitation in Russia, made him appear menacing to Germans. Later Bismarck admitted, "I could not invent Boulanger, but he happened very conveniently for me." By exaggerating the French lust for *revanche*, he sought to create a favorable environment for the Reichstag's renewal of the iron budget in 1887. And Boulanger, in turn, exploited this challenge by stressing within the French government the need for moving troops and matériel up to the border France shared with Germany. With each turn of the screw the tension mounted on both sides of the frontier.[33]

During the winter of 1886–1887 Germany faced one of the most dangerous situations in its modern history. If the chauvinists behind Boulanger seized power in Paris, the struggle of 1870–1871 might well be renewed, and, if Austria and Russia became embroiled in war over Balkan issues, Germany would be under great pressure to commit itself to one side or the other. If these crises occurred simultaneously, Germany would be confronted with a two-front war that would test to the limit its military strength and national will. The danger was real, but Bismarck's exploitation of it in domestic politics may have increased its urgency and its hazards.

The Septennat Election of 1887

On November 5, 1886, the first day of a new legislative year, the government presented to the Reichstag a bill calling for an extension of the military bud-

[31] GP, VI, 96–98, 156–168; Lucius, Bismarck-Erinnerungen, p. 366.

[32] GP, VI, 170–175; Lucius, Bismarck-Erinnerungen, 357; GW, VIII, 550: Helmuth Rogge, Holstein und Hohenlohe (Stuttgart, 1957), pp. 264–265.

[33] A.J.P. Taylor, The Struggle for Mastery in Europe, 1848–1918 (Oxford, 1954), pp. 308–309; Seager, Boulanger Affair, pp. 48–51.

get for another seven years, beginning April 1, 1887. The peacetime strength of the army was to be increased by 41,135 men to a total of 468,409. This increase was not exceptional, being in accord with the constitution, which fixed the size of the army at 1 percent of the population as determined by the latest census (1885). Nor was the cost out of line, being estimated at 24,000,000 marks annually in new money, with a single start-up appropriation of 24,200,000 marks.[34] The extraordinary aspect of the bill of November 1886 was its timing. The current *Septennat*, passed in 1880, was not due to expire until March 31, 1888. Hence the bill of 1886 was one year ahead of schedule. Since the Reichstag election of 1884—held long before Bulgaria and Boulanger appeared on the horizon—Bismarck had foreseen that renewal of the *Septennat* would be an ideal issue for dissolving the Reichstag and conceivably staging a *Staatsstreich*. Rising international tensions merely increased its value for such a purpose. If necessary, Bismarck told Mittnacht in December 1885, he would dissolve parliament "six times in succession."[35]

Even without the European crisis, renewal of the *Septennat* would have produced a major dispute between the government and the Reichstag. All parties of the oppositional majority—centrists, left-liberals, social democrats, Poles, Guelphs, Alsace-Lorrainers—had voted against the two previous *Septennat* bills. Since 1867 left-liberals and democrats had agitated for annual military budgets; to them the "iron budget" was the most hated feature of the 1867 constitution. Had the *Septennat* come up for renewal in the halcyon years of 1883–1884, the opposition might have stood firm. But in 1886–1887, with Boulanger making headlines in France and scare rumors, probably of governmental origin,[36] spreading through the German press, it was a formidable issue sufficient to shake even the most obstinate of Bismarck's opponents. Hence Stauffenberg proposed in behalf of the Freedom party an amendment granting the increase for only three years. As pressures mounted during the third reading of the bill, Windthorst offered five years, a compromise that Miquel, speaking for the national liberals, advised Bismarck to accept. But the chancellor was fully determined to force an election.[37]

On the day after arriving from Friedrichsruh, the prince, "looking well" and speaking "more quickly and lively than he had for a long time," reviewed the situation for the cabinet. Even the seven-year law, he told the ministers, was an unjustifiable limitation of the Kaiser's authority. If the bill failed to pass, the power to fix the size of the army would revert to the monarch. To grant the necessary funds would then be the "duty" of the Reichstag. From Rome he had heard, he continued, that Windthorst intended to drag out the

[34] *SBR* (1886–1887), Anlagen, Nos. 11, 46.

[35] Heinrich Heffter, *Die Kreuzzeitungspartei und die Kartellpolitik Bismarcks* (Leipzig, 1927), p. 82.

[36] Lucius, *Bismarck-Erinnerungen*, p. 367.

[37] Heffter, *Kartellpolitik*, pp. 82–83. Hans Herzfeld, *Johannes von Miquel* (Detmold, 1938), II, 94–95; Bussmann, ed., *Herbert von Bismarck*, pp. 409–412.

debate until the Prussian government came through with further revisions of the May laws. But Bismarck had persuaded the pope not to let the centrist leader grab the glory for reestablishing peace between church and state. Reportedly he had told Rome that no coercion was needed to gain additional revisions of the May laws. Leo had responded by ordering his nuncio in Germany to influence the Center party to accept the *Septennat*. The Guelph fund, Bismarck hinted to the ministers, had been in part responsible for this success. (Indeed Cardinal Galimberti was on the Guelph fund payroll.) Yet Bismarck did not expect or want the Center to follow the pope's advice. This was an issue, he told the cabinet flatly, upon which an election had to be held.[38] "We will strengthen the army even without the Center," he had told Rome, "and if need be without the Reichstag."[39]

When Bismarck appeared in the Reichstag to defend the *Septennat* on the second reading of the bill (January 11, 12, 13, 1887), every seat was filled; thousands had waited for hours hoping for gallery seats. The chancellor, looking fresh and vigorous,[40] used the chamber as a forum to speak to the nation and to Europe. On the eleventh he delivered for two hours a masterful review of his foreign policy. In order to secure for Germans the right "to live and breathe as a great nation," he declared, the Kaiser had fought two great wars. As a satiated state, whose primary goal was consolidation, the German Reich had striven to preserve the peace of Europe for sixteen years. To this end it had entered into a close relationship with Austria, but also with Russia. This same combination of three powers had preserved the peace for thirty years after 1815, a period of great economic, scientific, and technical progress. Whether Europe would again enjoy such a long period of peace was difficult to say, but it was the goal of German policy. Relations with Russia were as friendly as they had been earlier under Alexander II; Germany had nothing whatever to gain from conflict with Russia. It could not be assumed that Russia was courting France as a potential ally against Germany. Who ruled in Bulgaria was of no interest to Germany; over such an issue Berlin would never quarrel with Russia. The problem of war and peace lay not between Germany and either of its two allies, but between the allies themselves. German foreign policy was engaged in the effort to reduce their frictions.

Relations with France, he contended, had a different character, and their deterioration was the reason for early presentation of the military bill. Generations of Germans had been compelled to defend the western frontier against France. Were these struggles finally at an end? "Neither you nor I can

---

[38] Cabinet meeting of Jan. 9, 1887. Lucius, *Bismarck-Erinnerungen*, pp. 351–352. The official minutes of this meeting are much longer than Lucius's account, but also less revealing. *DZA* Merseburg, Rep. 90a, B, III, 2b, Nr. 6, Bd. 99.

[39] Bismarck to Schlözer, Jan. 2 and 10, 1887. GW, VIc, 351–352; Bussmann, ed., *Herbert von Bismarck*, pp. 401–402.

[40] GW, VIII, 549.

know the answer to that question. I can only express the presumption that they are not over. Otherwise the entire character of the French and all of the relationships on the border would have to be different." Preventive wars were unjustifiable; only God could foresee their outcome. But an attack from France could not be discounted—whether in ten days or ten years depended upon which government was in power in France. "Parliamentary strategists" underestimated the military power of France. By rejecting the bill, they and not the government would assume responsibility for future defeat. A victorious France would demand much more than merely the return of Alsace-Lorraine; Hanover would be reconstituted, Schleswig lost to Denmark, and burdensome conditions imposed on Prussian Poland.

Having painted this threatening picture, Bismarck proceeded to demonstrate to the deputies the weakness of their constitutional position. He developed a new "gap theory" akin to that of 1862–1866, citing the most prestigious authorities on constitutional law (Ludwig von Rönne and Paul Laband) to prove his point. If, owing to disagreement between Bundesrat and Reichstag, the military bill should fail, the authority to establish the size and financial support of the army would revert to the Kaiser. The government would be compelled, furthermore, to turn to the Prussian Landtag for funding. The actual issue, he charged, was whether Germany was to have a "Kaiser's army" or a "parliamentary army" dependent upon the whims of shifting majorities. Rather than accept the latter, the governments would appeal to the voters. After three more days of debate (chiefly an oratorical duel between Bismarck and Windthorst), the chamber voted 183 to 154 in favor of Stauffenberg's proposed three-year budget, the Center voting with the majority.[41]

As he neared the age of seventy-two, Bismarck, his health restored by a sure-fire issue, dealt the Reichstag opposition the hardest blow in its history. Immediately after the votes had been counted, he read the Kaiser's order dissolving the chamber. On emerging from the parliament building, the chancellor was greeted by thunderous applause and thousands of waving hats. The throng that had gathered followed his carriage through the streets to his quarters in the Wilhelmstrasse.[42] Not since July 1870 had Germany witnessed such a scene. Clearly the voters could now be expected to repudiate the opposition.

In preparation for the election to be held on February 21, 1887, an "election cartel" was formed by the three parties favoring the *Septennat*: conservatives, free conservatives, and national liberals. This was the combination that Bismarck had sought to bring together in the election of 1884. During the intervening years the national liberals, purified of democratic elements by the secession of 1881 and deprived of any possibility of reunion with them by the

---

[41] BR, XII, 155–278; SBR (1886–1887), pp. 69–115, 327–433.
[42] BR, XII, 278; SEG (1887), p. 7.

left-liberal fusion of 1884, had found common cause with the two conservative parties on many issues. Now they were eager to consolidate that alliance
by shutting out the possibility of a conservative-Center alliance. Ultraconservatives of the *Kreuzzeitung* variety still balked, to be sure, at the idea of close
cooperation with liberals of any stripe. But their voices were stilled by the
opportunity presented by the *Septennat* election of 1887.[43] In the cartel agreement the three parties pledged to accept no candidates uncommitted to the
Septennat, to contest no districts already held by deputies representing one of
the cartel parties, and to find common candidates for constituencies held by
opponents of the *Septennat*, or, if that proved to be impossible, to support the
strongest candidates in the runoff elections. In conducting the campaign, the
cartel parties would avoid attacking each other in the press and public meetings.[44]

Stoked by the official press, the consuming issues of the election were foreign danger and national patriotism. Acceptance or rejection of the *Septennat*
was the only measure of a candidate's fitness. Wilhelm, whose eightieth year
as a soldier had been celebrated with pomp and circumstance on January 1,
1887, informed the nation how "deeply and painfully" he had been hurt by
the bill's rejection.[45] On January 31 the free conservative *Post* published a
lead article, "On the Razor's Edge," that warned of approaching war. Rumors
that the Prussian Landtag, which convened (January 15) on the heels of the
Reichstag's dissolution, was to receive a bill calling for a war credit of
300,000,000 marks circulated through the press and created panics on both
the Berlin and Paris stock exchanges. In early February 72,000 reservists were
called up for practice maneuvers in Alsace-Lorraine. Miquel and Bennigsen
happily exploited the issue, with Bennigsen speaking of a second war for Alsace-Lorraine as a "historical necessity."[46]

Although he had appeared in the Prussian Chamber of Deputies only twice
since 1881 (both times in 1886), Bismarck now converted it into a forum
from which to attack the centrists and left-liberals, whom he accused of undermining social and political order by cooperating politically with social
democrats.[47] In early February he released surreptitiously to the press copies
of two notes, dated January 3 and 21, 1887, from Cardinal State Secretary
Jacobini to the papal nuncio at Munich, in which the pope advised centrists
to support the *Septennat*.[48] He aimed to embarrass Windthorst and Franckenstein who had withheld Leo's advice from their own comrades. But Wind-

---

[43] Heffter, *Kartellpolitik*, pp. 68ff.

[44] SEG (1887), p. 60.

[45] SEG (1887), pp. 1–2, 63–64.

[46] Walter Bussmann, *Das Zeitalter Bismarcks* in Leo Just, ed., *Handbuch der deutschen Geschichte*
(3d ed., Constance, 1956), III (3), 233.

[47] BR, XII, 279ff. See also Bismarck to Schlözer, Jan. 15 and 17, 1887. GW, VIc, 352–355.

[48] SEG (1887), pp. 67–68, 80–81, 83; GW, VIII, 550.

BISMARCK PLAYING ON THE OFFICIAL PRESS. *LE GRELOT*, PARIS, FEBRUARY 6, 1887.

thorst, no mean political tactician himself, escaped the noose by pointing out that in the second note the cardinal had responded to warnings from Franckenstein that the issue might break up the party by asserting that its continued existence was essential to Catholic interests. In a major speech delivered at Cologne, Windthorst made the preservation of the Center his campaign slogan.[49]

So aroused was the public by the *Septennat* issue that 77 percent of the electorate voted on February 21, 1887—21 percent more than in 1881 and nearly 17 percent more than in 1884. Windthorst's strategy paid off, for the

---

[49] Heffter, *Kartellpolitik*, p. 85; SEG (1887), pp. 78–79.

Center maintained its strength of 98 seats, losing only one constituency while attracting 226,000 more voters than in 1884. The chief losers were the Freedom party (from 67 to 32) and the Social Democratic party (from 24 to 11), despite a strong gain in the latter's popular vote (from 550,000 to 763,100). Except for the Danes and Alsatians, who remained steady at 1 and 15 seats, the minor parties also suffered, the Poles falling from 16 to 13, the Guelphs from 11 to 4, and the German Peoples party, a small caucus of 7 south German democrats, vanishing. Predictably the victors were the German Conservative party (from 78 to 80), the Free Conservative party (from 28 to 41), and especially the National Liberal party (from 51 to 99). Among the winning national liberals were Bennigsen, who returned to political life, and Johannes Miquel, who had not held a Reichstag seat since 1877. So effectively did the national liberals exploit the national issue that they polled 1,678,000 votes as against 997,000 in 1884. With 220 out of 397 seats the cartel parties controlled the chamber. As long as the coalition held together, the Center had lost the swing position between alternative majorities that had made it so potent in the chamber since 1881.[50]

Ludwig Bamberger, prominent in the Secession and the Freedom party, concluded that the result was not accidental. "Although it was accomplished by crude cunning and coercion, I say to myself: The new representation is the true expression of German popular will. Junkerdom and the Catholic church both know very clearly what they want, while the burghers [Bürgertum] are childishly innocent, politically naive, and in need of neither justice nor freedom. Junkerdom and Catholic church will join hands, and the burghers will get what they deserve, with the national liberals contributing the political music. Il faut que les destins s'accomplissent. The crown prince is now relieved of all embarrassment. He will do what Bismarck wants."[51] For Bismarck, however, the victory was not great enough. The Reichstag, he declared, "must still become quite different and much better."[52]

More Germanization

The continuing presence of Danish and French protesters in the German Reichstag after the election of 1887 spurred Bismarck to accelerate the Germanization of both minorities. The late 1870s and 1880s was a period of growing tension in North Schleswig. With Bismarck's blessing the provincial authorities fought Danish agitation by expelling Danish journalists and actors who nurtured cultural ties with the homeland, threatening innkeepers who permitted public meetings on their premises, denying reentry to youths who

[50] Bernhard Vogel, Dieter Nohlen, and Rainer-Olaf Schultze, Wahlen in Deutschland: Theorie-Geschichte-Dokumente, 1848–1970 (Berlin, 1971), p. 290; Heffter, Kartellpolitik, pp. 85–86.
[51] To Franz von Stauffenberg, Feb. 25, 1887. HW, II, 429; see also pp. 431–432.
[52] To Lucius, Feb. 23, 1887. Lucius, Bismarck-Erinnerungen, pp. 371–372.

had crossed the border to evade the Prussian military draft, putting pressure on mixed communities to choose German as the language of instruction, dismissing pro-Danish teachers and school inspectors, and replacing county counselors who were insufficiently aggressive.[53] Judging by optimistic reports from provincial and district authorities to Berlin and a decline in the voting strength of the Danish party (from 18,725 in 1871 to 11,616 in 1886), these tactics, supplemented by the benefits of economic growth attributable to union with Germany, had some effect in softening Danish intransigence.[54]

But then the Bismarck government threw away its gains by applying in North Schleswig the same rigid school policy inaugurated in the east. On December 18, 1888, German was made the language of instruction in all subjects but religion; religious instruction in German was mandated for two hours a week on the middle and upper levels, Danish to be used in the remaining four hours only on the request of parents. This "fateful" measure, which was opposed by the Provincial Governor-General Georg von Steinmann, revived and reinvigorated the Danish opposition. In the *Wählerverein für Nordschleswig*, founded in 1888 and supplemented by a network of local patriotic clubs, the Danes found a new defender for their interests. A confrontation began between Dane and German that did not die until the plebiscite of 1920 restored North Schleswig to Denmark.[55]

Chlodwig zu Hohenlohe-Schillingsfürst, who succeeded to the governorship of the Reichsland on Manteuffel's death in 1885, resolved to conduct the office like a "responsible minister" rather than a "constitutional monarch." He reversed the policy of his predecessor, relying on the bureaucracy rather than on notables. Hohenlohe was favorably impressed by the friendly recep-

[53] Reports of *Regierungspräsidenten* of Schleswig, DZA Merseburg, Rep. 2.2.1., Bde. 16588 and 16589; also miscellaneous correspondence, DZA Potsdam, Reichskanzlei, 1409, pp. 1–18v. Oswald Hauser, *Preussische Staatsräson und nationaler Gedanke* (Neumünster, 1960), pp. 47–61.

[54] Reports of *Regierungspräsidenten* of Schleswig. DZA Merseburg, 2.2.1., Vols. 16588, 16589. See also Otto Brandt, *Geschichte Schleswig-Holsteins* (4th ed., Kiel, 1949), pp. 195, 202.

[55] Brandt, *Geschichte Schleswig-Holsteins*, pp. 202–205; Troels Fink, *Geschichte des schleswigschen Grenzlandes* (Copenhagen, 1958), pp. 167–196; Hauser, *Preussische Staatsräson*, pp. 81ff., 211–212. The superintendent of schools in Schleswig, who was not consulted, regarded the order as disastrous for the German cause. Theodor Kaftan, *Erlebnisse und Beobachtungen* (Kiel, 1924), pp. 207–235. Drafted in the *Kultusministerium* in Berlin, the order came at a time when Bismarck was eager to encourage better relations with Denmark. To this end he eased restrictions on reentry by Danish emigrants into northern Schleswig and abruptly halted plans for a German celebration on the anniversary of the victory at Düppel. See the exchange of correspondence between Berchem, Herrfurth, and Bismarck, Aug. 27, 30, and Sept. 4, 1888. DZA Merseburg, Rep. 77, Tit. 4030, Nr. 1. Also Bismarck to Herrfurth, Dec. 12, 1888. DZA Merseburg, Rep. 77, Abt. 50, Nr. 84, Bd. 3. That this policy did not mean a relaxation of the struggle against Danish resistance is evident from Bismarck's advice to Herrfurth on October 11, 1889. He wrote that Danish citizens who agitated for resistance candidates in the Reichstag election should be "mercilessly expelled." DZA Potsdam, Reichskanzlei, Nr. 1409, pp. 41–52. This was Bismarck's final word as chancellor on the subject of the Danish minority.

tion initially accorded him in the Reichsland. He was also gratified by the popular enthusiasm with which the Kaiser and crown prince were greeted on their official visit to Strassburg, Metz, and other localities in September 1886. One of his first acts was to restore the Strassburg city council, which had been dissolved in 1873 after conflicts with the government. The municipal elections of 1886 produced cooperative majorities in Strassburg and Metz, although the results in upper Alsace were unsatisfactory.[56]

The Reichstag election of 1887, however, shattered every illusion about the progress of assimilation. Anticipating war and return of the French, the electorate overwhelmingly returned protest candidates, among whom were many extremists.[57] At a cabinet meeting in March 1887 the chancellor warned his colleagues that the French would invade Alsace if Boulanger came to power. "But there is no harm in that. Instead it would be militarily useful to draw the French out of their fortifications. If Alsace should be laid waste, there would be no harm in that either. In view of the recent elections Alsace does not deserve any better; nor do we need to consider any special indemnification afterward. It is true that they have voted thus out of anxiety, in order not to be subjected to revenge on the part of the French, but they still deserve punishment." Two weeks later he discussed the matter again, confirming the "complete fiasco of the administration up to this point. . . . He declared himself in favor of reconstituting the dictatorship, abolishing the territorial assembly, the governorship, and the governor's cabinet. He prefers a three-fold partition between Bavaria, Baden, and Prussia, rather than annexation by Prussia, although there will be no objection to the later in the Bundesrat. The formation of a Prussian province would be the simplest solution."[58]

But the Kaiser resisted these draconian measures. He remembered scenes from his visit in September 1886: waving handkerchiefs and cheering crowds at the military parade in Strassburg, the torchlight procession past the governor's palace, Alsatian villages decorated in his honor. These were the memories he wished to "carry with him to the grave." For once Wilhelm's will prevailed and Bismarck chose a more moderate course: to Prussianize the Reichsland by "purifying" its bureaucracy and shifting legislation from the Reichsland assembly to the Reichstag.[59] Over Hohenlohe's vigorous objec-

[56] GW, VIc, 218–321; VIII, 527–529; Karl Stählin, Geschichte Elsass-Lothringens (Munich, 1920), pp. 239ff. In his role as "responsible minister," Hohenlohe resisted pressure from Holstein, local military commanders, and others to take more vigorous action against pro-French dissidents. Rogge, Holstein und Hohenlohe, pp. 249–263.

[57] This was Hohenlohe's analysis of the voters' motives. DZA Potsdam, Reichskanzlei, 182, pp. 82–82v. Hohenlohe's reports in 1886 had glowed with assurances over the progress of the "German cause" in the Reichsland. Ibid., pp. 3–17v, 30–41.

[58] Lucius, Bismarck-Erinnerungen, pp. 373, 375–376, 379–380; GW, VIII, 560.

[59] Lucius, Bismarck-Erinnerungen, p. 379. Cabinet meeting of Mar. 27, 1887. DZA Merseburg, Rep. 90a, B, III, 2b, Nr. 6, Bd. 99; DZA Potsdam, Reichskanzlei, 182/1, pp. 1–4, 14–15, 63–73. See also Rogge, Holstein und Hohenlohe, pp. 282–287.

tions he insisted on a new system of passport controls that made it difficult for French citizens either to reside in or visit the Reichsland. By inhibiting personal and commercial traffic between France and Alsace-Lorraine, he hoped to speed the process of assimilation. "For eighteen years we have vainly tried to accomplish that by courtship. . . . Gratitude is alien to the Gallic character." The French must be made aware that their frontier was no longer the Rhine, but the Vosges. "The traditional commercial intercourse with Paris and France is freighted with political sympathy." Hence French firms doing business in the province were to be deprived of their contracts and the investments of French capitalists liquidated.[60] At Bismarck's direction new tax laws were drafted whose purpose was to ease the burden of poorer citizens, spare farmers and estate owners, and injure wealthy "Parisians," whose income stemmed from investments in French securities.[61] Yet he rejected a proposal of Hohenlohe to employ in Alsace-Lorraine an economic measure being used in Posen against the Poles: the purchase for resale to "old Germans" of estates owned by French-speaking citizens. German investors, he declared, would be reluctant to purchase property that might soon be lost to France. "Return this to me," he scrawled on the document, "after the next war, if we are then still in possession [of Alsace-Lorraine]."[62]

Had the French attacked in 1887, Bismarck would have treated Alsace-Lorraine as "enemy territory"—no differently than in the campaign of 1870.[63] Without waiting for the attack, he ordered the arrest of Alsatian members of the Déroulède's League of Patriots, who were suspected of plotting to destroy railway lines. No evidence was found, but repression continued with the help of a new political police: house searches, arbitrary arrests, expulsion of agitators, dissolution of organizations, banning of newspapers.[64] The disaffected,

[60] GW, VIc, 391–392. Cabinet meetings of Apr. 12 and May 13, 1888. DZA Merseburg, Rep. 90a, B, III, 2b, Nr. 6, Bd. 100. Rogge, Holstein und Hohenlohe, pp. 292–297, 313–325.

[61] DZA Potsdam, Reichskanzlei, 193, pp. 200–205v (Scholz to Bismarck, May 25, 1887); 194, pp. 10–11 (Scholz to Bismarck, July 4, 1887), pp. 51–53 (Rottenburg to Hohenlohe, Sept. 3, 1887), pp. 139–140v (Schwarzkoppen to Boetticher, Aug. 12, 1888). Later it will be shown that this program, intended here to speed assimilation of the Reichsland, was in line with Bismarck's general tax reform plan for all Germany after 1875.

[62] DZA Potsdam, Reichskanzlei, 183, pp. 43, 50–53v (Bismarck to Hohenlohe, Jan. 12, 1889); also GW, IVc, 405–406. This episode illustrates some of the frustrations that Bismarck's subordinates encountered in their effort to execute his wishes and avoid his wrath. Bismarck had sent to Hohenlohe newspaper clippings in which a private citizen urged such a project. Assuming that Bismarck was genuinely interested, Hohenlohe promptly set his officials to work. After two months they produced a detailed plan, which was abruptly shelved after a swift reading by the chancellor. DZA Potsdam, Reichskanzlei, 183, pp. 25–33 (Bismarck to Hohenlohe, Oct. 25, 1888), pp. 42–49 (Hohenlohe to Bismarck, Dec. 28, 1888).

[63] DZA Potsdam, Reichskanzlei, 190, pp. 61–66 (Hohenlohe to Bismarck, with Bismarck marginal note, Mar., 1887).

[64] DZA Potsdam, Reichskanzlei, 190, pp. 31–100 (exchange of letters between Bismarck, Schelling, Hohenlohe, Moltke, and Schellendorff, Feb. 11 to Apr. 13, 1887); GW, VIc, 360,

Bismarck concluded, were chiefly young people; by contrast, youths in the rest of Germany were the most enthusiastic supporters of the Reich. None of those arrested, he noted further, was a veteran; evidently the army was doing its job in the assimilation process, but the schools were not. The culprits were female teachers who were either pro-French or were dependent, because of low salaries, upon pro-French mayors and Catholic clergymen, who supplemented their incomes.[65] This chain of reasoning led to a salary increase for teachers and changes in the government's language policy in the schools. German was made the sole language of instruction in professional schools, including those training teachers. The use of French in elementary and secondary schools was drastically reduced. French was banned from the proceedings of district and local governmental bodies. German-speaking pastors were chosen for Protestant churches.[66] In February 1888 Bismarck and Hohenlohe resolved "to work with every available means for the expulsion of the French language as far as possible from the schools, churches, and from civil life altogether in Alsace-Lorraine." What he had begun in Posen, Bismarck now wanted to attempt in the Reichsland.[67]

At a pessimistic moment in 1871 Bismarck suspected that he had created in the west "a new Posen, with France in its rear."[68] As frustrations mounted, he fantasized about drastic solutions. "We made a mistake in Alsace and Lorraine," he said in 1873, "in that we did not completely drive out the entire pro-French population. With them no understanding is possible. If we must

391–392, 401–402, 420–421; VIII, 677; Dan P. Silverman, *Reluctant Union: Alsace Lorraine and Imperial Germany, 1871–1918* (University Park, 1972), pp. 51–60.

[65] *DZA* Potsdam, Reichskanzlei, 196, pp. 7–9 (Rottenburg to Hohenlohe, May 18, 1887).

[66] *DZA* Potsdam, Reichskanzlei, 196, pp. 13–14 (Hohenlohe to Bismarck, Dec. 22, 1888), pp. 27–30v (Bismarck to Hohenlohe, Dec. 29, 1888); 183, pp. 12–12v (Verwaltungsbericht, May 25, 1888), pp. 71–72v (Verwaltungsbericht, Jan. 28, 1890). See also Silverman, *Reluctant Union*, pp. 76–77.

[67] The proposition appears in a previously unknown dispatch to Hohenlohe drafted and signed by Franz von Rottenburg at the chancellor's request. (The passage is important enough to be quoted here in the original.) An article published in the Paris newspaper Le Correspondent on September 10, 1886, had brought it to Bismarck's attention that political circles in France regarded the French language as the most effective barrier to the "Entwicklung des Deutschthums." "Die Lektüre des Aufsatzes hat bei dem Herrn Reichskanzler den Gedanken angeregt, ob es nicht zweckmässig sein würde, in Elsass-Lothringen mit allen zu Gebote stehenden Mitteln auf die möglichste Verdrängung der französischen Sprache aus Schule, Kirche und dem bürgerlichen Leben überhaupt hinzuwirken. Bezüglich der polnischen Sprache ist in unseren östlichen Grenzbezirken in dieser Richtung bereits vorgegangen." *DZA* Potsdam, Reichskanzlei, 196, pp. 10–11 (Rottenburg to Hohenlohe, Feb. 20, 1888), pp. 11–11v (Rottenburg to Gossler, Feb. 20, 1888). Hohenlohe responded favorably. *DZA* Potsdam, Reichskanzlei, 182/1, pp. 94–95v (Hohenlohe to Rottenburg, Feb. 28, 1888). Simultaneously Bismarck made the same proposal to *Kultusminister* Gossler with regard to the Walloon population on the Belgian border. *DZA* Potsdam, Reichskanzlei, 196, pp. 11–11v (Rottenburg to Gossler, Feb. 20, 1888). Gossler's response could not be located. Drafts of the Rottenburg dispatches are in *DZA* Potsdam, Reichskanzlei, 182/1, pp. 91–93v.

[68] *DDF*, I, 64ff.

again take away provinces from France after another war—provinces that were once German, such as Burgundy—we must adopt a different principle. We must remove the French population completely, shove them ahead of us as it were, and then colonize the country, attract immigrants from Germany (Mecklenburg and Westphalia), and give each several acres of land as they do in America. That will be the best protective wall against France. Only then will it be possible gradually to make Alsace and Lorraine all German again."[69] "If only we were living in the time of Charlemagne," he mused in 1887, "we could move the Alsatians to Posen and the inhabitants of Posen to the region between the Rhine and the Vosges, or create an uninhabited desert between ourselves and the French. As it is, however, we must try something else."[70]

The Bismarck government was not the only one to seek internal consolidation through forced ethnic assimilation in the nineteenth century. France had followed such a policy with regard to German-speaking Alsatians before 1870, Denmark with regard to Germans in Schleswig-Holstein before 1864. And the Russification and Magyarization programs instituted by the governments in St. Petersburg and Budapest in the 1870s and 1880s were notorious. Hence Bismarck and his conservative colleagues were very much "children of their times." They swam with the current, not against it, as Bismarck's historians were once prone to believe. Germanization was vital to the achievement of his general aim of consolidating the German Reich. There is no truth to the assertion that he sought a "symbiosis of peoples" in central Europe.[71] While he stopped short of the assumption that ethnic assimilation required the liquidation of minority languages, he certainly hoped and strove for a steady growth of the German language at the cost of minority tongues. He applauded the prospect that one day they might be reduced at least to the size of the small Wendish and Slavic enclaves that were still to be found in the trans-Elbian region. The assimilation policy of the Bismarck government proved to be largely ineffective before the Paris Peace Conference ended Germany's minority problems. What the policy's failure did produce among Germans was a general sense of frustration out of which eventually came a determination to seek the expansion of Germanism by more violent means. The ultimate result was a bitter harvest, of which Bismarck would certainly have disapproved but for which he cannot be cleared of all responsibility.

The Cartel Reichstag

During the election campaign Bismarck asserted "categorically" that "there has been no discussion of any kind about an attack on the existing election

[69] Heinrich E. Brockhaus, *Stunden mit Bismarck, 1871–1878* (Leipzig, 1929), pp. 80–81.

[70] Moritz Busch, *Tagebuchblätter* (Leipzig, 1899), III, 219.

[71] Hans Rothfels, *Bismarck: Der Osten und das Reich* (Stuttgart, 1960), pp. 94–95, and *Bismarck und der Staat* (2d ed., 1954), pp. xli–xliii.

law."[72] The statement was false.[73] Yet the electoral victory of 1887 robbed him for the time being of his best justification for more drastic action. Once again German voters had given him a Reichstag majority that conformed to his expressed wishes. During March 7–11, 1887, the chamber responded to the public mandate by accepting the *Septennat* with minimum debate. In the final balloting the bill passed by a vote of 227 to 31. The minority consisted entirely of left-liberals, since the Center party abstained, and the ethnic parties did not attend. Franckenstein explained the Center's position: While recognizing the need for an increased army, centrists were unwilling to surrender the budget rights of parliament for a period of seven years.[74] Again the Center had demonstrated its unwillingness to accept direction from Rome on an issue unconnected with church affairs.

Passage of the military bill raised once more the question of new taxes. Since 1883 the imperial revenues flowing to the states and local governments under the Franckenstein clause and *Lex Huene* had consistently exceeded the amount of state assessments (*Matrikularbeiträge*) flowing in the opposite direction. Yet this would not have been the case if the Reich had not borrowed heavily to cover fiscal deficits produced chiefly by military, naval, and colonial expenses.[75] Increased military expenditures meant that parliament must grant new taxes or face either a huge increase in the imperial debt or a decline in revenue-sharing from the Reich and an increase in state assessments. In past years Bismarck had attempted to exploit such situations by forcing through the Reichstag his "tax reform," including an imperial tobacco or liquor monopoly, a reduction of direct taxes on income and property, and a diminution of the fiscal power of both the imperial and Prussian parliaments. During the election campaign, however, Bennigsen had emphatically declared that national liberals would accept neither of the two monopoly proposals.[76]

Hence Bismarck was compelled in 1887 to face the likelihood that to insist on either monopoly proposal would destroy the parliamentary majority he had gone to such extremes to create. Yet he was teased by the possibility that the rest of his reform program was feasible. In a cabinet meeting on March 1, he asked whether it would not be "tactically correct" to propose new taxes on a large number of items. "Each of the different interests is willing to cooperate

[72] To Chamber of Deputies, Jan. 24, 1887. *BR*, XII, 300. See also Busch, *Tagebuchblätter*, III, 211–213.

[73] See Lucius, *Bismarck-Erinnerungen*, pp. 352, 366; *GW*, VIII, 549; Bussmann, ed., *Herbert von Bismarck*, p. 418.

[74] *SBR* (1887), pp. 16–22, 38–48, 72–93. During the election the Center had supported progressive candidates in runoff elections in which they had no chance of success themselves. Lucius, *Bismarck-Erinnerungen*, p. 371; *HW*, II, 429–430.

[75] Wilhelm Gerloff, *Die Finanz- und Zollpolitik des deutschen Reiches* (Jena, 1913), pp. 191, 521–522; *RGB* (1887), pp. 308–328.

[76] Hermann Oncken, *Rudolf von Bennigsen* (Stuttgart, 1910), II, 533.

in taxing others. But if only *one* object is in question, they will all be opposed to it." Scholz objected that this procedure would merely "unsettle the different interests" by renewing the debate over tax proposals that the Reichstag (and the special interests) had previously rejected. It was better, he declared, to concentrate on closing the deficit in the imperial budget than to engage in another futile attempt to put through the prince's program. Although Bismarck would have preferred to tilt at the windmill one more time, he yielded to Scholz's judgment, which was supported by other cabinet members. He no longer insisted that the government must, as a matter of duty, present to parliament tax proposals that had no chance of acceptance.[77]

In 1887–1888 the government and Reichstag met the costs of new armaments primarily with massive loans, amounting to 218,389,000 marks at 3.5 percent. (The largest amount previously borrowed had been 79,107,000 at 4 percent in 1879–1880.)[78] Although they ultimately increased the Reich's income significantly, new taxes granted by the "cartel Reichstag" in 1887 served primarily the causes of tax reform (the sugar tax bill) and agrarian first aid (the liquor tax and grain tariff bills). The need for a reform of sugar taxation was undisputed. Under existing law the tax on domestic sugar production was levied on the quantity of sugar beets used rather than on the sugar produced or on its consumption. Technical progress in the refining of beet sugar had greatly increased the yield per ton of sugar beets, with the consequence that the tax yield dropped dramatically from about 50,000,000 to 15,000,000 marks. While preserving tax rebates on exports, the act of July 9, 1887, began the taxation of refined sugar, increasing the tax yield, as forecast, to 52,100,000 marks in 1889.[79]

The debates on the new liquor tax and grain tariffs were preceded by heavy pressure from agrarian interest groups. Since 1885 farmers and estate owners had become increasingly concerned over the near collapse of the prices they received for liquor and grain.[80] "The protective tariff on grain," read one widely distributed complaint, "has not helped, because it should have been three times higher. Further tariff increases were not undertaken, and duties on wool were rejected. Agriculture is being left to its fate, and 28 million rural workers, small landowners, and big landowners are approaching ruin by

[77] Cabinet meeting of Mar. 1, 1887. DZA Merseburg, Rep. 90a, B, III, 2b, Nr. 6, Bd. 99. Other sources show how tenaciously Bismarck continued to hold to his finance plans (including the monopolies). BR, XII, 140–141, 282–283; GW, VIII, 568–569.

[78] Hans Blömer, "Die Anleihen des deutschen Reiches von 1871 bis zur Stabilisierung der Mark 1924" (unpublished dissertation, Bonn, 1946), pp. 90–91.

[79] Richard Müller, *Die Einnahmequellen des Deutschen Reiches und ihre Entwicklung in den Jahren 1872 bis 1907* (Mönchen Gladbach, 1907), pp. 16–17; Gerloff, *Finanz- und Zollpolitik*, pp. 191–192; RGB (1887), pp. 253–272.

[80] On a scale of 1913 = 100, agrarian prices had declined as follows from 1881 to 1887: 91, 83, 81, 78, 76, 71, and 70. Alfred Jacobs and Hans Richter, *Die Grosshandelspreise in Deutschland von 1792 bis 1934. Sonderhefte des Instituts für Konjunkturforschung*, vol. 37 (Berlin, 1935), p. 83.

giant steps. At present prices the costs of production are higher than the return. A bad harvest could bring about the complete bankruptcy of agriculture in one year. . . . Distilleries bring in so little today that the distillery tax can no longer be paid. In spite of this price decline, which is leading us to certain bankruptcy, we must pay the old land and building taxes, as well as the income taxes. . . . Rural workers, small and large landowners! Your existence is at stake. Unite and sign petitions to the Chamber of Deputies, demanding that we be freed finally from this unjust burden."[81] The petitions came and likewise resolutions from the Prussian Chamber of Deputies (launched by conservatives and centrists) demanding redress.[82] In early March 1887, shortly before the new Reichstag met, the Congress of German Farmers added its weight to the agitation.[83]

Bismarck, no less than other estate owners, suffered from the decline in grain and alcohol prices during the mid-1880s. From scattered sources it would appear that this was a period of strain on his personal finances.[84] Still, even he now found the heavy pressure of special interests unpleasant. The new liquor tax bill introduced by the government in May 1887 had the dual purpose of producing about 96,400,000 marks in new revenues and of serving the interests of rural distillers in eastern and southern Germany. Among its highly complicated provisions was a duty of 50 pfennig per liter to be paid by small rural distilleries and of 70 pfennig per liter to be paid by large urban distilleries.[85] In the cabinet Bismarck actually spoke against the proposed aid to small distillers, even while swiftly calculating for the benefit of the ministers its meaning for his own operations.[86] And yet he did not make a cabinet

[81] Anonymous (Ein Landwirth), "Nothschrei der Landwirtschaft über ungerechte Steuern!" (printed in Bromberg, no date). DZA Potsdam, Reichskanzlei, 2088, p. 130.

[82] SEG (1887), pp. 109–110; SBHA (1887), II, 1047–1078; Anlagen, Vol. III, Nos. 165 and 176.

[83] SEG (1887), pp. 87–88.

[84] In March 1887 Wilhelm von Kardorff reported, "Bismarck is forced to pour large sums of money into his estates this year." Kardorff, a leading free conservative in the Reichstag, often conferred with the chancellor on political and economic matters. A Silesian estate owner and industrialist, Kardorff believed that bimetallism was as important as protectionism for agrarian recovery, but had no success in his effort to convince Bismarck of the necessity of monetizing silver. Threatened himself by bankruptcy, he found Schadenfreude in Bismarck's financial difficulties. Siegfried von Kardorff, Wilhelm von Kardorff: Ein nationaler Parlamentarier im Zeitalter Bismarcks und Wilhelms II., 1828–1907 (Berlin, 1936), p. 196. Bleichröder's correspondence reveals that Bismarck had heavily mortgaged Varzin (425,850 marks) and Schönhausen (259,400 marks). Rantzau to Bleichröder, Oct. 11 and Nov. 25, 1886. Bleichröder Archive, Box 4. The Varzin paper mill destroyed by fire was not fully insured, and its reconstruction cost 57,471 marks, another drain on his resources. Moritz Behrend to Bleichröder, July 27, 1887. Ibid., Box 4. In April 1887 Bismarck had to make a hasty trip to Friedrichsruh, because his manager there, Head Forester Peter Lange, had extended excessive credit (40,000 marks) to English customers, from whom it would be expensive to collect. Lucius, Bismarck-Erinnerungen, p. 382.

[85] SBR (1887), IV, Aktenstück No. 90.

[86] Cabinet meeting of Apr. 9, 1887. Lucius, Bismarck-Erinnerungen, p. 382.

issue of the question, and the cartel parties and the Center passed the measure over the objections of the liberals and socialists, who denounced this "love token" for small distillers.[87] "The distillery act helps greatly and will soon raise estate prices prodigiously," rejoiced Wilhelm von Kardorff, who had nearly been compelled to sell his Silesian property.[88]

As minister of agriculture Lucius resented the prodding of conservative Prussian landowners in the Chamber of Deputies for increases in grain tariffs. Bismarck also complained of "agrarian greediness." But they yielded, nevertheless, and the minister of finance rejoiced at the fiscal prospects.[89] When finally introduced in the fall of 1887, the bill proposed to increase again the tariffs on wheat and rye—from 3 to 6 marks per ton—and to raise significantly the rates on other agrarian products.[90] Even free conservatives found the proposed rate on grain excessive. An amendment introduced by Windthorst reduced the new rate to 5 marks per ton, and the bill passed with the support of conservatives, free conservatives, centrists, and about twenty national liberals.[91]

With the tariff act of 1887, protectionism reached a high point in the German Reich. Once again agrarian interests had demonstrated their political power and the industrialists their tolerance of agrarian interests. The injured parties were the urban lower classes, who were denied cheaper food, and merchants importing agrarian products. Although skeptical of both the need and value of the new tariff, Bismarck acquiesced. Yet this did not save him from the wrath of landowners dissatisfied with the extent of their gains. In late October he was again attacked in the pages of *Kreuzzeitung* for betraying conservative interests.[92]

The Mediterranean Agreement

That Bismarck pointed to France rather than Russia as the chief danger to Germany's security in his speech of January 11, 1887, was owing to an apparent turn for the better in German-Russian relations. Inspired by news of the French-Russian rapprochement, he had made yet another effort in the fall of 1886 to convince Petersburg of the value of German friendship. Germany was willing, he told the Russians, to accept any candidate nominated by Russia for the vacant Bulgarian throne. "We have absolutely nothing against Russia's

[87] *SBR* (1887), I, 491–548; II, 878–1002, 1089–1116.
[88] Kardorff, *Kardorff*, pp. 192–193, 199.
[89] Cabinet meeting of May 4, 1887. Lucius, *Bismarck-Erinnerungen*, p. 386. See also his discussion with Rottenburg, Oct. 10, 1887. *Ibid.*, p. 398. Bismarck spoke for the bill in the Reichstag (*BR*, XII, 427ff.) and congratulated Lucius on his skillful defense of it (*GW*, VIc, 373–374).
[90] *SBR* (1887–1888), III, Aktenstück No. 22.
[91] *SBR* (1887–1888), pp. 47–107, 173–278, 309–340; *RGB* (1887), pp. 533–534.
[92] Lucius, *Bismarck-Erinnerungen*, p. 400; *Neue Preussische Zeitung*, No. 250, Oct. 26, 1887.

Bismarck as Hypnotist

THE EYE ON FRANCE

1872	1882	1887	18??
WITH	WITH	WITH	WITH
GOODWILL	CAUTION	MISTRUST	???

THE EYE ON PARLIAMENT

WINDTHORST EATS THE *SEPTENNAT*; KARDORFF REACHES FOR THE LIQUOR TAX BILL; A DAZED RICHTER CONTEMPLATES THE SCENE WITH DISTASTE. WILHELM SCHOLZ IN *KLADDERADATSCH*, 1887.

going to Constantinople and taking the Dardanelles."[93] In Russia opinion was still divided on the value of the Berlin connection. The journalist Katkov agitated against renewal of the Three Emperors League and for recovery by Russia of a free hand in foreign affairs. His views were shared by Ignatyev, Saburov, and others, while Giers and the brothers Paul and Peter Shuvalov clung to the traditional alliance with the central European powers.

In early January 1887 Peter Shuvalov arrived in Berlin bearing a letter from the tsar that requested of the Kaiser a commitment (easily granted) against Battenberg's return to the Bulgarian throne. While there, Shuvalov discussed with Bismarck the basis for a "dual entente" to replace the Three Emperors League. The agreement would have provided for the benevolent neutrality of Russia in the event of war between Germany and France and of Germany in the event Russia was "obliged to assure" closure of the Straits. Both powers recognized that the existence of Austria-Hungary was necessary to the maintenance of the European balance of power. Germany accepted Russia's "exclusive" influence in Bulgaria (and Rumelia), and both powers recognized the necessity of preserving Serbia's independence under King Milan.[94] But this démarche had not been authorized by Alexander III, who received it coldly on the ambassador's return to Petersburg. At a council meeting on January 20 the tsar rejected both of the contradictory policies being urged on him, that is, alliance with France or Germany. For many weeks the direction of Russian policy was uncertain. Was the tsar being indecisive or was he waiting, as Schweinitz thought, to see what would come of the mounting tension between Berlin and Paris? As the days went by without word from Petersburg, Bismarck grasped that he had been too sanguine: "No answer is still an answer."[95]

The prospect of serious trouble with France, coupled with uncertainty about Russia's course, compelled Bismarck to take the Italian connection more seriously. The Triple Alliance was destined to expire in May 1887, and the Italians spurred Bismarck's interest in its renewal by revealing to Berlin recent overtures from Paris for a settlement of France's differences with Italy in the Mediterranean. Italy's new foreign minister, Count Nicolis Robilant, had attacked his predecessors as profligates for having yielded so much in the original treaty, and he was determined now to strike a harder bargain. The Austrians left the negotiations in Bismarck's hands, which were remarkably open. He listened receptively to Robilant's desire for a guarantee of military support if France should try to take Tripoli (Bismarck: "highly unlikely") and for a voice in future decisions of the dual powers relating to the Balkans. Nor did he balk when the Italians presented a treaty draft that extended the guar-

---

[93] Bussmann, ed., *Herbert von Bismarck*, pp. 395–396, 406–407; GP, VI, 98–103.
[94] GP, V, 84–120 (especially 108, 117), 160–166, 212–215.
[95] Bussmann, ed., *Herbert von Bismarck*, p. 429; GP, V, 118–120, 218–220.

antee to Morocco. Germany, he declared, could not stand idly by in the event of war between France and Italy, whatever its origin.[96]

The Austrian government, however, was leery of such new commitments, particularly since Italy promised no equivalent return (Bismarck: "neutrality is one already"). Kálnoky was annoyed at Bismarck's persistent refusal to assure Austria of German support in the event of an Austrian war with Russia over Bulgaria and was as unwilling as before to become involved in a war against France in behalf of the interests of her two allies. In mid-January 1887 Kálnoky, who believed war imminent between France and Germany, bluntly refused the Italian proposals, advocating instead a simple renewal of the agreements of 1882.[97]

Kálnoky's adamancy produced despondency in the German foreign office, but Bismarck simply conceded the legitimacy of the Austrian position and found a way out of the impasse. He proposed that the treaty of 1882 be renewed but supplemented by separate agreements among the three powers. Actually he believed that multiple agreements would be "more important to us" than the old treaty. On February 20, 1887, the treaty of 1882 was extended another five years. A separate treaty between Austria and Italy provided that the powers would use their influence to maintain the territorial status quo "in the regions of the Balkans or of the Ottoman coasts and islands in the Adriatic and in the Aegean Sea." But if this should become impossible "in consequence of the action of a third power or otherwise" and, if either of the two contracting powers should find it necessary to modify the status quo by carrying out "a temporary or permanent occupation," they would reach prior agreement with each other on the basis of "reciprocal compensation." The German-Italian pact differed in that the two states agreed to use their influence to oppose any territorial modification injurious to the interests of either power "on the Ottoman coasts and islands in the Adriatic and the Aegean Seas," with no reference either to the Balkans or to contingent compensations.[98]

The remarkable aspect of this agreement was Germany's commitment to support Italy militarily in the event that Rome should be compelled to fight to safeguard its position in the Mediterranean against French expansionism in Morocco and Tripoli. Under the threat of a two-front war against France and Russia, Bismarck, who had earlier regarded the Italian alliance with contempt, came close to permitting its conversion from a defensive into an offensive alliance. Like Austria in 1866, France must be faced with the necessity of defending its southern frontier against Italy in the event of war with Germany. For Bismarck this gain was evidently greater than the risk that Ger-

[96] GP, IV, 181–209.

[97] GP, IV, 210–237; VI, 170–172.

[98] GP, IV, 240–251, 257–260; Alfred Pribram, The Secret Treaties of Austria-Hungary, 1879–1914 (Cambridge, Mass., 1920), I, 104–115.

many's new commitments to Italy might involve Germany in a future war of North African origin for purely Italian interests.

In view of what we have learned about Bismarck's tactical system in foreign affairs since 1870, it comes as no surprise that, as the German link to Petersburg weakened, he turned westward again seeking in Britain a potential replacement for Russia in the combination of three out of five great powers that was his key to German security. In this quest he was assisted by growing friction between Britain and France, another phenomenon of the Boulanger epoch. During the autumn of 1886 the British had made repeated efforts to reach an understanding with Austria over Balkan issues, but both Bismarck and Kálnoky were wary of London's continuing efforts to seduce Austria into taking the lead in any joint diplomatic action against Russia. Bismarck's objective was to get Britain instead to take the initiative in bolstering Turkey against Russia in the Near East and to follow Germany's leadership in strengthening Italy against France.

During that critical winter of 1886–1887, the Freycinet cabinet in Paris provided London with a motive for yielding to these enticements by vigorously opposing Britain's consolidation of its position in Egypt, which Freycinet publicly declared to be the key to mastery over the Mediterranean. Germany, Bismarck told the British, had nothing to gain by war against either France or Russia and could not risk a conflict in order to block Russian aims in the Near East or French objectives in Egypt. But British interests were directly involved in both instances. Hence it behooved Britain to join Italy in blocking France's expansion in North Africa and to join Austria and Italy in checking Russian expansion into the Balkans and toward the Straits. British sea power and German military power would hold France in check, while Austria, Italy, and England did the same for Russia. The balance of power would be "complete" and peace preserved.[99]

The force of these arguments enabled Bismarck to become the catalyst for the formation of the First Mediterranean Agreement, by which the British government associated itself through Italy with the central powers in seeking to preserve the status quo in the Black, Adriatic, Aegean, and Mediterranean seas (specifically Egypt, Tripoli, Cyrenaica, and "every other point" on the North African coast). The notes exchanged between Rome and London on February 12, 1887, did not establish a formal alliance. They contained pledges of mutual support in the event that either power found itself at odds with a third, pledges that were regarded by both sides in that threatening situation as tantamount to an alliance.[100]

The agreement was not intended to be the prelude to action but rather a

[99] GP, IV, 118–120, 263–294, 300–311, 323–324.

[100] GP, IV, 311–313; Pribram, Secret Treaties, I, 124–133; Hans Rothfels, Bismarcks englische Bündnispolitik (Berlin, 1924), pp. 101–115.

deterrent to France in the Mediterranean. By drawing Britain into the defense of Italy, Bismarck eased the burden upon Germany of supporting Italian interests in North Africa under the German-Italian pact signed eight days later, a fact that explains his willingness to yield to Robilant's demands. With British naval power filling the vacuum in the Mediterranean, he could rest easier about making commitments to Italy that, if not evaded, could have been fulfilled only by military action in the north. During March 1887 Britain and Austria with Bismarck's encouragement, entered into discussions that led to Austria's adherence by an exchange of notes to the Mediterranean agreement (with emphasis placed on the eastern rather than the western Mediterranean). In May Spain, seeking support against France, also adhered to the agreement in an exchange of notes with Italy.[101] By the late spring of 1887 France was hedged about in every direction by a formidable combination of military and naval power. To challenge it would have been an act of supreme folly.

The Reinsurance Treaty

Of the two crises in foreign affairs that Germany faced in 1886–1888 that with France was probably the less dangerous. Despite public adulation of Boulanger and the efforts of French chauvinists to exploit it, the French government had little desire to initiate a war against Germany. Foreign Minister Émile Flourens was outraged when he heard that Boulanger had tried to establish independent contacts with Russia. And yet he was also disturbed by reports that the Germans were themselves preparing an attack on France. Flourens thought it prudent to seek assurances of Russian neutrality and moral support in the event of an unprovoked German attack on France, but the results were vague.[102]

In April 1887 the arrest on German soil of Guillaume Schnaebelé, a French frontier official suspected by the Germans of espionage, aroused France's patriotic press to a new frenzy of denunciation. Boulanger and Premier René Goblet favored an ultimatum to Berlin calling for the official's release. But their colleagues in the French cabinet refused to take this step, and Bismarck, who no longer had need of such an issue, secured Schnabelé's release when the French proved that he had crossed the border by official invitation and hence under a safe-conduct.[103] On May 16, 1887, Boulanger's anxious colleagues precipitated a cabinet crisis that forced him out of office. He left the Ministry of War with the greatest reluctance, determined one day to return to it. Since that was unlikely to happen with the cooperation of the parties in

---

[101] GP, IV, 315–331; Pribram, Secret Treaties, I, 116–123.
[102] Kennan, Decline of Bismarck's European Order, pp. 266–288.
[103] GP, VI, 182–192, 204.

power, the general had little choice but to bargain and conspire with parties of the opposition. The critical issue now was whether Boulanger would become a greater threat to the government out of office than in.[104]

Contrary to the criticisms of some contemporaries and later historians, Bismarck's diplomatic performance in 1886–1887 was masterful. With undiminished virtuosity he fashioned a consistent policy capable of counteracting dangers on two potentially intersecting fronts. Germany had to avoid a two-front war that would divide its armies, dissipate its strength, and involve it in a prolonged struggle of attrition without the prospect of decisive victory over either foe. Above all, Germany had to avoid a war from which it had nothing to gain worthy of the sacrifices the struggle would impose and whose outcome and consequences no one could foresee.

Whenever the occasion demanded, he continued to insist in Vienna that the terms of the Dual Alliance did not require Germany to support Austria in an offensive war against Russia over the Balkans. Yet he encouraged the Austrians to secure from Britain and Italy the support that Germany could not offer, and he had to be prepared for the possibility that their collaboration would produce a war with Russia. By keeping a free hand in the east, he calculated, Germany could hold the French in check in the west. But if France attacked, he believed (March 1887) it "very likely" that the two wars could be fought separately.[105] By fostering but not participating in the English-Italian-Austrian agreements, furthermore, he kept the door to Russia open, if only slightly, and thereby avoided the destruction of that flexible position between east and west that was vital to his political strategy.

Like the Triple Alliance, the second Three Emperors League was destined to expire in 1887. Hence Bismarck watched the struggle between Giers and Katkov for primacy over Russian policy with keen interest. Whether Giers, the conservative advocate of a continuing relationship with Germany, or Katkov, the patriotic advocate of a free hand for Russia, would win out in the counsels of Alexander III was the critical issue upon which the peace of Europe depended in 1887. On February 20, the date of the renewal of the Triple Alliance, an article published in *Nord*, a Belgian newspaper known to be a mouthpiece of the Russian government, seemed to indicate that Katkov had won. It warned that, if Germany should seek to crush France, Russia would not remain neutral as it had in 1870. To protect France from being weakened any further, Petersburg would avoid conflict with Vienna and London and let events in Bulgaria take their course.

Bismarck reacted by reassuring Russia that Germany had no intention of attacking France and that, even if provoked by France into a war, would grant her a lenient peace, like that given Austria in 1866. "France's continuing

---

[104] Seager, *Boulanger Affair*, pp. 57–69.
[105] GP, IV, 321–323.

existence as a great power, like that of every other great power, is a necessity for us, because, if for no other reason, we need in certain situations a maritime counterweight to Great Britain." Germany, he said, would not be averse to a renewed entente with France even closer than that under the Ferry government. Simultaneously the prince returned to his earlier policy of encouraging the Russians to slake their thirst for influence and security by seeking an agreement with Turkey permitting Russian occupation of key points on the Dardanelles.[106] If the crisis of 1887 was to end in frustration for Russia, in other words, Alexander must be led to believe that England and her allies were responsible for it—not Germany, which had not joined the Mediterranean agreement and even looked with benevolence upon Petersburg's ambitions for a wider sphere of influence in the Balkans.

In March 1887 the tsar finally called a halt to Katkov's attempts to dictate Russian foreign policy through the press. His personal reproofs to the journalist and to those, like Saburov, who aided the journalist from within the government meant victory for Giers, who had steadfastly refused to believe those who insisted that Germany intended to attack France and that Russia must seek the latter's alliance. Giers would have preferred simply to renew the Three Emperors League, but first he sought evidence of Germany's good faith by asking Bismarck to "second" Russia's demand that Bulgaria accept a regent chosen by Petersburg. Bismarck accepted with alacrity and even sent son Herbert, state secretary in the German foreign office, to persuade the London government of the wisdom of such a step. Although Salisbury agreed, the Russians had no effective means for forcing their candidate on Sofia, and nothing came of the proposal. Bismarck's compliance made it easier for Giers to present to Alexander III the case for renewal of the Three Emperors League. But Giers could not overcome Alexander's unwillingness to perpetuate the relationship with Austria. All that the minister obtained was a commitment by Alexander to observe the "spirit" of the treaty after it lapsed. During May 11–18 and June 11–12, 1887, Bismarck and Paul Shuvalov, Russia's ambassador in Berlin, negotiated a separate agreement that became known as the "reinsurance treaty."[107]

In this secret pact, signed on June 18, 1887, and scheduled to last for three years, the two powers declared that, if either should "find itself at war with a third great power," the other would maintain benevolent neutrality and seek to "localize the conflict." But this commitment would not apply in a war against either France or Austria begun by one of the contracting powers. Germany recognized "the rights historically acquired by Russia in the Balkan Peninsula and particularly the legitimacy of its preponderant and decisive influ-

---

[106] Kennan, *Decline of Bismarck's European Order*, pp. 298ff.; GP, V, 215ff.; VI, 177–178.

[107] GP, V, 167–176, 220–229, 256; Hans Hallmann, ed., *Zur Geschichte und Problematik des deutsch-russischen Rückversicherungsvertrages von 1887* (Darmstadt, 1968), pp. 74–94.

ence in Bulgaria and Eastern Rumelia." The two powers agreed to oppose "any modification of the territorial status quo" in the Balkans without their prior accord. They affirmed "the European and mutually obligatory character of the principle of the closure of the Straits of the Bosphorus and the Dardanelles" and agreed to warn Turkey against permitting an infraction of that principle by a belligerent power. In "additional and ultrasecret protocols," however, Germany agreed to support, "as in the past," Russia's effort to "reestablish a regular and legal government in Bulgaria" and to give "moral and diplomatic support" for any measures the tsar might deem necessary to defend the entrance to the Black Sea, "the key to his empire." The treaty, Herbert Bismarck judged, was "rather anodyne." "It puts some pressure on the tsar and should, if matters become serious, keep the Russians off our necks six to eight weeks longer than otherwise would be the case. That is worth something."[108]

Once again Bismarck appeared to have restored the preferred combination of three in an unstable system of five great powers. But at what cost?[109] No treaty concluded by Bismarck has been subjected to greater scrutiny and more controversy than the reinsurance treaty of 1887. Was it compatible with Germany's obligations to Austria under the Dual Alliance of 1879? During the negotiations with Paul Shuvalov Bismarck (with Austria's agreement) enlightened the Russian government concerning the terms of that alliance (except for its duration). "Honor and propriety," he declared, required that "the cards be put on the table," even though the evidence of Germany's continuing relationship to Austria was not beneficial to the cultivation of that with Russia. It was the Russians, furthermore, who insisted that the reinsurance pact be kept secret from other powers, including Austria.[110]

Was the reinsurance treaty incompatible with the Dual Alliance as seen from the Austrian standpoint? Since 1879 Bismarck had repeatedly warned Vienna that the alliance did not obligate Germany to support Austrian policy in the Balkans, and, but for one brief interval, he had never ceased to advance the proposal that the Balkans be divided into spheres of influence, the western half to Austria, the eastern half to Russia. The areas mentioned in the reinsurance treaty (Bulgaria, Eastern Rumelia, and the Straits) all fell within the Russian sphere. If Franz Joseph should learn of the treaty, Bismarck maintained, the result would not be uneasiness but relief.[111]

Was the reinsurance treaty compatible with the Mediterranean agreement signed only a few months later? Obviously the latter had been designed to

---

[108] GP, V, 229–232, 239–255; S. Goriainov, "The End of the Alliance of the Emperors," *American Historical Review*, 23 (1917–1918), pp. 333–339; Bussmann, ed., *Herbert von Bismarck*, pp. 457–458.

[109] For a sampling of contrasting opinions on this subject, see Hallmann, ed., *Rückversicherungsvertrag*, pp. 257–258.

[110] GP, V, 221, 233–243, 251; Hallmann, ed., *Rückversicherungsvertrag*, pp. 79–81.

[111] GP, V, 265–268.

freeze the status quo in the Balkans in view of the Russian threat, and now in the reinsurance treaty Germany approved Russia's ambition to expand its influence and potential military action to include the Straits. Since Germany was not a signer of the Mediterranean agreement, it can be argued that even here there was no formal incompatibility. But Germany had been a prime mover of that agreement, and from that standpoint it can be said that Bismarck was guilty of bad faith toward Russia and England. Still he signed the reinsurance treaty knowing that English and Austrian opposition to Russia's aims in the eastern Balkans would nullify the effect of the German commitment. Whatever may be said on the issue of faith and honor, the two treaties served not only Germany's interests but also Europe's by keeping France and Russia apart for the time being, by frustrating the war hawks in both countries, and by stabilizing the balance of power in such a way as to preserve the peace in the most threatening international crisis Europe experienced between 1871 and 1914.

Even so, the question remains whether the reinsurance treaty, even if it had been renewed by Bismarck's successors in 1890, could have halted for long the erosion of German-Russian relations. That deterioration began in the late 1870s as a by-product of the diplomatic conflict between Russia and Austria in the Balkans. Bismarck had long understood that this was the neuralgic point in the relationship, and we have seen how he sought during these years to reduce its dangers for the link to Russia by insisting that Germany had no interests in that region, by refusing to back Austria's ambitions there, and by continually promoting a division of the region into mutually exclusive spheres of influence. But he could not secure by this route the satisfaction of Russian pride and ambition for expansion in the Near East because of the incompetence of the tsarist government, which first overreached itself in the Treaty of San Stefano and then did not know how to exploit even the still substantial gains made at the Congress of Berlin.

That influential Russians, inside and outside the government, blamed Bismarck for their disasters was not the consequence of intrigues, of which they unjustly accused him, but of the steadily increasing personal dominance he had established over the diplomatic processes of the European balance of power during a quarter of a century in office. Diplomatic finesse, political vision, and narcissistic self-assertion had elevated him to the pinnacle of European politics. To repeat Katkov's observation, he appeared to "possess the talisman before which all obstacles dissolve and all locks open." Such a reputation has a high cost. Bismarck was held responsible for whatever happened—or failed to happen—in Europe. To the Russians the German chancellor now appeared to be an evil genius who was to blame for their continuing frustrations and humiliations. If Russia's goals were not achieved, it was because Bismarck had somehow blocked their accomplishment by intriguing

behind the scenes or by failing to use his formidable talents for their achievement.

Ironically the free hand that Katkov demanded for Russia in 1887 echoed
the demand that Bismarck had made for Prussia three decades earlier. Both
called for a loosening of the conservative ties that bound their countries to
other great monarchies in central Europe, and both called for rapprochement
with France as the best way to attain the political maneuverability that, it was
presumed, must lead to success in their objectives. But there was a difference.
Katkov was a clever Russian journalist, Bismarck the most astute diplomat of
his time. Public speculation in Russia about the possible corrosive effect of a
Russian free hand on the solidity of Germany's alliance with Austria merely
strengthened it and sent both powers looking for additional allies.

Politics and Economics

In recent years historians of international politics have begun to search for
other, more material causes for the widening gulf between Berlin and Petersburg that ultimately ended in the Franco-Russian alliance of 1894 and the test
of strength between rival alliances that came in 1914–1918.[112] Nothing yet
produced by this effort has succeeded in replacing the view that conflicting
political interests and judgments concerning those interests by rulers, statesmen, generals, journalists, and other manipulators of government policy and
public opinion were primary. Still lacking is direct evidence that material
concerns influenced the actual decision makers sufficiently to cause them to
give precedence to economic-financial over power-political interests. The
most that can be said is that the continuing problems of the depression of the
1870s, its aftereffects in the 1880s, and the defensive measures taken by European governments in behalf of important economic interest groups contributed in a secondary way during the late 1880s to the divisiveness that weakened the Three Emperors League.

Russian industry was hard hit by the sagging European economy of the late
1870s, and Russia's entrepreneurs, like their counterparts elsewhere, redou-
bled their efforts to obtain tariff protectionism. As war with Turkey loomed
in 1876, Minister of Finance Mikhail Reutern sought to strengthen the Rus-

---

[112] See, for example, Sigrid Kumpf-Korfes, *Bismarcks Draht nach Russland: Zum Problem der
sozial-ökonomischen Hintergründe der russisch-deutschen Entfremdung im Zeitraum von 1878 bis 1891*
(Berlin, 1968); Horst Müller-Link, *Industrialisierung und Aussenpolitik: Preussen-Deutschland und
das Zarenreich von 1860 bis 1890* (Göttingen, 1977); Hans-Ulrich Wehler, "Bismarcks späte Russ-
landpolitik 1879–1890," in his *Krisenherde des Kaiserreiches 1871 bis 1918: Studien zur deutschen
Sozial- und Verfassungsgeschichte* (Göttingen, 1970), pp. 163–180; Helmut Böhme, "Die deutsch-
russischen Wirtschaftsbeziehungen unter dem Gesichtspunkt der deutschen Handelspolitik
(1878–1894)," in Karl Otmar Freiherr von Aretin and Werner Conze, eds., *Deutschland und
Russland im Zeitalter des Kapitalismus, 1861–1914* (Wiesbaden, 1977), pp. 173–206.

BISMARCK'S ROLE IN THE 1887 CRISIS—A GERMAN VIEW. "EUROPE'S CENTRAL SWITCHMAN" DIVERTS
THE ENGINE "REVENGE" TO CLEAR THE WAY FOR THE ENGINE "PEACE." WILHELM SCHOLZ IN
KLADDERADATSCH, 1887.

sian treasury by requiring tariff payments in gold rather than paper rubles, a
measure equivalent to a 30 to 50 percent increase in tariff rates on imported
goods. As Russia's major trading partner, Germany was particularly hard hit
by this decision. More dependent than ever on exports after the crash of
1873, German industrialists and financiers had found in Russia, whose industrial development lagged far behind that of western Europe, a surrogate market for their products and investment capital. In the mid-1870s 24 percent of
German exports went to Russia (about 35 percent of all Russian imports),
whereas Russia sent 34 percent of its exports to Germany (8.6 percent of
German imports). Russia bought primarily industrial, Germany primarily agricultural products.[113] The interests most injured by this trade were Russian
industry (Moscow region) and German agriculture (east-Elbian region). For
reasons already explained the German tariff act of 1879 provided more protection for industry than for agriculture. As a consequence, the statute affected western European countries more than it did Russia.

In Russia the agitation by industrialists and their journalistic allies (Katkov
in the van) for still more protection and the government's search for new
revenue with which to repair the fiscal damage of the Russian-Turkish war led
in 1881 to an increase of 10 percent in new duties on manufactured goods.

---

[113] Kumpf-Korfes, *Draht nach Russland*, pp. 7–9; Jürgen Kuczynski and Grete Wittkowski, *Die
deutsch-russischen Handelsbeziehungen in den letzten 150 Jahren* (Berlin, 1947), p. 26.

BISMARCK'S ROLE IN THE 1887 CRISIS—A FRENCH VIEW. THE SEA MONSTER REACHES OUT FROM THE
RHINE TO DISTURB A PROMISING RELATIONSHIP BETWEEN FRANCE AND RUSSIA. FROM A CONTEMPO-
RARY FRENCH BROADSHEET.

Further increases came in 1884 (10 percent) and 1885 (20 percent), with the consequence that Russia's share of all German exports sank from 40 to 4.5 percent between 1880 and 1885, chiefly at the cost of German textile, iron, and machine industries. Bismarck's desire to preserve the "line to Petersburg" in foreign policy led him to give up the idea of retaliatory tariffs directed specifically against Russia. Russia was, nevertheless, the country most affected when Germany tripled (1885) and then doubled (1887) general import duties on foreign grain.[114]

And yet the adverse effect of these statutes upon Russian grain exports to Germany was temporary. Russia supplied 36 percent of German grain imports in 1880, 40 percent in 1886, and 53 percent in 1888. Of the two major export crops, rye reached a high of 566,242 tons (66,800,000 marks) in 1884, declined to 329,425 tons (32,000,000 marks) in 1886, but recovered to 470,430 tons (42,300,000 marks) in 1888 and 920,189 tons (98,500,000 marks) in 1889; wheat also reached a high of 325,872 tons (49,200,000 marks) in 1884, fell to 141,819 tons (20,700,000 marks) in 1886, but recovered to 153,996 tons (22,200,000 marks) in 1888 and 301,247 tons (42,000,000 marks) in 1889. Despite their tariff walls, Russia and Germany remained important trading partners in world commerce. Of Germany's total imports in 1889, Russia supplied 13.5 percent, second only to Britain's 16.5 percent. But Russia had fallen to sixth place among Germany's foreign customers, purchasing 6.0 percent of Germany's exports, behind Great Britain (20.0 percent), Austria-Hungary (10.5 percent), the United States (12.1 percent), the Netherlands (7.9 percent), and France (6.5 percent).[115] Given its practical effect, Germany had more cause to complain about Russia's protectionism than Russia about Germany's.

The link between producers and consumers of both industrial and agrarian products was not the only area of economic interdependence—and friction— between Germany and Russia in the 1870s and 1880s. Since 1857 German financiers had found Russia's voracious need for industrial capital a lucrative source of investment. According to the best estimate, German financiers had by 1876 invested 900,000,000 marks (417,000,000 rubles) in state guaranteed loans for the construction of Russian railways. Germans are believed to have invested another 30,000,000 rubles in Russian banks and industrial enterprises during these years of favorable political relations between the two countries. By providing a hothouse for native industry, Russia's protective tariffs of the 1880s stimulated the export of German capital in search of high rates of return. Although the flow of capital for railway construction lessened during the 1880s, the total figure is still believed to have been close to the

[114] Kumpf-Korfes, *Draht nach Russland*, pp. 13, 16–17, 50–51.
[115] Das Kaiserliche Statistische Amt, *Statistisches Handbuch für das deutsche Reich* (Berlin, 1907), Part II, 152–159, 516–523, 528–531.

417,000,000 rubles of the 1870s. Investments in Russian industry (sometimes in the form of satellite companies) reached in 1890 an estimated 79,000,000 rubles (the largest, at 36.7 percent, of any European country).[116]

These investments were far exceeded by Germany's involvement in Russia's state finance. By 1886 the Russian government had accumulated a massive national debt of 6,488,000,000 rubles as a result of the Crimean War, the Polish rebellion of 1863, the Russo-Turkish war of 1877–1878, the occupation and development of new territories acquired in Central Asia and the Far East, and the subvention of railways and industries. Of this debt (whose servicing was at 264,000,000 rubles, the largest single item in the annual budget), about 2,000,000,000 rubles were held by foreign creditors, mostly Germans (about 1,200,000,000 rubles). Because of the piecemeal way these obligations had accumulated, the debt was expensive to administer and service, leading successive Russian ministers of finance in the 1880s to seek from Berlin bankers massive new loans with which to refinance and convert the Russian public debt.[117]

Bismarck was sensitive to material and financial questions in his negotiations with Russia during 1885–1887, and yet there can be no doubt that political and military issues were primary in his calculations and that the needs of Russian grain producers and shippers as well as the fiscal needs of the Russian state were also for him weapons in the struggle to restrain Russian imperialism in the Balkans and preserve European peace. Mounting signs in early 1886 that the Russian government might respond to more protectionist demands from industrialists caused Bismarck to direct the foreign office's chief expert on economic policy, Count Maximilian von Berchem, to draft a memorandum (*Promemoria*) proposing that Germany threaten retaliatory tariffs and hindrances to Russia's debt conversion. In May Bismarck instructed the embassy in Petersburg to utter the first of these threats, holding the second in reserve. In return for Germany's neutrality on the Bulgarian question, he told Shuvalov, Russia should halt for at least five years further increases in its duties on manufactured goods and abolish its discriminatory differential rates on Silesian coal imports. Otherwise Germany would be compelled to increase its duties on Russian grain, timber, and swine. During the last half of 1886 negotiations with the Russians on tariff policy made no progress because Bismarck refused to make concessions on grain and timber tariffs, while Shuvalov, Giers, and Bunge were unsuccessful in their attempts to stem the tide of protectionism in Russia.

Meanwhile, Bunge failed in his extended negotiations with Berlin bankers for a conversion of the Russian public debt. Rumors of war and discourage-

[116] Joachim Mai, *Das deutsche Kapital in Russland 1850–1894* (Berlin, 1970), pp. 109–110, 222–224; Valentin S. Djakin, "Aus der Geschichte der russisch-deutschen Wirtschaftsbeziehungen," in Aretin and Conze, eds., *Deutschland und Russland*, pp. 164–166.

[117] Kennan, *Decline of Bismarck's European Order*, pp. 223–227.

BISMARCK EXPLAINING A POINT TO WILHELM I. THE SCENE IS THE KAISER'S FAMED CORNER OFFICE AT
THE PALACE, WELL KNOWN TO MOST BERLINERS (FROM THE SQUARE BELOW). PAINTING BY KONRAD
VON SIEMENROTH (1887).

ment from the Wilhelmstrasse sufficed to disinterest the bankers in the project. The consequence was a sharp decline in the price of Russian securities on the Berlin exchange. At the end of 1886 N. K. Bunge, regarded as pro-German and proagriculture, was replaced at the Finance Ministry by Ivan Vishnegradsky, a staunch protectionist with close ties to Russian industry. During 1887 both Germany and Russia resorted to another round of tariff increases.[118]

Increasing economic frictions were an undercurrent in Germany's relations with Russia during these years. At the beginning of an *"exposé"* of November 1887, in which he briefed Kaiser Wilhelm for an approaching talk with Tsar Alexander, Bismarck explained the relationship between economic and political affairs in German foreign policy. "We are far from complaining about tariff and legislative measures that affect the material interests of Germany. Those are questions of domestic politics that every government must regulate according to its needs. Differences over customs and other matters have always existed—for sixty to seventy years—without weakening our political and personal intimacy. The latter has been compromised only by an unjust assessment in Russia of our attitude at the Congress of Berlin, refusal of the government publicly to correct that assessment, and the encouragement and support given the French menace that threatens us by the organs of the press and Russian government, including the ministers except for M. de Giers."[119] That the economic affairs of Russia and Germany were so intertwined might, under differing political conditions, have dictated accommodation rather than divergence. But political friction tended during 1887–1890 not only to prevent the accommodation but also to deepen the divergence.

[118] Kennan, *Decline of Bismarck's European Order*, pp. 228–229; Kumpf-Korfes, *Draht nach Russland*, pp. 51–61; Müller-Link, *Industrialisierung und Aussenpolitik*, pp. 286–302.

[119] The *Exposé* composed for the Kaiser is dated Nov. 10, 1887—the day of the *Lombardverbot* (to be discussed later)! GP, V, 320; see also pp. 307–308, 312–314, and especially GP, VI, 324.

BOOK THREE

Decline and Fall,

1888–1890

The greedy element always gains the decisive preponderance among the great masses. It is in the interest of the masses themselves to desire that this conquest occur without dangerous acceleration and without wrecking the wagon of state. Whenever the latter happens, nevertheless, the cycle of history will always return in a relatively short time to dictatorship, despotism, and absolutism, because in the end even the masses have a need for order. And if they do not recognize this a priori, they will eventually see it themselves after manifold ad hominem disputes. They will then purchase order with dictatorship and Caesarism, voluntarily surrendering that measure of freedom that is justified and worth preserving; namely, the measure of freedom that the European society of states can tolerate without getting sick.

—*Bismarck in* Gedanken und Erinnerungen

✠

※※※

The Year of Three Kaisers

HE PERIOD of relatively good health for Bismarck that began in the late spring of 1886 continued through the *Septennat* election in February 1887 and the legislative victories that followed. In January 1887 he did complain to Busch of chest pains, which he attributed to a "lung inflammation," a self-diagnosis that Busch doubted, because "he looked quite healthy and rosy."[1] In March Crown Prince Rudolf of Habsburg found him looking well, although thinner than expected and short of breath at the end of a long talk.[2] By April satisfaction over his recent domestic political victory had begun to fade, and again he complained about ailments, insomnia, and overwork imposed by colleagues.[3] By May rheumatism afflicted various parts of his body and in the summer facial neuralgia returned to plague him, hindering speech, chewing, and yawning. In June Lucius reported that for sleep he frequently resorted to morphine, which Schweninger finally had to forbid.[4] As in the previous year he sought relief by fleeing from Berlin to Friedrichsruh (June 16–July 12), Varzin (July 14–August 11), Kissingen (August 13–September 8), and back to Friedrichsruh (September 13–January 28). On these journeys he stopped briefly in the capital; his longest stay (November 15–22) was made necessary by the visit of Tsar Alexander III.[5] The occasion demanded standing, speaking, and gustatory "excesses" that left him exhausted. Again Schweninger administered morphine to induce sleep. The chancellor left Berlin on November 22 to avoid all contact with the Reichstag, which convened two days later.[6]

In the country Bismarck's daily life followed a set routine. To get seven hours of sleep cost him eleven to twelve hours in bed. During the day four hours were spent in the open air, walking, riding, or driving. Three to four hours of work were still the most he could manage. Instructions and dispatches had to be dictated to his aides. To affix his signature so that it looked authentic required great effort with his weakened fingers. Standing was diffi-

---

[1] Moritz Busch, *Tagebuchblätter* (Leipzig, 1899), III, 211.

[2] GW, VIII, 557.

[3] Busch, *Tagebuchblätter*, III, 218.

[4] GW, VIc, 361; Freiherr Lucius von Ballhausen, *Bismarck-Erinnerungen* (Stuttgart, 1920), pp. 392, 394, 395, 406.

[5] Horst Kohl, ed., *Fürst Bismarck: Regesten zu einer wissenschaftichen Biographie des ersten Reichskanzlers* (Leipzig, 1892), II, 439ff.

[6] Walter Bussmann, ed., *Staatssekretär Graf Herbert von Bismarck: Aus seiner politischen Privatkorrespondenz* (Göttingen, 1964), p. 482.

cult, and, while indoors, he had to lie on a sofa. No business was permitted during the evening hours; after dinner he read light novels and smoked his four pipefuls, finding the narcotic effect soothing, the smoke distracting.[7] When Schweninger was absent, his old eating habits returned. Admonishments from Johanna had little effect; he kept "right on eating huge portions" of every dish.[8] The doctor had forbidden alcohol at mealtime, but the prince made up for that during his daily drive with bottles of beer concealed under the coachman's seat.[9]

"I am very dependent on the course of business," he wrote son Bill in late 1887. "If it is wearisome or troublesome and superfluous, I sleep badly and am then tired and dissatisfied with myself and others. After a good night the world looks different to me, and I can walk and ride like a robust old man." Two weeks later he told Prince Wilhelm that he was so exhausted by "pains and insomnia" that he found it difficult to master the daily flow of business. "Every exertion increases this weakness."[10] Friedrichsruh, he claimed, was ideal for him. Fast communication with Berlin kept official business flowing, while the distance enabled him to avoid dinners, receptions, and unwelcome guests.[11] By the end of 1887, however, even country life had begun to pall. "It does not much matter to me whether I am here or there [Berlin]," he wrote to Bill. "Wretched politics has deprived me of pleasure in the hunt, in socializing, and in music, and gradually I will lose my love for field and forest. I don't cling so much to country life as in earlier years. Unfortunately, the inner emptiness is increasing and the bodily strength is declining. But that is natural and ultimately bearable."[12] In this mood and condition he endured the grand finale of the diplomatic crisis of 1885–1887 whose peaceful resolution was in large part owed to his undiminished diplomatic skill. From March to June 1888 his strength and nerves were severely taxed by Kaiser Wilhelm's death after a brief illness, the final illness and death of Friedrich III, and the succession of Wilhelm II.

Grand Finale of the Eastern Crisis

The exclusion of Boulanger from the French cabinet formed on May 16, 1887, and the signing of the reinsurance treaty on June 18 did not end the dual crisis with France and Russia. The general's continuing popularity with

[7] GW, VIII, 587, 592, 620; XIV, 985. Hans Rothfels, ed., *Bismarck-Briefe* (Göttingen, 1955), pp. 413–414.

[8] GW, VIII, 643, 648–649. Even when Schweninger was present, he occasionally took advantage of the doctor's short-sightedness to sneak a forbidden portion. GW, VIII, 582–583.

[9] GW, VIII, 646, 671–672.

[10] Bussmann, ed., *Herbert von Bismarck*, p. 456; GW, XIV, 982; VIc, 382.

[11] GW, VIII, 587.

[12] GW, XIV, 982.

the volatile Parisian public caused the government to transfer him to a remote command in the Auvergne. On the day of his departure thousands stormed the railway station and blocked the train with their bodies. Boulanger had to be smuggled out of Paris by a different route. In exile he wooed and won royalist financial and political support. His cause was helped by a sordid scandal that tangentially involved and forced the resignation of President Jules Grévy, an event that discredited the republic and strengthened rightist political movements. The possibility grew that Boulanger might rally a coalition of dissident forces eager to sweep the republicans out of the Élysee.

The menace of the Boulanger movement for Germany stimulated public agitation in Russia among those who wished to reorient Russian foreign policy away from Berlin. The death of Katkov on August 1, 1887, removed from the scene the most eloquent spokesman for this viewpoint. Yet Déroulède, who attended the funeral, was well received by Russian generals and officials, and Russian newspapers continued to propagate Katkov's views, but in more radical form. Katkov had written of the need for a "free hand"; they advocated openly an alliance with France. Within the government were powerful men who shared their advocacy—Minister of Interior Tolstoy, Minister of War Wannowsky, Chief of the General Staff Obruchev, Minister of Finance Vishnegradsky, and Director General of the Holy Synod Pobedonostsev (whose advice to the tsar went far beyond church affairs). Since Giers clung to his earlier policy, the issue now was whether Alexander III would listen to him or them. Bismarck warned that a mistrustful Germany would be compelled to seek allies, strengthen its armed forces, and reduce its support for Russian policy in Bulgaria and Constantinople.[13]

Once certain that Battenberg would not return, the Bulgarians elected (July 3, 1887) Prince Ferdinand of Saxe-Coburg-Kohary to the vacant throne. Ferdinand was an officer in the Austro-Hungarian army, and the Russians regarded him as a puppet of the Habsburg government. Bismarck resolutely refused to support the Coburg candidacy and backed subsequent Russian efforts to unseat Ferdinand and install a pro-Russian regent. But he adamantly refused, as in the past, to take the initiative the Russians tried to thrust on him, not only because German interests were not directly involved, but also because he feared that, if the initiative failed, Germany would draw the blame. When it appeared as though the Russians might invade Bulgaria, he urged Austria to exercise restraint. Let the Russians become militarily engaged in Bulgaria, he argued again, and they would be far more vulnerable to Austrian pressure. "The eastern question is a game of patience [Geduldspiel]. Whoever can wait will win."[14] Continuing attacks in the Russian press and repeated requests from Alexander III for German support (showing that the

[13] GP, V, 295–312, 315–318; VI, 110ff.
[14] GP, V, 160–206; quotation on p. 195.

tsar had expected far more from Germany than the wording of the reinsurance treaty required) led Bismarck to encourage the signers of the Mediterranean agreement to strengthen their alliance. To that end Bismarck joined Austria and Italy in supporting British efforts to negotiate favorable terms with the Porte for the eventual withdrawal of British troops from Egypt.[15]

By supporting Britain in Egypt, Russia in Bulgaria, and Austria in Serbia, Bismarck strove to maintain the balance between the great powers and thereby hold open Germany's options. In August 1887 Lord Salisbury, again prime minister, threatened to upset the balance in Britain's favor by suggesting vaguely that England might come to terms with Russia, which could only mean the surrender of Constantinople and the Straits to the latter. Bismarck detected Salisbury's probable motive—to make Germany more amenable to English policy by threatening rapprochement with Russia and conceivably with France.[16]

The great powers, Bismarck meditated, were engaged in a waiting game— France for Germany's involvement with Russia, Russia for Germany's involvement with France, Britain for Germany's involvement with either or both. To deflect Salisbury's maneuver was not difficult. Bismarck replied that Germany would be pleased to second a British initiative to come to terms with Russia in the Balkans but not at the cost of Austria. To prevent Austria from outbidding Britain in competition for Russia's favor, he proposed an agreement between the three powers to demarcate spheres of influence in the Near East. Italy, he suggested, might be bought off with Abyssinia. France was the only bellicose power in Europe; its isolation would secure the peace. France would never enjoy Russian support for an attack on Germany, but, even if this most improbable event should happen, Germany could deploy a million soldiers on each frontier and in alliance with Austria would not be in a desperate situation. His bluff called, Salisbury retreated from his suggestion, and Bismarck likewise backed off. Germany, he declared, was interested in a Balkan settlement only if Britain took the initiative and if it included Austria and Italy.[17]

The continuing pressure from Russia, the diminished but still active threat of Boulanger, the signs of rapprochement and even collaboration between Russia and France, and the uncertainty of Salisbury's course—all of these factors compelled Bismarck to cement further the relationship with Austria. At Bad Gastein in August 1887 the Kaisers Wilhelm and Franz Joseph met for

[15] William L. Langer, *European Alliances and Alignments* (2d ed., New York, 1950), pp. 428–429; Hajo Holborn, ed., *Aufzeichnungen und Erinnerungen aus dem Leben des Botschafters Joseph Maria von Radowitz* (Stuttgart, 1925), II, 265–269. Owing to French and Russian opposition, the convention negotiated by Sir Henry Drummond Wolff remained a dead letter with the consequence that the British occupation of Egypt was perpetuated.

[16] GP, IV, 335–337, 339, 342–343; V, 186.

[17] GP, IV, 337–349.

that purpose, and the Austrians were gratified to hear Wilhelm advocate vigorously the alliance he had opposed in 1879. And yet Bismarck remained adamant in his determination not to support any aggressive action by Austria in the Balkans unless supported by Britain. To shore up the defenses against Russian expansion in that region, an extended Mediterranean agreement was the proper instrument, not the Dual Alliance. The Mediterranean agreement had to be given a capacity for action in the Near East as potent as that already gained for the western Mediterranean. The succession of Francesco Crispi as Italian prime minister and foreign minister on August 8 offered an opportunity. Crispi had long agitated for a more positive role for Italy in the Mediterranean and North Africa; commercial and political frictions with France made him eager to establish still closer relations with Britain and the central powers.[18]

Bismarck received Crispi on October 1–3, 1887, at Friedrichsruh and readily accepted the minister's proposal that the Triple Alliance be buttressed by a military convention. Germany, Bismarck declared, wanted peace but did not fear war. It had the capability to put into the field one and a half million men immediately, three million ultimately, and hence could meet any test of strength against France and Russia. Yet he also stressed again that Germany had no interest in blocking Russia from Bulgaria or even the Straits. Such conquests could only weaken Russia by thinning out the forces defending its frontier against Austria. Germany would not participate in such a conflict as long as France remained quiet. But Crispi took a different view, as Bismarck undoubtedly foresaw. Once in possession of Constantinople, Russia would be the "master of the Mediterranean" and hence dominant not only in the Near East but also in Europe. The interested powers must prevent Russia from exploiting the continuing decay of the Ottoman Empire. In reply Bismarck expressed pleasure that Italy, Austria, and Britain had joined hands in the eastern question. He urged Crispi to cooperate with Kálnoky in preserving the peace in that region, a task that could perhaps be "the subject of a special treaty." If peace could not be preserved, Germany would act as the "rear guard" of its allies.[19]

Evidently on Vienna's initiative the representatives of Austria, Italy, and England at Constantinople drafted an agreement, whose purpose was to bolster Turkey against Russia by guaranteeing the status quo in the eastern Balkans. Before acceding to this extension of the Mediterranean coalition, however, the Salisbury government wanted information from Bismarck on two subjects: the actual terms of the Austro-German alliance of 1879, showing

[18] Langer, *Alliances and Alignments*, pp. 432–433, 445–446; GP, VI, 24–28; W. N. Medlicott, "The Mediterranean Agreements," *Slavonic Review*, 5 (1926), pp. 66–68, and "Austria-Hungary and the War Danger of 1887," *Slavonic Review*, 6 (1927), pp. 437–441.

[19] GW, VIII, 571–577; GP, IV, 351–352; VI, 228–229; Thomas Palamenghi-Crispi, ed., *The Memoirs of Francesco Crispi* (London, 1912), II, 211–222.

the extent of Germany's commitment to the Habsburg monarchy, and assurances that, when Kaiser Wilhelm died, his heir apparent (Prince Wilhelm of Prussia), would not change the direction of German policy. (Wilhelm's pro-Russian sympathies were well known.) Bismarck readily complied with the first request, since he had already informed the Russian government of the terms of the Dual Alliance during the negotiation of the reinsurance treaty.[20] On November 22, 1887, he transmitted to London, in reply to the second request, another of those masterful dispatches carefully calculated to disarm the recipient.

By this "most unusual step" he explained why future German monarchs, whatever their personal sympathies, could not deviate from the established course. None could impose war on a nation of 50 million people without convincing them of its necessity. An army based on universal service could not be sent into battle for purely dynastic purposes as in earlier times, but only to defend the fatherland, its independence, and its newfound unity. The German empire had three great powers on its open frontiers. Without an unweakened Austria as an ally, Germany would be isolated vis-à-vis France and Russia. England, Austria, and Germany were "saturated" powers and hence pacific and conservative in foreign policy. England and Austria accepted Germany's new status, but France and Russia did not. French hostility could be explained by its centuries-old tradition of aggression toward Germany and by the "national character" of its people. Russia was being propelled toward war by radical dissidents who wanted to embarrass the tsarist regime, monarchists who wanted to suppress radicalism and distract liberals from constitutional reform, and generals eager to further their careers.

To restrain bellicose neighbors, he continued, Germany needed allies. If compelled to fight alone, however, its situation would not be desperate. But even a successful war would be a "great calamity" that Germany would try to avoid by accommodating Russia. If supported by friendly powers with similar interests, any German Kaiser would want to defend the independence of those powers that were also satisfied with the status quo in Europe. Germany would avoid war with Russia as long as that course was compatible with German honor and security and the independence of Austria-Hungary was not jeopardized. He hoped that those powers that, unlike Germany, had interests to defend in the Near East would combine to keep the Russian sword in its scabbard or to deflect it if a rupture came. Germany would remain neutral unless Austria's independence were threatened by Russian aggression or England or Italy were invaded by French armies.[21]

This document is remarkable for its many combinations—contingent threat, promise without commitment, self-reliance without boastfulness,

[20] GP, IV, 353–356; 367–373.
[21] GP, IV, 376–380.

independence and cooperativeness, freedom and necessity, frankness and vagueness—all bound together by a persuasive logic specially designed for the recipients. And yet the document was notably consistent with the policy Bismarck had enunciated on many other occasions in London, Petersburg, Vienna, Rome, Paris, and even in the Reichstag and inspired press. At Downing Street it achieved his purpose by enabling Salisbury to persuade his colleagues to conclude the Second Mediterranean Agreement by an exchange of notes with Kálnoky and Crispi on December 12 and 16, 1887. The purport of this agreement was that the three powers would not tolerate a change in the status quo of the Near East as established in earlier treaties and would not permit Turkey to part with either its remaining rights in Bulgaria or its sovereign power over the Straits. The three signatory powers would defend the independence of Turkey and the integrity of its territories.[22] Although Salisbury insisted that the treaty remain secret in order to avoid a stormy debate in the British Parliament, he, Crispi, and Kálnoky had already delivered speeches establishing the determination of their countries to defend Bulgaria against any breach of the treaties in which it figured.[23] Their common position was publicly known, even though their actual commitments were not.

During the last half of 1887 relations between Germany and Russia continued to deteriorate despite the reinsurance treaty. The Russian press continued to hammer away at Germany and Austria for their presumed intrigues against Russia in securing the election of Ferdinand and stiffening Bulgarian resistance. "My father," Herbert wrote to Bernhard von Bülow (counselor of embassy in Petersburg), "is *really* embittered, and I almost more so, by Russian shamelessness, which has now reached its apogee." On his father's orders Herbert sought to "electrify" Giers with a double barrage of protest (through the embassies in Berlin and Petersburg) against the continuing failure of the Russian government to check anti-German excesses of its press and officials. Germany, they said, could no longer accept lame excuses that the tsar was apathetic, his ministers in disarray, the press unimportant.[24]

Since June the Berlin stock market had been unsettled by government-inspired newspaper stories about the instability of Russian securities, whose prices declined accordingly, along with the value of the ruble. On November 10, 1887, the German government, acting on Bismarck's advice, ordered the *Reichsbank* to cease using Russian securities as collateral (the famous *Lombardverbot*)—a practice unique to the *Reichsbank* among European banks. Sell orders inundated the bourse and the price of Russian state bonds fell dramatically. By this maneuver Bismarck wished to make it difficult for Petersburg to finance the military campaign forecast by the Prussian general staff for the

---

[22] GP, IV, 381–394; Alfred Pribram, *The Secret Treaties of Austria-Hungary, 1879–1914* (Cambridge, Mass., 1920), I, 124–133; Medlicott, "Austria-Hungary," pp. 84–86.

[23] Langer, *Alliances and Alignments*, p. 441.

[24] Bussmann, ed., *Herbert von Bismarck*, pp. 472–475; GP, V, 293–296.

following spring. But he also hoped to demonstrate again the indispensability of German friendship for Russia. Here also economics yielded to politics rather than the reverse. Low prices in Berlin enabled Russian capitalists to repurchase their securities at favorable rates but also forced the Russians to turn to other markets, particularly Paris, in search of new credits and capital. German financiers lost and French financiers gained a profitable source of investment. And the switch to Paris reinforced the arguments of those in both France and Russia who believed their two countries were destined by an identity of interests to ally in European politics.[25]

On the day after the *Lombardverbot* Bismarck took the train to Berlin to confer with Alexander III on the state of German-Russian relations. For four months the tsar and his family had been visiting relatives in Copenhagen, and the European press had speculated avidly on whether he would use the opportunity for a state visit in Germany. Measles delayed the Romanov family's departure from Copenhagen until mid-November. Rather than risk a rough North Sea voyage the tsar returned by rail via Berlin, where he paused for eleven hours on November 18, just long enough to pay his respect to the Kaiser, give Bismarck an audience, and attend a state dinner (at which Bismarck, to his outrage, was placed out of the tsar's earshot). The audience lasted one and a half hours, during which the tsar chain-smoked nervously, showing, so Bismarck thought, the consequence of having been so long in "entirely Guelphish company, particularly that of [Denmark's] Queen Louise." With him tsar Alexander carried four incriminating letters, purportedly written by Prince Alexander of Bulgaria, that contradicted Bismarck's repeated assertions that he had not promoted the Coburg candidacy to the throne in Sofia. The tsar already had reason to believe that the documents were forgeries, and Bismarck convinced him that this was indeed the case.

During the rest of the interview Bismarck, according to his own account, criticized Russian journalists and generals, whose chauvinistic agitation made it difficult for Germany to remain friendly. Sooner or later their calumnies, if unchecked, might force the Russian government into a war that could only "unleash revolutions in more than one country." Respect for Russian power compelled Germany to seek allies everywhere. With a well-trained army of four million men (including reserves), Germany would find such a war "ruinous but not desperate." Alexander promised to discipline Russia's press and bureaucracy. He averred, furthermore, that he would never attack Germany, that he had no interest in allying with France, and that he would have nothing to do "with that animal Boulanger." But the tsar complained bitterly about Austria's conduct, whereupon Bismarck reminded him of Germany's

[25] GP, V, 327, 330–337; VI, 3ff.; Bussmann, ed., *Herbert von Bismarck*, p. 456; SEG (1887), p. 157; George F. Kennan, *The Decline of Bismarck's European Order: Franco-Russian Relations, 1875–1890* (Princeton, 1979), pp. 342–346; Ludwig Raschdau, *Unter Bismarck und Caprivi* (Berlin, 1939), pp. 18–19.

obligation to defend Austria against Russian attack.[26] After Alexander's train had clattered eastward into the night, Bismarck sought, by publicizing both the forgery and the tsar's reassuring words, to advertise the divergence between the tsar's own friendly demeanor toward Germany and the hostile intrigues of those seeking to change it.[27]

The chancellor, however, had cause to worry about intrigues in his own camp, emboldened by his extended absence from Berlin at a critical time. During the final months of 1887 German and Austrian generals judged that Russia was preparing for war in early 1888 and believed the moment to be favorable for preventive action by the dual powers. Helmuth von Moltke, chief of the Prussian general staff, and Count Alfred von Waldersee, army quartermaster-general, advocated a winter campaign to forestall the Russian attack. But again Bismarck rejected a "prophylactic attack" and urged Austria to avoid all provocation, while strengthening its forces on the Galician frontier. Once more the Austrians were reminded that the alliance of 1879 provided only for a defensive war against Russian aggression. The Austrians, he believed, should avoid any "aggressive action" against Russia unless absolutely certain that England would participate. In that case "the whole picture" would change, and Austria could risk war with Russia even without German participation.[28]

On November 24 the German government presented to the Reichstag a new military bill, which proposed to extend the age limit for service in the reserve to forty-five and thereby add 600,000 men to the German army in the event of mobilization. At Crispi's suggestion negotiations were begun in late October 1887 for an agreement providing for the transport and deployment

[26] GP, V, 313, 320–324, 338–350; Lucius, Bismarck-Erinnerungen, pp. 404–405; Bussmann, ed., Herbert von Bismarck, p. 482.

[27] SEG (1887), pp. 180–184.

[28] GP, VI, 21, 24–29, 302, 309; Ferdinand von Schmerfeld, Graf Moltke: Die deutschen Aufmarschpläne 1871–1890. Forschungen und Darstellungen aus dem Reichsarchiv (Berlin, 1929), pp. 137–146; Heinrich Otto Meisner, ed., Denkwürdigkeiten des General-Feldmarschalls Alfred Grafen von Waldersee (3 vols., Stuttgart, 1922–1923), I, 333–339, 421–423; Radowitz, Aufzeichnungen und Erinnerungen, II, 277; Wilhelm von Schweinitz, ed., Denkwürdigkeiten des Botschafters General von Schweinitz (2 vols., Berlin, 1927), II, 350–351, 353, 355; Norman Rich and M. H. Fisher, eds., The Holstein Papers: The Memoirs, Diaries and Correspondence of Friedrich von Holstein, 1837–1909 (4 vols., Cambridge, Eng., 1955–1963), III, 233–254; Bussmann, ed., Herbert von Bismarck, pp. 488–496. Canis's thesis—that Bismarck wished Austria to undertake war against Russia without the expectation of German support, a conflict that would have "opened the way" for a German preventive attack on France—is interesting but improbable. Bismarck was too conscious of the imponderables that arise once large armies begin to march to have considered unleashing simultaneously two wars of this magnitude on the European continent in the expectation that they would remain separate. His vision of Germany's security focused on the preservation of the balance of power system, which would have been gravely disturbed by the victory of either of the eastern great powers over the other. See Konrad Canis, Bismarck und Waldersee (Berlin-East, 1980), pp. 207–240.

of Italian armies to the Rhenish and Rumanian frontiers on the outbreak of war. Vienna proposed similar discussions between the Prussian and Austrian general staffs. On December 17 the Prussian generals met with the Kaiser to discuss the Russian danger. Wilhelm agreed to the military negotiation, but minimized the Russian danger. At Friedrichsruh Bismarck was vexed by the interference of the generals in his foreign policy prerogatives and alarmed by the inclusion in the conference (on Waldersee's initiative) of the impression-able Prince Wilhelm. He too agreed to the military talks with Austria, but as a demonstration of Germany's good faith. When the German officers assigned to the negotiation permitted themselves to be drawn into a discussion of mil-itary cooperation in an offensive strike against Russia, he objected vigorously. To him this constituted an expansion of the casus foederis and an unallowable intrusion by the military into the political sphere. The consultation ceased, much to the distress of Franz Joseph, Kálnoky, and the Austrian generals. On February 3, 1888, the Austro-German treaty of 1879 (minus the article limit-ing it to three years) was published, on Bismarck's insistence, to end specu-lation in the Hungarian parliament on whether Austria could expect German support in a war with Russia. Hungarians were gratified to learn that the treaty was defensive in import, while Russians were sobered by the revelation that they were its object.[29]

Three days later Bismarck, in defending the military bill, delivered to great applause in the Reichstag another memorable speech, in which he recounted in detail his version of Germany's disappointing relationship with Russia over two decades and why it had led to the Austrian alliance. Although the two-hour speech was generally conciliatory, the peroration reverberated like a cannonade through the German and European press: "We Germans fear God and nothing else in the world!" The rest of the sentence—"and it is precisely the fear of God that leads us to love peace and to nurture it"—was soon for-gotten. Afterward Bismarck walked back to the chancellery with difficulty through streets choked by cheering crowds. Herbert cleared the way with back and elbows. It was, he said, "as though war had been declared." Two days later the Reichstag approved the military bill without further debate.[30]

In his speech and in dispatches Bismarck asserted that Germany relied on tsar Alexander's word that Russia did not intend to attack Germany. Indeed, he appears not to have doubted that Alexander himself was peacefully in-clined. The relocation of military garrisons from Russia's interior to the Polish and Galician frontiers that aroused the generals of the dual powers was for Alexander a purely defensive move necessitated by the inferiority of Russia's

[29] GP, V, 282–290; VI, 23, 55–87, 229–261. GP, VI, 65–69; Rich and Fisher, ed., Holstein Papers, III, 233–243; Waldersee, Denkwürdigkeiten, I, 340–341; John Alden Nichols, The Year of the Three Kaisers: Bismarck and the German Succession, 1887–88 (Urbana, 1987), pp. 70–77.

[30] BR, XII, 440–477; SEG (1888), p. 43; Bussmann, ed., Herbert von Bismarck, pp. 504–505.

transport system.[31] Even the most rabid war hawks in Russia, moreover, could scarcely remain unimpressed by mounting evidence that Russia would face most of Europe, if it should undertake to solve the Balkan conundrum by attacking Austria. In that event Germany would stand beside Austria, and behind both would stand England, Italy, and the minor powers of the Mediterranean agreement (a treaty whose existence was unknown but suspected). At one juncture Bismarck even threatened to "stir up the Chinese" against Russia![32]

Faced by such a massive opposition, what was the value to Russia of republican France? The chastened mood that followed these revelations reinforced the position of Giers, who had never wavered in his conviction that Russia's best course was to remain in harmony with Germany and Austria. As the spring of 1888 approached, Giers turned to Berlin for assistance in the Bulgarian affair and received it within the limits Bismarck had long ago established.[33] Although Ferdinand remained on his throne, despite Russian efforts to unseat him, there was no longer any threat that Alexander III would respond to the pressures of chauvinists willing to defy most of Europe in a madcap effort to rescue Russia's "honor" in the Balkans.

The centrality of Bismarck's role throughout the European crisis of 1885–1888 is beyond question. Either directly or indirectly he was responsible for the network of treaties and agreements from whose restraints no aggressive power could escape without catastrophic results. Formally at least, the reinsurance treaty secured Germany against an offensive, though not a defensive, French–Russian alliance. Together the reinsurance treaty and Austro-German alliance established that neither Russia nor Austria could attack the other and expect German support; Germany would support the attacked power; whoever the attacker, Germany would permit neither combatant to suffer a draconian peace that would greatly reduce its weight in the European balance of power. The Mediterranean agreement and subsidiary arrangements presented Russia with the certainty that any attempt to overwhelm Bulgaria or Turkey would set in motion an opposing coalition that, even without German participation, made victory unlikely. Bismarck's aim was primarily that of securing Germany against attack from any direction. To attain that goal it must arm but also ally, avoid wars fought either for preventive purposes or for

[31] GP, V, 324–328; VI, 34–35, 45–51; Schweinitz, *Denkwürdigkeiten*, II, 359–360. Bussmann, ed., *Herbert von Bismarck*, pp. 498–499.

[32] Waldersee, *Denkwürdigkeiten*, I, 334–335. How far Bismarck was willing to go at critical moments in his search for allies can be seen in his consideration of a German-Turkish alliance in 1883 and 1887. GP, III, 263; V, 251. Beginning in 1878 he nurtured the relationship with the Ottoman Empire, including the assignment of German officers and officials as advisers to the Porte (after 1882) and a limited encouragement to German bankers eager to invest in the Baghdad railway after 1888. See Hajo Holborn, *Deutschland und die Türkei, 1878–1890* (Berlin, 1926).

[33] Bussmann, ed., *Herbert von Bismarck*, pp. 506–508; GP, V, 278–279; Schweinitz, *Denkwürdigkeiten*, II, 360–361.

non-German interests, and make certain that, if war came, it would be fought on battlefields remote from Germany's frontiers and be concluded without critical damage to the European balance of power. Bismarck's adroit pursuit of these ends—more than any other factor in the situation—preserved the fragile peace of Europe in the greatest and most complex international crisis since 1815.

With remarkable consistency Bismarck kept insisting that Russia be permitted to satisfy her ambitions in the eastern Balkans. And yet he was so uncertain about Russian policy toward Germany, despite the reinsurance treaty, that he encouraged the powers of the Mediterranean agreement to restrain the tsarist government from taking such a step by solidifying their coalition with further agreements. He urged both sides to pursue their interests, knowing that those interests were in conflict and that the result was likely to be a stalemate in which Russia, as the potential aggressor, would be the frustrated party. He was disinclined to believe that the result would be war, for he judged that Alexander III would not go to that extreme, especially since even the crudest comparison of forces, finances, and domestic stability would show the probability of failure. Even if folly prevailed and war came over the Bulgarian issue, the initial battlefield would be remote from Germany's frontiers, and Germany, by remaining out of the fray, would retain a position of some maneuverability, providing options that might well enable her to limit the struggle in the end. That limitation would preserve the existence of the great powers and likewise the European balance of power system, which was Germany's best chance for survival in the European game of power politics.

Kaiser Friedrich III

In late 1887 Kaiser Wilhelm I reviewed the fleet at Kiel. Determined that sailors on the passing warships should actually see their sovereign, he stood on the open deck of a dispatch boat in raw weather and came away with a severe cold, from which he never fully recovered. On March 3, 1888, another severe throat inflammation led to pneumonia; six days later he died, two weeks short of his ninety-first birthday. In recent months he had become increasingly frail, so inclined to stumble and fall that he had to be constantly attended. To his distress he was unable to maintain his old work routine. Although long expected, Wilhelm's passing was still for Bismarck a personal tragedy. On March 8 he conferred with the Kaiser for the last time—about relations with France and Russia. During the night he was summoned to the palace, where he sat for a few hours by the dying monarch's bedside. At dawn he came away "nervous and depressed," unable to sleep. Later that day he was compelled to give the bad news officially to the Bundesrat and Reichstag, suppressing tears only with great effort. That night he slept with the aid of morphine.[34] To the public the sudden death of a monarch who had ruled for nearly three decades, who had led his country in three wars, and whose person had come to symbolize Germany's unity and power, came as a profound shock. The trauma was heightened by the knowledge that Wilhelm's successor, Crown Prince Friedrich Wilhelm, was already deathly ill.

In January 1887 Crown Prince Friedrich Wilhelm first showed signs of hoarseness, whose persistence led to the summoning of a series of physicians and the detection of a growth on the larynx. Ernst von Bergmann, a celebrated surgeon, advised its removal by an external operation known as thyrotomy. To save him anxiety the patient was not to be told in advance. Here Bismarck intervened and got the Kaiser to demand the crown prince's consent.[35] More physicians were summoned, but all agreed that the growth was

FUNERAL PARADE OF WILHELM I, MARCH 16, 1888. (LANDESBILDSTELLE BERLIN.)

[34] Karl Heinz Börner, *Wilhelm I: Eine Biographie, 1797–1888* (Cologne, 1984), pp. 272–273; *SEG* (1888), pp. 54–55; Horst Kohl, ed., *Anhang zu den Gedanken und Erinnerungen von Otto Fürst von Bismarck* (Stuttgart, 1901), II, 544ff.; Bussmann, ed., *Herbert von Bismarck*, pp. 508–509.

[35] *GW*, XV, 446. Some evidence suggests that Bismarck, skeptical of surgeons as usual, wanted to hinder the operation itself, for it was better to "fall into the hands of God than of men." H. J. Wolf, *Die Krankheit Friedrichs III und ihre Wirkung auf die deutsche und englische Öffentlichkeit* (Berlin, 1958), pp. 10–12, 99–101. If so, his skepticism was not unjustified. Bergmann had performed the operation he advised seven times. Of five cases requiring total removal of the larynx, two had died within two weeks, three within six to eighteenth months. Of the two cases requiring only partial removal, one had died after three months; the other survived. Bergmann's results were reported to be above average at the time. *Ibid.*, p. 85.

cancerous and the operation necessary. Still, only one of the doctors was a throat specialist. Before anything drastic was done, it was decided to consult Sir Morell Mackenzie, a Scottish physician practicing in London and reputedly the best laryngologist in Europe. Two biopsies were taken and examined by Rudolf Virchow, an eminent pathologist, who found no malignancy. Whether they had been taken from the affected place was uncertain. Mackenzie, however, found his skepticism concerning the original diagnosis confirmed. He asserted that the patient could be cured without an operation. Later, when Friedrich Wilhelm's condition worsened, the physicians began to argue. The dispute, which had a national as well as professional character, helped neither the patient nor the cause of historical accuracy.[36]

At the time (May 1887) it was only natural that emperor, empress, crown prince, and crown princess should have accepted Mackenzie's opinion, especially after two later biopsies also produced negative results. On June 3 Friedrich Wilhelm embarked for Britain to attend Queen Victoria's jubilee, then proceeded to the Tyrol, and, when the weather turned bad, to Baveno, Venice, and San Remo. Despite extensive treatment by Mackenzie, improvements were only temporary, and in early November a sudden turn for the worse led Mackenzie to concede that he might have erred. More doctors were summoned. Again an operation was considered. The radical procedure now required would, even if successful, have left the patient permanently voiceless. Friedrich Wilhelm refused the operation. He preferred to die rather than reign as a "mutilated Kaiser." The malignant cells continued to multiply, and a tracheotomy was required to prevent strangulation.[37] In this pathetic condition Kaiser Friedrich III returned to Berlin on March 11 to take up residence at the palace of Charlottenburg. One of his first acts was to request that Bismarck remain in office.

The political views of Friedrich and his relationship to Bismarck have been the subject of considerable speculation. Because of his liberal associations and his daring criticism of the government in 1863,[38] it is often assumed that the tragedy of German liberalism was the longevity of Wilhelm I and the prema-

[36] Wolf, *Krankheit Friedrichs III*, pp. 117ff. The illness and the medical and political disputes that attended it have been the subject of extensive and often impassioned literature. See Frederick Ponsonby, ed., *Letters of the Empress Frederick* (London, 1929), pp. 224ff.; Egon C. Corti, *The English Empress* (London, 1957), pp. 235ff.; Michael Freund, *Das Drama der 99 Tage: Krankheit und Tod Friedrichs III* (Berlin, 1966); Erich Eyck, "The Empress Frederick," *The Quarterly Review*, 289 (1951), pp. 355–366. It appears, however, that Crown Princess Victoria, "the English Empress" as her detractors called her, has been unfairly made the villainess of the drama. The crown prince's German doctors, not she, selected Mackenzie. That she preferred to believe his assurances that the ailment was nonmalignant and curable is understandable. Wolf, *Krankheit Friedrichs III*, pp. 43ff., 90ff.; Nichols, *Year of Three Kaisers*, pp. 19ff.

[37] Wolf, *Krankheit Friedrichs III*, pp. 25, 56, 90; HW, 272; Ernst Feder, ed., *Bismarcks grosses Spiel: Die geheimen Tagebücher Ludwig Bambergers* (Frankfurt a. M., 1933), p. 478.

[38] See vol. 1, pp. 174–177, 211–215.

ture death of Friedrich III. Had Wilhelm died in 1878 of Nobiling's gunshot or earlier of natural causes, Friedrich would have dismissed Bismarck—so the scenario goes—appointed a liberal cabinet, and begun the conversion to parliamentary government. The power Bismarck had both preserved and acquired for the Hohenzollern monarchy would have become the instrument of its liberalization.[39] Before Friedrich's own death the system would have been irreversibly changed, presuming that their "vassal's loyalty" would have sufficed to prevent ultraconservatives, reactionary officials, and army officers from staging a coup.

These presumptions place too much confidence in Friedrich's liberalism, steadfastness of purpose, and clarity of political understanding. As a child, he was raised in a divided home, frightened by the sternness of his father and aware that his mother, the Weimar princess, judged her son to be of mediocre intellect. After 1855 his father-in-law, Prince Albert, consort of Queen Victoria, became his mentor in liberal politics. In these early years Friedrich Wilhelm, freed by marriage from the highly conservative atmosphere of the Prussian court and a frequent visitor in England, embraced liberalism with the zeal of a religious convert. But Albert died in 1861, the year Wilhelm I ascended the Prussian throne. Friedrich Wilhelm's liberalism, furthermore, was limited in its goals, like that of his associates and of the moderate liberal movement as a whole—aspiring toward German national unity, constitutionalism, centralization, the rule of law, economic freedom, and freedom of opinion, but not necessarily toward parliamentary government.[40]

Like right-wing liberals in general, Friedrich Wilhelm was powerfully influenced by the achievement of many of these objectives under Bismarck's leadership. There could be no doubt that the man in the Wilhelmstrasse had brought the Hohenzollern dynasty to a new peak of power and glory. A handsome man of kingly stature and appearance, the crown prince had great reverence for the Hohenzollern tradition, the trappings of kingship, and the majesty of empire. Evidence of this can be seen in his obsession with the imperial title ("Kaiser madness," Bismarck called it) during 1866–1871, his absorption in the heraldry and ceremony of the coronation of 1871, his readiness, if necessary, to use force in 1870–1871 against south German governments, and his thoughts about reducing the monarchies created by Napoleon to the status of grand duchies.[41] Yet he had sufficient modesty to realize that as a com-

[39] The persistence of his view can be seen in Felix von Eckardt, *Ein unordentliches Leben: Lebenserinnerungen* (Düsseldorf, 1967), p. 13.

[40] For accounts of Friedrich Wilhelm's development, the influences upon him, and the nature of his views, see Andreas Dorpalen, "Emperor Frederick III and the German Liberal Movement," *American Historical Review*, 54 (1948–1949), pp. 1–31; Nichols, *Year of Three Kaisers*, pp. 7ff.

[41] Vol. 1, pp. 499–500; Dorpalen, "Emperor Frederick III," pp. 19–21. In anticipation of his coming reign the crown prince proposed to Bismarck that he take the title Friedrich IV, thus identifying the second with the first (medieval) empire. But Bismarck replied emphatically that

manding general in 1866 and 1870 he owed his martial successes to the brilliance of subordinates, particularly General Blumenthal, his chief of staff.[42]
Hans Delbrück, family tutor and later an eminent historian, wrote of him,
"He was somewhat more progressive and tolerant than the groups that customarily surround a prince and king, but he remained basically the Prussian
officer." In the struggles over the iron budget he stood on the side of the
crown. "We must never have a parliamentary army," he told Delbrück.[43]

During the 1870s the crown prince maintained contacts with important
liberals, particularly those in the middle of the movement (for example,
Forckenbeck). Like them, he hoped to reunite the liberal parties.[44] But Forckenbeck's attempt to rally all liberals to the cause of free trade in May 1879
proved belated and futile. Nor did the Secession of 1881 succeed in becoming
the nucleus of a liberal reunion. During these critical years the middle group
from which Friedrich Wilhelm might have drawn his cabinet declined in
number, importance, and political clout. The Secession itself was swallowed
up by progressives in the fusion of 1884. Eugen Richter, who became the
practical dictator of the new Freedom party, was not one with whom Friedrich
Wilhelm could have governed. The polarization of German politics left him
without a base for the political course he might have followed.

Naturally the crown prince's views were a matter of concern and anxiety
for the Kaiser. After recovering from Nobiling's buckshot in 1878, Wilhelm
tried repeatedly to ascertain his son's views, but "Fritz" was silent or evasive.
Bismarck sought to still the father's anxiety by questioning the crown prince's
"basic" liberalism. The chancellor predicted that Friedrich Wilhelm, if he
should start off on a liberal course as Kaiser, would soon abandon it.[45] Bismarck's assessment of Friedrich Wilhelm was based not only on his longtime
study of the crown prince's character and attitudes but also on the conver-
gence of their views concerning the eastern crisis in the late 1870s and on the
necessity of the Austrian alliance. During the 1880s Bismarck repeatedly asserted in private that the crown prince had asked him to remain in office when
the throne changed hands.[46] In 1885, when Wilhelm's end appeared near,
the chancellor and heir to the throne conferred, and Friedrich Wilhelm expressed his satisfaction over the concurrence of their views. Yet Bismarck was
leery of "experiments" in which he might be asked to participate under the

the two empires had no connection with another, advising the numeral III, which Friedrich
would bear as king of Prussia. Lucius, *Bismarck-Erinnerungen*, p. 423.

[42] Christoph von Tiedemann, *Sechs Jahre Chef der Reichskanzlei unter dem Fürsten Bismarck*
(Leipzig, 1910), p. 215.

[43] Quoted in Dorpalen, "Emperor Frederick III," p. 25.

[44] Dorpalen, "Emperor Frederick III," p. 23; Bamberger, *Bismarcks grosses Spiel*, pp. 331–332;
Hermann Oncken, *Rudolf von Bennigsen* (Stuttgart, 1910), II, 425.

[45] Bismarck to Wilhelm I, July 13, 1879. GW, VIc, 159–160.

[46] Busch, *Tagebuchblätter*, II, 577; III, 88, 94–95, 139, 164–165, 192, 202, 216; GW, VIII,
535.

new regime. He laid down two conditions: "that you want to follow a German rather than a non-German policy and that you do not wish to introduce a parliamentary government." Friedrich Wilhelm dismissed both propositions with a wave of his hand. "No thought of it!" he said.[47]

As he passed his fiftieth year and neared the throne, Crown Prince Friedrich Wilhelm did not possess the firmness of political conviction and self-confidence to chart a new course. In 1884 the liberal deputy Karl Schrader, once a political intimate, wrote to Stauffenberg, "You want to know something about the political views of the crown prince. I am afraid I can tell you less about them than I used to, for I have seen neither him nor the crown princess for a long time. They have become very careful in their contacts with liberal people; it seems that word has been passed around to avoid everything that might annoy Bismarck."[48] The heir to the crown sought in advance of his advent to power to make sure that the man who had directed Prussian and German politics for more than two decades would remain in the driver's seat. He shrank from the awesome responsibility of becoming the world's most powerful ruler (measured by autocratic authority and military and industrial strength) with new and untried hands on the throttle. What he had decided in health became doubly necessary in sickness.

Ninety-Nine Days

Bismarck often said that he would decline to remain in office after Wilhelm's death, that he was too old and ailing to serve under a new monarch and wanted only to retire in peace to his estates.[49] But as the time approached, he began to speak also of his duty as a royal vassal to respond to the king's command![50] On March 11, 1888, he met Kaiser Friedrich's train, returning from San Remo, at Leipzig and was "repeatedly embraced and kissed" by the new monarch. On the following day the official *Reichsanzeiger* printed two proclamations: one addressed "To my people!", the other "To my dear prince!" They were well written, not the work of a sick man; in fact, they had been drafted in 1885 by Friedrich in collaboration with close friends (Albrecht von Stosch, Heinrich Geffcken, Franz von Roggenbach, Heinrich von Friedberg,

[47] Lucius, *Bismarck-Erinnerungen*, pp. 324, 338, 396; GW, XV, 445.

[48] To Stauffenberg, Aug. 21, 1884, HW, II, 417–418; translation from Dorpalen, "Emperor Frederick III," p. 24.

[49] Busch, *Tagebuchblätter*, II, 577; III, 88, 164–165, 192; GW, VIII, 410, 441; Lucius, *Bismarck-Erinnerungen*, pp. 359–360.

[50] GW, XIV, 963–964; Moritz Busch, *Bismarck: Some Secret Pages of His History* (New York, 1898), II, 395. Whatever the unconscious motivation, the sentiment was probably a genuine expression of Bismarck's royalism. Despite all that divided them, he was deeply moved—to the point of tears—by the news that Friedrich Wilhelm's illness was terminal. Philipp zu Eulenburg-Hertefeld, *Aus 50 Jahren* (Berlin, 1923), pp. 139–140.

BISMARCK AS HAMLET AT THE CASKET OF WILHELM I. *LE DON QUICHOTTE*, PARIS, MARCH 17, 1888.

and Baron von Stockmar).[51] Both documents stressed the continuity of the new regime with the old. The first spoke of the great achievements of Wilhelm I, of the "position of power" united Germany had attained that fulfilled the yearnings and exceeded the hopes "of every German heart" and also of the following years of peace that had fortified the solidarity of the empire. "I have received all of the rights and duties that are associated with the crown

[51] Martin Philippson, *Das Leben Kaiser Friedrichs III* (Wiesbaden, 1908), p. 412; Bussmann, ed., *Herbert von Bismarck*, p. 510.

of my house. I am determined to preserve those rights faithfully in the time given to my government by God's will." His powers would be used to promote peace and the public welfare and he expected to rely on the "inseparable union between prince and people, which, independent of every change in the life of the state," had always been the foundation of the Hohenzollern crown.

His message to Bismarck paid tribute to the adviser who had given direction to German policy under Wilhelm I. The established constitutional order must be protected as much as possible from shocks resulting from frequent changes in the laws and institutions of the state—especially in the powers of the states, the Reichstag, and the crown. He was determined to hold constitutions inviolable, to preserve the Hohenzollern tradition of religious toleration, to promote the economic welfare of all classes, to seek social reform within the possibilities open to the state, to make higher education available to ever wider circles of the population, to consider any proposal (including a curb on the independent power of local governments to impose taxes) for financial reform that did not impose new burdens, to promote art and science, and to lead the country, with the trusting cooperation of all classes, to new heights of achievement.[52]

Certainly there was little in either document (except perhaps the proposal for more higher education) to cause Bismarck concern. On March 13 he reported to the Prussian cabinet, "I feel relieved of the great concern I had that I would have to fight with a dying man against inappropriate intentions even to the point of demanding my release from office. Everything is going easily and pleasantly with his majesty, like a *jeu de roulette*. . . . The Kaiser wishes to make no changes at all in the cabinet, neither do I. This is no time to change course. In view of his earlier utterances in younger years, there was reason to fear he would pursue all kinds of deviant aims—but I do not fear that any more!"[53] Yet on March 22 he informed the ministers that "the existence of the cabinet is most seriously in question." In nine days the relationship between palace and chancellery had changed.

One issue concerned the power of the Kaiser under the imperial constitution. Friedrich refused to sign two bills passed by the Reichstag. The first extended for two years the antisocialist act (Puttkamer demanded five, but the national liberals insisted on two); the second, initiated by the cartel parties themselves, amended the constitution to prolong the interval between Reichstag elections from three to five years. As Bismarck saw it, the Kaiser's reasons for opposing these statutes were the same as those expressed in the debates by the left-liberal opposition; in addition, Friedrich suspected that the government had coerced the Reichstag impermissibly to secure passage. On

---

[52] *SEG* (1888), pp. 59–62.

[53] Lucius, *Bismarck-Erinnerungen*, p. 433. The official minutes of these meetings do not contain these remarks.

March 21 Bismarck drove to Charlottenburg to deliver his response. To Kaiserin Victoria, who received him, he declared that the cabinet could not accept such a reversal of policy; furthermore, the refusal to sign was contrary to the constitution. The Kaiser had no veto power; once the Prussian government through its delegation to the Bundesrat had voted for a bill, the Kaiser could not legally withhold his signature after it had been passed by both chambers.

Victoria appeared astonished at this unexpected lesson in German constitutionalism. She disappeared into the Kaiser's sickroom and returned in a few minutes with Friedrich's signature still wet on both documents. Again Bismarck smelled feminine intrigue—an attempt by Victoria, supported by three women who attended her that day (Anna von Helmholtz, Baroness von Stockmar, and Henriette Schrader), to intervene between Kaiser and cabinet. Later we shall see that on March 21 he succeeded in wresting from Friedrich and Victoria an order giving Crown Prince Wilhelm, at this point a devoted admirer of the chancellor, extensive powers to deputize for his father. By inserting Wilhelm into the decision process, Bismarck erected another barrier against possible liberal "experiments" by Friedrich, Victoria, and Victoria's feminine coterie. Still he felt as though he and his colleagues "were on infirm footing—standing on a snowbank that can melt away any day."[54]

The metaphor was apt. Early March 1888 was one of the coldest on record, and snow lay in great heaps along the streets of Berlin. At month's end a sudden thaw overfilled the river beds of northern Germany, including the Wipper at Varzin. Flood waters carried away all of the prince's mills, including the newly reconstructed Hammermühle.[55] Simultaneously he had to scramble to keep his political footing.

As Bismarck foresaw, the abdication of Prince Alexander of Battenberg in Bulgaria revived the "Battenberg marriage" project and made it all the more troublesome. Kaiserin Victoria assumed the abdication would remove the political obstacle to the marriage of "Sandro," as he was affectionately known at the palace, to Princess Viktoria.[56] Aware that her time on the throne would be short, she wanted to assure her daughter's happiness. But Bismarck still argued that the marriage would contaminate Germany's relations with Russia. While at Berlin in November 1887 Tsar Alexander showed some continuing sensitivity on the subject of Battenberg. And yet, to Bismarck's vexation, the tsar and Foreign Minister Giers showed no disposition to validate Bismarck's claim that the marriage would be adversely received in Petersburg. On the contrary, Giers appeared to be amused by Bismarck's predicament. Only

---

[54] For Bismarck's account to the Prussian cabinet of the events of March 21, see Lucius, *Bismarck-Erinnerungen*, pp. 437–439; *DZA* Merseburg, Rep. 90a, B, III, 2b, Nr. 6, Bd. 100.

[55] Lucius, *Bismarck-Erinnerungen*, pp. 437, 445; Busch, *Tagebuchblätter*, III, 226.

[56] Rantzau to Herbert Bismarck, Nov. 3, 1885. Bussmann, ed., *Herbert von Bismarck*, pp. 332–333. On the Battenberg marriage affair, see p. 221.

KAISERIN VICTORIA, AS CROWN PRINCESS, IN 1883. (BILDARCHIV PREUSSISCHER KULTURBESITZ.)

PRINCESS VIKTORIA OF PRUSSIA.

(SÜDDEUTSCHER VERLAG.)

ALEXANDER I, PRINCE OF BULGARIA, ABOUT 1890.

(ARCHIV FÜR KUNST UND GESCHICHTE, BERLIN.)

when informed by Ambassador Paul Shuvalov that Bismarck intended to resign over the issue did Alexander, who preferred to keep him in office, declare the marriage "prejudicial" to German-Russian relations.[57]

Obviously the main obstacle to the Battenberg match was no longer Russia but Bismarck. The aging master of *Realpolitik* could not tolerate the prospect of losing his dispute with "the women" at Charlottenburg. In early April he took the issue to the public in inspired, polemical articles in the *Kölnische Zeitung* and other newspapers.[58] Naturally he also summoned Moritz Busch, who was, as always, glad to assist. When they met, the journalist complimented the chancellor on looking "quite well," but Bismarck denied it, complaining of "nervous excitement and sleeplessness," which he attributed to overwork and "the people at Charlottenburg." "Only opium and morphine help me to get any sleep. . . . The doctors urge me to go to the country. Schweninger prophesies that, if I don't do it, I will be afflicted by all kinds of nervous illnesses, including typhus [sic]." He needed, furthermore, to inspect the ruins of his mills at Varzin, whose reconstruction was expected to cost hundreds of thousands. But he could not leave Berlin for fear of what might happen behind his back. His problem was not the new Kaiser, "who is reasonable and shares my views," but "the women who want to have a share in the government." For three and a half years the "present empress" had actively promoted the Battenberg marriage. Queen Victoria—"fond of matchmaking like all old women"—was using the Battenberg affair to drive a wedge between Russia and Germany. It was necessary to protect Friedrich III from "martyrdom" at the hands of his wife. If she won on the marriage issue, this "young and impetuous" woman would prevail in other matters. Bismarck would resign rather than allow Germany to be used by "this Englishwoman," who had always been "a channel for English influence here, an instrument for the furtherance of English interests."[59]

Kaiserin Victoria had replaced the dowager Kaiserin Augusta as the chief object of Bismarck's political misogyny, and against her, as earlier against Augusta, he was willing to inflame German public opinion. Hatred of women with political influence was not, however, the only source of Bismarck's vendetta against the Battenberg marriage. As crown prince, Friedrich III had originally considered the match a mésalliance and was annoyed that the subject kept reappearing. And yet his attitude changed after Prince Alexander's military exploits in 1885–1886, and the prince's courageous return to Sofia for a more dignified abdication made him something of a popular hero in

[57] GP, VI, 281–298; Schweinitz, *Denkwürdigkeiten*, II, 363–365.

[58] Lucius, *Bismarck-Erinnerungen*, pp. 445–448. For excerpts from the press discussion, see SEG (1888), pp. 73–81.

[59] Busch, *Tagebuchblätter*, III, 226–235; Busch, *Secret Pages*, II, 412–420. Both editions of this work must be used here, since the German editors cut out passages they evidently considered defamatory of Kaiserin Victoria.

Germany. According to Prince Wilhelm, who was decidedly opposed to his sister's proposed marriage, his father had shocked their Baden relatives in September 1886 by describing Alexander as a "highly talented prince with outstanding capabilities both as an officer and as a statesman, who must be considered as a prospect for high positions in Germany." As Friedrich Wilhelm neared the throne, reports were widespread that he intended as Kaiser not only to approve the "Battenberg marriage" but also to appoint Alexander governor of the Reichsland (Bismarck: "Only over my dead body"). Some thought it conceivable that the dethroned Sandro might one day resurrect as German chancellor. Friedrich III was in no condition to press for the marriage, but he yielded to his wife's entreaties and his testament instructed Crown Prince Wilhelm as a matter of "filial duty" to insure his sister's happiness. But Wilhelm II ignored the will and forbade the marriage. Sandro consoled himself by wedding an actress.[60]

Another problem that tortured Bismarck's nerves during these weeks was the question of rewards—and punishments. Friedrich wished to begin his reign, as was customary, by elevating some aristocrats to higher titles and by ennobling some persons prominent in government, scholarship, and business, for example, Eduard Simson, Rudolf Gneist, Werner Siemens, and Karl Stumm. (Bismarck favored even more ennoblements than Friedrich proposed in the expectation that greater accessibility would make the nobility more popular.) In addition, the Kaiser proposed to decorate some persons of achievement, including friends and political allies. Among them were names to which Bismarck strongly objected: Rudolf Virchow, Theodor Mommsen, Albert Hänel, Max von Forckenbeck, Baron von Stauffenberg, Georg von Bunsen, and Karl Schrader. All had injured Bismarck in some way over the years by their liberal politics. To him their decoration could only be read as a justification for their opposition to his regime. The most he was willing to concede were medals to Virchow and Forckenbeck, but only for the former's achievements as a scientist and the latter's services to city government.[61] Another issue was Friedrich's desire to dismiss the court preacher and anti-Semitic political agitator Adolf Stöcker. Bismarck's personal distaste for Stöcker was counterbalanced by the preacher's effectiveness in combating liberals and

[60] Bussmann, ed., Herbert von Bismarck, pp. 310–312, 340–341, 377–389, 415– 418. See also Philippson, Leben Kaiser Friedrichs, pp. 425–426; Lucius, Bismarck-Erinnerungen, p. 447; Ponsonby, ed., Letters of Empress Frederick, pp. 293–304, 321; SEG (1889), p. 30. By his marriage Alexander intended to end all speculation concerning his return to Sofia. He abandoned the Battenberg name, took the title Graf von Hartenau, and petitioned Kaiser Franz Joseph for a commission in the Austro-Hungarian army. But he did return to Sofia after all—on his death in 1893 to be buried in Sofia with pomp and circumstance as the "Prince of Bulgaria." Egon C. Corti, Alexander von Battenberg: Sein Kampf mit den Zaren und Bismarck (Vienna, 1920), pp. 335–340.

[61] Lucius, Bismarck-Erinnerungen, pp. 448–450, 453–454; GW, VIc, 389–390; Philippson, Leben Kaiser Friedrichs, p. 421.

socialists ("His mouth is like a sword"). In a Crown Council Friedrich settled for a directive compelling Stöcker to choose between his official position and his political activism—a choice that Stöcker evaded after Friedrich's death. At Easter the Kaiser wished to include in the customary amnesty imprisoned social democrats as well as petty criminals. In this, too, he did not succeed.[62]

Still another issue arose to disturb the last days of Friedrich III. In the footsteps of the Reichstag, the Prussian Chamber of Deputies, followed by the House of Lords, passed a statute extending the interval between Landtag elections from three to five years. In this case the king clearly had the power of veto. For weeks the responsible minister, Puttkamer, delayed presenting the bill to Friedrich for his signature. When he did, the monarch refused to sign. He had a strong distaste not only for the statute, which he thought would weaken parliament, but also for Puttkamer, who, more than any other member of the cabinet, symbolized the reaction of the 1880s. In the waning days of the Landtag session, Rickert and Richter exploited a disputed election (that of the minister's brother Puttkamer-Plauth) to expose again the fear tactics used by the Ministry of Interior to influence the outcome of Prussian elections. In addition, Richter criticized caustically the "hateful manner" in which the cartel press had recently attacked the Kaiserin Victoria.

The signature that he refused Puttkamer, Friedrich gave one day later (May 27) to his old friend Minister of Justice Friedberg. On that evening Bismarck returned from two weeks at Varzin and in his next audience with the Kaiser (May 29) inexplicably undid Friedberg's work. In contrast to Friedrich, he believed the statutes would strengthen the lower chamber. Hence the prince urged Friedrich to show cabinet and chamber who was king in Prussia. "If you believe yourself in the right, you can still prohibit publication." On the note pad that was his only means of communication the monarch replied, "Then I would like not to publish the statute." Before leaving the palace Bismarck sat in the adjutants' chamber describing what had occurred, "merry as an ensign, joking and drinking cognac."[63]

The prince's ministerial colleagues were astounded, particularly Friedberg. "Have I become senile," the minister asked, "or is it someone else!" What, Lucius asked himself, did Bismarck want? When the cabinet discussed the episode on June 1, Bismarck appeared "uncomfortable and even embarrassed." All of his colleagues sided with Friedberg, who maintained that the statute must be published; to delay publication would damage the governmental process itself in the eyes of the public. Bismarck's discourse generally wandered from the subject, although he castigated Richter for his criticism

---

[62] Cabinet meeting of March 22, 1888. *DZA* Merseburg, Rep. 90a, B, III, 2b, Nr. 6, Vol. 100. Crown Council meeting of Mar. 23, 1888. *DZA* Merseburg, Rep. 90a, B, III, 2c, Nr. 3, Bd. IV. Lucius, *Bismarck-Erinnerungen*, pp. 439, 443–445; Philippson, *Leben Kaiser Friedrichs*, pp. 421–422.

[63] Lucius, *Bismarck-Erinnerungen*, pp. 454–455, 458–460; *SBHA* (1888), pp. 1651–1677.

and Puttkamer for his procrastination.[64] In the press there was open speculation over a crisis between crown and cabinet that could only end in Puttkamer's dismissal. But on June 4 Bismarck told Lucius, "In the present circumstances we must all hold firmly together and not let a single person be
expelled. She [Victoria] wants to offer a sacrifice to her progressive friends,
because she is in some things not compos mentis. . . . I will hold tightly on
to my chair and not give it up, even if they want to throw me out." At the
palace there was confusion over why Friedberg could have pressed for a decision with which Bismarck disagreed. In the end Puttkamer was the sacrificial
lamb. The law was published, the minister dismissed; the rest of the cabinet
remained in office.[65]

Friedberg was uncertain whether Bismarck's action on May 29 was the result of a deep-laid plot or sudden inspiration.[66] If the prince's ulterior motive
was, as some suggest, to get rid of Puttkamer, that could have easily been done
without the donnybrook he produced and without putting the monarch, to
whom he had so recently given a lecture on German constitutional law, in a
dubious legal position, that is, a refusal to promulgate a law properly passed
and signed. Bismarck's action was a callous and frivolous deed, creating an
unnecessary crisis that plagued the last hours of a ruler who was desperately
trying, with admirable success, to die like a soldier-king—erect, dignified,
conscientiously fulfilling his duties, uncomplaining to the end. On June 13,
less than a week after the resolution of the last cabinet crisis, Kaiser Friedrich
began to fail. Two days later he was dead. He had reigned but ninety-nine
days.

Prince Wilhelm

As it gradually became apparent during 1887 that Friedrich Wilhelm, if he
ascended the throne at all, was destined to have a short reign, the attention
of those who sat in or hovered about the seats of power in Berlin began to
focus upon his eldest son, Prince Wilhelm. Born in 1859, the first of eight
children, Wilhelm was an impressionable child at the time of the wars of
unification and ascended the throne at the age of twenty-nine. Some of the
experiences that went into the formation of his character are evident, particularly as related by his mother in lengthy letters to Queen Victoria.

His birth was difficult, leaving the infant with an injured left arm (damaged
shoulder socket and torn muscles). Attempts at electrical and other means of

---

[64] Lucius, *Bismarck-Erinnerungen*, p. 456; DZA Merseburg, Rep. 90a, B, III, 2b, Nr. 6, Bd.
100.

[65] Lucius, *Bismarck-Erinnerungen*, pp. 457–462. The motivation given by Friedrich for Puttkamer's dismissal was dissatisfaction with the minister's defense of his use of government pressure
to influence the election of Puttkamer-Plauth. *Ibid.*, p. 461.

[66] Lucius, *Bismarck-Erinnerungen*, p. 455.

therapy were painful and useless.[67] The crown princess, who delivered children almost annually after his birth, left him largely in the care of nurse and governess. In October 1864 was born Sigismund, her fourth child and third of her four sons, who died at twenty-one months. The mother mourned the dead infant as "more to me than its brothers and sisters," as cleverer than either of his older brothers, "Willy and Henry." "I thought he was going to be like Papa [Prince Albert]. Fritz and I idolized him."[68] Thereafter she is said to have taken a greater personal interest in her oldest son, who was already seven when Sigismund died.[69]

In May 1870 the crown princess wrote, "Wilhelm begins to feel being behind much smaller boys in every exercise of the body—he cannot run fast, because he has no balance, nor ride, nor climb, nor cut his food, etc."[70] On Willy's thirteenth birthday, she wrote of his "winning" ways. "He is not possessed of brilliant abilities nor of any strength of character or talents, but he is a dear boy, and I hope and trust will grow up a useful man. He has an excellent tutor, I never saw or knew a better, and all the care that can be bestowed on mind and body is taken of him. I watch over him myself, over each detail, even the minutest, of his education, as his Papa has never had the time to occupy himself with the children. These next few years will be very critical and important for him, as they are the passage from childhood to manhood. I am happy to say that between him and me there is a bond of love and confidence, which I feel sure nothing can destroy. He has very strong health and would be a very pretty boy were it not for that wretched unhappy arm which shows more and more, spoils his face (for it is on one side), his carriage, walk and figure, makes him awkward in all his movements, and gives me a feeling of shyness, as he feels his complete dependence, not being able to do a single thing for himself. It is a great additional difficulty in his education, and not without its effect on his character. To me it remains an inexpressible source of worry! I think he will be very good-looking when he grows up and he is already a universal favorite, as he is so lively and generally intelligent."[71]

Mirrored here is a strong maternal ambivalence. Willy was not very talented, yet generally intelligent; more and more disfigured, yet potentially handsome; without strength of character, yet potentially a useful man; dominated by a mother who, although aware of the danger of dependence, prescribed in minute detail how he was to grow up; sired by a father who had

[67] Recollection of Count August Eulenburg, Apr. 20, 1875. Lucius, *Bismarck-Erinnerungen*, p. 74.

[68] To Queen Victoria, June 18 and 26, 1866. Ponsonby, ed., *Letters of Empress Frederick*, pp. 60–62.

[69] Michael Balfour, *The Kaiser and His Times* (London, 1964), p. 75.

[70] To Queen Victoria, May 28, 1870. Ponsonby, ed., *Letters of Empress Frederick*, p. 68.

[71] To Queen Victoria, Jan. 28, 1871. Ponsonby, ed., *Letters of Empress Frederick*, pp. 119–120.

CROWN PRINCESS VICTORIA AND PRINCE WILHELM, 1876.

little time for him, yet nurtured by a tutor who became a father surrogate. Like his wife, Friedrich Wilhelm felt the need to reassure himself of the boy's affection. In his diary on Willy's thirteenth birthday he wrote, "Thank God there is between him and us, his parents, a simple, natural, cordial relation, to preserve which is our constant endeavour, that he may always look upon us as his true, his best friends."[72] "The dream of my life," the crown princess wrote to Queen Victoria, "was to have a son who should be something of what our beloved Papa was, a real grandson of his, in soul and intellect, a

[72] Quoted in Ponsonby, ed., *Letters of Empress Frederick*, p. 118.

grandson of yours."[73] Willy was expected to be another Prince Albert, the wise and moderate counselor of kings and queens on the ways of constitutional government, more an English- than a Prussian-style monarch.

Until 1870 the two royal princes, Wilhelm and Heinrich, were tutored in English by Thomas Dealtry and in French by a Mademoiselle d'Arcourt. Dealtry insisted that they read the classics of English history and literature and memorize appropriate passages.[74] The tutor who remained with them longest (1866–1879) and had the greatest impact upon Willy was Georg Hinzpeter. A devout Calvinist, Hinzpeter took his task seriously, beginning lessons at 6:00 A.M. in the summer, 7:00 A.M. in the winter and continuing twelve hours a day. He was a firm believer in classical education as a source of discipline, problem solving, and "harmonious development" of the intellect. Hinzpeter's responsibilities reached beyond the classroom. He taught Willy to ride by brutally hoisting him on a pony without stirrups again and again until finally the crippled boy stopping falling. On Wednesday and Saturday afternoons Hinzpeter took the royal princes into mines, factories, galleries, and museums in the effort to broaden their perspectives. Yet the tutor was never fully satisfied with his "beloved problem child." "He never learnt the first duty of a ruler, hard work."[75]

In September 1874 the crown princess wrote, "The emperor's interest is warm, but alas his influence on the child's education, whenever he enforces it, is *very hurtful!*"[76] The Kaiser wanted his grandson to complete his education in Berlin, where he would be surrounded at court with influences his majesty thought salubrious, his parents harmful. Victoria and Friedrich Wilhelm had their way, sending both princes away for three years to a public school, the *Gymnasium* at Kassel, to finish the classical education Hinzpeter had begun.[77] Willy graduated tenth in a class of seventeen. Afterward he followed his father's example by spending two years at the University of Bonn. There he joined one of the more chauvinistic student corps, the Borussia, although excused from dueling. He heard lectures on history, philosophy, law, art, politics, economics, government, and science—a wide variety of subjects for a man with a limited attention span. At the age of twenty in 1879 he began two years of active military service as a lieutenant (a rank he had held since the age of ten) in the elite guard regiment at Potsdam. As he

[73] To Queen Victoria, Apr. 23, 1887. Ponsonby, ed., *Letters of Empress Frederick*, p. 215.
[74] Thomas Dealtry to Crown Princess Victoria, Apr. 30, 1870. Ponsonby, ed., *Letters of Empress Frederick*, pp. 67–68.
[75] Balfour, *The Kaiser and His Times*, pp. 68, 76–78, 81.
[76] To Queen Victoria, Sept. 1, 1874. Ponsonby, ed., *Letters of Empress Frederick*, p. 135.
[77] Ponsonby, ed., *Letters of Empress Frederick*, p. 118; Egon Corti, *The English Empress: A Study in the Relations between Queen Victoria and her Eldest Daughter, Empress Frederick of Germany* (London, 1957), p. 194.

emerged from this experience in 1881 at the age of twenty-two, his mother concluded, "This son has never been really mine."[78]

After 1880 Prince Wilhelm's alienation from his parents became increasingly evident. His secret engagement that year to Princess Auguste Viktoria of the house of Augustenburg, daughter of the hapless claimant to the Schleswig-Holstein succession in 1864, was an act of independence. Yet his parents were pleased by the choice and helped overcome the Kaiser's opposition. His mother was a little regretful that he married so young, having seen so little of the world, but noted that when traveling "he did not care to look at anything, took no interest whatever in works of art, did not in the least admire beautiful scenery," and never consulted a guidebook about what was worth seeing.[79] Freed from the parental household by marriage, Prince Wilhelm rejected everything his mother seemed to stand for, particularly the export to Berlin of English ideas on government and foreign policy. Ultimately he concluded that she "hates me like nothing else in the world,"[80] while she regarded him as immature, rude, and arrogant.[81]

Destined by heritage to be a soldier-king, this Hohenzoller had neither the physical nor intellectual attributes for the task. He took refuge in the Prussian-Hohenzollern tradition: orthodox conservatism (now wedded to German nationalism) in politics, elitism in social outlook and behavior, an autocratic conception of his office as King-Kaiser, and an excessive reverence for the military. In public and before the camera his face assumed a theatrically taut, stern, and masculine expression; offstage his disposition was generally relaxed and amiable, although excitable, and his conduct sometimes vulgar and juvenile. In a stable personality like Wilhelm I there was no apparent gap between the public and private person. He was what he was expected to be and what he thought himself to be. But in Prince Wilhelm the gap was huge. The Princess of Pless said of him, "He was such a good actor; he could make himself do anything." Sarah Bernhardt got on with him "splendidly, for aren't the two of us both troupers."[82] The woman Prince Wilhelm married, unlike his mother and both grandmothers, had no interest in politics. A boring conversationalist, she was often said to have been selected primarily for childbearing. Over ten years she gave birth to seven children (six sons and one daughter). In his memoirs Bismarck wrote enigmatically that the young Kaiser had a "strong sexual development."[83] He was in a good position to know, having

[78] Balfour, The Kaiser and His Times, pp. 79–82; Corti, English Empress, p. 213.

[79] To Queen Victoria, Mar. 26, 1880. Ponsonby, ed., Letters of Empress Frederick, pp. 175–180.

[80] Arthur von Brauer, Im Dienste Bismarcks (Berlin, 1936), p. 284.

[81] Ponsonby, ed., Letters of Empress Frederick, pp. 214ff.

[82] Balfour, The Kaiser and His Times, pp. 82–86.

[83] GW, XV, 545.

had with son Herbert the task of buying off at least one of the prince's impor-
tunate mistresses.[84]

Although Prince Wilhelm had a quick mind and fluent tongue, his powers
of concentration were poor and his judgment of character execrable. The circle of men who gathered around him speedily noted and made use of his need
for approval. He became an easy victim for flatterers and sycophants. During
the early 1880s both Bismarck and Wilhelm's parents thought that the prince
ought to be separated from the clique of officers at Potsdam who were his
favorite companions and that he should be initiated in the internal affairs of
the monarchy on every level beginning with the county *Landrat* and ending
with the ministries in Berlin. But the prince received only periodic briefings

FOUR GENERATIONS, 1882: KAISER WILHELM I, ATTENDED BY CROWN PRINCE FRIEDRICH
WILHELM AND PRINCE WILHELM, WITH PRINCE WILHELM'S FIRST CHILD. (BILDARCHIV
PREUSSISCHER KULTURBESITZ.)

[84] John C. G. Röhl, "The Emperor's New Clothes: A Character Sketch of Kaiser Wilhelm II,"
in John C. G. Röhl and Nicolaus Sombart, *Kaiser Wilhelm II: New Interpretations* (Cambridge,
Eng., 1982), pp. 26, 44–46.

by the former minister Achenbach, now governor-general of Brandenburg province. Not until the fall of 1887, when his succession appeared imminent, did Prince Wilhelm begin to spend several days a week in the Ministry of Finance, where Scholz took care that the work given him was not too dull. "The prince has quick comprehension and remembers what he hears, but his knowledge of general state affairs is very small. His occasional utterances and questions show that the intellectual circle in which he has lived until now is completely alien to such matters."[85]

Earlier Bismarck had begun to involve Prince Wilhelm in foreign affairs, much to the displeasure of his parents. In 1884 he, rather than the crown prince, was chosen to represent the Kaiser at the celebration in St. Petersburg on the coming of age of Crown Prince Nicholas. His age and politics made him appear the better choice, and indeed Prince Wilhelm, carefully coached by Bismarck, made a favorable impression on Alexander III. "Willy" and "Nicky" also got on well. In 1886 Prince Wilhelm, not his father, attended the meetings the Kaiser held with Franz Joseph at Gastein and Alexander III at Skierniewicz. In December of the same year the Kaiser granted the prince's request for access to current foreign office documents. On each occasion the parents were indignant, but their protests were overridden.[86] If, as they believed, Prince Wilhelm was "as blind and green, wrong-headed and violent on politics as can be,"[87] it was indeed time that he received some training in the conduct of foreign affairs.

After it became evident in Berlin that the crown prince was terminally ill, Bismarck drafted for Kaiser Wilhelm's signature a proclamation dated November 17, 1887, conferring on his grandson the power to act as his deputy (Stellvertreter) in the event of incapacitation.[88] At San Remo news of this document was taken as proof that Kaiser and chancellor were seeking to force Friedrich Wilhelm to renounce the succession.[89] During the ninety-nine days Friedrich was compelled, nevertheless, to request that some of his duties be

[85] GW, XV, 455. Adolf von Scholz, Erlebnisse und Gespräche mit Bismarck (Stuttgart, 1922), pp. 80–81; Lucius, Bismarck-Erinnerungen, p. 411.

[86] GW, XV, 455–456; GW, VIc, 347–348; GP, V, 55–61, 63–65; Balfour, The Kaiser and His Times, pp. 99–100; Bussmann, ed., Herbert von Bismarck, pp. 370–371, 384, 388–389, 391–392; Nichols, Year of Three Kaisers, pp. 27–30.

[87] To Queen Victoria, Aug. 11, 1886. Ponsonby, ed., Letters of Empress Frederick, pp. 206–207. See also Crown Prince Friedrich Wilhelm to Bismarck, Sept. 28, 1886. GW, XV, 456. When told that in Friedrich Wilhelm's judgment Prince Wilhelm was too "immature" for political responsibility, Kaiser Wilhelm I responded, "My grandson is to my great joy unusually mature. . . . My son has never been so mature." Bussmann, Herbert von Bismarck, pp. 403, 415–416.

[88] SEG (1888), p. 58. The document was initiated not by Bismarck but by General Emil von Albedyll, chief of the military cabinet. He warned the chancellor that the Kaiser could be found "dead in bed" at any time. Herbert Bismarck to his father, Nov. 14, 1887. Bussmann, ed., Herbert von Bismarck, pp. 480–481.

[89] Ponsonby, ed., Letters of Empress Frederick, pp. 261–262.

delegated to his son. And yet Bismarck and Prince Wilhelm insisted on renewal of the far-reaching decree of November 17. Prince Wilhelm wanted it understood that, if he actually assumed power as deputy, he would follow his own, not his father's policies. In pressing the point in their audience on March 21, 1888, Bismarck reminded Victoria of that episode in 1863 when her husband had openly disagreed with his father's policies. Victoria and Friedrich could not expect from their own son, in other words, more self-effacement than Friedrich himself had shown while crown prince. The Kaiser signed the document.[90] That Puttkamer took so long to present to him the statute extending the interval between Prussian elections was undoubtedly owing to the belief that Friedrich's demise was nearer than it proved to be. Wilhelm's signature either as deputy or as Kaiser would have been no problem.

On June 14 Friedrich III received Bismarck for the last time. Taking his wife's hand, the monarch placed it protectively in that of the chancellor, a symbolic act that may explain why he yielded so much during his final weeks.[91] Yet this did her little good after her beloved "Fritz" passed away. On orders from the new Kaiser a regiment of hussars "appeared unmounted with rifles in their hands from behind every tree and every statue" to cordon off the palace. The widow, her younger children, and staff were forbidden to leave before all private and state papers had been located and seized.[92]

Friedrich was hardly buried when the surgeon Bergmann publicly attacked the laryngologist Mackenzie for malpractice, and the press pilloried the bereaved empress for favoring British medicine and mismanaging her husband's care.[93] Neither her son, who may have believed the charge, nor Bismarck, who knew better, intervened to stop the slander. An autopsy (expressly forbidden by Friedrich before his death) confirmed the presence of cancer. To demonstrate that "German science" could have kept Friedrich alive, Bergmann is said to have performed for his students a thyrotomy on another patient showing the same symptoms. The patient died.[94] The "English empress" was forced to move out of her last home, Friedrichskron (Neues Palais) located in the park at Potsdam; she was denied residence at Sans Souci in the same park, and eventually chose virtual exile at Homburg in Hesse far from Berlin.[95]

[90] Lucius, Bismarck-Erinnerungen, pp. 437–439.

[91] Ibid., pp. 464–465.

[92] Corti, English Empress, pp. 302–303; Balfour, The Kaiser and His Times, pp. 118–119. According to Herbert Bismarck, the widowed Victoria was cooperative, ordering boxes of documents returned for inspection that Kaiser Friedrich had sent to England in 1887 as "property of my wife." Bussmann, ed., Herbert von Bismarck, p. 519.

[93] Wolf, Krankheit Friedrichs III, pp. 124ff.

[94] C. L. Schleich, Besonnte Vergangenheit (Berlin 1921), pp. 219ff. But see also Wolf, Krankheit Friedrichs III, pp. 78ff., who questions the accuracy of Schleich's memoirs.

[95] Corti, English Empress, pp. 306–308.

Webs of Intrigue

The tensions that developed between palace and chancellery during the short reign of Friedrich III cannot be dismissed as the work of his wife. Nor can Bismarck's effort in the public press to establish a contradiction between the good German Kaiser and the bad English Kaiserin be accepted as anything but a caricature. That Victoria may have tried too hard to shield her dying husband from unnecessary distresses and burdens is probable. But there is no evidence that she did not interpret or relay correctly her husband's wishes. Nor can it be assumed that Kaiser Friedrich, had he been blessed with a longer reign, would have been able to retain Bismarck for long as chancellor. The difficulties that arose, despite Friedrich's long expressed intention to work with Bismarck in following the policies of Wilhelm I, suggest the contrary. The old chancellor and new Kaiser were sufficiently opposed in temperament and in political outlook that the Bismarck government could not have lasted with Friedrich on the throne. Yet the probable consequence of Bismarck's departure would have been a change in government, not in the constitution. Friedrich III would never have willingly surrendered the important powers he inherited. Instead, he would have chosen ministers of a "new era" type, perhaps with some left-liberal representation. Since the era of Stein and Hardenberg it had repeatedly been demonstrated that even an autocratic government could pursue liberal policies with liberal ministers, but without the sacrifice of its essential authority.

Months before the deaths of both Wilhelm I and Friedrich III there were signs that Bismarck might also have difficulty remaining in office even under the future Wilhelm II. As it became apparent that his succession was near, Prince Wilhelm naturally became the object of considerable attention from those who hoped to use him for their own purposes. One of them was Waldersee, quartermaster-general of the Prussian army and soon to be Moltke's successor as chief of the Prussian general staff. As already shown, the chancellor's coup against Minister of War Kameke in 1883 was followed by the success of Waldersee and Albedyll in establishing the independence of the general staff and military cabinet from the Ministry of War.[96] Waldersee cultivated close relations with Holstein and Hatzfeldt in the Imperial Foreign Office and established, through correspondence with German military attachés in embassies abroad, a private channel for political reporting and even for transmitting his political views to foreign governments. While Bismarck strove to preserve the peace of Europe during the crises of 1887–1890, Waldersee concluded, as noted earlier, that conflict with Russia was inevitable and that Germany and Austria should initiate it for prophylactic reasons. In December 1887 Bismarck rebuked him sharply for interfering in foreign policy

[96] See pp. 38–39.

through his Austrian contacts.[97] Had he remained in office, Bismarck would have been compelled to smash Waldersee's personal diplomatic corps, as did his successor Caprivi after Waldersee's fall from grace in 1891.

Bismarck was probably correct in suspecting that Waldersee aspired to supplant him as chancellor on the succession of Prince Wilhelm. Since 1883 Waldersee and his American-born wife had cultivated the friendship of Prince Wilhelm and Princess Auguste. The wives had in common an intense piety and a familial relationship through marriage (the countess's first husband was an Augustenburg). Through them Prince Wilhelm had become interested in Pastor Adolf Stöcker and his work as head of the Berlin city mission (*Stadtmission*), which dispensed charity, religion, and anti-Semitism to the capital's lower classes. (In 1885 Prince Wilhelm had saved Stöcker from dismissal as court preacher by a personal appeal to Wilhelm I.)[98] In their political discussions Waldersee undoubtedly insinuated his conviction that Bismarck at age 72 and Kaiser Wilhelm at 90 were no longer able to cope with the necessities of state in either domestic or foreign affairs.

In October 1887 Prince Wilhelm told Minister of Finance Scholz that no one, not even the mighty chancellor, should be regarded as indispensable and that, once Bismarck was gone, some of his powers must be restored to the monarch. During that fall Waldersee urged Prince Wilhelm to seek admission to the Kaiser's audiences with ministers and generals. Hence it was that Prince Wilhelm appeared unexpectedly in the audience on December 17, 1887, at which the generals sought to persuade the Kaiser to cooperate militarily with Austria against Russia and to which Bismarck so strenuously objected. Under Waldersee's influence, it appeared, Prince Wilhelm had joined the war hawks.[99]

Waldersee was merely the most visible threat to Bismarck's position. Behind the scenes were others, of whom in earlier times the chancellor would surely have become more aware and against whose influence he might have been more effective. The coterie that was to have the greatest influence on his ouster in 1890 consisted of Friedrich von Holstein, privy counselor and future "gray eminence" of the foreign office; Count Philipp zu Eulenburg, secretary of the Prussian legation at Munich, who had been in regular contact with Prince Wilhelm since 1885 and was soon to become his closest friend; and ultimately Baron Adolf Marschall von Bieberstein, Baden's representa-

---

[97] Waldersee, *Denkwürdigkeiten*, I, 340–341. See also Gordon A. Craig, *The Politics of the Prussian Army, 1649–1945* (Oxford, 1955), pp. 266–270; Nichols, *Year of Three Kaisers*, pp. 67–75. Bismarck's effort to unseat Waldersee as quartermaster general was halted by Moltke, who declared him indispensable. "He knows no one abler." Bussmann, ed., *Herbert von Bismarck*, p. 506.

[98] Heinrich Heffter, *Die Kreuzzeitungspartei und Bismarcks Kartellpolitik* (Leipzig, 1927), pp. 103–104.

[99] Scholz, *Erlebnisse und Gespräche*, pp. 82–83; Nichols, *Year of Three Kaisers*, pp. 67–72.

tive in Berlin, whose sovereign, the Grand Duke of Baden, was to play a significant role in the climactic events of March 1890.

Since 1886 Holstein, Eulenburg, and Marschall had become increasingly convinced that Bismarck was no longer equal to the demands of his office, that in both foreign and domestic affairs his course was dangerous for Germany.[100] They were opponents of Bismarck's seemingly pro-Russian policy in the Balkans, which they anticipated would weaken the Dual Alliance. In domestic affairs their attention was focused on Bavaria, where they feared the fall of the pro-Prussian cabinet of Baron Johann Lutz and its replacement by an ultramontane and particularist government. From such a development they anticipated a chain reaction in both domestic and foreign affairs—the loosening of federal relationships and new challenges to Prussian leadership, the weakening and perhaps liquidation of the alliance with the anticlerical government of Italy. Yet their intrigues against the chancellor were muted as long as he based his parliamentary power on the cartel parties, which the coterie regarded as the principal barrier to the chain reaction they foresaw and the only practical foundation for the future personal rule of Wilhelm II. They became desperate and dangerous to Bismarck only when they began to detect an inclination on his part to sacrifice the cartel in favor of a conservative-centrist majority.[101]

Outside the government and in the public press the chief threat to Bismarck's position came from ultraconservatives. For them the brilliant recovery of the National Liberal party in the election of 1887 was hardly a cause for joy. They had entered the cartel only with the greatest reluctance, had sacrificed a number of constituencies to national liberal candidates, and lost their role in the "Berlin movement" that challenged left-liberal domination of the capital. Known as the "Kreuzzeitung group" or "party" (the journal's editor, Baron Wilhelm von Hammerstein, was their chief spokesman), the ultras feared the revival of Bennigsen's "crazy ideas about 'constitutional' guarantees."[102] In the spring of 1887 the ultras, led by Hammerstein and Hans von Kleist-Retzow, tried and failed to exploit the new political power of the conservatives as a whole to make the Protestant church hierarchy administratively and financially independent of the state. Bismarck sharply denounced this "criminal" attack upon the *summus episcopus* of the king and upon the authority of the state. Unable to dominate the German Conservative party, which followed the progovernment leadership of Otto von Helldorf-Bedra, the ultras now sought in their relationship to the future Kaiser the political

[100] Rich and Fisher, ed., Holstein Papers, II, 274ff.; Eulenburg-Hertefeld, Aus 50 Jahren, pp. 134ff., 146–147.

[101] John C. G. Röhl, "The Disintegration of the Kartell and the Politics of Bismarck's Fall from Power, 1887–1890," The Historical Journal, 9 (1966), pp. 60–89.

[102] Herbert to Wilhelm von Bismarck, Mar. 4, 1887. Bussmann, ed., Herbert von Bismarck, p. 430; Heffter, Kreuzzeitungspartei, pp. 82ff.

clout they lacked in parliament. For this they possessed a convenient channel in the persons of Count Waldersee and Adolf Stöcker.[103]

The Waldersee–Stöcker Meeting

Months before Prince Wilhelm ascended the throne as Wilhelm II occurred an incident that exposed before all Germany the character of the struggle that had already begun for the mind and favor of the future Kaiser. On November 28, 1887, Prince and Princess Wilhelm participated in a meeting held under their auspices at Waldersee's official residence for the purpose of raising money for Stöcker's city mission. Among the dignitaries who attended were the Prussian ministers Puttkamer and Gossler, Chief of the Military Cabinet Albedyll, President of the Reichstag Wilhelm von Wedell-Piesdorf, conservative deputies (particularly ultras), conservative journalists (including Hammerstein), but also some national liberals (notably Robert von Benda and David Hansemann). Several of those present spoke in behalf of the mission's efforts to preserve social order through Christian revivalism, but naturally Prince Wilhelm's brief remarks received primary attention. As reported in the *Kreuzzeitung*, he praised the "Christian-social idea," with its emphasis upon loyalty to the Protestant church and to "legal authority and love for the monarchy." By merely uttering the term "Christian-social," the prince identified himself with Stöcker and his political movement.[104] To Herbert Bismarck he spoke privately of the pastor as having "something of Luther" in him.[105]

Prince Wilhelm, Waldersee, and the other participants did not anticipate that the "Waldersee–Stöcker meeting" would become within days the subject of widespread public and private discussion and debate in Germany. Liberal journalists, Eugen Richter's *Freisinnige Zeitung* in the lead, picked up the story from perfunctory accounts in the conservative press and subjected the future Kaiser to his baptism of fire in the newspaper press.[106]

Bismarck reacted sharply. "Those who wear skirts (women, clerics, judges) are incompetent in politics, and one must cut off all relationships with anyone who favors their ideas. Stöcker must withdraw from princes and politics. Prince Wilhelm has the most reactionary impulses."[107] On December 11 and 14 the *Norddeutsche Allgemeine Zeitung* carried two unsigned, acid attacks on Stöcker composed by Franz von Rottenburg, chief of the Imperial Chancel-

---

[103] Heffter, *Kreuzzeitungspartei*, pp. 90–99, 102–103; BR, XII, 390ff.; GW, VIII, 563; Hans Leuss, *Wilhelm Freiherr von Hammerstein* (Berlin, 1905), pp. 50–54.

[104] Heffter, *Kreuzzeitungspartei*, pp. 104–105; SEG (1887), p. 190.

[105] GW, XV, 459.

[106] For an account of the public debate, see Nichols, *Year of Three Kaisers*, pp. 32–43, and "Bismarck and the Accession of Frederick III," *Studies in Modern European History and Culture*, I, pp. 112–118; SEG (1887), pp. 199–201.

[107] Lucius, *Bismarck-Erinnerungen*, p. 409.

WILHELM II AS CROWN PRINCE.

lery. In view of the newspaper's semiofficial character, this was taken as a signal from Friedrichsruh. The cartel newspapers joined the hue and cry of the left-liberal journals. All Germany was treated to the spectacle of a broad-scale assault upon the clerical-conservative circle that, it was openly charged, deliberately exploited the sympathies of Prince Wilhelm for reactionary purposes. When the free conservative *Post* condemned "*Muckerei und Stöckerei*," the campaign got its slogan.[108]

For the first time the man who was soon to ascend the German throne found himself in the eye of a journalistic storm. His first private reaction was to assert that Jews should be banned from journalism. Even Puttkamer, the cabinet's most reactionary member, was shocked by this remark and reminded the prince that the nation's industrial code guaranteed freedom of occupation. The young Hohenzoller replied, "Then we will get rid of it." At Christmas, however, he was reported as protesting plaintively, "I am no anti-Semite."[109] He waited for open support from Friedrichsruh, but none came, and he suspected Herbert to be the author of the articles in the *Norddeutsche Allgemeine*.[110]

On December 21, 1887, Prince Wilhelm indignantly protested to Bismarck

[108] SEG (1887), pp. 199–201; Heffter, *Kreuzzeitungspartei*, pp. 106–108.
[109] Lucius, *Bismarck-Erinnerungen*, pp. 410–411.
[110] Waldersee, *Denkwürdigkeiten*, I, 346–354.

the "untruths" being spread about a charitable venture without partisan character, in which Stöcker was to play no major role. It was intended to be a weapon against anarchism and social democracy. Not until January 6 did Bismarck compose his reply. Bad health, he wrote, was responsible for the delay; a full response would require a historico-political book, which he was in no condition to write. National patriotism, not Christianity, was the best antidote against urban socialism and democracy. The prince's primary concern must always be to uphold the monarchical principle. Voluntary organizations such as the city mission could never supply a lasting foundation for monarchy. By association with them a future Kaiser could be contaminated by their failure. Did the prominent persons who attended the Stöcker meeting do so out of commitment to its cause or a desire to ingratiate themselves with the Kaiser? None could qualify for the task of governing the country. Talkers, clerics, and women were of limited effectiveness in politics. After ascending the throne, Prince Wilhelm must be in a position to use men and parties in alternation. "I have nothing against Stöcker; to my mind his only shortcoming as a political figure is that he is a cleric and his only shortcoming as a cleric is that he is involved in politics." Stöcker's energy and oratorical skill were commendable, but his successes were temporary, and he was associated with ultraconservative elements that were divisive and made governing more difficult. Social reform could be achieved only through the king, state, and legislative process. In response, Prince Wilhelm tried to preserve his dignity by refusing to surrender his patronage of the city mission. By persuading Stöcker to resign as its chief, he expected to still all criticism—"if not, then woe to them [the critics] when my time comes to command."[111]

Holstein found it "incredible" that the chancellor should use the public press to censure a young prince, "whose ignorance had involved him in this affair." The proper medium would have been a private letter or an audience, not the columns of the Norddeutsche. "For the sake of the chancellor," Wilhelm bleated to Hinzpeter, "I have (so to speak) for years locked myself out of my parent's house. So I did not deserve such treatment from the chancellor, of all people." To others he burst out, "The chancellor cannot go on enjoying the power he wields at present; he simply must realize there's still a Kaiser." Pounding the table, he blustered, "He'd better remember that I shall be his

[111] GW, XV, 460–470. When Bismarck wrote on January 6, he was in receipt of yet another letter from Prince Wilhelm, dated November 29, in which the prince enclosed the draft of a proclamation that he proposed to send to Prussian legations at the capitals of the Reich's lesser states, where it would be ready for immediate delivery to their monarchs on Wilhelm's succession to the throne. His "uncles" were to be given no time to brood over the elevation of so young a prince to the imperial dignity; it must be presented to them as a fait accompli. Bismarck was quick to see that the prince's proclamation would not solve a problem but create one. He advised the prince to burn the draft without delay, lest it become known prematurely and give offense to rulers who had no thought of resisting his succession. That ended the matter. Ibid; also Nichols, Year of Three Kaisers, pp. 58–66.

master." In a calmer moment he declared, "I shall not manage without the chancellor at first, but in due course I hope the German Reich will be sufficiently consolidated to be able to dispense with Prince Bismarck's cooperation."[112]

That Wilhelm I died before Friedrich III compelled Prince Wilhelm and the ultras to close ranks with the Bismarcks for the time being. During the ninety-nine days all had the same objective—to forestall any liberal "experiments."[113] On April 1, 1888, the heir to the throne toasted the chancellor on his seventy-third birthday in the flamboyant style and military imagery that were to become all too familiar to the coming generation of Germans. "To employ a military metaphor, I see our present situation as that of a regiment charging in battle. The commander of the regiment has fallen; the next in command rides on, although badly wounded. The soldiers look at the flag, whose bearer waves it high. Thus does your serene highness hold the imperial banner above us. May you—such is our most sincere wish—be granted still for a long time [the task] of holding aloft the imperial flag together with our beloved and honored Kaiser. God bless and protect him and your serene highness."[114]

[112] Holstein diary, Feb. 4, 1888. Rich and Fisher, eds., *Holstein Papers*, II, 362–363.

[113] Philipp Eulenburg claimed to have patched up the relationship between Prince Wilhelm and Herbert in December 1887. Eulenburg, *Aus 50 Jahren*, pp. 156–158.

[114] SEG (1888), p. 72.

CHAPTER TEN

✦✧

Growing Frictions

ERHAPS [the liberals] are out in their reckoning," Bismarck mused in 1882, "and a long-lived sovereign may be followed by a short-lived one. It seems to me as if this might be the case. He who would then ascend the throne is quite different. He wishes to take the government into his own hands; he is energetic and determined, not at all disposed to put up with parliamentary co-regents, a regular guardsman! Philopater and Antipater at Potsdam! He is not at all pleased by his father's association with the professors, with Mommsen, Virchow, and Forckenbeck. Perhaps he may one day develop into the *rocher de bronze* of which we stand in need."[1] What Bismarck did not foresee in 1882 was that the same autocratic temperament that would make parliamentary "experiments" impossible under Wilhelm II could jeopardize his own position as chancellor and minister-president. In late 1887 the prince already regarded Bismarck's accumulated power as injurious to the monarchy, had begun to consider possible replacements, and had been aroused to fury in one instance by the chancellor's heavy-handed treatment.

A Generation Gap

As his time to ascend the throne approached, nevertheless, Prince Wilhelm could not bring himself to dispense with the assistance of the seventy-three-year-old statesman who had governed Prussia and Germany for more than a quarter of a century. Like Friedrich III, he lacked the self-confidence to chart a new course with an untried navigator. That there were so few, if any, qualified successors was in large part Bismarck's own doing. But he had also become in the public mind a fixture of the Wilhelmstrasse. After so long a time it was difficult to conceive of the chancellorship without the man who had created it. The aging Junker was the vital link to the great era of German unification and to the political and military achievements Germans celebrated annually on *Sedantag* and almost every day in the classrooms and lecture halls of patriotic teachers and professors. Like Wilhelm I, Bismarck had become a living symbol of Germany's new power and influence in the world. And so for nearly two years after Wilhelm ascended the throne the old chan-

[1] Moritz Busch, *Bismarck: Some Secret Pages of His History* (New York, 1898), II, 325. The German edition has been purged of a passage critical of Friedrich III in the same paragraph. See Moritz Busch, *Tagebuchblätter* (Leipzig, 1899), III, 88–89.

cellor remained in power, despite mounting restlessness among those in high places who wished to see him gone.

"If I was younger and able to be with him every day, as I did with the old emperor, I would twist him around my finger," Bismarck meditated in December 1889, "but as it is he lets himself be influenced by individual people, by adjutants, especially by the military."[2] During the summer that began with the death of Friedrich III, the chancellor left for Friedrichsruh on July 12, 1888, not much later than usual; he remained there until January 10, 1889, skipping his usual stays in Varzin and Kissingen. In 1889 he summered at Varzin (June 8–August 10) and spent the rest of the year in the Sachsenwald (August 20, 1889–January 24, 1890), returning but twice to Berlin to confer with visiting rulers (August 10–20 and October 9–16, 1889).[3]

Apparently the long vacation in late 1888 and his initial satisfaction with Wilhelm II improved his condition. In mid-January 1889 Lothar von Schweinitz found him in better health and humor than for many years, "drinking and laughing a lot." But dietary indiscretions were again frequent. Baroness von Spitzemberg watched at a midday meal as "one thing after another wandered into his stomach"—lobster, breast of goose, *Gänsesulz*, sprats, herring, smoked meat, and turkey-hen. The old maladies flared up intermittently: rheumatism, facial neuralgia, insomnia, and the injured leg (at one point dangerously inflamed). The sources contain more references to the use of morphine and opium for sleep.[4] In Berlin the rumor began to circulate that he had become addicted, an insinuation that Schweninger indignantly denied.[5]

Long vacations and health problems reduced still further Bismarck's appearances in parliament. In the Landtag he appeared not at all during 1887–1890, except on ceremonial occasions, such as the proclamations of the succession to the throne of Friedrich III and Wilhelm II. The Reichstag heard him speak only once (a two-hour speech on foreign policy) during the session

[2] Rudolf Vierhaus, ed., *Das Tagebuch der Baronin Spitzemberg* (Göttingen, 1960), p. 264.

[3] Horst Kohl, ed., *Fürst Bismarck: Regesten zu einer wissenschaflichen Biographie des ersten Reichskanzlers* (Leipzig, 1892), II, 462–495.

[4] Wilhelm von Schweinitz, *Denkwürdigkeiten des Botschafters General von Schweinitz* (Berlin, 1927), II, 373; GW, VIc, 418; VIII, 643, 646–649, 656, 661, 709; XIV, 985, 992; Busch, *Secret Pages*, II, 432, 455, 506.

[5] Norman Rich and M. H. Fisher, eds., *The Holstein Papers: The Memoirs, Diaries and Correspondence of Friedrich von Holstein, 1837–1909* (4 vols., Cambridge, Eng., 1955–1963), II, 362; GW, VIII, 709; Karl Alexander von Müller, *Mars und Venus: Erinnerungen, 1914–1919* (Stuttgart, 1954), pp. 80–81. On January 4, 1890, the Kaiser asked Boetticher to ascertain on the next trip to Friedrichsruh whether the rumor of Bismarck's addiction was true. On January 7 Boetticher put the question to Schweninger, who appears to have given an untruthful answer: "for years the prince has abstained from any use of morphine. When he cannot sleep, I give him paraldehyde, a medicine that does not affect the nerves!" Georg Freiherr von Eppstein, *Fürst Bismarcks Entlassung* (Berlin, 1920), pp. 77–78.

of 1887–1888. During the early months of 1889 he did take part five times in important debates on colonial affairs, foreign policy, and old-age and invalid insurance. In the final legislative year (1889–1890) of his chancellorship the Reichstag saw nothing of him.[6] Franz von Rottenburg, who acted as Bismarck's personal secretary at Friedrichsruh, told Lucius in early October 1889, "Bismarck is no longer what he was and is losing freshness and energy. He is limiting himself and his influence to the most pressing matters, and he exercises that influence less often."[7]

Not all of Bismarck's activities during these many months were worth his efforts. In September 1888 the *Deutsche Rundschau* published excerpts from Friedrich III's war diary of 1870–1871, revealing his critical view of Bismarck's solution to the German question. Although he knew that the document was genuine, the chancellor promptly denounced it as a forgery.[8] But Heinrich Geffcken, a Strassburg historian and former friend of the dead monarch, authenticated the document and admitted publishing it. He was promptly indicted for revealing state secrets! He tried to flee, but was arrested and imprisoned pending trial.[9] In January 1889 the Imperial Supreme Court dismissed the charge as unsubstantiated. Dissatisfied with the scales of justice, Bismarck persuaded Wilhelm to publish the charges in the official *Reichsanzeiger* and to transmit to the Bundesrat supporting documents, including sequestered copies of Geffcken's private correspondence. Having failed in the courts, Bismarck thought to prove his case against Geffcken in the public press.[10] Here he violated his own injunction—"Never shoot at sparrows with cannon!" After listening to the chancellor claim that the "legend" of Friedrich's liberalism "must be destroyed," lest it endanger the monarchy, Hohenlohe wrote in his diary, "He gave me the impression of a man not quite sound mentally."[11]

Even while the Geffcken case was pending, Bismarck launched in the *Kölnische Zeitung* (December 16, 1888) an attack upon Sir Robert Morier, British ambassador to Russia. Morier, it was asserted, had expected to be named ambassador to Germany in view of his good relationship with Friedrich III, established during Morier's earlier service as first secretary of the British Embassy in Berlin. But the succession of Wilhelm II had, the article inferred, ended his candidacy for the Berlin post and led instead to his appointment in Petersburg. In the course of the Geffcken investigation, it continued, German authorities had learned that during the war of 1870 Morier, then British

[6] *BR*, XII, 425ff.

[7] Freiherr Lucius von Ballhausen, *Bismarck-Erinnerungen* (Stuttgart, 1920), p. 505.

[8] *GW*, VIc, 395; XIV, 988; Busch, *Tagebuchblätter*, III, 240–243.

[9] *SEG* (1888), pp. 133–142.

[10] *SEG* (1889), pp. 4–5, 9.

[11] Friedrich Curtius, ed., *Memoirs of Prince Chlodwig of Hohenlohe-Schillingsfuerst* (New York, 1906), II, 411.

envoy in Hesse-Darmstadt, had passed information on German troop movements by way of London and Paris to Marshal Bazaine, the French commander at Metz, costing the army of Crown Prince Friedrich Wilhelm heavy casualties during the investment of that fortress.[12]

But Morier had been forewarned in July 1888 of this calumny and had already obtained from Bazaine, then in exile at Madrid, a declaration that the charge was a "clumsy invention." On publication of the Kölnische Zeitung article, Morier sent the denial to Herbert Bismarck, state secretary in the German foreign office, with the request that he "as a gentleman and man of honor" publicly repudiate the article. When Herbert refused in an impertinent, two-sentence letter composed on Christmas Day in Friedrichsruh, Morier released the exchange of letters between himself, Bazaine, and Herbert to the press.[13] According to Lothar von Schweinitz, Morier suddenly became popular in Petersburg, where he had previously been "hated," was defended by "the whole of England, where he had few friends, and at the same time gained the support of independent German newspapers." For Bismarck it was a public relations debacle that shook the public's faith in his "political infallibility."[14]

Poor Geffcken could not draw upon such support. Exculpated by the courts, he emerged from prison a broken man, addicted to the barbiturates sold him for insomnia. In a narcotic stupor he knocked over a petroleum lamp at his bedside and perished in the flames.[15] His fate aroused memories of Bismarck's persecution of Arnim, his ugly defamation of Lasker's memory, and other similar episodes. By the ferocity of his attack upon Geffcken Bismarck drove a nail into his own political coffin. Among the documents Bismarck published on the Geffcken affair was a memorandum from the chancellor to Wilhelm II asserting that Friedrich III as crown prince had been denied access to information about current negotiations—to prevent "indiscretions" reaching the English court, which sympathized with France.[16] This unnecessary assault upon the dead Kaiser and his widow enabled the Kreuzzeitung to editorialize that "monarchical sentiment" was being injured by public debate over such matters as the Geffcken affair. Although this issue of the newspaper was first confiscated by the police and later released without explanation, the argu-

---

[12] SEG (1888), p. 198.

[13] SEG (1889), pp. 2–4. On Herbert's animus toward Morier, see Walter Bussmann, ed., Staatssekretär Graf Herbert von Bismarck: Aus seiner politischen Privatkorrespondenz (Göttingen, 1964), pp. 252–253.

[14] Schweinitz, Denkwürdigkeiten, II, 374, 378–381.

[15] Felix von Eckardt, Ein Unordentliches Leben: Lebenserinnerungen (Düsseldorf, 1967), pp. 11–13.

[16] The fateful sentence was inserted by Bismarck in the original draft, perhaps as a stroke against the Prince of Wales, an advocate of the Duke of Cumberland's claim to the throne of the German principality of Brunswick. Otto Gradenwitz, Bismarcks letzter Kampf, 1888–1898: Skizzen nach Akten (Berlin, 1924), pp. 21–34.

ment was not lost on Wilhelm II.[17] Bismarck had forgotten that blood is thicker than ink.

Perhaps the most serious consequence of Bismarck's diminished presence and declining involvement in important governmental affairs during 1888–1889 was his loss of personal contact with the Kaiser. During the early years of his association as chancellor with Wilhelm I, he had been at the Kaiser's side as much as possible, particularly during critical periods when the monarch might be vulnerable to hostile influences. Now his constant presence was even more necessary, for at age twenty-nine Wilhelm II was far less experienced and more impressionable than Wilhelm I had been when he ascended the throne. Furthermore, the new ruler was a child of the railway and steamship age, to whom frequent, long-distance travel was a natural way of life and for him a psychological necessity. Keeping up with Wilhelm II would have been difficult even for a healthy chancellor. The Kaiser drifted restlessly over the European continent in the evident need to show himself in his new dignity to foreign rulers, courts, and peoples: to Petersburg, Stockholm, Copenhagen (July 14–31, 1888); to south German courts, Vienna, and Rome (September 26–October 21, 1888); to England (July 31–August 7, 1889); and to Monza, Athens, and Constantinople (October 17–November 10, 1889).

On most of these trips Herbert, upon whom his father had come increasingly to rely, acted as surrogate chancellor. Through him Bismarck instructed Wilhelm II on his policies and received reports on what passed between the Kaiser and foreign rulers and statesmen. Eventually, the chancellor hoped, Herbert would succeed him and assure the continuity of his course.[18] Naturally Herbert's role aroused jealousy and concern among ministers, privy counselors, and courtiers, particularly among those who suffered from his arrogance and bad manners. There was indignant talk of a "Bismarck dynasty" and of *Hausmeiertum*.

Initially Herbert was impressed with Wilhelm's performance as Kaiser. "Our new master," he wrote in June 1888, "is entirely on top of the matter, also calm and objective." In October Herbert was still of this opinion. By July 1889, however, he was highly alarmed, reporting to his father that the young Kaiser conducted business in a "hasty, disjointed manner," because he lacked a solid comprehension of the issues gained by study and reflection. Wilhelm II did not like to read lengthy documents. When presented with more than four handwritten pages, he would invariably demand an oral summary. He was averse to memoranda containing analyses and argumentation, preferring narratives and, above all, newspaper articles. Philipp Eulenburg observed that

---

[17] SEG (1889), pp. 10–13. Hans Leuss, *Wilhelm Freiherr von Hammerstein* (Berlin, 1905), p. 64. As crown prince Wilhelm had himself accused his mother of transmitting to the English government information gained from dispatches sent to Friedrich III at San Remo. Bussmann, ed., *Herbert von Bismarck*, p. 485.

[18] GW, VIII, 622; Busch, *Secret Pages*, II, 511.

the Kaiser, on receiving dispatches, always read the newspaper clippings first and laid aside written reports. "Thus it appears that his majesty forms his opinions on the basis of *oral* communications and conversations and is intermittently influenced by press attitudes."

Herbert came to the same conclusion, noting that, when forced to read documents, the Kaiser was inclined toward contradiction and obstinacy, expressed in harsh marginalia. "In oral communication his majesty is always very polite and obliging."[19] By the summer of 1889 the relationship between Kaiser and chancellor was already coming unglued as differences and misunderstandings, many petty in themselves, accumulated. At fault was Bismarck's remoteness from the scene, even more than the intrigues of ambitious foes and the uncertainty of officials and ministers, who felt that their careers depended on guessing correctly which way the dice would fall. One source of friction and intrigue was foreign policy.

Division on Foreign Policy

Fortunately for Germany the critical periods in the eastern and western segments of the prolonged crisis of 1886–1889 came at different times. The crisis over Bulgaria and the Straits reached its climax in late 1887 and early 1888, that between France and Germany over Alsace-Lorraine and *revanche* in the last half of 1888 and early 1889. By retiring Boulanger from the army in March 1888, the French government left the general legally free to run for public office. As a candidate in successive by-elections for seats in the National Assembly, he demonstrated his personal popularity. Monarchists, Bonapartists, clericals, left-leaning republicans, and ultrapatriots of varied political sentiments swarmed to his support. On January 27, 1889, Boulanger brought this informal plebiscite to its apogee by winning a large majority in a normally republican district of Paris itself. Recent research has exposed the myth that only the general's indecision stood in the way of a successful coup d'état on the evening of the election. Although he welcomed rightist support and financing (some of it American in origin), Boulanger remained committed to republicanism. He took up the cause of revisionism, attracting the support of those who disliked antidemocratic features of the 1875 constitution.

What Boulangism offered was a rallying point, not a program, for many political fragments whose only common cause was the desire to exploit general dissatisfaction with a government that remained inactive in a time of economic adversity and social distress. After the election the government launched a counterattack against the general, who was accused of plotting

---

[19] Bussmann, ed., *Herbert von Bismarck*, pp. 518, 529, 539–540. Bismarck warned a subordinate that Wilhelm II tended to put aside unread any reports that he found too long. Schwarzkoppen to unknown *Geheimrat* in Reichskanzlei, Jan. 21, 1890. DZA Potsdam, Reichskanzlei, 446, pp. 134–134v.

against the constitutional order. He fled the country to avoid arrest. In September the Boulangists were badly defeated in a general election. Boulangism was not viable without Boulanger. The spook was gone.[20]

During the climactic year of the Boulangist movement (March 1888 to March 1889) Bismarck could not be sure that the French would not prove the accuracy of his assessment of their "character." Crispi, too, was apprehensive. Rumors that Italy had allied with Germany and Austria in a triple alliance and with Austria and Britain in another compact were bruited widely in the

THE TRIPLE ALLIANCE—A FRENCH VIEW. *LE GRELOT*, PARIS, JUNE 30, 1889.

[20] Frederic H. Seager, *The Boulanger Affair: Political Crossroad of France, 1886–1889* (Ithaca, 1969), pp. 167–261; Theodore Zeldin, *France, 1848–1945: Politics and Anger* (Oxford, 1979), pp. 277–281.

European press and diplomatic channels. Naturally this news stimulated the interest of the Paris government in a Russian alliance, but the Petersburg government and Russian press reacted coolly. The French financial market was the only source of assistance to the Russian treasury in its struggle to maintain the value of the ruble and Russian state bonds. Even so, France's internal instability made an alliance now seem like an "absurdity" to the Russians.

By encouraging the Vatican in its ambition to restore papal sovereignty over Rome, the Quai d'Orsay found a way to make life uncomfortable for Crispi and his colleagues. On March 1, 1888, the French government broke off negotiations for a new trade treaty with Italy, and the result was a trade war catastrophic for Italy's exports and public finance. Crispi believed the French were preparing to attack, and London was also alarmed to the point of sending a naval squadron to Genoa with Bismarck's encouragement. These events forced the British and Italians to reconsider their requirements for naval bases, warships, and armaments, beginning a new round in the European arms race.[21]

The reinsurance treaty, Triple Alliance, Mediterranean agreements, and Russia's declining interest left France completely isolated. In Berlin there was again speculation about the possibility of a preventive strike. Even Bismarck fed the discussion in ways that have puzzled historians. In May 1888 he insisted over Hohenlohe's objections on imposing passport restrictions upon foreigners (mostly French) wanting to visit Alsace-Lorraine. In that same month he informed Crown Prince Wilhelm, who had converted from Russophilism to Russophobia after his visit to Petersburg in September 1886, that France was a better target than Russia for a preventive war.[22] On May 13, 1888, he told the Prussian cabinet that, "as things stand, it is no longer necessary to avoid war with France with such care." War would come if Germany merely let another "Schnaebelé case" run its course. If Germany became entangled in war with Russia, France would be on her back; but war with France would not necessarily involve Russia. "While the old Kaiser was on the throne, one could no longer bring about a war, and the same is true of the present peaceful and very sick ruler. But once the young and militant crown prince ascends the throne, the situation will be different." This was, he cautioned, merely an "observation of natural history," not an intention. Prince Wilhelm would have no difficulty deciding for a war if it was needed. Hence war need not be avoided "so anxiously and conscientiously as in the past."[23]

On May 16 the crown prince confided to Waldersee "under the seal of

[21] William L. Langer, *European Alliances and Alignments* (2d ed., New York, 1956), pp. 472, 479–480; George Kennan, *The Decline of Bismarck's European Order: Franco-Russian Relations, 1875–1890* (Princeton, 1979), pp. 379–391; GP, VI, 206–215.

[22] GP, VI, 215–218, 302–309; Bussmann, ed., *Herbert von Bismarck*, p. 504; Hohenlohe, *Memoirs*, II, 395–399.

[23] Lucius, *Bismarck-Erinnerungen*, p. 452.

secrecy" that Bismarck had decided "not to shun war with France any more."
But Waldersee told Herbert Bismarck a few days later that the French had
"little desire" for war and were not ready for one. He speculated that the
chancellor had merely tried to be "pleasant" to the militant heir to the throne
and get him "in hand" by declaring that he would not accept further provocations from France.[24] Waldersee recognized the tactic, for it was the reverse
of his own. Bismarck was seeking to break the general's hold on the bellicose
imagination of the heir to the throne.

The only positive preparations that Bismarck made for trouble with France
during 1888–1889 were diplomatic rather than military and were designed to
tighten still further the straitjacket of her isolation. After Wilhelm's succession in June 1888, he persuaded the new king and Kaiser to make his first
state visit to Russia, accompanied by Herbert, for the purpose of cementing
relations with the tsar and his government. In briefing the young Hohenzoller, he again described the tactic of balanced alternatives that had made
him the arbiter of European politics: A French-Austrian-Russian coalition
against Germany could be more easily established now than in the time of
Frederick the Great; to avoid it Germany must maintain good relations with
either Russia or Austria; to be firmly allied to both was desirable but difficult
in view of their mutual antagonism; close relations with one of those powers
did not necessarily mean enmity toward the other; Germany could and must
prevent either one from disturbing the peace by combining with the other,
but only Austria had shown a willingness to cooperate to that end; if unable
to retain the friendship of both powers, "we must at least keep what we have."

Austria was, he continued, less demanding than Russia because its sympathies for Germany were shared by its people and were not dependent upon
the goodwill of its ruler as in Russia. Germany could not support Russia in the
eastern question where Austria's vital interests were affected; hence she could
support Russian aspirations "in the eastern area" (including the Black Sea,
Constantinople, and the Straits). Possibly Austria had an interest in hindering Russian expansion there, but in that case she must find other allies. The
acquisition of Constantinople would weaken Russia by bringing her into conflict with England and perhaps France. Although willing to support Petersburg, Germany must avoid every initiative, lest Russia, whose vanity was easily aroused, conclude that Germany itself had need of Russian support. On
the contrary, Germany had no demands or requests to make, whether of an
economic, military, or political character. Russia must understand that Germany was without need or fear, but also peace-loving and friendly.[25]

As Bismarck advised, Wilhelm went to Russia on a courtesy call without

[24] Heinrich O. Meisner, ed., *Denkwürdigkeiten des General-Feldmarschalls Alfred Grafen von
Waldersee* (Stuttgart, 1923), I, 399–401.
[25] GP, VI, 311–314.

any political objective. But Giers was not content to let the occasion pass without a political discussion with Herbert. The Russian minister made the usual complaints about Austrian intrigues in the Balkans and the intransigence of Prince Ferdinand in Bulgaria, and Herbert reiterated the standard reply: While unwilling to act in Russia's behalf, Germany would support any Russian initiative in the Bulgarian question. While denying any expert knowledge of tariff questions, Giers lamented that the "stepped up economic struggle of our times influences the political attitudes of peoples" and expressed an interest in a trade treaty. Herbert reiterated with precision his father's view "that the economic and political relations between large states have in themselves nothing to do with one another. At times of the most intimate relations between Prussia and Russia we have always had complaints about economic difficulties. More than sixty years ago at a time of extremely close friendship between our monarchs those difficulties even led to prohibitions [*Sperrmassregeln*], from which we are at this time far away. Those measures had no effect on the intimacy of the political relationship, and they need not do so now." Herbert reported that his personal reception by Alexander III

BISMARCK AND WILHELM II AT FRIEDRICHSRUH, OCTOBER 30, 1888. (BILDARCHIV PREUSSISCHER KULTURBESITZ.)

was informal and friendly and asserted that the tsar seemed pleased by the conduct of Wilhelm II.[26]

The visit, however, did not cure Wilhelm II of Russophobia. On the contrary, he expected war with either France or Russia by the end of 1888. German generals were also apprehensive, for the Russian army resumed redeployment of its troops from the interior to the Austrian border. Bismarck too was uneasy about Russian intentions, and his disquietude was reinforced by the news that the French were again pouring massive sums into fortifications and armaments. Under these circumstances Bismarck's course was predictable; he turned to England. Through Count Hatzfeldt, the German ambassador in London, he urged the British in late August 1888 to strengthen their military preparedness; those powers that wanted peace—Germany, Austria, Italy, and England—must restrain those that lusted for war—Russia and France. In January 1889, as the Boulanger campaign moved toward a climax in Paris, he formally proposed to Salisbury a German-British treaty providing for a common defense against French aggression "for a definite period of time." Although a secret treaty ("if it were possible") would do much to assure victory, only an open treaty approved by the British Parliament and known by the Reichstag could be expected to hinder war. If diverging interests forced England to go to war against Russia or the United States (or both), the conflict would be critical for Britain only if France should join her enemies. But France could hardly do so if threatened by a German army of one million men. In Europe neither France nor Russia would disturb the peace if Britain would "certainly and immediately" come to the assistance of the attacked. Bismarck preached to the converted, for Salisbury already believed that "France is, and must always remain, England's greatest danger." The prime minister asked for time in which to sound out his colleagues.[27]

For months Bismarck had already been engaged in the endeavor to improve the Kaiser's image in London and to remove sources of friction between the two powers. In March 1889 he sent Herbert to the British capital to seek a settlement of the problem of Samoa. (The result was a tripartite conference in Berlin that led to the Samoa treaty between Britain, Germany, and the United States on June 14, 1889.) In London Herbert listened sympathetically to Joseph Chamberlain's proposal that Britain cede Helgoland to Germany in exchange for Southwest Africa! (Bismarck considered the matter not yet "ripe" for concrete discussion.) On this visit Salisbury reported to Herbert that his colleagues believed a German-British alliance would be "most healthy for both countries and for European peace" but the moment was "inopportune," for the issue would break up the government's parliamentary majority. Salisbury uttered a few deprecatory words about parliamentary democ-

[26] GP, VI, 320–337, also V, 320.
[27] GP, IV, 399–404.

racy, which "damned his country to such impotence" in foreign affairs. The prime minister rejoiced, however, that Britain and Germany could for the time being "go hand in hand"; he appreciated that Berlin demanded nothing more at present. In June Queen Victoria delighted her nephew Wilhelm by naming him Admiral of the Fleet, and in August a German squadron anchored at Cowes, while Britain's newest admiral, resplendent in the "uniform of Nelson," watched the British fleet pass in review before the queen.[28]

Naturally the signs of rapprochement between Britain and Germany aroused suspicion in Russia. For Bismarck, of course, the démarche was just one more maneuver in his favorite tactic of balanced alternatives—that of restraining a potential foe by demonstrating Germany's capacity to find allies. As the Boulangist danger subsided, the necessity for exercising the option passed, and he let it lapse. In Petersburg he insisted that the rapprochement with Britain was aimed only at France and had no significance for Russia. Indeed, if the discussion with Salisbury had become concrete, he would have excluded from the agreement any promise of support for British policy in the Balkans and at the Straits. In this regard his policy toward Britain would have been no different from that toward Austria under the alliance of 1879. Despite all their suspicions concerning Bismarck and Germany, the tsar and Giers were unwilling to part with the reinsurance treaty, which was destined to lapse in 1890. They looked forward to its renewal.[29]

At the end of his chancellorship Bismarck's seesaw tactic still functioned, fluctuating up and down as the balance threatened to tip in one direction or another. Where Bismarck's diplomatic tactics ultimately failed was in the mind and understanding of the Kaiser. Wilhelm II did not have the experience, temperament, and intelligence to grasp the subtleties of Bismarck's course in foreign affairs. His grandfather had also never fully understood it, but, whatever his doubts, the old Kaiser had always, if only at the final moment, placed his trust in Bismarck's skill. Hovering around his grandson, however, were those, particularly Waldersee, who undermined that trust by insinuating that the old chancellor no longer understood the realities of European politics and that his foreign policy was confused and contradictory.[30] In Herbert's mind they were "unconscionable troublemakers" who aroused the Kaiser unnecessarily about even minor issues of foreign policy.

One such issue was an attempt by the Russian treasury to convert at a lower rate of interest a series of state railway bonds with approaching due dates. When asked by Bleichröder, Bismarck did not object to the conversion, and

[28] GP, IV, 404–410; Langer, Alliances and Alignments, pp. 493–494.

[29] Schweinitz, Denkwürdigkeiten, II, 374–375, 392, 396ff.

[30] Waldersee, Denkwürdigkeiten, II, 42, 48; Hajo Holborn, ed., Aufzeichnungen und Erinnerungen aus dem Leben des Botschafters Joseph Maria von Radowitz (Stuttgart, 1925), II, 296–297; Norman Rich, Friedrich von Holstein: Politics and Diplomacy in the Era of Bismarck and Wilhelm II (Cambridge, Eng., 1965), I, 249–250.

the "elders' council" of the Berlin stock exchange approved. The Kaiser wanted the conversion blocked, arguing that Russia would use the 20 million marks in annual savings (Bismarck: "?") for military purposes. Even Herbert sided on this issue with the Kaiser, influenced evidently by hatred for Bleichröder, that "dangerous Jew" and "avaricious Semite," whom he accused of being more interested in earning millions than in Bismarck's and the country's good (Bismarck: "Who wouldn't be?"). As long as no one knew what was going to happen in France, his father replied, it was best to avoid antagonizing Russia. Yet he did appease the Kaiser by causing the *Norddeutsche Allgemeine Zeitung* to advise German investors to exercise the option of redemption rather than conversion.[31]

Another issue brought to the Kaiser's attention by dissidents was the adverse reaction of south Germans to the government's attempt to interdict the flow of socialist newspapers from Switzerland, where many German socialists had sought refuge from the antisocialist statute. In April 1889, August Wohlgemuth, a German police inspector charged with the investigation of this traffic, was lured into Switzerland by German exiles, arrested on arrival as an agent provocateur by provincial police, and imprisoned for ten days. Bismarck saw in this episode an opportunity to reinforce the conservative bond with Russia, pending the results of his overtures to England. Alexander III and Giers, already aroused by Switzerland's hospitality to Russian nihilists experimenting with bombs, readily agreed to join in delivering to Berne an identical note of protest (subsequently joined by Austria).[32]

Bismarck, however, had a second objective in which Russia and Austria were evidently reluctant to cooperate. He expected that the three powers, by their common front toward Switzerland on the terrorist issue, would make the Berne government see the wisdom of cooperating with Berlin in its efforts to interdict socialist agitation. But both Petersburg and Vienna softened the effect of the note by the low-key manner in which their envoys delivered it in Berne and by refusing to permit its publication. Bismarck proceeded independently by tightening passport and customs controls at the border and abrogating a treaty of 1876, which had eased for Swiss citizens the restrictions on foreigners living in Germany. This action also had an ulterior objective. Since the Treaty of Frankfurt (1871) contained a "most favored nation" clause, French citizens had been able to exploit the Swiss-German treaty of 1876 to reside in Alsace-Lorraine, and their presence there had become in Bismarck's view an obstacle to the Germanization of the Reichsland's population.[33]

[31] Bussmann, ed., *Herbert von Bismarck*, pp. 535, 538–542; Waldersee, *Denkwürdigkeiten*, II, 54–59.

[32] Bismarck to Boetticher, June 26, 1889. GW, VIc, 414–415.

[33] Hansjörg Renk, *Bismarcks Konflikt mit der Schweiz. Basler Beiträge zur Geschichtswissenschaft*, vol. 125 (Basel, 1972), pp. 128ff., 331ff.

When seen in all of its ramifications, Bismarck's campaign against Switzerland in 1889 shows that he had not lost his capacity for striking simultaneously several targets in a single action. But it also revealed a diminished capacity for calculating all of the serious side effects that the action might produce. The campaign against Switzerland injured commercial and tourist relations with Switzerland in the German border states. The citizens and governments of Baden and Württemberg did not appreciate the sacrifice they were asked to make in behalf of *die grosse Politik*. Among the angered was Grand Duke Friedrich of Baden, who protested vigorously and persistently to his nephew, the Kaiser, that the action was excessive and even dangerous economically and politically, for it might cause the Swiss to side with France in a future war. "Even Herbert," the grand duke told Hohenlohe, "says he can no longer understand his father, and many people are beginning to think that [his father] is no longer quite right in the head."[34]

Worse still, the Swiss affair showed how weakened Bismarck's position had become. Through Herbert (and Holstein) he was warned that those with access to the Kaiser were using the Russian conversion and the Swiss border incidents to injure his standing with the Kaiser. Insecure ministers were trying to use these issues to force a "chancellor crisis" in the expectation that it would improve their own situations. But Holstein doubted that it would "get as hot as is cooked"; the intriguers knew they would have to wait for "the psychological moment." Herbert believed Waldersee to be the chief culprit and was deeply concerned. Without his father's guidance an "immature and inexperienced" Wilhelm II, advised by ambitious *homines novi* of poor judgment, could soon produce a "great war." But his father affected indifference: "If our lord and master does not want to continue with me, nothing can be done about it."[35]

When the Kaiser departed on a cruise in Scandinavian waters in late July 1889, Herbert was not along, and he feared the effect of that "chatterbox," the Russophobe Waldersee, on the monarch's views. Herbert took comfort in the fact that Russia's Crown Prince Nicholas was a guest—proof that Wilhelm II did not want war and still clung to the chancellor's leadership. But the young prince and his entourage proved to be poor company. They developed "hydrophobia" and left the trip prematurely. Apparently on the tsar's instructions, furthermore, Nicholas had avoided talk about politics, in preference to weather and hunting (Bismarck: "was predictable"), a severe disappointment to the Kaiser who had hoped to influence him. "I have definitely given up on

[34] Walther Peter Fuchs, ed., *Grossherzog Friedrich I. von Baden und die Reichspolitik 1871–1907* (Stuttgart, 1975), II, 628–670; Friedrich Curtius, ed., *Denkwürdigkeiten des Fürsten Chlodwig zu Hohenlohe-Schillingsfürst* (Stuttgart, 1906), II, 456–457; Renk, *Bismarcks Konflikt mit der Schweiz*, pp. 335–357.
[35] Bussmann, ed., *Herbert von Bismarck*, pp. 538–544.

the Russians," Wilhelm told Herbert, "I will remain courteous to the last, but I do not expect anything from Russia any more."[36]

In October 1889 Tsar Alexander, returning to Petersburg from Copenhagen after an autumn visit with his relatives, stopped off in Berlin. Although irritated that the tsarina avoided the German capital by taking ship to Königsberg, Wilhelm's demonstrative hospitality did make a positive impression on the tsar. But the Kaiser overdid it by inviting himself to Russia for a return visit. When he heard of this, Bismarck was alarmed. He knew that Wilhelm's success with Alexander would be temporary and easily destroyed by too much contact. The "aggressively friendly" Hohenzoller, who liked nothing better than travel and state visits, could easily exhaust the patience of the "defensively mistrustful" Romanov, who much preferred the comfort of family life to official entertainment. During his audience with Alexander at Berlin, Bismarck had to exert himself to convince the tsar that Wilhelm's recent visit to England and his projected trip to Athens and Constantinople had no political import. His persuasion was wasted when Wilhelm, while in Greece, reviewed the British fleet at Piraeus and engaged the Prince of Wales in discussions on the subject of sea power in the Mediterranean. This seeming demonstration of solidarity with Britain in a critical region was disturbing to the Russians, and the tsar spoke of Wilhelm as "an ill-bred and faithless youngster."[37]

Yet Alexander's trust in Bismarck grew in ratio to his distrust of Wilhelm, and in December 1889 the tsar first broached a renewal of the reinsurance treaty. In February 1890 Bismarck succeeded in gaining the Kaiser's approval for the renewal. But by that time the relationship between Kaiser and chancellor had deteriorated to the point where every aspect of state policy, including foreign affairs, was affected.[38] Bismarck's assumption that good relations with Russia were a 'fixed and unchanging" necessity for German foreign policy that no monarch could arbitrarily change was soon to be put to the test.

Defeat of the Ultraconservatives

Once Wilhelm II's grandfather and father had left the scene, Bismarck was the only father figure left against whom Willy could rebel. His feelings toward the aging chancellor had all of the ambivalence characteristic of the Oedipal problem. He stood in awe of the statesman who had created—by "blood and iron," it was said—the power that was now constitutionally his, but resented the schoolmasterly way in which the chancellor often instructed him in its

[36] Ibid., pp. 540–541, 544–545, 547.

[37] Ibid., pp. 547–549; GP, VI, 359–362; GW, XV, 559–560; Waldersee, Denkwürdigkeiten, II, 70–73; Hans Übersberger, "Abschluss und Ende des Rückversicherungsvertrages" in Hans Hallmann, ed., Zur Geschichte und Problematik des deutsch-russischen Rückversicherungesvertrages von 1887 (Darmstadt, 1968), pp. 313–317.

[38] Langer, Alliances and Alignments, pp. 496–498; Wilhelm von Schweinitz, ed., Briefwechsel des Botschafters General von Schweinitz (Berlin, 1928), pp. 264–265.

proper use. Toward this insecure young man, whom he knew to be "lacking in moderation and balance" and whose best friend said he was "notably young for his years," Bismarck often adopted the same pedagogical manner that he often used toward subordinates, ministers, and parliaments.[39] If Wilhelm felt the need for guidance in the beginning, he still resented the dependence it implied. He liked to compare himself to Frederick the Great, who was born on January 24, just three days short of Wilhelm's own birthday, and had ascended the throne and begun a major war at the age of twenty-eight.[40]

As long as the chancellor and Kaiser, and those to whom the latter listened, were in general agreement on the direction of German policy, these latent feelings were not disruptive. Prince Wilhelm's flirtation with the ultras in the Waldersee meeting affair appears to have been but a temporary and innocent aberration from political views that he had held since 1886. In that year he had been delighted by the discredit into which the centrists fell by combining with left-liberals and socialists in opposing the Septennat. "May the day soon come," he exulted to Eulenburg, "when the Grenadier Guards purge the place with bayonets and tambours." He was equally pleased by the formation of the cartel and by its victory in the election of 1887.[41] On the day before he succeeded to the throne in 1888, the crown prince told Bismarck, "I want to govern along the lines established by my grandfather, respecting the rights of sovereigns and legislatures, finding support not from the extremists but from the cartel parties. The ultraconservatives will never be a majority and will usually be led by an extreme wing that is half crazy and too limited."[42] In July the Austrian ambassador reported, "The intimacy of the present ruler with the first counselor of the crown is so close that it is scarcely capable of improvement. There is a veritable honeymoon of respect, affection, trust, and understanding."[43]

[39] GW, VIII, 672–673; Helmut Krausnick, Neue Bismarck-Gespräche (Hamburg, 1940), pp. 60–62; Philipp zu Eulenburg-Hertefeld, Aus 50 Jahren (Berlin, 1923), pp. 222–224. In 1888 Bismarck showed some awareness of the problem, when he advised Finance Minister Scholz not to send to Wilhelm II an instruction from the cabinet on what actions required a ministerial countersignature. "In view of his majesty's character it would not have the right effect if the form of address used were that of a ministerial lesson in public law. In the peculiarities of his character lie many inconveniences for us and for later ministers perhaps but also such great advantages for the country and for the monarchy that I do not see it as our task to engage him with polemical sharpness in a personal matter." Aug. 2, 1888. GW, XIV, 986–987.

[40] At the end of his letter of December 21, 1887, to Bismarck, Prince Wilhelm wrote, "In the event [war] should occur, you should not forget that the hand and sword of a man is ready who is very conscious that Frederick the Great is his ancestor and that Frederick fought armies three times as large as those we now have against us. And do not forget that this man has not gone through ten years of hard military training for nothing!" GW, XV, 463–464.

[41] Quoted in John C. G. Röhl, "Disintegration of the Kartell and the Politics of Bismarck's Fall from Power," Historical Journal, 9 (1966), pp. 68–69.

[42] Lucius, Bismarck-Erinnerungen, p. 465.

[43] Quoted in Heinrich Heffter, Die Kreuzzeitungspartei und Bismarcks Kartellpolitik (Leipzig, 1927), p. 137.

As his first official act, Wilhelm II wished to reinstate Puttkamer as Prussian minister of interior. But Bismarck persuaded him to delay the appointment, which would have been widely regarded as an "act of impiety" against his father's memory. The Kaiser appointed Ernst Herrfurth, a liberal official, on an interim, ultimately permanent basis.[44] According to Bismarck, the Kaiser himself initiated the appointment of Rudolf von Bennigsen as governor-general of the province of Hanover, a decision intended to demonstrate his support of the cartel.[45] That autumn Wilhelm confirmed a decision by the Prussian cabinet to back Gossler in summoning the liberal church historian Adolf Harnack to join the theological faculty of the University of Berlin, an appointment opposed by the conservative general council of the Evangelical church. In late August he let it be known in the press, although somewhat circumspectly, that he disapproved of anti-Semitic agitation. During the fall campaign for the election of the Prussian Chamber of Deputies, he authorized a free conservative deputy, Count Hugo Douglas, to deny that he had ever had direct dealings with Stöcker or the anti-Semitic movement.

All of these actions were interpreted as an endorsement of Bismarck and the cartel parties and ipso facto a defeat for ultraconservatives and orthodox clericals in the struggle for the favor of the new ruler. In November 1888 the Prussian electorate appeared to approve Wilhelm's course. The "middle parties" of the cartel (free conservatives and national liberals) were strengthened by twenty seats in the Chamber of Deputies at the cost of left-liberals and German conservatives.[46]

Undeterred by the Kaiser's defection, Stöcker proceeded in early 1889 to found a newspaper, Das Volk, which printed veiled attacks on the chancellor for debasing the national character, confusing the public, and even undermining the monarchy itself. At this juncture the controversial preacher made himself vulnerable to counterattack by engaging in a public feud with another orthodox cleric in which each accused the other of lying. Through the chief of his civil cabinet, Hermann von Lucanus, the Kaiser reproved the church's general council for not stopping the feud, which was damaging to the prestige of the church, and ordered Stöcker to surrender either his position as court preacher or his political activity. In April 1889 Stöcker responded that he would give up politics, from which he no longer derived any pleasure. "To organize a conservative-Christian opposition" was impossible. Still, he delayed acting on his choice for some months while waiting to see what fortune the Kreuzzeitung would have in yet another assault upon the Bismarck government.[47]

[44] Lucius, Bismarck-Erinnerungen, pp. 464–465, 471; Heffter, Kreuzzeitungspartei, pp. 120–121.

[45] Lucius, Bismarck-Erinnerungen, p. 477; GW, VIII, 615–616.

[46] Heffter, Kreuzzeitungspartei, pp. 140–143; SEG (1888), p. 121; Röhl, "Disintegration of the Kartell," p. 72.

[47] Heffter, Kreuzzeitungspartei, pp. 165–167. Kronratsprotokolle. DZA Merseburg, Rep. 90a, B, III, 2c, Nr. 3, Bd. 4, pp. 172–173.

Stöcker's political demise, which Waldersee attributed to Bismarck's influence on Wilhelm II, left the *Kreuzzeitung* as the only remaining center of ultraconservative opposition. In its pages Hammerstein raged at the suppression of his political ally and questioned whether there remained any force capable of defending the "old principles" of conservatism against the chancellor's pressure. But Hammerstein too fell victim to a rebuke from the Kaiser, which appeared in the official *Reichsanzeiger* on October 3, 1889. "His majesty sees in the cartel a political structure that corresponds to the principles of his government. He cannot harmonize the way in which the *Kreuzzeitung* attacks the cartel with the respect owed to his imperial highness and our constitutional institutions."[48] This public intervention by the ruler in a political dispute was without parallel in the history of the Prussian-German constitutional monarchy.

By winging the ultraconservatives Bismarck did not cripple Waldersee. After Friedrich's death the general was openly discussed in the press as a future chancellor and as a member of the "war party" at court.[49] In the past Bismarck had enjoyed only limited success in his attempts to separate the monarch from close associates, particularly generals. Sensing the danger to himself of an unsuccessful attack on Waldersee, the chancellor extended the hand of friendship. "I feel that I have won my campaign," the general exulted in his diary. "Bismarck has indicated that he will never ask Kaiser Wilhelm II to get rid of me and now prefers to be my friend."[50] Waldersee's appointment as chief of the general staff in August 1888 and member of the House of Lords in January 1889 seemed to be further proof of a secure future. "The Kaiser wishes," he mused, "that I have a look at what goes on outside the area of purely military affairs and counts on me as an adviser in domestic and foreign policy if the occasion should arise. I have gained this impression over a long period of time. He covers himself by gaining the views of many observers of our development. For a year this has been the subject of gossip but also of serious discussion, and it can be proved that the chancellor has many times regarded me as a rival."

And yet Waldersee was not sure that he wanted to be the immediate successor of a world-historical figure like Bismarck. Before assuming that awesome responsibility, he thought, perhaps it was better to let "one or more successors break their necks."[51] Waldersee decided on caution for the time being, lest he undermine himself by intriguing against the prince. Two futile efforts to save Stöcker demonstrated the limits of his political influence. During 1889 he avoided the catastrophe of the *Kreuzzeitung* by disassociating himself from the ultras and supporting the Kaiser in his enthusiasm for the cartel

[48] *Ibid.*, pp. 167, 175–178; Leuss, *Wilhelm Freiherr von Hammerstein*, pp. 61–70; Lucius, *Bismarck-Erinnerungen*, pp. 502–503.

[49] Gradenwitz, *Letzter Kampf*, pp. 76–77; SEG (1888), pp. 97, 101; (1889), pp. 107, 125–126.

[50] June 22 and July 10, 1888. Waldersee, *Denkwürdigkeiten* I, 405–406, 412.

[51] *Ibid.*, I, 413ff.; II, 33–36.

parties.[52] Meanwhile, he waited for Bismarck to stumble and fall or succumb to the ravages of age and illness.

Ironically Bismarck's dual success in defeating the *Kreuzzeitung*-Stöcker faction and in keeping Wilhelm II committed to the cartel parties contributed in the end to his own undoing. What was for him a temporary majority, to be exploited as long as it remained amenable to his purposes, became for Wilhelm II the only conceivable basis for his government.[53] Although the chancellor had striven for years to bring the national liberals (purged of their left wing) into alliance with the free conservatives and German conservatives (preferably purged of their right wing), he never looked upon this combination or any other as permanent. Such an attitude would have been inconsistent with his view of the relationship between government, parliament, and parties and with his practice of exploiting party cleavages to create alternative majorities in the chamber. As related earlier, he told the Prussian cabinet in 1884 that he could govern with the national liberals only "until they again become too strong and uppity."[54]

During 1889 the repeated public and private assurances of the Kaiser's favor ("The cartel is as necessary for internal peace as is the Triple Alliance for external peace")[55] emboldened leaders of the National Liberal party to believe that they might be able to achieve in harmony with the Kaiser what they had never been able to coerce from the chancellor. Miquel exulted to Bennigsen, "Our ideas have found firm support in our young Kaiser"; he predicted that the Kaiser's patronage would bring the national liberals to power.[56] Throughout most of their party's history, leaders of the national liberal movement had hoped to achieve influence over the executive power of the Prussian-German state not by changing the system itself but through ministerial appointments by the monarch. During Bismarck's first decade as chancellor they had found a surrogate for that control in Bismarck's willingness to follow a liberal, procapitalist economic policy. In the chancellor crisis of 1877–1878 their hopes and expectations had reached a new peak, only to fall again. After ten years of renewed frustration they now found in Wilhelm II a possible instrument for the fulfillment of their ambitions and interests. As the ultras came under fire from the Kaiser during 1889, national liberals began to differ openly with Bismarck. This was particularly true of Miquel, increasingly the party's most influential spokesman. The Bismarck era was patently about to end; perhaps the time of the national liberals had finally come.

Among the important reforms advocated by Miquel and his associates was

[52] *Ibid.*, I, 352–354, 377ff., 413; II, 3ff., 38ff., 43ff.; Heinrich Otto Meisner, ed., *Aus dem Briefwechsel des Generalfeldmarschalls Alfred Grafen von Waldersee* (Berlin, 1928), I, 301–303, 310–315. Heffter, *Kreuzzeitungspartei*, pp. 168, 180–181.

[53] Bussmann, ed., *Herbert von Bismarck*, pp. 548–549, 554–555.

[54] See pp. 173–174.

[55] Herbert to Otto von Bismarck, Oct. 5, 1889. Bussmann, ed., *Herbert von Bismarck*, p. 549.

[56] Sept. 1, 1888. Hermann Oncken, *Rudolf von Bennigsen* (Stuttgart, 1910), II, 547.

a major reform of the Prussian tax system. They wished to replace the anti-quated class and classified income taxes with a single income tax based on progressive rates, self-assessment, and exemption of low-income groups. A vigorous supporter of the old-age and invalid insurance act, Miquel (a member of the *Verein für Sozialpolitik*) was critical of Bismarck's unwillingness to extend social reform to include labor protection, urban housing, and labor representation. Miquel was also opposed to Bismarck's seemingly pro-Russian stance in Balkan affairs and was privately an advocate of preventive war, a view that enabled Holstein to bring him into contact with Waldersee.[57] During the summer of 1889 colonial zealots, a strong faction in the National Liberal party, became aware of Bismarck's waning enthusiasm for imperialism; a fierce debate erupted between the *Kolonialzeitung* and the *Norddeutsche All-gemeine Zeitung* over the government's refusal to support the Emin Pascha expedition to the upper Nile.[58]

Miquel's tactic for undermining Bismarck was to exploit every opportunity publicly to flatter "our young, energetic Kaiser." "The nation's trust in the Kaiser has grown from day to day as we see him, like his distinguished ancestors, holding the reins of government with unflagging zeal and untiring attention to duty." Fundamentally disillusioned about the value of party politics and of the parliamentary system, Miquel preached a kind of enlightened absolutism, by which he hoped to outbid everyone, Bismarck included, in gaining the attention and appreciation of the Kaiser.[59] At the end of October Bennigsen raised the old demand for a constitutionally responsible imperial cabinet, or at least for a responsible minister of finance to cope with the Reich's growing budget and debt.[60] In a circular letter Heinrich Patzig, the party's general secretary, is said to have warned against "too far-reaching support for a rapidly aging chancellor."[61]

Scholz's Initiative on Tax Reform

That Bismarck's hand was no longer so firm on the throttle is also evident in the conduct of a colleague. Since appointment as Prussian minister of finance in 1882, Adolf Scholz had shown little inclination toward independence in

[57] Hans Herzfeld, *Johannes von Miquel* (Detmold, 1938), II, 133ff.; Waldersee, *Briefwechsel*, pp. 303, 310–317.

[58] SEG (1889), p. 140.

[59] Herzfeld, *Miquel*, II, 156–160. At an informal beer hall meeting of national liberal deputies, Miquel is said to have astonished and antagonized his colleagues, especially Bennigsen, by loudly declaring that the National Liberal party was guilty of too much self-abnegation. The time had come to demand concessions in return for support, both in matters of personnel and legislation. Wilhelm Mommsen, *Bismarcks Sturz und die Parteien* (Berlin, 1924), p. 22.

[60] SBR (1889–1890), I, 52–58. For Bismarck's reaction to this demand, see Gradenwitz, *Letzter Kampf*, pp. 82–83.

[61] Herzfeld, *Miquel*, II, 161. Miquel is said to have inspired Patzig's circular letter. Mommsen, *Bismarcks Sturz*, p. 23.

the conduct of his office. For that reason Bismarck later praised him as the only finance minister with whom he had worked in harmony.[62] After the debacle of the liquor monopoly in 1886, however, Bismarck's interest in fiscal matters had visibly slackened. The successive protective tariffs adopted since 1879 had proven to be excellent finance tariffs. From 104,300,000 marks in 1878 customs revenues rose to 288,000,000 marks in 1888 and 349,900,000 marks in 1889. Supplemented by other new taxes of smaller yield the tariffs increased the total revenue of the Reich in the same years from 350,700,000 marks to 579,300,000 marks and 707,300,000 marks. Through the Franck-enstein clause and the Lex Huene the indirect taxes of the Reich had become a major source of income for state and local governments. Payments to the states in excess of assessments paid by the states to the Reich rose from a low of 5,400,000 marks in 1887 to 70,000,000 marks in 1888 and 139,700,000 marks in 1889.[63] The financial crises that Bismarck had earlier attempted to exploit as leverage for his tax proposals no longer existed. During the rest of his chancellorship Bismarck undertook no new initiatives toward the goal he had sought for so long: abandonment by the Prussian state of direct taxes on income and real estate.

Among parliamentary deputies, journalists, political economists, fiscal experts, and involved public officials it was increasingly recognized that the German-Prussian system of taxation was badly in need of repair. In 1887 the Prussian Chamber of Deputies again resolved "by great majority" that the growth of indirect taxation made the reform of direct taxation in Prussia an "unavoidable necessity." But as in 1883–1884 public discussion of the issue ignited conflicts between agrarian and industrial interests, between east and west, about the character of the reform to be undertaken. Both interest groups recognized that the existing tax system was inequitable, that the burden of supporting the state (especially the cost of military expansion) was carried by German consumers, meaning chiefly the lower classes. But they disagreed on what else was to be done. Agrarians continued to demand and financiers and industrialists to resist the imposition of taxes on corporate and unearned capital income.[64] Without skillful and forceful leadership from Bismarck and the Prussian Ministry of Finance, the dam against change could not be broken. Bismarck was the principal obstacle.

In January 1889 Adolf Scholz, impelled by the public discussion and probably by advice from subordinates in the Ministry of Finance, presented to the

[62] GW, XV, 385–386.

[63] Richard Müller, Die Einnahmequellen des Deutchen Reiches und ihre Entwicklung in den Jahren 1872 bis 1907 (Mönchen Gladbach, 1907), pp. 62–63.

[64] Debate of May 12, 1887. SBHA (1887), pp. 1205–1234; Anlagen, Nos. 126, 201; Henry Axel Bueck, "Bericht über die Sitzung des Ausschusses am 20. Februar 1889," in publication No. 20, Verein zur Wahrung der wirtschaftlichen Interessen von Handel und Gewerbe (Berlin, 1889), p. 47.

Prussian cabinet the lengthy draft of a Prussian tax reform modeled after that unsuccessfully submitted to the Landtag in 1883–1884. Although Bismarck, whose health had reached its nadir in late 1883, had little to do with the drafting of the earlier bill, he had raised no objections at that time to its basic features. But five years later he disputed in acerbic marginalia on Scholz's draft proposal both the necessity and character of the reform.[65] Incomes under 1,200 marks (brackets one through four of the class tax) were to be tax free (Bismarck: "How expensive?"). Incomes from 1,200 to 9,500 marks (brackets five through twelve of the class tax and one through eight of the classified income tax) were to be taxed progressively at 1 to 3 percent (Bismarck: "What is the cost of the progression?"). Incomes above 9,500 marks were to be taxed at the existing rate of 3 percent. Deductions of 100 marks were permitted for each family member (Bismarck: "33 percent!"). Extenuating circumstances (educational costs of children, support for impoverished relatives, sickness, debts, accidents) could be taken into consideration to the point of cancelling the entire tax on incomes of less than 1,800 marks and up to half the tax on incomes between 1,800 and 9,500 marks (Bismarck: "a lot of room for arbitrary decisions!"). Self-assessment was required (Bismarck: "Over the sources of the income or its amount?") from persons with incomes of more than 3,000 marks—except for incomes derived from personally cultivated or managed farms and forests, which were to be assessed by a local commission "because of the difficulty of filling out the tax declaration" (no comment from Bismarck).[66]

Scholz's memorandum and draft bill recognized serious inequities in the structure of existing taxes on personal income. An income of 1,200 marks, Scholz declared, was insufficient to cover the necessities of a family, as was shown by the continuing high number of foreclosures for nonpayment of the class tax. In 1887–1888 (October 1 to September 30) the percentage of persons in bracket three (900 to 1,050 marks) who were victims of attachments was 11.7 in the cities and 1.79 in rural areas, in bracket four (1,050 to 1,200 marks) 7.24 and 1.27, in brackets five through twelve (1,200 to 3,000 marks) only 4.27 and 0.37. Income tax relief for the poor had been an announced purpose for expanding the Reich's indirect taxes. To remove brackets three and four from the tax rolls, a proposal that had encountered heavy opposition in the Chamber of Deputies in 1883, would cost 5,536,000 marks (Bismarck: "A lot of money"), a loss that Scholz believed affordable in view of "the generally favorable fiscal situation" (Bismarck: "Will it last?").[67] In 1889 declining interest rates led Scholz to conclude (Bismarck: "Unfortunately") that the tax on unearned capital income (*Kapitalrentensteuer*) proposed in 1883 was

[65] Scholz to Bismarck, Jan. 4, 1889. DZA Potsdam, Reichskanzlei, 2089, pp. 111–115.
[66] *Ibid.*, pp. 37, 79.
[67] *Ibid.*, pp. 38, 44.

"inopportune" (Bismarck: "An increase in property taxes even more so"). In the discussions of 1883–1884, Scholz recalled, the point had been made that to tax corporate income would constitute double taxation (Bismarck: "Landowners are taxed three-fold").[68]

Bismarck's reaction to Scholz's tax plan of January 1889 shows again the poverty of the chancellor's understanding of public finance and his limited comprehension of the social issues with which it was intimately connected. He rejected the progressive income tax as wrong in principle, asserting that even the moderate progression for low-income groups proposed by Scholz led "into the path of socialism." He was not opposed in principle to double taxation. On the contrary, he continued to insist on higher rates for income from invested capital as against income from "real labor" and for income from foreign investments as against domestic investments. "The income tax cannot be considered apart from the property tax. Income from land is affected by both."[69] The liquidation of surtaxes levied on the land and building taxes by local tax authorities must precede income tax reform. To end this "abuse" he proposed local taxes on corporate income and a reduction in public expenditures for public education. "We are producing not only in our *Gymnasien* and middle schools, but also in our elementary schools a higher quantity of culture than we can make use of in the normal development of life." Like Russia, Prussia and Germany were threatened by an overproduction of educated people. The state was itself creating the dissatisfactions with which it would ultimately have to cope.[70]

Apparently Scholz did not disclose to Bismarck in advance the details of his reform plan, a dereliction that in earlier years had cost ministers like Camphausen and Hofmann their posts. Under Wilhelm II, however, Bismarck could no longer dispose of ministers so easily. When he returned to Berlin on January 10, 1889, the chancellor found that the Kaiser and Prussian cabinet had generally agreed on Scholz's initiative.[71] On January 14 Wilhelm II committed the government to more income tax relief for low-income groups in his speech from the throne opening the Prussian Landtag.[72] Isolated within the government, Bismarck launched a counterattack in the Chamber of Deputies. While Scholz and his colleagues were still deliberating on the details of the government's bill, the centrist deputy Karl Huene introduced a bill, drafted in collaboration with Bismarck, that would have required the

[68] *Ibid.*, pp. 1, 38–39.

[69] "Bemerkungen Seiner Durchlaucht zu dem neuen Einkommensteuer-Entwurf," Jan. 18, 1889. DZA Potsdam, Reichskanzlei, 2089, pp. 111–115.

[70] Bismarck to Scholz, Jan. 22, 1889. GW, VIc, 406–408.

[71] Cabinet meetings of Mar. 18 and Apr. 7, 1889. DZA Potsdam, Reichskanzlei, 2090, pp. 70–83.

[72] SEG (1889), p. 6.

transfer of one-half of the revenues from land and building taxes to local governments (*Kommunalverbände*)—in preparation for the ultimate transfer of the entire tax.[73]

The revival of this old demand, highly popular among big landowners seeking relief from surtaxes and city governments seeking new revenues, jeopardized Scholz's reform bill by depriving the treasury of money destined for income tax relief. Scholz's response was to incorporate Huene's proposal into the government bill; to pay for it, he reduced the cost—and benefits—of income tax relief by lowering exemption from the class tax to 900 marks (300 marks below the income long regarded as necessary for a minimal standard of living) and reducing the range of deductions allowed the taxpayer. In this form the bill was again accepted by the Prussian cabinet and the Kaiser.[74] Before it could be officially presented to the Landtag, however, Bismarck persuaded the cabinet to obtain from the Kaiser an order abruptly closing that body. The deliberations on the income tax reform and on other pending issues, he argued, would adversely affect the coming Reichstag election.[75] On April 30, 1889, the deputies returned from a long Easter vacation and to their astonishment were sent home again without explanation.[76]

For more than a decade Bismarck had repeatedly striven for major changes in Prussian and German tax laws. As a result of those efforts, the imperial system of indirect taxation, particularly tariffs on mass consumption items, had been developed at the cost of consumers, particularly those of low income who bore a disproportionate share of the tax burden. Relief from the Prussian class and classified income taxes, which would have compensated Prussian workers and the lower middle class somewhat for this sacrifice, had been only partially achieved. The flow of revenue from the Reich to state and local governments (Franckenstein clause and *Lex Huene*) had not sufficed to end the hated surtaxes, whose liquidation had always been a major purpose of the reform.

When the issue of tax reform came up again in December 1889 during the final months of his chancellorship, Bismarck again insisted that tax relief for landowners must take precedence over any other proposal for direct tax reform. The use by local governments of real estate taxes as the basis for surtaxes was "more oppressive, unjust, and alienating than all the faults of the income and class taxes." To him the surtaxes represented "the annual renewal of the inequity in taxation that began with the introduction of the land tax in

---

[73] Huene to Bismarck, Mar. 2 and May 4, 1889. *DZA* Potsdam, Reichskanzlei, 2090, pp. 6–11, 26–27.

[74] Cabinet meeting of Apr. 7, 1889. *Ibid.*, pp. 79–83. Scholz to Bismarck, Apr. 13, 1889. *Ibid.*, pp. 65–70.

[75] Cabinet meeting of Apr. 20, 1889. *Ibid.*, pp. 84–85.

[76] *SEG* (1889), pp. 61–63.

1861."[77] Bismarck demanded that tax relief for landowners have priority over tax relief for low-income groups, although in the months since the closing of the Landtag on April 30 Germany had experienced widespread labor unrest. His views on tax reform, coupled with his views on social reform during that period, are graphic evidence of his increasing rigidity and declining capacity for realistic judgments.

[77] Scholz to cabinet, Dec. 1889. DZA Potsdam, Reichskanzlei, 2090, pp. 95–106. Bismarck to Scholz, Dec. 26, 1889. GW, VIc, 423–425. See also BP, I, 310.

❖❖❖

CHAPTER ELEVEN

Division on Social Policy

The Great Strike of May 1889

URING the month in which the Reichstag passed the old-age and invalid insurance act, German industry experienced the largest mass work stoppage in its history. It began spontaneously on May 3 in the northern sector of the Ruhr basin and spread like a tidal wave over the Ruhr to nearby Aachen, the Saar basin, Saxony, and Silesia. The wave peaked in the Ruhr on May 13, elsewhere later in the month. At the high point about 97,000 miners (86 percent of the work force) were on strike in the Ruhr, 2,465 (40 percent) at Aachen, 12,000 (46 percent) in the Saar, 10,000 (over 50 percent) in Saxony, 10,000 to 12,000 in Lower Silesia (about 75 percent), and 13,300 (about 32 percent) in Upper Silesia.[1] Clashes at Gelsenkirchen on May 4 left two policemen badly wounded. On the following day troops were deployed to protect mine properties, a step that some authorities believed to be unnecessary and provocative. By the strike's end (about June 1) forty-five persons were dead, the largest number (seventeen) in the Ruhr, thirteen in Silesia.[2] The dispute flared up repeatedly during the following months and likewise the danger of further walkouts. Coal miners were not, furthermore, the only disaffected laborers in Germany during 1889–1890. Work stoppages also occurred in other industries and continued for months. By April 1890 the number of strikes had reached 715 and strikers 289,300 (including thousands of workers in the building, textile, and metal working trades).[3]

Since 1887 the business cycle had been on the upswing, engendering among businessmen new optimism and among workers resentment that they were not included in the benefits. In the Ruhr production soared from 28,500,000 tons in 1886 to 33,900,000 tons in 1889 and its value from 134,700,000 marks to 185,000,000 marks, while labor's wages as a percentage

---

[1] Karl Oldenberg, "Arbeitseinstellungen in Deutschland," *Handwörterbuch der Staatswissenschaften* (2d ed., Jena, 1898), pp. 749, 761, and "Studien über die rheinisch-westfälischen Bergarbeiterbewegung," in Gustav Schmoller, ed., *Jahrbuch für Gesetzgebung, Verwaltung und Volkswirtschaft im Deutschen Reiche*, Neue Folge, XIV (1890), 925–928. The exact figures are not known, since statistics on work stoppages were not systematically kept before 1890. See Klaus Tenfelde and Heinrich Volkmann, eds., *Streik: Zur Geschichte des Arbeitskampfes in Deutschland während der Industrialisierung* (Munich, 1981), pp. 260–261, 287–294. The statistics used here have been informed by figures provided by Detlev Puls.

[2] Information provided by Detlev Puls.

[3] Oldenberg, "Arbeitseinstellungen," p. 761.

of that value fluctuated downward (57.7 in 1886, 56.0 in 1887, 55.3 in 1888, 57.0 in 1889).[4] Between 1886 and 1889 shift wages paid to skilled and experienced workers increased from 2.92 to 3.42 marks; to the least skilled, from 1.00 to 1.12 marks. Annual living costs for a family with three children were estimated at 1,067 marks, a figure that even skilled workers, the underground hewers and haulers, had difficulty attaining. As demand for coal increased, overtime shifts of two to four hours were common, six to eight hours possible. Often they were compulsory, since workers who sought to leave the mine at shift's end found the lift not operating. Newly arrived, single workers from eastern farms and villages had the greatest struggle for survival. At the bottom of the pay scale, most of these *Kostgänger* found work in the newly opened mines in the northern region of the Ruhr basin. Their inexperience and the pressure to increase production raised the accident rate.[5]

Although unplanned and unexpected, the Ruhr strike wave was preceded for months by meetings at which disaffected workers aired their grievances. The demands that emerged became the demands of the strikers: a flat 15 percent increase in wages for all workers, abolition of overtime labor (up to sixteen hours), reduction of the normal working shift from ten or more to eight hours portal to portal, and improvements in working conditions (including an end to mistreatment by brutal supervisors). The chief motivation of the strike was higher wages, although once an increase was promised, the discussion shifted to other issues, especially working hours and overtime.[6]

To employers and the government the May uprising came as a shock. Although aware of the agitation that preceded it, neither was prepared for what happened. Naturally the mine owners were anxious about the safety of their facilities (which proved to be unjustified), the cost of interrupted production (soon reimbursed by rising prices accelerated by the strike), and the demands themselves (an unwelcome precedent if the strike were successful). They denounced the strike as illegal and the demands for a percentage wage increase and shorter working hours as unjustified. Wages, they declared, would naturally follow the upward trend of the economy. If the strikers would return to work, they could expect higher wages.[7] On every level of the government

[4] Max Jürgen Koch, *Die Bergarbeiterbewegung im Ruhrgebiet zur Zeit Wilhelm II.* (1889–1914) (Düsseldorf, 1954), pp. 139–140.

[5] *Ibid.*, pp. 17–19; Hans Georg Kirchhoff, *Die staatliche Sozialpolitik im Ruhrbergbau 1871–1914. Wissenschaftliche Abhandlungen der Arbeitsgemeinschaft für Forschungen des Landes Nordrhein-Westfalen*, vol. 4 (Cologne, 1958), pp. 82–84.

[6] Koch, *Bergarbeiterbewegung*, pp. 34–35; Kirchhoff, *Staatliche Sozialpolitik*, pp. 48ff.; Oldenberg, "Studien über die rheinisch-westfälischen Bergarbeiterbewegung," pp. 189–191; Otto Hue, *Die Bergarbeiter* (Stuttgart, 1913), II, 354ff.

[7] Declaration of the *Bergbaulicher Verein* in Dortmund on May 11, 1889. Koch, *Bergarbeiterbewegung*, pp. 54–55. Also unidentified businessman to Rottenburg, May 10, 1889; F. A. Krupp to Rottenburg, May 11, 1889: Herrfurth to Bismarck (concerning the Dortmund conference), May 11, 1889. DZA Potsdam, Reichskanzlei, 444, pp. 24–26v, 62–63v, 70–95v.

there was a division of opinion both on the tactics to be followed in handling the strike and on the merits of the miners' cause. In the first days of the strike this was evident in the reactions of local officials in the Ruhr. In the province of the Rhineland Baron Hans von Berlepsch, governor (*Regierungspräsident*) of the Düsseldorf district, resisted the demand for troops on the grounds that their presence would provoke local miners, who were normally law abiding. Instead he reinforced the local police, who were familiar to the strikers. His counterpart at Arnsberg in the province of Westphalia, Governor Alfred von Rosen, called in the army, and the result was bloodshed. By mid-month soldiers had fired on a number of occasions, leaving nine dead and fifteen wounded.[8]

At Berlin differences of opinion on merits and tactics quickly developed between Kaiser and chancellor. When the Kaiser received the news, he was at Kiel, and, without consulting Bismarck, he ordered (May 6 and 7) the provincial governments to report to him directly and continually on all developments. When he returned to the capital, Wilhelm conferred not with the chancellor but with his former tutor Hinzpeter, and on May 11 he ordered Robert Eduard von Hagemeister, governor-general (*Oberpräsident*) of Westphalia, to "coerce" the managers and directors of the coal companies to increase wages "immediately" in order to end the strike and avert a "national calamity." If they did not comply, he would withdraw the troops.[9]

Bismarck, who was ignorant of these initiatives, had already declared his position in a cabinet meeting on May 9. Although initially inclined to declare martial law, he had concluded that the time was not "yet" ripe for such a step. The complaints of the workers were not groundless; for example, by exacting fines from workers who refused overtime work, the owners had violated the spirit of the law. The government should stay neutral in the dispute, while seeking privately and publicly (in the unofficial press), to convince mine owners that they should make concessions. Bismarck was no longer eager for a quick end to the strike, whose "sad effects," he declared, might have a salutary effect on liberal opposition to renewal of the antisocialist laws.[10] In what others perceived to be a "calamity" Bismarck saw the possibility of political gain.

At the next meeting of the cabinet (May 12) the Kaiser appeared, unannounced and unexpected, to preside over the discussion on the strike. In his

[8] Kirchhoff, *Staatliche Sozialpolitik*, pp. 53–54; Wolfgang Köllmann and Albin Gladen, eds., *Der Bergarbeiterstreik von 1889 und die Gründung des "Alten Verbandes" in ausgewählten Dokumenten der Zeit* (Bochum, 1969), p. 13.

[9] Wilhelm II to Hagemeister, May 11, 1889. DZA Potsdam, Reichskanzlei, 444, p. 111.

[10] DZA Potsdam, Reichskanzlei, 444, pp. 19–21v, 1889. Excerpts from the cabinet minutes have been published by Paul Grebe, "Bismarcks Sturz und der Bergarbeiterstreik vom Mai 1889," *Historische Zeitschrift*, 157 (1938), pp. 89–90, and Michael Stürmer, ed., *Bismarck und die preussisch-deutsche Politik (1871–1890)* (Munich, 1973), pp. 273–275.

opening statement Bismarck dealt with the issues between workers and owners in an evenhanded way. The miners had the right to strike and could not be compelled to return to work, but the state must protect property and persons, including the right of nonstrikers to work, and it must aid industries adversely affected by the work stoppage; the companies had helped workers to survive bad times, and now their managers understandably wished to make the best of returning prosperity; while the workers' pay was not too low and their hours not too long, company profits justified pay raises; some improvements in working conditions (such as overtime shifts and entry and departure time) could be made. For workers to gain their ends quickly and easily by breach of contract would set a bad precedent. It would be politically useful, furthermore, if the strike were not ended swiftly; the "liberal bourgeoisie" must "feel" the consequences and be disabused of the assumption that social democracy was a greater threat to the government than to themselves.

When the chancellor finished, Wilhelm II summarized for the ministers the alarming reports he had received from Hagemeister and Rosen in Westphalia. The strike movement was growing, mobs were intimidating nonstriking workers, ironworks were shutting down for lack of fuel, more battalions and squadrons were needed to protect mine properties. At bottom, he declared, foreign owners of coal mines were responsible for the situation, for they were interested only in maximum profits, not the welfare of the worker or the public. There was evidence that a general strike, planned for June, had broken out prematurely. The movement, Wilhelm concluded, was not social democratic; owners must be put under pressure to satisfy the justified demands of the workers. The strike was "threatening" and must be ended before the coal shortage "disarms us" by immobilizing the railways and the fleet. To this end, he had "ordered" Hagemeister and his subordinate *Landräte* to put pressure on mine owners to grant pay increases. The government must act as an arbitrator; legislation was needed to reestablish its control over the mining industry.

In reply, Bismarck doubted that the strike endangered Germany's defensive capabilities, for the state railway administration had sufficient coal reserves for a mobilization. But the strike, if successful, would encourage Germany's enemies to assume that they could exploit such "calamities." He "rejoiced" at the proposal to strengthen state supervision of the mining industry. "I would regard an expropriation of coal mining companies (namely, the foreign ones)—a conversion to state ownership of coal production—as an indispensable need and a goal to be striven for."[11]

[11] *DZA* Merseburg, Rep. 120, BB, VII, 1, 3, Bd. 5; Grebe, "Bismarcks Sturz," pp. 90–92; Stürmer, *Preussisch-deutsche Politik*, pp. 275–277. The details and opinions expressed by Bismarck in the cabinet meetings of May 9 and 12 reflected the varied reports he received from officials in the Ruhr basin through Minister of Interior Herrfurth and Minister of Public Works Maybach. Although the mining authority (*Bergamt*) maintained the strike was organized and unjustified, the governor of Westphalia (Hagemeister) and *Landrat* at Gelsenkirchen reported that the strike

Kaiser and chancellor were on a collision course, the monarch pressing for a quick conclusion to the strike at the cost of the owners, his chief minister arguing for neutrality in order to let the strike take its course—for the education of the "liberal bourgeoisie." And yet Bismarck made it clear that he was not opposed to intervention as such. Although we have no recorded reactions from the ministers present, his willingness to regard expropriation of mining companies as a "goal" and "indispensable need" ought to have astounded them. Perhaps they dismissed it as merely a debating point, an effort to outbid the Kaiser in the game of anticapitalistic rhetoric and terminate the discussion? The chancellor's inconsistency about whether all, or only foreign-owned, firms were in question leaves an impression of improvisation. According to Lucius, Bismarck found it "no easy task" to cope with the Kaiser's "stormy effusion." After the monarch left the meeting, the prince remarked to his colleagues, "The young master has Friedrich Wilhelm I's conception of his authority and power, and it is necessary to protect him from excessive zeal in this regard."[12]

Privately Bismarck was outraged by the revelation that the young master was giving orders to and receiving reports from provincial officials behind the backs of his responsible ministers. In an official report, signed by the entire cabinet and heavily larded with the standard phrases of deferential etiquette, Bismarck summarized for Wilhelm II the decisions reached in the cabinet meeting and then noted that the governor-general of Westphalia had no legal authority to coerce mine owners. Withdrawal of the troops would expose to the wrath of the strikers persons who were not responsible for the work stoppage; the destruction of machines and pumps would lead to the flooding of the mines and harm "the national capital" of the entire country.[13] To the unfortunate Hagemeister he dispatched a coded telegram in which he icily declared that ministers could not assume responsibility for actions taken by subordinates without their prior knowledge and approval.[14]

Another incident in mid-July shows how sensitive Bismarck was on the issue of the Kaiser's disregard for constitutional procedures. On July 17 a telegram arrived in Berlin from Governor Berlepsch reporting another strike in the Dahlbusch mine at Essen. Bismarck advised Interior Minister Herrfurth, Berlepsch's superior, not to intervene "for the time being," unless "special orders arrive from the Kaiser." The conditional clause was necessary, for a copy of the telegram had been sent to the Kaiser, who was absent from Berlin. Bismarck had to consider the possibility that Wilhelm II would again by-pass

movement was not the consequence of social democratic agitation and "not entirely without justification." DZA Potsdam, Reichskanzlei, 444, pp. 4–26v.

[12] Freiherr Lucius von Ballhausen, *Bismarck-Erinnerungen* (Stuttgart, 1920), pp. 496–497.

[13] Cabinet to Kaiser, May 13, 1889. DZA Merseburg, Rep. 120, BB, VII, 1, Nr. 3, Bd. 5; DZA Potsdam, Reichskanzlei, 444, pp. 110–122v; Grebe, "Bismarcks Sturz," pp. 92–95.

[14] Kirchhoff, *Staatliche Sozialpolitik*, p. 59.

official channels by going over the heads of his chancellor and cabinet. To Herrfurth the prince wrote dryly, "It is not advisable to send reports like this to his majesty, the Kaiser, without *petitum*, certainly not in a situation, in which his majesty can feel compelled to make decisions without his responsible advisers and without any expert advice other than the wording of the telegram. Under such circumstances his majesty cannot be expected to reach a decision, and to send him such a communication could easily be interpreted by him as a criticism of his absence."[15] To keep Herrfurth from triggering another independent action by the Kaiser, Bismarck pointed out how, given Wilhelm's temperament, the attempt might boomerang.

In the coalfield strike of May 1889 Wilhelm II had shown his compulsion for direct rule, and lower officials of the Prussian monarchy had readily responded to his impetuous initiative. The issue that surfaced here was portentous. For the time being, however, it resubmerged. In the audiences he granted on May 14 and 16 to separate delegations of miners and mine owners Wilhelm adhered fairly well to the policy of neutrality Bismarck had laid down in the cabinet meeting. On receiving the miners' petition, he promised to investigate their grievances and demands. But he also chastised them for breach of contract, harassment of nonstrikers, and opposing state authority. Should public order be disturbed or the strikers combine with social democrats, the Kaiser would intervene with all the power at his command—"and that is great!"[16]

That the delegation's visit in Berlin bore fruit was not owed to the government but to two deputies of the Freedom party who brought the three miners into contact with Friedrich Hammacher, national liberal Reichstag deputy and chairman of the mine owners' association (*Bergbauverein*). The result was the "Berlin Protocol" of May 15. In this agreement the delegation gave up the 15 percent pay increase in favor of an "appropriate raise" considering the recent rise in the price of coal. The normal shift was conceded to be eight hours, but not portal to portal; entry and exit were calculated as "ordinarily" not more than thirty minutes. Overtime shifts were restricted to "exceptional cases" subject to prior approval by a committee elected yearly by the workers. Although the delegation made major concessions, they gained in the consul-

[15] Herrfurth to Bismarck, June 13, 1889; Berlepsch to Herrfurth, July 17, 1889; Bismarck to Herrfurth, July 19, 1889. *DZA* Potsdam, Reichskanzlei, 445, pp. 23–26v, 83, 86–87.

[16] *GW*, VIc, 412; *SEG* (1889), pp. 64–65. Before publication the Kaiser's remarks to the workers' delegation were censored in accordance with Bismarck's wishes. Herrfurth to Bismarck, May 14, 1889. The Kaiser's actual remarks may have included some positive statements about the justice of the strikers' cause. The final version was sent to Bismarck but not, it would appear, to the Kaiser, although there is no record of a protest by Wilhelm II. *DZA* Potsdam, Reichskanzlei, 444, pp. 128–133. In petitioning the king, Ruhr workers followed an old custom embedded in the Prussian tradition of the *Ständestaat*. Klaus Tenfelde, *Sozialgeschichte der Bergarbeiterschaft an der Ruhr im 19. Jahrhundert* (2d ed., Bonn, 1981), pp. 593–597.

tative committee a potential instrument for collective bargaining, which the owners had resolutely refused to consider in the strikes of 1872.[17]

This agreement was already known on the following day, when the Kaiser, acting on Bismarck's advice, met the owners' delegation headed by Hammacher. At this meeting Wilhelm declared that the workers had made a good impression on him, that they had refrained from contact with the social democrats, and that he had no doubt that they represented the Ruhr workers. He lectured the owners on the wisdom of maintaining contact with their workers and listening to their concerns and on their duty to the state and society to look after their employees' welfare. "Workers read newspapers and know how their pay stands in relationship to corporate profits." His "royal duty" compelled him to support the efforts of employers and employees to reach agreement.[18]

The owners' delegation read into Wilhelm's oblique words about "maintaining contact" and "listening" an approval of the provision for workers' committees in the Berlin Protocol. In great alarm they hastened to the chancellery. Although Bismarck refused to see them, they talked with Rottenburg and came away with the impression that the chancellor was opposed to the arrangement. Meeting at Essen on May 18, the coal-mining association reviewed the agreement and struck out the offending clause. What remained was a prohibition against overtime shifts without prior agreement between management and workers, but with no procedure for negotiating the agreement. Strike leaders raised no strong objections to this amendment, for the establishment of committees (an idea introduced into the Berlin negotiations by the left-liberal deputies who arbitrated the protocol) had not been among their original demands and its importance was not yet appreciated.[19]

Aftermath of the Strike

The Kaiser's warnings to both sides and the negotiations and agreements that followed acted as a damper on the strike movement in the Ruhr. The workers assumed that their representatives had won significant concessions from the owners. But disputes soon arose over the proper interpretation of the Berlin Protocol and the version of it accepted by the mine owners' association at Essen. The wording of the clause on entry and exit time was ambiguous: Workers understood it to mean one-half hour altogether; owners, one-half hour in each direction. Some managers, moreover, violated the agreement by discharging strike leaders, continuing coerced overtime shifts, and denying

[17] *SEG* (1889), pp. 65–66; Oldenberg, "Studien über die rheinisch-westfälischen Bergarbeiterbewegung," pp. 202–203.

[18] *SEG* (1889), pp. 70–71.

[19] Koch, *Bergarbeiterbewegung*, pp. 38–39. Their followers in Dortmund were, however, very disappointed by the concession. Köllmann and Gladen, eds., *Bergarbeiterstreik*, pp. 176–230.

pay increases. The strikers' central committee called for another walkout to begin on May 27. Hagemeister ordered the committee arrested and recommended a declaration of martial law.[20] But the Kaiser, chancellor, and cabinet were unanimously opposed; they concluded that the governor was too much under the influence of Westphalian mine owners, and he was replaced by Konrad von Studt. Again Bismarck argued that the strike should be permitted to "burn out," for the sobering effect it would have on both sides. "The liberal bourgeoisie must be cured of the opinion that it was not their affair and that a restoration of order was the task of the government." Faced by an ultimatum from the owners, the workers went back into the mines at the end of the month. But the issue continued to fester. The rest of the year was marked by scattered strikes and general unrest not only in the mines but also in other sectors of German industry.[21]

In the waning days of the May strike Bismarck yielded to requests for a general inquiry to be executed by the ministries of the interior and public works through their respective subordinate agencies (the provincial governments and regional mining authorities).[22] The principal role of the *Oberbergamt* for the Ruhr region in the conduct of the inquiry tended to prejudice its findings from the start. Attacked by an editorial in the *Kreuzzeitung*, the agency had already publicly condemned the strike as illegal and unjustified. Under pressure from the Prussian cabinet, especially Maybach, the board of enquiry did seek to conduct a palpably impartial investigation by gathering testimony during June and July from all quarters, workers as well as owners. Although the resulting report contains much useful evidence and appears to reflect the actual flow of events, the board's residual bias is evident in its procedure. The request for worker and owner representation on subcommittees was rejected, and state officials remained in control of the investigation— essentially judges of their own cause. In the final stages, furthermore, managers were permitted to reply point by point to the testimony of workers, who had no opportunity for rebuttal. Among the recommendations three were designed to help close the gap between management and labor in the coalfields: obligatory company (house) ordinances subject to review by state mining authorities; committees to represent labor; arbitration courts also functioning as conciliation agencies. Neither the workers nor the owners were satisfied with the results. Historians are inclined to regard the report as an

[20] DZA Potsdam, Reichskanzlei, 444, pp. 198–199v, 228–229, 241–245, 249–251v; GW, VIc, 413 fn.

[21] Cabinet meetings of May 25 and 27, 1889. DZA Potsdam, Reichskanzlei, 444, pp. 236–240v, 294–302; Lucius, *Bismarck-Erinnerungen*, pp. 498–499; SEG (1889), pp. 74–75, 145ff.

[22] Herrfurth to Rottenburg, May 26, 1889. DZA Potsdam, Reichskanzlei, 444, pp. 241–242v. Berlepsch had urged such an inquiry as early as May 14, but Bismarck had opposed it on the grounds that the strikers would await its outcome before returning to the mines. The strike would be prolonged. *Ibid.*, pp. 164–167v.

honest effort to understand the events of May, inevitably biased, however, by the promanagement perspectives of the participating commissioners.[23]

The government's enquiry was not completed until November 1889. Meanwhile, Bismarck launched his own investigation. In mid-May he evidently discussed the general problem with a subordinate, Privy Counselor Baron Carl von Gamp, one of the authors of the accident insurance act of 1884. He commissioned Gamp to write a memorandum on the government's options for either preventing or minimizing the consequences of major strikes in the coal-mining industry.[24] Gamp's memorandum (dated May 27) is studded with marginalia, showing Bismarck's immediate reactions to the counselor's propositions. Many strikes, Gamp asserted, could be avoided by the prompt rectification of justified grievances, particularly those arising from harsh treatment by low-level officials of the mine companies (Bismarck: "certainly; cf. junior officers in the army"). As a solution Gamp recommended the obligatory creation of workers' committees, like those already created by benevolent employers (Bismarck: "Pless"), and of state conciliation agencies (Einigungsämter). Another step would be to restrict or prohibit the employment of "half-grown" workers, who, having the least to lose, usually played the leading role in strikes (Bismarck: "correct"); the sons of miners living at home could be excepted (Bismarck: "correct"). Gamp recommended immediate (Bismarck: "and sharper") punishment of strikers who resorted to violence (Bismarck: "pressure to strike is itself a kind of incitement to violence"), although the judicial system was much too slow (Bismarck: "unfortunately true") for this to be an effective deterrent. Criminal punishment for breach of contract, on the other hand, would not be very successful (Bismarck: "Prohibition against reemployment of the convicted in coal [mines]. Coal is an existential necessity, and production must be in reliable hands"). Employers guilty of breach of contract must also be punished (Bismarck: "cer-

---

[23] Denkschrift über die Untersuchung der Arbeiter- und Betriebsverhältnisse in den Steinkohlenbezirken, published as a special supplement to the Reichs- und Staatsanzeiger, Jan., 20, 1890, republished in Zeitschrift des Oberschlesischen Berg- und Hüttenmännischen Vereins, 29 (Feb. 1890), pp. 57ff. A complete copy (with appendices) of this important document can be found in GSA, Rep. 84a, 11400, pp. 239ff (113 pages). For contrasting judgments on the impartiality of the investigation, see Koch, Bergarbeiterbewegung, pp. 43–44; Kirchhoff, Staatliche Sozialpolitik, pp. 75–85; and Max Quarck, "Die preussische Bergarbeiterenquête vom Jahre 1889," Archiv für soziale Gesetzgebung und Statistik, 3 (1890), pp. 162–179.

[24] Gamp was the author of a book, Die wirtschaftlichen und sozialen Aufgaben, that advocated the decentralization of industrial production from the great cities to the country, where the owners would find cheaper land, the workers a healthier environment and cheaper living. The book also favored compulsory social insurance for workers under the paternalistic protection of the state. When he became aware of the book and its thesis, Bismarck obtained Gamp's transfer from the Prussian railway administration to the Ministry of Commerce in 1882 and additionally to the Reich Office of the Interior in 1883, where he was one of three key officials charged with the drafting of social insurance statutes. Walter Vogel, Bismarcks Arbeiterversicherung: Ihre Entstehung im Kräftespiel der Zeit (Braunschweig, 1951), pp. 102–108.

tainly"), but this might be easily abused by litigious workers and partisan judges, exacerbating labor relations (Bismarck: "right"). In any case judicial proceedings would be ineffective against mass strikes.

But what then would and would not be effective in the case of mass strikes? Not to be recommended was the reaction of the Prussian state railways, which had belatedly (after May 20) sought to keep consumers like Friedrich Krupp in production by reducing freight rates on coal and coke shipped more than 350 kilometers from operating mines in Upper Silesia. This measure had increased the coal shortage by encouraging unaffected firms to increase their coal purchases at the lower rates. Gamp found other proposals more promising: (1) Prepare in advance to transport coal swiftly from operating coalfields to the regions normally supplied by the struck mines (Bismarck: "Applies only to sporadic, not general strikes, which are the dangerous ones"). (2) Encourage cities, railways, gasworks, and corporations that were accustomed "to live hand to mouth" from coal stocks to build up reserves sufficient to last three months without resupply. This could be done by ordering the state railway administration to grant longer freight credits and, during the summer months, lowered rates even to small firms (Bismarck: "That means direct financial support") with special regard for individual cases (Bismarck: "far-reaching"). (3) Legally compel coal-mining companies to establish coal reserves sufficient to last three months in the general (Bismarck: "their own") interest and compensate them (Bismarck: "?") financially for the expense. (4) Have the state take control over mines idle for more than four weeks (Bismarck: "obligatory?"); after all, owners had themselves been known to go on strike either by refusing to accept the settlements of labor disputes drafted by conciliation agencies or by conspiring with their competitors to stop production in order to drive up prices (Bismarck: "Copper ring!"). (5) If all else failed, prohibit the export of coal (Bismarck: "right"); the need to protect national productivity outweighed whatever damage the prohibition would do to private interests (Bismarck: "Yes").

Finally Gamp reached his climactic proposal: Convert the entire coal-mining industry to state ownership. Workers in state-owned mines were much more reluctant to strike than those in private industry; they were better protected against arbitrary dismissals and bad treatment; they saw themselves as state officials. No high dividends, furthermore, aroused their lust for more pay. Because the state did not have to consider the interests of investors, it could for the public good even give in to unjustified demands by workers. At the current prices of their shares on the stock market, the Westphalian mining companies were worth 840,000,000 marks, the Upper Silesian companies 400,000,000 marks. With their acquisition the entire industry most essential to national productivity and the general welfare would be withdrawn from private hands and private speculation. But if considerations of either principle or finance made this impossible, the acquisition of a "few good mines in Westphalia" (heavily underlined by Bismarck) would enable the state to exercise a controlling influence over the wages and working conditions of coal miners. The moment was not propitious (Bismarck: "No"), however, to initiate a public discussion either of the advisability of building stockpiles of coal, which might stir workers to renew the strike, or of state acquisition of the coal mines, which would lead speculators to drive up the price of company shares.[25]

Judging from his underlining in the text and the cryptic and approving marginalia that he scrawled with sweeping hand (many unrecorded here), Bismarck's interest in Gamp's memorandum reached a climax at the point where the counselor argued for the sequestration or purchase of the nation's coal mines. Here is the proof that his remark to the Kaiser and cabinet on May 12 was not just a debater's point, a bluff suddenly conceived and as quickly forgotten, but a proposition to be seriously considered. In the domestic crisis of May 1889 Bismarck conceived yet another state-socialist notion of major dimensions, one which, had it been known, would have created an uproar in the boardrooms of industrial capitalism.

Kaiser and Chancellor Drift Apart

The coal strike of 1889 shows what profound changes had occurred in the work force since the abandonment of state direction in the mining act of 1865. Liquidation of the state's traditional patriarchal role in the processes of production had left mine workers subject to the interests and whims of the owners and their managers. What governed their fate was no longer the conception of a "just wage" but the "law of supply and demand" in the labor market, a theory that established the value of a worker's labor no differently than it did the value of the goods he created.

To the more literate workers of the 1880s, to those who in the Kaiser's own words could "read newspapers" and learn about company profits and investor dividends, it appeared that they were not receiving a fair share of the wealth their hard hands produced. The transition from small to big industry had transformed working and living conditions and likewise the values and expectations of the worker. A new proletarian consciousness was in the making, one that neither the owners nor the officials who supported their cause could comprehend.[26] To them the strike was a strange and unpredictable phenomenon, better explained by conspiracy than by rational cause. Social democratic propaganda, ultramontane malevolence, and the agitation of outsiders had corrupted workers by arousing undue expectations. Why else would coal miners strike at a time of returning prosperity and increasing pay? "The true

[25] Gamp to Bismarck, May 27, 1889. DZA Potsdam, Reichskanzlei, 444, pp. 264–293v.

[26] See Tenfelde, *Bergarbeiterschaft an der Ruhr*, pp. 573–597.

explanation of the strike in the Rhineland-Westphalian coalfields," reported the Dortmund Chamber of Commerce, "is not poverty, not hunger pay, not the eight-hour shift, but the next Reichstag election."[27]

In the cabinet meetings of late May Bismarck and Wilhelm II were at least outwardly in agreement on how to handle the strike. Bismarck had success-fully marshaled the cabinet to his support in objecting to Wilhelm's experi-ment in personal government through Hagemeister and his subordinate county counselors. Wilhelm's audiences with representatives of workers and owners, on the other hand, had had a positive effect on both sides, and the Hohenzoller could congratulate himself on having performed to great ap-plause the role of king and Kaiser as he perceived it. In the months that followed, however, Kaiser and chancellor drew steadily apart as they tried to assess the meaning of the strike for the social policy of the government. The split was not merely one of personal temperament and differing conceptions of the monarch's constitutional role, but also of contrasting views of the social reality that had given rise to the strike in the first place. Once the immediate crisis of the strike was over, Bismarck began to lose the balanced perspective he had shown in mid-May, tilting increasingly in the direction of the owners, while Wilhelm returned to a course sympathetic to the mine workers, from which Bismarck had only momentarily diverted him.

Bismarck's long absence from Berlin in 1889–1890 (June 8–August 10, Au-gust 20–October 9, October 16–January 24) reduced his contact with subor-dinates and his awareness of the Kaiser's attitude and the influences at work on it. On the day before his departure for Varzin, the prince informed the officials at Düsseldorf and Münster of his intention to dispatch Gamp on a fact-finding tour of the Ruhr basin for the purpose of determining how to prevent a repetition of the recent strike.[28] On July 7 Gamp reported that he had returned and was ready to present his information and conclusions, but Bismarck was in no hurry to receive him. The counselor was told on July 26 and again on September 5 to wait until the chancellor returned from leave.[29] Gamp finally received his interview on October 15, nearly three months after the completion of his tour.[30]

It can be assumed that Gamp summarized on that occasion what he wrote in his official report (dated November 1889): the housing, wages, and work-ing conditions of Ruhr miners were generally good, compared with those of

[27] Report of the Dortmund chamber of commerce, June 13, 1889, with marginalia by Bis-marck. DZA Merseburg, Rep. 120, BB, VII, Fach 1, Zu Nr. 3, Bd. 1, pp. 8–12v. On the "pro-letarianization" of the miners see Hue, *Bergarbeiter*, pp. 1–258.

[28] Bismarck to Studt and Berlepsch, June 7, 1889; Bismarck to Seydewitz, June 25, 1889; Rottenburg to Gamp, June 25, 1889. DZA Potsdam, Reichskanzlei, 445, pp. 12–12v, 65–66.

[29] Gamp to Bismarck, July 7, 1889; Rottenburg to Gamp, July 26, 1889; Rottenburg to Magde-burg, Sept. 5, 1889. DZA Potsdam, Reichskanzlei, 445, pp. 74, 91, 138.

[30] *Ibid.*, p. 145

other workers; since 1877 employers had been plagued by low prices for coal and had not yet begun at the time of the strike to profit from price increases; mine managers had lost contact with their workers by paying no attention to their complaints during April; this had enabled the few socialists in the mines to gain influence; with the help of young miners and Polish workers they had spread the strike movement over the entire region; another general and long-lasting strike might well occur as the weather improved in the spring of 1890; a strike was not the only way in which the flow of fuel to private and public enterprises could be interrupted—coalitions of mine owners posed the "same danger"; only by owning mines could the state be sure of obtaining supplies of coal sufficient to fuel its public facilities and military establishment; state-owned mines were largely confined to Upper Silesia and the Saar valley, and only by obtaining a large mining property in Westphalia could the state be sure of influencing coal prices and workers' circumstances.[31] Before distributing the report, Bismarck had Rottenburg excise from it all references to Gamp's proposals for action, limiting the document entirely to "facts and wishes of workers and employers."[32]

When the official enquiry conducted by the ministries of the interior and public works was finished at the end of November, the prince passed over Theodor Lohmann to designate Gamp as one of two Ministry of Commerce officials to participate on the panel of officials designated to evaluate it.[33] By this route Gamp's personal investigation was, in effect, submerged in the larger enquiry.[34]

While Gamp waited in Berlin nearly three months for the opportunity to deliver his report in person, Bismarck listened at Varzin and Friedrichsruh to advice from other sources. One of these was Friedrich Vohwinkel, lumber wholesaler at Gelsenkirchen to whom Bismarck sold pit props from the saw-mills at Friedrichsruh. This business relationship enabled Vohwinkel to relay to the chancellor the complaints of Ruhr mine owners about the conduct of public officials during the May strike.[35] After a meeting with Bismarck, ap-

---

[31] "Denkschrift betreffend die Ausstandsbewegung der Grubenarbeiter (und die Massregeln zu ihrer Bekämpfung)." DZA Merseburg, Rep. 120, BB, VII, 1, Nr. 3, Bd. 8, pp. 14–15, 19–59.

[32] Rottenburg to Bismarck, Nov. 15, 1889. DZA Potsdam, Reichskanzlei, 445, pp. 268–268v.

[33] Magdeburg to Bismarck, Nov. 25, 1889; Rottenburg to Magdeburg, Nov. 26, 1889. DZA Potsdam, Reichskanzlei, 445, pp. 270–272; Magdeburg to Maybach and Herrfurth, Dec. 2, 1889. DZA Merseburg, Rep. 120, BB, VII, 1, Nr. 3, Bd. 1, p. 38. Maybach to Bismarck, Dec. 7, 1889. Ibid., Vol. 8, pp. 141–142.

[34] Herrfurth to Bismarck, Dec. 12, 1889, and to Schelling, Dec. 18, 1889. DZA Merseburg, Rep. 120, BB, VII, 1, Nr. 3, Bd. 8, pp. 189–190.

[35] On Bismarck's business relations with Vohwinkel, see Fritz Stern, Gold and Iron: Bismarck, Bleichröder, and the Building of the German Empire (New York, 1977), pp. 297–299. During the strike Friedrich Krupp had been the conduit to Bismarck for the complaints of Ruhr industrialists, made unhappy by Hagemeister's attempt to mediate between owners and strikers. They desired the appointment of a special commissar with authority over the entire coalfield and greater sym-

parently at Varzin, Vohwinkel dispatched a memorandum containing seven documents provided by mine owners (among them, Hugo Stinnes and Emil Kirdorf), describing alleged cases of incompetence or partiality toward workers by low-level state officials (a *Landrat*, three mayors, a police commander, a police commissioner, a Hussar commander).[36] Bismarck forwarded these charges to the relevant ministries for investigation; unfortunately for Vohwinkel and his informants, they were not substantiated.[37] Meanwhile, Vohwinkel had brought to Bismarck's attention a report by the director-general of the Dahlbusch mine at Essen, where over two thousand workers walked out on July 16 (the third work stoppage at this mine). According to the director, the strike had been caused by the systematic agitation of a few miners belonging to the "radical party," whose leader had been fired for "publicly slandering the mine manager." Dismissed workers, furthermore, were spreading dissatisfaction among the workers by obtaining peddling licenses, which permitted them to propagate their views from door to door; to stop this Vohwinkel recommended new restrictions on peddling licenses, an idea that Bismarck quickly approved and presented on August 17 to the cabinet, which ordered an investigation.[38]

From these or other contacts in industry Bismarck also heard that British coal companies had exploited the German strike to increase their share of the German market, raising the question whether imports should not be curbed. But the Ministry of Commerce reported that the increase in British imports had begun before the strike.[39] In October three important organizations representing German entrepreneurs (the Central Federation of German Industrialists, the Association for the Promotion of the Economic Interests of Trade and Industry in Berlin, and the Association for the Promotion of the Economic Interests of Rhineland and Westphalia) sent delegations to Britain to find out how their counterparts in that country avoided strikes. Their reports were duly forwarded to the chancellor at Friedrichsruh.[40]

---

pathy for the interests of the owners. Krupp to Rottenburg (*Mein hochverehrter Freund*), May 11, 1889. DZA Potsdam, Reichskanzlei, 444, pp. 62–63v. Krupp also complained about the "clumsiness" of the Prussian state railway administration in accommodating the needs of industrialists in search of coal. Krupp to Rottenburg, May 12, 1889. *Ibid.*, pp. 134–135v.

[36] Vohwinkel to Bismarck, June 21, 1889; Rottenburg to Herrfurth, July 2, 1889. DZA Potsdam, Reichskanzlei, 445, pp. 31–32v, 69–69v.

[37] Schelling to Bismarck, July 16, 1889; Herrfurth to Schwarzkoppen, Aug. 30, 1889; Rottenburg to Herrfurth, Sept. 5, 1889. DZA Potsdam, Reichskanzlei, 445, pp. 124–128, 137–137b, 138a.

[38] Vohwinkel to Bismarck, Aug. 10, 1889; Bismarck to cabinet meeting of Aug. 17. DZA Potsdam, Reichskanzlei, 445, pp. 93–110, 129.

[39] Rottenburg to Magdeburg, Aug. 27 and Sept. 11, 1889; Magdeburg to Bismarck, Oct. 11, 1889. DZA Potsdam, Reichskanzlei, 445, pp. 139–139a, 162–176.

[40] Bueck to Rottenburg, Oct. 28, 1889. DZA Potsdam, Reichskanzlei, 445, pp. 177–217; 446, pp. 35–70.

Bismarck Diagnoses the Strike

From official reports and private letters that crossed his desk Bismarck concluded that the strikes in Westphalia and Silesia were for the most part traceable to young workers, recent migrants to the coalfields from the provinces, particularly Poles.[41] Restricted to the less skilled, low-paying jobs (particularly the transport of coal to the surface), these young, newly arrived workers were reputed to have terrorized older, native miners, drawing them unwillingly into the movement. Bismarck asked the ministries of interior and public works to determine whether these young firebrands could not be brought under control by "prophylactic" measures directed at them through parents or guardians, who could be held accountable for their actions.[42] The response to this request was meager: a report from Herrfurth on the legal aspects of the proposal and statistics from the Ministry of Public Works on the number of minors working in the coalfields (20 percent of the work force).[43] What the chancellor needed most, however, was not numbers but evidence of patterns of conduct. He sent the statistics to the provincial governors of Westphalia and the Rhineland, inquiring to what degree youthful workers had influenced the development of the strike and whether the agitation came from resident or recently arrived minors, assuming in the former case the likely connivance of parents or guardians. Finally, he wanted the governors' views concerning the "paternal power or authority" exercised by independent adults over minors working in the coalfields.[44]

The responses to these questions were patently not what Bismarck expected. In late October the governor-general of the Rhine province reported that in all but one of the coal-mining districts within its borders (Düsseldorf, Trier, and Saarbrücken) adult workers had taken the lead in the strike; to the extent that minors were involved they had been "shoved to the fore" by older men; only at Aachen, the smallest of the Rhineland coalfields, had younger

---

[41] Herrfurth to Bismarck, May 11, 1889. DZA Merseburg, Rep. 120, BB, VII, 1, Nr. 3, Bd. 5, pp. 54ff.; Bismarck to Maybach and Herrfurth, May 24, 1889. GW, VIc, 412–413; Vohwinkel to Bismarck, June 21, 1889. DZA Potsdam, Reichskanzlei, 445, pp. 31–32v.

[42] Bismarck to Maybach and Herrfurth, May 24, 1889. GW, VIc, 412–413. Earlier he ordered the deportation of foreign workers involved in the strike movement. DZA Potsdam, Reichskanzlei, 444, pp. 126–126v.

[43] The statistics showed that out of 207,700 workers studied 40,796 were minors; that 35,600 minors (144,000 adults) resided within 5 kilometers of the mine and presumably lived at home; that 3,602 minors (15,147 adults) lived outside that range but within the same province as the mine; that 717 minors (1,955 adults) were officially resident in Prussian provinces other than their place of work; that 385 minors (2,746 adults) came from states other than Prussia, 227 minors (2,332 adults) from other countries. Ministry of Public Works to Bismarck, Aug. 23, 1889. DZA Potsdam, 445, pp. 130–133.

[44] Rottenburg to Kayser and Kayser to Magdeburg, Sept. 2, 1889. DZA Potsdam, Reichskanzlei, 445, pp. 135–136.

workers led the action.[45] In mid-December Bismarck extended his inquiry to the Silesian coalfields. From reports available to him, he now said, it appeared as though the moving force in the Silesian strikes had been adult agitators and labor leaders (*Vertrauensmänner*), who had strongly influenced young workers.[46]

From these actions it is apparent that Bismarck diagnosed the May strikes as a superficial, not a structural phenomenon, symptomatic of the common cold rather than heart disease. If the cause were superficial, then likewise the cure. If a few dismissed workers were peddling their nostrums of discontent door to door, an artful interpretation of, or amendment to, the industrial code would suffice. If the youths who shoved the coal carts to and from the mine lifts and entrances were responsible, they could be brought under control by holding their parents and guardians accountable for the damage done. If Polish and German migrant workers were the root of the problem, they could be purged from the coalfields.

But then there was the problem of "agitators" who stirred up normally placid workers and focused their discontents on concrete demands. From early May the attempt within the Prussian government to identify and categorize them was unceasing. To have discovered that the culprits were social democrats would have been alarming, but also useful for the renewal and stiffening of the antisocialist act. Provincial and district authorities reported that neither the social democrats nor their sympathizers were responsible for the strike, although they naturally sought to lead it.[47] Strikers in Westphalia began their meetings with a patriotic cheer for the Kaiser and applauded arriving troops, singing "*Heil dir im Siegerkranz.*" Only 3,300 of 104,000 proletarian voters in the Ruhr region had voted social democratic in the last election. Press reports forwarded to Bismarck attributed the strikes to "ultramontane troublemakers."[48] General Emil von Albedyll, commander of the seventh army corps, was soon convinced that the strike was the result of a conspiracy planned and introduced into the region by newly arrived outsiders unacquainted with the traditions and problems of the miners. Although Bismarck was little impressed with the political reporting of the military ("not a military question"), Albedyll's belief that the older, long-resident, professional miners had been "coerced" into striking fitted the prince's old assumption that the Prussian-German masses were loyal to the existing order and that all social

[45] *DZA* Merseburg, Rep. 120, BB, VII, 1, Nr. 3, Bd. 8, pp. 144–183, 192–194.

[46] Rottenburg to Magdeburg, Dec. 17, 1889. *DZA* Merseburg, Rep. 120, BB, VII, 1, Nr. 3, Bd. 8, pp. 191–192.

[47] Hagemeister to Herrfurth, May 7, 1889. *DZA* Potsdam, Reichskanzlei, 444, pp. 13–14.

[48] Herrfurth to Bismarck, May 11, 1889. *DZA* Merseburg, Rep. 120, BB, VII, 1, Nr. 3, Bd. 5, pp. 54ff. Herrfurth to Bismarck, June 1 and 7, 1889. *DZA* Potsdam, Reichskanzlei, 445, pp. 1–2, 13–14.

and political difficulties stemmed from demagogic politicians and political agitators who deceived and misled the common people.[49]

Given that assumption, it is understandable why, once the mass strike had dissolved and the crisis waned, the chancellor should have turned away from most of the options outlined in Gamp's memorandum of May 27. No longer was there any thought of liquidating private enterprise in the coal-mining industry. Even the proposal for worker committees was now too radical for Bismarck, as is shown by his reaction to Berlepsch's desire to hold economic conferences at Düsseldorf on "how to prevent large-scale strikes and, should they occur, end them as soon as possible." Periodic economic conferences (*Wirtschaftliche Conferenzen*) with representatives from management, workers, and the state had been authorized for Düsseldorf in 1886 as surrogate for a business chamber (*Gewerbekammer*), which the provincial Landtag had refused to accept.[50] Berlepsch (with the approval of the provincial governor) proposed to put before the conference a subject not originally included in that directive and, furthermore, to enlarge for this occasion the number of worker representatives from five to twenty.[51] Bismarck responded that he did not believe "we could learn very much from workers" and that in any case as much could be learned from five as from twenty. He feared that such conferences would merely encourage "utopian ambitions" and proposed that instead Berlepsch privately seek the unmitigated views of "a few insightful workers and employers notably friendly to workers," avoiding publicity at all costs.[52]

At Bismarck's request Berlepsch wrote an opinion on the matter, in which he pointed out that statutory and voluntary organs existed through which industrialists, merchants, farmers, and artisans could make their wishes known and give expert advice to the government on matters affecting their interests, but factory and mine workers had no equivalent channel "free from agitational influences." To provide a "loyal representation of workers' interests" in the economic conferences at Düsseldorf was particularly appropriate since the district contained the largest concentration of factory workers in

---

[49] Verdy to Albedyll, May 11, 1889; Albedyll to Ministry of War, July 11, 1889. DZA Potsdam, Reichskanzlei, pp. 444, 56–57; 445, pp. 112–123. Albedyll to Wilhelm II, June 1, 1889. DZA Merseburg, Rep. 120, BB, VII, Fach 1, Zu Nr. 3, Bd. 1, pp. 4–6.

[50] See pp. 157–158, fn. 43.

[51] Berlepsch to Bismarck, Herrfurth, Scholz, Maybach, and Lucius, May 22, 1889. DZA Merseburg, Rep. 120, BB, VIa, 13, I, Bd. 2, pp. 83–84; Magdeburg to Bismarck, June 16, 1889, *ibid.*, pp. 97–98; Magdeburg to Bismarck, June 16, 1889, *ibid.*, pp. 97–98. Participating in the economic conferences at Düsseldorf were representatives from agriculture (8), artisanry (8), industry and mining (10), commerce (6), and "other individually suitable personalities" (5). The first question it discussed was whether the living conditions of workers in the district could be improved by state ordinances. Berlepsch to Puttkamer, June 7, 1887. DZA Merseburg, Rep. 120, BB, VIa, 13, 1, Bd. 1, pp. 303–320v.

[52] Rantzau to Magdeburg, June 19, 1889; Magdeburg to Berlepsch, June 25, 1889. DZA Merseburg, Rep. 120, BB, VIa, 13, 1, Bd. 2, pp. 100–101.

Prussia. In an effort to meet Bismarck's objections Berlepsch refined the proposal by proposing that the twenty worker representatives be considered as an *Arbeiterkammer*, whose participation would be limited to "preliminary discussions" with the representatives of big business. Worker representatives could be carefully chosen from "the large number of intelligent and understanding workers" who were unlikely to voice "unlimited wishes and utopian ambitions." By presenting "carefully prepared" bills, the government could also hold the discussion, which was not public, within "the limits of the attainable and possible." He anticipated that in a month the official and unofficial enquiries then under way would recommend the creation of conciliation agencies. He would prepare a bill for it, to be discussed by the Düsseldorf economic conferences, but otherwise let the matter of worker representation rest for the time being.[53]

Berlepsch sent his original proposal also to the ministers of public works, agriculture, interior, and finance. Maybach, Lucius, and Scholz dodged the issue by agreeing to wait upon Bismarck's response before giving their own opinions.[54] But Maybach joined Herrfurth in advancing other suggestions for dealing with the strike question. He proposed to create a legal basis for state intervention in conflicts between workers and owners by requiring every mining firm to submit to state mining authorities for their review and approval all work regulations governing the conduct of workers and their relations with management. This would have resurrected a requirement of the old system of state paternalism abolished by the statute of 1865. (Bismarck: "Could the same be required of all industrial firms?") Another issue was whether to erect conciliation agencies or arbitration courts, chaired by state mining officials, whose decisions could be appealed in the law courts. Since the regulation of relationships between workers and employers in mining affected industrial relations generally, a legislative prerogative of the Reich, the best solution might be to effect changes in the imperial industrial code (Bismarck: "*la mer à boire*").[55]

The delegation of disturbed owners that rushed to the chancellery after their audience with the Kaiser on May 16 got the impression from Rottenburg that Bismarck opposed any form of worker representation in the coal mines. But they were wrong, for he did not reject this option when Gamp proposed it in his memorandum of May 27. On the contrary, his cryptic marginal comment ("Pless") shows that he was aware of a successful model for such committees in the Silesian mines of the Prince of Pless. Gamp pointed out, fur-

[53] Berlepsch to Bismarck, Aug. 5, 1889. DZA Merseburg, Rep. 120, BB, VIa, 13, I, Bd. 2, pp. 92–95.

[54] Maybach, Lucius, and Scholz to Bismarck, July 22, 1889. *Ibid*, pp. 91–92.

[55] Herrfurth and Maybach to Bismarck, June 18, 1889. DZA Merseburg, Rep. 120, BB, VII, Fach 1, Zu Nr. 3, Bd. 1, pp. 1–3. On the distinction between *Einigungsämter* and *Schiedsgerichte*, see Kirchhoff, *Staatliche Sozialpolitik*, pp. 86–87.

thermore, that workers had been known to accept temporary overtime shifts of up to sixteen hours, when management convinced their representatives of the necessity (Bismarck: "and when they earn *more* than during the day").[56] In his response to Maybach and Herrfurth, moreover, he declared conciliation agencies or arbitration courts permissible, but insisted that participating workers be over 25 years of age. To seek imperial legislation imposing such an institution upon all German industries was neither necessary nor advisable. Rapid passage of a Prussian statute regulating working conditions in the coal industry was "not excluded." The coal shortage had demonstrated the urgency of such legislation as a supplement to relevant paragraphs of the industrial code. Arbitration courts were easier to introduce in coal mining than in other branches of Prussian industry, for they were compatible with existing "traditions and organizations" there.

But the chancellor frowned on obligatory work ordinances subject to review by state mining officials. That might lead to a similar requirement in other industries. The result would be a deep intrusion into the "private relations between employers and their workers." A worker who felt oppressed by a mining ordinance would blame the state agency that authorized it. Furthermore, effective state control over the ordinances was not feasible. And yet he agreed to the suggestion that the gendarmerie and police forces in the coal-mining areas should be reinforced in order to reduce future reliance on the military in time of crisis.[57] Maybach and Herrfurth were evidently reluctant to surrender the proposal for state supervision over obligatory "house ordinances" in the coal-mining industry, but they agreed to leave the matter in abeyance until completion of official enquiries then in progress.[58]

The Reins Grow Slack

During the last six months of 1889 Bismarck leaned increasingly toward the side of the owners in labor disputes. In reacting to Vohwinkel's report that the strike in mid-July at the Dahlbusch mine had started as a protest against the dismissal of a mine leader accused of libeling the management, Bismarck wrote, "If the mine administration should no longer have the freedom to dismiss a worker without the consequence of a general strike, that would mean the establishment of mass rule, which would present a great danger for public

---

[56] *DZA* Potsdam, Reichskanzlei, 444, pp. 3–6.

[57] Bismarck to Maybach and Herrfurth, July 10, 1889. *DZA* Merseburg, Rep. 120, ad BB, VII, 1, Nr. 3, Bd. 1, pp. 27–31v. The factual information that informed this document is to be found in Magdeburg to Bismarck, June 26, 1889. *Ibid.*, pp. 17–24.

[58] Maybach and Herrfurth to Bismarck, Aug. 13 and Nov. 20, 1889. *DZA* Merseburg, Rep. 120, ad BB, VII, 1, Nr. 3, Bd. 1, pp. 33–37v.

life."[59] In December he took the same position with regard to a strike by factory workers at Lückenwalde in the Potsdam district, where four thousand
workers protested the employment of scab workers. Bismarck maintained that
employers must be able to hire whom they pleased.[60] The congealing of his
antilabor position is seen most clearly, however, in his reaction to the revelation that the mine owners, once the May strike was over, had formed a
secret agreement not to hire any worker who either had been discharged by
another firm or had voluntarily left its employ. Their purpose was dual: to rid
themselves of labor activists and to prevent a competition for labor that would
drive up wages while they met the surging demand for coal built up during the
strike. At Friedrichsruh in early December he must have first learned from the
newspapers of the growing unrest in the coalfields and of the efforts of regional
officials to quiet it, an involvement of which he thoroughly disapproved.

On December 1, three thousand miners assembled at Essen and resolved to
strike over the blacklist on the following day. Their leaders persuaded them
to negotiate first, but the mine owners' association refused to participate.
More and larger meetings of Ruhr miners (four thousand in Dortmund) on
December 5 and 7 finally convinced the owners at Essen of the wisdom of
abandoning the blacklist. The mine owners' association ratified the decision
at a meeting attended by Berlepsch, now governor-general of the Rhineland,
the Düsseldorf district governor, the local *Landrat*, the lord mayor of Essen,
and three miners' representatives. The officials communicated the decision to
the miners' representatives and warned that, if the miners should strike despite the owners' declaration, they could expect "no sympathy" from the government. During these anxious days Rhineland and Westphalian officials
were active behind the scenes in mediating between owners and workers in
order to avoid a repetition of the massive strike of May. On December 10
Berlepsch instructed his officials that it was not enough to wait until miners
made their grievances publicly known; they must remain in frequent contact
with labor leaders to learn their grievances before miners reached the point of
open protest. But they must also warn the workers against violating the truce
just arrived at, stressing the determination of the owners to abide by their
promises.[61]

Bismarck regarded the involvement of officials in resolving labor-manage-
ment frictions as proof of their partiality toward labor and a departure from
his policy of nonintervention. He received from Herrfurth and Maybach official confirmation of the secret blacklist agreement, but was unimpressed.[62]

[59] Vohwinkel to Bismarck, Aug. 10, 1889; Bismarck to cabinet meeting of Aug. 17. DZA
Potsdam, Reichskanzlei, 445, pp. 93–110, 129.

[60] Hue de Grais to Herrfurth, Dec. 5, 1889; Bismarck to Herrfurth, Dec. 13, 1889. DZA
Merseburg, Rep. 120, BB, VII, 1, Nr. 3, Bd. 8, pp. 129–130, 134–138.

[61] SEG (1889), pp. 145–147; Kirchhoff, *Staatliche Sozialpolitik*, pp. 91–122.

[62] Herrfurth to Bismarck, Dec. 7, 1889; Studt to Herrfurth, Dec. 4, 1889; Maybach to Bis-

The government, he asserted, could not compete with socialist and ultramontane parties for the favor of workers at the cost of law and justice. Its authority must shield both parties in their rights. Although an agreement to blacklist employees was "perhaps not useful," it was no more illegal than a strike. Like their workers, employers had a right to strike. (Lockouts were common in England.) For the government to leave the path of nonpartisanship in order to appease labor by yielding to its wishes would harm the capacity of industry to provide work, reducing the number of employed workers and their pay. It would also give workers the feeling that the government feared their power and needed their friendship. Their heightened self-importance would result in bigger demands. Industrialists feared—so they had told him—that, if they failed to yield to "government insinuations," they would be refused any support in the event of a renewal of "tumultuous events." He regarded this fear as a reflection on the honor of the state.[63]

Herrfurth's response to this criticism was masterful. He expressed satisfaction that his own position in the matter, the instructions he had given to his subordinate officials, and their actual conduct corresponded with the prince's views! He too regarded state intervention in labor relations, where no violation of law occurred, as unjustified (Bismarck: "Good"). But recognition of these principles, he continued, did not exclude intervention when public peace, order, and safety were threatened by massive work stoppages or when the welfare of large regions and the state's operating capacity were jeopardized. The owners' blacklisting agreement had existed for six months without any reaction from officials. The authorities had undertaken their mediation only when confronted with the threat of another massive strike—leaving aside the issue of whether or not it was justified (Bismarck: "But that is decisive and salient")—and after receiving requests from both sides (Bismarck: "?"). Their successful mediation had not only warded off a dangerous strike but also established the basis for a "longer armistice and perhaps a lasting peace" (Bismarck: "?"). "Nonpartisan" (Bismarck: "?") mediation by the Oberpräsidenten Berlepsch and Studt had been praised by both sides and had "strengthened" (Bismarck: "?") trust in the government.[64]

Bismarck's marginalia show that he read the document with increasing fury. While claiming to act in full accord with Bismarck's "principles," the minister approved and defended an action they contradicted. Under Wilhelm

marck, Dec. 7, 1889. Eilert to Maybach, Dec. 5, 1889. DZA Merseburg, Rep. 120, BB, VII, 1, Nr. 3, Bd. 8, pp. 97–105, 109–119, 141–142.
[63] Rottenburg to Magdeburg, Dec. 10, 1889; Bismarck to Maybach, Dec. 13, 1889; Rottenburg to Magdeburg, Dec. 9, 1889; Bismarck to Herrfurth, Dec. 13, 1889. DZA Merseburg, Rep. 120, BB, VII, 1, Nr. 3, Bd. 8, pp. 120–126, 130–132, 134–138. Bismarck to Herrfurth, Dec. 15, 1889; Rottenburg to Boetticher, Dec. 19, 1889. GW, VIc, 422–423. Herrfurth to Bismarck, Dec. 17, 1889. DZA Potsdam, Reichskanzlei, 446, pp. 5–13.
[64] Herrfurth to Bismarck, Dec. 17, 1889. DZA Potsdam, Reichskanzlei, 446, pp. 20–23v.

I no minister would have dared to give such a response to the mighty chancellor. It confirmed Bismarck's suspicion that Herrfurth, confident of the Kaiser's backing, was following a divergent course, not only in this but also in other matters.[65] One day after the receipt of Herrfurth's explanation, Bismarck dictated a letter to Boetticher that reveals a growing awareness that he was losing control over the governmental apparatus and its social policy. While claiming that he intended no "recrimination over what had occurred," he declared it "absolutely necessary that provincial governors not correspond directly with his majesty, the Kaiser and king." Even if Wilhelm II should command them to send their reports directly to him, the documents must go first to the minister of the interior. Otherwise the governors would usurp the role of minister.

Bismarck's problem, however, was not the provincial governors but the minister of interior who approved their actions. His only hope for bringing Herrfurth into line was to convince Wilhelm II that the course they were following was dangerous. He ordered Boetticher to draft a personal report to the sovereign (Immediatbericht) and sketched out what it should contain. "We are cultivating in the workers a great danger that will ultimately be felt not only at the polls but also in the army. The efforts of workers to obtain ever more pay for ever less work has no limits." The costs of production would make German industry uncompetitive against foreign producers, as in the period after liquidation of the iron tariffs. This time the "cure" could not be effected by protective tariffs, but only by force (Vergewaltigung). The provincial governors had intervened in behalf of workers, who were not wise and independent enough to resist the blandishments of social democratic and ultramontane enemies of the monarchy. Labor movements of the kind Germany was experiencing would be led by social democratic extremists ultimately, if not currently. The government could not let itself be led by workers without falling into danger. The recent conduct of the government—"in the persons of the provincial governors"—was injurious to the interest of state. The government could not run after the workers, and the workers could not pari passu negotiate with the Kaiser through the royal governors. "If we let the mistake they began exert an influence, its consequence can only be corrected later by hard and perhaps bloody disciplinary measures." To curry favor with the coal miners would not influence an election because of their small

[65] The suspicion arose when Wilhelm II recanted his earlier decision to reappoint Puttkamer to the Ministry of Interior, from which he had been dismissed by Friedrich III. Bismarck suspected that Herrfurth had consolidated his position by pursuing in harmony with Wilhelm a reform of rural local government, which Bismarck vigorously opposed. From an official metallographed questionnaire distributed by the interior ministry and brought to Bismarck's attention by a delegation of Schönhausen peasants, Bismarck had concluded that Herrfurth was actually preparing the reform without cabinet approval, another indication of Wilhelm's willingness to work through unconstitutional channels. GW, XV, 485–486.

number in the total population. But the reaction against an illegal partisanship for workers against employers might be important in determining the outcome. Despite the seriousness of Bismarck's objections, this document contained no threat of resignation, of the kind that Bismarck had so often used to coerce his colleagues and the sovereign during the reign of Wilhelm I.[66]

Even as this document was drafted, Maybach and Herrfurth yielded either to Bismarck's pressure or to their own second thoughts. On December 19 they ordered provincial authorities to cease conferring with labor representatives; the commitment of mine owners to abolish the blacklist on terms acceptable to workers had ended the occasion for government intervention. Although Berlepsch and Studt did not cease to work on plans for some form of corporate representation for the Ruhr's workers, they were for the moment powerless to effect it—at a time when the socialist movement and its labor union auxiliary began to penetrate the Ruhr in earnest.[67] That the Prussian minister of commerce (the title and capacity under which Bismarck often corresponded with them) accepted only one of the proposals sent to him (conciliation agencies and arbitration courts) and persisted in seeking repressive rather than structural remedies for the problems posed by the coal miners' strike was frustrating to Prussian officials who believed in the state's obligation to establish an institutional channel for the resolution of differences between labor and management. Those who were privy to the correspondence must have been appalled, furthermore, by the degree to which the prince sided with employers on the critical issue of lockouts and blacklisting. Naturally they were cheered by the knowledge that the Kaiser had a different view.

On returning from Constantinople in November, Wilhelm II talked a lot about strikes and labor legislation. "Very much has to be done," Lucius heard him say, "to stop capital from devouring labor. Not all industrialists are like Krupp and Stumm, who take good care of their workers. Most exploit workers ruthlessly and ruin them. I regard it as my duty to intervene here and to make sure that the people are not oppressed and do not strike. The corporations don't care for their workmen; many are foreign-owned."[68]

---

[66] Rottenburg to Boetticher, Dec. 19, 1889. DZA Potsdam, Reichskanzlei, 446, pp. 20–23v. The contents of this document were summarized by the editors of Bismarck's collected works, who chose to leave out the phrase "harte und vielleicht blutige Massregeln." GW, VIc, 423. Neither this author nor, apparently, the editors could find the final version of the *Immediatbericht* in the files; it may have been countermanded.

[67] Kirchhoff, *Staatliche Sozialpolitik*, p. 95.

[68] Lucius, *Bismarck-Erinnerungen*, p. 505.

✠✦

CHAPTER TWELVE

Kaiser or Chancellor?

Y THE END OF 1889 Bismarck appears to have given up the idea that industrial labor could be integrated into a German national consensus based on the Prussian-German establishment. Since 1863 he had intermittently pursued that objective by both reform and repression—*Zuckerbrot und Peitsche*. As the end of his career approached, the old chancellor was increasingly inclined to rely on the whip; at the beginning of his reign, the young Kaiser preferred to offer more sweets. Continuing social unrest created a fresh sense of urgency for many Prussian officials and ministers. But so also did the approach of Reichstag elections on February 20, 1890, and the threatened dissolution of the cartel, whose survival Wilhelm II and his circle of confidantes regarded as vital to the legislative success of his government. From Friedrichsruh Bismarck sought to orient the sense of developing crisis in Berlin with a Christmas message to Wilhelm II: "I hold internal struggles as obviously more likely than foreign wars, and I deplore especially that I am no longer as robust for such a fight as I was in 1862. My strength is declining, but what I have left I will gladly expend in your majesty's service, as long as that is your highness's will."[1]

Collision Course

On convening in October 1889, the Reichstag received a government bill that would have permanently renewed the antisocialist statute, due to lapse on September 30, 1890, and increased the powers of regional authorities to imprison and exile agitators. During the ensuing debates the national liberals not only rejected the new features of the statute but also refused to renew the provisions of the old law that provided for regional banishment of radicals. In the view of Miquel and his associates use of this power by the police had merely spread the infection of subversion into areas hitherto germ free. They chose the path of reform over coercion, confident in the knowledge that this was also the desire of Wilhelm II.[2]

---

[1] Bismarck to Wilhelm II, Dec. 29, 1889. GW, XIV, 996. Six months earlier (July 8, 1889) he had written, "I regard wars with foreign powers as less dangerous in the long run than the poison being spread within the country among the naive masses by way of social democracy." Quoted in Hansjörg Renk, *Bismarcks Konflikt mit der Schweiz. Basler Beiträge zur Geschichtswissenschaft*, vol. 125 (Basel, 1972), p. 347.

[2] SBR (1889–1890), pp. 117–190, 1152–1199, 1225–1255, Anlagen, Nos. 37, 104; Hans Herzfeld, *Johannes von Miquel* (Detmold, 1938), II, 162ff. For Bismarck's role in shaping the bill

In 1888 Bismarck had maintained that to let the watchdog die was better than to pull its teeth. Once the public had experienced the excesses of the mob, aroused by anarchists and revolutionaries, it would accept even more drastic measures than were now proposed.[3] This was still his position in the winter of 1889–1890. Hence he resolutely refused to take the initiative in forging a compromise among the cartel parties that would have permitted passage of a toothless statute; nor would he even say in advance whether such a statute, once passed, would be accepted by the government. His aim was to force the Reichstag to assume full responsibility for the chaos he believed would result either from rejection of the statute or passage of an inadequate one. If chaos came, the fears it would engender among people of property and those who put a higher premium on social order than on social justice would produce the proper climate for public acceptance of a *Staatsstreich*.

Bismarck's actions during the fateful winter that ended with his dismissal from office can only be understood against the background of his obstinate determination to pursue this course, even if it meant the breakup of the cartel and conflict with the Kaiser. He was probably truthful in saying that he wished to preserve the cartel but not at the cost of dependence upon its national liberal component. He wanted good relations with the Kaiser but not at the cost of postponing what he believed to be an inevitable crisis in German internal affairs.[4] Consciously or unconsciously, he may have wanted to produce such an emergency in the expectation that most would recognize that he alone had the prestige and personal authority to master it. Once more he would prove to the world, even to Wilhelm II and the sycophants who inflated the Kaiser's ego, that the old chancellor was indispensable after all. In the quiet of Friedrichsruh he gathered strength for yet another battle, one that would determine whether his evaluation of his own importance to the monarchy and Germany would be shared by the Kaiser, the government, the parties, and the people.

Bismarck's remoteness from the scene of political maneuver and his seeming inflexibility produced confusion among the cartel parties. Bennigsen, Kardorff, and Helldorff worked for a compromise, which was not impossible in view of their decision to renew the cartel for the Reichstag election in Feb-

---

see Freiherr Lucius von Ballhausen, *Bismarck-Erinnerungen* (Stuttgart, 1920), p. 491; GW, VIc, 409–410; Otto Gradenwitz, *Bismarcks Letzter Kampf, 1888–1898* (Berlin, 1924), pp. 78–79.

[3] Bismarck to cabinet, Aug. 6, 1888. GW, VIc, 392–393.

[4] The mood in which Bismarck approached the February election can be seen in remarks recorded by Baroness Spitzemberg, December 7, 1889. "One must always reckon with the possibility of a hostile majority; one can dissolve [parliament] three, four times, but in the end you have to smash the pots. Such problems as how to cope with social democracy and what to do about the relationship between the parliaments and individual states cannot be solved without bloodshed any more than could the problem of German unity. And when it comes to the use of violence the young master is easy to . . ." Here the prince broke off in mid-sentence—the unspoken words "too weighty to utter." Rudolf Vierhaus, ed., *Das Tagebuch der Baronin Spitzemberg* (Göttingen, 1960), p. 266; GW, VIII, 673–674.

BISMARCK IN THE REICHSTAG, EARLY 1889. (BILDARCHIV PREUSSISCHER KULTURBESITZ.)

ruary. Except for the ultras, conservatives of all hues were willing to sacrifice the banishment paragraphs. German conservatives insisted, however, that the government declare its willingness to accept the amendment before the debate.[5] On November 25, 1889, Helldorff journeyed to Friedrichsruh to appeal for the chancellor's support. But Bismarck adamantly refused to give up the banishment paragraphs. Finally he did say, to Helldorff's astonishment, that "preservation of the cartel was more important to him than the entire antisocialist act."[6] Although unwilling to grease the wheels of compromise, in other words, he was likely to ride along. To participate in weakening the bill, he explained later, would "cut off" the possibility of ultimately seeking even more stringent measures.[7]

Helldorff and his colleagues refused to shoulder a responsibility Bismarck evaded. When the national liberals voted with the majority to strike out the banishment paragraphs in a crucial committee meeting on December 4, the German conservatives, under considerable pressure from the ultras, rejected the entire statute. On this ballot they would have been in the majority had not Windthorst, sensing an opportunity to drive a wedge into the cartel, reversed the centrist position and voted for the weakened statute. In this form the bill was reported out of committee to the Reichstag's plenum for a third reading in late January 1890.

The new strike wave that began in December 1889 continued into 1890, spreading out from the coalfields (individual strikes) into other branches of German industry.[8] As reports of renewed labor unrest in Prussia's most industrialized regions arrived at the Berlin ministries in December and January, the sense of crisis in May was reborn. But Germany's chancellor, hours away amid the rustling evergreens of the Sachsenwald, was seemingly unperturbed by the course of events. He instructed his colleagues not to intervene in these struggles but to "let the strikes burn themselves out."[9] To protect workers at the cost of the owners, he declared, would shake the trust of the "more intelligent circles in the stability and judiciousness" of the government. "This has all the more to be avoided, since our laws already tend to place the decisive power of the state in the hands of the lower classes, who are least equipped to judge

[5] Herzfeld, Miquel, II, 165–166; Georg von Eppstein, ed., Fürst Bismarcks Entlassung (Berlin, 1920), pp. 123–131.

[6] Gradenwitz, Letzter Kampf, pp. 79–80; Wilhelm von Schweinitz, Denkwürdigkeiten des Botschafters General von Schweinitz (Berlin, 1927), II, 391–392.

[7] Bismarck to cabinet, Jan. 10, 1890; Bismarck to Herbert Bismarck, Jan. 23, 1890. GW, VIc, 426–427.

[8] The total number of work stoppages in 1889 has been calculated at 280; in 1890, at 390. Klaus Tenfelde and Heinrich Volkmann, eds., Streik: Zur Geschichte des Arbeitskampfes in Deutschland während der Industrialisierung (Munich, 1981), p. 294.

[9] DZA Merseburg, Rep. 120, BB, VII, 1, Nr. 3, Bd. 8, pp. 120–122, 129–130, 191–192, 210, 219, 234, 248, 281, 284, 287; DZA Potsdam, Reichskanzlei, 446, pp. 134–134v.

political matters and cannot measure the dangers that the pursuit of their special interests holds for the general welfare of the state."[10]

Since the May strike, Wilhelm II had begun to question the adequacy of the social reforms of the 1880s and to consider further governmental action in areas that Bismarck had declared out of bounds: wages, hours, Sunday rest, child and female labor, working and living conditions. On returning from his voyage to the Middle East in early November, the Kaiser discussed the issue with a number of individuals, including court painter August von Heyden, industrialist Count Hugo Douglas, and Wilhelm's childhood tutor Georg Ernst Hinzpeter. Although trained in philology, Hinzpeter had long been interested in urban social problems and had contacts with Catholic circles influential in formulating the Center party's position on social issues. Evidently at the Kaiser's suggestion, the pedagogue composed an extensive memorandum on the labor question, which became the basis for Wilhelm's discussions with others. In late December the Hohenzoller sent the memorandum to Minister of Interior Herrfurth, who handed it on to Karl Heinrich von Boetticher, state secretary of the Imperial Office of the Interior and Puttkamer's successor as vice-president of the Prussian cabinet. At the end of December the document reached Rottenburg, Bismarck's secretary and aide at Friedrichsruh, who found the memorandum "too simple." He did not present it to Bismarck and advised Boetticher not to do so.[11]

Hence Bismarck did not know what was brewing in the Kaiser's mind until January 6, 1890, when Boetticher finally arrived in the Sachsenwald. Both the vice-president and Holstein, who helped prepare him for the interview with Bismarck, feared that the developing breach between Kaiser and chancellor would adversely affect the cartel in the approaching elections on February 20.[12] Bismarck rejected Boetticher's plea for "concessions" to the Kaiser on the question of "worker protection." Later Bismarck publicly castigated Boetticher, whose career he had furthered over many years, for forgetting that as state secretary and vice-president his job was to represent the views of the chancellor to the Kaiser, not the reverse. What was needed, the prince asserted, was not concessions to workers potentially harmful to business, but defense against the advance of social democracy, which had become "in the highest degree" a "question of war and peace, not law, in internal affairs."[13]

[10] Rottenburg to Magdeburg, Dec. 10, 1889. DZA Merseburg, Rep. 120, BB, VII, 1, Nr. 3, Bd. 8, pp. 120–122. This passage, dictated by Bismarck to Rottenburg, does not appear in the final versions of his responses to Herrfurth and Maybach for which it was originally intended. See p. 345, fn. 57.

[11] Hermann Bollnow, "Wilhelms II. Initiative zur Arbeiterschutzgebung und die Entlassung Bismarcks," in Hermann Bollnow et al., *Aspekte sozialer Wirklichkeit* (Berlin, 1958), pp. 100–101.

[12] Norman Rich, *Friedrich von Holstein: Politics and Diplomacy in the Era of Bismarck and Wilhelm II* (Cambridge, Eng., 1965), I, 263–265.

[13] GW, XV, 482–484; Johannes Penzler, ed., *Fürst Bismarck nach seiner Entlassung* (Leipzig, 1897–1898), VI, 358–359.

Rebuffed in Friedrichsruh, Boetticher turned for advice to the Grand Duke of Baden and for help to the Saxon government. The German medium-sized states presented a possible way out of the dilemma. Prussia could not present reform legislation to the Bundesrat without Bismarck's consent—or resignation—but other German states were free to do so. The logical state was Saxony, which had a progressive record in the field of worker protection. King Albert was eager to offer the Saxon model to the Reich and was encouraged by Wilhelm II and Boetticher to take the initiative with support from Baden and perhaps Bavaria.[14]

Meanwhile, two other initiatives got under way. The ubiquitous Holstein engaged Franz Fischer, lawyer and Berlin correspondent for the *Kölnische Zeitung*, to write a memorandum on the social question for transmittal to Philipp zu Eulenburg, the Kaiser's close friend and confidante. But Eulenburg, who also regarded Hinzpeter's memorandum as primitive, had launched his own quest for expert advice. After talking the matter over with the Kaiser during a walk in the Tiergarten, Eulenburg turned to Privy Counselor Paul Kayser, formerly of the Imperial Agency for Social Insurance and now a counselor in the political division of the Imperial Foreign Office, who wrote yet another exposé, which he also showed to Holstein. Through Kayser's work Eulenburg hoped to supply the Kaiser with concrete, practical, and informed proposals, more realistic and presentable than the impressionistic meditations of Hinzpeter. A copy of the Kayser–Holstein report went to Baron Adolf Marschall von Bieberstein, Holstein's friend and Bundesrat plenipotentiary for Baden, who communicated the contents to the Grand Duke of Baden.

By now the cost of Bismarck's long absence from Berlin and his separation from the Kaiser was evident. The Kaiser was being influenced by persons unqualified either by station and experience or constitutional "responsibility" to advise the ruler on matters of state policy. The Kaiser's lust for ideas and information about the labor question offered opportunities to those eager to advance their careers and influence. And yet it is undeniable that those involved in what Bismarck branded as self-serving intrigue and even conspiracy were also genuinely concerned about the direction of public policy under his faltering leadership. They were disturbed by the government's immobility on the subject of further social reform and signs of increasing restlessness among workers, the electorate, and political parties.

At the center of the developing Fronde were Holstein and Eulenburg; associated with them in varying degrees were Boetticher, Marschall, Grand Duke Friedrich of Baden (the Kaiser's uncle), and King Albert of Saxony. Eulenburg and Holstein were alarmed over Bismarck's seeming vacillations in both foreign and domestic policy. And yet they seem to have had no candidate in mind for his replacement. Instead they expected to use the authority

---

[14] Ernst Gagliardi, *Bismarcks Entlassung* (Tübingen, 1927), I, 25–26.

of the Kaiser, with whose capacities they were not yet disillusioned, to rectify the chancellor's "errors." To this end they encouraged Wilhelm to establish direct contact with ministers, officials, and parliamentary leaders in order to bypass Bismarck, who, they hoped, could be eased out of his Prussian offices and as chancellor gradually restricted to foreign affairs. At the same time they feared that the process of transition might proceed too swiftly. Until he was ready to govern, Wilhelm needed the protective shield of Bismarck's prestige and influence.[15] In early 1890 this uneasy balance was constantly threatened by both Bismarck's obstructionism and Wilhelm's impetuosity. On the evening of January 23 Holstein thought it wise to warn Herbert that his father's position was being undermined. The bitterness in the Reichstag was spreading to the electorate, not to speak of the Kaiser and his circle. "The idea persists that Prince Bismarck does nothing himself and prevents others from doing anything, and unless this idea is killed at the source it will before long materially alter the prince's position, *inside* Germany at least."[16]

Defeat of the Cartel

Finally the Kaiser ran out of patience. With the election less than one month away he could not wait for the legislative process to grind out its results in Bundesrat and Reichstag. But he must also have asked himself why he should surrender to the king of Saxony and his government the appreciation of German workers and the glory of achieving industrial peace. Why not issue to the nation a bold proclamation such as that with which his grandfather had begun the campaign for social insurance in 1881? On January 23 Wilhelm II abruptly summoned a Crown Council for the following day to discuss "my ideas on the labor question."

With the Kaiser's approval and Herbert's encouragement Bismarck had remained at Friedrichsruh during January. But now it was obvious to Herbert that his father must hear in person what the Kaiser had to say about the social question rather than read about it later in the minutes. Bismarck agreed, and Herbert arranged for an audience between chancellor and Kaiser to occur one hour before the council meeting. The purpose was to enable them to reach an understanding on the issues. "I do not expect it," Herbert advised his father, "to be difficult at all."[17] For a septuagenarian in poor health January 24

[15] John C. G. Röhl, *Germany Without Bismarck: The Crisis of Government in the Second Reich, 1890–1900* (London, 1967), pp. 27–34; Isabel V. Hull, *The Entourage of Kaiser Wilhelm II, 1888–1918* (Cambridge, Eng., 1982), pp. 80–84.

[16] Rich, *Holstein*, I, 264–266; Heinrich O. Meisner, ed., *Denkwürdigkeiten des General-Feldmarschalls Alfred Grafen von Waldersee* (Stuttgart, 1923), II, 76–77, 85–87.

[17] Walter Bussmann, ed., *Staatssekretär Graf Herbert von Bismarck: Aus seiner politischen Privatkorrespondenz* (Göttingen, 1964), pp. 554, 559–560. See also Eppstein, ed., *Bismarcks Entlassung*, pp. 87–88, 122–124. From an analysis of the telegrams exchanged between Berlin and

was a long, exhausting day, and the physical strain may well have influenced the outcome. Rising early, Bismarck took the train to Berlin, arriving at 1:50 P.M. At 3:00 he met the cabinet; at 5:30, the Kaiser alone; at 6:00, the Crown Council. In the cabinet meeting the prince persuaded the ministers to procrastinate on the issue of social reform until concrete proposals could be prepared. But the chancellor was alone in insisting that the government refuse to declare in advance whether it would accept a weakened antisocialist bill. Boetticher warned that without such a declaration conservatives would vote in the plenum against the entire bill, ensuring its defeat. The meeting ended in a "very tense mood." So also did the brief audience with the Kaiser, of which we have no record other than the Kaiser's assertion that Bismarck admitted wanting the antisocialist bill to fail because he desired a sharper one.[18]

The Kaiser began the Crown Council with a long exposé about the unhealthy development of German industry in comparison with the English.[19] German industrialists, with a few praiseworthy exceptions, had not taken care of their workers, but had "squeezed them like lemons and left them rotting on the manure pile." Recent strikes showed the degree of alienation existing between worker and employer, whose fruit was the spread of socialism. Revolutions stemmed from the failure to make timely and reasonable concessions. As necessary reforms he listed the restriction of Sunday and night labor; female and child labor; workers' committees to supplement factory inspectors; conciliation and arbitration boards; conversion of state-owned enterprises into model projects providing savings banks, churches, schools, and hospitals for workers, who would also have the opportunity to become state officials. "I want to be *roi des queux*; the people must know that their king is concerned about their welfare." January 24, he reminded the ministers, was the birthday of Frederick the Great, who had done much for the peaceful development of

---

Friedrichsruh on January 23, Gradenwitz concluded that at this stage the Kaiser tried to keep Bismarck away from the capital until the last minute. *Letzter Kampf*, pp. 91–102; GW, VIc, 427–428. But there is also evidence that Bismarck remained away from Berlin during the winter in order to avoid confrontation with the Kaiser on the labor question. Gagliardi, *Entlassung*, I, 50–52; Freiherr von Maltzahn-Gültz, "Bismarck: Persönliche Erinnerungen an ihn," in Arthur von Brauer, Erich Marcks, and Karl Alexander von Müller, eds., *Erinnerungen an Bismarck* (Stuttgart, 1915), p. 117.

[18] Lucius, *Bismarck-Erinnerungen*, pp. 505–507; GW, XV, 491; Gagliardi, *Entlassung*, I, 33–35; Hans Rothfels, "Zur Bismarck-Krise von 1890," *Historische Zeitschrift*, 123 (1920), pp. 267–296.

[19] There are several sources for what transpired in the Crown Council. Naturally the official protocol leaves out the dramatic moment—Bismarck's threat of resignation. See Eppstein, ed., *Bismarcks Entlassung*, pp. 157–165. The best record is that of Lucius, ed., *Bismarck-Erinnerungen*, pp. 507–509, but see also the recollections of Bismarck in *Gedanken und Erinnerungen* (GW, XV, 491–495), of Herbert (*ibid.*, pp. 592–595), and of Boetticher (Eppstein, ed., *Bismarcks Entlassung*, pp. 42–47). For the memoranda that the Kaiser brought with him and were read aloud, see Eppstein, ed., *Bismarcks Entlassung*, pp. 146–155. A good summary of the entire proceeding is Gagliardi, *Entlassung*, I, 35–42.

the country. As the cabinet had agreed, Bismarck handled the issue in dilatory manner, insisting that it be studied before measures were recommended.

As tension mounted, the Kaiser shifted to the antisocialist statute, insisting
that the banishment paragraphs be stricken in order to save the cartel. "The
antisocialist law contains the minimum powers needed by the government,"
Bismarck responded. "Presumably we will have to request more powers later.
To indicate now that one can get by with less will undercut such a request."[20]
A bad law would damage the government in the elections; failure of the law
would not endanger the cartel. The chancellor's voice began to rise. "I cannot
prove that to yield on this point would have fateful consequences for his majesty, but I believe it on the basis of many years of experience. If his majesty
has a different opinion on such a weighty question, then I am obviously no
longer the right person for my position. If the [antisocialist] statute lapses, we
must do our best without it and let the waves go higher. Then we may have a
conflict."[21] Wilhelm had already given his answer to this proposition in a
prepared statement read earlier in the meeting. "It would be lamentable if I
were to color the beginning of my government with the blood of my subjects!
My dearest wish is to avoid that as long as is possible. No one would ever
forget that I did that, and all of the expectations that have perhaps been
placed on me would be converted into their opposite. I cannot and will not
be forced into such a situation. Whoever intends to be honest with me must
do everything possible to avoid such a misfortune."[22]

Asked their opinions, the other ministers hedged, unwilling to break the
bond of collegial solidarity by siding with the Kaiser against the minister-
president. No vote was taken and no decisions reached. "We parted," said
Lucius, "with our differences unresolved, with the feeling that an irreparable
breach had occurred between sovereign and chancellor. His majesty exerted
himself, it is true, to be friendly toward the prince, but he was boiling. At
any rate he possesses great self-control." In private the monarch was less composed. He accused Minister of War Julius von Verdy du Vernois, whom he
had recently appointed to replace Bronsart, with "desertion" and threatened
him with balled fist.[23]

Next day the Reichstag faced the moment of truth on the antisocialist act.
Beforehand Helldorff went to Bismarck and Bennigsen to Lucius for instructions, but both came away empty-handed.[24] The statute was rejected by an
overwhelming majority (169 to 98) composed of all colors in the political

[20] From the official protocol. Eppstein, ed., *Bismarcks Entlassung*, p. 163.

[21] Lucius, *Bismarck-Erinnerungen*, p. 509.

[22] Memorandum of Jan. 21, 1890. Eppstein, ed., *Bismarcks Entlassung*, pp. 152–153.

[23] Lucius, *Bismarck-Erinnerungen*, pp. 509, 511; Philipp zu Eulenburg-Hertefeld, *Aus 50 Jahren*
(Berlin 1923), p. 227; Gagliardi, *Entlassung*, I, 53–56.

[24] Lucius, *Bismarck-Erinnerungen*, p. 510.

spectrum from conservative to socialist.[25] At the end of September 1890 Germany was to be without an "exceptional law" against socialists for the first time since 1878. Historians still differ on who was responsible for the collapse of the cartel on such an important issue. Does the blame belong to Bismarck, who stubbornly refused the declaration demanded by conservatives? To Helldorff, who either failed or did not want to understand Bismarck's hints that the government would not reject the amended statute? To the ultras, who were pleased at the opportunity to bust the cartel? Whoever was actually responsible, the deputies of the cartel parties were inclined to place the blame on Bismarck's head. In the Reichstag and Prussian ministries the feeling developed that Bismarck had lost the capacity for leadership.

Nearly two months were to pass before Bismarck's final resignation, but it seems clear that the Crown Council of January 24 made his departure inevitable. He had dealt the German Kaiser a humiliation to be neither forgiven nor forgotten. Wilhelm II was outraged to discover that Bismarck's hold over the ministers appeared greater than his own. What had the chancellor said to the ministers that afternoon, he asked Verdy, to cause them all to look "whipped"?[26] In the days that followed, to be sure, both men made an effort at reconciliation. Bismarck admitted to his colleagues on January 26 that he had "gone too far." One had to put up with the moods of a ruler as with good and bad weather. "I love him as the son of his forefathers and as sovereign." Next day the cabinet trooped into the palace to greet the monarch on his birthday. Kaiser and chancellor shook hands heartily. "I hope," Wilhelm said, "to have the cooperation and support of the prince for a long time."[27]

With relief Lucius concluded that the storm had "cleared the air," but the atmosphere was still charged with unresolved tensions. In the council on January 24 the Kaiser had proposed a solemn proclamation to dramatize his interest in the social question before the approaching Reichstag election.[28] Bismarck failed to dissuade him but edited the draft, which he found too far-reaching. On February 4 the Kaiser signed two rescripts. One, addressed to the chancellor, called for a European conference in Berlin at which Europe's industrialized nations would seek common agreement on social reform (the aim was to equalize the burden and hence prevent any state from gaining a competitive advantage for its manufacturers). The other rescript, addressed to the Prussian ministers of commerce and public works, directed them to prepare legislation providing for more social insurance, creating a system of labor representation for the ventilation of proletarian grievances, and regulating the time, hours, and conditions of labor. Bismarck included a summons to the Prussian State Council to deliberate on the Kaiser's proposals—in the

[25] SBR (1889–1890), pp. 1253–1255.
[26] Lucius, Bismarck-Erinnerungen, p. 511.
[27] Ibid., pp. 511–513; Eppstein, ed., Bismarcks Entlassung, pp. 48–49.
[28] Eppstein, ed., Bismarcks Entlassung, pp. 152–155.

hope that it would oppose or dilute them. That the documents were drafted in a form that did not require the chancellor's countersignature was quickly noted in the press.[29] After a parliamentary dinner on February 4 the Kaiser sat in one corner, the chancellor in another, each attended by a group of deputies. While the former explained the necessity of more protection for labor, the latter deplored the consequences. "The Kaiser likes me," Bismarck jested, "but I cannot impress him."[30]

Meanwhile the chancellor was busy trying to plug other holes in the dike. Through Boetticher he heard of Saxony's plan to introduce bills for labor protection in the Bundesrat. On January 30 he told Dresden's envoy that in that case he would immediately resign all of his offices. "The social question cannot be solved with rosewater; for that you need blood and iron." If this continued, Hinzpeter would be the next imperial chancellor. Rather than precipitate a breach between Kaiser and chancellor, the Saxons backed off despite Wilhelm's prodding.[31] Ignorant of Wilhelm's plans, Switzerland had also called for an international congress on the social question to be held at Berne. Bypassing his own foreign office, Wilhelm II urged the Swiss to abandon their project in favor of his own. Bismarck countered by maintaining that the two projects were not mutually exclusive; to the Swiss he denied that the Berlin conference had a diplomatic character and attributed to it a very limited agenda. The Swiss (and the foreign powers whom they invited to Berne) found themselves in the peculiar, unenviable position of having to take sides in a German domestic quarrel. They wisely chose to appease the thirty-year-old Kaiser, with whom they must reckon for years to come, and not the seventy-five-year-old chancellor, who could be gone tomorrow.[32]

Bismarck's flanking tactics were accompanied by a deceptive retreat on the main front. In the cabinet meetings on January 24 and 26 he announced his intention to resign all posts and functions except the chancellorship and foreign affairs. The latter he could not relinquish, for no one could inherit the trust he had established in London, Vienna, and even Paris (he did not in-

    [29] GW, XV, 498–503; VIII, 686; SEG (1890), pp. 19–21; Eppstein, ed., Bismarcks Entlassung, pp. 166–172. On the origin of the rescripts, see Bollnow, "Wilhelms II. Initiative," pp. 107–113.

    [30] BP, I, 308–312; III, 221ff.

    [31] GW, VIII, 679–683; VIc, 429–430; Eppstein, ed., Bismarcks Entlassung, pp. 50–52; Gagliardi, Entlassung, I, 56ff. After his failure to move the Saxon government to action in an audience on January 31 with Count Hohenthal, Dresden's representative in Berlin, Wilhelm summoned Leo von Caprivi to Berlin, where the monarch ordered the surprised general to prepare himself for the eventuality that he would become chancellor. The chancellor's office would, however, be diminished, for Wilhelm would himself govern the country after Bismarck's departure. Ibid., pp. 85–86.

    [32] Gagliardi, Entlassung, I, 321–370; Gradenwitz, Letzter Kampf, pp. 136–139. Eulenburg, Aus 50 Jahren, pp. 231–233. For other delaying tactics by Bismarck, see his report to the Kaiser of Feb. 26, 1890. GW, VIc, 432–433.

clude Petersburg). His colleagues interpreted this to mean that he would disengage himself from the internal affairs of both Prussia and the Reich. On
January 27 he did relinquish the Ministry of Commerce, to which the Kaiser,
on Bismarck's recommendation, appointed Berlepsch, then governor-general
of the Rhineland.[33] Yet it was ten days (February 3) before Bismarck actually
offered to the Kaiser his resignation as minister-president and Prussian foreign
minister. Boetticher was to assume the former office, Herbert the latter, in
addition to their posts as imperial state secretaries. The changes were to be
announced on election day, February 20.[34]

On February 12, however, Bismarck reneged on both resignations. This
reversal is hardly surprising in view of what we know of his psychology, but
narcissism also has its reasons. Even the Kaiser gave him one. When Bismarck
formally presented his resignations on February 3, Wilhelm II did not follow
the scenario of Wilhelm I—no protests, entreaties, certainly no tears, just
nodding assent. And yet this young Hohenzoller could not quite face the
consequences of his own decision. He asked, "But you will still defend the
military bills, won't you?"[35]

In addition to the increases already granted in 1887 and 1888, Wilhelm II
and his minister of war wanted to enlarge the German army by another
80,000 men and strengthen the field artillery at an ultimate annual cost of
about 120,000,000 marks. In the Kaiser's anxiety to make sure that Bismarck
would steer these bills through parliament, the chancellor found the leverage
he needed to get the monarch's consent to another antisocialist law. Hence
on February 12 he proposed to remain as minister-president "until the first
votes of the new Reichstag over the military bills and the renewal of the antisocialist law have been won or lost." Then, he said, he would give way in
May or June to a military man (he proposed General Leo von Caprivi), who
would be more suited to hold the post "during possible struggles with the
socialist movement and repeated dissolutions of the Reichstag." The Kaiser
looked disappointed, but he agreed. "Then everything will stay for the time
being as it has been."[36]

There was, however, more to Bismarck's reluctance to surrender his Prussian posts than merely the question of securing passage of the new military
and antisocialist bills. On February 10 the Bavarian delegate to the Bundesrat, Count Hugo von Lerchenfeld-Koefering, found him considering how he
could enhance his position as chancellor, particularly within the Bundesrat,

---

[33] Lucius, *Bismarck-Erinnerungen*, pp. 509–510.

[34] In his memoirs Bismarck dated this resignation February 8, but contemporary evidence suggests that the correct date was February 3. He did not inform the cabinet until February 9. *GW*,
XIV, 997; XV, 596; VIII, 693–694; Lucius, *Bismarck-Erinnerungen*, pp. 515–516.

[35] *GW*, VIII, 684; XV, 505.

[36] *GW*, XV, 505–507; VIc, 430. On the military bill, see Johannes Ziekursch, *Politische Geschichte des neuen deutschen Kaiserreiches* (Frankfurt a. M., 1925–1930), II, 439–441.

in order to compensate for the loss of his Prussian positions. Bismarck discussed several combinations, but they all rotated, Lerchenfeld observed, around the problem of control over Prussia's votes in the Bundesrat, with which the prince said he "wanted nothing more to do." But what would he do if the Prussian votes were cast contrary to his wishes? That was the critical issue.[37] As long as Herbert held the cabinet post of Prussian foreign minister, of course, the answer was clear. And yet Bismarck could not free himself from the suspicion that by giving up the minister-presidency he was surrendering a fundamental bastion of power. On February 16 Herbert reported to brother Bill that their father "seemed to have found the separation of Reich and Prussian affairs to be impracticable, since he does not want to be Boetticher's subordinate and is thinking now of a full resignation about April 1."[38]

The election of February 20, 1890, seemed to confirm Bismarck's surmise that stormy weather lay ahead. Lacking an international crisis like that of 1887 to bolster it, the cartel suffered a catastrophic defeat. Of 7,261,600 votes cast, 4,658,900 went to opposition parties. Seats controlled by the coalition fell from 220 to 135, the greatest losses being suffered by national liberals (from 99 to 42) and free conservatives (41 to 20). The Freedom party, on the other hand, recovered from 32 to 66 (approximately their strength in 1884–1887), and the Center reached its peak strength in the imperial era (98 to 106). The moral victors of the election of 1890, however, were the social democrats. While electing only 35 deputies (up from 11), they attracted an astonishing 1,427,300 voters (nearly twice the number of 1887), giving them the largest constituency of any German political party. By comparison, the gain in Freedom party voting strength was modest (from 973,100 to 1,159,900 voters).[39]

The election results of 1881, 1884, and 1890 suggest that, without the pressure of a foreign crisis ruthlessly exploited by the government, the majority of the voting electorate (71.5 percent of those eligible in 1890) was oppositional, although for varied reasons. Bad weather had produced a mediocre harvest in 1888 and a worse one in 1889, driving up grain prices by about 25 percent and cattle prices by about 19 percent in three years.[40] The rise was also attributed to the steep increase in agrarian tariffs granted by the cartel in 1887. The "love tokens" granted big landowners in the liquor tax bill of the same year also created resentments. For the urban lower classes the facts of

[37] GW, VIII, 684–687.

[38] Bussmann, ed., Herbert von Bismarck, p. 562.

[39] Bernhard Vogel, Dieter Nohlen, and Rainer-Olaf Schultze, Wahlen in Deutschland: Theorie-Geschichte-Dokumente, 1848–1970 (Berlin, 1971), pp. 290–291.

[40] Hans W. Graf von Finckenstein, Die Getreidewirtschaft Preussens von 1800 bis 1930. Vierteljahreshefte zur Konjunkturforschung, Sonderheft No. 35 (Berlin, 1934), p. 56; Alfred Jacobs and Hans Richter, Die Grosshandelspreise in Deutschland von 1792 bis 1934. Sonderhefte des Instituts für Konjunkturforschung, vol. 37 (Berlin, 1935), p. 83.

everyday life—the cost of bread, sausage, and liquor—counted for more than social insurance benefits and promises of protective legislation. The collapse of the great strike of May 1889 and the lockouts that followed left a bitter legacy. The lengthening of the legislative term from three to five years sponsored by the cartel was treated as a curtailment of democracy. These were issues upon which the social democrats thrived, despite the antisocialist statute. These issues may have brought to the polls thousands who did not vote in 1887 either because they were too young or too disinterested, while other thousands, who had been mobilized by patriotic issues in 1887 to vote for the cartel, remained away.[41]

Bismarck was hardly alone in believing that Germany stood on the threshold of a major social and political crisis.[42] The question was how to meet it. Should proletarian unrest be quelled by more social legislation or by more police repression? How, furthermore, was the government to cope with a hostile majority in the Reichstag? With another period of fruitless conflict in prospect, had not the time come for the series of dissolutions and elections that Bismarck had long foreseen as the prelude to a *Staatsstreich*?

To the Ides of March

Later Bismarck stated that he was well aware by this time that the "Kaiser wanted to be rid of me." The chancellor who had mused so often about the virtues of country life, had spoken remorsefully of politics as having "devoured all the carps in my pond," had bitterly complained of the burdens and responsibilities of public office, had repeatedly offered his resignation to a monarch who he knew would not accept it, and had asserted as recently as July 6, 1889, that he regarded with indifference Wilhelm's desire to rule alone—this chancellor now refused to bow out gracefully when his time had obviously come. In his memoirs he described himself as heroically determined not to yield to cowardice, as committed by love of the throne and fears for the future to defend the monarchy until "every means" had been exhausted.[43] Seen in more human terms, his compulsive need for power led him to cling in desperation to the handholds at the summit, even as they crumbled in his grasp and his body commenced to slide.

[41] Wilhelm Mommsen, *Bismarcks Sturz und die Parteien* (Berlin, 1924), pp. 14ff., 61–65, 78ff. Bismarck chose to blame the cartel's defeat on the Kaiser's two manifestos of Feb. 4. Moritz Busch, *Bismarck: Some Secret Pages of His History* (New York, 1898), II, 512–513.

[42] See, for example, the pessimistic letter of Wilhelm von Rauchhaupt to Hammerstein, Feb. 20, 1890. Without yet knowing the results of the voting, the leader of the conservative caucus in the Prussian chamber judged that the campaign itself showed that "huge masses of the population are consciously turning away from the monarchy." Hans Leuss, *Wilhelm Freiherr von Hammerstein* (Berlin, 1905), pp. 83–84.

[43] GW, XV, 504ff.; Bussmann, ed., *Herbert von Bismarck*, p. 542.

On February 25, 1890, Bismarck outlined to Wilhelm II his battle plans for the coming months. The election results made it all the more imperative that he retain his Prussian offices long enough to secure "our future against the socialist menace." He would, however, support the Kaiser's social reform program, once clarified by the Prussian State Council and approaching international conference. If unrest, even uprisings, should occur, he asked, was Wilhelm prepared to shoot? "Yes," the Kaiser replied. In that event, Bismarck continued, he would demand from the new Reichstag both the army bill and a new and more stringent antisocialist statute, giving police the power not only to banish agitators from cities and regions within Germany, but also to expel them from the country and deprive them of citizenship. Since the Reichstag would certainly reject both bills, the government must be prepared for repeated dissolutions. They parted with a hearty handshake and Bismarck's battle cry, "No surrender!" Returning to the Wilhelmstrasse, Bismarck exulted to Rottenburg, "The Kaiser is ready to fight; then I can remain at his side."[44]

By pumping bellicosity into the monarch's veins Bismarck evidently thought he had gained the same psychological hold on Wilhelm II that he had won over Wilhelm I in their famous audience of September 22, 1862. He had no reason to doubt the grandson's susceptibility to the use of force. On election day Wilhelm II had ordered the troops put on alert. From Waldersee he had warnings similar to those from Bismarck: The Reichstag would certainly not grant the military bill; in the long run repeated dissolutions would not suffice; the only choice would be to abolish universal male suffrage, a task for which the general offered his services.[45] To what thoughts of courage and violence Wilhelm II was able to elevate himself the German public learned on March 5, 1890, when he toasted the estates of Brandenburg province. Celebrating the long association of the Hohenzollern dynasty with Brandenburg, he declared that he, like his forefathers, looked upon his country and people as talents (in the biblical sense) entrusted to him by God, talents whose increase was his task and for which one day he would have to give reckoning. If "serious times" lay ahead, he expected to depend upon his loyal Brandenburgers. "Those who want to help me are heartily welcome, whoever they are, but those who oppose me in this work I shall crush."[46]

Even as he strove to restore harmony with Wilhelm II, Bismarck sensed that he was becoming increasingly isolated. On February 18 he made unex-

---

[44] What happened in the audience of February 25 must be pieced together from several accounts, some stemming from Bismarck, others from Wilhelm II; GW, XV, 508; Eppstein, ed., Bismarcks Entlassung, p. 84; Gradenwitz, Letzter Kampf, pp. 140–141; Eulenburg, Aus 50 Jahren, pp. 293–294; Waldersee, Denkwürdigkeiten, II, 106–107. See also the summary in Egmont Zechlin, Staatsstreichpläne Bismarcks und Wilhelms II., 1890–1894 (Stuttgart, 1929), pp. 32–35.

[45] Waldersee, Denkwürdigkeiten, II, 105–106; Zechlin, Staatsstreichpläne, p. 32.

[46] SEG (1890), pp. 33–34.

pected social calls on Waldersee and Moltke. Waldersee, who was not at home, exclaimed in his diary: "The chancellor wanted to visit me! I didn't trust my ears when I heard that. For years he has made no visits whatever, and now he drives to me and the field marshal in order to call. He is indeed becoming weak." Waldersee heard from Moltke that Bismarck had groused about the Kaiser, grumbled about the incapacity of Prussia's ministers, and was so distressed generally that the old field marshal felt obliged to console him and urge him to remain in office. On February 19 the Dowager Kaiserin Victoria was also startled when Bismarck and Johanna came seeking an audience. She asked what she could do for him. "I want only sympathy," was the answer. For one and a half hours he emptied his heart to her as he had to Moltke. But when he lamented the burden he was still compelled to bear, the empress made the innocent mistake of advising him to retire. That was not what he had come to hear. At about this time the chancellor also conferred seriatim with all of his former subordinates in the Ministry of Commerce, some of whom he hardly knew by name. Here too he seemed to be seeking support for his decision to remain in office.[47]

On February 26, one day after Bismarck talked Wilhelm II into a shooting mood, the prince already regretted his concession on social policy. Early that morning Boetticher, who had heard of the concession from the Kaiser, came happily to invite the chancellor to lunch. But he found Bismarck in "the worst possible mood." Did the minister really believe, the prince asked, that he would ever consent to such measures? Later that morning Bismarck attended, contrary to his announced intention, the first session of the Prussian State Council. Scribbling on the margin of the document under discussion ("quack," "humbug," "casuistry"), he kept silent until the Kaiser, who presided, put the first issue under discussion (Sunday labor) to a vote. Ministers, the chancellor observed, could not vote in a body whose function it was to give them advice. "Another stumbling block placed in my way," the Kaiser muttered to Boetticher.[48]

By then it was obvious that under the firm leadership of the Kaiser this "servile" body would endorse the monarch's social program. At the luncheon hosted by Boetticher, the chancellor sat stone-faced, uncommunicative, and patently out of sorts. Afterward he did not return to the session, but wandered off through the corridors of the Ministry of Interior "like a ghost, his expression blank, without apparent purpose, opening a door here and there and looking inside. Startled clerks moved respectfully out of his way." Through a side entrance he reached the quarters of the foreign office, where he paused in the offices of top officials (including Holstein), grumbling again about the

---

[47] Waldersee, Denkwürdigkeiten, II, 103–104; Gagliardi, Entlassung, I, 153–154.

[48] Penzler, ed., Bismarck nach seiner Entlassung, VI, 341; GW, VIc, 432; Eppstein, ed., Bismarcks Entlassung, pp. 58–60.

Kaiser's conduct and his own fate, even to those who on the previous day had heard him say that the conflict had been resolved. News of the chancellor's unprecedented peregrination spread quickly and led some gossips to speak of the onset of senility.[49] Bismarck had always been a chronic complainer, but never before had he exhibited such a need for consolation and reassurance, even from strangers and former enemies.

Bismarck faced the crisis he expected in 1890 by pursuing simultaneously two alternative routes: the search for a new majority in the Reichstag willing to come to terms with the government and preparation for a *Staatsstreich* either as a threat with which to expedite the formation of that majority or as an action to be carried out if the threat should fail. Since 1878 he had repeatedly dealt, publicly as well as privately, with the possibility of a coup and hinted at the form it might take, namely, a dissolution of the Reich by its member states and its replacement by an assembly based on corporative representation. Since January Herbert and Ludwig Raschdau had been researching at Bismarck's request the legal questions involved. The central issue was whether the Reich's "members" were the federated states or their rulers and the senates of the free cities. Bismarck himself had once taken the first position, which had support in the writings of Paul Laband, an authority on constitutional law. But now he took the contrary view, dismissing Laband's opinion as unfounded. (By coincidence the issue had come to a head in connection with the impending extinction of the ruling dynasty of the principality of Schwarzburg-Rudolstadt.)[50]

In an audience on March 1 Bismarck obtained the Kaiser's agreement to his latest interpretation, which on the following day he developed at length in a cabinet meeting.[51] What the princes and free cities had granted, he asserted, they could also take away. To what end? "In this way it would be possible to be rid of the Reichstag if the elections continue to turn out badly."[52] But he also described to the ministers other possible actions of less drastic character: The king of Prussia could lay down the imperial crown; Prussian ministers and imperial officials would no longer be sent as Prussian delegates to the Bundesrat, giving the Reichstag opposition nothing but "anonymous majorities" to attack; the Reich chancellor himself need not be a member of that body, except as its presiding officer.

On March 2 Bismarck, whatever his private doubts, acted as though he and the Kaiser were of one mind on the course to be steered. He told the assembled ministers that a "homogeneous cabinet" would be necessary to carry out the struggle for the protection of royal prerogatives. Prussian officials must be reminded of the royal order of January 4, 1882, requiring their positive sup-

[49] Gagliardi, *Entlassung*, I, 167–171.
[50] Zechlin, *Staatsstreichpläne*, pp. 38–41, 177–178; GW, VIc, 433–434.
[51] For the minutes of this cabinet meeting, see Zechlin, *Staatsstreichpläne*, pp. 178–184.
[52] This sentence was stricken from the minutes by Bismarck. *Ibid.*, pp. 43, 184.

port of progovernment candidates at election time. The ministers themselves must keep in mind the cabinet order of 1852, which required them (except for the minister of war) to consult with the minister-president before making presentations to the king.[53]

Bismarck's attempt to tighten the bolts and stop the leaks that had eroded his authority in recent months was necessary, but dangerous. Wilhelm's aspirations to reestablish "personal rule" required direct access to royal and imperial officials. The phrase "my ministers" was for him a real, not a theoretical expression. On two occasions he strode into cabinet meetings unannounced, spurs jangling, to hear the discussion.[54] As shown, he was angered on January 24 by the unwillingness of the ministers to break ranks and side with him against the chancellor.[55] Bismarck, on the other hand, had been miffed by the readiness of his colleagues on February 9 to accept his resignation from the cabinet and later by their evident disappointment over his reversal of that decision. Ministers and officials dreaded being whipsawed between two masters competing for their loyalties, and they were highly unsettled by Bismarck's tergiversations, by his increasing rigidity on such vital matters as social and tax reform, and by signs of decay in his capacity for leadership.

Particularly vulnerable was Boetticher, in whom Wilhelm II found a cooperative instrument for the pursuit of his plans for labor reform, much to Bismarck's vexation. As vice-president of the Prussian cabinet and an imperial state secretary deputized to act for the chancellor, Boetticher's task had been to relieve Bismarck of many routine duties during his long absences. As deputy he presided over the Bundesrat and defended government policy in the Reichstag. As vice-president he also supervised the meeting of the state council on the labor issue. During February Bismarck found occasions to

[53] For remarks not included in the minutes, see GW, XV, 509; Lucius, *Bismarck-Erinnerungen*, p. 519. On the cabinet order of 1852, see Gradenwitz, *Letzter Kampf*, pp. 111–119; SEG (1890), p. 47. A week earlier he had already reminded the new minister of commerce of the order's existence. Only the foreign office, he declared, could issue invitations to an international conference on labor protection. Bismarck to Berlepsch, Feb. 24, 1890. GW, VIc, 431–432. On February 18, he had stressed to the heads of imperial agencies that the chancellor alone had the right of direct access to the Kaiser. GW, VIc, 430.

[54] Lucius, *Bismarck-Erinnerungen*, pp. 496–514. Since ascending the throne, Wilhelm II had replaced a number of cabinet members with persons more sympathetic to his program. In Jan. 1889, he abruptly dismissed Minister of Justice Heinrich Friedberg, replacing him with Hermann von Schelling, state secretary of the Imperial Office of Justice. After several clashes with Bronsart, he replaced him as minister of war with Verdy du Vernois, reputedly Waldersee's candidate. Although Bismarck nominated him, Berlepsch was strictly Wilhelm II's choice as minister of commerce. In late February the Kaiser, without prior consultation, announced his intention to replace Berlepsch as governor of the Rhineland with Johannes Miquel, who declined. Lucius, *Bismarck-Erinnerungen*, pp. 482, 488–489, 492–494, 516.

[55] Eulenburg, *Aus 50 Jahren*, pp. 227ff. The Kaiser said of the cabinet he inherited, "The ministers are certainly not my ministers; they are the ministers of Prince Bismarck." Eppstein, ed., *Bismarcks Entlassung*, p. 47.

charge him with exceeding his authority. Particularly galling was Boetticher's failure as vice-president to lead the expected chorus of dismay in the cabinet over Bismarck's announcement on February 9. Naturally the prince presumed that Boetticher coveted the minister-presidency and chancellorship, which was probably not the case. With savage irony he once challenged Boetticher to make up his mind whether he wanted to be minister-president of Prussia or state secretary in the interior department (his permanent post). Boetticher replied, "The latter."

On March 3 Bismarck learned that Count Wilhelm von Hohenthal, Saxony's minister in Berlin, had delivered to the Kaiser and Boetticher copies of his government's renewed proposal for labor reform, preliminary to its formal presentation to the Bundesrat. Bismarck summoned Hohenthal and forcefully reminded him that such proposals could reach the Bundesrat only through the chancellor, its presiding officer under the constitution. In addition, he denounced the Kaiser's reform plans as misconceived, a product of the Hohenzoller's lust for popular applause that was alienating the propertied classes and weakening the position of chancellor. The time was not far off, he lamented, when the army could no more be depended upon, and that would seal Germany's fate. He had, he said to Hohenthal, lost all confidence in Boetticher and would reassume the powers he had delegated to that official under the statute of 1878, including the duty of chairing Bundesrat sessions. Afterward Bismarck denounced Boetticher to the Kaiser for "insubordination and falsehood." Wilhelm's response was to confer on the threatened minister the treasured Order of the Black Eagle (March 9).[56]

Having gained the endorsement of the state council, Wilhelm wished to introduce his labor reforms immediately into the Reichstag, but Bismarck insisted that this would be premature in view of the international congress scheduled for Berlin in late March. The Kaiser interpreted this maneuver as just one more effort at sabotage. Meanwhile, news of the chancellor's discourse about "reconstructing" the cabinet and a possible *Staatsstreich* rippled through the upper circles of the government.[57] Holstein and Marschall interpreted it as a perfidious attempt on Bismarck's part to fortify his authority at the cost of the Kaiser, a development from which they expected a host of evils in both domestic and foreign affairs. Resolved to "rescue the Kaiser," Marschall tried to persuade Wilhelm II not to go through with the antisocialist bill, even if it meant dismissing the chancellor. Holstein and Marschall alerted Helldorff, leader of the German conservatives and supporter of the cartel (still Wilhelm II's ideal majority), who went to the palace on March 4 to reinforce Marschall's protest. Marschall—who had acted with the approval

[56] Lucius, *Bismarck-Erinnerungen*, pp. 518–519; Gagliardi, *Entlassung*, I, 167–168, 195–203, 209, 219; Eppstein, ed., *Bismarcks Entlassung*, pp. 64–65, 177–178; GW, XV, 509.

[57] John C. G. Röhl, "Staatsstreichplan oder Staatsstreichbereitschaft? Bismarcks Politik in der Entlassungskrise," *Historische Zeitschrift*, 203 (1966), p. 617; Gagliardi, *Entlassung*, I, 204.

of his superior, the Grand Duke of Baden—wrote in his diary, "Kaiser is firm in his readiness to break."[58]

On that same day the Hohenzoller demanded that Bismarck abandon the antisocialist bill, expecting him to refuse and resign. But the chancellor evaded the trap. To the consternation of the Kaiser and his advisers, he agreed to withdraw the bill.[59] Evidently he calculated that the military bill alone would suffice to provoke the crisis that would certainly take precedence over the social reform upon which the Kaiser had staked his bid for personal popularity. At any rate he now pushed zealously for early introduction of an uncompromising bill into the Reichstag. On March 12 he obtained from Minister of War Verdy the draft of a directive from the Kaiser to regional military headquarters (*Generalkommando*) giving instructions on actions to be taken in the event of a declaration of martial law: suspension of constitutional liberties, arrest of agitators, suppression of newspapers and literature dangerous to public safety, formation of military courts, advance printing of proclamations, preparation of quarters for the jailed, and deployment of sufficient forces to meet uprisings.[60] To his enemies at court Bismarck's intent seemed clear: "The bill for worker protection is to be nullified, the Reichstag blown into the air. Then will come the moment when the propertied classes will see that the chancellor alone can rescue them from danger."[61]

Also on March 12 Bismarck met with Windthorst to discuss the possibility of forming a parliamentary majority that would include the Center party. Since the election the possibility of a clerical-conservative majority had been hinted at in the *Norddeutsche Allgemeine Zeitung* (a trial balloon?) and openly discussed in the *Kreuzzeitung* and other journals. Now Bismarck learned Windthorst's terms: repeal of the expatriation act, weakening of the notification requirement (*Anzeigepflicht*), readmission of the Jesuits, and, in general, restoration of the status quo ante in Catholic affairs. "It should be feasible," Bismarck is said to have replied. "Not, of course, all at once, but step

---

[58] John C. G. Röhl, ed., *Philipp Eulenburgs politische Privatkorrespondenz* (Boppard am Rhein, 1976), I, 477, 493–496.

[59] Röhl, "Staatsstreichplan oder Staatsstreichbereitschaft," pp. 623–624.

[60] Marschall to Eulenburg, Mar. 12, 1890. Eulenburg, *Privatkorrespondenz*, I, 495. Röhl gave credence to the motives attributed to Bismarck by the camarilla of Holstein, Eulenburg, Marschall, and the Grand Duke of Baden, that is, destruction of the cartel, creation of a conservative-clerical majority, consolidation of his personal authority, prevention of Wilhelm II's personal rule. But their view of Bismarck's motives was not necessarily accurate. Nor can it be assumed that the fall of the anticlerical Lutz government in Bavaria was intended by Bismarck or that it would have had the domino effect that the camarilla foresaw: an ultramontane cabinet in Munich, loosening of the federal bonds of the empire, loss of the Italian alliance, alienation of Austria, etc. See John C. G. Röhl, "The Disintegration of the *Kartell* and the Politics of Bismarck's Fall from Power, 1887–1889," *The Historical Journal*, 9 (1966), pp. 60–89, and "Staatsstreichplan oder Staatsstreichbereitschaft," pp. 610–624.

[61] Mommsen, *Bismarcks Sturz*, pp. 112ff., 123ff.

by step." Windthorst, also alarmed over the prospect of disorder, had reason at this juncture to keep his old enemy in power. During the election campaign he had been careful not to close the door to cooperation with Bismarck. And yet he sensed the untenability of the prince's situation. Afterward he remarked to a political ally, "I have just come from the deathbed of a great man." Indeed, this negotiation, inconclusive though it was, had a poisonous effect. Conservative party leaders withdrew their support, Helldorff describing Bismarck to the Kaiser as a "national calamity."[62] Nor were the national liberals, who were increasingly conscious of the necessity of choosing between Kaiser and chancellor, pleased at his overtures to the centrists. Even the free conservatives, badly diminished by the election, had grown uncertain in their old role as the "Bismarck party *sans phrase*." Within both the government and the Reichstag Bismarck was effectively isolated.

The aging lion was cornered. Wilhelm II, given a few hours, could now muster the courage to deliver the coup de grace. On the morning of March 14 Bismarck requested an audience, intending to report on the talk with Windthorst. The Kaiser let him wait. At 8:30 A.M. on March 15 the monarch sent word that he would call on the chancellor in thirty minutes. Bismarck had to be awakened to receive this news and, in all probability, faced the Kaiser without breakfast. Wilhelm II revealed that he already knew of the negotiation with Windthorst ("Didn't you have him thrown out the door?") and that it had been mediated by Bleichröder ("Jews and Jesuits" cling together). He disputed the chancellor's right to negotiate with party leaders without permission and insisted on rescinding the cabinet order of 1852, newly reinvoked by Bismarck on March 2. In the Kaiser's version of this audience—perhaps more revealing of himself than of Bismarck—Wilhelm II asked how he could avoid dealing directly with the other ministers, since the minister-president was absent "in Friedrichsruh most of the time." According to Wilhelm, the question provoked a fit of anger. Bismarck slammed a file of documents on the table, and the Kaiser gripped his saber as though to defend himself. Then, according to Wilhelm II, the old man "grew soft and wept." The Kaiser went on to say that he wished to reduce the demands made in the military bill to the point required to find a majority. With that decision he effectively deprived Bismarck of the only remaining issue upon which the prince could have initiated a quarrel with the Reichstag.

Shifting to foreign affairs, Bismarck made a last-ditch attempt to persuade Wilhelm to give up his plan for a second state visit to Russia. According to a report received from Hatzfeldt in London, he declared, the first visit had been adversely received by the tsar. Wilhelm demanded that the report be read to

[62] SEG (1890), pp. 29, 36ff.; Wilhelm Schüssler, *Bismarcks Sturz* (Leipzig, 1922), pp. 156–164; Margaret Lavinia Anderson, *Windthorst: A Political Biography* (Oxford, 1981), pp. 384–389; Eduard E. Hüsgen, *Ludwig Windthorst* (Cologne, 1907), pp. 335–345.

him and, on Bismarck's demurral, seized it. While the Hohenzoller read, Bismarck meditated that death is the traditional reward for messengers who bring bad news.[63] For the first time the Kaiser's prerogative in foreign affairs now became an issue. Deeply wounded by Hatzfeldt's report, Wilhelm II was vulnerable later that day to Waldersee's denunciation of the government's Russian policy.[64] Consular reports from Kiev of purported Russian troop movements on the Austrian frontier caused him to dispatch to the chancellor an accusatory note (March 17) demanding to know why such reports, which showed that the Russians were deploying their forces for war, had previously been withheld from him; it was "high time" the Austrians were warned to take countermeasures. In a reply written on the same day Bismarck refuted both the Kaiser's charge of delinquency and his conclusion that Russia was preparing for war. On that morning Russian Ambassador Count Paul Shuvalov had arrived from Petersburg with authority to negotiate a renewal of the reinsurance treaty, due to expire within a few months.[65]

Meanwhile, Bismarck had maneuvered to find the most advantageous ground for the final skirmish. He got it on March 16, when General Wilhelm von Hahnke, who had replaced Albedyll as chief of the military cabinet, arrived with the Kaiser's demand that the cabinet order of 1852 be invalidated. Again Bismarck refused, but still he did not react to the monarch's effort to goad him into resigning. On the morning of March 17 Hahnke returned with word that the Kaiser expected the chancellor at the palace that afternoon, resignation in hand. Bismarck replied that bad health prevented him from complying! Instead he met the Prussian cabinet for the last time, hoping perhaps that the shock of his imminent departure on such an issue would produce a common front.

To the ministers he declared that his health was "now good"; he had no desire to live an "idle life" but had to retire, for he had lost the king's confidence in both foreign and domestic affairs. That the conflict now extended to foreign affairs was news to the ministers. Boetticher, seconded by Scholz, hoped that a compromise could be found, enabling Bismarck to remain in charge of foreign affairs. Gossler and Minister of Justice Hermann von Schelling chose to believe that the differences stemmed from a "misunderstanding," which could be clarified. Both Verdy and Berlepsch denied having violated the cabinet order of 1852; the former had limited his direct contacts

---

[63] For Bismarck's version of his audience with Wilhelm II, see his memoirs. GW, XV, 512–515. For Wilhelm II's account, see Eulenburg, *Aus 50 Jahren*, pp. 235, 243–244; and especially Waldersee, *Denkwürdigkeiten*, II, 114–116.

[64] GW, XV, 517–519; GP, VI, 362–366. The reports had arrived at the foreign office on March 15. Bismarck had selected five containing military information to be sent to the Kaiser. The remaining fifteen were politically and militarily unimportant. GP, VI, 362–363 (fn.).

[65] GW, XV, 516–522, 570–574; GP, VI, 364–366; Eppstein, *Bismarcks Entlassung*, pp. 67–95, 179–188.

with the Kaiser to military affairs; the latter, to the imperial rescript of February 4, a document issued before he had assumed office. Verdy averred that he had heard nothing recently from Wilhelm II about the possibility of war with Russia. Scholz, Maybach, and Lucius suggested that a misfortune could be averted only if the ministers joined Bismarck in resigning. But the proposal fell flat. That evening the ministers met informally at Boetticher's house without Bismarck and accepted their host's argument that resignation *in corpore* was not in the Prussian tradition.[66]

While they met, Hermann von Lucanus, chief of the civil cabinet, came to the chancellery to ask on the Kaiser's behalf why Bismarck had not at least sent the document he could not personally deliver. The prince replied that it must first be put in publishable form! The Kaiser had the power, of course, to discharge him without a formal request, but Wilhelm II was eager not to appear ungracious before German public opinion. On the following morning General Leo von Caprivi appeared in the Wilhelmstrasse as the new chancellor. While Caprivi took charge of the government in the adjoining rooms, Bismarck sat at his desk drafting and editing the document that would explain to posterity that his insistence on constitutionalism had led to his fall from office. To invalidate the cabinet order of 1852 meant a return to absolutism in Prussia. Without it neither ministerial responsibility nor a unified governmental policy was possible, both of which were essential attributes of a constitutional state. Until now his authority had rested on his many years in office and the trust placed in him by the late (*hochselige*) Kaisers Wilhelm I and Friedrich III. No longer possessing that trust, he had found it necessary to remind the ministers of the order of 1852. His successors would be even more dependent upon the order, if the government was to remain cohesive. Nor would it be possible to retire from his Prussian posts and remain as imperial chancellor. Even if it were practicable to separate domestic from foreign policy—which he doubted—he could not accept the responsibility for the direction Wilhelm II now wished to pursue in foreign affairs. He had the impression, he concluded, that Wilhelm no longer had use for his experience and talents as a statesman. That being the case, he could retire from office without fearing that the public would judge that decision to be premature.[67]

On the afternoon of March 18 Bismarck finally finished and signed his "re-

[66] GW, XV, 521–522; Vlc, 435–438; Busch, *Secret Pages*, II, 513ff.

[67] SEG (1890), pp. 44–45; Mommsen, *Bismarcks Sturz*, pp. 140 ff; Eppstein, ed., *Bismarcks Entlassung*, pp. 189–194, 199–202. According to one account, Lucanus, on hearing of Bismarck's intent to publish the letter of resignation, reminded the chancellor that such an action was prohibited by the "Arnim paragraph." This amendment of the penal code, for which Bismarck was himself responsible, provided for the prosecution and imprisonment of officials who misused government documents. The sources do not tell us whether Bismarck actually decided against publishing the letter of resignation because of this warning. Manfred Hank, *Kanzler ohne Amt: Fürst Bismarck nach seiner Entlassung, 1890–1898* (Munich, 1977), p. 190.

quest for release from office" with the familiar long vertical strokes of his pen. Forty-eight hours later Hahnke and Lucanus arrived at the chancellery with the Kaiser's acceptance. "My dear prince! It is with deepest emotion that I see from your request of March 18 that you have decided to resign from the positions you have occupied for so many years with incomparable success." He had hoped, the message continued, not to have to face the idea of parting from the prince "in our lifetimes." "With troubled heart" he had reconciled himself to the idea, but only in the knowledge that Bismarck's "wish" was irreversible and in the expectation that "your counsel and prowess, your faithfulness and dedication" would remain available "to me and the fatherland." In equally flowery language he paid tribute to the prince's achievements for Prussia, Germany, and the Hohenzollern dynasty, as well as his "wise and active policy" in behalf of peace, a policy that would be Wilhelm's "guide for the future." In conclusion, he conferred on Bismarck promotion to colonel-general of the cavalry (rank of field marshal-general), the title "Duke of Lauenburg," and "my lifesize portrait."[68]

Into Exile

As he approached his seventy-fifth birthday, Bismarck's aging body, weakened by persistent maladies and indulgences, and his nervous system, tortured by excessive burdens and narcissistic rage, were close to collapse. Under similar circumstances most persons would have long since abandoned the race or at least passed the baton to someone else and retired to the peace and quiet of the countryside. Bismarck not only clung to every shred of authority that he possessed but also persuaded himself that he was needed more than ever. During 1889–1890 the prince sought, whether consciously or unconsciously, to convince the man upon whom his continuation in office depended that Germany was approaching simultaneous crises in several interrelated arenas: the mines and factories, where labor's demands, bolstered by socialist leadership, must ultimately be met by violence; the schools, where advanced education was producing a spoiled generation of potential nihilists; the voting public, where socialist agitation among the working classes was undermining their traditional and natural loyalty to the monarchy and their acceptance of the Prussian-German establishment; and the Reichstag, where the government could find no lasting majority to support its policies, especially renewal of an undiluted antisocialist statute.

Fifteen years earlier, Bismarck had likewise concluded that internally Germany needed a change of front that would stabilize and consolidate the Reich. Although in desperately poor health in 1875, he had thrust aside serious thoughts of retirement. In the quiet of his country estate he had conceived a

---

[68] Gagliardi, *Entlassung*, I, 153, 170–171.

new line of march that, despite many checks and failures, altered German public life significantly over a period of years. In 1889–1890 he perceived new dangers that required, he believed, yet another change of front, one that would produce a still greater transformation in German government and society than that of 1875–1880. The continuing wave of labor unrest marked by persistent strikes revealed, he concluded, a limitless appetite among workers for improvements in their condition that must one day be met by "hard and perhaps bloody disciplinary measures."[69]

Meanwhile, the government must not alienate capital by intervention and mediation. Labor's violence would frighten the "liberal bourgeoisie" into supporting the continuation of repressive measures against socialists. The collapse of the cartel and its defeat at the polls would bring about a political crisis to match the social one. As Bismarck peered into the future, he saw disruption in the marketplace, nihilism in schools and universities, chaos in parliament, and carnage in the streets—all leading to the likely necessity of a *Staatsstreich* that would fundamentally transform the character of the Reichstag from a parliament into a corporative diet. Only he, the creator of the German Reich, had the personal authority, political wisdom, and tactical skill to master the crisis and refound the empire.

Conceivably this warning of coming events and the measures they required was merely a tactical maneuver in the developing struggle between Kaiser and chancellor, an attempt by Bismarck to make himself indispensable to a young and inexperienced monarch. Consciously or unconsciously, he may have had such a purpose. Still, this would not exclude the possibility that Bismarck's concern was also genuine, that he actually believed that the time had come for an internal "preventive war," that is, a fundamental revision of the governing basis of the German Reich. If this be true, its full significance for Bismarck's political outlook has not been fully appreciated. During the last half of 1889, Bismarck abandoned his lifelong faith in the continuing loyalty of the German masses to the Hohenzollern monarchy and the social-political establishment that was its power base. He lost, in other words, his long-held conviction that by widening that base to include other large interest groups— German nationalists (through unification and centralization), industrial and finance capitalism (first through laissez-faire, later through protectionism), factory and mine workers (through social insurance), and all of these groups

[69] Rottenburg to Boetticher, Dec. 19, 1889. DZA Potsdam, Reichskanzlei, 446, pp. 20–23v. On Apr. 16, 1890, Bismarck received the directors of the Central Federation of German Industrialists at Friedrichsruh. As reported by Thomas Hassler, Bismarck told them that earlier he had regarded labor's striving for a "better and more beautiful life" as "justified." But now the workers, inspired by "envy" (a weakness in the German character), wanted the "millenium." By raising demands that industry could not satisfy short of self-destruction, they had become "dangerous to the security, even to the existence of the state." "Aufzeichnungen über Bismarck und den Centralverband deutscher Industrieller," *Tradition*, 7 (1962), pp. 227–228.

by other measures of more peripheral character—he could build a national social and political consensus that would consolidate, fortify, and preserve externally and internally the Reich he had created. The strikes of 1889, following on the heels of the last of the social insurance laws, convinced him that nothing more was to be gained by concessions to the working class, that the elite groups of Prussian-German society must consolidate behind a purified governmental apparatus (Reichstag, bureaucracy, schools, and universities) before its final bastion, the army, was infiltrated and corrupted by disloyalty, protest, and rebellion. Protected externally by close relationships with two other conservative European great powers, Germany could put its internal affairs in order without outside interference.

Diminishing vigor made Bismarck all the more eager to get on with the task of initiating an internal "preventive war," for the opening stage of which he believed he had the necessary stamina. Here he was guilty of the kind of presumption—assuming for himself the power to perceive God's will in the course of history—that he had deplored as sacrilege in foreign affairs. Wilhelm II and his advisers can hardly be blamed for their unwillingness to share this apocalyptic vision. The critical question, however, was whether they could provide for Germany a coherent and consistent leadership superior to that of the aging and enfeebled chancellor whom they discarded. Unfortunately for Germany, this was not to be the case.

Bismarck fell victim in the end to the authority that he had spent the whole of his career to protect and enhance. Wilhelm II dared to get rid of him because Bismarck no longer had any base of political support. Before the election of February 20 Bismarck had launched rumors of another "chancellor crisis" in the official press. But the German public had long since become deadened to this appeal.[70] A whole generation had grown up since the man from Schönhausen had taken charge of the government. Even the opposition found it hard to believe that the master of *Realpolitik* would not succeed in holding on. Nor could most visualize who would take the place he vacated; no one of comparable stature and charisma was on the horizon.

Yet the reaction to Bismarck's fall in press and parliament was feeble.[71] After twenty years of peace and security, the empire for whose creation so much blood, iron, and gold had been expended was now accepted as an established reality, which would survive, whoever was at the helm. In the Reichstag a few words from the presiding officer marked the event; in the Prussian Chamber of Deputies, none at all. The stock market, one measure of the national pulse, yielded a little ground, soon regained. Newspapers with good connections to the ex-chancellor (including the *Norddeutsche Allgemeine*

[70] Lucius, *Bismarck-Erinnerungen*, p. 517; GW, VIII, 688; Mommsen, *Bismarcks Sturz*, pp. 66ff.
[71] Mommsen, *Bismarcks Sturz*, pp. 44ff., 66ff., 125ff.; Gagliardi, *Entlassung*, II, 325–389. See also Karl Lange, *Bismarcks Sturz und die offentliche Meinung in Deutschland und im Auslande* (Berlin, 1927), pp. 17ff.

Zeitung) quickly made known without attribution the prince's version of his resignation, but anonymous reports in the press carried less weight with the public than the Kaiser's laudatory message. Wilhelm II won handily the first round in the contest for public opinion.[72]

During the days that followed his resignation both Bismarck and the Kaiser were careful to preserve the dictates of protocol. Bismarck gave a parting dinner for ministers and state secretaries, paid his respects to the Dowager Kaiserin Victoria and the Kaiser (one hour), drove to a restaurant in the Grünewald to say goodbye to its proprietor (his former chef), distributed silver goblets to his bodyguards and office personnel at a public ceremony in front of the chancellery, called on Moltke, and visited the sarcophagus of Wilhelm I in Charlottenburg, from which he returned to the chancellery, eyes brimming with tears. At the dinner he singled out Caprivi for friendly attention. But those whom the prince suspected of having played a role in his downfall—Boetticher, Marschall, and the Grand Duke of Baden—were coldly, even cuttingly, received when they called to take leave of him. Bismarck's formal visits to the royal palaces drew cheering crowds, a disturbing sign to the progovernment press.

But these ovations were far overshadowed by what occurred on Bismarck's departure from Berlin for Friedrichsruh on March 29. From the chancellery

BISMARCK'S DEPARTURE FROM BERLIN, MARCH 29, 1890.

[72] Hank, *Kanzler ohne Amt*, pp. 190–207.

to the Lehrter railway station the avenues were choked with people, shoulder to shoulder, all windows and balconies occupied. "Like a flood the crowd surged toward the carriage, surrounding, accompanying, stopping it momentarily, hats and handkerchiefs waving, calling, crying, throwing flowers. In the open carriage, drawn by the familiar chestnut-colored horses, sat Bismarck, deadly pale, in his cuirassier uniform and cap, Herbert at his side, before them a large black mastiff [popularly dubbed 'the *Reichshund*']—all three covered with flowers, to which more were constantly being added." At the station waited an honor guard of cuirassiers, Chancellor Caprivi, Prussian ministers, imperial state secretaries, the diplomatic corps, and officers of the imperial army headquarters. But Germany's dynasties were represented only by Prince Max of Baden, and there was no sign of the Kaiser. The sounds of *Die Wacht am Rhein* and the national anthem filled the air, along with cries of "Come again!" and *Auf Wiedersehen!* Bismarck quickly mounted the steps of his private car, retreated briefly from view and then returned, eyes filled with tears, a finger raised to his mouth as though to quiet the tumult. Leaning forward, he shook hands with Caprivi, and the train began to move.[73]

[73] Spitzemberg, *Tagebuch*, pp. 275–276; Hank, *Kanzler ohne Amt*, pp. 22–29.

BOOK FOUR

After the Fall,

1890–1898

He was subconsciously conservative and consciously constructive, an inventor of the simplest fundamental ideas, but not a person to be bound by principles. [He was] natural, changeable, even unpredictable, yet inexhaustible of insight and maneuver. Thus he had an unbelievable influence upon his time. He could drive men ahead of him, hither and thither. Each time he invoked the highest motives. He was monarchist and democrat, Prussian and German, free trader and protectionist, capitalist and state socialist. He was all of these things and yet fully sincere at the same time. For that reason everyone held him, at one time or another, for unfaithful, for they all wanted to claim him permanently as their own. But he took what he found, destroyed what disturbed him, and exploited every principle that existed.

—*Friedrich Naumann in*
April 1915

✠

CHAPTER THIRTEEN

++

Leader of the Opposition

ISMARCK'S final state paper, had it been published, would have
warned the public that he did not intend to disappear into the dark,
never to be heard from again. It was to have announced the beginning of a new struggle to be conducted not in the hidden corridors
of power, but at center stage before the German public. The dismissed chancellor, who had been busy for weeks with plans for a possible coup d'état,
intended now to present himself to the country as the protector of constitutionalism against absolutism. Not only that—he intended to unsettle Germany and all Europe with the news that the inexperienced ruler of the most
powerful nation on the continent was embarking on a direction in foreign
policy that his chief minister, a world-recognized authority on diplomacy,
could not condone. Naturally, Wilhelm II suppressed the document. What
the public learned instead was that the chancellor had repeatedly asked the
Kaiser to release him from office (reasons unspecified) and the request had
been graciously and reluctantly granted.[1]

Even when the circumstances of his departure became known, many continued to believe that the ex-chancellor might be recalled to power in the
event of a major crisis, which he alone had the authority to master. In Berlin
this possibility was dreaded by those who had profited from his fall or were
suspected in Friedrichsruh of having contributed to it. But Bismarck denied
any such ambition. Like Metternich after 1848, he was satisfied to sit in the
parterre while others took the stage. "You can let yourself be thrown out of
the house but once." Burning with resentment over his dismissal (for such it
was), Bismarck was, nevertheless, not content to observe the drama in silence. He had paid for his ticket, he said, and had a right to criticize.[2] The
spontaneous ovations during his last days in Berlin demonstrated what resources remained to him for salving his injured narcissism, avenging his humiliation, and ultimately attacking the government's "new course." What to
Bismarck was the satisfaction of a psychological necessity seemed to many
others a pathetic and unedifying spectacle. He disdained the dignified role of

---

[1] SEG (1890), pp. 44–45; Georg von Eppstein, ed., *Fürst Bismarcks Entlassung* (Berlin, 1920),
pp. 189–194, 199–202.

[2] GW, IX, 167, 347; XIII, 412, 428, 532; Heinrich O. Meisner, *Denkwürdigkeiten des General-
Feldmarschalls Alfred Grafen von Waldersee* (Stuttgart, 1923), II, 202, 224–226; Arthur von
Brauer, *Im Dienste Bismarcks* (Berlin, 1936), p. 358.

an elder statesman and became an outspoken and often outrageous critic of government policy.[3]

Search for a Forum

During the months that followed his dismissal Bismarck's health appears to have steadily improved. Although sometimes bothered by neuralgia, aggravated by occasional gustatory excesses in Schweninger's absence, he looked well to his guests during the summer at Friedrichsruh and Kissingen. An American visitor, the railway tycoon Henry Villard, found him thinking seriously about a voyage to the United States offered by the Hamburg-America Line. Again walking and horseback riding became his chief pastimes. Conversation with journalists and prominent visitors was another source of recreation, offering an outlet for his views, memories, and resentments. And yet Bismarck was bored. Farming, he complained, did not keep him sufficiently busy or interested. "One passion always consumes the others. Politics was my last. It has absorbed everything else."[4] But where could he find a forum suitable for its pursuit? He had always maintained that parliament's most valuable function was to criticize unwise policies of the government (inapplicable to himself) and had on occasion used it as chancellor to rid himself of inconvenient colleagues.[5]

Bismarck possessed a seat in the Prussian House of Lords but dismissed that chamber as a dead end. Two days after his return to Friedrichsruh, the prince spoke privately of standing for the Reichstag, and on May 22 he publicly hinted at his availability for a by-election. In desperation Herbert pleaded with his father not to expose himself to "his enemies and the general knavishness" of Berlin politics. Not until February 1891 did the prince accept an offer (from the national liberal committee of a Hanover election district) and only then with the understanding that he need not actually appear in parliament. In the by-election held on April 15, 1891, Bismarck gained only 43 percent of the vote in an apathetic election in which only 55 percent of the electorate cast ballots; with support from the Guelph party, whose candidate withdrew, he won the following runoff election with 10,549 votes over 5,504 for his

[3] Bismarck's last years were best described by Manfred Hank, *Kanzler ohne Amt: Fürst Bismarck nach seiner Entlassung, 1890–1898* (Munich, 1977). First published in a typescript edition complete with footnotes, the book was republished commercially under the same title in a limited edition without footnotes (Tuduvverlag, 1980). All references here are to the first edition. Hank's volume will not be easily surpassed by other historians. Thoroughly grounded in new research, particularly in the Bismarck family archive, the work is skillfully written and contains many perceptive judgments.

[4] Waldersee, *Denkwürdigkeiten*, II, 202; GW, IX, 3, 11–13, 31–32, 36, 67, 72.

[5] See vol. 2, pp. 154–155. On coming to power in 1862, he said, his task had been to strengthen the crown; now the time had come to reenforce parliament. GW, IX, 32, 118–119, 347–348; XIII, 431.

BISMARCK RETURNING TO THE SACHSENWALD AS WOTAN CLAD IN A BEARSKIN. *FIGARO*, VIENNA,

MARCH 1890.

social democratic opponent.[6] The possibility that he might speak in the Reichstag on some crucial issue sent shivers up the spines of his enemies in the Berlin government. But he never did. Although tempted to participate in the Reichstag debate on the German-Austrian trade treaty, Bismarck yielded to the entreaties of Johanna, Herbert, and Schweninger not to honor that "accursed" body with his presence. He feared to appear there "like Banquo's ghost" or a "person with the plague."[7]

Clearly Bismarck was ambivalent about whether to return to the Reichstag in a new role, that of opposition deputy rather than chancellor. He was still driven by a compulsion to exert his will over the political process, to batter and confound those whose views differed from his own. And yet he also felt a sense of resignation, born of a grudging recognition that he could never as a deputy influence the chamber in the way he had as chancellor. His only chance perhaps was to join the Reichstag as the leader of a new party. During 1892 the possibility arose, when seventy-seven prominent persons—including bankers, industrialists, professors, journalists, and literators—signed the founding platform of a proposed "National party." In December 1892 they sent a delegation to Friedrichsruh, which was coldly received. Herbert found the plan "utopian" and premature. The "pathetic Germans," he said, must suffer much more before they could be brought to "emancipate themselves from their shoemaker mentality." Initially Bismarck agreed with Herbert, but in January 1893 he let himself be persuaded to edit the party platform—an uncompromising declaration of war on the government's "new course." One of the prerequisites for the party's success was in Bismarck's opinion the creation in Berlin of a sympathetic newspaper. But the newspaper did not materialize soon enough; the founding in February 1893 of an agrarian league (Bund der Landwirte) absorbed a potential constituency for the proposed party; enthusiasm waned, and by summer the party project was dead.[8]

In the newspapers Bismarck found a forum more suitable than parliament for defending his personal interests and advancing his views on public policy. At this he was hardly a neophyte. Within weeks after his dismissal he began to grant interviews, particularly to foreign journalists beginning with the New York Herald.[9] To his open annoyance, those newspapers previously accessible to his influence, particularly the Norddeutsche Allgemeine Zeitung, quickly sev-

---

[6] Hank, Kanzler ohne Amt, pp. 258–270; Wolfgang Stribrny, Bismarck und die deutsche Politik nach seiner Entlassung, 1890–1898 (Paderborn, 1977), pp. 73–100.

[7] GW, IX, 118–119, 178–179, 347; XIII, 428–430; Wolfgang Windelband, ed., Johanna von Bismarck: Briefe an ihren Sohn Wilhelm und ihre Schwägerin Malwine von Arnim Kröchlendorff geb. von Bismarck (Berlin, 1924), pp. 87–88; Sidney Whitman, Personal Reminiscences of Prince Bismarck (New York, 1903), pp. 27–28.

[8] Hank, Kanzler ohne Amt, pp. 150–156, 282–285, 669–672; Stribrny, Bismarck und die deutsche Politik, pp. 169–174.

[9] Heinrich von Poschinger, ed., Fürst Bismarck: Neue Tischgespräche und Interviews (Stuttgart, 1895–1899), pp. 272–263.

GERMAN CORPS STUDENTS PAYING HOMAGE TO BISMARCK AT BAD KISSINGEN, AUGUST 10, 1891.
STANDING ON THE RIGHT IN A DARK SUIT, HAND ON HIP, IS COUNT HARRY VON KESSLER, WHO
DESCRIBED THE "DELIRIUM" OF THAT DAY IN HIS MEMOIRS. OUT OF POWER, HE WROTE, BISMARCK
HAD BECOME POPULAR "FOR THE FIRST TIME SINCE 1870, PERHAPS FOR THE FIRST TIME EVER."
HARRY GRAF VON KESSLER, *GESICHTER UND ZEITEN: ERINNERUNGEN* (BERLIN, 1962),
PP. 250–266. (BILDARCHIV PREUSSISCHER KULTURBESITZ.)

ered the connection under official pressure. But he soon found a substitute in
the *Hamburger Nachrichten*, which became his principal mouthpiece. Its political editor, Hermann Hofmann, was a regular visitor at Friedrichsruh, carrying away with him notes, drafts, and background information that soon
appeared in articles widely read and reprinted throughout Germany and Europe.[10] Whatever their convictions, Hofmann and his publisher were hired
guns, paid off by increased circulation and heightened prestige. In addition,
Hofmann, who lived beyond his means, received subsidies in the form of
loans that he could never repay, not the only instance in which Bismarck's
private purse became a partial substitute during these years for the Guelph
fund of earlier times. In Maximilian Harden Bismarck found a journalistic ally

[10] We have two collections of the newspaper articles Bismarck is said to have written or inspired during these years: Hermann Hofmann, ed., *Fürst Bismarck, 1890–1898* (2 vols., Stuttgart,
1913), and Johannes Penzler, ed., *Fürst Bismarck nach seiner Entlassung* (7 vols., Leipzig, 1897–
1898). After a critical comparison of these works Hank concluded that Penzler's volumes are the
more reliable. Hank, *Kanzler ohne Amt*, pp. 176–180; see also pp. 719–773.

of different caliber. Founder and editor of Zukunft, Harden was a brilliant, if convoluted, writer, an independent man of fearless rectitude, and a thorn in the flesh of the Kaiser and his government. For nearly two years (1892–1894) he frequently visited Friedrichsruh, finding in Bismarck a valuable ally but not a master.[11]

In southern Germany Bismarck found another willing collaborator in Hugo Jacobi, chief editor of the Münchener Allgemeine Zeitung, owned by the famous publishing house of J.G. Cotta with whose chief, Adolf Kröner, Bismarck soon contracted to publish his memoirs. But Kröner was less firm than Jacobi in his willingness to affront the Kaiser and his supporters by becoming a link in the "Bismarck press." Jacobi left the editorship to become the newspaper's correspondent in Berlin, where he strove to persuade Bismarck and wealthy members of the "Bismarck Fronde" (Count Guido Henckel von Donnersmark, the Duke of Ujest, Prince zu Fürstenberg, Adolf von Hansemann, and others) to purchase the newspaper, which was losing money, and relocate it in Berlin, which lacked a newspaper sympathetic to the ex-chancellor's interests. There it would have become the principal mouthpiece of the proposed Nationalpartei. But the project foundered when the foreign office got wind of it and launched a counteroffer, which, however, Caprivi refused to fund. Friedrich Alfred Krupp, in whom the consortium had hoped to find a partner, betrayed the membership to the Kaiser, who vented his displeasure. Kröner took the newspaper off the market, aided perhaps by a subsidy from Gerson Bleichröder.[12]

Finally the consortium, led by Henckel, succeeded in purchasing the Berliner Neuesten Nachrichten and installed Jacobi as editor. Unable to face the Kaiser's reproaches, Ujest and Fürstenberg deserted the partnership before the purchase was concluded in December 1893, but even Henckel, the largest and most persistent investor, began in March–April 1894 to wither before the attacks of Holstein, which nearly culminated in a duel. Ultimately Jacobi found that his services to the Bismarcks could not shield him from a harsh rebuke out of Friedrichsruh via the Hamburger Nachrichten, when he failed to comprehend and follow the prince's altered course toward Wilhelm II in 1894.[13]

Hofmann, Harden, and Jacobi were the most important channels through

[11] Hank, Kanzler ohne Amt, pp. 122–147. On Harden and his relationship to Bismarck, see Harry F. Young, Maximilian Harden, Censor Germaniae (The Hague, 1959), pp. 36ff.

[12] Walther Peter Fuchs, ed., Grossherzog Friedrich I. von Baden und die Reichspolitik 1871–1907 (Stuttgart, 1980), III, 366–368; Fritz Stern, Gold and Iron: Bismarck, Bleichröder, and the Building of the German Empire (New York, 1976), p. 277.

[13] Hank, Kanzler ohne Amt, pp. 149–159, 666–668; Waldersee, Denkwürdigkeiten, II, 312, 315; Norman Rich, Friedrich von Holstein: Politics and Diplomacy in the Era of Bismarck and Wilhelm II (Cambridge, Eng., 1965), I, 410–415; Norman Rich and M. H. Fisher, eds., The Holstein Papers: The Memoirs, Diaries and Correspondence of Friedrich von Holstein, 1837–1909 (4 vols., Cambridge, Eng., 1955–1963), III, 466–474.

which Bismarck brought his views and interests to the attention of the public. On a less regular basis he employed many other journalists, pamphleteers, historians, and literators for that purpose. To be invited to Friedrichsruh for an interview was a flattering opportunity for struggling newspapermen, whose desire to exploit the connection was no less avid than that of the host. One was Moritz Busch, Bismarck's old *Leibjournalist*, who came away with copious verbatim notes (on one occasion with unauthorized copies of documents he had been given merely to read). Others earned the right to such visits by favorable articles, brochures, and even books about the ex-chancellor, the receipt of which at Friedrichsruh sometimes triggered an invitation and interview.

At Friedrichsruh these writers and journalists were known as the "diaspora press," to be exploited at every opportunity to exalt the chancellor's image, discredit his foes and critics, and advance his views on past and present affairs. Father and son strove to keep these sometimes unsavory scribblers under control by punishing their indiscretions with public denials and their deviations with the threat of excommunication. After faithfully executing the ex-chancellor's wishes, they were sometimes disavowed when, by some miscalculation in Friedrichsruh, the public reaction to their publications was adverse.[14]

Fate of the Caprivi Government

Initially Bismarck regarded the appointment of Caprivi as the one favorable outcome of the dismissal crisis. On the morning after his resignation he hosted Caprivi for breakfast and a long talk. Evidently Caprivi listened, and Bismarck voiced to others the conviction that the general intended no major changes in policy.[15] But this turned out to be their only consultation, and, even before the deposed chancellor left Berlin, a major change in foreign policy was under way. On March 23, 1890, Caprivi conferred with Holstein and others about the reinsurance treaty, which Giers and Shuvalov were eager to renew. He was persuaded that the treaty contradicted Germany's commitments to Austria and would become highly embarrassing to Berlin if disclosed by Russia. Caprivi readily agreed to let the treaty lapse, and the Kaiser, who had already informed the Russian ambassador that it would be renewed, reversed himself. Unlike Bismarck, Caprivi said, he could not juggle five glass balls simultaneously—at the most two. He sought greater simplicity and clar-

---

[14] Hank, *Kanzler ohne Amt*, pp. 89–114.

[15] Horst Kohl, ed., *Fürst Bismarck: Regesten zu einer wissenschaflichen Biographie des ersten Reichskanzlers* (Leipzig, 1892), II, 499; GW, IX, 33, 58, 89, 179; XIII, 411, 416; Ernst Gagliardi, *Bismarcks Sturz* (Tübingen, 1927), II, 420–421. Later Bismarck complained to Waldersee and Brauer that Caprivi had not asked to be briefed by his predecessor on a single question. "If I bought a farm, I would at least think it wise to consult a little with the previous owner about the property." Waldersee, *Denkwürdigkeiten*, II, 202; Brauer, *Im Dienste Bismarcks*, p. 364.

THE *SCHLOSS* AT FRIEDRICHSRUH FROM THE PARK SIDE.

BISMARCK AT FRIEDRICHSRUH, JULY 7, 1890.

ity in Germany's foreign relations, and he achieved it. Abandoned by Berlin, the tsarist regime reluctantly came to terms (1894) with republican France.[16] Germany was no longer one of three in a system of five great powers.

What most attracted Caprivi's interest in foreign affairs was the negotiation of trade treaties with neighboring states, particularly Austria. "An alliance and a tariff war with Austria are incompatible . . . the object is to consolidate central Europe economically into a trading area for German industrial exports and against the brutal tariff barriers of Russia and of North America." Confronted with a downswing in the business cycle, bad harvests, and sharply increasing grain prices, he negotiated a series of reciprocal trade treaties with Austria, Belgium, Italy, and Switzerland that reduced duties on wheat and rye from 5 to 3.5 marks per 1,000 kilograms in return for lowered duties on German manufactured goods. In order to ease the distress of lower-class bread-eaters and win applause from manufacturers, Caprivi injured the interests of agrarian landowners, including Bismarck. This was the issue that, more than any other, galvanized a new opposition to the government. Although they now had a common enemy, the trans-Elbian landlords who dominated the new *Bund der Landwirte* were loath to ally with Bismarck, who urged them to abandon traditional conservative politics and broaden their political base by appealing to the farmers of western and southern Germany.[17]

Caprivi took office determined to defuse explosive issues and attain stability and tranquility in internal affairs. To this end the antisocialist statute would be permitted to expire without fanfare on September 30, 1890, increases in military spending held to a minimum, the Kaiser's program for labor protection implemented, and remnants of the Kulturkampf laws jettisoned. During the spring the Bundesrat accepted a bill initiated by the Reichstag to end the banishment of priests. A bill introduced in the Prussian Chamber of Deputies would have restored to the Catholic church the income from sequestered church funds (it failed of passage because centrists demanded the return of the funds themselves). After a protracted struggle Caprivi succeeded in gaining Wilhelm's approval of a "little army bill," containing compromises palatable to the Reichstag majority, which passed it on June 28, 1890. During that same month the Reichstag passed a bill creating industrial arbitration courts; in January 1891, a labor protection statute that largely abolished Sunday labor

---

[16] Wilhelm von Schweinitz, ed., *Denkwürdigkeiten des Botschafters General von Schweinitz* (Berlin, 1927), II, 396–407; Sergei Goriainov, "End of the Alliance of the Emperors," *American Historical Review*, 23 (1917–1918), pp. 340–345; Rich, *Holstein*, I, 308–319; Rich and Fisher, eds., *Holstein Papers*, I, 130–131; GP, VII, 4–11, 30–37, 47–49. George Kennan doubts that the line to Petersburg, seriously weakened by growing public hostility, could have been long preserved. But its voluntary surrender by Germany, its greatest beneficiary, was certainly an act of folly. George F. Kennan, *The Decline of Bismarck's European Order: Franco-Russian Relations, 1875–1890* (Princeton, 1979), pp. 398–424.

[17] J. Alden Nichols, *Germany after Bismarck: The Caprivi Era, 1890–1894* (Cambridge, Mass., 1958), pp. 139–153; Penzler, ed., *Bismarck nach seiner Entlassung*, V, 3–4, 16–17, 54–56.

and limited the workday of children under fourteen to six hours (when excused from school), of children between fourteen and sixteen to ten hours,
and of women to eleven hours. A reorganization and enlargement of the factory inspection system was achieved in 1892.

And yet Germany's workers were disappointed by the failure of the government to support and the Reichstag to pass restrictions on the working hours
of adult males (a principal demand of 1889) and to introduce a bill providing
for worker committees to represent labor in negotiations with both employers
and government agencies. The Kaiser had committed himself to both reforms
in his message of February 4, but employers were vigorously opposed, including the powerful Central Federation of German Industrialists. The labor bills
presented to the Prussian chamber by Caprivi and Berlepsch, furthermore,
would have penalized workers for breach of contract, intimidating nonstrikers, and inciting strikes, provisions that the chamber's majority refused to
accept.[18]

Boetticher, Herrfurth, Berlepsch, Lohmann, Miquel, and Gossler gained
the opportunity under Caprivi to seek reforms that Bismarck had either
blocked or would have blocked had they been proposed in his time. In November 1890 Caprivi presented to the Prussian Chamber of Deputies five bills
of major significance: conversion of the class and classified income taxes into
a single, progressive income tax based on self-assessment; reform of the inheritance tax by eliminating duties on small estates under 1,000 marks, abolishing tax exemptions on larger estates, and imposing a new tax on invested
capital; transfer of the land and building taxes from the Prussian state to communal governments (to cover increasing expenditures for schools), the lost
state revenue to be replaced by new agrarian tariffs to be levied by the Reich
with yields to be shared with the states; a uniform law (as against the usual ad
hoc regulations) to define the role of the state in the supervision of the public
schools and the role of the churches in shaping religious instruction; and extension of the county government reform accomplished by Friedrich Eulenburg in 1872 to Prussia's seven eastern provinces. To Caprivi these bills—all
of which had been under discussion in the Prussian ministries during Bismarck's last years, some even with his approval—formed a single package.
Their purpose was not only to bring greater order in the tax and budget structure of the government, but also to redistribute the tax burden upward, improve the organization and financing of public schools, and secure a uniform
system of local self-government throughout the Prussian monarchy.[19]

Caprivi's expressed aim (compared at the time to the goals of Stein and
Hardenberg) was to defeat the socialist movement by appeasing the disaffected and inculcating a "love of the state" capable of withstanding the blandishments of social radicalism. "The government can subjugate and suppress,

[18] Nichols, *Germany after Bismarck*, pp. 70–84.
[19] *SBHA* (1890–1891), Anlagen, Nos. 5, 6, 7, 8, 10.

but that is not the end of the matter; the injuries with which we are confronted can only be healed from within." The general spoke the language of
love and peace but also that of violence. The nation, he declared, was again
at war—this time against a domestic not a foreign foe, one no less dangerous
than those fought on the battlefields of the past. The very existence of "the
state and culture" was at stake. Parties and factions must forget their differences and unite to save the fatherland. To preserve order and protect property
the state did not need more power; what it needed was the united support of
its people.[20]

Here Caprivi, not unlike Bismarck in earlier years, began the quest for a
national consensus behind the existing social and political order or, to put it
another way, the enlargement of the Prussian-German establishment to include all major interest groups. The goal that Bismarck abandoned in late
1889 was revived by Caprivi and his colleagues, to be achieved not by acts of
suppression but by reforms and concessions that the prince found unacceptable and even dangerous.

Another change of course that aroused contempt in Friedrichsruh was the
general relaxation of executive control over the imperial and Prussian administration. General Caprivi wished to make room for the initiatives of his colleagues and subordinates by disassembling the "chancellor dictatorship." The
consequence was what Bismarck had foreseen: internecine struggles between
and within ministerial bureaucracies, eventually intrigues against the chancellor himself. The issue that brought these tendencies into the open was a
surprising one—the school reform bill of 1891–1892. Under the leadership of
the Center party Catholics had resisted the school bill of November 1890 as
insufficient for the restoration of clerical control over religious instruction.
Kultusminister Gossler resigned and was replaced by Count Robert von Zedlitz-
Trützschler, a conservative, who erred in the opposite direction. A former
governor of Posen, Zedlitz had disagreed with Bismarck's Polish policy; as
minister he restored Polish as the language of religious instruction in the
schools of Posen and West Prussia; the capital funds sequestered during the
Kulturkampf were released to the Catholic church; and a Pole was appointed
archbishop of Posen and Gnesen. But he also produced a school reform bill
so sympathetic to the interests of the clerics that it was passionately defended
by centrists and conservatives and opposed by free conservatives, national
liberals, and left-liberals—a resurrection of the old Kulturkampf alignment.[21]

Within the Prussian cabinet Caprivi, who needed the support of the Center
to secure passage of a new army bill in 1892, had been opposed on the school
bill by Minister of Finance Johannes von Miquel, who needed liberal votes
for the completion of his income tax reform. Miquel finally signed the school

[20] SBHA (1890–1891), pp. 12–15.
[21] For a summary of the school bill controversy, see Nichols, Germany after Bismarck, pp. 158–
191.

bill, risking the respect of his former colleagues in the leadership of the National Liberal party. During the cabinet discussion he offered his resignation (the Kaiser refused) and leaked the story to the press in order to restore his liberal credentials with the public. The Kaiser was also uncomfortable with Caprivi's desire to govern with a conservative-centrist alliance and intervened to announce on January 23, 1892 (a significant anniversary) to the leaders of the cartel parties over a beer at Zedlitz's house that he would never accept a school reform passed only by conservative and centrist votes. Heated debates reminiscent of the Kulturkampf followed in the Chamber of Deputies.[22]

Waldersee's diary records the scene within the government. "A deplorable game of intrigue is going on, in which Caprivi, Boetticher, Miquel, Zedlitz, and Lucanus are all trying to go their own separate ways; none trusts the other, none really knows what the Kaiser wants, especially how far he wants to go, and all suspect other influences which they don't quite know about." At a Crown Council on March 17, 1892, the Kaiser demanded that the bill be amended to make it acceptable to the cartel parties. Afterward Zedlitz resigned and then Miquel. On March 18 (another significant anniversary) Caprivi, furious over the Kaiser's repeated interventions, also offered his resignation. Wilhelm II deserted the scene for his hunting lodge at Hubertusstock.[23]

In the following days the government, press, and public were left wondering what the outcome would be. Rumors even spread that Bismarck was to be recalled. Ultimately Caprivi remained as chancellor but surrendered the minister-presidency to Count Botho Eulenburg, who withdrew the school bill. Zedlitz was replaced, while the wily Miquel, considered indispensable for the completion of the tax reform, was persuaded to return. The consequence of these developments was the separation of the imperial and Prussian governments. Caprivi retained the post of Prussian foreign minister, but attended cabinet meetings only when Reich affairs were discussed. In 1894 he abolished Bismarck's order of 1885 that channeled all communications between Prussian ministries and Reich agencies through a small bureau in the Imperial Foreign Office that housed the "Prussian foreign ministry." The formal power of the Prussian minister of foreign affairs to instruct the Prussian vote in the Bundesrat—once the linchpin of the Bismarck "dictatorship"—was abandoned.[24]

[22] Nichols, Germany after Bismarck, pp. 163–167; J.C.G. Röhl, Germany without Bismarck (London, 1967), pp. 77–84; SBHA (1892), pp. 17–19, 89–241, 1162, Anlage No. 9 with amendments.
[23] Waldersee, Denkwürdigkeiten, II, 232–233; translation in Nichols, Germany after Bismarck, p. 178.
[24] Hans Goldschmidt, Das Reich und Preussen im Kampf um die Führung (Berlin, 1931), pp. 90–91, 311–312, 324–327.

BISMARCK IS COMING! THE RUMOR PUTS CAPRIVI (CENTER) AND OTHERS TO FLIGHT; RICHTER PRE-
PARES FOR COMBAT. *DER FLOH*, VIENNA, MAY 1891.

As Bismarck had foreseen, the consequences of this abdication were severe. The Prussian cabinet and its ministers were now free to pursue the interests of Prussia without much consideration for those of the Reich. The chancellor and imperial agencies could no longer count on the support of Prussia's representatives in the Bundesrat. The federal bonds began to loosen as other states followed Prussia's example. Within the Prussian government the regulation of 1852 no longer bound ministers to seek the agreement of the minister-president before approaching the crown. The same was true of the imperial government, where Caprivi's control was constantly threatened by the Kaiser's direct and often arbitrary dealings with the chancellor's subordinates and by the plots among those subordinates that the Kaiser's intervention inevitably spawned. The governmental system lost coherence and coordination; it became the victim of conflicts, intrigues, personal ambitions, and bureaucratic particularism.[25]

The situation was ideal for the restoration of monarchical rule, but ironically the school bill crisis had shown that the man who yearned for that role was incompetent to play it. During 1890–1892 Wilhelm repeatedly depicted himself in oratorical flourishes, relentlessly reported in the press, as a divine-right ruler possessing the unimpeded power to direct the course of the government, even if it meant ordering soldiers to fire upon their fathers. The possibility that Bismarck, after his election in April 1891, might appear at the head of an opposition party in the Reichstag aroused the Kaiser to new heights of anger and bluster. "The Reich has but one ruler, and I am he," he pontificated to Rhenish industrialists, "I tolerate no other." In June 1891 the Kaiser told his commanding generals that his patience with Bismarck was running thin; if provoked further, he would not hesitate "simply to send the prince to Spandau prison." Wilhelm II had begun to think and talk like an absolute monarch on the model of Frederick the Great, but his equivocation and ultimate veto in the school bill affair had shown him to be unsteady at the helm, shifting this way and that under the winds of contradictory influences. He was, his mother wrote, a "big baby."[26]

In retrospect, it is difficult to see why so much was expected of Caprivi. His reputation as an able general and military administrator was well deserved, but no prior experience had prepared him for the political role that now, to his surprise and dismay, was thrust upon him. His belief that honorable men of goodwill in cabinet and parliament would provide the political support he needed for policies obviously beneficial to the commonweal was typical of a military man accustomed to rely upon such qualities in his fellow officers. But this "battlefield theory," as Bismarck scornfully termed it,[27] did not comport with the interest-bound politics of a mature parliamentary system. His delegation of authority to subordinate ministers and officials, while laudable in some respects, could not be harmonized with the complicated constitutional structure that Bismarck had devised; the result was lack of coordination and leadership.

[25] Nichols, *Germany after Bismarck*, pp. 85–191; Röhl, *Germany without Bismarck*, pp. 85ff.

[26] SEG (1891), 80–82; Walther Peter Fuchs, ed., *Grossherzog Friedrich I. von Baden und die Reichspolitik 1871–1907* (Stuttgart, 1980), III, 73; Frederick Ponsonby, ed., *Letters of the Empress Frederick* (London, 1928), pp. 434–435.

[27] Hank, *Kanzler ohne Amt*, p. 195.

One cement holding the government together was fear that its collapse would leave the Kaiser with no choice but to recall the Bismarcks, one or both, to the Wilhelmstrasse. Careers would be jeopardized. The Kaiser himself, Holstein foresaw, might be one of the victims—subjected to "constitutional thumbscrews of the Belgian kind."[28] Since neither Wilhelm II nor his ministers could tolerate a Bismarck restoration, it behooved them to deactivate the ticking bomb in Friedrichsruh. A reconciliation would at least prevent the "nasty old man" from becoming the rallying point for the disparate forces of the opposition. In early May 1892 the Kaiser made an overture by congratulating Herbert on his approaching marriage to Hungarian Countess Marguerite Hoyos. But attempts at rapprochement were cut short when it was learned in Berlin that the marriage would take place not in Fiume, the bride's hometown, but in Vienna and that the ex-chancellor intended to visit Dresden and Munich on the way to and from the wedding.[29]

Bismarck Idolatry

So advanced was the paranoia in Berlin that the decision for Vienna, actually made by the bride's family, was credited to the ex-chancellor. The prince, it was assumed, intended to make of the wedding a political demonstration in the capital of Germany's closest ally. On the contrary, Bismarck feared to embarrass Kaiser Franz Joseph, particularly if his presence in Vienna should become the occasion for demonstrations by German-national factions hostile to the imperial government of Count Eduard von Taaffe. And yet the date of the wedding, June 21, 1892, coincided unhappily with Franz Joseph's presence at Schönbrunn, June 11–25. Custom demanded that Germany's ex-chancellor request by way of his country's ambassador in Vienna, Prince Reuss, the opportunity for a courtesy call on the Austrian Kaiser. From Fiume Herbert made soundings in Vienna and reported to his father that Franz Joseph welcomed the request.[30]

On June 9 Wilhelm II and Caprivi launched a determined effort to prevent an audience. The chancellor reported to Prince Reuss that no reconciliation was under way. If approached by Bismarck or his family, the ambassador was to limit his response to formalities and evade the expected wedding invitation; embassy personnel were to do the same. Kálnoky and Franz Joseph were to be informed of this instruction and assured that Bismarck would never again influence German policy. Copies of this "Uriah letter" were sent to the principal German courts, obviously to discourage their participation as well.[31]

[28] Röhl, Germany Without Bismarck, p. 83.

[29] Hank, Kanzler ohne Amt, pp. 327, 372–382.

[30] Hank, Kanzler ohne Amt, pp. 327–345.

[31] Otto Gradenwitz, Akten über Bismarcks grossdeutsche Rundfahrt vom Jahre 1892 (Heidelberg, 1922), pp. 4ff.

But this message was exceeded by far in ferocity and impact by the letter that Franz Joseph received on June 14 from Wilhelm II. The German Kaiser advised his "true friend" not to make difficulties for him and his government by receiving this *"disobedient subject* until he comes to me and says peccavi." Not satisfied with this communication, Wilhelm II repeated the same in still stronger terms to the Austrian military attaché in Berlin: "Bismarck was always a Russian, is a Russian, and will always be Russian and in his heart a decided enemy of Austria." Reluctantly Franz Joseph decided to follow the advice he received.[32]

From the documents we now know that the architect of the intervention by Caprivi and the Kaiser was the "gray eminence" of the foreign office, Holstein (with help from Philipp Eulenburg and Privy Counselor Alfred von Kiderlen-Wächter), whose mutual anxiety at the prospect that the Bismarcks might return to power or at least influence reached a new peak with the rumors of reconciliation. They fantasized that Bismarck would even seek the favorable mediation of the Austrian Kaiser and the King of Saxony in his feud with Wilhelm II. Bismarck began his journey to Vienna on June 18 with some trepidation, for Herbert had already warned of the cold shoulder to be expected at the Vienna court. At Dresden, where he spent the night, he received confirmation from Herbert of Franz Joseph's embarrassed decision not to receive the contumacious Hohenzollern vassal.[33]

To the courts of Germany and Austria Bismarck was a pariah in 1892; to the public he was a hero, one of the greatest in German history. His progress from Friedrichsruh over Berlin to Dresden and from there to Vienna, where he remained until June 22, and finally to Munich and Bad Kissingen can only be described as an unprecedented triumph. Deprived of any need for moderation, he enjoyed to the full the roaring applause of huge crowds that met him at every stop in Germany and even Austria. They swept aside the police barricades, surging to the train or carriage, shouting their adulation, competing to press or kiss his hand, and burying him and Johanna with flowers. Everywhere the iron chancellor appeared in Vienna—whether on courtesy visits to friends and diplomats or in public places such as the Rathaus, Prater amusement park, a theater exhibition, a folk music performance, and the *Pavillion des Münchener Bürgerbräus*—his presence aroused excitement and ovations. This popular reception was uninfluenced by the boycott efforts of the Berlin government, which only became known on June 21 in the pages of the *Allgemeine Zeitung*. The article included the text of Caprivi's order of June 9

---

[32] Hans Schlitter, ed., "Briefe Franz Josefs I. und Kaiser Wilhelms II. über Bismarcks Rücktritt," *Österreichische Rundschau*, 58 (1919), pp. 98–108; Eduard von Wertheimer, "Ein k.u.k. Militärattaché über das politische Leben in Berlin," *Preussische Jahrbücher*, 201 (1925), pp. 269–272.

[33] Hank, *Kanzler ohne Amt*, pp. 335–346. From sources in the family archive in Friedrichsruh Hank has disproved the assumption that Bismarck deliberately planned the tour of 1892 as a political stroke against the Kaiser and his government. *Ibid.*, pp. 368–369.

made available by the Princess Reuss, wife of the German ambassador in Vienna, without her husband's knowledge, a case of feminine intrigue of which for once Bismarck did not complain.[34]

While in Vienna Bismarck sought to avoid any appearance of endorsing the cause of German-national, anti-Semitic extremists, but they came calling in a procession of sixty carriages, staged a near riot in the streets against police restraints, and on the day of his departure assembled at a way station along the track to sing *Die Wacht am Rhein* and celebrate "the founder of the German Reich" (Bismarck: "Say, rather, 'Founder of the German-Austrian alliance' "). At every opportunity Bismarck testified to his "sympathy" for Austria and loyalty to the "indissoluble" German-Austrian alliance. This was also the basic theme of his interview with the editor and publisher of Vienna's *Neue Freie Presse*, to whom he made clear his resentment at the treatment accorded him by the Berlin government. Germany, he declared, was a saturated power and had nothing to gain through war. His effort to maintain good relations with Russia, now abandoned by his successor, had also been in Austria's interest. He had, he declared, "no more personal obligations toward the present personalities [in Berlin] and toward my successor. All bridges have been broken."[35]

At Munich on June 24–26, the public reception, which began at the railway station on his arrival well after midnight, was no less ear-splitting than in Vienna. The Bavarian Prince Regent had retreated to his mountain castle, but the city government defied the official boycott. The authorities at the Rathaus received him with ceremony and opened for his signature the Golden Book, in which but ten months earlier Wilhelm II had written, "*Suprema lex regis voluntas.*" Wherever he appeared on those two days—Rathaus, Hofbräuhaus, reception by the elite club Allotria, the glass palace museum (where he paused longest before Rocholl's *König Wilhelms Ritt um Sedan*)—popular enthusiasm was the same. On both evenings huge parades arrived in the square before his quarters (Lenbach's house)—sixteen hundred torches borne by students in corps uniforms, bands, speeches, serenades, and inevitably the singing of *Die Wacht am Rhein* and *Deutschland, Deutschland über alles*. After the hurrahs had faded away on the night of the twenty-fifth, the crowd remained in the streets, until informed by the mayor that the prince had retired.

His departure at noon on June 26 was the occasion for yet another massive demonstration. The locomotive of his special train was draped in garlands, his salon car filled with flowers. On his arrival at Augsburg the shouts of the multitude accompanied his progress to the Rathaus, where a chorus of seven hundred voices waited to entertain him. In Würzburg that afternoon he was received by the rector and senate of the university surrounded by a crowd of

[34] Hank, *Kanzler ohne Amt*, pp. 347–363; Penzler, ed., *Bismarck nach seiner Entlassung*, III, 293–328.

[35] GW, IX, 214–219; XIII, 442–445; Penzler, ed., *Bismarck nach seiner Entlassung*, III, 312, 321.

eight thousand citizens. In garrison cities the officer corps met him at the railway station and along the track en route stood groups of people, waving and shouting as the train passed. That evening he arrived at Bad Kissingen, with aching hands, "glowing cheeks, and sparkling eyes," to meet yet another ovation and a fierce bombardment of flowers that left him slightly wounded in one eye.[36] At Kissingen, where he remained until July 30, the ovations continued whenever he was sighted by the public, and the demands of his cure did not prevent him from addressing visiting delegations from towns and villages for miles around.[37]

And so it went for the rest of his travels that summer and autumn; from Kissingen via Jena, Halle, and Magdeburg to Schönhausen (where he spent six days), through Berlin (thousands waited at the railway stations, although train schedule and route were unannounced). Nothing could keep the crowds from assembling—not streaming rain, police barricades, official boycott, time of day or night—to demonstrate their affection and respect. Now that the "Uriah letter" and its effect in Vienna was publicly known, the crowds seemed all the more determined not to be deterred by official displeasure. Bismarck's journey through Brandenburg and Pomerania was marked by ovations at every station until his arrival on August 8 at Varzin, where he remained for several months, avoiding the cholera in Hamburg and recovering from a journey that, while strenuous, had visibly rejuvenated him. On December 3 he passed through Berlin once more, again to the plaudits of thousands at barricaded railway stations, en route to Friedrichsruh and the end of a triumphal progress such as would have pleased the most demanding Roman emperor. Along the way he was not loath to make known to journalists and audiences his differences with the Caprivi government on matters of policy, his desire for a strong and effective Reichstag to oppose the government, and his disdain of those who had categorized him "among those personalities whom one may not receive."[38]

Reconciliation

Without seeking it, Bismarck had become a German national hero, a symbol of the unity and greatness of the German empire and, beyond that, of the

---

[36] Hank, *Kanzler ohne Amt*, pp. 353–364; GW, XIII, 446–451; Johanna von Bismarck, *Briefe*, pp. 89–90; Penzler, ed., *Bismarck nach seiner Entlassung*, III, 328–345.

[37] In his memoirs Harry Kessler described in disgust mixed with awe the behavior of the crowds at Kissingen and Bismarck's manipulation of them. At a reception for leaders of a large delegation of university students, "His conversation was dazzling, possessing a colorfulness and plasticity such as I have subseqently seldom experienced. Unfortunately no written description can give anyone a grasp of its unique spell. It consisted of a masterful linguistic imagery in combination with a partly conscious, partly unconscious theatrical skill." Harry Graf Kessler, *Gesichter und Zeiten: Erinnerungen* (2d ed., Berlin, 1962), pp. 250–266.

[38] Hofmann, *Fürst Bismarck*, II, 90; Hank, *Kanzler ohne Amt*, pp. 364–371; GW, IX, 221–243; XIII, 451–480; Penzler, ed., *Bismarck nach seiner Entlassung*, IV, 32–264.

BISMARCK SPEAKING AT JENA TO A TYPICAL THRONG ON HIS "GREAT GERMAN TOUR" IN THE SUMMER OF 1892.

national identity of all German-speaking people, an identity that transcended the political frontiers that still divided them. What the masses saw and cheered was not his politics—which were still focused in foreign affairs on the necessity of maintaining those frontiers and in domestic affairs on the necessity of preserving the elitist Prussian-German establishment—but the symbolic man, who seemed to embody in his person the virtues of all that was German. If he did not seek it, he certainly enjoyed, even bathed in, the spontaneous outpouring of public adulation that surfaced on his departure from Berlin in March 1890, on his "great German tour" of 1892, and on his birthdays and other occasions thereafter.

Bismarck seems to have known that this type of adulation could not be channeled into a political force capable of shaking governments and changing policies. While in power, his personal charisma (and political tactics) had not enabled him to dominate the electoral and parliamentary process for long periods. Nor had he scored an overwhelming victory in his election to the Reichstag in 1891. Hence in December 1892, upon returning to Friedrichsruh from his triumphal journey, Bismarck did not leap at the chance to endorse the nascent National party. For all of his anger at Wilhelm II and palace coterie, furthermore, he seems to have been at bottom ambivalent about the desirability of a full-scale attack upon or even permanent estrangement from the king and Kaiser. Despite some sniping at the monarch, he continued even after 1892 to concentrate his attacks primarily on Caprivi and other ministers. Bismarck was a monarchist and his devotion to the crown outweighed, if only slightly, his disappointment over the man who wore it.[39]

Eventually the Vienna affair and its aftermath proved to be a mere interruption in the process of reconciliation that both the Kaiser and Bismarck basically desired. The dispute had become a public scandal that threatened the prestige of the Prussian-German establishment, forcing people of prominence to take sides; those who attempted neutrality were in danger of being ground up between the millstones of Berlin and Friedrichsruh.[40]

Members of the Bismarck Fronde wavered, unsure whether they could best influence the "new course" by opposing or coming to terms with the government. The prerequisite for the latter was peace between the palace and Friedrichsruh. Around the Kaiser, furthermore, were many who sensed that Wilhelm was losing the battle for public esteem. The Hohenzoller's public boasts about his personal rule uttered in thoughtless oratorical excesses and the uncertain course of his government under Caprivi, with whom Wilhelm himself was now disillusioned, were costly to his popularity. The monarch's success in getting the Austrian and German courts and governments to give the cold shoulder to the man who had unified Germany in three successful wars and dominated European international politics for nearly three decades was seen as petty and unworthy. Wilhelm II was rapidly squandering what sympathy he had gained by his efforts to achieve social justice and peace at the outset of his reign, while the astounding demonstrations of Bismarck's popular ap-

[39] Bismarck's ambivalence toward Wilhelm II comes out clearly in a remarkable interview with Hans Kleser, editor of the *Westdeutsche Zeitung*, May 31, 1892, shortly before the trip to Vienna. GW, IX, 203–209.

[40] The source that mirrors most clearly the embarrassment produced by the quarrel is the remarkable diary of the Baroness von Spitzemberg. *Higachen* (as she was affectionately known to the Bismarcks) continued to circulate in both camps, deploring the estrangement, trying her best to effect a reconciliation, while confiding to her diary her disgust with both parties. Rudolf Vierhaus, ed., *Das Tagebuch der Baronin Spitzemberg* (Göttingen, 1960), pp. 279ff. Arthur Brauer attempted to maintain his relationship with Bismarck, but suffered the consequences in Berlin. *Im Dienste Bismarcks*, pp. 356–365.

peal showed how quickly the public had forgotten the unpleasant side of the ex-chancellor's own regime. The prince's image improved as the Kaiser's worsened.[41]

Even before the last of the labor protection statutes was passed, Wilhelm II had soured on the subject of social reform. The proclamation of February 4, 1890, in which he had placed so much store, did not appear to affect the outcome of the Reichstag election held later that month, in which the voting strength of the social democrats increased by 87 percent. The unsatisfactory outcome of the strikes of 1889 opened the way for social democrats to penetrate the coal-mining regions and organize the workers; their far-reaching demands (including a 50 percent pay increase and nationalization of the mines) alarmed owners and cooled somewhat the zeal for reform in Berlin.[42] If less in magnitude, the strikes of 1890 in German industry were greater in number than those of 1889. A walkout at Gelsenkirchen in March 1890 inspired the Kaiser to instruct his generals to "use the repeating rifles freely at the first opportunity." In August a social democratic assembly in Berlin was attended by rioting, causing the Kaiser such anxiety that he interrupted army maneuvers to dispatch a brigade to reinforce the police. In the winter of 1892–1893 several thousand workers struck the Saar coal mines, more evidence of continuing labor unrest.[43] To Wilhelm II, who liked fast fixes, all of this was proof that the proletarians were no longer worthy of his attention.

Meanwhile, he had become increasingly dissatisfied by the difficulties encountered by Caprivi in securing passage of a new military bill calling for major increases in manpower and expenditures. In order to secure liberal votes in the Reichstag, the general agreed to a reduction from three to two years in the length of military service and from seven to five years in the length of the "iron budget"—concessions accepted by the Kaiser only with the greatest reluctance and repeated equivocations. Even so it required a dissolution and fresh election in 1893 to procure a slim majority for the bill. Although the socialist deputies voted consistently against the statute, it was

---

[41] Ponsonby, ed., *Letters of Empress Frederick*, pp. 427–434; Waldersee, *Denkwürdigkeiten*, II, 242–247; Siegfried von Kardorff, *Wilhelm von Kardorff: Ein nationaler Parlamentarier im Zeitalter Bismarcks und Wilhelms II.*, *1828–1907* (Berlin, 1936), pp. 239, 259–270; Count Bogdan Hutten-Czapski, *Sechzig Jahre Politik und Gesellschaft* (Berlin, 1936), I, 159–160; Johannes Haller, *Aus dem Leben des Fürsten Philipp zu Eulenburg-Hertefeld* (Berlin, 1924), pp. 97–104; Fritz Hellwig, *Carl Ferdinand Freiherr von Stumm-Halberg, 1836–1901* (Berlin, 1936), pp. 432–437; Rich, *Holstein*, I, 386–388; Brauer, *Im Dienste Bismarcks*, pp. 374–375; Hank, *Kanzler ohne Amt*, pp. 372ff.

[42] Hans Georg Kirchhoff, *Die staatliche Sozialpolitik im Ruhrbergbau 1871–1914* (Cologne, 1958), pp. 96ff.

[43] Klaus Tenfelde and Heinrich Volkmann, eds., *Streik: Zur Geschichte des Arbeitskampfes in Deutschland während der Industrialisierung* (Munich, 1981), p. 294; Graf Erhard von Wedel, ed., *Zwischen Kaiser und Kanzler: Aufzeichnungen des Generaladjutanten Grafen Carl von Wedel aus den Jahren 1890–1894* (Leipzig, 1943), pp. 63–64. Where now, Wedel asked himself, is that lofty statement "that he would not besmirch the first years of his reign with the blood of his subjects"?

the Freedom party, which divided on the issue, that suffered most from the appeal to the electorate.

During 1894 European governments were shocked by an upsurge in anarchist terrorism that included the assassination of French President Sadi Carnot. German postal authorities discovered bombs in two packages addressed to the Kaiser and chancellor. Wilhelm II demanded a highly punitive law to protect "religion, decency, and order" against the parties of subversion. But Caprivi could not produce a majority in parliament for the bill, and the Kaiser and his entourage began to consider the possibility of a *Staatsstreich* to revise the constitution in league with the federated dynasties and governments. Wilhelm II had reversed himself on the most basic issue of internal policy; his position was now essentially that which Bismarck had held in 1890.[44]

Although both sides had reason to seek an end to the public quarrel, neither Bismarck nor Wilhelm was willing to accept a loss of face by making the first overture. But time ran in Bismarck's favor. He could sit in Friedrichsruh, continuing to attack the concessions of the Caprivi government—in economic, educational, religious, ethnic, social, military, financial, administrative, and foreign affairs—that ran counter to policies he had followed during nearly three decades in power, while Wilhelm had to worry with increasing intensity that the "nasty old man" would die unreconciled. In late August 1893 Bismarck fell ill at Kissingen—sciatica, lumbago, and pneumonia (followed during the winter by influenza and a chronic shortness of breath). In September his condition improved, but an insect sting produced a spreading infection that delayed his departure until October 7.

The prince's indisposition was kept secret for a time. Wilhelm, who had ordered Schweninger to report any deterioration in the prince's condition, sensed a conspiracy to "present me with a dead Bismarck." Even so, he could not be persuaded to send a sympathetic message of inquiry or concern; he was still smarting over recent speeches and newspaper articles by the ex-chancellor criticizing Caprivi's decision to separate the Prussian and German governments and urging south German particularists to oppose the centralization of executive authority under the Reich. On September 18, 1893, Caprivi, Rottenburg, Boetticher, Botho Eulenburg, and August Eulenburg discussed the practicability of conducting a house search at Friedrichsruh during the interval between Bismarck's death and funeral for the purpose of confiscating public and private papers that, if published, might injure the Kaiser and his government.[45] (Did they know of the cache of letters, reputedly documenting

---

[44] Röhl, *Germany without Bismarck*, pp. 85–117; Nichols, *Germany after Bismarck*, pp. 192–340.

[45] Ernst Schweninger, *Dem Andenken Bismarcks* (Leipzig, 1899), pp. 15–16; GW, XIII, 512–517; Penzler, ed., *Bismarck nach seiner Entlassung*, V, 116–131; Hank, *Kanzler ohne Amt*, pp. 389–391.

some of Wilhelm's sexual adventures, that are said to lie even today in the safe at Friedrichsruh?)[46]

Finally Caprivi persuaded Wilhelm to send a message from Güns in Hungary, where the monarch was the guest of Kaiser Franz Joseph during army maneuvers, expressing concern about Bismarck's health and offering him the use of a Hohenzollern residence in central Germany for his convalescence. Bismarck replied with thanks that he preferred Friedrichsruh. When this exchange was published, Wilhelm judged from the deprecating reaction of the "Bismarck press" that his overture had not moved the prince toward recon-

THE FAMILY CIRCLE AT FRIEDRICHSRUH, 1893. *SITTING, FROM LEFT:* KUNO ZU RANTZAU (STEPSON), HERBERT VON BISMARCK (SON), FRAU VON LENBACH, MARIE ZU RANTZAU (DAUGHTER), JOHANNA VON BISMARCK, OTTO VON BISMARCK. *STANDING, FROM LEFT:* DR. CHRYSANDER (PHYSICIAN AND SECRETARY), THE RANTZAU CHILDREN, THEIR TUTOR, WILHELM VON BISMARCK (SON), ERNST SCHWENINGER (PHYSICIAN), MARGUERITE VON BISMARCK (HERBERT'S WIFE), FRANZ VON LENBACH (PORTRAIT PAINTER). (STÄDTISCHE GALERIE IM LENBACHHAUS.)

[46] John C. G. Röhl, "The Emperor's New Clothes: A Character Sketch of Kaiser Wilhelm II," in John C. G. Röhl and Nicolaus Sombart, *Kaiser Wilhelm II: New Interpretations* (Cambridge, Eng., 1982), p. 26.

ciliation. Indeed, Johanna, Herbert, and Bill regarded the "Güns dispatch" with disdain.[47]

At the end of 1893 the mood was the same in both Friedrichsruh and Berlin. Wilhelm waited for Bismarck to confess his sin and seek absolution; the Bismarcks, for the Kaiser to admit error and seek forgiveness. The Kaiser, vexed by reports that Herbert and Bill had treated the Güns dispatch as comedy, rebuffed suggestions that he visit the prince in Kissingen or Friedrichsruh. And yet the thought still nagged him that he might be confronted suddenly with a dead Bismarck. Hence it was that Herbert, much to his astonishment, was invited to attend the annual *Ordensfest* in Berlin on January 21, 1894. As a former minister, a Reichstag deputy, and possessor of the star (with chain) to the Hohenzollern *Hausorden*, he was entitled to an invitation, although none had come in recent years. In all likelihood the moving force behind this decision was Philipp zu Eulenburg in alliance with Count August zu Eulenburg, court master of ceremonies, and Count Cuno von Moltke, wing adjutant to the Kaiser. Philipp realized that the feud with the Bismarcks had become costly to his friend the Kaiser.

At the celebration the Kaiserin Victoria and other members of the royal family spoke with Herbert, but the Kaiser snubbed him. Chastened by August Eulenburg and Cuno Moltke, Wilhelm wrote on that same day a letter to Bismarck, which Moltke personally carried to Friedrichsruh, wishing him speedy recovery from an attack of the grippe and, to that end, sending a bottle of the finest Rhine wine from the palace cellar. Not a muscle twitched in Bismarck's face as he read the message and then, after asking Moltke to relay his thanks to the Kaiser, expressed regret that he could not do so personally. Moltke took the hint and urged the prince to favor Berlin with a visit. After a show of hesitation Bismarck agreed. Johanna, who could never forgive and never forget, was appalled; she telegraphed to Herbert for help, but his intervention came too late. On the morning of January 23 Moltke brought Bismarck's response—birthday greetings! In his telegraphed reply Wilhelm II expressed his "great surprise and joy" at the tidings of Bismarck's impending visit. Technically neither side had initiated the visit, but the public did not doubt that it was the Kaiser. And such were the benefits that the palace saw no purpose in denying it.[48]

On January 26, 1894, Bismarck, wearing his general's uniform, entrained for Berlin, a journey that proved to be in many respects the reverse of that on March 22, 1890. Six white-clad maidens, strewing flowers, preceded him to

[47] Hank, *Kanzler ohne Amt*, pp. 392–395; SEG (1893), pp. 128; Eduard von Wertheimer, "Neues zur Geschichte der letzten Jahre Bismarcks," *Historische Zeitschrift*, 133 (1925), pp. 235–245; Penzler, ed., *Bismarck nach seiner Entlassung*, V, 133–141.

[48] Hank, *Kanzler ohne Amt*, pp. 396–404; Ludwig Raschdau, *Unter Bismarck und Caprivi: Erinnerungen eines deutschen Diplomaten aus den Jahren 1885–1894* (Berlin, 1939), pp. 329–331; SEG (1894), p. 30; Penzler, ed., *Bismarck nach seiner Entlassung*, pp. 182–183; Waldersee, *Denkwürdigkeiten*, II, 304–305.

the railway station, where hundreds from the village, the area, and Hamburg had gathered to see him off. En route applauding crowds gathered at every stop. In Berlin thousands waited at the Lehrter station to greet him. On the platform was a delegation of officers from the imperial headquarters and Prince Heinrich (the Kaiser's brother), who drove Bismarck in a closed carriage (much to the public's disappointment) to the palace through crowded streets decorated with flags and banners. They were accompanied by a squadron of cuirassier guards, who had been ordered to stop any attempt by the crowd to unharness the horses and pull the carriage.

As the procession passed, the crowds closed in behind and followed through the streets to the palace, where Bismarck reviewed an honor guard (not in full ceremonial uniforms) to the blare of band music and the roar of the multitude. Afterward he slowly ascended the stairs, Prince Heinrich at his side, and entered the palace. There he greeted the assembled officers of the army command and entered the reception room, where the Kaiser, obviously nervous, shook his hand and kissed him on both cheeks. The double doors were closed. What the two men said to each other in the next ten minutes, no one ever learned.

The military-ceremonial character of the visit was preserved during the rest of the day, which ended with a banquet, after which the prince returned,

BISMARCK APPROACHING THE BERLIN PALACE ON THE ARM OF PRINCE HEINRICH FOR HIS MEETING
WITH WILHELM II, JANUARY 27, 1894. (BILDARCHIV PREUSSISCHER KULTURBESITZ.)

again to thunderous applause, to his salon car for the trip back to Friedrichs-ruh. This time the Kaiser drove with him (again in a closed carriage), assisted his descent, walked deferentially on his left, kissed him repeatedly on both cheeks, and waved until the train disappeared into the darkness. The Kaiser received him that day like a foreign potentate; the crowd, like a conquering hero. But of politics the Kaiser offered not a word; Bismarck had expected none.[49]

Amid the general euphoria some in both camps were disappointed by the "reconciliation" and apprehensive about its consequences. In the government it raised the dread possibility (Holstein and Marschall) that the Bismarcks would return to power or at least influence. Opponents of the regime (Harden) feared an end to Bismarck's collaboration. But neither the Kaiser nor Bismarck conceived of the event in this way. In his "return visit" at Frie-drichsruh on February 19 Wilhelm treated the ex-chancellor, who had never advanced beyond the rank of lieutenant on active duty, like a retired general. His gift, sent in advance, was an expensive military cloak (cut and sewn from measurements secretly taken while Bismarck was in Berlin) and his talk was not of politics but of the advantages of the new field uniform and pack being introduced into the army. One witness detected an undiminished, crackling tension. With great effort each restrained a burning desire to tell the other what he actually thought. "One minute longer and they would have ex-ploded." And so the relationship remained until the end of Bismarck's life.

On birthdays and anniversaries of significance the Kaiser sent greetings and presents and the prince responded in kind. Publicly the Kaiser demonstrated his devotion in other ways, sponsoring and contributing to Bismarck memo-rials and referring to his heroic greatness in occasional speeches. At the palace the theatrical "reconciliation" was regarded as a public relations victory. Wil-helm was widely applauded in the streets and in the press for taking the ini-tiative to end the quarrel. But the Kaiser was well aware that the "old Wal-lenstein in the Sachsenwald had not laid down his weapons." Indeed, he had not. On February 14 Bismarck merrily drank with Maximilian Harden the gift bottle of wine ("Lacrimae Caprivi," a wit dubbed it) that Cuno Moltke had brought from Wilhelm in January.[50]

[49] Hank, *Kanzler ohne Amt*, pp. 404–408; Helmuth von Moltke, *Erinnerungen, Briefe, Doku-mente, 1877–1916* (Stuttgart, 1922), pp. 165–176; Spitzemberg, *Tagebuch*, pp. 320–321; Rasch-dau, *Unter Bismarck und Caprivi*, pp. 331–332; Alexander von Hohenlohe, *Aus meinem Leben* (Frankfurt, a. M., 1925), pp. 262–264; Brauer, *Im Dienste Bismarcks*, pp. 392–393; Penzler, ed., *Bismarck nach seiner Entlassung*, V, 204, 212–215.

[50] Hank, *Kanzler ohne Amt*, pp. 410–414; Fürstin Marie Radziwill, *Briefe vom deutschen Kai-serhof, 1889–1915* (Berlin, 1936), pp. 84–85; Young, *Harden*, p. 44. The wine was Steinberg Kabinett Trockenbeerenauslese (1862). Lamar Cecil, *Wilhelm II. Prince and Emperor, 1859–1900* (Chapel Hill, 1989), p. 222.

CHAPTER FOURTEEN

Legend in His Own Time

Creating the Legend

HE PRESS WAR that Bismarck began after his departure from Berlin in 1890 was devoted not only to an assault on the policies of his successors but also to the defense of his own career. During the remaining years of his life stories appeared in the press and in parliament that were potentially damaging to his public image. Through Harden's *Zukunft* and Hofmann's *Hamburger Nachrichten* Bismarck (or Herbert) defended his version of the events involved or denied their occurrence altogether.

Rumors of serious conflicts between Bismarck and Helmuth von Moltke were met with a flat denial. Their differences had always been courteously resolved. Bismark's troubles with the military had come only from the "demigods" of the general staff, who lacked "the capacity to become full gods." It was also bruited that Bismarck was guilty of serious improprieties in the use of the Guelph fund. Bismarck responded that he had employed the fund only against the country's foreign foes, never against domestic opponents. If all documents concerning the fund were made public, his detractors, not he, would be embarrassed. Bismarck was himself the source of the story that implied he had falsified the Ems dispatch in editing it. But Caprivi, eager to defend Germany against the charge of war-mongering, read both the original and the edited dispatches to the Reichstag in order to show that no falsification had occurred. Herbert resented Caprivi's "patronizing" air, and his father, preferring the legend to the truth, kept the implication of a falsification alive by reiterating his version of the episode in his memoirs.[1]

The Harry von Arnim affair resurfaced with the publication of Hans Blum's *Das deutsche Reich zur Zeit Bismarcks*, a hagiography written with Bismarck's connivance, which charged that Arnim had intentionally delayed an early payment of the French war indemnity in order to benefit from a speculation on the bourse. Although Bismarck had merely suspected, never proved, Arnim's involvement in such a speculation, he failed to correct the passage in

[1] Manfred Hank, *Kanzler ohne Amt: Fürst Bismarck nach seiner Entlassung, 1890–1898* (Munich, 1977), pp. 208ff; Johannes Penzler, ed., *Fürst Bismarck nach seiner Entlassung* (7 vols., Leipzig, 1897–1898): (Ems dispatch) IV, 187, 221–222, 228–231, 244–248, 286–288, 293–334, 334; (Moltke) IV, 21–22, 326–328, 349–358; (Guelph fund) III, 112, 130–132, 243, 288–289, and IV, 324–326. On the Guelph fund, the Ems dispatch, and Bismarck's conflicts with Moltke and his generals, see vol. 1, pp. 424–425; 462–469; 362–363, 474–480.

BISMARCK AT FRIEDRICHSRUH, 1895.

Blum's book. Arnim's son demanded a retraction, threatening an unspecified retribution. But Bismarck replied only indirectly through anonymous articles in the *Hamburger Nachrichten* and *Zukunft* in which he sought to shift the blame for the ferocity of the judicial prosecution of Arnim on to Holstein and Bülow, his subordinates in the foreign office. That the persecution of the Catholic church had gone so far in the Kulturkampf Bismarck blamed on Kutusminister Adalbert Falk; Bismarck had gone along with the May laws only "out of comradeship." Nor was he responsible for Falk's resignation, which he blamed on ugly attacks by that "old frigate," Kaiserin Augusta. The prince took credit not only for calling off the Kulturkampf, blaming it on the collapse of liberal support, but also for preserving its most important achievements. His attitude toward the social insurance acts was similar. He admitted having provided the impulse for the legislation but denied all responsibility for the "patchwork" statutes produced by bureaucrats, state governments, and the Reichstag. Boetticher, he charged, had more influence on the result than the chancellor himself.[2]

During his years in power Bismarck's public speeches were limited to the Landtag and Reichstag. Press and parliament were the vehicles through which he sought to influence the public mind. Unlike his English, French, and Italian counterparts, he did not head a political party that demanded his active participation at election time in mobilizing public opinion. As a grand seigneur holding high office the thought would never have entered his mind that he should speak on any issue before mass meetings or public assemblies. But this rapidly changed after his departure from office, much to the surprise and even shock of palace and government in Berlin. Friedrichsruh quickly became a mecca for delegations not only from Hamburg and the surrounding region but also from more distant cities and districts and eventually from the German populations in foreign lands, especially Austria, but also Russia and the United States. Many brought gifts—honorary citizenships from cities, honorary degrees from universities, ceremonial cups, and ornately engraved and sculptured plaques. Others arrived bearing torches or accompanied by choirs or bands to perform the traditional rituals for an honored person.

From March 1890 through 1895 Bismarck received and spoke to about 150 such audiences, numbering from dozens to thousands. Most speeches were delivered to delegations at Friedrichsruh, some at Kissingen, and no less than twenty-five at railway stations, city halls, and public squares on his "great German tour" of 1892. At Friedrichsruh he generally addressed his audience from a low balcony, accompanied by members of his household and visiting

---

[2] Hank, *Kanzler ohne Amt*, pp. 134–149, 208ff.; Penzler, ed., *Bismarck nach seiner Entlassung* (Arnim) V, 167–176, and VII, 224, 234; (Kulturkampf), II, 61–62, IV, 124–125 and VI, 3–7; (Social insurance), VI, 148–149, 160–165, 371–372. On the conflict with Arnim and the origins of the Kulturkampf, see vol. 2, pp. 179–213, 228–233. On the origins of the social security system, see this vol. pp. 150–162.

dignitaries. On these occasions he sometimes merely expressed his thanks and appreciation for the pilgrimage, but often he delivered a political message, hammering home his views on domestic and foreign affairs and the policies appropriate to them, striking an occasional patriotic note, reiterating the refurbished version of his career (particularly his lifelong German patriotism), occasionally reflecting philosophically on the nature of politics and statecraft. Over the years thousands shared these contacts with the great man and heard his message.[3] Through the newspapers his speeches reached a much wider audience, numbering into millions. To guarantee the proper message, attending journalists were screened, their stenographic notes and summaries reviewed and revised before release.[4]

Bismarck's eightieth birthday in 1895 became the occasion for a celebration of unprecedented proportions. From March to June Friedrichsruh was the destination of no less than thirty-five special trains bearing more than fifty delegations, ranging from over four hundred members of the Landtag and Reichstag to four thousand students (in corps uniforms) from all parts of Germany. The pilgrims included the capped and gowned rectors of all universities and most technical schools, city delegations bearing more honorary citizenships, Hamburg's citizens in a traditional torchlight procession, representatives of German rulers and foreign governments, and the German chancellor himself. The most significant visit, however, was that of the Kaiser on March 26. Accompanied by the crown prince, minister of war, and commandant of the imperial army headquarters with wing adjutants, the Kaiser on horseback with spiked helmet and glistening breastplate led a small army of infantry, artillery, hussar cavalry, and, naturally, the Halberstadt cuirassiers (Bismarck's regiment). Banners streamed and bands blared as this force was deployed in an open field to be reviewed by the prince, attired in general's uniform and driven in a small open carriage. While cannon thundered from the park, Wilhelm II dined at Bismarck's table and again spoke not of politics but of military affairs. It satisfied him to treat Germany's most experienced statesman like a military puppet, knowing that an innocent public would praise their ruler for his reverence and magnanimity. Bismarck suffered this charade with inner vexation and outward resignation.

By the end of June Bismarck had spoken to about thirty-five of the visiting delegations, finding something amenable and appropriate to say to each group along with his political or patriotic message. Outside the high brick wall that sheltered the manor and its park, throngs of visitors intermixed with curio hawkers, overwhelmed the village, and on April 1 spilled over into the park itself, where six military bands provided entertainment. Well over a thousand gifts were registered by aides at the manor house. Within a few days post and

[3] GW, XIII, 405–620; Hank, Kanzler ohne Amt, pp. 687–696.
[4] Hank, Kanzler ohne Amt, pp. 115–116.

THE KAISER VISITING BISMARCK AT FRIEDRICHSRUH (MARCH 26, 1895) BEFORE HIS EIGHTIETH BIRTH-
DAY. (BILDARCHIV PREUSSISCHER KULTURBESITZ.)

telegraph offices were inundated by several thousand packages, nearly 10,000 telegrams, and 450,000 postcards, letters, and publications.

Bismarck's eightieth birthday was celebrated not only in Friedrichsruh, but also in the beflagged and decorated streets of Hamburg, Berlin, and other cities. At Berlin imperial, Prussian, and city agencies marked the day, and the Kaiser invited high officials, ministers, and members of the Bundesrat, Reichstag, and Landtag to a palace banquet. In most German states flags were flown, public buildings decorated, school let out, and ceremonies held. By one count sixty-four German cities, fifteen Austrian cities, and many German communities abroad celebrated in one way or another, not to speak of the many small towns and villages in Germany and the hundreds of German clubs (eighty in the United States) in cities around the world. The fabled Kyffhäuser mountain was visited, likewise the great Niederwald memorial on the Rhine. Everywhere newspapers wrote of him, whether in praise or criticism. Bismarck's eightieth birthday took on the character of a national holiday of the kind usually reserved for Sedan Day and the anniversaries of reigning monarchs.[5]

Until 1895 Bismarck out of office was hardly less of a presence in German

[5] Hank, *Kanzler ohne Amt*, pp. 574–591, 698–708; Penzler, ed., *Bismarck nach seiner Entlassung*, VI, 2–181; Werner Pöls, "Bismarckverehrung und Bismarcklegende als innen-politisches Problem der Wilhelminischen Zeit," *Jahrbuch für die Geschichte Mittel- und Ostdeutschlands*, 20 (1971), pp. 183–201.

EIGHTIETH BIRTHDAY CELEBRATION. GERMAN STUDENTS IN CORPS UNIFORMS AT FRIEDRICHSRUH,
APRIL 1, 1895.

EIGHTIETH BIRTHDAY CELEBRATION. BISMARCK SPEAKS TO A DELEGATION OF AUSTRIAN GERMANS
(STYRIA) FROM A BALUSTRADE ON THE PARK SIDE OF THE MANSION AT FRIEDRICHSRUH, APRIL 15, 1895.

public life than Bismarck as chancellor. His press activities, speeches, and appearances were a frequent annoyance to his successors in Berlin. They (and the Kaiser) could do little without considering what opportunities for mischief their actions might offer to the giant in the Sachsenwald. Without the responsibility for governing, he had the capacity to make things difficult for those who did.

For Bismarck's old opponents in the Reichstag and Landtag—the centrists, left-liberals, and socialists—the feud between Berlin and Friedrichsruh was often embarrassing. Although the centrists soon made their peace with Caprivi and became supporters of the monarchy and the existing order, socialists and radical liberals could not come to terms with either camp. While opposed to the regime, they had suffered too much at the hands of Bismarck to ally with him against a common foe. The reconciliation of 1894 submerged the continuing tensions within the ruling establishment, a great relief for those who placed the demands of patriotism over those of principle and self-interest. For those outside the establishment, however, the blossoming of Bismarck idolatry must have been a severe trial. During the tour of 1892 their discordant whistles were stifled by the roar of enthusiastic throngs. We can assume that the growing legion of socialist workers and their leaders stayed away from the celebrations; certainly their newspapers (chiefly *Vorwärts*) remained unswayed.

The attitudes of left-liberals were evident in the actions of the Berlin city assembly, one of their long-standing political strongholds, which voted on March 14 in secret session 56 to 34 against joining with the city council in a common greeting to Bismarck on his birthday. On March 23 Albert von Levetzow, president of the Reichstag, asked the chamber to authorize such a salutation, although soundings had already shown that the majority was opposed; the result was a brief but noisy debate in which the resentments of centrists, left-liberals, and socialists came to the surface. In alliance with Poles, Guelphs, and Alsatians, they rejected the proposal, 163 to 146. The debate spilled over into the newspaper press on the following days. Wilhelm II, already calculating the profit to be derived from such a scandal, called for a dissolution of the chamber, but the Prussian cabinet had no desire to turn to the voters for what would have constituted a plebiscite on Bismarck's popularity. Where would the Kaiser and they be if he won? Bismarck himself was indifferent to these demonstrations of bad will; from that source he had expected nothing else.[6]

Reflections and Reminiscences

During these same years Bismarck was sporadically at work on what ultimately proved to be the most powerful image maker of all, his memoirs. He had toyed

[6] Hank, *Kanzler ohne Amt*, pp. 578–581; SBR (1894–1895), pp. 1671–1676; Penzler, ed., *Bismarck nach seiner Entlassung*, VI, 70–83.

with the idea of such a work since the 1870s. But active preparations began only in late 1888, when he charged Moritz Busch with the preliminary task of sorting and ordering the necessary documents at Friedrichsruh and Varzin.[7] Little progress had been made by March 1890, when the problem of sources became acute. On March 16 Busch found Bismarck in his chancellery office surrounded by boxes of papers and a half-empty filing cabinet, concerned that the contents would be sequestered before he could bring them to safety. According to Holstein, Herbert, who continued to function as foreign secretary until his own resignation was accepted on March 26, ordered stacks of document files delivered to his quarters until Caprivi forbade it.[8]

It is unclear what father and son managed to bring with them in the many chests of household goods, including hundreds of bottles of wine, that were shipped from the Wilhelmstrasse to Friedrichsruh. But it did not suffice to document even the important episodes that the prince wished to relate. In any case Bismarck preferred to rely primarily on his memory, which was very selective. Ultimately his choice of a collaborator was not Busch, the journalist, but Lothar Bucher, his long-time secretary and aide who had retired from the foreign office in 1886. In July 1890 he signed a contract with the publisher Cotta of Stuttgart, providing for six volumes with a royalty of 100,000 marks each. The royalty was meager, but so were the prospects, for the contract relieved the prince of all liability in the event that the work were never written.[9]

Bucher soon had reason to doubt that the memoirs would ever be finished. At seventy-three years, the former radical of 1848 was plagued by gout, bent and worn by years of dedicated service. He was also a highly intelligent, learned, and independent soul, whose conception of the memoirs differed radically from that of his master. His idea was to produce an objective and balanced historical work based not only on Bismarck's memory but also upon such documents as were available. Bismarck, on the other hand, viewed his memoirs as one more opportunity to shape the image of himself and his works that he wished to imprint on the public mind. It was just another stroke in his ongoing struggle against critics, detractors, and the "new course." Bucher's occasional attempts to keep Bismarck on the track of historical veracity went unheeded, even in instances, such as the Hohenzollern candidacy to the

[7] Moritz Busch, *Tagebuchblätter* (Leipzig, 1899), II, 487 (fn.), III, 94, 253–267, 314–315. Busch was interrupted briefly on October 29 and sent to Hamburg for the day because the Kaiser was expected. "Otherwise," Bismarck explained, "he will ask who that is and what he is doing here. I will have to tell him, which will make him curious. Then he will confiscate the whole business, and that would not suit me well at all." *Ibid.*, III, 261.

[8] Busch, *Tagebuchblätter*, III, 275–281; Norman Rich and M. H. Fisher, eds., *The Holstein Papers: The Memoirs, Diaries and Correspondence of Friedrich von Holstein, 1837–1909* (4 vols., Cambridge, Eng., 1955–1963), I, 149.

[9] Gerhard Ritter, "Zur Entstehungsgeschichte des Werkes," *GW*, XV, iv–viii; Hank, *Kanzler ohne Amt*, pp. 231–235.

Spanish throne, in which Bucher himself had been personally involved. "It is not only that his memory is inadequate and his interest in the finished parts small," Bucher fretted, "but that he also begins to distort intentionally, even when the facts and events are clear. In no instance does he want to have been involved in anything that was unsuccessful."[10]

Also distressing to the patient but ailing secretary was the slowness with which the work proceeded. Often he sat, pencil poised, ears attuned, before a blank pad of paper, while the prince reclined in his chaise longue, absorbed in newspapers, incoming mail, or other matters of lesser moment. Bismarck's dictations followed no chronological pattern, but wandered from subject to subject. Afterward Bucher had the task of separating and reassembling the text, divining the author's intent, correcting and implementing.[11] For this he was an ideal, if grumbling, collaborator. By May 1892 the draft of *Erinnerung und Gedanke* (subsequently renamed *Gedanken und Erinnerungen*) was complete. But the prince was already concerned about the frankness with which he had described his relationships with and opinions about living personalities. "I have seen three kings naked." To tell the world how they actually looked would violate principle, and yet silence was also impossible. If published posthumously, people would say, "There you have it; now it comes from the grave; what a dreadful old man!"[12]

That May Bucher, suffering from a painful bladder ailment, went on leave in search of a cure. In October he died alone in a hotel room on Lake Geneva. His loss was mourned at Friedrichsruh. Without him there could be no thought of additional volumes. To Adolf Kröner's vexation, furthermore, Bismarck made little progress thereafter in preparing the existing manuscript for publication. The ex-chancellor's illness at Bad Kissingen in August–September 1893 added to the publisher's anxiety and the urgency of his appeals. Kröner did succeed in gaining the prince's permission to set type, but only for the first volume. In early October the galley proofs arrived at Friedrichsruh. But again Bismarck introduced many changes—corrections of style, orthography, and typography, striking some lines and amending others.[13] In 1894 the surface "reconciliation" with Wilhelm II intervened to slow his progress. It no longer seemed politically expedient to launch an open attack on the Kaiser and his new ministers.

Several Bismarcks contested with one another during these years. Bismarck, the realist, was eager to expose the incompetence of his successors; Bismarck, the narcissist, lusted to reveal how shabbily he had been treated; Bismarck, the pedagogue, wished to instruct the next generation on the prin-

[10] Hank, *Kanzler ohne Amt*, pp. 235–237; Busch, *Tagebuchblätter*, III, 303–307, 310–311, 321–324, 330–332.

[11] Ritter, "Entstehungsgeschichte des Werkes," *GW*, XV, x–xi.

[12] *GW*, IX, 111; Busch, *Tagebuchblätter*, III, 314–315; Hank, *Kanzler ohne Amt*, p. 238, fn. 1.

[13] Hank, *Kanzler ohne Amt*, pp. 237–240.

ciples of German foreign policy; Bismarck, the monarchist, was reluctant to damage the dynasty's public image. The last of these Bismarcks seems to have predominated, but only marginally so and certainly not to the point that he contemplated abandoning the memoir project. His continuing ambivalence is evident in his failure to make any clear and firm decision on when the work was to be published. In Bucher's time he apparently wanted the second volume to appear "posthumously." Subsequently he spoke of delaying publication of volume one until his death; volume two, until the death of Wilhelm II. And so the corrected galley proofs of volume one and the manuscript of volume two still lay at Friedrichsruh when he died on July 30, 1898.[14]

Three day after Bismarck expired, Adolf Kröner altered Friedrichsruh to expect the page proofs for volume one. When they arrived, Herbert saw that the pages did not contain the corrections that Bismarck had made in the galley proofs, which had never been returned to Cotta. Furthermore, Bismarck himself had often complained of gaps in the narrative he and Bucher had produced. And so Herbert called in Horst Kohl, a *Gymnasium* professor in Chemnitz and editor of several of Bismarck works. With Herbert's cooperation, Kohl fleshed out volume one, writing an introduction, inserting letters from the Friedrichsruh family archive, and adding a large number of footnotes. But he also made stylistic and factual "corrections," some needed, many not. As a result of Kohl's additions, volume one reached a size that made advisable its division into two volumes. The memoirs became a three-volume work.[15] Volumes one and two were published simultaneously with remarkable speed at Stuttgart on November 30, 1898. Volume three, to which Kohl was not given access, was not published until 1921.[16]

The news that Bismarck was at work on memoirs was not secret for long. At least forty-three publishing houses (including some in the United States) wrote to Friedrichsruh to inquire. In 1895 rumors in the press that the work was finished led the new chancellor, Prince Chlodwig zu Hohenlohe-Schillingsfürst, to attempt with threats and offers (500,000 marks) to purchase the publication rights to the work from the Cotta Verlag through a blind consortium. The work could then be "corrected" and rendered harmless for publication in the *Allgemeine Zeitung*. But Kröner was not foolish enough to take a course that would obviously have involved him in legal difficulties with Bismarck; nor could he be brought to part with a book from which the Cotta firm stood to make millions.[17]

Indeed, *Gedanken und Erinnerungen*, when finally released at the end of

[14] GW, XV, xxiii, 449, 455.
[15] GW, XV, xxiii–xxvi.
[16] GW, XV, xxvi.
[17] Hank, *Kanzler ohne Amt*, pp. 233–234; Alexander von Müller, ed., *Fürst Chlodwig zu Hohenlohe-Schillingsfürst: Denkwürdigkeiten der Reichskanzlerzeit* (Stuttgart, 1931), pp. 74, 83–85, 113–114.

November 1898, became one of the most successful ventures in the history of the German book trade. The first printing of 100,000 copies was quickly exhausted despite its high price (20 marks for the cloth, 30 marks for the leather edition), and so likewise was the second printing of 200,000. The translated work was quickly published in several countries. In 1905 Cotta published a "folk edition" edited by Kohl and in 1913 a "new edition."[18] Publication of volume three in 1921 sparked renewed interest in the entire work, which was republished several times during the next fifty years in both full and abridged editions.[19]

Naturally Bismarck's "reflections and reminiscenses" made waves. Those whose reputations were attacked and their defenders were outraged and not reluctant to challenge the accuracy of the work. On the basis of other sources and archival research historians have also challenged part or all of most chapters. Much of the content, furthermore, had already been related by the prince in parliamentary speeches, private conversations, and inspired newspaper articles. Despite its lack of objectivity and the patchwork origins of the work (still evident in the final version), the volumes had impact because of their uniqueness and their revelation of the character and concerns of one of the most significant figures of modern history. Ludwig Bamberger (journalist, banker, and left-liberal opponent of the ex-chancellor) wrote of it as a "rich historical, political, and psychological monument to the strength of the human spirit and character" and a contribution to world literature that would have been even greater had it been objectively written.[20] And Nietzsche, one of Bismarck's severest critics, admitted with a blush that it was a "good" book.[21] Undoubtedly thousands who bought this "German bible" had little chance of understanding what it related. Perhaps they had no intention of reading it all; it was a book to own and put on the shelf, like Goethe's *Faust* and *Dichtung und Wahrheit*.

Delays in the writing and publication of the memoirs frustrated the initial purpose of their composition—that of supplying the Bismarck camp with a significant weapon in the public struggle against foreign and domestic policies of Caprivi's "new course." By the time volumes one and two appeared Caprivi had been out of office for five years, Wilhelm II had lost his enthusiasm for social reform, the reinsurance treaty with Russia was gone beyond recall (Russia was already allied with France), Caprivi's attempt to reduce agrarian protectionism had been frustrated by the determined opposition and political influence of the landlord lobby, and the first steps had been taken toward

[18] Hank, *Kanzler ohne Amt*, pp. 243–245; GW, XV, xxvi, fn. 89.

[19] On the publication of volume three, see Hank, *Kanzler ohne Amt*, pp. 246–257.

[20] Hank, *Kanzler ohne Amt*, pp. 168, 256–257; Ludwig Bamberger, "Bismarck Posthumus," *Die Nation*, 16 (Berlin, 1898–1899), p. 145.

[21] Quoted in Harry Graf Kessler, *Gesichter und Zeiten: Erinnerungen* (2d ed., Berlin, 1962), p. 250.

construction of a high seas fleet and the inauguration of *Weltpolitik*. The revelations concerning Wilhelm's incompetence came in volume three published after the monarchy had fallen and Wilhelm was in exile—far too late to have any practical value. What *Gedanken und Erinnerungen* could still accomplish, however, was no less important to Bismarck and son Herbert: namely, the molding of Bismarck's image in the public mind and in history itself.

What emerged was the self-portrait of a great statesman, a German patriot who had used his talents to unify the nation and consolidate and fortify that unity over great obstacles, including the misunderstandings and malevolent opposition of ministers, party leaders (conservatives as well as liberals), subversives and dissidents (ultramontanes and socialists), kings and Kaisers, their wives, and their courts. This statesman had been ungraciously dismissed at a perilous time and without explanation, the victim of conspiracies in high places by men jealous of his power and eager to advance their own careers. Interspersed among these charges were general observations about the nature of political life, the conduct of foreign policy within the European balance of power system, and the value of constitutional monarchy (in contrast to Wilhelm II's "personal rule") as a barrier to revolution and mass dictatorship. Reflections take precedence over reminiscences in Bismarck's memoirs.[22]

Gedanken und Erinnerungen was not the only work that contributed to the Bismarck legend. Long before the prince had retired from office the hagiographers were busy, celebrating his person and his career, with or without his cooperation. Historians and documentary editors did their part. One editor was Heinrich Ritter von Poschinger, privy counselor of the Imperial Office of the Interior, who in the period 1882–1911 published no less than ninety-six volumes in seventy publications. Among them were multivolume collections of documents, interviews, and remarks by Bismarck on diplomatic, economic, and political affairs that are still indispensable to the historian, despite the many "corrections" they received in Friedrichsruh. Just as industrious and more reliable than Poschinger was Horst Kohl, who edited fourteen volumes of Bismarck's parliamentary speeches (1892–1905), a daily chronicle of Bismarck's life to 1890, a yearbook devoted to documents by Bismarck and articles and poetry about him, two volumes of letters exchanged by Bismarck, Wilhelm I, and others, a volume of Bismarck's letters to Johanna as bride and wife, and other works.

Neither of these indefatigable workers escaped occasional censure from Friedrichsruh when they overstepped their bounds or tried to associate their work too closely with the Bismarcks. But neither did the journalist Moritz Busch, who exploited his privileged relationship with the great man over more than quarter of a century by publishing their interviews in diary form,

[22] For a critical analysis of the memoirs, see Otto Pflanze, "Bismarck's *Gedanken und Erinnerungen*," in George Egerton, ed., *Political Memoirs* (forthcoming).

first in England and then in Germany.[23] Hermann Hofmann too exacted his price by publishing an account of his relationship with Bismarck and republishing without authorization the articles in the *Hamburger Nachrichten* he claimed Bismarck had written or inspired. Many others of higher status, who had known Bismarck in one context or another—former ministers, diplomats, and officials (or their heirs)—did the same. Among them were Lucius, Tiedemann, Scholz, Brauer, Roon, Waldersee, Schweinitz, and Hohenlohe. Often they used his name in their titles, but, even when they did not, his actions and words were omnipresent in their texts.

Bismarck's effort to shape the image of himself that he wished to project to the German people and the world could be seen as an act of megalomania, a desire to establish his place in history. His actions can be partially explained, it is true, by his injured narcissism, by his resentment over the circumstances of his departure from office, the "ingratitude" of Wilhelm II, and the "disloyalty" of ministers and officials who had failed to support the chancellor at a critical time. And yet it would be wrong to assert that Bismarck was driven by a manic desire for vainglory and even historical immortality. He was not a demagogue, staging, promoting, or just inviting mass demonstrations for the purpose of ego aggrandizement. His was a more modest compulsion—the need for self-assertion in the political process, the same thirst for domination and control that had been evident throughout his life. And that compulsion had a rational purpose: the consolidation, fortification, and perpetuation of the social and political order he had served. It can also be argued that he was by now justifiably concerned about the immaturity and perhaps even mental stability of the occupant of the imperial throne.[24] Deprived of his command over the political apparatus and faced with foreign and domestic policies of which he disapproved, Bismarck used the only recourse available to him by carrying on the struggle through the newspaper press, public speeches, and his memoirs.

The most significant aspect of the developing Bismarck idolatry of the 1890s is to be found not in the motivation of Bismarck himself but of the masses who participated in the ovations accorded him. The image of the "iron chancellor" that moved them was in the end not of Bismarck's creation. What stirred them was the need for a romantically conceived national hero, a liberating myth on the order of Siegfried, Frederick Barbarossa, and Fred-

---

[23] Hank, *Kanzler ohne Amt*, pp. 95–114.

[24] In this Bismarck was hardly alone. "The phrase current among all parties in the Reichstag: 'That the behaviour of the Kaiser can only be explained pathologically,' is taking effect quietly but devastatingly, like a miasma. For the time being this feeling is not being expressed openly because the present government, i.e., Hohenlohe and Marschall, have won a position for themselves; people have confidence in them and regard them as security against the imperial nervousness. But if the present government disappears, we will experience something to reckon with." Holstein to Philipp Eulenburg, Nov. 24, 1896. Rich and Fisher, eds., *Holstein Papers*, III, 655.

FASHIONING THE LEGEND—BISMARCK AS PHOTOGRAPHED AND AS PAINTED. FRANZ VON LENBACH
WAS A PIONEER IN THE USE OF PHOTOGRAPHS FOR PAINTING PORTRAITS. THE PHOTOGRAPH WAS
TAKEN AT FRIEDRICHSRUH ON FEBRUARY 2, 1896; THE PAINTING, ALTHOUGH UNFINISHED, WAS SIGNED
BY LENBACH IN THAT YEAR. HIS BRUSH TRANSFORMED THE IMAGE OF AN OLD AND AILING MAN,
WHOSE EYES HAVE LOST THE FIRE OF COMBAT, INTO A STATESMAN, WHOSE UPLIFTED EYES LOOK TO
THE FUTURE WITH FOREBODING. (STÄDTISCHE GALERIE IM LENBACHHAUS.)

erick the Great capable of elevating them above the mundane routine of daily
life and resolving insecurities born of a fast-changing economy and society.
In Bismarck they found living proof that the "German spirit" was still capable
of greatness. No longer need they look to a mythical past, or even to the
actual past of the twelfth and eighteenth centuries, to find their hero. The
mighty chancellor who had united Germany in three overwhelmingly successful wars (in which the achievements of diplomacy outshone those of the
sword) and dominated German and European politics for nearly two decades
thereafter was still alive, a vital presence who could still be seen and applauded, either in the streets and at railway stations or on pilgrimages to
Friedrichsruh, and whose views could still be read in the daily press.

The need to believe the legend and worship the myth became all the
greater as the reading public became disillusioned with the reigning monarch,
whose posturing and outrageous oratory made him seem a pygmy in comparison with the giant whom he had driven from office, a man of empty words in

contrast to the man of great deeds, a man whose pretensions for his grandfather (whom he futilely tried to dub "Wilhelm the Great") and for himself
(cast in the image of Frederick the Great) showed no understanding of monarchy's role in the modern age.[25] The more Wilhelm II tried to construct a
powerful image for himself and his dynasty, the greater that of Bismarck became. What Bismarck fostered for immediate political objectives in the 1890s
went far beyond his purposes. It struck a responsive chord in the minds of
millions that resonated long after he was dead and buried.

The Clock Winds Down

Bismarck's eightieth birthday celebration was the final, climactic event of his
life. Signs that the clock was already winding down in the Bismarck household had been evident for several months. In the spring of 1894 Johanna's
health began to fail. Consistent to the end, she did not participate in the
"reconciliation" of that year. Her anger at the Kaiser, Boetticher, and all
others whom her husband and oldest son believed responsible for the dismissal
remained unabated. The welfare of *Papachen*, Herbert, Bill, and Marie re-

[25] No one understood this better than the Kaiser's mother, whose letters to Queen Victoria are
full of laments about her son's incomprehension. "He does not understand what a constitution
is." Frederick Ponsonby, ed., *Letters of the Empress Frederick* (London, 1928), pp. 427–436.

mained her sole concern, more important to her than her own aches and pains, which she tried to conceal. In July the household began its annual migration from Friedrichsruh to Schönhausen to Varzin. A half-hour before their arrival at the Pomeranian estate, an ancient chestnut tree collapsed in the park. "A bad omen," Bismarck said. "Not all who came here are likely to leave Varzin alive."

In early October Johanna's close friend and companion, "Auntie" Reckow, died, and Johanna soon followed. Schweninger had diagnosed dropsy, and the disease left her increasingly weak. Early on the morning of November 27, 1894, she gave her daily instructions for the management of the household and then drifted away in the arms of her daughter. On Schweninger's orders Bismarck was not awakened. Toward 9:00 A.M. he shuffled into her bedroom in slippers and pajamas to find her gone. The iron chancellor wept inconsolably. The future, he wrote soon afterward, was now empty for him. "Life is a continuing process of burning, and what I possess for consumption by the flames is almost gone."[26]

He would have preferred, he said, to spend the rest of his days at Varzin, where Johanna's zinc casket lay surrounded by wreaths in a small garden house to await his own demise. But Schweninger persuaded him to avoid the harsh Pomeranian winter. Henckel von Donnersmarck offered his Berlin mansion to the prince as a residence, which produced another fright in the Wilhelmstrasse. But the Kaiser voided this possibility by insisting to Bill that the prince, if he came to Berlin, must be a guest at the royal palace. To Bismarck this was more intimidation than invitation. He would not be a "prisoner" spied upon by every palace lackey. And so Bismarck spent the several months of his eightieth birthday celebration in Friedrichsruh.[27]

Wilhelm II was still troubled by a deep ambivalence toward the "old man" in the Sachsenwald. He had learned both the cost of slighting and the benefits of embracing the prince; and yet the Kaiser and his associates were vexed by the knowledge that, as long as Bismarck was alive, Friedrichsruh would be regarded both in Germany and abroad as a second capital of the Reich. What emanated from there in the way of releases to the "Bismarck press," speeches to visiting deputations, interviews with journalists, and the like could compete with the palace and government in Berlin for the attention of the world.

In June 1894 Wilhelm, irritated by Bismarck's attacks on Boetticher and his claims to have had a part in planning the Kiel Canal, decided to issue a warning. He chose as his messenger none other than Bill Bismarck, whom he had recently promoted to governor-general of the province of East Prussia.

[26] Hank, Kanzler ohne Amt, pp. 575–576; Ernst Westphal, Bismarck als Gutsherr: Erinnerungen seines Varziner Försters (Leipzig, 1922), pp. 133–135; Arthur von Brauer, Im Dienste Bismarcks (Berlin, 1936), pp. 394–395; Penzler, ed., Bismarck nach seiner Entlassung, V, 284, 345–351; GW, IX, 394; XIV, 1017.
[27] Hank, Kanzler ohne Amt, pp. 576–577.

Instructed by Chancellor Hohenlohe, Bill arrived in Friedrichsruh bearing the advice that Bismarck should cease attacks on the government in the interest of avoiding further friction with the Kaiser. Bismarck was "first astounded and then amused" by the presumption. "They don't know me very well; to such an unreasonable demand I would only answer as did Götz von Berlichingen." The Kaiser's revenge was to avoid any mention of Bismarck's name in connection with the ceremonies at the opening of the Kiel Canal in June. In general, however, his tactic was to maintain the outward appearance of complete harmony by sending a steady stream of greetings on special occasions (birthdays, Christmas, New Year's, Sedan Day), solicitous telegrams, presents, decorations (*Pour le Mérite* and the new *Wilhelms-Orden*), and invitations that the recipient's health, if nothing else, would not let him accept (opening of the Kiel Canal, laying the cornerstone of the memorial to Wilhelm I, anniversaries of Sedan and the Frankfurt peace, autumn army maneuvers, launching of the battleship *Bismarck*). Among the presents were pictures of the fleet's new warships, about forty in all.

In returning from Kiel to Berlin on December 16, 1895, the Kaiser stopped off in Friedrichsruh on short notice, presenting the prince with yet another naval picture book. As before, the Hohenzoller avoided the subject of politics, but Bismarck found a way to get to him. After lunch over cigars he reminisced about Napoleon III, to whom he claimed to have uttered some good advice: "It would be good to surround yourself with a wall of ministers in order to ward off the first thrust. Otherwise, the people will make you responsible for every sign of bad weather."[28]

There was more to the Kaiser's visit than met the eye. During the final months of 1895 Wilhelm's relationship to the Prussian cabinet reached a new flash point. Only one year had passed since Hohenlohe replaced Caprivi as chancellor and Botho Eulenburg as minister-president. Under Hohenlohe's weak leadership the reunion of those offices did little to end the near anarchy in government. Far from exercising a controlling influence, furthermore, the Kaiser's vacillating inconsistencies, general tactlessness, and autocratic interventions in both domestic and foreign affairs had brought many (including Holstein) to the point of questioning his sanity. In the fall of 1895 the entire cabinet combined to force the resignation of Minister of Interior Ernst von Köller, who had betrayed their trust by leaking information about cabinet deliberations. The Kaiser, who valued Köller, was outraged by the cabinet's invasion of the royal prerogative to appoint and dismiss ministers. By stopping at Friedrichsruh without informing Hohenlohe and listing Bill Bismarck as a potential successor to Köller, the Kaiser vented his anger.[29]

---

[28] Hank, *Kanzler ohne Amt*, pp. 592–596; Helmuth von Moltke, *Erinnerungen, Briefe, Dokumente, 1877–1916* (Stuttgart, 1922), pp. 203–210.

[29] J. C. G. Röhl, *Germany without Bismarck* (London, 1967), pp. 118–171; Norman Rich,

One way to keep the cabinet in line, ironically, was to threaten a Bismarck restoration. To that end Wilhelm was compelled to show again and again that he was no longer at odds with the man who had first tried to limit his authority over Prussian ministers and Reich officials. And so the flow of gifts and recognitions of one kind or another continued from the palace in Berlin to the *Schloss* in Friedrichsruh. In the summer of 1896 the Kaiser volunteered to be godfather to Bill's son Nicholas, Bismarck's first male grandchild in the male line, and shortly afterward, on hearing rumors that Bismarck was seriously ill, he summoned Bill to express his concern. Bismarck responded to these overtures in the flowery language protocol demanded of a subject communicating with his sovereign.[30] But Wilhelm II found out how little this meant when, on October 24, 1896, the *Hamburger Nachrichten* carried a story revealing the terms of the reinsurance treaty with the statement that Caprivi had rejected Russia's wish to renew it in 1890.

In the Wilhelmstrasse this inexplicable revelation produced consternation. No immediate motivation could be discerned, and Bismarck himself appears to have been surprised by the commotion it caused in the press. The foreign office exercised damage control in Vienna and Petersburg, while Wilhelm II raged that the government must proceed against the *Hamburger Nachrichten* "by all legal means." But cooler heads prevailed, and the government restricted itself to press and parliament. In the Reichstag Herbert was compelled to listen to debates in which centrists and left-liberals condemned his father's action, while the parties of the cartel and anti-Semites defended it, chiefly on the grounds that Bismarck could do no wrong. Hohenlohe and Holstein reflected with alarm on the growth of a "Bismarck cult" so powerful that the government had to rely upon such allies. In November the beehive was disturbed once again by a newspaper report that the tsar had intended to stop in Friedrichsruh during a September visit in Germany but had been dissuaded by a "high-placed quarter."[31]

One way to combat Bismarck's influence was to exalt the achievements of Wilhelm I and minimize those of his chancellor. In the draft of a proclamation deposited in 1895 in the base of a "national monument" to be erected in honor of "Wilhelm the Great," the Kaiser excised a reference to "the great chancellor" and substituted for Bismarck's "incomparable deeds" the phrase

Friedrich von Holstein: Politics and Diplomacy in the Era of Bismarck and Wilhelm II (Cambridge, Eng., 1965), II, 484–543; Hohenlohe, *Denkwürdigkeiten der Reichskanzlerzeit*, pp. 123–124.

[30] Hank, *Kanzler ohne Amt*, pp. 595ff.

[31] Walther Peter Fuchs, ed., *Grossherzog Friedrich I. von Baden und die Reichspolitik 1871–1907* (Stuttgart, 1980), III, 561–563; Penzler, ed., *Bismarck nach seiner Entlassung*, VII, 106–107; Count Bogdan Hutten-Czapski, *Sechzig Jahre Politik und Gesellschaft* (Berlin, 1936), I, 301–307; Rich and Fisher, eds., *Holstein Papers*, III, 654–656; Hohenlohe, *Denkwürdigkeiten der Reichskanzlerzeit*, pp. 270–278.

"energetic support."[32] In February 1897 Wilhelm II again chose the Brandenburg provincial diet for an oratorical effort of consequence. The first great
Kaiser of the new German Reich, he intoned, would have achieved sainthood
in the Middle Ages and his reliquiae would have attracted pilgrims from all
countries. The coming struggle against subversive attacks upon the very foundations of the state could be successfully fought only by remembering the man
to whom Germany owed its unity, who by God's grace had able advisers to
assist him in executing his task, advisers who were, however, mere "handy-
men and pygmies" (in the printed version "but tools for the fulfillment of his
desires"). So massive and diverse was the adverse reaction to this effort to
rewrite recent history that Bismarck could instruct the *Hamburger Nachrichten*
to remain silent.

Wilhelm II was astonished that the German people could prefer to be governed by a mere minister rather than by a ruler born to his station and summoned to his responsibilities "by the grace of God."[33] The Bismarck cult had
more popular appeal than the Hohenzollern. During ceremonies (March 21–
23, 1897) marking the centennial of the birth of Wilhelm I, Wilhelm II
avoided all mention of Bismarck. When the national monument was un-
veiled, what the public saw was an equestrian statue decorated not with im-
ages of ministers and generals, but with carved angels, lions, banners, can-
nons, and the like. On April 1 the Kaiser failed to send birthday greetings to
the ex-chancellor. But thousands of telegrams and letters and many gifts
poured into Friedrichsruh. Among the many guests who arrived there in these
days were the viceroy of China, king of Siam, two German grand dukes, the
sons of Prince Albert of Hohenzollern, and many former ministers, generals,
and officials.[34]

The Clock Stops

Despite these episodes, Bismarck had perceptibly declined in health and com-
bativeness since the death of Johanna at the end of 1894. The fall of Caprivi,
Boetticher, and Marschall had deprived him of favorite targets. The new
chancellor, Hohenlohe, was after all an old associate, who, furthermore,
twice made pilgrimages to Friedrichsruh to visit his old chief.[35] Schweninger
reported that his patient was in frequent pain, usually confined to a wheelchair. The stream of delegations and visitors had to be curtailed. In December
1897 Prince Heinrich stopped off en route to join the fleet destined for Kiao-
chow and reported to his brother that "it is coming to an end there." That
moved the Kaiser to demonstrate to the public once again what reverence he

[32] Hank, *Kanzler ohne Amt*, pp. 594–595.
[33] Hank, *Kanzler ohne Amt*, pp. 612–617.
[34] Hank, *Kanzler ohne Amt*, pp. 617–618.
[35] GW, IX, 405–408, 416–417.

had for the man he had come to hate. To his entourage he explained that he wanted to find out personally when the prince's death was to be expected. Again Bismarck agreed to receive him, much to Herbert's disgust. On December 15 the Kaiser and entourage spent one hour and fifteen minutes in Friedrichsruh, long enough for dinner, during which he again evaded his host's effort to engage him in political discussion by telling barracks jokes and anecdotes. In March, on the sixtieth anniversary of Bismarck's army commission, he proposed to reenact the military charade of 1895 by filling the Friedrichsruh meadow with troops and cavalry, but word came back that the prince's health would not permit it. In private Bismarck referred to the Kaiser as that "dumb kid."[36]

With Johanna's death the Bismarck household lost its nucleus. Servants, housekeepers, family members quarreled, and disorder reigned. Bismarck himself both profited and suffered from the chaos. In late 1896 Schweninger diagnosed gangrene in the left foot but managed to keep the disease under control. Although in pain much of the time and often dosed with morphine, Bismarck refused to take the condition seriously. By manipulating the servants, he satisfied his wants in food and drink and refused the prescribed massages and footbaths. The doctor's order that he "stand up and walk despite the pain" were in vain. Only Schweninger could scold him into submission, and Schweninger could not be constantly in residence. Anger and rebellion alternated with submission and depression. Bismarck was a pain-ridden, lonely man, tired of life and inclined now to reflect more on events of his youth than on current affairs. But he did follow the uproar in France over *J'accuse* and the Dreyfus case. This aroused his interest in Émile Zola, whose novels he read, complaining about excessive detail and description.

In the spring of 1898 he managed a few excursions to view his beloved trees and to inspect the rye fields. But as summer progressed he was reduced to a wheelchair in the park, finally in July to house and bedroom, afflicted by recurrent fever, difficulty in breathing, and periods of deep sleep bordering on unconsciousness. Excruciating pain produced cries and tears, and the patient begged for a revolver. On July 28 Schweninger managed to get him on his feet and, fortified by a glass of champagne, to the dinner table, where his family enjoyed for the last time a nearly typical evening, as Bismarck showed some of his old brilliance of mind and spirit. Afterward sitting in his usual place, he read newspapers, smoked three pipefuls, and conversed vibrantly.

During the next forty-eight hours his condition rapidly worsened. A lung edema forced him to struggle for breath; he became feverish, lost consciousness at times, and was often incoherent while awake. On July 30 Rudolf Chrysander, the resident doctor cum secretary, applied hot sponges to the upper torso and injected morphine to ease the pain. Schweninger, who had opti-

36 Hank, *Kanzler ohne Amt*, pp. 621–623; GW, XIII, 488–489.

mistically left for Berlin on the twenty-eighth, was recalled to find that he could do nothing but make the patient comfortable. Just short of midnight, in the eighty-third year of his life, Bismarck drew his last breath.[37]

Two years before his death, Bismarck had made his final preparations. Above all, he wanted to prevent the Kaiser or anyone else from making a spectacle of his funeral. In this he was not mistaken. On his summer voyage in Norwegian waters, Wilhelm II, suspecting that Herbert and Schweninger were concealing the worst, had already begun to discuss what was to be done.

FUNERAL PROCESSION FOR JOHANNA AND OTTO VON BISMARCK AT FRIEDRICHSRUH, MARCH 16, 1899. KAISER WILHELM II CAN BE SEEN IN MILITARY CAPE AND HELMET IMMEDIATELY BEHIND THE SECOND CASKET. FORESTERS OF THE SACHSENWALD PROVIDE THE HONOR GUARD FOR JOHANNA; A DELEGA-TION OF CUIRASSIER OFFICERS (IN WHITE UNIFORMS), FOR THEIR HONORARY COMMANDER.

[37] Hank, *Kanzler ohne Amt*, pp. 624–632; Hermann Hofmann, ed., *Fürst Bismarck, 1890–1898* (2 vols., Stuttgart, 1913), I, 203–204, 241–246; Ernst Schweninger, *Dem Andenken Bismarcks* (Leipzig, 1899), pp. 15–16; Sidney Whitman, *Personal Reminiscences of Prince Bismarck* (New York, 1903), pp. 291–304.

Informed of the end by telegram on July 31, he ordered all flags at half-mast, directed the ship southward at full speed, and telegraphed his condolences to Herbert. "Germany's greatest son," he said, must be buried in the Berlin cathedral "by the side of my ancestors"; the finest artists would design the sarcophagus, and the burial would be a memorable event.

On arriving at Friedrichsruh on August 2, Wilhelm II embraced Herbert, kissed him on both cheeks, and excitedly spilled out his plans and desires. But Herbert coolly cited the deceased's testament: no postmortem, no death mask, no drawings, and no photographs; burial at a site he had chosen on the rising ground above the manor. The massive casket of dark oak had already been sealed in preparation for the funeral service, which lasted but a few minutes. Within a half-hour, the Kaiser was back on the train and off to Berlin, where a few days later a memorial service was held at the Kaiser Wilhelm memorial church. The Kaiser, Kaiserin, and many other dignitaries attended. At Wilhelm's direction the imperial loge was reserved for the Bismarck family. It remained empty.

The burial at Friedrichsruh did not occur until March 16, 1899, just two days short of the ninth anniversary of Bismarck's dismissal from office. On that day the Kaiser followed the caskets of Otto and Johanna von Bismarck in a short procession that wended its way from the manor house through the gate in the red brick wall, across the railway tracks, and up the slope to a small mausoleum newly constructed in romanesque style. Engraved on the prince's plain sarcophagus was the epitaph he had specified: "A loyal German servant of Kaiser Wilhelm I."[38] From the grave Bismarck had the last word in his dispute with Wilhelm II.

[38] Hank, *Kanzler ohne Amt*, pp. 634–635.

⊹

Conclusions

Personal power, even the most inspired, has an incalculable dimension.

Every good deed that issues from it is a medallion bearing

on the reverse side a contrary possibility.[1]

OST OF WHAT Bismarck created disappeared within fifty years of his death. The country he united was divided after 1945, this time into two states, each seeking its own version of the state-nation. Prussia's eastern provinces, whose potential loss so concerned Bismarck, belong to Poland and Russia, and Prussia itself, like Carthage, has disappeared from the map. The Habsburg Empire, whose preservation he believed vital to German security, is no more, and likewise tsarist Russia. The constitution Bismarck drafted for a united Germany disappeared under the impact of the First World War—liquidated by the Hindenburg–Ludendorf dictatorship in 1917, a hasty conversion to parliamentary democracy in 1918, and adoption of the Weimar constitution in 1919. The monarchical order that he believed vital to the internal stability of the three central and east European empires has disappeared, and likewise the aristocratic latifundia that were its economic and social backbone. Some members of the old aristocracy (including Bismarck's great-grandchildren at Friedrichsruh) still have land and social status in West Germany, and many others have found niches in West German business and professional life that keep them in the upper stratum of society. But the traditions that guaranteed their privileged position in government and the armed services vanished along with the society that created and preserved them. Bismarck would find little that is familiar in contemporary Germany—with one exception: The social insurance system to which his initiative gave birth is still in place, though much modified, and has been copied widely throughout the western world. And yet, ironically, this was an achievement on which Bismarck placed little store, for it failed to achieve his immediate objective. Not a line did he devote to it in his memoirs.

Did Bismarck himself contribute to the ultimate destruction of his handiwork? This is the critical and quite unavoidable question that every historian of modern Germany must face.

[1] Ludwig Bamberger, "Zum Jahrestag der Entlassung Bismarcks," *Gesammelte Schriften* (Berlin, 1897), V, 335. Originally published in *Die Nation*, 1891.

A "White Revolutionary"?

By now it should be obvious that, fundamentally, the accelerating progress of economic and social change in the modern world is what doomed the Bismarckian system. Looking backward, it is inconceivable that the social and political order of Germany in the nineteenth century could have long survived in the twentieth, even without the catastrophes of two world wars. However much they accelerated the process of change, the wars did not create it. No contemporary was more conscious than Bismarck of the forces that were transforming his world and of their potential consequences for the society in which he was born. Like Franklin Delano Roosevelt, the American president with whom he is most comparable, he sought to modify the system in order to save it.

Nineteenth-century Germany has often been portrayed as the story of liberty frustrated. Repeatedly—1819, 1848, 1866—history reached a turning point and failed to turn. The authoritarian state survived when it should have expired. This concentration of interest on social, political, and ideological weaknesses of German liberalism has obscured a story of equal, perhaps greater importance—that of the strength and vitality of German conservatism, both in its institutions and its ideology. The essential Prussian establishment managed to endure long after the time when, by all the laws of dialectical materialism, it ought to have perished.

A favorite way of explaining this survival is by reference to Bismarck's "white revolution" or "revolution from above."[2] Implicit in the term is an assumption that Bismarck's "revolution" was unique. But was it? To understand him and his significance, one must put his career in perspective by taking a long look backward. Since the seventeenth century the Hohenzollern monarchy had been the principal instrument of change in Prussian society. Over a period of two hundred years it had transformed a backward (even by the standards of that age) social and political order by suppressing the feudal powers and liberties of the aristocracy in central governmental affairs. Suppression required creation. New military and governmental institutions were needed to create and administer the central power that the suppression of the feudal estates made possible. In its search for revenue with which to support the army, the bureaucracy not only created new forms of taxation but also assumed the function of directing the economy and as a consequence the responsibility for economic development.

---

[2] Henry A. Kissinger, "The White Revolutionary: Reflections on Bismarck," in *Daedalus*, 97 (1968), pp. 888–924; Lothar Gall, *Bismarck: Der weisse Revolutionär* (Frankfurt a. M., 1980), translated as *Bismarck: The White Revolutionary* (2 vols., London, 1986); Wolfgang Sauer, "Probleme des deutschen Nationalstaates," in Helmut Boehme, ed., *Probleme der Reichsgründungszeit 1848–1873. Neue wissenschaftliche Bibliothek* (Köln, 1968), pp. 448–479; Hans-Ulrich Wehler, *Das deutsche Kaiserreich 1871–1918* (Göttingen, 1973), translated as *The German Empire, 1871–1918* (Dover, 1985); Ernst Engelberg, *Bismarck: Urpreusse und Reichsgründer* (Berlin, 1985).

This revolution from above during 1640–1740 was not unique in Europe in the age of absolutism, but it was the most successful of its kind in terms of efficiency, infrequent corruption, and general professionalism. Under Frederick the Great the revolution was extended to the field of foreign affairs by the wars against Austria, whose ultimate resolution established Prussia for the first time as a European great power. Within decades after this accomplishment the social and political order upon which it was based proved to be inadequate for the task of preserving what Frederick the Great had created. Crushed by Napoleon, Prussia was reduced to the status of a minor power and compelled to support her conqueror's attack on Russia in 1812. Under these conditions leadership passed from the Hohenzollern dynasty to the state bureaucracy; monarchical absolutism gave way to bureaucratic absolutism. The reforms of the Stein–Hardenberg era have to be regarded as yet another revolution from above, one that stabilized the Prussian establishment for a few decades. The liquidation of serfdom, free sale of knights' estates, urban and provincial self-administration, cabinet government, modernization of the army, and freedom of occupation were just the most significant of the changes instituted by the monarchy at this critical time.

And yet the revolution of 1848 showed that a serious gap had emerged between the ruling order and a new society evolving under the impact of commercial and industrial change, a gap that the counterrevolutionary government could not ignore. The Manteuffel regime staged a revolution from above that began with a truly audacious move, the adoption of constitutionalism. How one judges this government depends on which side of the medallion is up: one face condemns the government for its coup against the revolution from below, denouncing as reactionary its adaptation of constitutionalism to conservative purposes; the reverse face looks upon the constitution of mixed powers as a great forward step in modernizing Prussia, a step that prepared the Berlin government for its future role of leadership in Germany. In many respects the ensuing reforms of 1850–1865—continuing progress toward peasant proprietorship, free enterprise (abandonment of the direction principle in heavy industry), successive renewals of the Zollverein (without Austria), and eventual commitment of the Zollverein to free trade—were merely logical extensions of the 1848–1850 revolution from above.

Seen in this light, Bismarck's unification of Germany was but the last of a long series of revolutionary acts by the Hohenzollern monarchy, its ministers and officials, stretching over a period of more than two centuries. By any standard of comparison the Prussian-German establishment demonstrated a remarkable capacity to stay afloat upon the rapids of economic, social, political, and intellectual change during the nineteenth century. Bismarck was but the last of a succession of rulers and statesmen who wittingly or unwittingly navigated around the shoals of rigidity and stagnation that could have

432   * After the Fall, 1890–1898 *

wrecked the enterprise of survival. From Stein to Bismarck they either appropriated or preempted the issues that elsewhere brought liberalism to power. This was the meaning of Bismarck's often quoted remark to Napoleon III that "only the kings make revolution in Prussia."[3]

Bismarck's contribution to that enterprise was the last, and for a very good reason. His revolution exhausted the possibilities of compromise. Any further democratization of the social and political order would have broken the power of the enlarged Prussian-German establishment, liquidating residual feudal institutions and traditions and, conceivably, endangering the capitalistic system that had become feudalism's partner in the serious game of survival. The establishment had run out of options.

The successive revolutions from above in Prussian history recounted here were of decreasing durability in their stabilizing effects. The military, administrative, and fiscal order established by Elector Friedrich Wilhelm I (1640–1688) lasted a full century after his death. The important changes in that system introduced by King Friedrich Wilhelm I (1713–1740) have to be regarded as a mere extension of his grandfather's work, and they stemmed more from the whims and dispositions of the ruler than from a compelling crisis in the society. The second revolution under Frederick the Great (1740–1788) lasted sixty years, from the Treaty of Dresden (1745) to the battles of Jena and Auerstädt (1806). The Stein–Hardenberg revolution (1807–1823) sufficed for twenty-five years (to the revolution of 1848); the "reactionary" revolution of 1848–1850, just fifteen years (to 1866). Although Bismarck's "white revolution" (1866–1879) lasted nearly four decades (to 1917), it was already in trouble after one decade.

In 1889–1890 the moment came for yet another white revolution, a bold new initiative bringing concessions that might have stabilized the system for another quarter century, perhaps longer, an initiative that would have incorporated into the system itself the possibility of evolutionary reform without revolution, whether white or red. Bismarck sensed the coming crisis throughout the 1880s, most intensely during his last months in office. But he had no solution for it except counterrevolution, a rolling back of the clock through the abandonment of universal, equal, and secret male suffrage and conversion of the Reichstag into a corporative diet. Even his most progressive act of statesmanship, the social insurance legislation of the 1880s, was intended to prepare the way for this retreat. From 1806 to 1871 Bismarck and his predecessors had met such crises by outflanking the foe, seizing the high ground that commanded the visible terrain ahead. But the strategy no longer worked, for it now demanded sacrifices that neither he nor his successors were willing to make. Bismarck's only solution was to retreat behind the battlements of privilege and raise the walls against an expected siege. To contemplate such

[3] GW, VIII, 459.

a step was a confession of failure. He had run out of compromises, but so also had the establishment itself. The statesmen who succeeded him had no other solution, for indeed there was none, given the values, traditions, and vested interests of the establishment. Social and political suicide was not an option.

Consequences in International Politics

Any discussion of Bismarck's impact upon German and European historical development must begin with the year 1866. Clearly the decision to provoke a war with Austria was his, and that decision did not arise from any necessity of Prussian or German politics. The struggle with Austria for economic control over Germany had been resolved in 1865 with the acceptance by the southern states of Prussia's free-trade treaty with France and renewal of the small-German Zollverein without the inclusion of the Habsburg Empire. The evidence does not support the belief of some that Bismarck required an external diversion to resolve Prussia's internal struggle between crown and parliament (the constitutional conflict). The assault on Austria was a war of aggression justified in the mind of its initiator only by considerations of power politics. He was convinced that Prussia must, in its own interest, increase its weight in the European balance of power, that its destiny was to dominate northern and perhaps southern Germany, and that the configuration of European politics, particularly after the Crimean War, favored the realization of the first stage of that objective. The wars of 1866 and 1870–1871 arose from Bismarck's personal assessment of Prussia's geopolitical situation. In the terminology of Morton White's version of "covering laws," Bismarck was the "abnormal" factor, the presence of which made the difference between war and peace.[4] If he had not been at the helm, the wars against Austria and France would not have occurred when and how they did. Perhaps they would not have occurred at all.

This leads to the further question: What were the consequences of those wars? In international politics the most striking answer is the final destruction of the territorial and political arrangements established by the Congress of Vienna in 1815. The German Confederation was abolished; in its place appeared a sovereign state, first the North German Confederation and finally the German Reich. Austria was expelled from Germany, the Habsburg Empire became the Dual Monarchy, Italian unification was largely completed. The war of 1870–1871 merely finished what was begun four years earlier in both Italy and Germany. With the acquisition of Venetia and Rome by Italy and Alsace-Lorraine by Germany the concept of national self-determination scored a significant victory over that of the balance of power as the organizing principle of international politics. From 1871 onward movements for national

---

[4] Morton White, *Foundations of Historical Knowledge* (New York, 1965), p. 126.

unity and independence gained momentum; their eventual consequence was dismemberment of the Habsburg and Ottoman empires.

It must be recognized, nevertheless, that Bismarck never intended or worked for this effect. He was never a convert to ethnic or cultural nationalism; he continued to think of the nation as an entity formed by the state. And yet he exploited ethnic nationalism as a moral force for legitimizing and consolidating the German Reich of 1871. If driven to it by the fortunes of war, he might well have exploited the national aspirations of Slavs and Magyars in the Habsburg Empire in 1866, as he did those of the Italians. But he also contributed to the growth of cultural nationalism within the German Reich by the policy he adopted toward its ethnic minorities. His policy of Germanizing Poles, Danes, and Frenchmen in the interest of consolidating the empire and solidifying its frontiers against foreign intervention boomeranged in the end, for it encouraged German intolerance toward other nationalities. Its natural consequence was to heighten the popular conviction in the superiority of German culture and its greater right to exist at the cost of others, a consequence that Bismarck himself would have deplored.

Was the erection of a closed national state in central Europe a necessity for Germans? As an autonomous movement German nationalism was patently lacking in vitality before 1870. For six decades German nationalists had been confronted with the challenging task of uniting a divided people, but only once, in 1848, did the ideal of national unity generate sufficient popular support for the attempt. Within weeks, however, the patriotic fervor evaporated. By May 1849 few were still willing to sacrifice for the cause. At other times the external stimulus of a crisis with France (1813–1815, 1840, 1859, 1867, and 1870–1871) succeeded in bringing life to the national movement. But only on the first and last of these occasions was anything accomplished, and this was due entirely to the leadership provided by the Prussian state, whose ministers exploited German national sentiment for their own political ends. The achievements of 1864 and 1866 were attained by the Prussian state over the bitter opposition of the German national movement. In 1864 the efforts of the Nationalverein to use popular agitation to realize the claims of the Prince of Augustenburg to Schleswig-Holstein ended in complete failure, and in 1866 German patriots could not prevent civil war over issues believed in the beginning to be alien to the national cause.

The common view of German nationalism as an irresistible current sweeping down the decades to fulfillment in 1870 was a fiction of nationalistic historians, derived from the hopes and aspirations of those kleindeutsch advocates, like Heinrich von Sybel and Heinrich von Treitschke, who were their intellectual forebears. Only under the stimulation provided by Bismarck for his own political ends did German nationalism generate a popular force capable of overwhelming the many barriers standing in its way: tradition, dynastic self-interest, state particularism, tribal prejudice and antagonism, reli-

DES HELDEN HEIMFAHRT.

BISMARCK'S FATE IN THE HEREAFTER —A GERMAN VIEW. A GERMANIC HERO ON A FLAMING "DRAGON SHIP" ASCENDS TO VALHALLA, WHERE WILHELM I (AS WOTAN) AND FRIEDRICH III (AS THOR) AWAIT HIM. *KLADDERADATSCH*, AUGUST 1898.

BISMARCK'S FATE IN THE HEREAFTER —A FRENCH VIEW. "HUMANITY" DIRECTS HIS SKULL TO THE SCRAP HEAP ALREADY OCCUPIED BY CAESAR, NAPOLEON, LOYOLA, BORGIA, AND OTHERS. *LE GRELOT*, PARIS, AUGUST 1898.

gious cleavage, and sheer lethargy. The assumption that German national
unity would have been achieved, for better or worse, at a later time under
other conditions and auspices is a counterfactual proposition unsusceptible to
proof.

It is conceivable, to be sure, that the economic depression that followed
the crash of 1873 would have produced greater pressures for economic and
political consolidation than the German confederation could have satisfied.
Whether the result of those pressures would have been greater accommodation between Austria and Prussia or friction and cleavage on the pattern of
1866 no one can know. Neither can we know whether the consequence of
either solution would have been more or less advantageous for the stability of
the European balance of power. The most that can be said is that Bismarck's
successes in foreign and domestic affairs during 1866–1871 closed off avenues
that would have remained open had he never come to power. And, barring
that, if in 1875 he had resigned and actually removed himself from the political scene (a most dubious condition), some of those options might have reappeared and been realized. Politicians become statesmen only through the exercise of political power. Whether liberal party leaders of the late 1870s had
that potentiality we will never know, for they did not get the chance.

But it is worth noting that the quest for national self-determination,
whether by a divided or a subject people, has seldom been achieved without
war. Britain fought hers in the seventeenth century, the Netherlands in
1568–1648, the United States in 1775–1783 and 1861–1865, France in
1792–1815, Italy in 1859–1866. The First and Second World Wars spawned
dozens of new national sovereignties throughout the world. Compared with
most of these struggles, the German wars of 1864–1871 were executed with
minimal violence and disruption. Whatever his motives (social as well as political), Bismarck's diplomacy was probably decisive in the preservation of
peace among the European great powers during the following two decades. He
convinced a skeptical Europe that he, and Germany, had no further expan-
sionist objectives. By preventing a major European war over the Balkan question in 1875–1878 and 1885–1888, he restrained for a time the destructive-
ness of forces he had earlier unleashed.

Consequences in Domestic Affairs

A resurgence of interest in social history has in recent years focused attention
on the combination of economic and social elites said to have been created
by the tariff act of 1879. By uniting the two elites of agriculture and finance
capitalism, Bismarck is believed to have forged an "alliance" of interest groups
that frustrated the development of political democracy in Germany, not only
under the Second Reich but also under the Weimar republic. To such a charge
he himself gave the answer in his metaphor of "the stream of time" that is

beyond the control of individual statesmen. All that the helmsman can hope for is an occasional, but always temporary, safe harbor. What Bismarck actually did in 1879 was to reinforce a rapprochement of the elite interest groups that had long been under way. And yet he was aware that the base they provided was too narrow and its cohesion too dubious to serve as the foundation of his government. He sought and failed to achieve a wider combination of interest groups, including Catholics and labor, that would have provided a general consensus behind the regime. He was defeated in that effort by his own temperament and tactics, which tended more toward the divisive than the conciliatory. He violated his own metaphor by attempting vainly to divert currents in the stream (the attacks on political Catholicism in the 1870s and social democracy in the 1880s). The stream flowed on.

Bismarck, it is often charged, designed a governmental system for the German Reich to suit his own talents, creating thereby a constitutional structure that no "ordinary man" (in Caprivi's words) could control. The constitutional balance of power that he devised in late 1866 has also been regarded as further proof of his genius for political realism. Indeed, the general features of that structure did take into account the existing powers and forces in German society, which had to be accommodated if German unification was to be accomplished. These were: the governments of the German states remaining after the annexations of 1866 (both inside and outside the North German Confederation); Prussia, whose army had won the war against Austria and whose hegemonic size and power made it the leading power in the union; the German nation in whose name and for whose union the war had ostensibly been fought; and, not least, Bismarck himself. To bring all of these factors into balance in a workable system of government was the task undertaken in the constitution of 1867. To have ignored either the wishes of the princes or the expectations of the public would have been unwise. And surely no one could reasonably have expected Bismarck to neglect the interest of the helmsman? Self-abnegation was not in his character.

To have factored all of these forces into the constitutional equation was a political achievement that demands recognition. That Bismarck's successors could not make the system function well was not a matter of their mediocrity in contrast to his genius. Clearly not, for Bismarck himself could not decide how to make it function. Throughout his career as chancellor he never ceased to tinker with the constitutional machine, deciding alternately to build up the Reich chancellery at the cost of the Prussian cabinet and the Prussian cabinet at the cost of the Reich chancellery, the Reichstag at the cost of the Bundesrat and the Bundesrat at the cost of the Reichstag. The same zigzag course can be seen in his decisions to resign, retain, and enlarge his position within the Prussian cabinet. These reversals, which continued to the very end of his chancellorship, stemmed in part from his accustomed political tactic, the provision for alternatives or balanced options, and the deliberately labile constitutional structure that he devised to accommodate it. But they also show some indecision on his part about what road to take in coordinating the dualistic structure that arose from Prussia's hegemonic position in the Reich.

Bismarck was but marginally more successful than were his successors in coping with this problem. Under Caprivi and Hohenlohe—the former talented but inexperienced, the latter experienced but untalented—it became clear that the structure tended to hinder more than advance the orderly transaction of government business in a rapidly changing economy and society. It lacked simplicity and symmetry of form, including clearly established channels of power and responsibility, and proved inadequate to the challenges posed by the First World War. The nagging constitutional problem of the relationship between the Reich and its hegemonic state survived the fall of the empire and continued to the end of the Weimar republic. That the problem endured so long shows that it arose more from the circumstances of Germany's unification under Prussian leadership than from any arbitrary arrangement decreed by Bismarck. He dealt with the real forces at hand, forced each to make the necessary compromises, and looked after his own interests as chancellor in the process.

Throughout Europe the constitutional system of mixed powers underwent changes in the nineteenth century that call into question its inherent stability as a governmental form. Either the power of the legislature penetrated the executive creating parliamentary government, or the reverse occurred with a consequent devitalization of parliamentary life. England, France, Italy, the Netherlands, and Scandinavian countries experienced the former process. In Prussia the possibility of such a development arose during the constitutional conflict of the early 1860s, but the chance was lost and the contrary current set in. Through the victories of 1866 and 1870 the essential features of the Prussian system, with some diminution of parliamentary authority, were extended over the rest of Germany. Another important consequence was the disorganization of the major political parties. Bismarck's manipulations fragmented the party structure and reduced the possibility of stable majorities. His stark realism weakened the attraction of political ideals and exalted in German political attitudes the prestige of power at the cost of principle.

"It was only through Bismarck," Bertrand Russell observed, "that German patriotism became respectable and conservative, with the result that many men who had been liberal because they were patriots became conservative for the same reason."[5] Before 1866 liberalism and nationalism, like conservatism and legitimism, had been companion movements. By his exploitation of German national sentiment to legitimate the expansion of Prussia in 1866 Bis-

---

[5] Bertrand Russell, *Freedom versus Organization, 1815–1914* (New York, 1934), pp. 362, 368; Herbert Michaelis, "Königgrätz: Eine geschichtliche Wende," *Die Welt als Geschichte*, 12 (1952), pp. 190ff.

marck expedited the realignment of these relationships. The founding of the German Conservative party in 1875 and the movement toward the right in the National Liberal party in the late 1870s signaled the appearance of a new combination in the German political consciousness: a conservative German nationalism. In the process German nationalism lost what remained of that humanitarian and cosmopolitan outlook that was its endowment from Herder and the ages of reason and romanticism.[6] His exploitation of German nationalism for imperialistic and authoritarian purposes is what makes Bismarck, like Napoleon III, a transitional figure between the politics of the eighteenth and twentieth centuries, between the age of aristocratic absolutism and that of authoritarian nationalism.

The effect of this ideological realignment can best be seen in the conversion of the German intelligentsia, chiefly the academic and professional elite, from opponents (on liberal grounds) to supporters of his government (on national grounds). To a generation steeped in Hegelian thought (if only in its neo-Hegelian form), the new German Reich, the Prussian *Machtstaat* at its core, appeared to be the moral and physical embodiment of the German *Volksgeist*. It was not an arbitrary, chance creation, but the natural fruit of the historical process and hence of God's will and plan. This conversion was Bismarck's most lasting accomplishment in his quest for a national consensus, for the attitudes it spawned dominated the academic profession (particularly the historians) throughout the Weimar period and into the early years of the Federal Republic of Germany.

Where he largely failed in his quest for consensus was in the effort to incorporate the urban working class. Repressive acts did not liquidate the socialist movement, and social reforms did not bind German labor to the established order. And yet the Kulturkampf did not produce the same consequence among German Catholics. Repression, it is true, did not destroy the Center party and its ultramontane leadership. But Catholics were not estranged from the empire. That the Center party became a major force in German parliamentary life with which Bismarck himself had to reckon perhaps made the difference. But it is also true that there was a persuasiveness about Bismarck's achievements and a majesty about the empire he created that had its effect

---

[6] See Manfred Rauh, *Föderalismus und Parlamentarismus im Wilhelminischen Reich* (Düsseldorf, 1973), and *Die Parlamentarisierung des deutschen Reiches* (Düsseldorf, 1977); Bernhard Mann, "Zwischen Hegemonie und Partikularismus: Bemerkungen zum Verhältnis von Regierung, Bürokratie und Parlament in Preussen 1867–1918," and Konrad von Zwehl, "Zum Verhältnis von Regierung und Reichstag im Kaiserreich (1871–1918)," in Gerhard A. Ritter, ed., *Regierung, Bürokratie und Parlament in Preussen und Deutschland von 1848 bis zur Gegenwart* (Düsseldorf, 1983), pp. 76–116; Volker R. Berghahn, "Das Kaiserreich in der Sackgasse," and "Politik und Gesellschaft im Wilhelminischen Deutschland," *Neue politische Literatur*, 16 (1971), pp. 494–506, and 24 (1979), pp. 164–195.

on Catholics and ultimately on socialists as well. Hence there came about the "civil peace" at the outbreak of war in 1914.

No subject in the history of the post-Bismarck era has engaged historians more than that of whether—and if not, why not—the constitutional order progressed toward parliamentary government.[7] By 1900 it was obvious to acute observers that change was needed. The monarchical authority, which was Prussia's lingering heritage from the era of absolutism and which Bismarck had done so much to protect and prolong in its postabsolutistic form, was in the hands of a ruler of questionable judgment and mental stability. In his unsteady hands was the power to make war, to negotiate peace, and to appoint and dismiss Prussian ministers, the imperial chancellor, and all high officials of the Prussian and imperial governments. At his command was the most potent war machine in the world, backed by one of the world's foremost industrial complexes. Under such unsettling leadership Germany began to seem to the outside world like the menace to European stability many foreign statesman had feared in the early 1870s. Under such circumstances even Bismarck urged the Reichstag to take a more positive role in governmental affairs.

Although Bismarck did not live to see it, the German Reichstag did become more active after 1900. And yet it never transgressed in any vital way on the boundaries he established for it in the constitutional balance of 1867. Formidable obstacles lay in the path of a conversion to parliamentary government. To accomplish that end would have required a conquest of the castle keep of the Prussian-German establishment (the Prussian House of Lords), as well as the encircling battlements (Bundesrat, Chamber of Deputies, cabinet, and king). This becomes evident when one examines, bastion by bastion, the successive defenses from the outer walls to the central tower.

Theoretically the power of *Kompetenz-Kompetenz* gave to the German Reich the legislative authority to supersede piecemeal the powers and functions of the federated governments, including Prussia. But this power could not be exercised without the consent of the Bundesrat, which was in theory the Reich's executive body with veto power over acts of the Reichstag. The Bundesrat was dominated by Prussia, which could be outvoted theoretically by the other state governments, although not actually so, given Prussia's superior weight in the governmental order. The Prussian vote was instructed by the Prussian foreign minister, but as a practical matter he could exercise that power only if he were also imperial chancellor, Prussian minister-president, and a Bismarck. Otherwise it would be wielded by the Prussian cabinet acting collegially. To control the Bundesrat liberals had to control the Prussian cabinet and that required a democratization of the Prussian constitutional order,

---

[7] See Bernhard Mann, "Das Herrenhaus in der Verfassung des preussisch-deutschen Kaiserreichs: Ueberlegungen zum Problem Parlament, Gesellschaft und Regierung in Preussen, 1867–1918," in Gerhard A. Ritter, ed., *Gesellschaft, Parlament und Regierung, Zur Geschichte des Parlamentarismus in Deutschland* (Düsseldorf, 1974), pp. 279–298.

specifically, parliamentary control over the Prussian cabinet. Before the Prussian Chamber of Deputies could be brought even to consider such a step, the three-class suffrage by which it was elected had to be replaced by universal, equal, and secret male suffrage and the electoral districts reapportioned—ending domination of the chamber by conservatives representing the landlords of eastern Prussia. But no such reform act could be passed in Prussia without approval by the House of Lords, in which those landlords and high aristocrats of the old establishment predominated. To break their resistance the king must appoint a sufficient number of new peers willing to outvote the Junker bloc—something Wilhelm II would never consent to do except under the most coercive conditions. The keep and with it the outer battlements appeared unassailable.

And yet the walls could have been breached by a determined Reichstag backed by massive and vocal public opinion in a threatening, near revolutionary situation. An internal crisis of this dimension could not, however, be generated spontaneously by any realizable combination of popular forces and parties in pre-1914 Germany. The social democrats had turned away in the 1890s from any commitment to revolutionary action and probably reached the pinnacle of their electoral appeal in 1912. Left-liberals were in any case too weak in popular support and political commitment to cooperate with socialists on the national plane. Neither centrists nor national liberals were to be had for such a venture. The opportunities (if such they really were) to force the abdication of Wilhelm II after the *Daily Telegraph* interview of 1908 and to curb the Prussian military after the Zabern incident of 1913 passed unused. Only a world war and impending German defeat could produce the crisis needed for a successful assault on Bismarck's fortress. And even then the first decision to act came from above rather than from below, from within the establishment, not from the Reichstag.

"What was . . . Bismarck's *political legacy?*" asked Max Weber in 1918. "He left behind a nation *totally without political education*, well below the level already attained twenty years earlier. Even more importantly, he left behind a nation *totally bereft of political will*, accustomed to expect that the great man at the top would provide their politics for them. And above all, a nation that, as a consequence of his abusive misuse of monarchical sentiment as a cover for the pursuit of his own power interests in the party struggle, had grown accustomed *to submit patiently* and fatalistically to whatever was decided for it in the name of 'monarchical government,' without criticizing the political qualifications of those who sat down in Bismarck's empty seat and took the reins of government into their own hands with such astounding nonchalance. This was the point of greatest damage by far. The great statesman left behind him *no* political tradition *whatever* to counteract that."[8]

[8] Max Weber, "Parlament und Regierung im neugeordneten Deutschland: Zur politischen Kri-

Some Speculations

In his *Politics* Heinrich von Treitschke wrote, "A monarch is competent to judge of external relations in a manner far beyond the scope of either private individuals or a republican government. A far-seeing policy is possible only to one who is the center of affairs. . . . Washington often and sadly declared that in his experience a sovereign people must suffer before it can be made to understand, and this dictum is confirmed by the War of Independence. Had the American people been guided by a right political judgment, that inevitable war would have broken out a generation earlier; but in fact they had to be forced into it by dire necessity. There is many a historical crisis of which it may be truly said that the decisive act could have been performed only by a monarch. Prussian policy up to 1866 could only have been carried out by a great king and a great minister, never by a republic."[9] To Germans who experienced the epoch 1848 to 1871 this was a natural, almost undeniable conclusion. And yet the combination of a "great king" and a "great minister" was a rare occurrence in the politics of monarchical absolutism. If Germans of the generation 1862–1890 were fortunate in enjoying such leadership, that cannot be said of the generations that preceded or followed. In the first half of the twentieth century Germany's reliance on authoritarian leadership led that country, Europe, and the world from one disaster to another, disasters that would have shocked Bismarck, Wilhelm I, and, perhaps, even Treitschke.

Whether the record would have been better with politically responsible statesmen at the helm no one can truly know. Again, this is a counterfactual speculation unsusceptible to proof. And yet the modern scientific mind resists the assumption, so acceptable to the Hegelian tradition, that what happens cannot be otherwise because man is subject to spiritual (and material) forces beyond his control. That contrary currents were demonstrably present in the stream of time gives us the freedom to speculate about what the German future might have been had Bismarck been merely a helmsman and not a builder of dikes and ditches capable of altering the channel.

For nearly three decades of generally expert leadership in foreign affairs Germany paid a high price in domestic affairs. That price was the sacrifice of more than a half-century of experience in self-government that could have given root to a liberal and democratic political tradition capable of withstanding the assault of totalitarianism. That most liberals were not yet ready to assume the responsibility for such a development is true. But had that responsibility been thrust upon them by the abdication of Wilhelm I in 1862 or by Bismarck's resignation in 1875 (in combination with an earlier succession to

---

tik des Beamtentums und Parteiwesens," *Gesammelte politische Schriften* (2d ed., Tübingen, 1958), p. 307. The italics are Weber's.

[9] Hans Kohn, ed., *Heinrich von Treitschke: Politics* (New York, 1963), p. 174. The translation has been improved.

the throne by Friedrich III), the course of German and European history might, conjecturally, have been different. As it was, the responsibility came to liberals and socialists in 1918–1919 only in the wake of a disastrous war and a dictated peace. Political parties, largely limited in the past to the negative role that Bismarck had assigned them, had suddenly to assume the task of governing under the most disadvantageous circumstances.

In a prophetic chapter of his memoirs Bismarck explained his general views on foreign policy. At the end he wrote, "International politics is a fluid element that solidifies under some conditions, but reverts on a change of atmosphere to its original diffuse state. The clause *rebus sic stantibus* is tacitly understood in all treaties that involve performance. The Triple Alliance is a strategic position, which—in view of the perils imminent at the time it was concluded—was both politic and feasible under prevailing conditions. It has been renewed from time to time, and it may be possible to renew it again, but no treaty between great powers is certain to last forever and it would be unwise to regard the alliance as affording a secure guarantee against all future contingencies that may modify the circumstances, necessities, and moods under which it was brought into being. Its importance is that of a strategic position in European politics taken in the light of the situation at the time it was concluded, but it does not constitute an eternal combination to be maintained against every conceivable change any more than were those earlier triple and quadruple alliances of recent centuries, especially the Holy Alliance and the German confederation. It does not dispense with the toujours en vedette."[10] Such was Bismarck's final judgment of the alliances with Austria and Italy.

With the abandonment of the reinsurance treaty in 1890, the character of the Dual Alliance between Germany and Austria began to change. One of three in a system of five great powers under Bismarck, Germany became one of two under his successors. In this situation Bismarck had always turned to England, and in the 1890s this option was still open. But the opportunity was squandered by the construction of Tirpitz's "risk navy," the blustering and threatening course pursued by Wilhelm II in the Boer War and two Moroccan crises, and general puffery about *Weltpolitik* during the post-1900 period. In Berlin the alliance with Austria became the "secure guarantee against all future contingencies" that Bismarck had characterized as "unwise." In 1914 the government's dependence upon Austria-Hungary as Germany's only ally and anxiety about the Habsburg empire's inner stability led Kaiser, chancellor, and chief of staff to urge the Vienna government to undertake the fateful ultimatum to Serbia. The leash that Bismarck designed to restrain Vienna in Balkan affairs was allowed to pull Germany itself into the abyss.

The European balance of power, it has been argued, was destabilized by the

[10] GW, XV, 416.

very creation of the German Reich of 1871, but this is hardly true. As long as German foreign policy remained defensive, the Reich had a stabilizing influence on European international politics. Germany became a menace to European stability only when its foreign policy assumed an offensive edge under Wilhelm II. The transition from defensive to offensive was gradual, reaching its climax only in August 1914 with Austria's ultimatum to Serbia. That action finally triggered the traditional restorative function of the European balance of power, that of restraining the aggressor and reestablishing an equilibrium. The major consequence of the two great wars that followed was the transformation of the European into a world balance of power. It is this new environment for the conduct of foreign relations that has so starkly revealed the ephemerality of Bismarck's achievement in foreign affairs.

Foreign policy is a matter of almost daily decision in a constantly fluctuating environment. Statesmen are forever in search of ways to resolve conflicts, but the resolutions they find, being temporary, are never solutions. Bismarck's assertion that alliances cannot be expected to outlast their purposes was not a cynical remark but a realistic judgment. Durable structures capable of effectively channeling the decision-making process have never been built in foreign affairs. Attempts to institutionalize international politics—the League of Nations, World Court, United Nations—have, without minimizing their importance for peripheral tasks, not changed the fundamental nature of the relations between states. But domestic politics have a different quality. Over many years individual and collective actions contribute to the development of structures that long determine how and by whom a country will be governed. And those actions can also influence in powerful ways the general political culture of a nation.

The Power of Personality

One of the great ironies of Bismarck's career is that the man who did not deliberately cultivate personal popularity, at least not while in office, and who in 1889 lost his lifelong faith in the instinctive loyalty of the masses to the monarchy should have become the most genuinely popular German statesman of all time. This was the significance of the outpouring of public respect and adulation on his departure from Berlin in 1890 and on his "great German tour" of 1892. What surfaced here was an evident need for additional psychological bonds capable of reinforcing the solidarity of a young state-nation still doubtful about its internal cohesion and external power. That the same need surfaced simultaneously among Austrian Germans shows how threatened they felt by the progress of self-development and self-assertion among their ethnic rivals within the Habsburg Empire. Bismarck became the universal symbol of all Germandom.

Within the Reich it is probable that the general acclaim penetrated deeply into the ranks of those who voted for opposition political parties while he was in power, for example, among Catholics and socialists who had experienced his heavy hand under the Kulturkampf and antisocialist laws. What the masses applauded was the developing legend rather than the reality. Memory tends to be selective, capable of ignoring or forgetting the unpleasant in the need to foster the benevolent. Man and myth became fused into a common image, and, as time passed, the image became more myth than man. The continuing influence of the mythic Bismarck can be substantiated in many sources, far more than can be introduced here. What cannot be measured—only conjectured or surmised—is its actual impact on the course of German history.

The era of Wilhelmian Germany was one of rapidly advancing prosperity (after 1893) and growing cultural pessimism. Writers and artists deprecated the growth of materialism and philistinism in the upper social strata. Critical journalists and commentators never ceased to deplore what they perceived as a dearth of effective political leadership in both parliament and government. The self-satisfaction of a bourgeoisie steadily growing in numbers and wealth was accompanied by a deep-seated fear of an alienated proletariat attracted in ever-increasing numbers to the Social Democratic party. Had Marx been right in his conviction that capitalism would self-destruct? Was the rising of the masses that would speed the collapse of the bourgeois world an immediate prospect? As the fears grew, Bismarck's genius seemed all the more apparent, his dismissal all the more tragic, the void he left behind all the more gaping. In this environment the Bismarck cult flourished. Maximilian Harden became its first high priest. He bemoaned the loss of the "dike captain" who alone, as even the "most stupid" now saw, could have shored up the dam against the coming flood. In Zukunft's pages Harden and others burnished unceasingly Bismarck's image as a great national hero. Borrowing from the "aesthetic Bonapartism of Nietzsche and Langbehn," they depicted the giant of the Sachsenwald as "the greatest and most fascinating phenomenon of the Germanic world" and "the fulfillment of the German spirit." When would Germany see his like again?[11]

Count Harry von Kessler, a sensitive observer, had opportunities to study Bismarck up close in the 1890s. Like most others, he did not escape the prince's charisma. And yet his reminiscences, published in 1935, described primarily its negative effects. Bismarck, he wrote, had to "brand everyone who did not side with him as disreputable, a criminal and traitor, in order that he could justify his hatred. The most dangerous consequence of this was that, because of the suggestive power of his personality, hundreds of thousands of

---

[11] Hans Dieter Hellige, "Einleitende Studie," in Walther Rathenau, Maximilian Harden, Briefwechsel, 1897–1920 (Munich, 1983), p. 123. Harden was hardly alone. After a chance meeting in the Grünewald park, Gerhart Hauptmann reported, "The impression this mighty warrior made on me was overwhelming." Ibid., p. 124.

little Bismarcks ran about, trying to hate like he did, sniffing everyone politically to determine whether he was a suitable object for fury. And so there
emerged an ever-present inquisition that spread a deadly climate over Germany, to which every independent political character fell victim. Bismarck
himself readily testified to this development. [His memoirs] assert that after
twenty-eight years as head of the state he was entirely surrounded by creatures
who betrayed him the moment they sensed his downfall was imminent. Those
who had been subject to his influence over a period of decades had all developed into brazen Judases!" Kessler deplored the decline of "free and upright"
personalities, a character type once nurtured by the neohumanistic culture of
the Goethezeit, whose influence was evident in the Prussian reformers of the
Stein–Hardenberg era and the movement for national unity at mid-century.
"What or who," he asked himself, was responsible for reversing the growth of
"free Germans"? "I found no other answer than—Bismarck."[12]

And yet we must not forget that Wilhelm II added another hue to this
picture. If Bismarck demanded obedience and loyalty, he had no need of
fawners and flatterers to exalt his self-esteem. He did not mistake subservience
for competence, although he often gave it a higher priority. "It was [the Kai-
ser], far more than Bismarck," wrote Norman Rich, "who fostered the quality
of groveling servility in the German administration and who would only tolerate sycophants or mediocrities in his immediate entourage and in the highest positions of the German government—including the German army."[13]

Heinrich Mann's Der Untertan is a devastating critique of Wilhelmian society and its values. The novel's protagonist, Diederich Hessling, epitomizes
the personality type known as "the bicyclist" (nach unten treten, nach oben
biegen). He apes the waxed mustache, arrogant demeanor, and autocratic posturing of the Kaiser, whose sentiments about "faithless workers," glories of
Weltpolitik, German greatness, and the like he incessantly mouths as the quin-
tessence of political wisdom. When the Kaiser rides through the streets, Hessling shouts his loyalty above the noise of the crowd and abuses bystanders
who do not share his ecstatic reverence. He interrupts his honeymoon in
Switzerland to pursue Wilhelm on a state visit to Rome, running after the
monarch's carriage in the streets, doffing his hat and crying out his homage

[12] Harry Graf Kessler, Gesichter und Zeiten: Erinnerungen (Berlin, 1962), pp. 178–187. A pam-
phleteer of the immediate postwar era wrote, "For half a century Bismarck imprinted on the
German people his spiritual stamp. . . . Involuntarily an entire folk copies its great men. This is
the only way to explain the colossal and, on the whole, regrettable change that came over the
Germans after 1871. Not only the German politicians, but also the German industrialist, the
German merchant, the traveling businessman, the professor—they all became little Bismarcks."
Professor Dr. Eugen Ehrlich, Bismarck und der Weltkrieg (Zürich, 1920), pp. 30–31.

[13] Norman Rich, Friedrich von Holstein: Politics and Diplomacy in the Era of Bismarck and Wilhelm
II (2 vols., Cambridge, Eng., 1965), II, 847; also John C. G. Röhl, "Kaiser Wilhelm II., Grossherzog Friedrich I. und der 'Königsmechanismus' im Kaiserreich," Historische Zeitschrift, 236
(1983), pp. 546–547.

and fealty for all to hear. Foreigners must be shown what loyalty the Kaiser inspires in his people. A doctor's degree (chemistry), awarded for a minimal performance at the university, provides Hessling with that treasured bourgeois surrogate for the predicate "von." Power comes to him at last as the inheritor of a small paper factory, whose foreman and workers he terrorizes in order to inculcate *deutsche Zucht und Sitte* and whose expansion he plans in search of "a greater place in the sun." Hessling adopts all the prejudices he thinks proper to his station: Jews are untrustworthy, Aryans are superior, socialists are "the enemy," the poor are unworthy, the unemployed are shiftless, liberals are losers, rank must be respected.[14]

That Bismarck and Wilhelm, so unalike as they were in most respects, could have had such an impact on the personal conduct of a meaningful number of people is, of course, unverifiable. And yet sensitive observers like Kessler and Mann must be paid their due. They and many others detected a downward current in the spiritual life of the German public of the Wilhelmian era, a moral deterioration that was both distasteful and threatening. And this suggests in turn that the problem was greater than Bismarck and Wilhelm II. If indeed a significant proportion of the public was so deeply influenced by these two personalities, that leads to the surmise that chancellor and Kaiser merely brought to the surface what was immanent—that is, culturally prepared—in the affected.

Man and Superman

In his autobiography the conservative Bavarian historian Karl Alexander von Müller testified to Bismarck's achievement in welding the fragments of the German nation together with spiritual as well as political bonds. "No one can understand the spirit and greatness of the German army in the First and, in part, the Second World War who has not witnessed that old Prussian spirit and its primal strength. I was born a south German and was un-Prussian to my innermost being. But we also were conjured deep into the magic circle by Bismarck and his Reich, and we saw in him—although not without reservations, not without concerns, not without desires for future change—the only possibility for German political unity and national consolidation."[15] Southern patriots voted their sentiments by erecting more memorials to Bismarck than to Wilhelm I. Although the memorials dedicated to the Kaiser were generally funded by state governments, those dedicated to Bismarck were financed by citizen groups, a more spontaneous demonstration of popularity.

The most grandiose plan for a national memorial to Bismarck was an-

[14] Heinrich Mann, *Der Untertan*. The novel was begun in 1907, but could not be published until 1918.

[15] Karl Alexander von Müller, *Aus Gärten der Vergangenheit: Erinnerungen, 1882–1914* (Stuttgart, 1952), p. 468.

nounced only months after his death. On December 3, 1898, a committee of university students issued a proclamation to the German people. "As the old Saxons and Normans once erected over the bodies of fallen warriors plain, undecorated rock columns topped by fiery beacons, we want to construct massive granite beacons in honor of Bismarck on all the heights of our homeland from which one can look out over our glorious German landscape." To be ignited annually on April 1 and also, "according to old Germanic custom," on June 21, the flames from these towers would be seen throughout the land. Bismarck was to be celebrated "like no German before him" as a perpetual witness to the nation's virtues—"devout love of fatherland, German loyalty to the death." More than 470 communities laid plans in 1899 to construct the pillars, although fewer than half were probably built.

In Berlin's great central park, the Tiergarten, the Reich government erected in 1901 a huge statue of Bismarck in full uniform intended as a "national memorial." But this was soon dwarfed by the granite statue (begun in 1901 and completed in 1906) that still looms over St. Pauli, suburb of Hamburg. Here Bismarck is depicted as Roland in medieval armor, hands resting on an enormous double-edged sword extending from toes to breast. The building committee and its architects wished to portray and obviously accentuate "the mounting popular consciousness of Bismarck's person gradually reaching the stage of the heroic." Intended by its designer to compete with the city's church spires, the statue was oriented not toward the city but toward the sea, "a giant symbol of the new German spirit, whose powerful wings spread out over the seas and which believes itself called to become a world power and a world culture."[16]

The greatest single monument of all was to have been erected as a "German national memorial" on the Elisenhöhe over the Rhine at Bingen in time to celebrate in 1915 the hundredth anniversary of Bismarck's birth. In 1909 a citizens' committee offered a prize of 20,000 marks for the best design, one that could satisfy, at a cost of no more than 1,800,000 marks, the people's yearning for a "monumental expression of their gratitude and veneration." No less than 370 designs were submitted. During 1911 they were reviewed by a jury of artists, architects, and laymen. Initially the jury's consensus was that none of the designs was outstanding, but, as the deliberations continued, unanimity disappeared. The jury divided into a majority favoring a design of more "lyrical" than "monumental" character and a minority favoring a grandiose design submitted jointly by Wilhelm Kreis, prizewinner of the great "battle of

[16] Thomas Nipperdey, "Nationalidee und Nationaldenkmal in Deutschland im 19. Jahrhundert," *Historische Zeitschrift*, 206 (1968), pp. 577–585; Hans-Günter Zmarzlik, *Das Bismarckbild der Deutschen—Gestern und Heute* (Freiburg, 1965), pp. 14–15. Manfred Hank lists 109 statues, 80 columns, 40 towers, 9 medallions, 7 fountains, 2 oak trees, but he makes no claim for completeness. *Kanzler ohne Amt: Fürst Bismarck nach seiner Entlassung, 1890–1898* (Munich, 1977), pp. 709–718.

THE "NATIONAL MEMORIAL" IN THE BERLIN TIERGARTEN. BISMARCK STANDS IN THE KÖNIGPLATZ GAZ-
ING AT THE VICTORY COLUMN (*SIEGESSÄULE*). HIS BACK IS TOWARD THE NEW REICHSTAG BUILDING—
A COINCIDENCE? THE SYMBOLIC FIGURES ARE AT CENTER SIEGFRIED, FORGING HIS SWORD; AT LEFT,
THE STATE'S AUTHORITY; AT RIGHT, THE STATE'S WISDOM. LIKE CARTOONISTS, ARTISTS (IN THIS CASE,
REINHARD BEGAS) AND THEIR PATRONS COULD CONCEIVE OF BISMARCK ONLY IN GARGANTUAN
TERMS. THE STATUE IS FORTY-NINE FEET TALL. PHOTOGRAPH BY E. GNILKA, ABOUT 1935. (BILDARCHIV
PREUSSISCHER KULTURBESITZ.)

nations" memorial at Leipzig, and Hugo Lederer, the designer of "Bismarck
as Roland." The committee decided for grandiosity. "The Bismarck idea has
something mighty, heroic about it; it reminds one of something ironclad, un-
bending." Lyrical classicism and poetic symbolism were out of place, regardless how elegant and beautiful.

The consequence of this decision was a donnybrook, marked by personal
attacks and venomous innuendo, that spilled over into the public press.
Throughout Germany and Austria, associations of artists and architects,
"even women's organizations," took sides. The nation was confronted with a

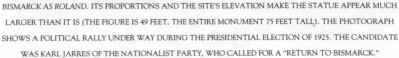

BISMARCK AS ROLAND. ITS PROPORTIONS AND THE SITE'S ELEVATION MAKE THE STATUE APPEAR MUCH
LARGER THAN IT IS (THE FIGURE IS 49 FEET, THE ENTIRE MONUMENT 75 FEET TALL). THE PHOTOGRAPH
SHOWS A POLITICAL RALLY UNDER WAY DURING THE PRESIDENTIAL ELECTION OF 1925. THE CANDIDATE
WAS KARL JARRES OF THE NATIONALIST PARTY, WHO CALLED FOR A "RETURN TO BISMARCK."

"shameful spectacle"; an undertaking to commemorate the unifier of Germany had disintegrated into squabbling factions of organizers, artists, architects, journalists, and the like. One of the organizers, Hermann Muthesius, regretted that the competition had occurred at an unfortunate moment when the "heroic," still overwhelmingly popular with the public, was going out of fashion among artists. A "lyrical, elegant, amiable" memorial, he wrote, was totally unsuited to its subject. "Only a great, heroic art can do justice to the memory of the greatest of all German heroes."[17] On April 1, 1915, no trum-

[17] Max Dessoir and Hermann Muthesius, *Das Bismarck-Nationaldenkmal: Eine Erörterung des Wettbewerbes* (Jena, 1912); Alfred Lichtwark and Walther Rathenau, *Der rheinische Bismarck* (Berlin, 1912).

pets blared and no speeches were heard on the Elisenhöhe at Bingen. Instead, cannon thundered at St. Mihiel on the western front. The memorial was never built.

Like the Sedan Day celebrations held every September to commemorate Napoleon's surrender in 1871, Bismarck's birthday on April 1 became an occasion for public celebrations and patriotic oratory. In 1913 the "Berlin Bismarck Committee" issued a summons: "Every year thousands of German men assemble to strengthen their faith in the future of the fatherland by remembering Bismarck. The German Reich faces great tasks. Surrounded by enemies, we must preserve what Bismarck fought to attain. At such a time Bismarck should be the focus of our thoughts! In view of his mighty deeds and remembering him in unswerving love and loyalty, we want to celebrate the day on which Bismarck was born to the German people." This almost religious appeal to the faithful filled the city's large Philharmonic Hall. At the lectern that day was Ludwig Bernhard, political science professor at the University of Berlin, who spoke on the "political culture of the Germans." "As we gather today to celebrate Bismarck, we do so in somber awareness that we still have much to expect from the dead Bismarck. We stand at the beginning of a time that should show how Bismarck will influence world history. Great men live twice! First, during their creative years on earth and, then again, after death. And Bismarck, the dead Bismarck, has yet another great task to fulfill."[18]

During the early stages of the First World War Germans were often told that they were fighting to defend Bismarck's legacy. Historians, journalists, and literati vied in describing and explaining this man whom Germany's youngest fighting men had never known. "Who was Bismarck?" asked Friedrich Naumann in 1915. "A man and a superman, a timely and a timeless phenomenon, a manager of small affairs and a conceiver of great goals. Already he has joined the gallery of our greatest forefathers, become a legend and a monument. Five million soldiers stand ready to defend with their blood what his hands created. We older people, who in our youth saw him before us in strength and fame, today let his image live again within us. And those of the younger generation, who witnessed only his declining and dying resonance, take time now in the midst of war to listen to *the* German statesman, the strongest political man of our people. Today all of the parties that he overpowered seriatim maintain a political truce in order to protect his Reich, because his Reich has become everyone's Reich. What he compelled the Germans to accept a half century ago is today worth 100,000 lives [a sad underestimate] to all of us without exception. . . . He is not for us any longer a

---

[18] Ludwig Bernhard, *Die politische Kultur der Deutschen: Festrede gehalten auf dem Bismarck-Kommers zu Berlin am 29. Maerz 1913* (Berlin, 1913).

disputed person but a national possession. He is not a party but the foremost of all Germans."[19]

"Has Bismarck's legacy, then, only now come up for discussion?" In 1916 the historian Erich Marcks answered this rhetorical question in his typically flowery prose. "From the war's beginning it has been our feeling—a most instinctive and general feeling—that his legacy is everywhere. This war is about his Reich. It is a war that he, like Moltke, foresaw as a threatening possibility. It is an attack on his work of 1866 and 1871. And we are conducting its defense with *his* means. All of those means have proven their worth: his Reich with the miracle of his constitution, which encloses within it, so firmly and yet so elastically, all of the vital forces of Germany—the peoples [Stämme], states, dynasties, all the diversity of our existence—in a steel-like restraint of unceasing, internal growth; the army, which he fought for and developed from 1862 to 1888 in a hundred domestic battles; the spirit, for which he fought with a hundred wounds, with entreaty and exhortation, in contest with the political parties and with the past—the spirit of unity, loyalty, devotion, and passion."[20]

Weimar and Beyond

Defeat in the First World War, collapse of the monarchy, and creation of the Weimar republic did not change the way most German academicians regarded Bismarck's heritage. On the contrary. The legend that the German army had not been defeated, the belief that Germany had been "stabbed in the back" by subversives, the general repudiation of "war guilt" and the Versailles treaty, the view that the republic was a foreign transplant ungrounded in the German political tradition, and a continuing reverence for the monarchical tradition (because of Bismarck and despite Wilhelm II)—all of these factors tended to keep the Bismarck legacy intact, particularly when nurtured by most historians.

In 1924 the liberal historian Walther Goetz rebuked his profession for its unwillingness to come to terms with the failures of the old regime. "The task of the historian is not cultivation of piety toward a misunderstood past, but the merciless search for truth. . . . German historical writing has since the time of the freedom movement been so closely associated with the monarchy and with the cult of the Hohenzollern dynasty that it has difficulty, both

---

[19] Friedrich Naumann, "Wer war Bismarck?" *Hilfe*, 21 (1915), republished in *Werke*, V, 533–542. Another publicist of 1915 who sought to bolster the German war effort with a historical message was Paul Rohrbach. Twice in the course of history, he wrote, the German people brought forth "mighty and fruitful personifications" of the idea of progress (that is, conservative revolutionaries)—one in the realm of the spirit, the other in the realm of power. The first was Luther; the second, Bismarck. *Bismarck und Wir* (Munich, 1915), p. 7.

[20] Erich Marcks, *Vom Erbe Bismarcks: Eine Kriegsrede* (Leipzig, 1916), pp. 10–11.

personally and thematically, in separating itself from these firmly rooted patterns of thought." Like all others, historians were affected by the overly ambitious and overly servile atmosphere of the age of Wilhelm II—to the point
of ignoring repeated Cassandra cries by Bismarck and other high-placed persons (*Wir gehen dem Abgrund entgegen!*) and being unwilling to question either
the monarchy's "legend" or its power to censor and censure. "To criticize
Bismarck's work was held, even in historian circles, to show a lack of national
patriotism." "The time has come," Goetz continued, "to examine with complete freedom and unremitting criticism the decades after the founding of the
Reich and to stop nowhere out of a false sense of piety. For nothing can save
us but the truth and the rebirth of the ideal of the upright character. There
are many who condemn the monarchy of Wilhelm II in body and soul and yet
remain silent in order not to injure the monarchical cause as such. . . . From
complete devotion to Bismarck and the house of Hohenzollern has come that
deep aversion to democracy characteristic of the German educated class as a
whole during the period 1871–1914." Goetz called upon historians to "open
their eyes and see the world as it really is." "We have been defeated by the
great democracies of the world." The idea and institutions of political democracy are the way of the future for Europe and the world. Historians must finally
grasp that the state of Bismarck and Wilhelm II could no more be resurrected
than that of Frederick the Great. "Preceptors of the nation!" Goetz cried out.
"Do you really think you are fulfilling an educational task when you command
history to stop its course and turn back to a prior condition?"[21]

But Goetz's appeal went unheeded. Seven years later, as Weimar neared its
end, a courageous young historian, Hajo Holborn, uttered a similar criticism
in Germany's most prominent historical journal. "The profound transforma-
tions experienced in all areas of intellectual, political, and social life as a
consequence of the world war have as yet scarcely touched the core of scholarly historical studies. The influence of old academic traditions and institutions has had the effect of making criticism of the customary methods, direc-
tions, and objectives of historical research and writing extremely rare. More
frequently expressed perhaps is a certain pride in how few of our inherited
ideals have to be sacrificed. To swim against the stream of time could be taken
as heroism. Insofar as these inclinations amount to a kind of professional 'Ni-
belungen loyalty,' which is basically just self-satisfaction, they can be seen as
symptomatic of a lack of scholarly awareness and of a methodological
thoughtlessness that threaten to be dangerous to our craft."[22] In the waning

---

[21] "Die deutsche Geschichtsschreibung der Gegenwart," in *Die deutsche Nation*, November 1,
1924, now in Walther Goetz, *Historiker in meiner Zeit: Gesammelte Aufsätze* (Köln, 1957), pp.
415–424.
[22] Hajo Holborn, "Protestantismus und politische Ideengeschichte: Kritische Bemerkungen
aus Anlass des Buches von O. Westphal 'Feinde Bismarcks,' " *Historische Zeitschrift* 144 (1931),
pp. 15–30.

months of the Weimar republic Holborn warned the academic profession that free scholarship could only survive in a free state. "Both are today exposed to the greatest danger."[23]

In the intellectual environment deplored by Goetz and Holborn, the Bismarck myth continued to prosper. Amid the chaos of post-1918 Germany—defeat and mutiny, revolutions and counterrevolutions, coups and counter-coups—Bavarian editor Paul Cossmann found solace in the thought that history could repeat itself. "If the primal force of his intellect made the rural Junker Bismarck the greatest statesman of his century, we may hope that, when the time comes, men will again be found who possess enough insight, courage, and strength to put an end to our distress. For it ought to console us that Bismarck was a German. In his personality we detect many characteristics that we can rightly regard as the roots of Germany's greatness. The folk still lives from which he came. Why should it not produce once more in our time of need a man who will fulfill our longings."[24] In 1922 writer Karl Groos reached the end of a book about Bismarck and "took leave of the man whose great picture looms, sad and wrathful, above the ruins of his work. Nothing like him will ever come again. But who wants to live without the hope that German soil may still contain the power to bring forth again a leader who will call to his people: 'Behind me lies the night, before me the day!' "[25]

In 1930 economist Edgar Salin, a disciple of Stefan George and addicted to Georgian hyperbole, wrote, "The strength of the Reich during the first decades of its existence stemmed less from the wording of the constitution than from the unpretentious, awe-inspiring person of the old Kaiser and the towering, heroic figure of the iron chancellor." Bismarck's brusque dismissal had "harmed, denied, and expunged from politics the purest of German public values—loyalty by and to the leader, ruler gratitude, and manly courage—and brought superficiality and mediocrity to power." The Bolshevik flood could be contained only "by a people capable of rejecting the enlightened secularization of the world, finding their way back to the buried wellsprings of their being, and honoring the future refounder of the state—a savior who will give new laws, worship authority, ennoble service, and create a living Reich with which to hold off the assault of the shapeless masses."[26]

What Cossmann, Groos, and Salin longed for became a reality for retired Lieutenant General Richard Kaden. A brigade commander at the battle of

[23] Hajo Holborn, *Weimarer Reichsverfassung und Freiheit der Wissenschaft*, in the series *Neues Deutschland* (Leipzig, 1933), 32 pages. See also his "Historische Voraussetzungen der Weimarer Verfassung und ihrer Reform," *Reichsverwaltungsblatt und Preussisches Verwaltungsblatt*, 53 (1932), pp. 921–924; and "Die geschichtlichen Grundlagen der deutschen Verfassungspolitik und Reichsreform," *Deutsche Juristenzeitung*, vol. 38, no. 1 (January 1, 1933), pp. 3–8.

[24] Paul N. Cossmann, ed., *Süddeutsche Monatshefte*, 19 (1921–1922), p. 122.

[25] Karl Groos, *Bismarck im eigenen Urteil* (Stuttgart, 1920), p. 247.

[26] Edgar Salin, *Die deutschen Tribute: Zwölf Reden* (Berlin, 1930), pp. 10–11, 50–51.

Verdun, Kaden concluded his memoirs in 1933 on a note of exultation. "How clearly the turn of fate of our people on January 30 confirms the old empirical principle, that only the leader, the single personality, never the masses, can bring liberation. And the German wants to be led despite everything—despite his tribal differences, despite his inclination to keep to himself, despite his critical and quarrelsome disposition. The right man, the personality, still always asserts himself. We saw that in Bismarck, now we see it again in Hitler, whose flaming battle cries, in combination with national sentiment and social understanding, have stirred up and united the masses.[27]

Hitler, too, often pontificated about the absence of a "towering personality" of Bismarckian proportions in the Weimar government. Both before and after his ascent to power, he found it useful to associate his own name and record with that of the first German chancellor. In 1925 he posed for a photograph with a drawing of the prince in the background; in the Brown House at Munich stood a statue of Bismarck, sword in hand, before massed flags; and in Hitler's chancellery office at Berlin a Lenbach portrait of him hung over the mantelpiece. At his own birthplace, Linz, Hitler celebrated Bismarck's birthday in 1938 by saying, "For us young Germans in my youth his name was a holy one." At Hamburg in February 1939—after pausing in Friedrichsruh to greet the family and lay a wreath at the tomb—he dedicated Germany's newest and largest battleship to the first German chancellor.

Hitler had studied Bismarck's memoirs during his imprisonment at Landsberg in 1924–1925 and had a more positive opinion of him than did most Nazi publicists and propagandists. Bismarck, he said in 1943, should not be reproached for failing to found "the Greater German Reich of today." The time had not been ripe for anything more. Bismarck's shortcoming, he liked to say, was his failure to unite Germany socially as well as politically. "The greatest German of modern times" had not known how to prevent or heal the split between bourgeoisie and proletariat that followed unification. He lacked "a real spiritual basis for such a struggle," that is, the concept of a truly national or *völkisch* state. No aristocrat, only a man from the masses could have grasped that. "Good old Bismarck had not the least notion of the Jewish problem." By praising Bismarck for his achievement, yet pointing to its limitations, Hitler sought to depict himself as a worthy successor. Standing on Bismarck's shoulders, he could survey more of the horizon and gain a greater vision and keener understanding of Germany's needs. What Bismarck had begun, Hitler presumed to be bringing to a triumphant conclusion. "Only a genius," he said, "can quite comprehend a genius."[28]

As the Cold War recedes, there are signs of a reawakening of the German

[27] Generalleutnant Richard Kaden, *In der alten Armee: Lebenserinnerungen aus Frieden und Krieg* (Groitzsch, 1933), p. 311.

[28] Herbert D. Andrews, "Hitler, Bismarck, and History." I thank the author for permitting me to see and quote from this interesting manuscript.

national consciousness. It ought not to surprise us if this development should bring with it a revival of the mythic Bismarck (this time, however, without the help of most historians). On June 17, 1982, the "Bismarck League" celebrated "the Day of German Unity" (anniversary of the 1953 uprising in East Berlin) at the mausoleum in Friedrichsruh. The address was delivered by Editor Hugo Wellums, who concluded (somewhat elliptically): "A new millennium will soon require a new testing period [Bewährung]: without order among peoples nothing will be achieved, for mankind alone offers no basis for the construction of states; and history is no vindication of the past, and it is not just a cemetery for elites. Indeed, history is above all a testing ground for elites and a challenge to coming generations. It is a perfidious lie that the youth of a people can live without models. One of the great models for our German people is Reich Chancellor Otto von Bismarck, whose memory we celebrate here on this Day of German Unity, in the hope that we will be given a political leadership that can learn from the errors and mistakes of the past [how] to overcome the ideological cleavages between left and right and to bring us together again in that unselfish dedication for which the life of Otto von Bismarck provides the precedent."[29]

It may be that Bismarck's most enduring consequence is his myth: the man of blood and iron, iron chancellor, mighty warrior, German patriot, and towering personality, who rescued the nation, in a time of great peril and against great odds, from the enemy within and the foe without and demonstrated for all time the indispensability of authoritarian rule in Germany. This image was sculpted less by Bismarck himself than by an intelligentsia steeped in Germanic mythology and lingering romanticism. The religious words and imagery chosen by the high priests of the Bismarck cult—*miracle, devotion, faith, sacrifice, savior,* even *resurrection*—as well as their manner of expression have an epiphanous quality. The "dead Bismarck" is invoked like a patron saint whose spiritual power will preserve the nation from evil. And the "living Bismarck" is presented like a messiah—rebuffed by nonbelievers, crucified by Wilhelm II, then universally recognized as savior. And the resurrection? Our evidence, admittedly sketchy,[30] suggests that many Germans were encouraged to believe that in times of internal crisis the nation would again find rescue in a hero of enormous narcissistic self-confidence, of autocratic and even dictatorial temperament, a man of genius who would end the nation's divisiveness and lead

[29] Hugo Wellems, *Bismarck und unsere Zeit, 17. Juni 1982 in Friedrichsruh* (Hamburg, 1982), p. 14. Wellums is editor-in-chief of the weekly *Ostpreussenblatt* and chairman of the *Staats- und Wirtschaftspolitische Gesellschaft e. V.*

[30] Research of more systematic character than has been undertaken here would, very likely, turn up many similar utterances in sources of the most varied sort—letters, editorials, memoirs, autobiographies, parliamentary debates, patriotic oratory, novels, poetry and song, magazine articles, newspaper editorials, and political commentary of every sort. For additional examples, see Zmarzlik, *Bismarckbild der Deutschen.*

it on to new heights of internal unity and external power. If so, the myth contributed to results that Bismarck in pessimistic moments dimly foresaw and would certainly have decried.

"For all their boasting, practical men do not know either men or the world; they do not even know the reality of their own works." To history is given the task of recovering and placing in context that of which historical figures are "conscious but not self-conscious." If they could return to life, "the geniuses of pure politics, the *fatalia monstra* recorded in histories, would be astounded to learn what they have done without being aware of it, and they would read of their own past deeds as in a hieroglyph to which they had been offered the keys."[31]

[31] Benedetto Croce, *La Storia come Pensiero e come Azione* (6th edition, Bari, 1954), p. 181.

✠ INDEX ✠